THE PREHISTORIC SOCIETY

IS THERE A BRITISH CHALCOLITHIC?

In memory of

Ian Alexander George Shepherd

This Volume is dedicated to the memory of Ian Alexander George Shepherd (1951–2009), who contributed so much to the study of Scotland's Chalcolithic and Bronze Age and who supported this book and the conference that gave rise to it.

Frontispiece: Ian, with wife Alexandra (Lekky, author of Chapter 17, far left) and colleague Moira Greig (centre) during the experimental cremation of a pig at Archaeolink, September 2004. Photo: Alison Sheridan

THE PREHISTORIC SOCIETY

Is there a British Chalcolithic?

People, place and polity in the later 3rd millennium

edited by

Michael J. Allen, Julie Gardiner and Alison Sheridan

Prehistoric Society Research Paper No. 4

THE PREHISTORIC SOCIETY
Series Editors: Michael J. Allen and David McOmish
Managing Editor: Julie Gardiner

OXBOW BOOKS 2012
Oxford and Oakville

Published by
The Prehistoric Society
and
Oxbow Books, Oxford, UK

Front cover: All Over Ornamented Beaker from a grave at Newmill, Perthshire © National Museums Scotland

Back Cover: Top: All Over Cord Beaker from Bathgate, West Lothian © National Museums Scotland; left: tanged copper blade from Sittingbourne, Kent © University of Birmingham Leverhulme Project, courtesy of the British Museum; and gold basket-shaped ornaments from Boltby Scar, Yorkshire © National Museums Scotland

Prehistoric Society Research Papers
ISSN 2040-5049
ISBN 978-1-84217-496-8

This book is available direct from:

Oxbow Books, Oxford, UK
(Phone: 01865-241249; Fax: 01865-794449)

and

The David Brown Book Company
PO Box 511, Oakville, CT 06779, USA
(Phone: 860-945-9329; Fax: 860-945-9468)

or from our website

www.oxbowbooks.com

Library of Congress Cataloging-in-Publication Data

Is there a British chalcolithic? : people, place and polity in the later 3rd millennium / edited by Michael J. Allen, Julie Gardiner and Alison Sheridan.
    p. cm. -- (Prehistoric society research paper ; no. 4)
Includes bibliographical references and index.
ISBN 978-1-84217-496-8
    1. Copper age--Great Britain. 2. Copper implements--Great Britain. 3. Metal-work, Prehistoric--Great Britain. 4. Great Britain--Antiquities. I. Allen, Michael J. II. Gardiner, Julie. III. Sheridan, Alison.
    GN778.22.G7.I7 2012
    936.1--dc23
                        2012010965

Printed and bound in Great Britain by
Short Run Press, Exeter

THE PREHISTORIC SOCIETY RESEARCH PAPERS

The Prehistoric Society Research Papers publish collections of edited papers covering aspects of Prehistory. These may be derived from conferences, or research projects; they specifically *exclude* the publication of single excavation reports. The Research Papers present the fruits of the best of prehistoric research, complementing the Society's respected *Proceedings* by allowing broader treatment of key research areas.

The Research Papers is a peer reviewed series whose production is managed by the Society.

Further information can be found on the Society's website (www.prehistoricsociety.org)

THE PREHISTORIC SOCIETY

The Prehistoric Society's interests are world wide and extend from the earliest human origins to the emergence of written records. Membership is open to all, and includes professional, amateur, student and retired members.

An active programme of events – lectures, study tours, day- and weekend conferences, and research weekends – allows members to participate fully in the Society and to meet other members and interested parties. The study excursions cater for all preferences from the relatively luxurious to the more economical, including highly popular student study tours. Day visits to sites are arranged whenever possible.

The Society produces two publications that are included with most categories of membership: the annual journal, *Proceedings of the Prehistoric Society* and the topical newsletter, *PAST*, which is published in April, July and November. In addition the *Prehistoric Society Research Papers* are published occasionally on which members may have discount.

Further information can be found on the Society's website (www.prehistoricsociety.org), or via the Prehistoric Society's registered address: % Institute of Archaeology, University College London, 31–34 Gordon Square, London, WC1H 0PY.

The Society is a registered charity (no. 1000567)

THE PREHISTORIC SOCIETY RESEARCH PAPERS

CONTENTS

LIST OF FIGURES AND TABLES

List of Figures

List of Tables

CONTRIBUTORS

Dr Michael J. Allen
Allen Environmental Archaeology, Redroof,
Green Rd, Codford, Wiltshire, BA12 0NW
and
School of Applied Sciences, Bournemouth
University, Fern Barrow, Poole, BH12 5BB
Email: aea.escargots@gmail.com

Prof. Dr Martin Bartelheim
Eberhard Karls Universität Tübingen, Schloß
Hohentübingen, Burgsteige 11, D-72070
Tübingen, Germany
Email: martin.bartelheim@uni-tuebingen.de

Dr Peter Bray
Research Laboratory for Archaeology and the
History of Art (RLAHA)
University of Oxford, Dyson Perrins Building,
South Parks Road, Oxford OX1 3QY
Email: peter.bray@rlaha.ox.ac.uk

Dr Joanna Brück
UCD School of Archaeology, Newman Building,
University College Dublin, Belfield, Dublin 4,
Ireland.
Email: joanna.bruck@ucd.ie

Dr Steve Burrow
St Fagans National History Museum, Cardiff,
CF5 6XB
Email: steve.burrow@museumwales.ac.uk

Neil Carlin
UCD School of Archaeology, Newman Building,
University College Dublin, Belfield, Dublin 4,
Ireland.
Email: neil.carlin@gmail.com

Dr Ros Cleal
The National Trust, Alexander Keiller Museum,
High Street, Avebury, Wiltshire, SN8 1RF.
Email: Rosamund.Cleal@nationaltrust.org.uk

Neil G.W. Curtis
University Museums, University of Aberdeen,
Marischal College, Aberdeen AB10 1YS
Email: neil.curtis@abdn.ac.uk

Dr Catherine Frieman
School of Archaeology and Anthropology,
The Australian National University, AD Hope
Building #13, Canberra, Act 0200, Australia
Email: cfrieman@gmail.com

Prof. Dr Harry Fokkens
Universiteit Leiden, Faculteit Archeologie,
Reuvensplaats 3–4, 2311 BE Leiden, Netherlands
Email: h.fokkens@arch.leidenuniv.nl

Dr Julie Gardiner
℅ Allen Environmental Archaeology, Redroof,
Green Rd, Codford, Wiltshire, BA12 0NW
Email: jpg.escargots@googlemail.com

Paul Garwood
Institute of Archaeology & Antiquity, Arts
Building, University of Birmingham, Edgbaston,
Birmingham, B15 2TT
Email: P.J.Garwood@bham.ac.uk

Dr Frances Healy
20 The Green, Charlbury, Oxon, OX7 3QA
Email: franceshealy@vodafoneemail.co.uk

Dr Volker Heyd
Department of Archaeology and Anthropology,
University of Bristol, 43 Woodland Road, Bristol
BS8 1UU
Email: volker.heyd@bris.ac.uk

Dr Mandy Jay
Durham University, Dept. of Archaeology, South
Road, Durham, DH1 3LE, UK
and
Max Planck Institute for Evolutionary
Anthropology, Dept. of Human Evolution,
Deutscher Platz 6, 04103 Leipzig
Email: Mandy.Jay@Sheffield.ac.uk

Jun.-Prof. Dr Tobias Kienlin
Institut für Archäologische Wissenschaftnm,
Ur- und Frühgeschichte, Ruhr-Universität
Bochum, Am Bergbaumuseum 31, 44791
Bochum, Germany
Email: tobias.kienlin@rub.de

Dr Raiko Krauß
Eberhard Karls Universität Tübingen, Schloß
Hohentübingen, Burgsteige 11, D-72070
Tübingen, Germany
Email: raiko.krauss@uni-tuebingen.de

Mark Maltby
School of Applied Sciences, Bournemouth
University, Fern Barrow, Poole, BH12 5BB
Email: mmaltby@bournemouth.ac.uk

Dr Stuart Needham
Langton Fold, North Lane, South Harting, West
Sussex, GU31 5NW
Email: sbowman1@waitrose.com

Prof. William O'Brien
Department of Archaeology, Connolly Building,
University College Cork, Cork, Ireland
Email: w.obrien@ucc.ie

Prof. Mike Parker Pearson
University of Sheffield, Dept. of Archaeology,
University of Sheffield, Northgate House, West
Street, Sheffield, S1 4ET, UK
Email: M.Parker-Pearson@Sheffield.ac.uk

Dr Joshua Pollard
Archaeology, Faculty of Humanities, University
of Southampton, Avenue Campus
Highfield, Southampton, SO17 1BF
Email: C.J.Pollard@soton.ac.uk

Dr Benjamin W. Roberts
Department of Prehistory and Europe, British
Museum, London, WC1B 3DG
Email: broberts@thebritishmuseum.ac.uk

Dr Alison Sheridan
Department of Archaeology, National Museums
Scotland, Chambers Street, Edinburgh, EH1 1JF
Email: a.sheridan@nms.ac.uk

†Ian Shepherd
Formerly of Aberdeenshire Archaeology Services,
Aberdeenshire Council, Planning & Economic
Development Woodhill House, Westburn Road,
Aberdeen, AB16 5GB

Alexandra (Lekky) Shepherd
509 King Street, Aberdeen, AB24 3BT
Email: Lekkwork2@aol.com

Dr Marc Vander Linden
School of Archaeology and Ancient History,
University of Leicester, University Road,
Leicester, LE1 7RH
Email: mmagvl1@le.ac.uk

Neil Wilkin
Institute of Archaeology & Antiquity, University
of Birmingham, Edgbaston, Birmingham, B15
2TT
Email: wilkin.neil@googlemail.com

Non-corresponding Contributors
Prof. Andrew Chamberlain
University of Sheffield, Dept. of Archaeology,
University of Sheffield, Northgate House, West
Street, Sheffield, S1 4ET
Email: A.Chamberlain@sheffield.ac.uk

Dr Janet Montgomery
Durham University, Department of Archaeology,
South Road, Durham, DH1 3LE
Email: janet.montgomery@durham.ac.uk

Dr Olaf Nehlich
Max Planck Institute for Evolutionary
Anthropology, Deutscher Platz 6, 04103 Leipzig,
Germany
Email: nehlich eva.mpg.de

Prof. Mike Richards
University of British Columbia, Department of
Anthropology, 6303 NW Marine Drive
Vancouver, British Columbia, V6T 1Z1, Canada
and
Max Planck Institute for Evolutionary
Anthropology, Deutscher Platz 6, 04103 Leipzig,
Germany
Email: Richards@eva.mpg.de

ABSTRACT

This volume brings together contributions from many leading authorities in 20 papers that address the question 'Is there a British Chalcolithic?' (*c.* 2450/2400–2200/2150 BC). This question was posed at a conference of the Prehistoric Society held at Bournemouth University in April 2009 and the volume contains a selection of key papers presented on that occasion, together with a number of commissioned additional contributions. The volume does not present a consensus view; rather, it has provided contributors with the opportunity to examine in depth a range of materials, issues, and themes, and to show just how much new information (particularly chronological and isotopic) has come to light in the last decade. The diversity of views expressed in these papers as to whether we should adopt a 'new' period classification for British Prehistory – ie, the Chalcolithic or Copper Age – reflects the lively debate surrounding this question.

The first four papers address the key subjects of definition, issues, and debate, with two advocating the use of the term 'Chalcolithic' and two rejecting it. Stuart Needham, presenting the original keynote paper from the conference, debates how the definition and labelling of this period are essential because it does mark a time of social and cultural change, distinguishable from what went before and from what happened once bronze began to be used. He sets out to characterise the British Chalcolithic by focusing on key aspects of the two cultural complexes that were involved – the insular Late Neolithic Grooved Ware culture and the continentally derived Beaker culture. A chronological framework for the British Chalcolithic is proposed, based on an examination of key Beaker-associated funerary assemblages, with the 23rd century BC marking a watershed, when Beaker use intensified and diversified. The overall trajectory of insular ceremonial monument construction throughout the 3rd millennium BC is set out and a process of its 'Beakerisation' is outlined. It is argued that the indigenous Late Neolithic traditions and those introduced with the use of Beakers and associated novelties coexisted and interrelated with one another from the outset, their fusion setting in train a highly dynamic situation as disparate interests were melded into common goals.

Ben Roberts and Catherine Frieman examine the concept of a distinctive British Chalcolithic from the perspective of the metal evidence, as viewed against the Continental Chalcolithic evidence and against their critique of the concept of a Continental 'Chalcolithic frontier'. They argue against the introduction of this period label for Britain on the grounds that it brings definitional baggage and untenable assumptions about the nature of society and the importance of copper use, derived from models developed for the Continental Copper Age. They also argue that the chronology of metalworking in Britain and Ireland is insufficiently well established to assess its social and economic importance.

Alison Sheridan continues the theme of definition by examining what we can and cannot say about traditions, practices, social relations and external contacts during the period between the 25th and the 22nd centuries BC, highlighting the outstanding research questions and the approaches that are needed to address them. The need for *a* term to describe this period is underlined, with 'Chalcolithic' or 'Copper Age', while being far from ideal, offering a pragmatic solution that is preferable to the commonly-used terms 'Late Neolithic–Early Bronze Age' or, even more erroneously, 'Early Bronze Age'. The period needs to be defined on its own terms, with its distinctive insularity and regional variability to the fore; we need to rid the term 'Chalcolithic' of the techno-cultural baggage (or rather clutter) that has grown up around its use elsewhere in Europe.

Peter Bray presents a chemical and chronological analysis of the British and Irish metalwork of the second half of the third millennium, in an attempt to explore how metal was viewed and used by the people who lived here. Applying new theoretical perspectives to a critical study of the huge database produced by the chemical characterisation studies over the last 60 years, his study includes new insights including the suggestion that Cornish copper was being exploited from an early stage. Bray argues against the use of the term 'British Chalcolithic' on the grounds that it implies a unified, coherent understanding of metal that simply does not exist.

The second group of papers provides a continental perspective and background with which to compare the British evidence. Marc Vander Linden discusses the possible impact of copper on the cultural and social history of Britain and Ireland, reviewing evidence from both sides of the Channel. He concludes that copper played only a very limited role in the re-establishment of cross-Channel contacts during the 'Bell Beaker Phenomenon' and that, although there was definitely a period of exclusive use of copper, its influence was insufficient to justify the definition of British Chalcolithic. Martin Bartelheim and Raiko Krauß discuss how, in large areas of Europe the appearance of metals occurred within a period of rapid evolution of technology, economy, society, and settlement structures. The production of metals, especially copper, and their use for symbols of prestige, was closely linked with the emergence of a complex economic and social organisation and became a defining factor for the Chalcolithic as an intermediate step from the Stone Age to the full Metal Ages. Volker Heyd picks up on this theme, describing how a long-term and ongoing evolutionary progress is attested for prehistoric Europe between the mid-5th and late 3rd millennium BC with deep-reaching social, economic, and ritual changes that transformed existing patterns. The Europe-wide Bell Beaker Phenomenon was the apex of this ideological domination which completed the process of the Chalcolithisation of Europe.

Harry Fokkens takes a closer look at the relationship between the Netherlands and Britain by revisiting the question of Beaker migration and the transmission of ideas and material culture in the light of recent finds and radiocarbon dates. Recent discussions have been based on the idea that Beakers and associated artefacts were prestige items – valuables that everyone adopted as soon as they were within reach. That would explain how (im)migrants could be responsible for bringing about culture change in, for instance, Britain, but it is argued here that this theory does not explain why other aspects of material culture, especially burial rites, were also adopted. Beaker burial assemblages in general do not represent the burials of prestigious Beaker People, but are constructed ancestral identities.

Tobias Kienlin questions our approaches to understanding early metalworking, arguing that notions of progress and evolution we use to account for long-term technological change falls short of representing a more complex ancient reality. We need to understand the technological choices taken through time by the countless individuals who depended on their local cultural background as much as they did on the laws of nature involved in the production and working of copper. Using examples from the Carpathian Basin and central Europe a brief review is presented of the development of metallurgical knowledge specific to the time and area under consideration and the need for a long-term perspective on the development of metallurgical knowledge emphasised.

The third section of the volume presents a series of detailed case studies from various parts of Britain and Ireland. Frances Healy discusses the Bayesian modelling of radiocarbon dates for articulated inhumations of the 4th–2nd millennia in England, demonstrating that Beaker burials of the later 3rd millennium seem to reflect a newly introduced continental tradition, rather than the revival of a long-lived insular one. This conclusion is reinforced by differences in demographic composition and burial context between Beaker and earlier articulated burials which suggests that the tradition may have persisted longest in southern

England. The lack of a Beaker element in the material culture from the Grime's Graves flint mines suggests that their exploitation may have been something of an assertion of old ways in the face of innovation. The focus moves north to Scotland in the late Ian Shepherd's contribution that examines the evidence for a Chalcolithic period in this part of Britain. Funerary practices, metalwork and pottery evidence are used to argue for a geographically extensive beginning to the 'Beaker phenomenon', with subsequent regionalisation highlighting differing responses. The possibility of continuing links with the continent, and particularly with the Lower Rhine, is discussed.

Steve Burrow reflects on the lack of prominence afforded to Wales despite its pivotal position between Ireland and other hotspots of late 3rd millennium BC archaeology. With the aid of 89 radiocarbon determinations, many of them obtained recently, he addresses themes including the introduction of copper mining, monumentality, the role of Beakers and the evidence for domestic occupation. He concludes that the evidence is currently insufficient to allow for a clear definition of a Welsh Chalcolithic. Moving across to Ireland, Neil Carlin and Joanna Brück examine settlement and ceremonial sites, mortuary and depositional practices over the period 2900–1700 BC to illustrate strong evidence for continuity between the Late Neolithic and Early Bronze Age. They argue that, in spite of the well-known early exploitation of Irish copper, metal had a very limited role in initiating and creating social change and that the term Chalcolithic is inappropriate in an Irish context. William O'Brien, in contrast, considers that the distinct period of metal production and use in Ireland from the 25th century was marked by a widespread adoption of copper and gold prior to the introduction of tin-bronze metallurgy, and that the concept of a Chalcolithic is entirely relevant. The Irish Chalcolithic was much more than a technological phase, but was a highly formative time of ideological change, social transformation and possibly language development.

Recent studies have examined the evidence of the actual people of this period through osteological and isotopic examination of human remains and via detailed studies of burial rituals, with particular emphasis on gender and age-related aspects and chronological developments. Mandy Jay and her collaborators on the *Beaker People Project* are investigating mobility, diet, environment, and subsistence for the Late Neolithic, Chalcolithic, and Early Bronze Age population of Britain using a number of research tools, but particularly isotopic analysis of bones and teeth. In this paper, preliminary results are presented mainly for individuals in Scotland and East Yorkshire. Various levels of mobility appear to be indicated. A chronological shift in carbon values may relate to changes in animal management strategies (eg, herd movements, grazing under forest cover, or provision of winter fodder). The general diet excluded significant levels of marine and other aquatic resources, regardless of the proximity of the individuals to the coast, and animal protein consumption (meat or dairy) is at relatively high levels.

Neil Curtis and Neil Wilkin report on the results of the complementary *Beakers and Bodies Project*, which focuses on individuals from north-east Scotland and the immediately adjacent regions of east-central Scotland and the Moray Firth area. They present several narratives/models to aid in understanding regional socio-cultural identities, changes, and networks of interaction during the Chalcolithic in this part of Britain.

Alexandra (Lekky) Shepherd presents the evidence for patterns of body orientation and Beaker style among the crouched inhumations of the British Chalcolithic–Early Bronze Age in two core areas of Beaker use, in north-east Scotland and east Yorkshire. She demonstrates predominant gender-defined burial patterns in these areas and looks in detail at the Beakers accompanying each burial in order to identify gender-specific indicators in their style and decoration. A series of case studies of paired inhumations indicates both conformities and variations in the observance of burial formalities and choice in the provision of accompanying pot. The study highlights the existence of cohesive ideologies and stresses the human dimension discernible within an otherwise technologically-defined period.

The final three papers in the volume look at the wider issue of the relationship between the economic, monumental and funerary use of landscape during the period in question.

Mike Allen and Mark Maltby attempt to examine the significant changes in farming and economy that is generally considered to accompany, if not enabled, the changes in social and artefactual assemblages. Paul Garwood examines the spatial distribution and frequency of early Beaker burial events in Britain considering the nature of early Beaker burials from a landscape perspective to show how a series of distinctive spatial strategies articulated relationships among monuments, spaces, people, and practices. These addressed tensions between past and present, foreign and native, reconfiguring past and present landscapes in efforts to delineate imagined landscapes of the future. Rosamund Cleal and Josh Pollard conclude the volume by revisiting and reviewing sequences in two of the most celebrated landscapes of Late Neolithic–Early Bronze Age Britain – Stonehenge and Avebury – in the period *c.* 2500–2200 BC. They consider a key problem in the identification of 'Chalcolithic' is that the term privileges metal over other material culture and concepts: it implies that metal is the catalyst and medium of changes so profound that they warrant the separate identification of a period as short as 200–300 years. Their argument is for a 'long view' – and that the appearance of Beaker-associated metal needs to be understood in the context of a series of changes and developments with their origins in the preceding centuries, and which continue into the full Early Bronze Age.

Résumé

Existe-t-il un chalcolithique britannique:
peuples, lieux et administration à la fin du
3ème millénnaire

Ce volume rassemble de grand nombre des
autorités principales en 20 articles qui s'adressent
à la question 'Existe-t-il un chalcolithique
britannique?' (*c.* 2450/2400–2200/2150 av.J.-
C.). On a posé cette question à une conférence
de la Société Prehistorique tenue en avril 2009
et le volume contient une sélection d'articles
clés présentés à cette occasion, ainsi qu'un
nombre de contributions supplémentaires qui
sont des commissions.Le volume ne présente
pas une vision consensuelle; au contraire il a
offert aux participants l'occasion d'examiner
en profondeur une gamme de matériaux, de
questions et de thèmes, et de montrer toute
l'étendue des nouveaux renseignements
(chronologiques et isotopiques en particulier)
qui ont vu le jour dans la dernièr décennie.
La diversité des points de vue exprimés dans
ces articles quant à l'adoption ou non d'une
nouvelle 'période' de classification pour
la préhistoire britannique, – c'est à dire le
chalcolithique ou âge du cuivre – reflète la
vivacité du débat autour de cette question
pendant la conférence.

Les quatre premiers articles traitent des
sujets clés de définition, questions et débat, deux
soutenant l'usage du terme 'chalcolithique' et
deux le rejetant. Stuart Needham débat qu'il
est essentiel de définir et de nommer cette
période parce qu'elle marque un moment de
changement social et culturel distinct de ce
qui existait avant et de ce qui s'est passé une
fois qu'on a commencé à utiliser le bronze
tandis que Ben Roberts et Catherine Frieman
examinent le concept d'un chalcolithique
britannique distinct de la perspective des
témoignages des métaux, tels qu'ils sont vus
contre les témoignages du chalcolithique
continental et contre leur critique du concept
d'une frontière chalcolithique continentale,
argumentant contre l'introduction de cette
nomenclature pour la Grande-Bretagne. Alison
Sheridan examine ce que nous pouvons et ne
pouvons pas dire des traditions pratiques, des
relations sociales et des contacts extérieurs
pendant la période entre le 25ème et le 22ème
siècles av.J.-C., soulignant les questions de
recherches non-résolues et les approches
nécessaires pour les régler, la période doit

être définie en ses propres termes. Peter Bray
présente une analyse chimique et chronologique
de la métallurgie britannique et irlandaise de la
deuxième moitié du 3ème millénaire, dans une
tentative d'explorer comment considéraient et
utilisaient le métal les peuples qui habitaient
là.Il argumente contre l'usage du terme
'chalcolithique britannique'.

Dans le second groupe d'articles Marc
Vander Linden discute de l'impact possible du
cuivre sur l'histoire culturelle et sociale de la
Grande-Bretagne et de l'Irlande, révisant les
témoignages venant des deux côtés de la mer.
Martin Bartelheim et Raiko Krauss discutent
comment, dans de grandes zones de l'Europe,
l'apparition des métaux s'est faite pendant une
période d'évolution rapide de la technologie,
l'économie, la société et les structures
des occupations et était étroitement liée à
l'émergence d'une organisation économique et
sociale complexe ; un facteur déterminant du
chalcolithique. Volker Heyd décrit comment
un progrès évolutif à long terme et continu
est attesté pour l'Europe préhistorique entre
le milieu du 5ème et la fin du 3ème millénaire
av. J.-C. Le phénomène des peuples à vases qui
a touché toute l'Europe fut le point culminant
d'une domination idéologique qui a mis fin
au procédé de chalcolithisation de l'Europe.
Harry Fokkens regarde de plus près la relation
entre les Pays-Bas et la Grande-Bretagne
en revisitant la question de la migration des
peuples à vases et de la transmission des
idées et de la culture matérielle à la lumière de
récentes trouvailles et de dates au C14, tandis
que Tobias Kienlin remet en question notre
approche pour comprendre les débuts de la
métallurgie, argumentant que les notions de
progrès et d'évolution utilisées pour expliquer
les changements technologiques à long terme
ne suffisent pas pour rendre compte d'une
réalité ancienne plus complexe.

La troisième section présente une série
d'articles de cas détaillées provenant de diverses
parties de la Grande-Bretagne et d'Irlande..
Frances Healy discute du modèle the Baysien
de datation au C14 des inhumations articulées
du 4ème–2ème millénnaire en Angleterre,
démontrant que les inhumations des peuples
à vases de la fin du 3ème millénnaire semble
refléter une tradition continentale introduite
récemment, plutôt que la réapparition d'une

insulaire à longue vie. Feu Ian Shepherd examine les témoignages d'une période chalcolithique en Ecosse, réexaminant les pratiques funéraires, la métallurgie et les témoignages de poterie pour argumenter en faveur d'un début géographiquement étendu de phénomène des peuples à vases avec une régionalisation ultérieure qui souligne les réactions diverses. Steve Burrow réfléchit sur l'absence de proéminence accordée au Pays de Galles malgré sa position de pivot entre l'Irlande et d'autres points chauds de l'archéologie de la fin du 3ème millénnaire av.J.-C. et il utilise 89 déterminations au C14 pour examiner divers thèmes, concluant que les témoignages sont actuellement insuffisants pour permettre de définir clairement un chalcolithique gallois. Pour l'Irlande, Neil Carlin et Joanna Brück examinent des sites d'occupation et cérémoniels, un mortuaire et des pratiques de déposition pour illustrer de solides témoignages de continuité entre le néolithique final et le début del'âge du bronze argumentant que le métal n'avait en fait joué qu'un rôle limité dans l'initiation et la création du changement social et que le terme Chalcolithique est inapproprié dans le contexte irlandais. William O'Brien, au contraire, considère que la période distincte de production et d'utilisation du métal en Irlande à partir du 25ème siècle fut marquée par une adoption très étendue du cuivre et de l'or avant l'introduction de la métallurgie de l'étain-bronze, et que le concept d'un chalcolithique est entièrement justifié.

Mandy Jay et ses collaborateurs sur le *Projet des peuples à vases* examinent la mobilité, la nutrition, l'environnement et la subsistance de la population britannique du néolithique final et du début de l'âge du bronze en utilisant en particulier l'analyse isotopique des os et des dents. Des résultats préliminaires présentés concernent essentiellement des individus écossais et de l'est du Yorkshire. Ils semblent indiquer divers niveaux de mobilité

et que l'alimentation générale excluait tout niveau significatif de ressources marines ou aquatiques. Neil Curtis and Neil Wilkin rendent compte des résultats du projet complémentaire *Peuples à vases et corps*, qui se concentre sur des individus venant de diverses parties de l'Ecosse. Ils présentent plusieurs histoires/modèles pour aider à comprendre les identités socio-culturelles régionales, les changements et les réseaux d'échange pendant le chalcolithique dans cette partie de la Grande-Bretagne. Alexandra (Lekky) Shepherd présente des témoignages d'exemples d'orientation des corps et de style peuples à vases parmi les inhumations accroupies du chalcolithique–début de l'âge du bronze britannique, démontrant la prédominance d'exemples d'inhumations définies par le sexe

Les trois derniers articles du volume considèrent la question plus étendue de la relation entre l'utilisation économique, monumentale et funéraire du paysage. Mike Allen et Mark Maltby revoient les données géoarchéologiques et les assemblages d'ossements d'animaux pour apporter des indications de changements significatifs quoique subtils, ayant résulté de, et pendant , la période des peuples à vases. Il est clair qu'il y a une augmentation de l'agriculture et des changements dans les pratiques de l'élevage. Paul Garwood examine la répartition dans l'espace et la fréquence des actes d'inhumation en Grande-Bretagne du point de vue du paysage pour montrer comment une série de stratégies spatiales particulières articulaient les relations parmi les monuments, les espaces, les gens et les pratiques. Rosamund Cleal et Josh Pollard concluent ce volume en revisitant et révisant des séquences des paysages de Stonehenge et d'Avebury.Ils argumentent en faveur d'une 'longue vue' – que l'apparition du métal associé aux peuples à vases doit être compris dans le contexte d'une série de changements et de développements ayant leurs origines dans les siècles précédents et qui continuent pendant tout le début de l'âge du bronze.

Traduction Annie Pritchard
14-02-2012

Zusammenfassung

Gibt es ein britisches Chalkolithikum? Menschen, Orte und Politik im späten 3. Jahrtausend

Dieser Band vereinigt zahlreiche führende Autoritäten in 20 Texten, die sich der Frage widmen: „Gibt es ein britisches Chalkolithikum?" (ca. 2450/2400-2200/2150 BC). Diese Frage wurde während einer Konferenz der Prehistoric Society im April 2009 gestellt, und der Tagungsband enthält eine Auswahl von Schlüsselvorträgen, die bei dieser Gelegenheit gehalten wurden, zusammen mit einigen weiteren nachträglich eingeworbenen Beiträgen. Der Band legt keine einmütige Sicht auf die Problematik vor; vielmehr wurde den Autorinnen und Autoren die Gelegenheit gegeben, eine Vielfalt an Material, Themen und Fragestellungen tiefergehend zu untersuchen und zu zeigen, wie groß der Umfang neuer Daten ist, insbesondere chronologische und isotopische, die im letzten Jahrzehnt gewonnen wurden. Die Vielfalt der Ansichten zur Frage, ob wir eine „neue" Periodenklassifikation für die britische Vorgeschichte annehmen, d.h. ein Chalkolithikum bzw. eine Kupferzeit einführen sollten, die hier vorgestellt wird, reflektiert die lebhafte Debatte, die während der Konferenz zu diesem Problem aufkam.

Die ersten vier Artikel beschäftigen sich mit den Schlüsselthemen der Definition, Fragestellungen und Erörterungsmöglichkeiten, wovon sich zwei für den Gebrauch des Terminus „Chalkolithikum" und zwei dagegen aussprechen. Stuart Needham diskutiert, dass eine solche Definition und Benennung dieser Epoche unerlässlich ist, da sie eine Zeit sozialen und kulturellen Wandels markiert, die deutlich unterscheidbar ist von dem Vorhergehenden wie auch von dem, was geschieht, sobald die Bronze in Gebrauch kommt. Dagegen untersuchen Ben Roberts und Catherine Frieman das Konzept eines unterscheidbaren britischen Chalkolithikums aus der Perspektive der Metallfunde und des Vergleichs mit den kontinentalen chalkolithischen Daten auf Basis ihrer Kritik des Konzepts einer kontinentalen „chalkolithischen Grenze", was sie zu dem Schluss führt, sich gegen die Anwendung dieses Epochenbegriffs auf Britannien

auszusprechen. Alison Sheridan untersucht die Möglichkeiten und Grenzen für Aussagen über Traditionen, Praktiken, soziale Beziehungen und äußere Kontakte zwischen dem 25. und 22. Jahrhundert BC, wobei sie die noch offenen Forschungsfragen und die Ansätze hervorhebt, die notwendig sind um diese Fragen zu beantworten; schließlich folgert sie, dass diese Epoche aus sich selbst heraus verstanden und definiert werden muss. Peter Bray legt eine chemische und chronologische Analyse britischer und irischer Metallurgie der zweiten Hälfte des 3. Jahrtausends vor in dem Versuch zu ergründen, wie die Menschen sich Metall gegenüber verhielten und es nutzten. Er argumentiert gegen eine Einführung des Terminus „Britisches Chalkolithikum".

Zu einer zweiten Gruppe von Beiträgen gehört Marc Vander Lindens Diskussion des möglichen Einflusses von Kupfer auf die Kultur- und Sozialgeschichte Britanniens und Irlands auf der Grundlage von Daten von beiden Seiten des Kanals. Martin Bartelheim und Raiko Krauß diskutieren das Erscheinen von Metall in einem großen Teil Europas während einer Periode rapider technologischer, ökonomischer, sozialer und siedlungsstruktureller Entwicklungen; diese Einführung der Metallurgie war eng verknüpft mit der Entstehung einer komplexen ökonomischen und sozialen Organisation, was ein definierender Faktor für das Chalkolithikum ist. Volker Heyd beschreibt, wie ein langzeitlicher evolutionärer Fortschritt für das prähistorische Europa zwischen der Mitte des 5. und dem späten 3. Jahrtausend BC festgestellt werden kann. Das europaweite Glockenbecherphänomen war der Höhepunkt einer ideologischen Dominanz, die den Prozess der Chalkolithisierung Europas vollendete. Harry Fokkens fokussiert auf die Beziehung zwischen den Niederlanden und Britannien, indem er die Frage der „Becher-Migration" neu beleuchtet und die Übertragung von Ideen und materieller Kultur im Licht neuer Funde und Radiokarbondaten betrachtet. Tobias Kienlin dagegen stellt unsere Ansätze zum Verständnis früher Metallurgie in Frage und argumentiert, dass Vorstellungen von Fortschritt und Evolution, die wir technologischem Wandel über lange

Zeiträume hinweg zugrunde legen, angesichts einer komplexeren vorgeschichtlichen Realität zu kurz greifen.

Die dritte Sektion präsentiert eine Reihe detaillierter Fallstudien aus verschiedenen Teilen Britanniens und Irlands. Frances Healy diskutiert die Bayessche Modellierung von Radiokarbondaten vollständiger Körperbestattungen aus dem 4. bis 2. Jahrtausend in England und demonstriert, dass Bechergräber des späten 3. Jahrtausends eine neu eingeführte kontinentale Tradition zu erkennen geben und nicht das Wiederbeleben einer lange bestehenden insularen Tradition. Der verstorbene Ian Shepherd untersucht die Hinweise für eine chalkolithische Periode in Schottland anhand von Bestattungssitten, Metallurgie und Töpferei; er spricht sich für einen geographisch extensiven Beginn des „Becher-Phänomens" mit anschließender Regionalisierung aus, die unterschiedliche Adaptionen erkennen lässt. Steve Burrow reflektiert über die mangelnde Beachtung von Wales, trotz dessen Schlüsselposition zwischen Irland und anderer Hotspots der Archäologie des 3. Jahrtausends, und er benutzt 89 Radiokarbonbestimmungen, um verschiedene Themen anzusprechen, die zu dem Schluss führen, dass gegenwärtig die Datenlage nicht erlaubt ein klares walisisches Chalkolithikum zu definieren. Für Irland untersuchen Neil Carlin und Joanna Brück Siedlungs- und Zeremonialplätze sowie Bestattungs- und Deponierungspraktiken um die Kontinuität vom Spätneolithikum zur Frühbronzezeit deutlich zu machen; sie argumentieren, dass Metall tatsächlich nur eine geringe Rolle dabei spielte sozialen Wandel auszulösen, und dass der Terminus „Chakolithikum" im irischen Kontext unpassend ist. Im Gegensatz dazu erwägt William O'Brien, dass die spezielle Phase der Metallproduktion und -nutzung in Irland seit dem 25. Jahrhundert durch die weitverbreitete Übernahme von Kupfer und Gold geprägt war, und dies vor der Einführung der Zinnbronzemetallurgie, weshalb das Konzept des Chalkolithikums absolut passend sei.

Mandy Jay und ihre Mitarbeiter im "Beaker People Project" untersuchen Mobilität, Ernährung, Umwelt und Subsistenz der spätneolithischen bis frühbronzezeitlichen Bevölkerung Britanniens und wenden insbesondere Isotopenanalysen von Knochen und Zähnen an. Vorläufige Resultate werden vor allem für Individuen aus Schottland und dem östlichen Yorkshire präsentiert. Verschiedene Ebenen von Mobilität scheinen erkennbar zu werden, während in der grundlegenden Ernährung keine signifikanten Spuren von marinen oder anderen aquatischen Ressourcen sichtbar werden. Neil Curtis und Neil Wilkin stellen die Resultate des komplementären „Beakers and Bodies Project" vor, das sich auf Individuen aus bestimmten Teilen Schottlands konzentriert. Sie entwerfen verschiedene Narrative bzw. Modelle, die helfen sollen die regionalen soziokulturellen Identitäten, deren Wandel sowie Interaktionsnetzwerke im Chalkolithikum in diesem Teil Britanniens zu verstehen. Alexandra (Lekky) Shepherd präsentiert Daten für bestimmte Regelhaftigkeiten in der Lage der Körper in Verbindung mit Becher-Stilen in Hockerbestattungen im britischen Chalkolithikum bzw. der Frühbronzezeit; sie kann hier demonstrieren, dass die Bestattungsmuster vor allem durch Gender definiert werden.

Die letzten drei Artikel dieses Bands widmen sich dem allgemeineren Thema der Beziehungen zwischen der ökonomischen, monumentalen und funeralen Nutzung der Landschaft. Mike Allen und Mark Maltby gehen die vorliegenden geoarchäologischen Daten und Tierknochenensembles durch um Hinweise auf signifikante, wenn auch dezente Änderungen zu finden, die während der und als Ergebnis der Becherperiode entstanden. Sie stellen eine klare Zunahme im Ackerbau fest und Änderungen in Tierhaltungspraktiken. Paul Garwood untersucht die räumliche Verteilung und Frequenz früher Becherbestattungen in Britannien aus einer Landschaftsperspektive um zu zeigen, wie eine Reihe unterschiedlicher räumlicher Strategien Beziehungen zwischen Monumenten, Räumen, Menschen und Praktiken ausdrückten. Rosamund Cleal und Josh Pollard schließen den Tagungsband ab mit ihrer Neubewertung der Landschaften von Stonehenge und Avebury. Sie sprechen sich für eine „lange Sicht" aus, d.h. dass das Erscheinen mit Bechern assoziierter Metalle im Kontext einer Reihe von Entwicklungen verstanden werden muss, deren Ursprünge in den vorangegangenen Jahrhunderten liegen und deren Wirkungen bis in die entwickelte Bronzezeit andauern.

ACKNOWLEDGEMENTS

The notion of discussing the British Chalcolithic was born from what Mike Allen and David McOmish perceived to be a lack among British archaeologists of engagement with, and consideration of, this concept and of its continental context. This volume derived from the successful conference held by the Prehistoric Society with the School of Applied Science, Bournemouth University in April 2008 which debated the subject. It was co-organised at Bournemouth by Eileen Wilkes and Mike Allen and fully supported by Professor Tim Darvill, to whom we are grateful. Many students at Bournemouth helped with the smooth running of the event, and our discussants, especially Brendan O'Connor, ensured lively debate that is reflected in these papers. Our thanks go to all of them and to the administrative staff who supported the conference.

The production of this volume has benefitted from constructive and apposite comments from an array of anonymous referees, readers, and advisors and from Clare Litt, our editor at Oxbow Books, to all of whom we give thanks. Special thanks are due to David McOmish for his editorial advice and assistance. We thank all the contributors for such excellent thought-provoking contributions and especially to those who, in the latter stages of production, turned revised papers and figures round so quickly and deftly. Our thanks too, to our typesetter, Julie Blackmore, and the rest of the team at Oxbow, for their continuing support for this series.

The Prehistoric Society is grateful for a substantial financial contribution towards the publication of this volume from Historic Scotland. We are also grateful for financial contributions from Aberdeenshire Council, the Marischal Museum of the University of Aberdeen, University College Cork, the Institute of Archaeology and Antiquity of the University of Birmingham and Department of Applied Science, Bournemouth University. Without these the cover price would be out of the reach of many students and young professional archaeologists.

One of the great supporters of the conference and, especially, of this volume was Ian Shepherd. He solicited the first financial contribution from his employers (Aberdeenshire Council) even before we had invited papers from all the contributors! He was always encouraging about the concept of the conference and especially this volume, and the editors, together with many of the contributors, are ever grateful for his support and greatly miss his further contributions to the debate.

EDITORS' PREFACE

The genesis of the conference which spawned this volume was a chance conversation between one of the editors (MJA) and David McOmish, conducted while registering late-comers to a Prehistoric Society day conference at the Society of Antiquaries in London in 2007. The same discussion also led to the proposal for a series of Research Papers (of which this volume is the 4th). The '*Is there a British Chalcolithic?*' conference, held at Bournemouth University on 18–20 April, 2008, attempted to address this question by examining what we can (and cannot) say about the period between the 25th century – when metal using and a range of other novel practices, objects, and ideas appeared in Britain and Ireland – and the 22nd century, when copper began to be alloyed with tin to create bronze, and to explore this period within its broader European context. Clearly this was a time of significant change, when not only metal-using but also a range of other novelties appeared on our shores from mainland Europe, including a new style of pottery (Beaker), novel archery paraphernalia and personal ornaments, and continental traditions of funerary practice. Here lies a curious paradox, for while continental colleagues have long been happy to use the term 'Chalcolithic' to describe the period of pre-bronze metal using on their side of the Channel, there has been a reluctance to embrace that term in Britain and Ireland, as Stuart Needham pointed out in his keynote speech (see Chapter 1), with commentators preferring to use terms such as 'Late Neolithic– Early Bronze Age', or the wholly inappropriate 'Early Bronze Age'. Not only that, but since Gordon Childe and Stuart Piggott wrote about British prehistory, firmly situating 'our' Neolithic and earlier Bronze Ages within their broader European context, in recent decades British archaeologists have tended to be more myopic and insular, often turning their back on continental prehistory. The suggestion, made by Abercromby and others, that the appearance of metalworking and other novelties in Britain and Ireland resulted from immigration by 'Beaker folk' had fallen into serious disrepute by the 1970s. However, the debate about agency and immigration was reignited in the early Noughties, when strontium and oxygen isotope analysis of tooth enamel from the so-called 'Amesbury Archer' near Stonehenge revealed that he must have been raised on the continent; current thinking, based on some of his grave goods as well as his isotopic signature, favours the northern edge of the Alps as an area of origin.

The popularity of the conference and the liveliness of the discussion provided ample proof that the time was ripe to revisit this topic. The Amesbury Archer discovery had prompted a major study of Beaker-associated (and other contemporary) human remains and their grave goods in Britain – Mike Parker Pearson's AHRC-funded *Beaker People Project* (see Jay *et al.*, Chapter 15). The radiocarbon dates obtained by this project added to those already obtained by the National Museums' Scotland dating programme, and further dates commissioned as part of Neil Curtis's Leverhulme-funded *Beakers and Bodies Project* for north-east Scotland (see Curtis & Wilkin, Chapter 16) have resulted in this region arguably becoming the best-dated Beaker province in the whole of Europe. At the same time, the developer-funded archaeology boom that formed part of the 'Celtic Tiger' in Ireland had been producing significant amounts of new information about the Beaker phenomenon there, and the task of synthesising these important data has fallen to Neil Carlin (see Carlin & Brück, Chapter 13). The findings of this work can now be compared with the evidence previously obtained from Billy O'Brien's seminal excavation work at the Beaker copper mine at Ross Island, Co. Kerry (see Chapter 14). In Wales, an area not traditionally associated with much Beaker evidence (but which was later to become an important copper – and probably also gold – producing area), staff at the Amgueddfa Cymru–National Museum Wales were quietly working away with colleagues in Groningen to improve the radiocarbon database for Beaker-associated activities (see Burrow, Chapter 12). And in England, in addition to the *Beaker People Project*, developments in Wessex (including Mike Parker Pearson's *Stonehenge Riverside Project*) were revealing a huge amount of new evidence about practices, beliefs and material culture over the 3rd millennium – including evidence for the construction of Silbury Hill *after* the appearance of Beakers and associated novelties (see Cleal & Pollard, Chapter 20). And John Hunter and Ann Woodward's Leverhulme-funded *Ritual in Early Bronze Age Grave Goods Project* was shedding new light on the artefacts associated with Beaker users in their graves, as well as those dating to the Early Bronze Age proper. All this research, and other work which is mentioned in this volume, had led to an explosion of data, much of it not yet published in its definitive form. The conference provided the opportunity for it to be aired and discussed, for the mechanisms of the appearance of Beakers and associated novelties to be considered, and for reactions to these novelties to be outlined. In doing so, the conference identified important lacunae in our knowledge: in the 40 or so years since Simpson's *'Economy and Settlement in Neolithic and Early Bronze Age Britain and Europe'*, little coherent research seems to have been undertaken on the nature of settlement and subsistence practices (as discussed by Allen & Maltby, Chapter 18). Similarly, it highlighted just how compartmentalised has been our research into this key period of prehistory, with some researchers focusing on funerary pottery, others on metalwork, etc. The need for an integrated and multi-scale approach was agreed by all the participants.

One important element of the conference was the need to consider the continent, not only as the area of origin for the novelties witnessed in Britain and Ireland, but also as a part of the world where the concept of a Chalcolithic has long been accepted. Having input from our continental colleagues proved to be a vital part of the discussion, since it offered a very different perspective. As Marc Vander Linden points out (Chapter 5), 'our' Chalcolithic – or rather, Chalcolithics, since the Irish situation differs from that of Britain – is a very different beast from the Chalcolithics seen on the continent, being much shorter and starting significantly later. He and our German colleagues (Chapters 6, 7, & 9) considered the meaning of the term and the appropriateness of applying it to the 25th–22nd centuries in Britain and Ireland. In mainland Europe, it comes with social, ideological, and economic baggage, since in parts of Europe (especially the south-east), copper production was a significant driver of other activity, and since the Chalcolithic has for some time been regarded as the period of Andrew Sherratt's 'Secondary Products Revolution', and associated with particular forms of hierarchical social organisation (although that formulation is beginning to be revised).

In the papers which follow, authors will debate at length whether this term is really applicable in a British and Irish context. Some will argue that, in the words of Cleal and Pollard (Chapter 20):

'it privileges metal over other material culture and concepts: it implies that metal is the catalyst and medium of change and that the change brought about by its adoption is so profound and rapid that it requires the relabelling of a period as short as 200–300 years'.

Others will contend that:

'there is still a need for chronological frameworks that have broader cultural meaning and emphasise parallel developments in western Europe in the later 3rd millennium. The value of a Chalcolithic is that it focuses our attention on what was an important transition period between two very different worlds' (O'Brien, Chapter 14).

At the beginning of the conference from which this volume arose we asked the question 'Is there a British Chalcolithic?' and the response was very mixed. After two days of lectures and much heated and lengthy debate we concluded with the same question. A show of hands revealed an almost 50:50 split between 'yes' and 'no'– a resounding 'don't know'! Since then, the contributors have had time to reflect further on the question and to develop their arguments for or against: some have hardened their beliefs, others have swayed … As a consequence, there is no consensus presented in these pages and, in some cases, similar evidence is used to develop very different and sometimes contradictory interpretations. To our minds, this is exactly how it should be. The late 3rd millennium was a period of complex and dynamic change and it is fitting that it should continue to engender lively and complex academic debate. As such, the contents of this volume fall precisely within the ethos of the Prehistoric Society's Research Papers series and we present them in the spirit of the Conference, for open discussion, debate, and consideration. We believe that there are seminal papers within these covers and we wait in eager anticipation to hear whether the term Chalcolithic becomes common parlance in the nomenclature of British prehistory.

Mike Allen, Julie Gardiner
& Alison Sheridan

FOREWORD

Mike Parker Pearson

About 30 years ago, the prehistorian Grahame Clark was asked to give a lecture to Cambridge University's student archaeological society. He was long retired and this was a retrospective on the development of archaeology and the challenges of the future. He felt very sorry, he said, for the students because, since his discovery of the Mesolithic, there were no more 'lost' periods of human evolution to be recovered. The main task of archaeology – mapping out the time frame of human history – was thus completed.

All these years later, it is refreshing to recognise the existence of a new period – the Chalcolithic – within British prehistory. Of course, the concept of the Chalcolithic has been known and applied within continental Europe for over a century, but its recognition as a distinct phase at the end of the British Neolithic is cause for excitement and debate.

At the moment, it seems that the British Chalcolithic may not have lasted very long, perhaps just 300 years from 2500 BC to 2200 BC, when bronze use became near-universal within Britain and Ireland. Of course, the dating of Britain and Ireland's earliest copper artefacts is problematic – recycling might well account for their scarcity in and even absence from the archaeological record during the mid-3rd millennium BC. The earliest copper artefacts such as axes tend to be found in contexts that are not amenable to radiocarbon dating.

There is a further problem of whether copper metallurgy was only adopted in Britain with the arrival of Beaker material culture, in particular the Beaker burials whose grave goods occasionally include copper knives, rings and awls. This funerary fashion's appearance in Britain is dated to within the period 2475–2315

cal BC (at 95% probability). It is impossible to know whether this is indeed the period in which the first metals were introduced to Britain, or whether they were introduced decades or even centuries earlier. The marks made by possible metal axe blades on chalk from the henge ditch at Durrington Walls can be dated to before 2460 cal BC. The presence of just one flint axe fragment among the 80,000 pieces of worked flint from the preceding settlement at Durrington Walls (beginning in 2525–2470 cal BC and ending in 2480–2440 cal BC, at 68% probability) raises the possibility that copper tools were widely in use at the beginning of the British Beaker period or even before.

Although we live with the legacy of earlier archaeologists' technologically defined prehistoric eras of stone, copper, and bronze, few would subscribe any more to Gordon Childe's brand of historical materialism in which metal technology was the motor of economic, social, and ideological transformation in later European prehistory. Over half a century later, a fully social archaeology has emerged, one which recognises the complexity of human agency and of our relationships with material culture. Yet we still struggle to explain the processes behind the profound changes in the 3rd millennium BC. Just how important was copper as an agent of social transformation? Within what social and economic conditions was metallurgy adopted? Do 'culture historical' migrationist interpretations offer sufficiently persuasive explanations for culture change?

The contributions to this book ask these and many more questions. They draw upon the analysis of styles and composition of ceramics and metal artefacts, new radiocarbon chronologies, landscape contexts of funerary monuments, isotopic analyses of human bones and teeth, and the evidence for land use and economy.

Evidence from this period is elusive and yet compelling. This was the time of Stonehenge and also the era when labour mobilisation for large-scale public works was replaced by the decentralised, perhaps more kin-based building of round barrows. Much research has gone into the reasons for, and development of, Stonehenge but there has been relatively little consideration of why it declined and how, or whether, the Beaker way of life may have been involved in its demise.

Only a small percentage of the population received funerary rites which are recoverable; the remainder are archaeologically invisible. Are the interred the elites of their day, or sectarians whose inhumation practices set them apart? Or groups whose choice of funerary rites meshed with neither social status, ethnic affiliation, nor religious belief? The Amesbury Archer – the most lavishly equipped Beaker burial in Europe – gives some idea of the degree to which portable wealth might have been accrued by certain individuals. The placing of 180 cattle skulls on a burial mound at Irthlingborough also shows how economic capital was similarly controlled and mobilised.

Dwellings from this period are largely invisible, leading some archaeologists to speculate that people lived in tents or in similarly ephemeral structures. However, recent excavations of houses at Durrington Walls and Marden henge are now providing a glimpse into this neglected aspect of life in the 3rd millennium BC. Beaker period houses are exceptionally rare anywhere in Europe; the Outer Hebrides of Scotland are one region where the remains of houses from this period have survived agricultural destruction yet still await investigation.

I mention these latter aspects because there is little coverage of them in this book, and researchers will wish to investigate them in years to come. For the moment, though, this book sets out the analytical frameworks, the regional syntheses, and the state of the art. It is a ground-breaking volume which addresses one of the most momentous changes in British and European society before the creation of the Roman Empire.

1

Case and Place for
the British Chalcolithic

Stuart Needham

A part of the late 3rd millennium BC, two to three centuries in duration (c. 2450/2400–2200/2150 BC), can be defined as the Chalcolithic, or Copper Age, terms that have historically been eschewed in British prehistory. However, the definition and labelling of this period are arguably essential if we are to lay terminological confusion to rest, and the growth of a reliable radiocarbon dataset eases the task of chronological definition. This contribution sets out to characterise the British Chalcolithic by focusing on key aspects of the two cultural complexes that were involved – the insular Late Neolithic Grooved Ware culture and the continentally derived Beaker culture, the latter initially brought by incomers and progressively adopted by indigenes. Early Beaker grave assemblages with distinctive goods are separated into three Association Groups, largely of temporal significance. The broad trajectory of insular ceremonial monument construction throughout the 3rd millennium BC is set out and the span of the Chalcolithic located within it. It is argued that, despite their radically different outlook on the world, these coexistent cultures interrelated with one another from the outset and thereby set in train a highly dynamic situation as disparate interests were melded into common goals. It is this dynamism as much as any other feature which characterises the British Chalcolithic.

Do we need a Chalcolithic? Why insert a period of relatively short duration into the broader trajectory of prehistory when we have managed without it for so long? One answer lies in terminologies and the way in which they affect mutual comprehension. It is no exaggeration to say that the later 3rd millennium has been dogged by terminological confusion more than any other period in British prehistory. Most prehistorians think in terms of the Late Neolithic extending down towards the end of the 3rd millennium, based on the continuation of certain 'type fossils' such as henges or Grooved Ware. Yet a new age of metal, Beakers and single graves was ushered in soon after the middle of that millennium and long unbroken sequences in these major cultural attributes often made it convenient to embrace their whole span as 'Early Bronze Age' (eg, Case 1966, 168ff). This problem was sometimes tackled head on, for example, Colin Burgess' nuanced definition of where the Late

Neolithic gave way to the Early Bronze Age (Burgess 1979). Substituting another oft-used label, the 'Beaker period', presents its own problems because it overlaps both the latest Neolithic and the material and sites that are accepted as classic Early Bronze Age. It is no wonder that it is difficult for anyone – whether specialist, generalist, or lay-person – to make sense of this crucial period of change with such divergent terminologies for what is the same bracket of time. It is a recipe for confusion at every deeper level of analysis and interpretation.

It is vital to emphasise at the outset, however, that if we dispense with these discordances in period name it does not exclude genuine overlap between quite different cultural manifestations. Period structures are of value precisely because they provide common templates against which the examination of cultural inter-relationships can take place. They facilitate rather than obstruct the inter-comparison of different specialist views on those relationships. And changes in prevailing interpretations of critical relationships may themselves act to modify the period framework. In this way it becomes evident that a defined period is itself always a part of the interpretative edifice; there is nothing inherent or immutable in any period definition.

The period that concerns us here is undeniably one of certain critical overlaps and thus unusual tempo-cultural complexity. It features certain cultural manifestations rooted in the previous era alongside others that are novel and yet others that anticipate important later developments. Indeed, it is this very overlap which has always excited considerable interest in the later 3rd millennium and might be more of a defining feature than any single material or behavioural attribute. Elsewhere, I likened the Chalcolithic to the European Renaissance, when sweeping change came in the arts, science, and technology, and in social, economic, and political institutions (Needham 2008). These two periods cannot be closely analogous for the obvious reason of their markedly different social contexts, but my point is that the Chalcolithic is likewise a period which saw radical change in many, perhaps most, aspects of culture. Moreover, it was dynamic and thus characterised as much by its rate of internal development as

its conformity to a period ethos. This aspect of marked change might encourage some to view it as a relatively drawn out 'transition', but it seems to the writer that this would be a travesty for it would undervalue the dynamic qualities of certain cultural situations relative to other, more static ones.

Historical perspectives

There has never been any generally accepted Copper Age or Chalcolithic for Britain despite widespread recognition of the utility of such a stage elsewhere in Europe (Gibson 1988; but see appendix I in Burgess 1992). There was even a long period of debate on whether there was a copper-using stage preceding that of bronze in Britain and Ireland. Space only permits the briefest of reviews of the relevant literature. As long ago as the mid-19th century Daniel Wilson believed there was a 'transitional age of copper' (Wilson 1851, 319–20; O'Connor 2008, 119), yet later, John Evans in his seminal work was doubtful of a discrete 'Copper Age' in Britain or even Europe (Evans 1881, 2, 455ff).

After the turn of the 20th century Oscar Montelius was convinced that Britain and Ireland, like much of continental Europe, had a 'Copper Age that ... could also be considered as the last part of the Stone Age' (Montelius 1909, 99). George Coffey, writing more specifically about the Irish evidence, accepted this position, although he questioned Montelius' absolute dating (1913, 3–4). He states explicitly that 'In Ireland the first metal used was copper' (*ibid.,* 6). Early metal analyses and a few key hoards were mustered to show that halberds were among the early types, alongside early styles of axe, knife and awl. A 'Copper period' was broadly accepted thereafter for Ireland (eg, Ó Ríordáin 1937, 305).

Meanwhile the lack of analyses for early British metalwork left Abercromby uncertain as to which objects were copper and which bronze (1912, 54) and in the following decades works by leading scholars continued to plunge straight into a full-blown bronze economy introduced from outside, even when aware that some early objects were of unalloyed copper (eg, Kendrick & Hawkes 1932, 99; Childe 1940, 112). This difference of perception between the two islands was only finally eroded by the first significant programme of metal analysis conducted under the auspices of the Ancient

Mining and Metallurgy Committee of the Royal Anthropological Institute during the 1950s. Nearly 100 objects of early type, from Britain as well as Ireland, were analysed and the majority proved to be of copper without tin. This culminated in explicit discussion of the 'metallurgy of copper' and recognition that this was established before the subsequent introduction of bronze alloying, the latter still within the currency of Beakers (Coghlan & Case 1957, 100).

From this platform, a copper-using stage became accepted at the beginning of the 'Bronze Age', even though there was often uncertainty over the degree of overlap with subsequently introduced bronze metallurgy (eg, Britton 1963; Piggott 1963; Case 1966; as well as Hawkes' unpublished but widely circulated Scheme for the British Bronze Age of 1960). For Dennis Britton, broad-butted axes and tanged flat daggers were the prime types of copper object belonging to a copper-using phase within a 'Late Neolithic' milieu, a cultural ascription for the earliest metalwork most often followed. Despite broad acceptance, there were still reservations about the strictness of the copper/bronze succession and a tendency for the time-span to remain compressed (Piggott 1963; Case 1966; Harbison 1969). Chronological compression arose partly from the view that the introduction of metals to Britain and Ireland could not have preceded the beginning of Reinecke's stage A in central European chronology, a view now overturned, but even more extreme effects arose from spurious cross-correlations between early metalwork and material in Wessex culture graves. Harbison, for example, considered that even the earliest Irish metal axe type (Lough Ravel) probably overlapped with early Wessex and he could not conceive of insular metallurgical origins before *c.* 1750 BC (1969, 72, 82).

Although cultural context had not gone ignored, up until this point the Chalcolithic question hung entirely on the metallurgical switch from copper to bronze. Colin Burgess changed all this in the 1970s. Not only did he de-couple the more tenuous comparisons made in previous research, but he also began by subdividing copper metalwork into two stages (Burgess 1974, fig. 26, 191–2). More fundamental in conceptual terms, however, was his developed thesis which broke away

from the assumption that metallurgical change was necessarily more important than other cultural change. By the end of the decade he had defined an early metal-using period – the Mount Pleasant period – to comprise not only three stages of copper use but also the succeeding first phase of bronze working (Burgess 1979; 1980). The early beginnings then envisaged for the Mount Pleasant period (cited at the time as *c.* 4100 BP, main intercept at around 2650 cal BC), were inspired by a few early and imprecise radiocarbon associations, and have since been tempered by much better dating evidence. But the principle Burgess set in defining periods on the basis of holistic cultural evidence is pivotal. Writing in the mid-1990s the present writer likewise put the earliest bronze metalwork in the *Metal-Using Neolithic* along with preceding copper metallurgy (Periods 1 & 2; Needham 1996, 123). However, the much augmented dating evidence now available has improved our understandings of alignments between different cultural manifestations and led to a modified configuration in this paper. Paradoxically, the phase of copper metallurgy can now be argued to coincide with other crucial cultural switches and *Chalcolithic* comes into its own as a fitting term.

Defining the Chalcolithic

The beginning of the Chalcolithic might be defined in one of two ways: either, the first appearance of the complete novelties – Beaker material culture including metalwork and Beaker ritual practices, especially burial; or alternatively, a point in time at which these became 'significant' (Gibson 1988, 193). Deciding between such options can be difficult. In pragmatic terms, the excellent archaeological visibility and distinctiveness of Beaker burials, Beaker material culture and the metalwork makes it easy to opt for 'first appearance' as the defining moment. This may actually make best sense also in historical terms. Evidence increasingly points to the first Beaker arrivals having been effectively simultaneous (in terms of archaeological chronologies) across large areas of Britain and Ireland and, given marked differences in virtually all aspects of culture (below), it is inconceivable that indigenous people would not immediately have taken note of the incomers. Beyond direct encounters, hearsay would inevitably spread word of the aliens far and wide, fast; the composite cultural picture in Britain would have changed rapidly on the first arrival of, or contact with, Beaker people. This is not a question of the indigenous Grooved Ware population immediately changing their ways, but rather the creation of a whole new reality of perceptions and relationships with the potential for both explicit and hidden effects.

Two variant historical trajectories need to be addressed for the beginning of the Chalcolithic. The first, much debated over the years (eg, Case 1966; Harbison 1979; Burgess 1979), is that metallurgy was introduced to Britain and (especially) Ireland prior to the arrival of Beaker people or the Beaker culture. This is difficult to accept or reject definitively because so much of the earliest copper metalwork has no association with other cultural material and no independent dating. But the typological arguments raised for such pre-Beaker introductions are at best ambiguous and as yet there are not even any recognised imports of pre-Beaker date.

The second variant trajectory involves the arrival of the distinctive Beaker cultural material *prior* to the first Beaker burials here, a case recently made for Beaker material at Stonehenge (Parker Pearson *et al.* 2007, 634). A steadily expanding culture will tend to have a 'bow-wave', regions beyond becoming aware of the material and ideological package and the people carrying it prior to any actual migration, settlement or assimilation. These can be deeply intertwined aspects of a single process of expansion; in the right circumstances fore-knowledge of the encroaching culture can be a major factor in drawing it ever further onward (Needham 2007a, 42). In such a model there is a time lapse between first discernible contact, which might result in exchanged material and ideas, and the first definitive adherence to the new cultural values (whether by incomers or indigenous people), but this may be brief in archaeological timescales.

For Britain there are still no occupation or ritual deposits containing Beaker material culture that can be securely dated earlier than the first Beaker burials. The specific case of two Beaker sherds in Q-hole 5 at Stonehenge should be reviewed given the uncertainties surrounding the site sequence and its absolute dating. These sherds are very small and the significance of their context is

equivocal; the published section (Sc45.4) shows an undifferentiated fill for the combined feature Q5/R5 (Cleal *et al.* 1995, 177, 246 fig. 141), which makes it impossible to judge whether they were incorporated in the fill during stone erection, demolition, or still later through soil processes. Moreover, the (empty) stone-hole for the later bluestone oval (WA3158) cuts right into the middle of Q5/R5 and evidently impinged on the section line; it is unclear whether the excavator fully unraveled, or understood the detailed stratigraphic interactions at this intersection (Cleal *et al.* 1995, 225–6) and it must remain a possibility that the Beaker sherds were introduced with the cutting or filling of WA3158 (*ibid.*, 219 fig. 120, 233 fig. 129, 246 fig. 141 Sc45.3).

So, setting aside the unproven variant trajectories, absolute dating of the beginning of the Chalcolithic still depends on the earliest reliable dating for Beaker graves. The later 3rd millennium is a particularly poor period for the calibration of radiocarbon dates, but the earliest graves seem to fall within the 25th century BC (Bayesian modelling of dates in Association Group 1a, Appendix 1.1✪). Within a century or two the first Beaker introductions had set in train irrepressible changes in the cultural landscape of Britain. Initially these were changes in scale or intensity – the escalation of Beaker-style burial and material culture in many areas and decline in the use of Grooved Ware and associated material goods. One change of extreme importance but difficult to pinpoint closely in time was the apparent Beaker 'appropriation' of the indigenous monument tradition (see below).

However, around the 22nd century BC there was a set of more marked changes, together suggesting more of a dislocation. There has long been a good case based on metal composition, typology and associations for a relatively swift switch to bronze metallurgy in Britain and Ireland (eg, Needham *et al.* 1989; although see an alternative view in Bray, this volume), a case now endorsed by a good number of critical dates associated with copper and the earliest bronze objects (Appendix 1.1✪; Tables 1.1 & 1.4). Dating evidence for the Grooved Ware 'package' suggests it had all but disappeared by this time, if dubious associations are dismissed (Garwood 1999). Indeed, Ann MacSween (2007) has noted that most reliable Grooved Ware radiocarbon dates in Scotland actually precede 2500 BC and therefore also the earliest Beakers, but dated sites there are few and, Littleour, Perthshire, at least seems to be well dated to the Chalcolithic as defined here (*ibid.*, 374 table 33.1).

Other key changes concern ceramics and associated burial rites. Just as Grooved Ware disappears, Food Vessels and, a little later, 'cinerary' Urns emerge fully fledged on the scene. The intriguing question of their stylistic origins is not of direct concern to this paper, but the temporally butting relationship to Grooved Ware seems to be beyond coincidence. I have suggested elsewhere that even though Beaker material culture, life-style, and ritual practices had become dominant in Britain (*Beaker as instituted culture* – Needham 2005, 209), they may never have been adopted by the total population. The new ceramic-cum-burial traditions were arguably a reaction from a rump of indigenous society which saw advantage in maintaining a degree of cultural autonomy (Needham 2007a).

Interestingly, these new ceramic-cum-burial developments do not appear to have been closely tied to the emergence of bronze metallurgy despite being more or less contemporary with it. There are only occasional examples of early associations between Food Vessels or Urns and bronze metalwork. Meanwhile, to take the regional example of north-east Scotland, one of the powerhouses of early bronze production, it was dominated by Beaker burials during Period 2 with very few Food Vessels (Simpson 1968, 204 fig 48; Curtis & Wilkin, this volume); here the new technology must have been adopted within a mature Beaker milieu even though bronze equipment was only rarely seen as a fitting funerary accompaniment in the region (Needham 2004). Of course, the adoption of bronze metallurgy may have had a different cultural background elsewhere.

The transition to bronze has traditionally been seen as a technological advance. But reconsideration of the Migdale–Marnoch production system of north-east Scotland (*ibid.*) suggested that it was more than this; rather, the new material was adopted as a means of creating a new regional identity and ideological power base and, through this, the region west of Aberdeen gained greater prestige relative to its neighbours. Such a model alters the significance of the metallurgical transition – social competition becomes as important a

factor as any technological advantage. This new slant on the switch to bronze and the fact that it was broadly synchronous with other important social or ritual changes does make the 22nd century BC look like a major fulcrum of change.

One major facet of funerary culture, the Beaker grave sequence, does not provide any obvious break at this point. Phase 2 (*Beaker as instituted culture*) of a three-fold phasing previously suggested (Needham 2005), is now seen to start a little earlier (Sheridan 2007) so the zenith of Beaker burial spans *c.* 23rd–20th centuries BC, and thus both the later Chalcolithic and the first bronze phase, Period 2. There may, however, be some differing regional trends (see below).

To summarise, by explicitly accepting the utility of a *Chalcolithic*, we are acknowledging a period for which the composite cultural landscape was radically different from what went before because of the introduction of a whole new component, that of Beaker culture. Likewise, we are saying this is not yet the classic Early Bronze Age – there is no consistent bronze alloying; there is no regular construction of round mounds for burial, nor therefore the development of barrow cemeteries proper (although Chalcolithic graves can cluster together); there are not yet the archetypal Early Bronze Age ceramic forms, Food Vessels and Urns. Defining a Chalcolithic gives us a way of resolving the terminological difficulties that derive from adherence to the Three-Age system (Table 1.2).

Beaker grave chronologies and assemblage definitions

An attempt was made in 2005 to make sense of radiocarbon dated Beaker graves, taking into account the patterns in artefact associations and proposing a new typological scheme for British funerary Beakers (Needham 2005). Since then many more dates have been generated, both *ad hoc* and through the *Beaker People Project* (BPP– I am grateful to Mike Parker Pearson for permission to draw on the dates generated so far) and the *Beakers and People* project (see Curtis & Wilkin this volume). It is too early to generalise across the whole sweep of the country and across the whole spectrum of funerary Beaker styles, but some summary comments are merited.

Site	Grave goods	Summary context	¹⁴C date BP	Cal date BC 1-sigma, 2-sigma	Key references
Boscombe Down West, Amesbury G85 (burial 2), Wiltshire	Dagger, wooden handle traces; bone socketed pommel; 3 slender bronze rivets (grip or pommel fixings); flint striker; sphagnum moss, yew leaves, *Mnium undulatum* and *Hypicum* leaves; organic remains of ?bag	Inh: male; in rectangular grave with traces of charred wood coffin/lining; SW quadrant of ring-ditch & denuded barrow (prob. later)	?3870±35 SUERC-26188 (GU-19937)	**2450–2290** 2470–2210	Newall 1930–2, 434–5; Moore & Rowlands 1972, 44 E, pl IIE; Gerloff 1975, no 66; BPP Sk310 Uncertainty as to whether sampled skull really from this context
Radley Barrow Hills barrow 3, Oxfordshire	Dagger	Inh: ?male; in sub-rectangular grave, centre of ring-ditch under mound remnant	3785±90 OxA-4355	**2395–2385** **2345–2125** **2090–2040** 2470–1970	Atkinson 1952–3, 23–4; Barclay & Halpin 1999, 152–3
Garrowby Wold 32 (burial 4), E Yorkshire	Dagger; bone slotted pommel	Inh: male; in grave, near centre of plough-denuded barrow	3729±29 OxA-V-2199-33	**2200–2125** **2090–2045** 2205–2030	Mortimer 1905, 146, fig 391; Gerloff 1975, no. 43; BPP Sk96
Rameldry Farm, Fife	Dagger; 5 jet conical buttons (1 with tin-inlaid decoration); 1 stone conical button (lizardite)	Inh: ?male; in stone-slab cist set in sub-rectangular grave	3725±40 GU-9574	**2200–2040** 2280–1980	Baker *et al.* 2003; Sheridan 2007, 185
Gravelly Guy (context 4013/12), Oxfordshire	Dagger with 6 copper rivets; antler tanged pommel; LN Beaker; flat medium–broad bracer (4-hole); sponge-finger; antler rod; flint scraper & flakes	Inh: male; in wooden chamber in grave, centre of ?annular palisade slot	3709±35 UB-3122	**2190–2180** **2140–2035** 2205–1980	Lambrick & Allen 2004, 51–61, 78 fig 2.18, 82–93
Gask Hill, Collessie, Fife	Dagger; gold corrugated sheet hilt band	Cremation in pit under SE quadrant of large cairn	Weighted mean: 3694±40, 3695±45 GrA-19054 (crem. human bone) 3690±80 OxA-4510 (hide from sheath)	**2140–2025** 2200–1960	Anderson 1876–8; Gerloff 1975, no. 84; Sheridan 2007, 185
Bught Park, Inverness, Highland	Dagger	Inh: male; in slab & dry-stone cist set in pit	3695±31 OxA-V-2247-48	**2135–2035** 2200–1975	Kirk & McKenzie 1953–5, 7–10; Henshall 1968, 190 no. 11, 179 fig. 40; Gerloff 1975, no. 75; Wilkin *et al.* 2009
Corkey, Co Antrim	Knife (Harbison: type Corkey); tripartite Food Bowl	Unburnt bones: in cist	3680±50 GrA-5409	**2140–1980** 2205–1930	Harbison 1969, no. 16; Ó Ríordáin & Waddell 1993, 85, 179 fig. 108; Brindley 2007, 55

Table 1.1: (this page and the following two pages) Radiocarbon dated graves with Period 2 (earliest bronze) daggers in Britain and Ireland. For dated graves of Period 1 (Chalcolithic), see Appendix 1.1①

Note: Dates are all on human bone unless otherwise specified. Calibrations use OxCal 4.1, but have been simplified: end dates have been rounded (usually outwards) to half-decades; discrete calibrated ranges coalesced for 2-sigma when over 25 years apart, but kept separate for 1-sigma when over 25 years apart; discrete ranges with minimal probability attached (<1%) are excluded. BPP – Beaker People Project; Inh – inhumation. Bayesian modelling of this data set, excluding Amesbury G85 and Manor Farm, gives a start boundary peaking at 2200 cal BC and an end boundary peaking in the mid-20th century cal BC. Some of the later dates, however, could individually indicate deposition early in Period 3.

Site	Grave goods	Summary context	^{14}C date BP	Cal date BC 1-sigma, 2-sigma	Key references
Shuttlestone Plantation, Parwich Moor, Derbyshire	Dagger, traces horn hilt; bronze flat axe-head with traces wood handle & leather; jet/shale disc bead; 'circular flint' (?scraper); remains skin clothing or shroud; fern fronds	Inh: male; on floor of grave under internal cairn within mutilated mound	3680±30 SUERC-26172 (GU-19924)	**2135–2025** 2190–1965	Bateman 1861, 34–5; M.A. Smith 1957, GB.19; Gerloff 1975, no. 54; Marsden 1977, 48; Vine 1982, 221; Needham *et al.* 2010, 369–71; BPP Sk 213
Aldro 116 (burial 2), E Yorkshire	Dagger; LC/LN Beaker on SE lip of grave – likely contemporary deposit	Inh: at base of oblong grave 'B', near centre of ring-ditch under barrow	3679±32 OxA-V-2199-43	**2135–2025** 2190–1960	Mortimer 1905, 54–5, figs 98–9; Gerloff 1975, no. 50; BPP Sk81
Gristhorpe, North Yorkshire	Dagger; whalebone socketed pommel; flint knife; 2 flint flakes (1 axe resharpening); birch-bark container; wooden waisted fastener; pig-fibula point/pin; foot bones of fox & pine marten (presumed furs)	Inh: male; in log coffin (oak), embedded in clay & covered by 'oak branches'; all under mound	3671±32 OxA-16844 (tooth dentine) [3590±100 HAR-4424 overlying oak branches]	**2135–1980** 2140–1950	Williamson 1872; Gerloff 1975, no. 55; N. Melton, C. Batt & A. Sheridan – pers.comm.
Foxley Farm (burial 15), Eynsham, Oxfordshire	Dagger; bone socketed pommel; Beaker (MC); frags 2 or 3 hollow bronze tubes – hilt studs or beads	Inh: male; in sub-rectangular grave; in 'flat' cemetery	3650±30 SUERC-26193	**2120–2095** **2040–1960** 2135–1935	Leeds 1938, 10, 18–9, 22 no. 15, 29 fig 6; M.A. Smith 1956, GB14; Gerloff 1975, no. 41; BPP Sk312
Lockerbie Academy (F33), Dumfries & Galloway	Dagger, in animal hide sheath; traces horn hilt plates; frags bronze corrugated hilt band; flint barbed-and-tanged arrowhead	No surviving skeletal remains; in sub-rectangular pit covered by capstone; possibly remains of ring cairn	3645±35 SUERC-19817 (animal hide)	**2120–2095** **2040–1950** 2135–1920	Kirby 2011
Lockington site VI (pit F5), Leicestershire	Dagger (Quimperlé type); 2 sheet-gold embossed armlets; sherds from lower bodies 2 Beaker vessels	Hoard in shallow oval pit (0.7 x 0.5 m) on line of palisade gully (int. diam. 37 m), N of centre; ring-ditch & mound later than palisade	3910±60 OxA-6173 3630±55 OxA-6447 (both on sheath remains (*Salix* sp.))	**2475–2300** 2570–2205 **2120–2095** **2040–1920** 2195–1875	Hughes 2000 Later of 2 dates favoured, but discrepancy unexplained
Candleston Castle, Merthyr Mawr, West Glamorgan	Dagger, in S. cell of cist; Food Vessel (or sherds of), in N. cell	Cremated bone: in long rectangular stone cist, poss. 2-phase	Weighted mean: 3620±25; 3630±35 GrA-27615 3605±35 GrA-27614	**2025–1945** 2035–1900	Gerloff 1975, no. 48; Savory 1980, 130 no. 326; Brindley 2007, 367
Carrick Drive, Dalgety Bay (cist 2), Fife	Dagger (early midrib type); animal limb bone; concentration of meadowsweet (*filipendula*)	Inh: male; in slab-cist; cup marked slab over S. corner	3610±30 OxA-V-2247-46	**2020–1930** 2035–1885	Proudfoot 1997, 10–20 (N. arrow incorrect in illus. 13); Wilkin *et al.* 2009

Site	Grave goods	Summary context	¹⁴C date BP	Cal date BC 1-sigma, 2-sigma	Key references
Hill of West Mains, Auchterhouse, Angus	Dagger (early midrib type); sheath-mount of horn with bone/ivory pegs. 2 further decayed bronze objects within external walling	Partly burnt bones in larger of double-compartment cist surrounded by stone walling; under turf mound & kerbed cairn	3610±50 GrA-19990	**2030–1900** 2135–1780	Henshall 1968, 180–1 no. 3; Gerloff 1975, no. 100; Sheridan 2007, 185
Moylough, Co Sligo	Dagger (slightly lenticular blade section) – heat-contorted blade often reconstructed as halberd, but better as dagger	Cremation in small stone-slab cist; decorated underside of capstone	3610±40 GrA-14775	**2025–1920** 2130–1880	Harbison 1969, no. 303; Brindley 2007, 372–3
Seafield West (context 232), Inverness, Highland	Dagger; flint flake	Inh (decayed): in log-coffin within sub-rectangular grave, W. of centre of ring-ditch; poss. cairn remnant	Weighted mean: 3600±30 GrA-27037/27039	**2020–1910** 2035–1885	Cressey & Sheridan 2003, 51–2, 56–63; Sheridan 2007, 185 Previous date of 3385±45 now thought problematic
Manor Farm (context SF 55), Borwick, Lancashire	Dagger; bronze flat axe	Inh: on OGS, close to centre of ring-cairn; under cairn infill	3450±70 HAR-5661 (animal bone) 3270±80 HAR-5628 (unburnt human bone)	**1880–1685** 1950–1540 **1630–1450** 1745–1405	Olivier 1987, 141 Dates always looked too late

Cal BC	'Perfect' [14]C BP	Period	Sub-period	Beaker sequence
Pre-2450/2400	Pre-3920	Late Neolithic		
2450/2400–2300	3920–3840	Chalcolithic	Earlier	1: pioneering
2300–2200	3840–3780		Later	2: fission horizon
2200–2150	3780–3730	Chalcolithic/EBA		2: floruit
Post-2150	Post-3730	Early Bronze Age		2: floruit 3: late use/re-use (post-1950 cal BC)

Table 1.2: An outline chronology for the British Chalcolithic
Note: the 'Chalcolithic/ Early Bronze Age' of *c.* 2200–2150 BC could represent either or both of: i) a genuine longish transition; ii) greater than usual overlap in radiocarbon determinations due to the transition being straddled by a calibration-curve wiggle

There are now a sizable number of dates for the Short-Necked (SN) Beakers that predominate in northern Britain; it is now clearer than ever that the great majority occupy a relatively contained chronological horizon, *c.* 2300–2100 BC (Sheridan 2007 and Curtis & Wilkin, this volume). A few later determinations probably indicate a 'tail' of later funerary use. Occasional earlier dates may be statistical outliers, but if the form *did* begin earlier, it would appear to have been sparse until after 2300 BC.

The picture for Low-Carinated Beakers (LC) now makes an interesting contrast. Despite virtual unanimity among Beaker researchers that this was probably the earliest funerary form in Britain, there has been no consensus on its longevity, not least because past radiocarbon results had not looked exclusively early (Needham 2005, 185, table 1); the situation was further confused by failure to distinguish between an early form and a particular decoration, all-over-cord. The still modest body of closely associated dates for LC Beaker graves points to a genuinely early *floruit*: eleven contexts, mainly but not exclusively from the south of Britain, have central determinations falling before 3845 BP (intercept date 2290 cal BC), and two others are only a little later (Table 1.3). Five still later dates are well spread; two should probably be suspended from serious chronological evaluation and another (Nether Criggie, Aberdeenshire) may involve multiple burial.

Although Mid-Carinated forms (MC)[1] can occur early, classically at Radley Barrow Hills, Oxfordshire, but now also at Thomas Hardye School, Dorset, to judge from radiocarbon dating and grave assemblage (Appendix 1.1☻), they were basically coming into funerary use as LC Beakers were phasing out. In reality this may simply reflect a subtle shift over time in the preferred position of the carination. They seem to peak at the beginning of the Early Bronze Age (Period 2), although the good number of MC vessels, including the specialised variant TMC (Tall Mid-Carinated), that are present in Association Groups Ib and Ic (Appendix 1.1☻) demonstrate their growing importance in funerary usage within the later Chalcolithic.

There are still no more than 20 Long-Necked Beakers (LN) dated, despite their large numbers in graves in southern Britain, but it is striking that there are no convincing early examples and they show a decided focus on central dates between 3800 and 3600 BP. On a minimal view this could mean a focus on 2200–2000 BC, though doubtless with distributional tails. This places them essentially in a post-Chalcolithic time-block, a position endorsed entirely by artefact associations. Dates for S-Profile (SP) Beakers are also insufficient, especially when divided into the significant form variants within the series. Many are probably also post-Chalcolithic, but there are undoubted examples from the Chalcolithic, occasionally from an early stage.

In summary, despite the explosion in well-dated Beaker graves since 2005, the pattern of funerary use remains little changed: there was an early phase when most were Low-Carinated, but probably supplemented by occasional Beakers of other forms drawn from the domestic repertoire; this was followed by a dramatic diversification of Beakers in funerary use, formerly dubbed the *Fission*

Site	Date BP	Lab ref	Cal BC 1-sigma, 2-sigma	Reference	Comments
*Radley Barrow Hills 919, Oxfordshire	3930±80 / 3990±80 / mean: 3960±57	OxA-1874 / OxA-1875	**2570–2350** / 2625–2285	Appendix 1.1 Ⓐ	2 burials treated here as contemporaneous (no observed recut) & their respective dates combined
*Chilbolton primary, Hampshire	3935±32 / 3740±80	OxA-V-2271-35 / OxA-1072	**2480–2345** / 2565–2300 / **2285–2030** / 2460–1940	Appendix 1.1 Ⓐ	The 2 dates fail the t-test at 5% confidence level (combined date: 3909±30; **2345**, 2475–2300 cal BC)
Upper Largie, Kilmartin, Argyllshire	3915±40	SUERC-15119	**2470–2345** / 2560–2285	Appendix 1.1 Ⓐ	Hazel charcoal dated – no bone survival
*Boscombe Down West, 1289, Wiltshire	3895±32 / 3877±33 / 3866±28 / mean: 3878±18	OxA-13541 / OxA-13540 / OxA-13623	**2455–2300** / 2460–2300	Appendix 1.1 Ⓐ	Last 2 dates on pig tusks
*Sorisdale, Coll, Argyll & Bute	3879±32 / 3884±46 / mean: 3881±27	OxA-14722 / BM-1413	**2455–2310** / 2470–2285	Sheridan 2007, 109	P. Ashmore increased error term on BM date to ±110
*Radley Barrow Hills (barrow 4A), Oxfordshire	3880±90	OxA-4356	**2470–2205** / 2580–2040	Appendix 1.1 Ⓐ	
*Upavon Flying School, Wiltshire	3873±28	OxA-V-2228-45	2455–2295 / 2465–2215	Goddard 1917; BPP Sk136	
Boghead, Fochabers, Morayshire	3867±70	SRR-687	**2465–2280** / **2250–2215** / 2560–2140	Burl 1984; Kinnes *et al.* 1991, 57	Charcoal from pit group with restorable LC vessel & other sherds; not as reliable as other dates listed here for dating the event; P. Ashmore increased error term to ±110
*QEQM Hospital (primary), Margate, Kent	3852±33	Wk-18733	2450–2210 / 2460–2205	Moody 2008, 80 fig. 35 right, 83 fig. 38, 85 fig. 39	
*Dornoch Nursery, Highland	3850±40	GrA-26515	**2450–2210** / 2460–2205	Appendix 1.1 Ⓐ	
*Boscombe Down Lower Camp, Wiltshire	3845±27	OxA-13624	2400–2385 / **2350–2210** / 2460–2205	Appendix 1.1 Ⓐ	Further dates for disarticulated remains in deposit are effectively contemporaneous (2) or earlier (2)
Aldro 116 (burial 3), E Yorkshire	3795±32	OxA-V-2199-44	**2290–2200** / **2165–2150** / 2345–2135	BPP Sk83; Mortimer 1905, 55, fig. 100; Clarke 1970, no. 1215, fig. 28	1 of 3 burials in 'grave C': ?set of intersecting graves; Beaker close to skull of individual dated
*Gene Function Centre, Oxford	3792±60	NZA-16624	**2340–2135** / 2460–2040	Boston *et al.* 2003; Needham 2005, 185	
Nether Criggie, Dunnottar, Aberdeenshire	3741±32	OxA-V-2166-46	**2200–2130** / **2085–2050** / 2280–2035	Sheridan 2007, 112; Kirk & McKenzie 1953–5, 1–6; Clarke 1970, fig. 322	Carinated Beaker 1 of 3 vessels in cist & no guarantee it was deposited with the individual dated. Kirk & McKenzie depict it with mid-carination (fig. 4.3), but Clarke shows it a little lower

Site	Date BP	Lab ref	Cal BC 1-sigma, 2-sigma	Reference	Comments
*Roundway G8, Wiltshire	3734±30	OxA-V-2228-40	2200–2130 2085–2050 / 2270–2030	Appendix 1.1⊛	
Stoneywood cist 1, Newhills, Aberdeenshire	3686±32	OxA-V-2172-25	2135–2030 / 2195–1965	Sheridan 2007, 101 fig. 11.6.6, 114	Sheridan lists this as a Short-Necked Beaker, but it appears to have deep concave upper body above moderate carination
*Radley Barrow Hills (4660), Oxfordshire	3650±50	BM-2704	2130–2085 2050–1945 / 2195–1890	Appendix 1.1⊛	Now looks too late
*Balksbury, Hampshire	3530±80	Har-5124	1960–1745 / 2130–1665	Cleal 1995	Radiocarbon determination too late

Table 1.3: (including opposite page) Revised list of dates for Low-Carinated Beakers. Dates on human bone unless stated otherwise. Those asterisked are the highest integrity contexts. BPP – Beaker People Project

Horizon (Needham 2005, 205–6 fig. 13) and now back-dated to broadly the 23rd century BC (Sheridan 2007, 99). It should not be assumed that phases of sudden change in burial customs were simultaneous across all regions; it is noteworthy that whereas the Short-Necked Beaker was adopted as the funerary norm in much of northern Britain in the middle of the Chalcolithic, the southern British response in the form of the Long-Necked Beaker may have occurred around a century later, at the end of the period.

The trends in funerary pot use come into sharper focus when considering the grave groups that contain distinctive artefacts – those that can be seen to have changed in form over time or in relation to their immediate associations. The 'key Chalcolithic grave groups' thus selected are summarised in Appendix 1.1⊛. They allow three association groups to be discerned for the Chalcolithic: Ia, Ib, and Ic. Also listed are eight noteworthy grave groups attributed just to the Chalcolithic, and the few Period 2 burials that included objects otherwise diagnostic of the Chalcolithic burials. As many as 50% of the graves listed are discoveries subsequent to Clarke's corpus (Clarke 1970). This much expanded dataset has allowed a fresh attempt at seeking patterns that might bear on either the temporal development of grave assemblages or more socially constructed choices (for example regional emphases). Variations in two of the more regular types covered in this list deserve amplification – tanged daggers/knives and bracers.

The current total of tanged copper daggers and knives stands at 37 coming from 34 sites; where context is known, they are mainly from burials (Table 1.4). This is a big increase since Gerloff's corpus (1975) and allows a new classification which will be detailed elsewhere. Variation in the hilt end is graphically summarised in Figure 1.1; although there is no uni-linear progression in tang shape and the addition of rivets, there are correlations with associations which support the argument for morphological development during the Chalcolithic. In particular, it is likely that riveted forms were added later in the period as suggested, for example, by Clarke (1970, 260–1). New finds have also led to the suggestion of rapid typological evolution from late tanged-and-riveted daggers of copper to the first butt-riveted ones of bronze; the

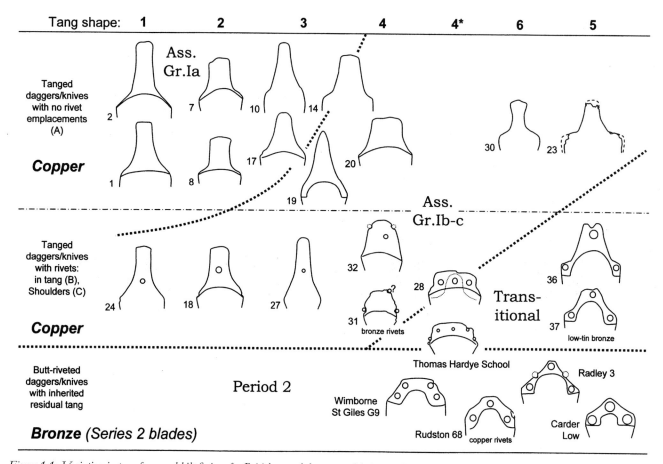

Figure 1.1: Variation in tang form and hilt fixings for British tanged daggers and knives; a few of the earliest bronze, butt-riveted types are also shown. The diagonal lines show the relationship to association patterns (see Appendix 1.1 ☺). Numbers indicate the finds upon which outlines are based, as listed in Table 1.4. Outlines are not to scale.

Tang shape definitions:1) Long, narrow, expanding trumpet-like to fairly sharp shoulders, 2) Moderately long and relatively broader, expanding trumpet-like to fairly sharp shoulders, 3) Long, expanding more steadily (trapezoid) to vestigial shoulders, 4) Relatively short and broad, approximately trapezoidal (variant 4*, very squat and actually proto butt-riveted), 5) Medium-length, approximately trapezoidal, with pronounced shoulders, 6) Medium-length, narrow waisted, with strong shoulders

transition is captured in the *Ferry Fryston* type dating to around the 22nd century BC (Needham 2007b).

There are some 25 associations in Britain between bracers and Beakers. A more comprehensive treatment of bracers has been prepared by Woodward and Hunter (2011), but it is worth showing here patterns in their funerary occurrence in terms of two attributes: firstly, cross-section, which is divided between flat to biconvex (*flat*) and concave/convex (*curved*), and secondly, outline proportions (Fig. 1.2). The concave/convex examples often show other refined features, such as gold stud-caps, neat beadings at the ends, or elegant waisting. One 'flat' example

from Barnack, Cambridgeshire, also has gold stud-caps. This simple categorisation takes no account of other features, notably the number of perforations which have often been used in past classifications (Woodward *et al.* 2006; Fokkens *et al.* 2008).

Flat narrow bracers are predominantly associated with Low-Carinated Beakers (4 of 5; Table 1.5), whereas broader flat forms have an equally strong association with Tall Mid-Carinated Beakers (4 of 6). There is also one curved bracer with this Beaker category, but otherwise virtually all of the curved examples (7 of 9) occur with Necked Beakers (SN, LN, IN). On a strictly temporal reading of this evidence, it is possible to suggest

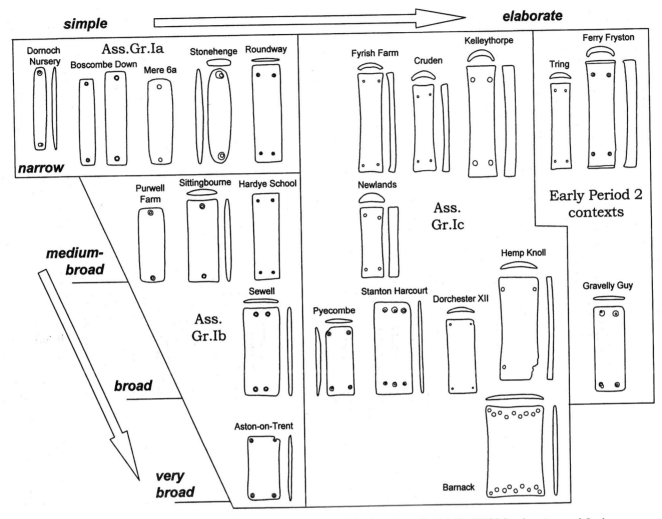

Figure 1.2: Variation in bracer form in relation to the Association Groups defined in Appendix 1.1 ☻. Width:length ratios are defined as: – narrow (≤ 0.29), medium-broad (0.30 – 0.39), broad (0.40 – 0.49), very broad (≥ 0.50)

that the first bracers introduced to Britain were narrow and of simple cross-section and that the subsequent development of more ostentatious examples ran along two paths simultaneously: i) the flat form was progressively broadened, ultimately creating the very broad, gold-embellished example at Barnack, Cambridgeshire; ii) the cross-section evolved (perhaps with some external stimulus) to a more complex concave-convex (or plano-convex) section, which would fit the curvature of an armband well; these vary in width but many classic examples are still 'narrow' in their proportions. This specific form was made from Group VI tuff from the Cumbrian massif (Woodward *et al.* 2006,

538) and the two lines of development had different regional emphases (*ibid*, 533–4).

A full summary of the occurrence of diagnostic object types in the grave groups listed in Appendix 1.1 ☻ is shown in Table 1.6. It can be suggested that objects eligible for well-furnished Beaker graves of the earliest phase could involve: Low-Carinated Beakers, simple tanged daggers and knives (A1, A2, A3), narrow flat bracers, copper or bone pins, and simple gold trinkets (disc- or basket-shaped). Pig tusks, Fire-lighting sets and bone or antler spatulae or rods were also most important in Association Group 1a. Beads of various materials may also be noted here, but they continue into Association Group 1b. Otherwise, however,

Site	Total length (recon-structed)	Blade width/ length ratio	Tang form	Metal compos-ition	Summary context	Key references
Association group Ia						
1. Roundway G8, Wiltshire	258	0.29	A1	BB	Burial of elderly male	Gerloff 1975, no. 1
2. Sutton Courtenay, Oxfordshire	161	0.35	A1	A	Presumed burial (Beaker sherd)	Gerloff 1975, no. 7; Kinnes 1994, A18
3. Hundon, Suffolk	>188	0.28–0.36	A1	A	Presumed burial (found with skull)	Gerloff 1975, no. 3; Kinnes 1994, A19
4–6. Boscombe Down West, (Amesbury Archer) Wiltshire	107.5 (110) 72.5 > 52	0.43 0.65 0.71	A1 A2 A2	BB As-only BB	Burial of adult male	Needham in Fitzpatrick 2011
7. Chilbolton, Hampshire	85	0.49	A2	A/BB mix?	Burial of adult male	Russel 1990; Kinnes 1994, A17
8. Auchterless, Aberdeenshire	230	0.29	A2	BB	Context unknown	Gerloff 1975, no. 2
9. Inverurie area?, Aberdeenshire	110	0.49	A2	BB	Context unknown	Gerloff 1975, no. 11
10. Mere 6a, Wiltshire	≥126	≤0.37	A3	Ag-As	Burial of adult male	Gerloff 1975, no. 6
11. Canterbury area?, Kent	≥111	≤0.46	A3		Context unknown	Gerloff 1975, no. 17
12. River Waveney, Stuston Common, Suffolk	98	0.40	A3	Sb-Ag	Found in river dredgings?	Pendleton 1999, 193
13. Radley 4660, Oxfordshire	> 52	< 0.67	A3/4	BB	Burial of adult male	Barclay & Halpin 1999, 60–5
14. Kenny Hill, Suffolk	301	0.25	A3/4		Surface find in arable field, 1942	Pendleton 1999, 148 no 181, fig. 44
15. Wellington Quarry, Herefordshire	c. 105		?1; highly decayed in ground		Decayed burial	Harrison *et al.* 1999
Association group Ib						
16. Thomas Hardye School (1643), Dorset	118	0.42	(A?)1		Burial of sub-adult/adult male	Smith 2000; Gardiner *et al.* 2007
17. Monkton Road Farm, Thanet, Kent	?	0.60	A3		Burial	Inf. Canterbury Archaeol. Trust (A. Richardson)
18. Sittingbourne, Kent	119 (122)	0.58	B2 (shoulder notches unlikely for rivets)	Blade: BB Rivet: BB	Burial of adult	Gerloff 1975, no. 13; Kinnes 1985, A13
Association group Ic						
19. Barnack, Cambridgeshire	130 (137)	0.50	A3 (+ Ω hilt line)	A	Burial of adult male	Donaldson 1977; Kinnes 1985, A7
20. Winterslow Hut, Wiltshire	135	0.39	A4	A	Burial (no sex/age given)	Gerloff 1975, no. 4
21. West Lilburn, Northumberland	≥ 45	≈ 0.60	(A)4		Burial of adult ?female	Collingwood 1946; Gerloff 1975, no. 240

Site	Total length (recon-structed)	Blade width/ length ratio	Tang form	Metal compos-ition	Summary context	Key references
22. Mid Torrs, Glenluce, Dumfries & Galloway	78 (85)	*c.* 0.63	(A4) – tang edges all lost		Context unknown?	Gerloff 1975, no. 238
23. Faversham, Kent	>237	<0.29	(A)5	BB	?hoard with halberd	Gerloff 1975, no. 5
24. Herringswell, Suffolk	185 (220–250)	0.26–0.31	B1		No context; found caught in agricultural machinery	Martin *et al.* 1993, 80 fig. 19A, 83
25. Shrewton 5k, Wiltshire	103	0.73	B(2/4)	BB	Burial of adult male	Gerloff 1975, no. 12; Green & Rollo-Smith 1984, 275–9, 294–5, 306–7
26. River Thames, Mortlake, London	88 (97)	≈0.48	B3	BB	River find	Gerloff 1975, no. 16
27. Whitby area?, North Yorkshire	100	0.88	B3		Context unknown	Gerloff 1975, no. 15
28. Castell Coch, South Glamorgan	>>80	0.37–0.54	B4* (+ Ω hilt line in one phase)	Blade: BB Rivet: BB	Hoard with 2 halberds	Needham *et al.* 1985, A1
29. Glenforsa, Mull	>90	?	B(4)		Presumed burial (found with 2 Beakers)	Gerloff 1975, no. 14
30–31. Dorchester XII, Oxfordshire	>92	<0.55	A6	Ni-Sb-Ag-As	Burial of adult ?male	Gerloff 1975, nos 10 & 239; Whittle *et al.* 1992, 175–84
	>54	<<0.89	C4	Rivets: **bronze** BB		
32. Kelleythorpe, Driffield (Mortimer barrow 138), East Yorkshire	87 (96)	0.61	C4	Rivet: Ag-Sb	Burial of adult male	Mortimer 1905, 271–83; Gerloff 1975, no. 237; Kinnes 1985, A11
33. Tavelty Farm, Aberdeenshire	>>32		Small frag. only	Copper	Burial of young adult ?male	Ralston 1996, 146 fig. 13; inf. T. Cowie
34. Pyecombe, West Sussex	–	–	Decayed in ground	Copper (traces)	Burial of adult male	Butler 1991
Transitional to Period 2 35. Massingham, Norfolk	215	0.28	C5 (+ Ω hilt line)		Surface find	Gerloff 1975, no. 19
36. Standlow, Derbyshire	150 (152)	0.41	C5 (+ Ω hilt line)	Blade: A Rivet: Ag-Sb	Presumed burial (excavated from cairn)	Kinnes 1985, A14
37. Ferry Fryston, North Yorkshire	159	0.41	C5 (+ Ω hilt line)	Blade & rivets: A – all **bronze**	Burial of adult male	Needham 2007b

Table 1.4: Copper Age tanged daggers and knives in Britain – a revised list. (Defined as series 1 blades in Needham in prep.). For those with known context, associations and radiocarbon dating see Appendix 1.1☉. Tang forms are illustrated in Figure 1.1. Key to metal compositions (see Needham 2002): A – Northover's A-metal; BB – 'Bell Beaker metal'; As-only – arsenic the only significant 'impurity'; others give significant impurities in descending order of magnitude, hence Ag-As – silver followed by arsenic

Beaker type	Flat bracers			Curved bracers
	Narrow	Medium –broad[3]	Broad & very broad	
Low-Carinated (LC)	4		?1[1]	
Mid-Carinated (MC)		1	?1[2]	
Tall Mid-Carinated (TMC)			4	1
S-Profile (SP)		1		1
Short-Necked (SN)	1	1		4
Intermediate-Necked (IN)				1
Long-Necked (LN)		1		2

Table 1.5: Associations between Beaker and bracer types. For relevant contexts see Appendix 1.1☺. 1 Aston-on-Trent: uncertain reconstruction, base missing – might alternatively be Mid-Carinated; 2 Sewell: carination only a little below middle (Relative Height of Carination = 0.45); 3 The uncertain association of a medium-broad flat bracer with MC and Globular SP Beakers at Brandon Fields, Suffolk, is excluded

Table 1.6: Distribution of selected types according to Association Group, as listed in Appendix 1.1☺ Key: [ ] – objects recorded as explicitly within the grave fill rather than around the body; ? – uncertainty in the identification of the object, rather than uncertainty of association (for which see details in listing); X – significant occurrence in Period 2 graves. Emboldened figures emphasise the most significant associations between object type and one or two Association Groups; these may be relate to short-lived currency and/or particular social-group preference

Object type	Ass Gr Ia	Ass Gr Ib	Ungr Chalc	Ass Gr Ic	Pd 2 listed	Pd 2 unlisted	Total
LC Beaker	**15 + 3?**	1					16 + 3?
Gold disc or basket ornament	**7**						7
Pin of copper or bone	**3**	1					4
Pig tusk/tooth (some worked/ modified)	**4 [+1]**				1		6
Copper tanged dagger/knife: types A1, A2, A3	**5**	1?		1			6 + 1?
Flat narrow bracer	**5**	1?		1			6 + 1?
Bone/antler spatula/rod	**5**		1		2		8
Pyrites/marcasite lump	**4**					X	4
Flint striker	**5**	[1]		1?		X	7
Bone simple belt-ring	2						2
Shale/jet belt-ring	1			1			2
Cushion-stone	2						2
Beads of gold, copper, shale or amber	3	2		1			6
Perforated disc/plaque, bone, stone, shale	2	1	1	3			7
Flint barbed & tanged arrowhead	10	2	1	6	3		22
SP Beaker, Low-bellied	2		3				5
LC/MC Beaker	1	2					3
MC Beaker	1	**4**					5
Bone magnifying-glass belt-ring	1	**3**					4
Bone tube-toggle		**3**					3
Flat (medium-) broad bracer		**7**		5	2		14
SP Beaker, mid-bellied		1	1	1			3
Copper tanged dagger/knife: types A4, A5, A6; all B & C		1	1	**6**			8
SN (& IN) Beaker				**15**			15
TMC Beaker				**6**			6
Bone ribbed belt-ring				**5**			5
Curved (narrow to broad) bracer				**8**	3		11
Bone/ivory/antler tanged pommel				2	2		4
Buttons, of amber, shale or jet				2	1	X	3
LN Beaker					**3**	X	3
Copper/bronze tanged dagger/knife: type C5					2		2
Amber belt-ring					**3**		3
Jet/shale pulley-ring					1	X	1
Bronze Series 2 dagger					1	X	
Battle-axe					1	X	
Stone sponge-finger					2	X	2

this group shows important modifications to the repertoire including a trend towards Mid-Carinated vessels, more fancy belt fittings (magnifying-glass and tube-toggle types), and broad bracers. The changes seen in Association Group Ic are perhaps more radical: systematic use of more 'developed' tanged daggers/knives, elaborate bracers, further modified belt fittings (ribbed type), the first pommels of bone-like materials and the first conical buttons, not to mention the obvious key switch to two different Beaker forms (SN, TMC).

Until more high-quality dates are accumulated for the Association Groups, the question of the degree to which they are strictly a temporal succession must remain open. Nevertheless, the particular formal and/or qualitative changes seen independently in three or more different types of object strongly suggest that there was at least in part a temporal shift from Group Ia to Ib to Ic, even if social and geographical realities meant that this was an eclipsing relationship. One further indication of a real social or temporal difference is that there appears to be a subtle shift in the mean orientation of male body position in southern British graves from NW/NNW in Association Group Ia to N in Association groups Ib/Ic (Table 1.7, cf. A. Shepherd this volume). This has not been suspected before because it relies on the fine grouping of a modest number of distinctive grave groups.

Copper axes and halberds were not placed in graves and space here does not permit their discussion. However, it needs to be remembered that they account for the great majority of Chalcolithic metal output and represent distinct deposition and belief sub-systems. Both types exhibit a spectrum of morphologies across Britain and Ireland and internal development of the types during the Chalcolithic is certainly feasible. However, the typological distinctions drawn by Burgess (1979) to create his three *copper* stages can be viewed in ways other than a temporal sequence (Needham 1996, 126; Rohl & Needham 1998, 85–6).

The indigenous monument sequence and the Beaker impact upon it

The focus here is on the more substantial monuments of the later Neolithic, Chalcolithic, and earliest Bronze Age. Excluded are simple and small post- or pit-rings, which have a longer chronology and potentially more diverse cultural and functional connotations (Gibson 1998). 'Hengiforms' – alternatively described as causewayed or segmented ring-ditches – can be seen as a different category of monument (Bradley 2007, 80; Bradley & Lamdin-Whymark 2009, although see also G. Barclay 2005). It is only necessary to summarise the historical trajectory, since henges, great henge enclosures, circles (timber and stone), and palisade enclosures have been well covered in the literature (eg, A. Harding & Lee 1987; Wainwright 1989; Burl 1976; Gibson 1998; 2004; Pitts 2000; J. Harding 2003; papers in Cleal & Pollard 2004; and Larsson & Parker Pearson 2007). The sites discussed in this section are listed in Appendix 1.2⊕ with any radiocarbon dates and key references. The objective is to tie the chronology of monument construction (and subsequent use) more closely to the sequence of material culture and graves. In fact very few sites have been dated with any precision as yet and many judgements on individual sites must therefore remain tentative.

It seems that both the circular enclosures that Jan Harding dubbed as 'formative henges' (Harding 2003, 10–20) and the first of the class 1 henges were in existence in the centuries around the turn of the 4th/3rd millennium BC. Stonehenge I, Wiltshire, and Flagstones, Dorset, are the earliest dated formative henges, while the Stones of Stenness, Orkney, Llandegai A, Gwynedd, and perhaps Balfarg Riding School, Fife (speculatively reconstructed in Needham *et al.* 2006, 22, fig. 17) are more or less contemporary henges. These sites fall towards the end of the period (*c.* 3400–2900 BC) during which *Impressed Wares* (Peterborough Ware) were in their *floruit* and at a time when Grooved Ware had already emerged in the north of Britain (Ashmore 1998; MacSween 2007).

The core time-block for the Late Neolithic in terms of the radiocarbon calibration curve falls between 2900 and 2470 BC (4250–3950 BP). By the beginning of this period Grooved Ware was well-established throughout Britain. The construction of timber circles and henges is best attested at this time at North Mains Ring A, Perth & Kinross, Dorchester site 3, Oxfordshire, Wyke Down, Dorset, and perhaps

Table 1.7: Orientations of burials in southern Britain (south of Humber–Mersey)
Key: F – female; I – infant; M – male; U – unknown sex

Head towards	Ass Gr Ia	Ass Gr Ib	Ass Gr Ic	Ungrouped
SE	F			M
SSE				FF
S		U		
SW				F
W	M			
WNW	M			
NW	MMMI		MM	
NNW	MMMM	M	M	M
N	M	M	U	
NNE		M	M	
NE		M	M?	

Balfarg, Fife (charcoal from packing of posts). However, these projects of moderate scale were now augmented, especially in the later part of the period, by grand enterprises – the great henge enclosures at Avebury, Wiltshire, and Mount Pleasant, Dorset, and the massive timber enclosures at Meldon Bridge, Scottish Borders, Dunragit, Dumfries & Galloway, Forteviot, Perth & Kinross (Kenny Brophy & Gordon Noble – pers. comm.), Hindwell II, Powys, and Greyhound Yard, Dorset. Such colossal monumental developments therefore clearly took place before the first evidence for Beaker contact.

Last, but not least, it is now possible to see the erection of the remarkable sarsen structures at Stonehenge (phase 3ii) as belonging to this aggrandising phase; feature WA2448, long assumed to be the ramp for erecting trilithon stone 56, has now been dismissed from this role (Parker Pearson *et al.* 2007). The feature and its radiocarbon-dated contents can now be divorced from the construction of the sarsen trilithons in particular and the sarsen settings in general. Only two radiocarbon determinations are left to date this phase, but they give a calibrated range of 2620–2480 cal BC (92% confidence; 4023±21 BP, UB-3821; 3985±45 BP, OxA-4840)

The dating evidence for a number of the sites listed in Appendix 1.2⊕ is ambiguous with regard to Late Neolithic or Chalcolithic, but there is little doubt that the kinds of enclosure established earlier continue to be constructed in the later 3rd millennium BC. The impetus for grand projects probably continued into the Chalcolithic. Further great henge enclosures – Durrington Walls and perhaps Marden, both Wiltshire – need not have been significantly later than Avebury and Mount Pleasant. The southern timber circle at Durrington (phase 2E) probably preceded the beginning of the Chalcolithic. Meanwhile, the Avebury landscape was elaborated by the construction of the West Kennet palisade enclosures (sites 1 and 2) and Silbury Hill phase 1; Bayesian analysis has suggested the beginning of mound construction at Silbury was most likely around the later 24th to earlier 23rd centuries BC (Bayliss *et al.* 2007), although subsequent work may already be pointing to the earlier of these two centuries (Leary 2010, 139). The inner mound defined on the basis of Atkinson's excavations (Silbury I – Whittle 1997; phase since sub-divided) was itself sizeable – around 30 m across and 6 m high – and recalls other great barrows which are associated with henges or other circular monuments (Thomas 2004, 104). Of these, the similar-sized Conquer Barrow on the western periphery of Mount Pleasant enclosure has yielded a slightly earlier date on an antler pick in the primary rubble of its ditch (4077±52 BP; 2870–2470 cal BC; BM-795; Wainwright 1979, 67, 186). The pick was dismissed in the excavation report as a redeposited object because it was assumed that the mound had to be later than the great enclosure but, in fact, there is no stratigraphic evidence for sequence. Julian Thomas has suggested, on the strength of OSL dating, that the 9 m high mound of Droughduil in the Dunragit complex, may also date to the Late Neolithic (Thomas 2004; http://www.arts.manchester.ac.uk/archaeology/research/dunragit/ accessed October 2010).

Some of these large mounds associated with ceremonial complexes therefore appeared prior to the phenomenal resurgence of round barrow construction associated with burials in the Early Bronze Age proper. This was not, however, the case at North Mains, where both the henge and the large mound seem to date to just after the end of the Chalcolithic (Barclay & Russell-White 1993), but even here the pairing may echo an association that had emerged earlier at other major complexes. It appears that monumental mounds, presumably inspired by Middle Neolithic antecedents in the landscape, first re-emerged as elements within ritual complexes and were only later given a more explicitly mortuary role.

Aspect	Late Grooved Ware	Early Beaker
Mortuary practice	Excarnation prob. the norm; occasional use of human skeletal material (eg cremated remains & infant burials) to mark particular observances/structures within ceremonial ambit	Definition of tiny mortuary plot, sometimes through enclosure but otherwise simply through grave & minor mound; minimal impact on landscape, but sites remembered through strong genealogical tradition
Cosmology	Framed by celestial observations made at special sites which served as 'world pillars': vertical axis of *access to origins*; ancestors continue to be relatively anonymous within a collective body	Centred on glorification of ancestors & ancestral line as represented by leader figures; strong horizontal dimension to *access to origins* created by dramatic territorial expansion over limited generations, further reinforced by dependency on widespread network for obtaining critical cultural resources
Scale of social gatherings	Medium- & large-scale periodic gatherings at ceremonial sites; feasting at some complexes	Smaller gatherings of kin-group; any larger gatherings would have to be drawn from much wider areas due to population dispersion
Nature of ceremonial	Processions to, around, & within henge monuments & circles: relating to seasonal cycle	Celebration of life of key social members who epitomise group as a whole: both at their death & subsequent remembrance
Social structure	Strongly hierarchical, as reflected in increasing selectivity of participants towards inner sanctums of ceremonial sites; structure founded on *ritual authority* & potentially, therefore, at least partly transmitted through schools of arcane knowledge	Widely scattered extended family units, each with leader: therefore very parochial leadership; however, a degree of ranking achieved between leaders on basis of heroic accomplishments, physical prowess & success in exchange/negotiation both within Beaker network & beyond
Inter-regional contact	Widespread amongst like-minded groups with similar cosmology & symbolic system: therefore essentially confined to Britain/Ireland	Concentrated within affinal groups: therefore widespread, but not necessarily dense network feathering out across W. Europe
Key status- & culture-defining artefacts	Edge-polished discoidal knives, highly finished stone maces, oblique arrowheads, polished bone skewer pins	Stone bracers, copper daggers & knives, barbed-and-tanged arrowheads, ornaments of exotic materials

Table 1.8: Comparison of some key aspects between late Grooved Ware and early Beaker culture groups

Modest-scale henges and circles such as Devil's Quoits, Oxfordshire (combined henge and stone circle), Maumbury Rings, Dorset, and Mount Pleasant site IV (possibly dating a pit circle prior to class 1 henge), cannot, on current evidence, be firmly ascribed to either the Late Neolithic or the Chalcolithic. However, Machrie Moor phase 2, Arran, Milfield North, Northumberland, Woodhenge, Wiltshire, Gorsey Bigbury, Somerset, and Condicote, Gloucestershire, seem best dated to the Chalcolithic or a little later. A few others are more securely post-Chalcolithic constructions, especially when radiocarbon evidence is reinforced by artefact associations as for the timber circles at Sarn y Bryn Caled site 1, Powys. The stone circles at Machrie Moor (phase 4) and the henges of Broomend of Crichie, Aberdeenshire, and North Mains, are also demonstrably late. At the latter site a deposit of cremated bones apparently sealed under the bank has been radiocarbon dated to 2200–1910 cal BC (3665±45 BP, GrA-24007) which implies the addition of the earthwork centuries after post-ring A had stood, even allowing for the latter having utilised mature wood (Barclay 2005, 86, 88).

At Mount Pleasant the reworking of the west

Figure 1.3: A model for cultural interaction during the Chalcolithic period.

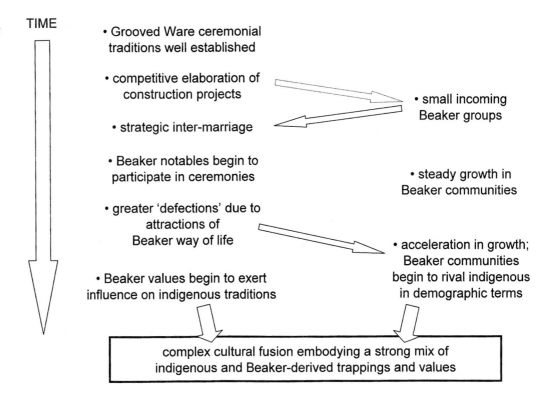

entrance of the great henge most likely took place around the end of the Chalcolithic or after, and the addition of a palisade enclosure within was seemingly a rare large undertaking of the Early Bronze Age proper. The other major site with evidence for significant structural modification at around this time is Stonehenge, with the phase 3iv bluestone settings (Bayliss *et al.* 1997).

There is still a tendency among some researchers to seek some critical influence exerted by early Beaker-using people on ceremonial monuments. This idea may have been encouraged by Beaker cultural debris at a number of henges, such as Gorsey Bigbury, Mount Pleasant, Balfarg, and Stonehenge, as well as by the proximity of Beaker burials to ceremonial sites. At Gorsey Bigbury, the radiocarbon dating and typology of the Beaker-associated deposits (predominantly Long-Necked vessels) in the secondary ditch silts suggests accumulation around Period 2 (ApSimon *et al.* 1976). At Mount Pleasant very little Beaker material relative to Grooved Ware was present in the earliest (ie, earlier Chalcolithic) contexts, but this proportion changed significantly in later stratigraphic

contexts (Longworth 1979). At Balfarg Riding School, there is a significant deposit of Beaker pottery high in the ditch fill (Barclay & Russell-White 1993); the assemblage looks relatively early with much all-over-cord decoration and a variety of pot profiles represented, but it need not belong to the beginning of the Beaker sequence. There is a second issue here too: the radiocarbon dating of the lower ditch silts and the internal rectangular timber structure alike indicate that the enclosure was in use in the centuries either side of 3000 BC, so it may actually have been a centuries-abandoned site by the time Beaker-using communities arrived in the area.

In the case of Stonehenge, Humphrey Case has taken the predominance of Beaker over Grooved Ware sherds to mean that it was essentially a Beaker monument in its stone phase (phase 3; Case 1997). However, this assumes that there would have been comparable material deposition patterns between the two very different ideologies of Grooved Ware and Beaker culture. If Stonehenge was in a dichotomous relationship with Durrington Walls during the Late Neolithic in the manner envisaged by Parker Pearson & Ramilisonina

(1998), then this provides an explanation for the dearth of contemporary artefact deposition; deposition at Stonehenge was instead focused on deposits of cremated human bone, for which three newly-obtained dates now confirm Late Neolithic phasing (Parker Pearson *et al.* 2009). Once Beaker attitudes came to prevail on the site, the attitude to depositing cultural debris (still only a very modest amount) may have changed. Unfortunately, the lack of precision regarding the chronology of the sequence combined with the small size of the Beaker sherds leave us unclear when exactly Beaker influence became important. Predictively, I would suggest that it was unlikely to have been at the beginning of the Chalcolithic when the Beaker population was very small and the indigenous Grooved Ware population was still revelling in its grand lithic achievement. Could the change have come after the burial of a key Beaker individual (sacrificial victim?) in the north-west ditch terminal around the middle of the Chalcolithic? (Appendix 1.1⊛).

While it is clear that Beaker culture 'infiltrated' the indigenous ceremonial scene, it is equally clear that it did not swing the monument tradition around to an entirely new direction. We have little chronological resolution on the timing of this process. If Beaker culture was rapidly expanding during the course of the Chalcolithic from a small *circumscribed and exclusive culture* (Needham 2005) in relation to the indigenous population to an *instituted culture* which had absorbed or infused much of that population, then the appearance of Beaker material on a given site may simply be a product of that change in majority cultural affiliation. Beaker material on a site right at the beginning of the Chalcolithic (if this were ever demonstrated to be the case) is likely to warrant a very different explanation from that occurring on a site for the first time towards the end of the period.

This brief review of the insular monument trajectory highlights that while some monuments saw manifest Beaker-isation during the course of the later 3rd millennium BC, there is no evidence that this took place early in the Chalcolithic. Moreover, the process gave rise neither to significant change in the nature of monument construction, nor to any outstanding novel achievements. If anything, the long-term impact of the cultural fusion of

the Chalcolithic was to curtail 'grand' projects (exception of Mount Pleasant palisade), to reduce the scale of traditional monuments more generally and, by Period 2 to turn their use more towards formal mortuary practice as that practice grew in intensity. The demise of these sites was not sudden and does not help define periods, but it is clear that there was a massive change in emphasis from beginning to end of the Chalcolithic.

Two contrasting cultures: Magnetic Monuments meet Mysterious Metals

If we are right to think in terms of two fairly discrete cultures rubbing shoulders in Britain during the Chalcolithic, was there a clash of cultures or a meeting of minds? There can be little doubt that the two cultures were poles apart at the point of their first interaction in the early Chalcolithic. Table 1.8 attempts to characterise a range of key aspects of society for the two cultures; this illustrates how fundamentally different they were from one another at every level. One could add more specific points such as the technology and design of ceramics. Consideration might also be given to the food economy, but this requires isolating very early Beaker elements from those that might already be complicated by processes of interaction and fusion. Obviously the importance of pigs for feasting at certain Grooved Ware sites stands out as a possible distinction.

The paradigm of the late 1970s and '80s promoted the introduction of Beaker cultural material as a ritual package adopted by native communities. From this point of view it was logical to see its introduction as being deeply intertwined with enhanced monumental expression; the adoption of new and exotic elements within traditional ceremonies could very easily have gone hand in hand with a competitive trend to elaborate further the stages of performance. However, if Beaker introductions were, instead, the result of small incoming groups of people who initially maintained a tightly circumscribed and quite alien culture, then the whole perspective changes. Firstly, their cultural outlook and belief system would not instantaneously have found a place in the monuments and ceremonies of the 'other lot'. Secondly, the incomers would not have had the appropriate skills and experience in mobilising large monument construction – there is no background for this among pre-existing Beaker groups anywhere in western Europe. And thirdly, there is the question why would a still flourishing and numerically dominant population suddenly defer to small bands of incomers in the conduct of their own, centuries-old traditions of belief? Any influence in the early days of contact would probably have been limited and we must give full credit to the indigenous communities for their achievements in this remarkable insular trajectory.

Several writers have commented on the distance at which early Beaker burials were set in relation to active ceremonial complexes (eg, Thorpe & Richards 1984). Of course, it might be argued that this was because henges were not traditionally places of burial, especially if we view the occurrence of deposits of cremated bones on a few sites as due to structured rituals other than formal burial. But a little later, Beaker and other formal burials *did* often come to be placed within the boundaries of ceremonial sites, so it is legitimate to ask: 'why not earlier?'. A case can be made for the early incomers sometimes being drawn towards the indigenous ritual complexes, but even so, they generally maintained a discreet distance. This relationship of 'looking on' is actually wonderfully conveyed by Jane Brayne's reconstruction painting of the Amesbury Archer (http://www.wessexarch. co.uk/projects/amesbury/archer.html). He, his companion and the equally celebrated Boscombe Bowmen were buried on the *opposite* side of the River Avon from the big joint ceremonial complex of Stonehenge-Durrington.

Why should the pioneering Beaker groups have been drawn towards ceremonial complexes at all, given their wholly different lifestyle and beliefs? First, of course, there might be a natural fascination with the spectacle of the ceremonies at these places. But I would argue that there was a more fundamental reason. Even though I have portrayed these communities as 'exclusive' and 'circumscribed', that does not mean they were hermetically sealed from the world around them; that world was totally dominated by indigenous people and the cultural landscapes they had created. Beaker people had to operate

within that world; they would probably have had to negotiate certain rights – notably occupancy rights. Furthermore, there could have been strong incentives for interaction from both sides in order to gain competitive edge over rival groups within their own respective cultures.

From the one side, it is hard to imagine that the elite of the Grooved Ware world would not have been impressed by copper and gold artefacts and would therefore have sought to enhance their individual standing by obtaining such items or at least associating with those who bore metal. These communities were already showing concern with artefactual finery of their own devising, notably highly polished stone mace-heads, flint discoidal knives and bone pins, and highly decorated pottery. Any cross-cultural transmission of rare metal objects would undoubtedly have been hard-won, not least because they were an integral part of *Beaker* identity; transmission would likely involve not just the object but some appreciation of how these objects were situated within the Beaker-constructed world.

Beaker people too had much to gain from successful liaison. A good relationship might ensure a relatively peaceable co-existence – we should not rule out some friction and violence, but there is little evidence for it – but beyond that it is quite possible that second and later generation Beaker individuals, if not first generation, would have begun to see advantage in being accepted within high-ranking indigenous circles (literally as well as metaphorically!). This could have included obtaining a notable position within the processional file. Not only would this have demonstrated enhancement for all who looked on, but it could also have given Beaker people more direct access to the gods and spirits of the land in which they had come to settle.

Taken together these kinds of incentives would, I think, be powerful forces for the establishment of *parleys* without instantly eroding the separateness of their respective existences and cultural identities. Such relationships would likely have led to periodic inter-marriage, most obviously at elite level, but there could have been other tiers of cross-marriage agreed within an established inter-communal relationship. It is perhaps hardly surprising that there was a degree of cultural fusion as the Chalcolithic wore on. Figure 1.3 summarises a possible model of interaction in which the Chalcolithic period is in essence one featuring the reconciliation of two contrasting cultures – a meeting of minds.

Acknowledgements

I am grateful to the conference organisers and a number of other individuals who have contributed in various ways towards this paper: Alistair Barclay, Brendan O'Connor, Paula Gentil, Mike Hamilton, Dave Mullin, Keith Parfitt, Mike Parker Pearson, Andrew Richardson, Alison Sheridan, Neil Wilkin, and Ann Woodward.

Endnote

1 A term now preferred by the writer to 'Weakly Carinated'; Mid-Carinated better encompasses the bulk of the carinated Beaker lineage once the Low-Carinated subset has been set aside. Tall Mid-Carinated Beakers (TMC), previously defined, are a specialised variant within the Mid-Carinated range.

Bibliography

Abercromby, J. 1912. *A Study of the Bronze Age Pottery of Great Britain and Ireland and its Associated Grave Goods.* Oxford: Clarendon Press

Anderson, J. 1876–8. Notes on the character and contents of a large sepulchral cairn of the Bronze Age at Collessie, Fife, excavated by William Wallace, Esq., of Newton of Collessie, in August 1876 and 1877. *Proceedings of the Society of Antiquaries of Scotland* 12, 439–61

ApSimon, A.M., Musgrave, J.H., Sheldon, J., Tratman, E.K. & Wijngaarden-Bakker, L.H. 1976. Gorsey Bigbury, Cheddar, Somerset: radiocarbon dating, human and animal bones, charcoals, archaeological reassessment. *Proceedings of the University of Bristol Spelaeological Society* 14, 155–83

Ashmore, P. 1998. Radiocarbon dates for settlements, tombs and ceremonial monuments with grooved ware in Scotland. In A. Gibson & D. Simpson (eds), *Prehistoric Ritual and Religion: essays in honour of Aubrey Burl*, 139–47. Stoud: Sutton

Atkinson, R.J.C. 1952–3. Excavations in Barrow Hills Field, Radley, Berks. 1944–45. *Oxoniensia* 17–18, 14–35

Baker, L., Sheridan, J.A. & Cowie, T.G. 2003. An Early Bronze Age 'dagger grave' from Rameldry Farm, near Kingskettle, Fife. *Proceedings of the Society of Antiquaries of Scotland* 133, 85–123

Barclay, A. & Halpin, C. 1999. *Excavations at Barrow Hills, Radley, Oxfordshire. Vol. I: the Neolithic and Bronze Age monument complex.* Oxford: Oxford University Committee for Archaeology, Thames Valley Landscapes

Barclay, G.J. 2005. The 'henge' and 'hengiform' in Scotland. In V. Cummings & A. Pannett (eds), *Set in Stone: new approaches to Neolithic monuments in Scotland*, 81–94. Oxford: Oxbow

Barclay, G. & Russell-White, C.J. (eds) 1993. Excavations

in the ceremonial complex of the fourth to second millennium BC at Balfarg/Balbirnie, Glenrothes, Fife. *Proceedings of the Society of Antiquaries of Scotland* 123, 43–210

Bateman, T. 1861. *Ten Years' Diggings in Celtic & Saxon Grave Hills, in the Counties of Derby, Stafford, and York, from 1848 to 1858.* London: George Allen & Sons

Bayliss, A., Bronk Ramsey, C. & McCormac, F.G. 1997. Dating Stonehenge. In B. Cunliffe & C. Renfrew (eds) *Science and Stonehenge*, 39–59. *Proceedings of the British Academy* 92

Bayliss, A., McAvoy, F. & Whittle, A. 2007. The World recreated: redating Silbury Hill in its monumental landscape. *Antiquity* 81, 26–53

Boston, C., Bowater, C., Boyle, A. & Holmes, A. 2003. Excavation of a Bronze Age barrow at the proposed Centre for Gene Function, South Parks Road, Oxford, 2002. *Oxoniensia* 68, 179–200

Bradley, R. 2007. *The Prehistory of Britain and Ireland.* Cambridge: Cambridge University Press

Bradley, R. & Lamdin-Whymark, H. 2009. Pullyhour – a signpost to the past. *PAST* 61, 3–5

Brindley, A. 2007. *The Dating of Food Vessels and Urns in Ireland.* Galway: National University of Ireland, Department of Archaeology; Bronze Age Studies 7

Britton, D. 1963. Traditions of metal-working in the later Neolithic and Early Bronze Age of Britain: part 1. *Proceedings of the Prehistoric Society* 29, 258–325

Burgess, C. 1974. The Bronze Age. In C. Renfrew (ed.), *British Prehistory: a new outline*, 165–232. London: Duckworth

Burgess, C. 1979. The background of early metalworking in Ireland and Britain. In M. Ryan (ed.), *The Origins of Metallurgy in Atlantic Europe: proceedings of the Fifth Atalntic Colloquium, Dublin, 1978*, 207–14. Dublin: Stationery Office

Burgess, C. 1980. *The Age of Stonehenge.* London: Dent

Burgess, C. 1992. Discontinuity and dislocation in later prehistoric settlement: some evidence from Atlantic Europe. In C. Mordant & A. Richard (eds), *L'Habitat et l'Occupation du Sol à l'Âge du Bronze en Europe*, 21–40. Paris: Comité des Travaux Historiques et Scientifiques; Documents Préhistoriques 4

Burl, A. 1976. *The Stone Circles of the British Isles.* New Haven: Yale University Press

Burl, H.A.W. 1984. Report on the excavation of a Neolithic mound at Boghead, Speymouth Forest, Fochabers, Moray, 1972 and 1974. *Proceedings of the Society of Antiquaries of Scotland* 114, 35–73

Butler, C. 1991. The excavation of a Beaker bowl barrow at Pyecombe, West Sussex. *Sussex Archaeological Collections* 129, 1–28

Case, H.J. 1966. Were Beaker-people the first metallurgists in Ireland? *Palaeohistoria* 12, 141–77

Case, H.J. 1997. Stonehenge revisited. *Wiltshire Archaeological and Natural History Magazine* 90, 161–8

Childe, V.G. 1940. *Prehistoric Communities of the British Isles.* London/Edinburgh: Chambers

Clarke, D.L. 1970. *Beaker Pottery of Britain and Ireland.* Cambridge: Cambridge University Press

Cleal, R.M.J. 1995. Beaker pottery. In G. J. Wainwright & S.M. Davies 1995, *Balksbury Camp, Hampshire: excavations 1973 and 1981*, 55–7. London: English Heritage Archaeological Report 4

Cleal, R.M.J. & Walker, K.E. with Montague R., 1995.

Stonehenge in its Landscape: twentieth century excavations. London: English Heritage Monograph 10

Cleal, R. & Pollard, J. (eds) 2004. *Monuments and Material Culture: papers in honour of Avebury archaeologist Isobel Smith.* Salisbury: Hobnob Press

Coffey, G. 1913. *The Bronze Age in Ireland.* Dublin: Hodges, Figgis & Co/London: Simpkin, Marshall & Co

Coghlan, H.H. & Case, H. 1957. Early metallurgy of copper in Ireland and Britain. Proceedings of the Prehistoric Society 23, 91–123

Collingwood, E.F. 1946. A prehistoric grave at West Lilburn. *Archaeologia Aeliana* (4th ser.) 24, 217–29

Cressey, M. & Sheridan, A. 2003. The excavation of a Bronze Age cemetery at Seafield West, near Inverness, Highland. *Proceedings of the Society of Antiquaries of Scotland* 133, 47–84

Curtis, N. & Wilkin N. this volume. The Regionality of Beakers and Bodies in the Chalcolithic of North-East Scotland. In M.J. Allen, J. Gardiner & S. Sheridan (eds), *Is there a British Chalcolithic?: place, people and polity in the later 3rd millennium.* Oxford: Prehistoric Society Research Paper 4

Donaldson, P. 1977. The excavation of a multiple round barrow at Barnack, Cambridgeshire, 1974–1976. *Antiquaries Journal* 57, 197–231

Evans, J. 1881. *The Ancient Bronze Implements, Weapons and Ornaments of Great Britain and Ireland.* London: Longmans

Fitzpatrick, A.P. 2011. *Amesbury Archer and Boscombe Bowmen. Early Beaker burials at Boscombe Down, Amesbury, Wiltshire, Great Britain.* Salisbury: Wessex Archaeology Report 27

Fokkens, H., Achterkamp, Y. & Kuijpers, M. 2008. Bracers or bracelets? About the functionality and meaning of Bell Beaker wrist-guards. *Proceedings of the Prehistoric Society* 74, 109–40

Gardiner, J., Allen, M.J., Powell, A., Harding, P., Lawson, A.J., Loader, E., McKinley, J.I., Sheridan, A. & Stevens, C. 2007. A matter of life and death: Late Neolithic, Beaker and Early Bronze Age settlement and cemeteries at Thomas Hardye School, Dorchester. *Proceedings of the Dorset Natural History and Archaeological Society* 128, 17–52

Garwood, P. 1999. Grooved Ware in southern Britain. In R. Cleal & A. MacSween (eds), *Grooved Ware in Britain and Ireland,* 145–76: Oxford: Oxbow Books/ Neolithic Studies Group Seminar Papers 3

Gerloff, S. 1975. T*he Early Bronze Age daggers in Great Britain.* Munich: Prähistorische Bronzefunde, VI, 2

Gibson, A. 1988. A summary of the transition from the Neolithic to Early Bronze Age in Great Britain. *Rassegna di Archeologia* 7, 193–210

Gibson, A. 1998. *Stonehenge and Timber Circles.* Stroud: Tempus

Gibson, A. 2004. Round in circles. Timber circles, henges and stone circles: some possible relationships and transformations. In R. Cleal & J. Pollard (eds) 2004, 70–82

Goddard, E.H. 1917. Early Bronze Age interment at the central flying school, Upavon. *Wiltshire Archaeological and Natural History Magazine* 40, 6–7

Green, C. & Rollo-Smith, S. 1984. The excavation of eighteen round barrows near Shrewton, Wiltshire. *Proceedings of the Prehistoric Society* 50, 255–318

Harbison P. 1969. The Daggers and Halberds of the Early Bronze Age in Ireland. Munich: Prähistorische Bronzefunde VI, 1

Harbison, P. 1979. Who were Ireland's first metallurgists? In M. Ryan (ed.), *The Origins of Metallurgy in Atlantic Europe: proceedings of the Fifth Atlantic Colloquium, Dublin, 1978,* 97–105. Dublin: Stationery Office

Harding, A. & Lee, G. 1987. *Henge Monuments and Related Sites of Great Britain.* Oxford: British Archaeological Report 175

Harding, J. 2003. *Henge Monuments of the British Isles.* Stroud: Tempus

Harrison, R.J., Jackson, R. & Napthan, M. 1999. A rich Bell Beaker burial from Wellington Quarry, Marden, Herefordshire. *Oxford Journal of Archaeology* 18, 1–16

Hawkes, C.F.C. unpubl. A scheme for the British Bronze Age. Address presented to the Council for British Archaeology, Bronze Age conference, London (dated 1960)

Henshall, A.S. 1968. Scottish dagger graves. In J.M. Coles & D.D.A. Simpson (eds), *Studies in Ancient Europe: essays presented to Stuart Piggott,* 173–95. Leicester: Leicester University Press

Hughes, G. 2000. *The Lockington Gold Hoard: an Early Bronze Age Barrow Cemetery at Lockington, Leicestershire.* Oxford: Oxbow Books

Kendrick, T.D. & Hawkes, C.F.C. 1932. *Archaeology in England and Wales: 1914–1931.* London: Methuen

Kinnes, I.A. 1985. *Beaker and Early Bronze Age Grave Groups.* British Bronze Age Metalwork, Associated Finds Series, A7–16. London: British Museum Publications

Kinnes, I.A. 1994. *Beaker and Early Bronze Age Grave Groups. British Bronze Age Metalwork, Associated Finds Series, A17–30.* London: British Museum Press

Kinnes, I., Gibson, A., Ambers, J., Bowman, S., Leese, M. & Boast, R. 1991. Radiocarbon dating and British Beakers: the British Museum programme. *Scottish Archaeological Review* 8, 35–68

Kirby, M. 2011. *Lockerbie Academy: Neolithic and Early Historic timber halls, a Bronze Age cemetery, an undated enclosure and a post-medieval corn-drying kiln in south-west Scotland,* 33–34. Scottish Archaeological Internet Report 46. www.sair.org.uk/sair46

Kirk, W. & McKenzie, J. 1953–5. Three Bronze Age cist burials in NE Scotland. *Proceedings of the Society of Antiquaries of Scotland* 88, 1–14

Lambrick, G. & Allen, T. 2004. *Gravelly Guy, Stanton Harcourt: the development of a prehistoric and Romano-British community.* Oxford: Oxford Archaeology, Thames Valley Landscapes Monograph 21

Larsson, M. & Parker Pearson, M. (eds) 2007. *From Stonehenge to the Baltic: living with cultural diversity in the third millennium BC.* Oxford: British Archaeological Report S1692

Leary, J. 2010. Silbury Hill: a monument in motion. In J. Leary, T. Darvill & D. Field (eds), *Round Mounds and Monumentality in the British Neolithic and Beyond,* 139–52. Oxford: Oxbow Books/ Neolithic Studies Group Seminar Papers 10

Leeds, E.T. 1938. Beakers of the Upper Thames district. *Oxoniensia* 3, 7–30

Longworth, I.H. 1979. The Neolithic and Bronze Age pottery. In Wainwright 1979, 75–124

MacSween, A. 2007. The Meldon Bridge period: the pottery from south and east Scotland twenty years on.

In C. Burgess, P. Topping & F. Lynch (eds), *Beyond Stonehenge: essays in honour of Colin Burgess*, 367–76. Oxford: Oxbow Books

Marsden, B.M. 1977. *The Burial Mounds of Derbyshire*. Privately produced

Martin, E. Pendleton, C. & Plouvier, J. 1993. Archaeology in Suffolk 1992. *Proceedings of the Suffolk Institute of Archaeology and History* 38 (1), 79–101

Montelius, O. 1909. The chronology of the British Bronze Age. *Archaeologia* 61, 97–162

Moody, G. 2008. *The Isle of Thanet from Prehistory to the Norman Conquest*. Stroud: History Press

Moore, C.N. & Rowlands, M. 1972. *Bronze Age Metalwork in Salisbury Museum*. Salisbury: Salisbury and South Wiltshire Museum

Mortimer, J.R. 1905. *Forty Years' Researches in British and Saxon Burial Mounds of East Yorkshire*. London: Brown & Sons

Needham, S.P. 1996. Chronology and periodisation in the British Bronze Age. In K. Randsborg (ed.), *Absolute Chronology: archaeological Europe 2500–500 BC*, 121–40. Acta Archaeologica 67

Needham, S.P. 2002. Analytical implications for Beaker metallurgy in North-west Europe. In M. Bartelheim, E. Pernicka & R. Krause (eds), *Die Anfänge der Metallurgie in der Alten Welt*. Freiberg: Forschungen zur Archäometrie und Altertumswissenschaf 1, 99–133

Needham, S.P. 2004. Migdale–Marnoch: sunburst of Scottish metallurgy. In I.A. Shepherd & G.J. Barclay (eds), *Scotland in Ancient Europe: the Neolithic and Early Bronze Age of Scotland in their European context*, 217–45. Edinburgh: Society of Antiquaries of Scotland

Needham, S.P. 2005. Transforming Beaker culture in north-west Europe; processes of fusion and fission. *Proceedings of the Prehistoric Society* 71, 171–217

Needham, S.P. 2007a. Isotopic aliens: Beaker movement and cultural transmissions. In Larsson & Parker Pearson (eds) 2007, 41–6

Needham, S.P. 2007b. The dagger blade and hilt furnishings from Site D (Ferry Fryston), burial 2245. In F. Brown, C. Howard-Davis, M. Brennand, A. Boyle, T. Evans, S. O'Connor, A. Spence, R. Heawood, & A. Lupton, *The Archaeology of the A1(M) Darrington to Dishforth DBFO Road Scheme*, 279–89. Lancaster: Oxford Archaeology North, Lancaster Imprints 12

Needham, S.P. 2008. In the Copper Age. *British Archaeology* (July/August 2008), 19–22

Needham, S.P., Lawson, A.J. & Green, H.S. 1985. *Early Bronze Age Hoards*. British Bronze Age Metalwork, Associated Finds Series A1–6. London: British Museum Publications

Needham, S.P., Leese, M.N., Hook, D.R. & Hughes, M.J. 1989. Developments in the Early Bronze Age metallurgy of southern Britain. *World Archaeology* 20, 383–402

Needham, S.P., Parfitt, K. & Varndell, G. (eds) 2006. *The Ringlemere Cup: precious cups and the beginning of the Channel Bronze Age*. London: British Museum Research Publication 163

Needham, S.P., Parker Pearson, M., Tyler, A., Richards, M. & Jay, M. 2010. A first 'Wessex 1' date from Wessex. *Antiquity* 84, 363–73

Newall, R.S. 1930–2. Barrow 85 Amesbury (Goddard's list). *Wiltshire Archaeological & Natural History Magazine* 45, 432–58

Olivier, A.C.H. 1987. Excavations of a Bronze Age funerary cairn at Manor Farm, near Borwick, North Lancashire. *Proceedings of the Prehistoric Society* 53, 129–86

O'Connor, B. 2008. 'Au silence et au travail': Evans and the Bronze Age. In A. Macgregor (ed.), *Sir John Evans 1823–1908*, 117–30. Oxford: Ashmolean Museum

Ó Ríordáin, S.P. 1937. The halberd in Bronze Age Europe: a study in prehistoric origins, evolution, distribution and chronology. *Archaeologia* 86, 195–321

Ó Ríordáin, B. & Waddell, J. 1993. *The Funerary Bowls and Vases of the Irish Bronze Age*. Galway: Galway University Press

Parker Pearson, M. & Ramilisonina 1998. Stonehenge and the ancestors: the stones pass on the message. *Antiquity* 72, 308–26

Parker Pearson, M., Cleal, R., Marshall, P., Needham, S., Pollard, J., Richards, C., Ruggles, C., Sheridan, A., Thomas, J., Tilley, C., Welham, K., Chamberlain, A., Chenery, C., Evans, J., Knüssel, C., Linford, N., Martin, L., Montgomery, J., Payne, A. & Richards, M. 2007. The age of Stonehenge. *Antiquity* 81, 617–39

Parker Pearson, M., Chamberlain, A., Jay, M., Marshall, P., Pollard, J., Richards, C., Thomas, J., Tilley, C. & Welham, K. 2009. Who was buried at Stonehenge? *Antiquity* 83, 23–39

Pendleton, C. F. 1999. *Bronze Age metalwork in Northern East Anglia. A Study of its Distribution and Interpretation*. Oxford: British Archaeological Reports, British Series 279

Piggott, S. 1963. Abercromby and after: the Beaker cultures of Britain re-examined. In I.Ll. Foster & L. Alcock (eds), *Culture and Environment: essays in honour of Sir Cyril Fox*, 53–91. London: Routledge & Kegan Paul

Pitts, M. 2000. *Hengeworld*. London: Century

Proudfoot, E. 1997. Short cist burials from Fife. Upper Kenly Farm, Belliston Farm and Dalgety Bay. *Tayside & Fife Archaeological Journal* 3, 1–21

Ralston, I.B.M. 1996. Four short cists from north-east Scotland and Easter Ross. *Proceedings of the Society of Antiquaries of Scotland* 126, 121–55

Rohl, B. & Needham, S.P. 1998. *The Circulation of Metal in the British Bronze Age: the application of lead isotope analysis*. London: British Museum Occasional Paper 102

Russel, A.D. 1990. Two Beaker burials from Chilbolton, Hampshire. *Proceedings of the Prehistoric Society* 56, 153–72

Savory, H.N. 1980. *Guide Catalogue of the Bronze Age Collections*. Cardiff: National Museum of Wales

Shepherd, A. this volume. Stepping out together: men, women and their Beakers in time and space. In M.J. Allen, J. Gardiner & S. Sheridan (eds), *Is there a British Chalcolithic?: place, people and polity in the later 3rd millennium*. Oxford: Prehistoric Society Research Paper 4

Sheridan. A. 2007. Dating the Scottish Bronze Age: 'There is clearly much that the material can still tell us'. In C. Burgess, P. Topping & F. Lynch (eds), *Beyond Stonehenge: essays on the Bronze Age in honour of Colin Burgess*, 162–85. Oxford: Oxbow Books

Simpson, D.D.A. 1968. Food Vessels: associations and

chronology. In J.M. Coles & D.D.A. Simpson (eds), *Studies in Ancient Europe: essays presented to Stuart Piggott,* 197–211. Leicester: Leicester University Press

Smith, M.A. 1956. *Grave Groups and Hoards of the British Bronze Age (2). Inventaria Archaeologica GB.14–18.* London: International Congress of Prehistoric and Protohistoric Sciences

Smith, M.A. 1957. *Bronze Age Hoards and Grave-Groups from the N.E. Midlands. Inventaria Archaeologica GB.19–24.* London: International Congress of Prehistoric and Protohistoric Sciences

Smith, R.J.C. 2000. Excavation of Neolithic and Bronze Age features at the Thomas Hardye (formerly Castlefield) School, Coburg Road, Dorchester, 1994. *Proceedings of the Dorset Natural History and Archaeological Society* 122, 73–82

Thomas, J. 2004. The later Neolithic architectural repertoire: the case of the Dunragit complex. In R. Cleal & J. Pollard (eds) 2004, 98–108

Thorpe, I.J. & Richards, C. 1984. The decline of ritual authority and the introduction of Beakers into Britain. In R. Bradley & J. Gardiner (eds), *Neolithic Studies: a review of some current research,* 67–84. Oxford: British Archaeological Report 133

Vine, P.M. 1982. *The Neolithic and Bronze Age Culture of the Middle and Upper Trent Basin.* Oxford: British Archaeological Report 105

Wainwright, G.J. 1979. *Mount Pleasant, Dorset: Excavations 1970–1971.* London: Report of the Research Committee of the Society of Antiquaries of London 37

Wainwright, G. 1989. *The Henge Monuments: ceremony and society in prehistoric Britain.* London: Thames & Hudson

Whittle, A. 1997. *Sacred Mound, Holy Rings. Silbury Hill and the West Kennet Palisade Enclosures: a Later Neolithic complex in north Wiltshire.* Oxford: Oxbow Monograph 74

Whittle, A., Atkinson, R.J.C., Chambers, R. & Thomas, N. 1992. Excavations in the Neolithic and Bronze Age complex at Dorchester-on-Thames, Oxfordshire, 1947–1952 and 1981. *Proceedings of the Prehistoric Society* 58, 143–201

Wilkin, N., Curtis, N., Hutchison, M. & Wright, M. 2009. Further radiocarbon dating results from the Beakers and Bodies project. *Discovery and Excavation in Scotland* 10, 216–8

Williamson, W.C. 1872. *Description of the Tumulus opened at Gristhorpe, near Scarborough.* Scarborough: Theakston (3rd edn)

Wilson, D. 1851. *The Archaeology and Prehistoric Annals of Scotland.* Edinburgh: Sutherland & Knox

Woodward, A, & Hunter, J. 2011. *An Examination of Prehistoric Stone Bracers from Britain.* Oxford: Oxbow Books

Woodward, A., Hunter, J., Ixer, R., Roe, F., Potts, P.J., Webb, P.C., Watson, J.S. & Jones, M.C. 2006. Beaker age bracers in England: sources, function and use. *Antiquity* 80, 530–43

2

Drawing Boundaries and Building Models: investigating the concept of the 'Chalcolithic frontier' in north-west Europe

Benjamin W. Roberts and Catherine J. Frieman

The concept of a Chalcolithic period is fundamentally underpinned by the adoption of copper metallurgy in the apparent absence of tin alloying. This technological definition has provided a framework upon which to propose ideas of Chalcolithic societies that are distinctive from their predecessors. In Britain, the early identification of copper-using communities did not lead either to the acceptance of a Chalcolithic or to any universal models of the groups involved as occurred throughout much of continental Europe. Instead Britain, together with the rest of north-west Europe, has been conceived of lying beyond a 'Chalcolithic frontier'. Examined from the perspective of the metal evidence, this oppositional perspective is flawed as it creates a world in which determinedly isolated Neolithic communities suddenly found migrants in their midst and consequently adopted metallurgy, thereby becoming socially and ideologically Chalcolithic. In this paper, we re-focus the Chalcolithic debates on the chronological, technological, and social contexts of the adoption of copper metallurgy which leads us to question the existence of a Chalcolithic frontier in prehistoric Europe and the utility of institutionalising a British Chalcolithic.

The concept of a Chalcolithic, Eneolithic, or Copper Age, distinct from the preceding Neolithic and subsequent Bronze Age, arose based on various excavations of European sites that contained copper but no bronze objects (Daniel 1975; Lichardus 1991; Lichardus-Itten 2006). The problems that these copper finds caused can be seen in the fragmented responses of scholars attempting to distinguish and name a new archaeological age within existing chronological frameworks. Each archaeologist developed his chronological theories based on their regional archaeologies leading to a Copper Age being proposed in Denmark (Vedel Simonsen 1813), Hungary (Von Pulsky 1884), France (Jeanjean 1884; Chantre 1885/6), and Iberia (Cartailhac 1886) as well as an Eneolithic in Italy (Chierici 1884); although the pan-European distribution of copper objects, including those in Britain and Ireland, was not ignored (Much 1885). The presence of copper objects and production practices in the absence of tin-bronze objects had long been recognised as having occurred throughout Britain (eg, Wilson 1851; Evans 1881; see O'Connor 2007). The excavation of copper and gold in Bell Beaker burials, and the acquisition and the recording of copper flat axes found in the landscape provided plentiful material evidence of an early phase of copper use as was observed by all subsequent scholars (eg, Montelius 1908; Kendrick & Hawkes 1932; Childe 1940; Burgess 1974; Needham 1996). The application of compositional analyses to the copper objects during the second half of the 20th century revealed not only the presence of relatively pure copper, but also arsenical and antimonal copper; compositions appearing with a frequency and consistency that, in certain instances, probably indicated that they were alloys rather than unintended by-products of smelting specific ores (eg, Coghlan & Case 1957; Rohl & Needham 1998; Northover 1999; Bray this volume). However, as we will demonstrate, the concept of a Chalcolithic has been used as a foundation to construct models of social and technological developments that involve, but are not explicitly linked to, copper metallurgy.

Across Europe, the Chalcolithic period is generally used as shorthand for a phase of growing social complexity, including new forms of social structure, the extension of exchange networks, and the adoption or development of new practices and technological innovations. In this paper we develop a critical review of the use of the concept of the Chalcolithic in Britain as compared to much of continental Europe, and discuss its social and technological implications. Furthermore, we address the recently proposed and influential model of a static 'Chalcolithic frontier' (Brodie 1997; 2001), by exploring its chronological, technological, and social basis and contrasting that with recent evidence from British, Irish and continental European sources. We acknowledge the utility of developing a better understanding of the archaeology of the 3rd millennium BC in Britain, particularly as regards its relationship to the end of the Stone Age and beginning of the Metal Ages. However, based on the myriad (and outdated) social implications of the term, the paucity of the British material record and the very real problems of developing a clear chronology for the mid-3rd millennium BC, we question the advisability of adopting a Chalcolithic period into British chronologies and institutionalising it alongside the Neolithic and Bronze Age in Britain.

British chronologies and the Chalcolithic

In Ireland and the British Isles, a copper industry distinct from bronze had been demonstrated to have existed, but was not attributed the chronological or social significance of other regional copper industries (Wilson 1851; Wilde 1863; Evans 1881). Even so, the lack of enthusiasm for a Chalcolithic period in Britain may result from the writings and influence of Oscar Montelius, who placed all copper-using periods throughout Europe within his scheme for the Bronze Age, naming them 'Bronze Age I' (Montelius 1885; 1903). In extending his chronological scheme to Britain and Ireland, he suggested that a copper-using phase was a part of the initial period 'Bronze Age I', as 'weapons and implements of stone were so common during the Copper Age that this period could also be considered as the last part of the Stone Age' (Montelius 1908, 99). Fox (1923, 53), following Montelius' (*ibid.*) general idea, designated this copper-using phase a 'Transitional Period' divided into a Copper Age and a Beaker Phase which preceded the onset of the Early Bronze Age proper. However, V. Gordon Childe subsumed these two periods under the broad umbrella of the Early Bronze Age (Childe 1930, 153–67). Neither the identification of a distinct copper-using period (eg, Burkitt *et al.* 1932) nor its inclusion in a broader period like the 'Bronze Age' (eg, Kendrick & Hawkes 1932) was universally accepted.

In a more detailed consideration of the evidence in Britain, Childe (1940) demarcated nine periods from the Neolithic to the Iron Age. The third comprised the Beaker culture which represented an invading people who brought copper metallurgy from the continent, and was divided into two phases on the basis of ceramic typologies (Childe 1940, 91–118). Hawkes's (1960) unpublished, yet highly influential, scheme proposed the idea of a British Copper Age, characterised by the use of Beakers and early copper axes, daggers, and halberds, and dated – presciently, in the absence of radiocarbon dates – 2500–2000 BC. Burgess's (1974) re-assessment of this framework in the light of radiocarbon dates enabled the independent confirmation that the earliest two metalwork stages (named after two hoards from Ireland: Castletown Roche and Knockague) could be partially distinguished

Implications	'Traditional' Chalcolithic	Chalcolithic as used in this paper
Social	• increasing social complexity • development of social hierarchies and elites • construction of monumental funerary architecture • increase in warfare and social violence	—
Technological	• domestication of the horse • development of wheeled vehicles • first phase of metal adoption process	• period of time when copper and copper-alloys (excepting tin-bronze) were in use
Economic	• increase in exotic, foreign materials • intensive, long-distance trade relations • "secondary productions revolution"	—
Chronological	• period of development between an ametallic Neolithic and a fully metal-using Bronze Age	—

from Beaker culture materials. In order to develop a broader synthesis, Burgess (1979; 1980) sought to rename the period, though he retained the metalwork phases, covering the problematic Neolithic–Bronze Age transition to the 'Mount Pleasant phase'. However, this general system of naming periods of several centuries after representative sites was not widely adopted, perhaps due to several of the selected type-sites being either unpublished or subsequently redated.

In more recent years, research into this period has yielded a much finer chronology of copper and gold use beginning in the mid-3rd millennium BC, and lasting several centuries prior to the regularisation of tin-bronze alloying (Needham 1996). Numerous terminological schemes remain in use, consequently, the earliest metal occurs in the 'Earlier Bronze Age' (Parker Pearson 1999) or the 'metal-using Neolithic' (Needham 1996); and one of the earliest, radiocarbon-dated, Bell Beaker

graves which, additionally, contains both copper and bronze objects has been placed in the 'Early Bronze Age' (Fitzpatrick 2002; 2011). Other scholars have sought to discuss the archaeological record of the broader stretch of time that encompasses the mid-3rd through mid-2nd millennia BC, arguing that seeking to find period divisions is unhelpful and distracting (eg, Bradley 2007, 88–177). Despite over a century of debate, there would seem to be little resolution in adding an explicitly Chalcolithic period into the chronological framework of British and Irish prehistory.

Envisioning Chalcolithic societies

The absence of a major period defined as occurring between the Neolithic and the Bronze Age in Britain meant that there has been no tradition of conceptualising a distinct Chalcolithic society. Any uniform, continental European perspective on the constitution

Table 2.1: Chalcolithic interpretations

of a British Chalcolithic society is further complicated by the absence of defined 'Copper Ages' in those countries surrounding Britain, including Scandinavia (Vandkilde 1996; Vandkilde *et al.* 1996), the Netherlands (Louwe Kooijmans 2005), Belgium (Vander Linden & Salanova 2004), Ireland (Brindley 1995; O'Brien this volume; Carlin & Bruck this volume), and, to an extent, much of France (Mille & Carozza 2009). In all of these areas, the earliest phases of copper use are included within the Neolithic which provides a far less distinctive framework for discussing a novel prehistoric society.

In reviewing the literature by continental scholars beyond north-west Europe, common societal themes emerge which unite perceptions of the period (Table 2.1), despite a wide chronological range with an Eneolithic beginning in Bulgaria at *c.* 4900 BC (Manolakakis 2006), a Copper Age beginning in Iberia at *c.* 3250 BC (Rovira 2002), and a potential Chalcolithic in Britain *c.* 2500 BC (see Lichardus 1991; Lichardus-Itten 2006). These continental themes include: increasing social complexity and the growth of new hierarchies (eg, Heyd 2007; Harrison & Heyd 2007); the construction of new social inequalities expressed in the rise of an elite (Guilaine 2006); the building of monumental structures and tombs (Lichardus-Itten 2006); a dramatic increase in the consumption of exotic materials, frequently over long distances (eg, Sherratt 1994); a growth of new networks of communication and exchange (eg, Vander Linden 2006); and an intensification of economic activity, particularly with regard to 'secondary products' (eg, Sherratt 1981; Harrison 1986) and the trade in salt (Weller 2002). It is also the period in which scholars have placed the domestication of the horse and the spread horse-riding and wheeled vehicles (eg, Bakker *et al.* 1999; Fansa & Burmeister 2004; Pétrequin *et al.* 2006; Anthony 2007; Primas 2007, though see Levine 2005); the spread of Indo-European languages (eg, Mallory 1989; Sherratt 1988; Anthony 2007); postulated a substantial increase in warfare, weaponry, and inter-group violence (eg, Guilaine & Zammit 2001; Fibiger in press a; in press b) and the migration of entire peoples (Childe 1950; Gimbutas 1953; 1981). V. Gordon Childe's (1944) declaration of technological stages as archaeological ages would seem to be very

far from being abandoned, even for a period whose definition beyond metallurgy can seem confused.

Rather than a Chalcolithic society of Britain, three traditional foci have dominated discussion of this period: Bell Beaker burials, metallurgy, and monuments. The introduction of Bell Beaker burials has been frequently cited as evidence for the invasion or migration of new elite people(s) from the continent (eg, Abercromby 1912; Childe 1940; Clark 1970; Case 1977); participation in an international network (eg, Clark 1976) resulting in the adoption of a standardised set of objects and practices (Burgess and Shennan 1976); the identification of a new elite in Britain (Clarke *et al.* 1985); intensification of exchange, interaction, and inter-marriage (Brodie 1997); and an early migration followed by localised adoption and adaptation (eg, Needham 2005). There are many variations on these themes that resonate throughout British and continental European Beaker research (see Brodie 2001; Nicolis 2001; Vander Linden 2006); but all argue that the mid-3rd millennium in Britain represented a period of increased interaction with continental communities leading to the adoption of the new practices, technologies, and objects bound up in the Beaker phenomenon.

Bound up within this debate is the prominence given to metallurgy which has long been argued to have arrived in Britain with Bell Beaker funerary practices. This situation creates the seductive model of Bell Beaker-using metallurgical prospectors arriving in Britain in search of fresh ore sources and being buried with the tools of their trade (eg, the Amesbury Archer: Fitzpatrick 2002; 2009; 2011). The short duration of copper metallurgy, only two to three centuries, rather than *c.* two millennia as throughout much of continental Europe, has provided insufficient evidence for any scholars to propose societal models involving metallurgy that transcend its probable Bell Beaker origins. By definition, Chalcolithic societies would not survive the widespread and comprehensive adoption of tin-bronze in Britain and Ireland around *c.* 2200 BC (Needham 1996; Bray this volume). This scenario stands in contrast to continental Europe where the adoption of tin-bronze is far patchier and more gradual. Tin-bronze is in evidence throughout Eastern and Central Europe from the early 3rd millennium (Müller 2002), but not fully adopted until the

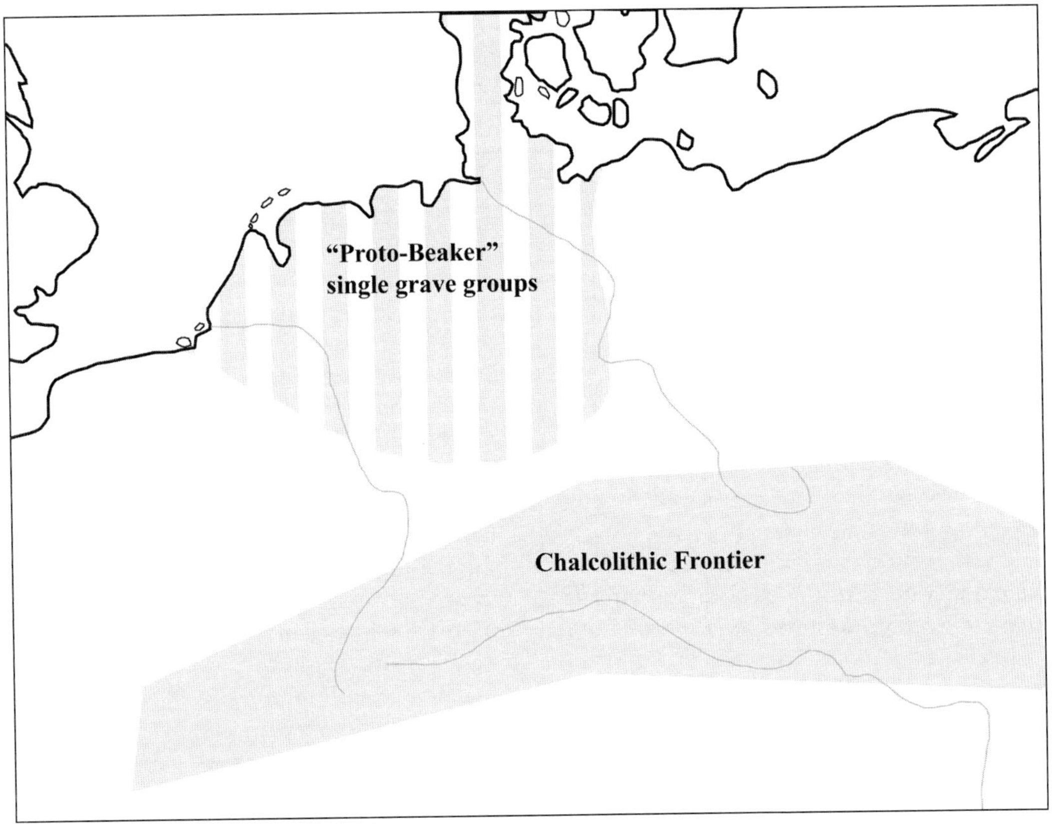

Figure 2.1: The Chalcolithic Frontier model (after Brodie 1997, fig. 1)

end of the 3rd millennium (Krause 2003); while, in Iberia, widespread bronze usage only occurred during the early to mid-2nd millennium (Fernández-Miranda *et al.* 1995). The growing scale of monument construction using earth, timber and stone throughout Britain during the 3rd millennium has also stimulated a variety of social models founded on the dynamics of building and using these sites. The sheer quantity of labour involved, together with the expertise required to erect these monuments led scholars to propose that communities were organised by leaders able to mobilise and direct large labour forces (eg, Renfrew 1973). This model has been challenged by others emphasising a less hierarchical social structure in which communities agree to participate in the creation and remaking of monuments that are subsequently used by elites (eg, Bradley 1993; Barrett 1994; Whittle 1997; Thomas 1999; Gibson 2005; Parker Pearson *et al.* 2007). The continental debates on horse domestication, Indo-European languages, salt production, warfare, and the secondary products revolution have not had as profound an impact on the discussion of the 3rd millennium in Britain despite, in certain

cases, extensive research (eg, Parker Pearson & Thorpe 2003; Heath 2009) – perhaps due to the relative paucity of data.

It is not that the idea of a Chalcolithic in Britain has only been championed at the margins – it has been proposed by figures as influential as Childe (1940) and Hawkes (1960), as well as more recently by Needham (2008) and Sheridan (2008). However, counterbalancing these proposals is a reluctance to create a Fourth Age to add to the deeply flawed Three Age system that scholars from Atkinson (1956) to Burgess (1980) to Bradley (2007) have criticised and taken great pains to avoid in their respective syntheses.

Is there a Chalcolithic frontier?

The idea of a 'Chalcolithic frontier' (Figure 2.1) as proposed by Brodie (1997) is an argument that Chalcolithic society, as represented by metal objects and metallurgy, did not spread immediately into north-west Europe from further south and east, but instead remained essentially static for around a millennium. This apparent impasse was only overcome with the development of exchange networks and inter-marriage between Chalcolithic and Neolithic communities which paved the way for the introduction of metallurgy, Bell Beaker burials, and, concomitantly, a Chalcolithic society into north-west Europe. This model appears to accommodate the many problems encountered by earlier scholars in seeking to relate British prehistory to the pan-European, Chalcolithic mainstream. It encompasses the large chronological delay and presents a simple and straightforward mechanism for the transmission of novel materials and objects which leads to a relatively rapid process of 'Chalcolithisation' over a few generations. However, there remain major problems in this model that undermine the validity of the interpretations it facilitates.

There is no indication that the definition of 'frontier' used in this model encapsulates the complexities inherent in the idea of a cultural boundary (eg, Green 1985; Lightfoot & Martinez 1995; Stark 1998; Lamont & Molnár 2002). Rather this frontier seems to derive intellectual inspiration from the culture-historical tradition by identifying distinct spatial and temporal groupings based primarily on artefact styles/typology and then searching for inter-connections (Roberts & Vander Linden 2011). The consequence is that the explanation for material change beyond the frontier is required to be an external event or process moving in a north-westerly direction, such as population movement, whether through migrations or inter-marriage. This idea is especially problematic as the Chalcolithic frontier it posits not only reinforces the opposition between Neolithic and Chalcolithic societies, but encourages also the idea that we are dealing two distinct and non-contiguous, though neighbouring, populations who suddenly 'find' each other after 1000 years. Furthermore, the social dynamics of the Chalcolithic frontier are unverifiable as the available scale of analysis, together with the quality of the data, makes the study of prehistoric inter-marriage highly problematic. The migration of populations remains a challenging hypothesis to demonstrate at a scale beyond the individual or small group, even using the isotopic analysis of numerous individuals (Roberts 2008a; 2009; Jay *et al.* this volume, although there are notable methodological problems inherent in this approach; Pollard 2011).

Beyond these concerns about the social theory underlying the Chalcolithic frontier model, a further problem is that it places metal at the centre of a value system predicated on the innate superiority of the new material. In this system, metal is deemed so desirable because of its physical properties, such as lustre and plasticity, as well as its functional properties which are presumed to be superior. Moreover it is assumed that a society that lacks metal does so because the technology is foreign and overly challenging. Thus, the presence of metal objects in an 'ametallic' society is framed as a significant technological and social event; and the presence of these objects in burial contexts is taken to mean that the deceased was a highly important, politically or cosmologically powerful individual. By elevating metal above other materials, it is taken out of its broader material, technological and social context – an approach with a great deal of historical precedent. The significance of metal in contemporary society means that its presence tends to be overemphasised rather than ignored; and, as a consequence, archaeologists studying this period tend to treat metal in isolation – as either the most or the least important material in a given assemblage. The apparent cessation of metal production or consumption in the archaeological record tends to be viewed negatively as relating to broader breakdowns in society or its inter-connectedness; and the visibility of metal in the archaeological record is rarely considered as an explanatory factor (Taylor 1999). In re-examining the role of early metal in prehistoric societies, we would argue that metal is not inherently valuable, but is valued and treated differently by each group of people who adopt it (see Thornton & Roberts 2009 and subsequent papers in *Journal of World Prehistory* 22 (3–4)). Neither copper nor gold, the two metals used earliest in north-west Europe, can be regarded as functionally superior to stone, bone, or wood for performing everyday tasks (Mathieu & Mayer 1997). The frequently cited lustre of the 'flashing blades' (Keates 2002), thought to provide the main attraction of copper, should be placed in the broader context of the many lustrous materials already in circulation, such as jadeitite axes (Pétrequin *et al.* 2002; 2008; Klassen 2004; Sheridan 2007), amber beads (Beck & Shennan 1991), and jet (Clarke *et al.* 1985; Sheridan & Davis 2002), all of which contributed 'supernatural power dressing' in life and death (Sheridan & Shortland 2003). The plasticity of metal is undeniable; however, there is no evidence to imply that it was exploited by the earliest metal-using communities (eg, Bray this volume). The technology to produce metal may well have been foreign compared to existing pyrotechnologies (Roberts 2008b); but the impetus to adopt aspects of metal technology developed out of pre-existing social structures (Ottaway & Roberts 2007). Similarly, the cessation of metal production or consumption should not be framed in terms of technological failure or social breakdown; rather, prehistoric communities made a choice to adopt and reject the material and technology. The apparent, metallurgical hiatus in north-west Europe that prompted Brodie (1997) and others to propose a frontier is actually typical of the broader pattern of punctuated adoption of metallurgy throughout Eurasia (Roberts *et al.* 2009), whereby metal is only adopted when there is a place for it. Objects without pre-existing cultural referents cannot, by definition, be adopted (Barnett 1953, 334–8); but new ideas can be developed to explain – and, consequently, socialise – the never previously encountered innovation (cf. Taylor 1999).

The reality of prehistoric metal adoption

The idea of a Chalcolithic implies many things about society; but, fundamentally, it refers to a period of time when copper and copper-alloys (excepting tin-bronze) were in use (see Table 2.1). According to this definition, there was a Chalcolithic in Britain *c.* 2500–2200 BC that involved the production, use, and deposition of copper, arsenical copper, and gold objects. The radiocarbon-dated evidence is comprised of objects from Bell Beaker graves (eg, O'Connor 2004; Needham 2005; Vander Linden 2006; Fitzpatrick 2011). These are used to bolster typological schemes for the majority of copper and gold objects which have little or no reliable context or provenience. There is currently no evidence for primary or secondary metal production in Britain for the centuries in question beyond an arsenical copper droplet from a midden at Northton, Isle of Harris, Scotland (Simpson *et al.* 2006). It is perhaps erroneous to compare this absence of evidence to Chalcolithic metal-producing sites in Iberia (eg, Montero-Ruiz 1994; Rovira

2002), southern France (Mille & Carozza 2009), or beyond (Bourgarit 2007; Roberts *et al.* 2009), given the potential archaeological invisibility of the smelting process in use in the mid-3rd millennium (Timberlake 2005).

Furthermore, there is evidence for the importation of copper objects into Britain from Ireland and the continent. This is demonstrated throughout western Britain by objects which appear to have been made from ores from the Ross Island copper mine in south-west Ireland which dates to 2400 BC (O'Brien 2004). In eastern Britain, the composition of metal objects is similar to the 'Bell Beaker metal' which is found throughout north-west Europe from 2600/2500 BC and probably derives from the combination of metal objects from several ore sources (Needham 2002). There is evidence for secondary metal production in the form of metal droplets in a hearth at the site of Val de Reuil, north-west France dating to the late 3rd millennium (Billard *et al.* 1991), but no confirmed primary metal production site beyond Ross Island, Ireland (O'Brien 2004). The only copper ores in north-west Europe outside Britain and Ireland are in Brittany; and there is currently no reliable evidence that they were exploited (Briard & Roussot-Larroque 2002).

Evidence for earlier metal in north-west Europe has been revealed in the dating of a burial at Vignely, north-west France to the mid-4th millennium BC – earlier than the oldest metal objects and metal production in southern France (Guilaine 1991; Mille & Carozza 2009). Its presence at the site is likely due to connections with communities on the northern European plain (Ottaway 1982; Klassen 2000; Krause 2003). The presence of similar copper trinkets at the site of Emmeln-2, western Germany, a presumed late 4th millennium megalithic burial mound (Schlicht 1968) indicates that metal circulation during this period occurred. However, while possible, there is currently no radiocarbon or typologically dated evidence to imply that there were metal objects in Britain during the late 4th through early 3rd millennia. If metal objects were known to the communities living in the British Isles at this time, they would probably only have been present on a very small scale and may not relate to later, archaeologically visible types

In light of this much less straightforward and

much smaller scale process of metal adoption, the effect of metal objects and metallurgy on prehistoric society needs to be re-evaluated. As discussed above, the presence of metal objects is frequently treated as a proxy for intensive, long-distance contact and exchange. While the presence of copper and gold objects without concomitant metal technology certainly indicates the existence of these sorts of trade networks, there is no evidence that metal was the motivating force behind their development. Not only was metal not the first material to be circulated over great distances around Europe, some non-metal objects, such as the previously mentioned jadeitite axes, were distributed even more widely. Furthermore, the manufacture of copper and gold does not require a complex, hierarchical production process. The identification, mining, processing, and smelting of the copper ores would have required verbal and visual instruction from an experienced practitioner (Roberts 2008a). However, the extent of any specialist control would be limited to the communication of these skills and does not translate immediately into elite control of the new technology or a social hierarchy founded upon it (cf. Kienlin 2008). The regional diversity in metal objects indicates that despite the 'foreign' introduction of metal production practices, the objects were shaped to the local and regional standards of the prehistoric communities (Roberts & Frieman forthcoming; Klassen 2000; Kienlin 2010).

The adoption of metal and metallurgy appears to have little initial effect on the variety of other types of objects and materials with which they were used. Archaeologists have traditionally identified a number of different stone, flint, and ceramic artefacts, contemporary with the earliest phases of metal use, as skeuomorphs (meaningful imitations) of metal objects. However, these so-called skeuomorphs can frequently be shown to stem more from pre-existing trends in stone-, flint-, and pot-making than from the adoption of metal (Frieman 2010; forthcoming a). For example, during the late 3rd and early 2nd millennia, complex necklaces made of jet beads were frequently deposited in burial contexts around the British Isles. These necklaces are often suggested to have been imitations of crescentic, hammered gold lunulae, of Irish origin (Craw 1928–9;

Sheridan & Davis 2002); but the very divergent depositional contexts, distributions, traces of usewear, and completeness of the two necklace varieties suggests that they developed independently of each other and functioned in different social spheres (Frieman forthcoming b; forthcoming c).

Discussion

Structuring prehistory through changes in stone and metal technology is deeply flawed and encourages a limited and biased understanding of the past. Almost since its inception, the Three (or Four) Age system has garnered as much criticism as it has acceptance (see Trigger 2006; Rowley-Conwy 2007); however, being thoroughly entrenched in the archaeological literature and serving as a useful, internationally understood shorthand, it remains in use. It could be argued that the addition of a Chalcolithic period in Britain might serve as a useful tool for drawing renewed archaeological attention to the highly dynamic 3rd millennium BC – a period traditionally dominated by studies of monuments, Beaker burials, and metal typologies. In other words, the idea of a British Chalcolithic could provide a focus for research into changes in monumentality, social structure, long-distance communication, treatment of the dead, and technology – including, but not centred on, the adoption of metal technology. The hope would be that a British Chalcolithic would reinvigorate debate and provide some much needed coherence between the all too separate worlds of Neolithic and Bronze Age scholarship. The richness of the archaeological record of the 3rd millennium in Britain is such that it seems to lend itself naturally to the construction of complex social models; yet, the Beaker- and metal-driven trajectory of much of the prior research into this period has been limited to the development of regressive models such as the 'Chalcolithic frontier' concept. In future, a broader material and regional approach to this period could potentially allow us great insight into the social and technological dynamism which become so visible at this time.

Yet, despite the heuristic potential of the concept of a British Chalcolithic, it remains difficult to identify – even in terms of metal technology. There is currently very little physical evidence of copper production in

Britain (although this is not the case for Ireland, see above), whether the mining or smelting of ore, that pre-dates the potential adoption of tin-bronze at *c.* 2200 BC (see Timberlake 2003; 2005; 2009). Moreover, the relatively small number of radiocarbon dates for copper objects together with the problems of their calibrated resolution resulting from the presence of a plateau in the calibration curve for the later 3rd millennium (Reimer *et al.* 2004) mean that any metal objects assigned to a proposed Chalcolithic would have to be identified typologically (eg, Needham 1979; 2005; Burgess 1979; Northover 1999). Further, the ability to recycle metal and to curate metal objects, as well as the potential for melting and re-use of the earliest tin-bronze objects, renders this chronology even fuzzier. Therefore, from a metallurgical perspective, the Chalcolithic is either a period that is too brief for current chronological resolutions or one that could have occurred earlier than we currently recognise. While there appears to be an ill-defined technological Chalcolithic in Britain, the social implications of early copper technology are much less clear-cut. The 3rd millennium BC was a period of dynamic change and intensive, long distance communication; but it is unlikely that metal was a causal factor. It is more likely to have been a symptom of broader patterns of interaction and change rather than a cause. Therefore, it represents an intensively researched source of data for understanding the dynamics of the prehistoric communities involved.

We agree with Ashmore's (2003, 40) assessment that 'period labels are particularly pernicious', and we must be wary of invoking evolutionary assumptions about social complexity and the nature of technological production. As we discussed above, traditionally 'Chalcolithic' implies a growth in social inequalities due to external interaction – an interpretation which is assumed rather than proven. Until the chronology of copper adoption and use in Britain can be refined, and in the absence of many of the social changes used in traditional definitions of the Chalcolithic phase, the institutionalisation of a Chalcolithic period within the British chronologies is suspect at best and highly problematic at worst.

Bibliography

Abercromby, J. 1912. *A Study of the Bronze Age Pottery of Britain and Ireland and its Associated Grave Goods*. Oxford: Oxford University Press

Anthony, D. 2007. *The Horse, the Wheel, and Language: how Bronze-Age riders from the Eurasian Steppes shaped the modern World*. Princeton: Princeton University Press

Ashmore, P. J. 2003. Terminology, time and space: labels, radiocarbon chronologies and a 'Neolithic' of small worlds. In I. Armit, E. Murphy, E. Nelis & D. Simpson (eds), *Neolithic Settlement in Ireland and Western Britain*, 40–6. Oxford: Oxbow Books

Atkinson, R.J.C. 1956. *Stonehenge*. London: Penguin

Bakker, J.A., Kruk, J., Lanting, A.E. & Milisauskas, S. 1999. The earliest evidence of wheeled vehicles in Europe and the Near East. *Antiquity* 73, 778–90

Barnett, H.G. 1953. *Innovation: the basis of cultural change*. New York: McGraw-Hill

Barrett, J.C. 1994. *Fragments from Antiquity: an archaeology of social life in southern Britain 2900–1200 BC*. Oxford: Blackwell

Beck, C. & Shennan, S. 1991. *Amber in Prehistoric Britain*. Oxford: Oxbow Books

Billard, C., Bourhis, J.-R., Desfosses, Y., Evin, J., Huault, M., Lefebvre, D. and Paulet-Locard, M.-A. 1991. L'habitat des Florentins à Val-de-Reuil (Eure). *Gallia Préhistoire* 33, 140–71

Bourgarit, D. 2007. Chalcolithic copper smelting. In S. LaNiece, D. Hook & P. Craddock (eds), *Metals and Mining: studies in archaeometallurgy*, 3–14. London: Archetype

Bradley, R. 1993. *Altering the Earth. The Origins of Monuments in Britain and Continental Europe*. Edinburgh: Society of Antiquaries of Scotland

Bradley. R. 2007. *The Prehistory of Britain and Ireland*. Cambridge: Cambridge University Press

Brindley, A. 1995. Radiocarbon, chronology and the Bronze Age. In J. Waddell & E. Shee Twohig (eds), *Ireland in the Bronze Age*, 4–13. Dublin: Stationery Office

Briard, J. & Roussot-Larroque, J. 2002. Les Débuts de la Métallurgie dans la France Atlantique. In M. Bartelheim, E. Pernicka & R. Krause (ed.), *The Beginnings of Metallurgy in the Old World*, 135–60. Rahden: Verlag Marie Leidorf

Brodie, N. 1997. New perspectives on the Bell Beaker Culture. *Oxford Journal of Archaeology* 16, 297–314

Brodie, N. 2001. Technological frontiers and the emergence of the Beaker culture. In Nicolis (ed.) 2001, 487–96

Burgess, C. 1974. The Bronze Age. In C. Renfrew (ed.), *British Prehistory: a new outline*, 165–221. London: Duckworth

Burgess, C. 1979. The background of early metalworking in Ireland and Britain. In M. Ryan (ed.), *The Origins of Metallurgy in Atlantic Europe*, 207–47. Dublin: Stationery Office.

Burgess, C. 1980. *Age of Stonehenge*. London: J.M. Dent

Burgess, C. & Shennan, S.J. 1976. The Beaker phenomenon: some suggestions. In Burgess, C. and Miket, R. (eds), *Settlement and Economy in the Third and Second Millennia BC*, 309–31. Oxford, British Archaeological Report 33

Burkitt, M.C., Childe, V.G., Fox, C., Hawkes, C., Kendrick, T.D., Leeds, E.T. & Raleigh-Radford, C.A. 1932. *A Handbook of the Prehistoric Archaeology of Britain: issued in connexion with the First International Congress of Prehistoric and Protohistoric Societies held in London, August 1–6 1932*. Oxford: John Johnson

Cartihallac, E. 1886. *Les Âges Préhistoriques de l'Espagne et du Portugal*. Paris: C. Reinwald

Case, H. 1977. An early accession to the Ashmolean Museum. In V. Markotic (ed.), *Ancient Europe and the Mediterranean: studies presented in honour of Hugh Hencken*, 19–34. Warminster: Aris and Philips

Chantre, E. 1885/6. *Âge du Bronze: recherches sur les origines de la métallurgie en France*. Paris: Baudry

Chierici, G. 1884. I sepolcri di Remedello nel Bresciano e i Pelasgi in Italia. *Bullettino di Paletnologia Italiana* 10, 133–64

Childe, V.G. 1930. *The Bronze Age*. Cambridge: Cambridge University Press

Childe, V.G. 1940. *The Prehistoric Communities of Britain*. London: Chambers

Childe, V.G. 1944. Archaeological ages as technological stages. *Journal of the Royal Anthropological Institute of Great Britain and Ireland* 74, 7–24

Childe, V.G. 1950. *Prehistoric Migrations in Europe*. Oslo: Aschehoug

Clarke, D.L. 1970. *Beaker Pottery of Great Britain and Ireland*. Cambridge: Cambridge University Press

Clark, D. 1976. The Beaker network – social and economic models. In J.N. Lanting & J.D. van der Waals (ed.), *Glockenbecher Symposion Oberried 1974*, 459–77. Haarlem: Fibula-Van Dishoeck

Clarke, D., Cowie, T. & Foxton, A. 1985. *Symbols of Power at the Time of Stonehenge*. Edinburgh: Her Majesty's Stationery Office

Coghlan, H.H. & Case, H. 1957. Early metallurgy in Ireland and Britain. *Proceedings of the Prehistoric Society* 23, 91–123

Craw, J.H. 1928–9. On a jet necklace from a cist at Poltalloch, Argyll. *Proceedings of the Antiquaries of Scotland* 63, 154–89

Daniel, G 1975. *150 years of Archaeology*. London: Duckworth

Evans, J. 1881. *The Ancient Bronze Implements, Weapons, and Ornaments of Great Britain and Ireland*. London: Longmans Green & Co.

Fansa, M. & Burmeister, S. (eds), *Rad und Wagen: der Ursprung einer Innovation im Vorderen Orient und Europa*. Mainz am Rhein: Verlag Philipp von Zabern

Fernández-Miranda, M., Montero-Ruiz, I. & Rovira, S. 1995. Los primeros objetos de bronce en el occidente de Europa. *Trabajos de Prehistoria* 52(1), 57–69

Fibiger, L. in press a. Investigating cranial trauma in the German Wartberg Culture. In R. Schulting & L. Fibiger (eds), *Sticks, Stones and Broken Bones. Neolithic Violence in a European Perspective*. Oxford: Oxford University Press

Fibiger, L. in press b. Misplaced childhood? Interpersonal violence and children in Neolithic Europe. In M. Smith & C. Knüsel (eds), *Traumatised Bodies: an osteological history of conflict from 8000BC to the present*. London, Routledge

Fitzpatrick, A.P. 2002. The Amesbury Archer: a well-furnished Early Bronze Age burial in southern England. *Antiquity* 76, 629–30

Fitzpatrick, A.P. 2009. In his hands and in his head: the Amesbury Archer as a metalworker. In P. Clark (ed.), *Bronze Age Connections: cultural contact in prehistoric Europe*, 176–88. Oxford: Oxbow Books

Fitzpatrick, A.P. 2011. *The Amesbury Archer and the Boscombe Bowmen: Bell Beaker burials at Boscombe Down, Amesbury, Wiltshire*. Salisbury: Wessex Archaeology Report 27

Fox, C. 1923. *The Archaeology of the Cambridge Region*. Cambridge: Cambridge University Press

Frieman, C. J. 2010. Imitation, identity and communication: The presence and problems of skeuomorphs in the Metal Ages. In B.V. Eriksen (ed.), *Lithic Technology in Metal Using Societies*, 33–44. Aarhus: Jutland Archaeological Society

Frieman, C. J. forthcoming a. *Innovation and Imitation: stone skeuomorphs of metal in 4th–2nd millennia BC northwest Europe*. Oxford: British Archaeological Report

Frieman, C. J. forthcoming b. Going to pieces at the funeral: completeness and complexity in British Early Bronze Age jet 'necklace' assemblages. *Journal of Social Archaeology*

Frieman, C. J. forthcoming c. Innovation and identity: the language and reality of prehistoric imitation and technological change. In J. Card (ed.), *Hybrid Material Culture: the archaeology of syncretism and ethnogenesis*. Carbondale, IL: Center for Archaeological Investigations

Gibson, A. 2005. *Stonehenge and Timber Circles*. Stroud: Tempus

Gimbutas, M. 1953. Battle Axe or Cult Axe? *Man* 53, 51–4

Gimbutas, M. 1981. The three waves of the Kurgan people into Old Europe, 4500–2500 BC. In R. Menk & A. Gallay (eds), *Anthropologie et archéologie: le cas des premiers âges des Métaux. Actes du Symposium de Sils-Maria, 25–30 septembre 1978*, 113–37. Archives Suisses d'Anthropologie générale

Green, S. 1985. *The Archaeology of Frontiers and Boundaries*. London: Academic Press

Guilaine, J. 1991. Roquemengarde et les débuts de la métallurgie en France méditerranéenne. In C. Eluère & J.P. Mohen (eds), *Découverte du Métal*, 279–94. Paris: Picard

Guilaine, J. (ed.), 2006. *Le Chalcolithique et la Construction des Inégalités*. Paris: Errance.

Guilaine, J. & Zammit, J. 2001. *Le Sentier de la guerre. Visages de la Violence Préhistorique*. Paris: Seuil

Harrison, R.J. 1986. The 'Policultivo Ganadero' or the secondary products revolution in Spanish agriculture, 5000–1000 BC. *Proceedings of the Prehistoric Society* 51, 75–102

Harrison, R.J. & Heyd, V. 2007. The transformation of Europe in the third millennium BC: the example of the Petit Chasseur I+III (Sion, Valais, Switzerland). *Prähistorische Zeitschrift* 82(2), 129–214

Hawkes, C.F.C. 1960. A Scheme for the British Bronze Age. Unpublished Paper

Heath, J. 2009. *Warfare in Prehistoric Britain*. Stroud: Amberley

Heyd, V. 2007. Families, prestige goods, warriors, and complex societies: Beaker groups of the 3rd millennium cal BC along the Upper and Middle Danube. *Proceedings of the Prehistoric Society* 73, 327–79

Jeanjean, A. 1884. L'âge du Cuivre dans les Cévennes. *Mémoires de l'Académie de Nîmes* 7, 491–506

Keates, S. 2002. The flashing blade: copper, colour and luminosity in north Italian Copper Age society. In A. Jones & G. MacGregor (eds), *Colouring the Past: the significance of colour in archaeological research*, 109–25. Oxford: Berg

Kendrick, T.D. & Hawkes, C.F.C. 1932. *Archaeology in England*. London: Methuen

Kienlin, T.L. 2008. Tradition and innovation in Copper Age metallurgy: results of a metallographic examination of flat axes from Eastern Central Europe and the Carpathian Basin. *Proceedings of the Prehistoric Society* 74, 79–108

Kienlin, T.L. 2010 *Traditions and Transformations: approaches to Eneolithic (Copper Age) and Bronze Age metalworking and society in eastern central Europe and the Carpathian Basin*. Oxford: British Archaeological Report S2184

Klassen, L. 2000. *Frühes Kupfer im Norden*. Århus: Århus Archaeology Monograph

Klassen, L. 2004. *Jade und Kupfer: Untersuchungen zum Neolithisierungsprozess im westlichen Ostseeraum unter besonderer Berücksichtigung der Kulturentwicklung Europas 5500–3500 BC*. Århus: Jutland Archaeological Society; Moesgård Museum

Krause, R. 2003. *Studien zur kupfer- und frühbronzezeitlichen Metallurgie zwischen Karpatenbecken und Ostsee*. Leidorf: Rahden/Westfalen

Lamont, M. & Molnár, V. 2002. The study of boundaries in the social sciences. *Annual Review of Sociology* 28, 167–95

Levine, M.A. 2005. Domestication and early history of the horse. In D.M. Mills & S.M. McDonnell (eds), *The Domestic Horse: the Origins, Development and Management of its Behaviour*, 5–22. Cambridge: Cambridge University Press

Lichardus, J. (ed.), 1991. *Die Kupferzeit als historische Epoche*. Bonn: R. Habelt

Lichardus-Itten, M. 2006. Le Chalcolithique: une époque historique de l'Europe. In Guilaine (ed.) 2006, 11–22

Lightfoot, K.G. & Matinez, A. 1995. Frontiers and boundaries in archaeological perspective. *Annual Review of Anthropology* 24, 471–92

Louwe Kooijmans, L.P. 2005. Hunters become farmers. Early Neolithic B and Middle Neolithic A. In L.P. Louwe Kooijmans, P.W. Van den Broeke, H. Fokkens & A. van Gijn (eds), *The Prehistory of the Netherlands*, 249–72. Amsterdam: Amsterdam University Press

Mallory, J.P. 1989. *In Search of the Indo-Europeans: language, archaeology and myth*. London: Thames & Hudson

Manolakakis, L. 2006. Varna et la Chalcolithique de Bulgarie. In Guilaine (ed.) 2006, 23–46

Mathieu, J.R. and Mayer, D.A. 1997. Comparing axe heads of stone, bronze, and steel: studies in experimental archaeology. *Journal of Field Archaeology* 24, 333–51.

Mille, B. & Carozza, L. 2009. Moving into the Metal Ages: The social importance of metal at the end of the Neolithic period in France. In T.L. Kienlin & B.W. Roberts (eds), *Metals and Societies: papers in honour of Barbara Ottaway*, 143–72. Universitätsforschungen zur prähistorischen Archäologie. Bonn: Habelt

Montelius, O. 1885. *Om tidsbestämning inom bronsåldern med särskild hänsyn till Skandinavien*. Stockholm: Kongl. Vitterhets Historie och Antiqvitets Akademiens Handlingar 30. Ny följd 10

Montelius, O. 1903. *Die Typologische Methode: Die älteren Kulturperioden im Orient und in Europa*. Stockholm: Asher

Montelius, O. 1908. The chronology of the British Bronze Age. *Archaeologia* 67, 97–162

Montero-Ruiz, I. 1994. *El origen de la Metalurgia en el Sureste Peninsula*. Almería: Instituto de Estudios Almeriense

Much, M. 1885. *Die Kupferzeit in Europa und ihr Verhältnis zur Cultur der Indogermanen*. Vienna: Kaiserlich-Königlichen Hof- und Staatsdruckerei

Müller, J. 2002. Modelle zur Einführung der Zinnbronze-technologie und zur sozialen Differenzierung der mitteleuropäischen Frühbronzezeit. In J. Müller (ed.), *Vom Endneolithikum zur Frühbronzezeit: Muster sozialen Wandels?*, 267–89. Universitätsforschung zur prähistorischen Archäologie 90. Bonn: Habelt

Needham, S.P. 1979. The extent of foreign influence on Early Bronze Age development in southern Britain. In M. Ryan (ed.), *The Origins of Metallurgy in Atlantic Europe*, 265–93. Dublin: Stationery Office

Needham, S.P. 1996. Chronology and periodisation in the British Bronze Age. *Acta Archaeologica* 67, 121–40

Needham, S.P. 2002. Analytical implications for Beaker metallurgy in North-West Europe. In E. Pernicka & M. Bartelheim (ed.), *The Beginnings of Metallurgy in the Old World*, 99–133. Rahden: Verlag Marie Leidorf

Needham, S.P. 2005. Transforming Beaker Culture in north-west Europe: processes of fusion and fission. *Proceedings of the Prehistoric Society* 71, 171–217

Needham, S.P. 2008. In the Copper Age. *British Archaeology* 101, 19–22

Nicolis, F. (ed.), 2001. *Bell Beakers Today: pottery, people, culture and symbols in prehistoric Europe. International Colloquium Riva del Garda (Trento, Italy), 11–16 May 1998*. Trento: Ufficio Beni Culturali

Northover, J.P. 1999. The earliest copper metalwork in southern Britain. In A. Hauptmann, E. Pernicka, T. Rehren & Ü. Yalçin (eds), *The Beginnings of Metallurgy*, 211–26. Bochum: Der Anschnitt

O'Brien, W. 2004. *Ross Island*. Galway: National University of Ireland, Bronze Age Studies 5

O'Connor, B. 2007. 'Au silence et au travail': Evans and the Bronze Age. In A. MacGregor (ed.), *Sir John Evans 1823–1908*, 116–30. Oxford: Ashmolean Museum

O'Connor, B. & Briggs, S. 2004. The earliest Scottish metalwork since Coles. In I.A.G. Shepherd & G. Barclay (eds), *Scotland in Ancient Europe: the Neolithic and Early Bronze Age of Scotland in their European context*, 205–16. Edinburgh: Society of Antiquaries of Scotland

Ottaway, B. 1982. *Earliest Copper Artifacts in the Northalpine. Region: their analysis and evaluation*. Bern: Schriften des Seminars für Urgeschichte der Universität Bern

Ottaway, B. and Roberts, B. 2007. The emergence of metalworking in Europe. In A. Jones (ed.) *European Prehistory*, 193–225. Oxford: Blackwell.

Parker Pearson, M. 1999. The Earlier Bronze Age. In J. Hunter & I. Ralston (eds), *The Archaeology of Britain*, 77–112. London: Routledge

Parker Pearson, M., Cleal, R., Marshall, P., Needham, S., Pollard, J., Richards, C., Ruggles, C., Sheridan, A., Thomas, J., Tilley, C., Welham, K., Chamberlain, A., Chenery, C., Evans, J., Knüsel, C., Linford, N., Martin, L., Montgomery, J., Payne, A., & Richards, M. 2007. The Age of Stonehenge. *Antiquity* 81, 617–39

Parker Pearson, M. & Thorpe, I. 2003. *Warfare, Violence*

and Slavery in Prehistory. Oxford: British Archaeological Report 1374

Pollard, A.M. 2011. Isotopes and impact: a cautionary tale. *Antiquity* 85, 631–638

Pétrequin, P., Cassen, S., Croutsch, C. and Errera, M. 2002. La valorisation sociale des longues haches de l'Europe néolithique. In J. Guilaine (ed.) *Matériaux, Productions, Circulations du Néolithique à l'Age du Bronze*, 67–98. Paris: Errance

Pétrequin, P., Arbogast, R-M, Pétrequin, A-M., Willigen, S. van & Bailly, M. (eds), 2006. *Premiers Chariots, Premiers Araires. La Diffusion de la Traction Animale en Europe Pendant les IVe et IIIe Millénaires Avant notre ère*. Paris: CNRS Editions

Pétrequin, P., Sheridan, J.A., Cassen, S., Errera, M., Gauthier, E., Klassen, L., Le Maux, N. & Pailler, Y. 2008. Neolithic Alpine axeheads, from the Continent to Great Britain, the Isle of Man and Ireland. *Analecta Praehistorica Leidensia* 40, 261–79

Primas, M. 2007. Innovationstransfer vor 5000 Jahren: Knotenpunkte am Land- und Wasserwegen zwischen Vorderasien und Europa. *Eurasia Antiqua* 13, 1–19

Reimer, P.J., Baillie, M.G.L, Bard, E., Bayliss, A., Beck, J. W., Bertrand, C., Blackwell, P.G., Buck, E.E., Burr, G., Cutler, K.B., Damon, P.E. Edwards, R.L., Fairbanks, R.G., Friedrich, M., Guilderson, T.P., Hughen, K.A., Kromer, B., McCormac, F.G., Manning, S., Bronk Ramsey, C., Reimer, R.W., Remmele, S., Southon, J.R., Stuiver, M., Talamo, S., Taylor, F.W., van der Plicht, J. & Weyhenmeyer, C.E. 2004. Marine04 Marine Radiocarbon Age Calibration, 0–26 Cal Kyr BP. *Radiocarbon* 46, 1029–1058

Renfrew, C. 1973. Monuments, mobilization and social organization in Neolithic Wessex. In C. Renfrew (ed.), *The Explanation of Culture Change: models in prehistory*, 539–58. Pittsburgh, University of Pittsburgh Press

Roberts, B.W. 2008a. Migration, craft expertise and metallurgy: Analysing the 'spread' of metal in western Europe. *Archaeological Review from Cambridge* 23(2), 27–45

Roberts, B.W. 2008b. Creating traditions and shaping technologies: Understanding the earliest metal objects and metal production in western Europe. *World Archaeology* 40(3), 354–72

Roberts, B.W. 2009. Production networks and consumer choice in the earliest metal of western Europe. *Journal of World Prehistory* 22, 461–81

Roberts, B.W. & Frieman, C. J. forthcoming. Early metallurgy in western and northern Europe. In C. Fowler, J. Harding & D. Hoffman (eds), T*he Oxford Handbook of Neolithic Europe*. Oxford: Oxford University Press

Roberts, B.W., Thornton, C.P. & Pigott, V.C. 2009. Development of metallurgy in Eurasia. *Antiquity* 83, 1012–22

Roberts, B.W. & Vander Linden, M. 2011. *Investigating Archaeological Cultures: material culture, variability and transmission*. New York: Springer

Rohl, B. & Needham, S. 1998. *The Circulation of Metal in the British Bronze Age: the application of lead isotope analysis*. British Museum Occasional Paper 102

Rovira, S., 2002. Metallurgy and society in Prehistoric Spain. In B.S. Ottaway & E.C. Wager (eds), *Metals and Society: papers from a session held at the European Association*

of Archaeologists Sixth Annual Meeting in Lisbon 2000, 5–20. Oxford British Archaeological Report S1061

Rowley-Conwy. P. 2007. *From Genesis to Prehistory. The Archaeological Three Age System and its Contested Reception in Denmark, Britain and Ireland*. Oxford: Oxford University Press

Schlicht, E. 1968. *Die Funde aus dem Megalithgrab 2 von Emmeln, Kreis Meppen: Studien zur Keramik der Trichterbecherkultur im Gebiet zwischen Weser und Zuidersee*. Neumünster: K. Wachholtz

Sheridan, J.A. 2007. Green treasures from the magic mountains. *British Archaeology* 96, 22–7

Sheridan, J.A. 2008. Towards and fuller, more nuanced narrative of Chalcolithic and Early Bronze Age Britain. *Bronze Age Review* 1, 57–78

Sheridan, J.A. & Davis, M. 2002. Investigating jet and jet-like artefacts from prehistoric Scotland: the National Museums' of Scotland project. *Antiquity* 76, 812–25

Sheridan, J.A. & Shortland, A. 2003. Supernatural power dressing. *British Archaeology* 70, 18–23

Sherratt, A. 1981. Plough and pastoralism: aspects of the secondary products revolution. In N. Hammond, I. Hodder & G. Isaac (eds), *Pattern of the Past: studies in honour of David Clarke*, 261–305. Cambridge: Cambridge University Press

Sherratt, A. 1988. The archaeology of Indo-European: an alternative view. *Antiquity* 62, 584–95

Sherratt, A. 1994. What would a Bronze Age world system look like? Relations between temperate Europe and the Mediterranean in later prehistory. *Journal of European Archaeology* 1(2), 1–57

Simpson, D.D.A., Murphy, E.M. & Gregory, R.A. 2006. *Excavations at Northton, Isle of Harris*. Oxford: British Archaeological Report 408

Stark, M.T. 1998. *The Archaeology of Social Boundaries*. Washington: Smithsonian

Taylor, T. 1999. Envaluing metal: theorizing the Eneolithic 'hiatus'. In S.M.M. Young, A.M. Pollard, P. Budd & R. Ixer (eds), *Metals in Antiquity*, 22–32. Oxford: Archaeopress

Thomas, J. 1999. *Understanding the Neolithic*. London: Routledge

Thornton, C.P. & Roberts, B.W. 2009. Introduction: the beginnings of metallurgy in the global perspective. *Journal of World Prehistory* 22(3), 181–4

Timberlake, S. 2003. *Excavations on Copa Hill, Cwmystwyth (1986–1999). An Early Bronze Age Copper Mine within the Uplands of Central Wales*. Oxford: British Archaeological Report 348

Timberlake, S. 2005. In search of the first melting pot. *British Archaeology* 82, 32–3

Timberlake, S. 2009. Copper mining and production at the beginning of the British Bronze Age new evidence for Beaker/EBA prospecting and some ideas on scale, exchange, and early smelting technologies. In P. Clark (ed.), *Bronze Age Connections: cultural contact in prehistoric Europe*, 94–121. Oxford: Oxbow Books

Trigger, B. 2006. *A History of Archaeological Thought* (2nd edn). Cambridge: Cambridge University Press

Vander Linden, M. 2006. *Le Phénomène Campaniforme dans l'Europe du 3ème Millénaire avant notre ère: synthèse et nouvelles perspectives*. Oxford: British Archaeological Report S1470

Vander Linden. M. & Salanova, L. (eds), 2004. *Le Troisième*

Millénaire dans le Nord de la France et en Belgique: actes de la Journée d'Études srbap-spf, 8 Mars 2003, Lille. Anthropologica et Praehistorica 115

Vandkilde, H. 1996. *From Stone to Bronze: the metalwork of the late Neolithic and earliest Bronze age in Denmark.* Aarhus: Jutland Archaeological Society 32

Vandkilde, H., Rahbek, U. & Rasmussen, K.L. 1996. Radiocarbon dating and the chronology of Bronze Age southern Scandinavia. *Acta Archaeologica* 67, 183–98

Vedel Simonsen, L.S. 1813. *Udsigt over Natjonalhistoriens ældste og mærkeligste Perioden.* Første Deel andet hæfte Copenhagen: Høfbogtrykker Christensen

Von Pulsky, F. 1884. *Die Kupferzeit in Ungarn.* Budapest: Friedrich Kilian

Weller, O. 2002. *Archéologie du Sel. Techniques et sociétés dans la Pré- et Protohistoire Européenne.* Rahden: Westfalen

Whittle, A., 1997. *Silbury Hill and the West Kennet Palisade Enclosures – a Later Neolithic Complex in North Wiltshire.* Oxford: Oxbow Books

Wilde, W. 1863. *A Descriptive Catalogue of the Antiquities of Animal Materials and Bronze in the Museum of the Royal Irish Academy.* Dublin: Gil

Wilson, D. 1851. *Prehistoric Annals of Scotland.* Edinburgh: Sutherland and Knox

3

A Rumsfeld Reality Check: what we know, what we don't know and what we don't know we don't know about the Chalcolithic in Britain and Ireland

Alison Sheridan

Should we create a specific label for the period between the 25th century BC, when metal-using and other novelties first appeared in Britain and Ireland, and the 22nd century, when bronze first started to be used here? And if so, should it be called the Chalcolithic? To address these questions, it is first necessary to take a critical look at how we characterise that period. This paper reviews what we do and do not know about what happened during those three or so centuries, concluding that this period does warrant a label of its own and taking the pragmatic view that 'Chalcolithic' is as good a term as any, but only if it is unshackled from the conceptual baggage that has grown up around its use on the continent. 'Our' Chalcolithic – or rather 'Chalcolithics', given the different trajectories in Britain and Ireland – is much shorter than, and different from, the Chalcolithics of continental Europe.

As is evident from the contributions to this volume, and from the lively discussions that characterised the 2008 conference that gave rise to this publication, the three or so centuries between the time that metal objects and a range of other novelties appeared in Britain and Ireland (25th century BC) and when bronze began to be used (22nd century BC, *pace* Bray this volume) offer much scope for debate. Much of this surrounds the appropriateness or otherwise of the use of the term 'Chalcolithic' (or 'Copper Age') to describe this period, but in essence there are two issues at stake: first, is this period sufficiently distinctive to warrant

it being given a label, to differentiate it from what had happened before and what happened afterwards? And secondly, if it is, then should 'Chalcolithic' be the term that is used to denote it? To prefigure what is set out below, the opinion of this author is 'Yes' and a conditional 'Yes'; but before we make these judgements, it is necessary to take a dispassionate view of what we actually know, and do not know, about traditions, beliefs, practices, material culture and inter-group relationships across Britain and Ireland during these few centuries. Since other contributions to this volume deal with specific aspects (eg, metallurgy) in detail, it is not proposed to offer a lengthy description here, but rather a brief critical overview.

What actually happened in Britain and Ireland between the 25th and 22nd centuries BC?

As Stuart Needham's contribution to this volume makes clear, it has been acknowledged for over a century that, onto the Late Neolithic scene in Britain and Ireland, there appeared some striking novelties, most notably the use of metal (copper and gold) and of a continental style of pottery (ie, Beakers). Thanks to significant recent advances in the radiocarbon dating of Beaker and non-Beaker associated material (the latter including the enormous mound at Silbury Hill, Wiltshire: Leary & Field 2010), and in the determination of patterns of movement through the application of isotopic analysis to human remains (see Jay *et al.* this volume), among other developments, we are now able to characterise the nature, timing, and tempo of this change in far more detail than hitherto, and also to assess its impact and reactions to it. The by-now infamous discovery that the 'Amesbury Archer' had been a long-distance immigrant from the continent (Chenery & Evans 2011), along with the discovery that copper was being mined *c.* 2400 BC by skilled, Beaker-using metalworkers at Ross Island in south-west Ireland (O'Brien 2004), reignited the long-standing debate about whether these novelties had been introduced by immigrants (eg, Case 1966; Clarke 1970; Burgess & Shennan 1976). As is clear from Harry Fokkens' contribution to this volume (and see below), that debate continues.

In order to clarify matters, we should review exactly what these novelties were, and set them against the background of Late Neolithic Britain and Ireland. The latter is characterised by its markedly insular dynamic, in which widely-separated communities the length of Britain (Parker Pearson 2007), and across the Irish Sea (Sheridan 2004), interacted with each other and shared specific practices that included the use of Grooved Ware pottery (Cleal & MacSween 1999) and the construction of ceremonial monuments such as timber circles (Gibson 1998), of which some were associated with solstitial ceremonies. Such interaction and activities had been underway since the beginning of the 3rd millennium,

when the use of Grooved Ware and associated beliefs and practices spread southwards from Orkney (Sheridan 2004). By the second quarter of the millennium, a process of escalating conspicuous consumption on monument construction is arguably discernible in Wessex (eg, with the erection of the Stonehenge sarsens and of enormous henge monuments such as Durrington Walls: Parker Pearson & Cox Willis 2011; Cleal & Pollard this volume), and this resonates with slightly earlier and/or contemporary developments in Orkney (on the Ness of Brodgar: Card 2010), if not elsewhere as well. In Wessex and Orkney the processes of monument construction and the ceremonies associated with them may well have involved the temporary agglomeration of several hundred people. Society would have been ranked, and the basis for temporal authority appears to have been control over access to and communication with the Otherworld of the ancestors and divinities. The symbols of power associated with this social system included maceheads of various shapes and carved stone balls (Figs 3.1, 1–2) – at least during the earlier part of the 3rd millennium – and imagery relating to cosmological beliefs includes the 'eyebrow' motif, which is found on a recently-discovered figurine from the Links of Noltland in Orkney (Fig. 3.1, 3), on a chamber tomb at Holm of Papa Westray South, again in Orkney (Fig. 3.1, 4), and the chalk 'drums' from an adolescent's grave at Folkton in Yorkshire (Fig. 3.1, 5; Longworth 1999). Prowess in archery was clearly also celebrated, as demonstrated for example by the exquisite, recently-discovered long-tailed oblique flint arrowheads from Marden henge (Fig. 3.1, 6; Leary *et al.* 2010). This is one of several pieces of evidence for skilled, and quite possibly specialist, production of flint artefacts, a practice that extends back into the 4th millennium (especially in Yorkshire: Manby *et al.* 2003).

The novelties that 'burst in' upon this scene from the 25th century are typified in the graves of the 'Amesbury Archer' and the 'Boscombe Bowmen' in Wiltshire (Fig. 3.2; see contributions in Fitzpatrick 2011 for detailed discussions of each component). These can be summarised as follows:

i.   new people: immigrants from the continent;

ii. continental funerary traditions, which

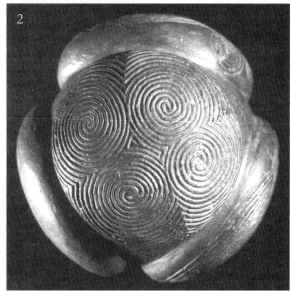

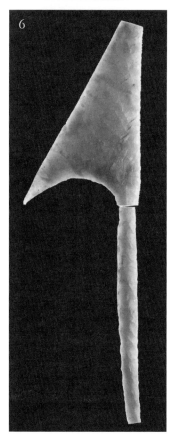

Figure 3.1: Late Neolithic material: 1. Stone maceheads, Egilsay (left) and Bloody Quoy (right), both Orkney; 2. Carved stone ball, Towie, Aberdeenshire; 3. Figurine from the Links of Noltland, Orkney; 4. Carvings of 'eyebrow' motif, Holm of Papa Westray South, Orkney; 5. Chalk 'drums' from Folkton, Yorkshire; 6. Long-tailed oblique flint arrowhead, Marden, Wiltshire. Photos 1,2 and 5: National Museums Scotland; rest: Crown copyright, reproduced courtesy of Historic Scotland (3 and 4; by Mike Brooks) and English Heritage (6; by Ian Leonard)

included an emphasis on male prowess in hunting and/or fighting skills in the portrayed funerary *persona* of the deceased;

iii. a novel style of pottery (Beaker), made according to continental tradition;

iv. novel archery paraphernalia: new styles of arrowhead (barbed and tanged, with hollow-based arrowheads also in use elsewhere); the use of stone wristguards (which, as Fokkens *et al.* persuasively argued in 2008, were probably principally objects of display); and new styles of belt ring (necessary to keep garments from interfering with the bow). The question of whether a new style of bow, the short composite recurve bow (Piggott 1971), had also been part of this set of novelties is discussed below;

v. continental-style ornaments and insular variants thereof (ie, the antler pendant from the Boscombe Bowmen grave and the pair of sheet gold basket-shaped hair ornaments from the Amesbury Archer grave);

vi. objects of copper and gold, and the knowledge of how to work metal.

To these can be added the aforementioned evidence for copper extraction from Ross Island, and for the manufacture of copper axeheads and other objects in south-west Ireland (O'Brien 2004) and their export to Britain (eg, Needham 2004).

Other Beaker-associated novelties were subsequently adopted from the continent, including the use of V-perforated buttons – a new style of garment fastener (although not exclusively used as such: I. Shepherd 2009) – and battle axeheads, a type of weapon/symbol of power that ultimately harked back to early 3rd millennium Corded Ware traditions on the continent (Roe 1966). These, like the use of Barbed Wire Beakers in and around East Anglia (Clarke 1970), attest to continuing or renewed contact with the near continent during the second half of the 3rd millennium (and indeed after 2000 BC, in the case of the Barbed Wire Beakers: van den Broeke *et al.* 2005, fig. 1.10).

Before considering the impact of, and reactions to, these novelties, some further comments will be offered to enlarge upon what we can say about them.

New people: immigrants from the continent

While, despite popular belief, the application of isotope analysis (principally of strontium and oxygen isotopes) to the study of human remains cannot pinpoint their area of origin precisely, there can be no doubt that the Amesbury Archer had not been brought up in Britain and must therefore represent a continental immigrant (Chenery & Evans 2011), perhaps from central Europe; Andrew Fitzpatrick favours Switzerland or environs as the candidate area of origin (Fitzpatrick 2011, 232–4). Chenery and Evans are more circumspect about the origin of the three adults among the 'Boscombe Bowmen' who have isotopic values characteristic of radiogenic rocks, citing various parts of Britain as geological candidate areas as well as south-east Ireland, Brittany and the Massif Central of France, parts of Portugal and the Black Forest (*ibid.*, 187). If the form of their grave and the associated artefactual assemblage are also brought into consideration, however, none of the British regions emerges as a plausible source area, whereas Brittany does (cf. Salanova 2000, fig. 6). Only one other individual can currently be pointed to as a potential continental immigrant on isotopic grounds, and that is the young adult buried at Sorisdale on the Hebridean island of Coll at some point between 2470 and 2215 cal BC (3879±32 BP, OxA-14722: Sheridan 2007, 109; 2008, 254), and whose isotopic signature suggests an origin in an area of Cenozoic or Cretaceous geology; the Netherlands cannot be ruled out as a possibility. Final publication of the *Beaker People Project* (see Jay *et al.* this volume) will reveal whether there are further candidates.

Other evidence for continental immigrants is more circumstantial, but nevertheless not to be ignored. Since there is not a shred of evidence for any interest in, or knowledge of, copper in Ireland prior to the establishment of the Ross Island mine, and since copper extraction requires an understanding of the requisite technological process, it is reasonable to assume that those miners had been immigrants. As argued by Billy O'Brien elsewhere in this volume (and see O'Brien 2004), on metallurgical grounds an area along the Atlantic façade (perhaps around the Gironde in France), rather than central Europe, seems the most plausible point of origin. This accords with Humphrey Case's reading of the 'Beaker phenomenon' in Ireland (Case 2001), which is distinctly different from that from most or all of Britain. (See O'Brien, and Carlin and Brück this volume).

A diversity of continental origins was also proposed in Stuart Needham's authoritative reconsideration of Beaker pottery (2005), and indeed in the author's own review of the earliest Beaker graves in Scotland (Sheridan 2008), it was argued that the Rhine Delta is a likely area of origin for at least some of Scotland's earliest Beaker-using inhabitants, on the grounds that both the Beakers and the style of grave have strong affinities with this area. Unfortunately, since most of the graves in question had consisted of organic containers dug into free-draining sediment, no traces of the bodies have survived to allow isotopic testing. Harry Fokkens (this volume) has argued that we may be dealing with selective adoption of continental practices and material culture by indigenous communities, rather than with Dutch immigrants, but this is arguably belied by the fact that the immediately preceding centuries saw no interest in the continent from any part of Britain and Ireland, (except, perhaps, for the Atlantic facade links suggested by the distribution of cup-and-ring rock art). It would be difficult to explain why, for example, people in Kilmartin Glen in western Scotland should suddenly have chosen to travel to the Rhine delta or thereabouts; by contrast, given our current understanding of Bell Beaker social dynamics in mid-3rd millennium north-west Europe, the undertaking of heroic long-distance journeys by high-status men and their retinues is perfectly plausible, as Laure Salanova has argued for some of the continental evidence (Salanova 2000; 2007; cf. Needham 2007).

This concept of the prestige-enhancing heroic journey of aristocratic men offers one mechanism to account for the appearance of Beakers and other novelties, and it accords with the life history of the Amesbury Archer, whose possessions from diverse geographical sources might conceivably have been acquired during such travels (unless the objects themselves had circulated). Furthermore, given the proximity of his grave to the major ceremonial centre of Stonehenge, it is not beyond the bounds of possibility that he and other continental immigrants could have returned across the sea and spread stories of the great midwinter ceremonies of Wessex, thereby attracting others to witness them.

Another mechanism that seems to have been in play was the search for copper (and arguably also gold). This, together with the 'heroic journey' idea, helps to account for the very wide distribution of early Beaker pottery in Britain and Ireland, extending as far north as Shetland (where a weathered sherd of All Over Cord-decorated Beaker has been found at Stanydale: Clarke 1970, 521). Overall, it appears that we are dealing with small numbers of immigrants, rather than waves of invaders (as portrayed, for example, by Abercromby in 1912) or entire communities of settlers (Piggott 1963, *inter alia*).

Continental funerary traditions

That we are dealing with more than one 'imported' funerary tradition is indicated by the fact that, in addition to the individual grave format as noted in the case of the Amesbury Archer and many other early Beaker-associated graves in Britain, there is also evidence for the use of a communal cist-like chamber (in the case of the Boscombe Bowmen) and, in Ireland, of megalithic wedge-shaped chamber tombs, usually for multiple interments. Much ink has been spilt on the degree to which these represent genuine novelties, with Alex Gibson (2007) citing indigenous precursors for aspects of the Beaker individual interment tradition, and pointing out that we are not dealing with a simple shift from a Neolithic tradition of communal interment to a Beaker tradition of individual burial, as many had previously asserted. However, while some similarities in practice undoubtedly existed – in just the same way as we can trace a shared interest in fancy archery gear – this does not mean that we are dealing with an unbroken tradition, in which Beakers and other exotic novelties were simply added to a pre-existing indigenous repertoire. Many of the *comparanda* cited by Gibson pre-date Beaker graves by several centuries, as he acknowledges, and the chronological discontinuity between superficially-similar practices is underlined by Frances Healy's chronological study (this volume). Indeed, funerary evidence associated with Grooved Ware or generally dating to the first half of the 3rd millennium is relatively rare, but where it exists, cremation tends to be the practice (at least as far as adults are concerned) – as shown, for example, by the deposits in the Aubrey Holes at Stonehenge (Parker Pearson & Cox Willis 2011). Furthermore, as Lekky Shepherd's research into Beaker-associated body orientation has shown (this volume), it appears that clear and gender-differentiated conventions regarding appropriate body positions were followed, and these find precursors in continental traditions. This supports the idea of the introduction (and subsequent adoption) of continental beliefs, as well as of practices.

The question of how and why wedge tombs came to be built in Ireland is complex, and is discussed elsewhere in this volume (eg, by O'Brien). Suffice it to note here that, unlike in the case of the individual and communal interment traditions mentioned above, this does not appear to represent the transplantation of a living continental tradition: the practice of constructing similar-looking *allées couvertes* in North-West France had ceased by the time wedge tombs started to be built (Brindley & Lanting 1992; O'Brien this volume), although bodies (with Beakers) were still being deposited in the French tombs (Salanova 2000, 20). The reason for this apparent adoption of a by-then ancient French monument type remains unclear.

An additional point to note is that, over the course of the three centuries between the 25th and the 22nd century, it is possible to trace not only developments within the individual interment tradition – with the use of timber chambers giving way to the use of cists in northern Britain, for instance – but also the use of some funerary monuments that have no connection with continental precursors, such as the recumbent stone circles of north-east Scotland (Bradley 2005). This will be returned to below. The re-use of many Neolithic funerary monuments in Scotland by Beaker users, in some cases as a process of sealing these ancient monuments, and not always accompanied by the deposition of bodies, is also well attested (eg, Henshall 1972; Lelong & MacGregor 2007, 88–91).

Beaker pottery

Needham's 2005 review of Beaker pottery development in Britain, as set against its continental Bell Beaker background, has clarified the typochronological sequence, and has highlighted the importance of the area between Normandy and the Lower Rhine as a 'fusion corridor' within which the earliest kinds of Beaker to be found in Britain emerged. The enhancement of the radiocarbon dating dataset since 2005, thanks mostly to the *Beaker People Project* (Jay *et al.* this volume) and the *Beakers and People Project* (Curtis & Wilkin this volume), has enabled further refinement of the scheme (Needham this volume), although, as noted below, all these studies have concentrated on Beakers from funerary contexts, and the overall Beaker ceramic repertoire (including purely 'domestic' forms: see Gibson 1982) needs to be subjected to the same close dating. For present purposes, three key points need to be noted. Firstly, the earliest Insular examples are the most similar to continental, 'international' style Beakers, in both design and technique of manufacture; subsequent developments represent a regional diversification (in both design and manufacture) away from the continental canon although, in certain areas, and at certain times, developmental trajectories suggest renewed acquaintance with continental Beakers (Piggott 1963; Clarke 1970; I. Shepherd 1986). Second, the very wide geographical spread of early Beakers in these islands is noteworthy, suggesting a diaspora-like arrival. It is, however, not evenly distributed: some parts of Britain (especially Wales and south-west England: Burrow this volume; Jones & Quinnell 2011, 208–10), and much of Ireland, have no or only a few early Beakers, and there is a marked coastal and riverine bias to the areas where such Beakers are found (cf. Clarke 1970, maps 1 and 2). Thirdly, the model for characterising Beaker use that Needham developed (and elaborated in this volume) seems to accord well with the evidence for all the concomitant novelties, at least as far as Britain is concerned. In other words, there was an initial phase, from the 25th century until *c.* 2300 BC, when Beakers and other novelties were relatively rare, widely spread and apparently not widely adopted by indigenous communities: this is his 'Beaker as circumscribed, exclusive culture' (Needham 2005, 209). Thereafter, between *c.* 2300 BC and *c.* 1950 BC (and spanning the initial use of bronze), the use of Beaker pottery and the other novelties became the social norm over much – but importantly not all – of Britain. (The areas of low or no Beaker use include Orkney, whose inhabitants appear not to have embraced this and the other

Figure 3.2 Items from the grave assemblages of the 'Amesbury Archer' (this page) and 'Boscombe Bowmen' (opposite page) both Wiltshire. Images: Wessex Archaeology

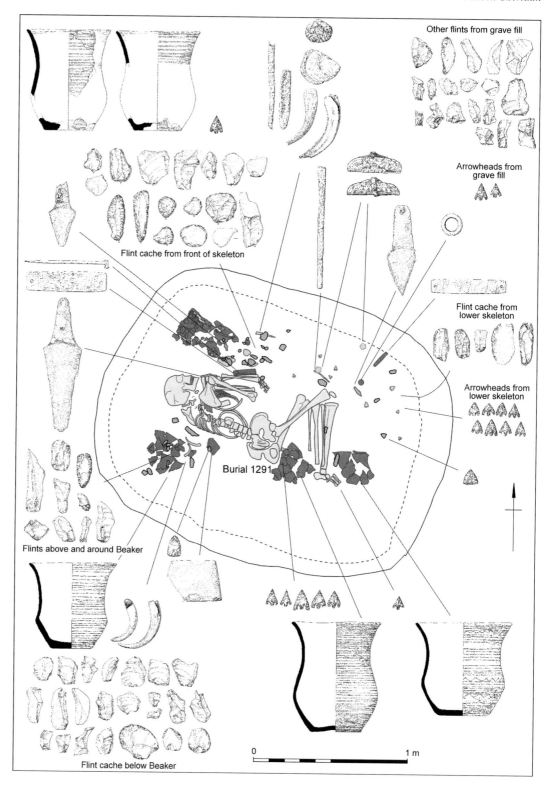

Other flints from grave fill

Arrowheads from grave fill

Flint cache from front of skeleton

Flint cache from lower skeleton

Arrowheads from lower skeleton

Burial 1291

Flints above and around Beaker

Flint cache below Beaker

0   1 m

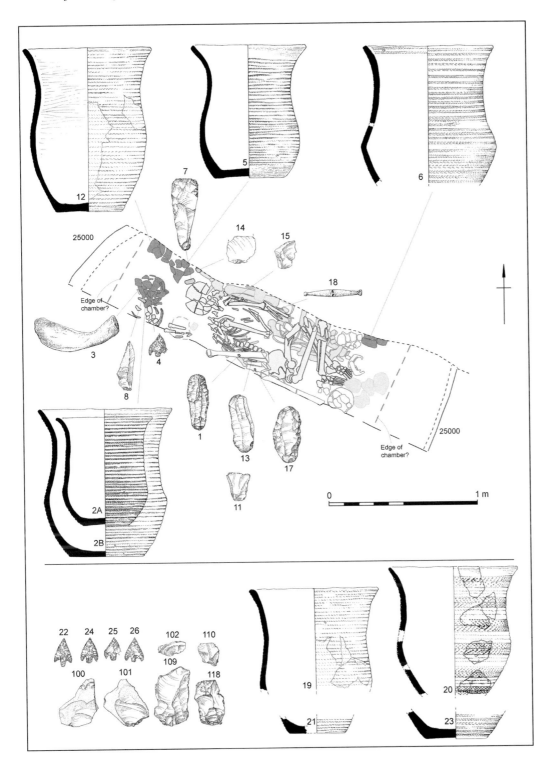

novelties to any great extent.) Many more, and diverse, Beakers were made and the associated funerary repertoire became enriched and socially differentiated: this is characterised as 'Beaker as instituted culture' (*ibid.*). From the 22nd century onwards, other kinds of pottery (notably Food Vessels and cinerary urns) began to be used alongside or instead of Beakers, and the practice of cremation rose in popularity. A final phase of Beaker use – 'Beaker as past reference' (*ibid.*) – is identified between the 20th and 18th/17th centuries, when for most of Britain (except where Barbed Wire Beakers were in use, evidently), the Beaker ceramic tradition was on the wane.

Novel archery paraphernalia

Not only can the continental precursors for the novel archery paraphernalia be identified clearly – as highlighted, for example, in Woodward and Hunter's comprehensive study of British wristguards (Woodward & Hunter 2011; cf. Roe 2011 on the Amesbury Archer's pair of wristguards) – but also, a clear process of elaboration over time can be identified regarding some of the object types, principally wristguards and belt rings. As with Beaker pottery, this represents a divergence away from continental precursors; and even though stone wristguards had probably always been prestige objects, the trajectory of their development shows that they became the subject of competitive conspicuous consumption, at least within Britain. Thus, the wristguard from Culduthel, Highland (Fig. 3.3, Woodward & Hunter 2011, 148) is one of 20 recorded examples made from tuff from Great Langdale (*ibid.*, fig. 10.2), most or all of which could have been made by a single, highly skilled stone carver. Its cachet is enhanced by having copper rivets capped with sheet gold. The adult male with whom the wristguard was found has been radiocarbon-dated (for the *Beakers and Bodies* Project) to 3735±35 BP (SUERC-26462, 2280–2030 cal BC at 2σ), and isotopic analysis of his molar enamel has suggested that he had probably come originally from north-east Ireland (Montgomery and Evans pers. comm.); this high-ranking man might have been involved with the import of Irish copper, via the Great Glen.

The detailed information that has emerged from this, and other recent research into archery paraphernalia (eg, concerning jet and jet-like belt rings: Sheridan & Davis 2002) confirms Needham's view that not only had Beaker-associated practices and material culture become embraced by many communities in Britain by the 23rd century BC; the vocabulary of esteem in which they were deployed was used to highlight social differences, in which some individuals were treated as being more important (at least in death, but also probably in life) than others.

Continental-style ornaments

It is not proposed to review the range of ornaments in use, since this will soon be documented in detail in the publication of a recent Leverhulme-funded research project, led by Ann Woodward and John Hunter, into Chalcolithic and Early Bronze Age grave assemblages in England. (See also the discussions included in Fitzpatrick 2011 regarding those associated with the Amesbury Archer and Boscombe Bowmen). Suffice it to note that the earliest Beaker-associated ornaments are relatively rare; are exclusively associated with men (plus one child), and include archery-related objects, as noted above; and are made from a relatively narrow range of materials (principally copper, gold, bone, and stone including Kimmeridge shale), with Whitby jet and amber not featuring to any significant extent. This contrasts with the situation post-2300 BC (and especially post-2200 BC when bronze started to be used, along with Food Vessels) when there was a proliferation and elaboration of jewellery and dress accessories and, for the first time, we find women being included within the system of status differentiation, and gender-specific forms of jewellery in use. It is at this time that Whitby emerges as an important centre of specialist production and export of jet jewellery, its products including V-perforated buttons (I. Shepherd 2009) and the spacer plate necklaces whose earliest versions, in northern Britain, most emphatically represent skeuomorphs of gold lunulae (*contra* Roberts & Friedman this volume; see Sheridan & Davis 2002).

Metal objects, metalworking, and metal extraction

Other contributions to this volume discuss aspects of this topic in detail, and add to the already considerable literature (as cited by the authors; see also Needham (2011) and La Niece

(2011) for detailed discussion of the copper and gold objects associated with the Amesbury Archer and his so-called 'Companion'). Key points are that the earliest metal objects (Fig. 3.4) are of copper and gold; that copper from Ross Island was being extracted and made into axeheads, knives, and halberds that were exported widely across Ireland and into Britain (Needham 2004); some copper objects, including the Amesbury Archer's knives, were imported from the continent; and recent research by Peter Bray has raised the intriguing prospect that Cornish copper was being exploited, contributing to the composition of some 'Bell Beaker' copper. The pre-Bronze Age gold objects include basket-shaped ornaments and so-called 'sun discs' – see below regarding lunulae – but while generalised continental ancestry for both these object types can be traced, the former clearly represent an insular variant. In the latest discussion of this artefact type (Needham 2011), the question is left open as to whether the source of inspiration had been central or Atlantic Europe. Issues of gold sourcing seem particularly complex, for reasons given below; perhaps all that can be said is that alluvial sources would have been used, and the relatively high copper content of the Amesbury Archer and Chilbolton basket ornaments raises the possibility that these could have been made from continental gold (La Niece 2011), whereas one or more insular sources are suspected for other gold artefacts.

The impact of, and reactions to, Beakers and Beaker-associated novelties

From the foregoing, it therefore appears that the novelties outlined above were probably introduced to Britain and Ireland by small numbers of individuals, coming from various parts of the near continent. While the exploitation of Ross Island copper will have created and satisfied the desire to possess objects of this curious and prestigious new material among the indigenous population, in other respects there does not seem to have been a widespread adoption of Beaker pottery use, or of the associated novelties, until perhaps two centuries after their initial appearance in Britain and Ireland. We are therefore not dealing with the wholesale transplantation of continental societies or values, even though this initial

exposure to foreign ideologies was ultimately to have a profound effect on many communities in these islands.

As far as can be judged, the responses to these continental novelties varied. In Wessex, as detailed by Cleal and Pollard's contribution to this volume, while illustrious foreigners such as the Amesbury Archer were accorded the right of burial according to their own tradition, the pre-existing dominant ideology of the Late Neolithic persisted for some time, with new monuments such as Silbury Hill (and indeed the Marlborough Mount: Pitts 2011) being constructed in post-contact times. That this continuity was a more widespread phenomenon is indicated by Needham's description (this volume) of the so-called 'Beakerisation' of indigenous monument types. The continuing use of Grooved Ware pottery post-contact is clearly demonstrated in East Anglia, where its use literally went underground in the flint mines of Grime's Graves (Healy this volume), at a time when Beaker pottery was being used in the settlements of the area.

Figure 3.3: Wristguard and rest of grave assemblage from Culduthel, Highland, Scotland. Photo: National Museums Scotland

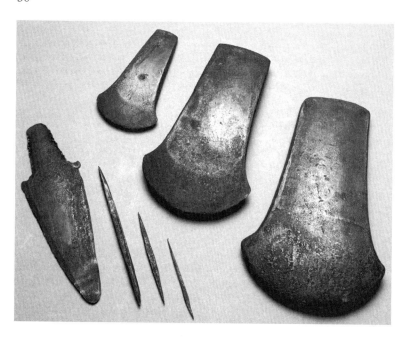

Figure 3.4: Selection of Chalcolithic copper objects: flat axeheads, 'dagger' or knife and awls from the hoard from Knocknague, Co. Galway, Ireland. Photo: National Museums Scotland

Elsewhere, in north-east Scotland, we see Beaker pottery being deployed in the distinctive and innovative funerary monuments of the local elite. These monuments (ie, the Clava ring cairns and passage tombs of the area around Inverness, and the recumbent stone circles of Aberdeenshire: Bradley 2000; 2005) show no continental ancestry. Later, in the same region of Scotland, a similar process of erecting monuments relating to particular individuals is seen at Broomend of Crichie where, at some time between 2150 and 1900 BC, a henge bank and ditch were constructed around a pre-existing arc of standing stones surrounding a Beaker-associated shaft grave (Bradley 2011, illus 2.9). Further afield still, in the Northern Isles we have already noted a reluctance to embrace Beakers and associated novelties in Orkney, where – thanks to the recent excavations at the Ness of Brodgar – we know that the pre-existing, Grooved Ware-associated Late Neolithic 'temple complex' there was remodelled and a major new ceremonial structure (Building 10) was constructed, and used for a massive feast around 2300 BC (http://www.orkneyjar.com/archaeology/2011/10/27/radiocarbon-dates-point-to-a-millennium-of-activity-on-the-ness-of-brodgar/) – all this without the hint of Beaker presence, save for a Beaker found near the socket of a standing stone nearby (Richards 2005, fig. 8.16). In Shetland, as in the Hebrides, domestic and funerary assemblages

indicate that the tradition of using Beaker pottery (and, in some cases, other novelties) took root and developed along local trajectories, with Shetland Beakers appearing in structures (such as Stanydale) that are emphatically local in their design and ancestry. (See Sheridan in press regarding Shetland Beakers, and Parker Pearson *et al.* 2004, 43–52 on South Uist).

What prompted Needham's 'fission horizon' around 2300 BC, when Beaker use became the norm in many parts of Britain, remains one of the many areas of uncertainty that will be touched upon in the following section; but as far as the eventual demise of Grooved Ware use (and of the ideology associated with it) is concerned, it may be that the competitiveness involved in its social dynamic in parts of Britain proved to be unsustainable in the long run. (A similar problem had been encountered by the passage tomb builders of late 4th millennium Ireland: Sheridan 2004.)

Areas of uncertainty, and what we don't know, about the period between the 25th and 22th centuries BC

While we now have a much clearer view of the 'Beaker Phenomenon' and reactions to it than we did just a decade ago, there still remain many areas of uncertainty, as other contributors to this volume point out. This section offers a snapshot of these.

The question of human movement as a mechanism for introducing novel ideas, practices, and material culture needs to be investigated in more detail. While some directions for the initial, 25th century movement of people from different parts of the near continent to different parts of Britain and Ireland have been mentioned, the question of subsequent (and indeed additional) links needs to be clarified, as does the directionality and nature of the interaction. In Ireland, for example, while the Ross Island metalworking evidence may point to Atlantic France as an area of origin, Irish Beakers include some forms that suggest some kind of contact with the Lower Rhine (eg, the large Pot Beaker from Cluntyganny, Co. Tyrone: Fig. 3.5, 1; Brennan *et al.* 1978; cf. Butler & Fokkens 2005, 374) and with central Europe (eg, polypod bowls in pottery and wood, with central Europe being the main, but not the only area of their use. Note the wooden (*Salix*

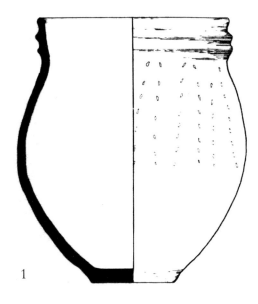

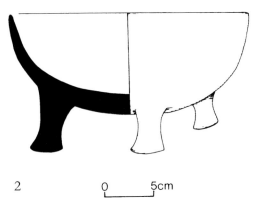

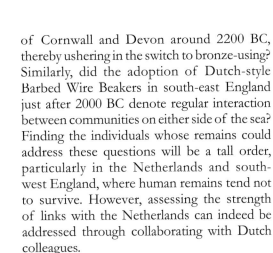

Figure 3.5: Left: Pot Beaker from Cluntyganny, Co. Tyrone (height 415 mm; from Brennan et al. 1978, reproduced by permission of the Ulster Archaeological Society); Right: Wooden polypod bowl from Tirkernaghan, Co. Tyrone (from Earwood 1992, reproduced by permission of the Journal of Irish Archaeology)

sp.) example from Tirkernaghan, Co. Tyrone, radiocarbon dated to 3960±100 BP (OxA-3013, 2860–2140 cal BC: Fig. 3.5, 2; Earwood 1992)). Furthermore, much more needs to be understood about the Atlantic strand that was involved with the introduction of Beakers and associated novelties to Ireland (and perhaps to parts of western Britain as well). As regards motives for immigration, does the model of 'heroic voyagers (mainly in Britain) and metal prospectors (in both Britain and Ireland)' account sufficiently well for the observed geographical spread of the novelties, or were additional motives and kinds of movement involved?

Regarding human movement after the initial appearance of Beaker novelties, while the isotope research on British bodies suggests that most movement was over short distances (Jay *et al.* this volume), with a few documented examples of longer-distance movement within northern Britain and between Ireland and Britain, what about the oft-claimed (eg, Shepherd 1986) connections between north-east Scotland and the Netherlands during the last quarter of the millennium? Did these involve movement of people from Scotland to the Netherlands, or *vice versa*, or both? How close are the claimed links between some short-necked Beakers from north-east Scotland and Dutch early Veluwe Beakers (Fig. 3.6, 1)? And are we to presume the existence of tin prospectors, perhaps from central Europe, who discovered the rich tin supplies

of Cornwall and Devon around 2200 BC, thereby ushering in the switch to bronze-using? Similarly, did the adoption of Dutch-style Barbed Wire Beakers in south-east England just after 2000 BC denote regular interaction between communities on either side of the sea? Finding the individuals whose remains could address these questions will be a tall order, particularly in the Netherlands and south-west England, where human remains tend not to survive. However, assessing the strength of links with the Netherlands can indeed be addressed through collaborating with Dutch colleagues.

In identifying the range of novelties associated with Beaker use it remains unclear as to whether the archery paraphernalia actually included the composite recurve bow, as Piggott had suggested in 1971. In the very rare instances where complete or fragmentary bows of this period have been found in Britain and Ireland, they have not been of this type (Fitzpatrick 2011, 161–3). Piggott had linked recurve bows with the idea of mounted archers, and until the recent radiocarbon dating of horse remains at Newgrange revealed them to be of Iron Age, not Beaker date (Bendrey 2012), it was assumed that domestic horses had been part of the Beaker 'Package'. The evidence in support of that hypothesis is now looking decidedly thin, relying on a single horse tooth from the Beaker settlement at Northton on Harris (Simpson *et al.* 2006), which is shortly to be submitted for radiocarbon dating to check whether it had been intrusive.

Many other chronological issues remain to be resolved. Despite the dramatic improvements in dating – with north-east Scotland now arguably being the most comprehensively-dated Beaker

*Figure 3.6: 1.
Short-necked Beaker
from Inveramsay,
Aberdeenshire, likened by
David L. Clarke (1970,
363) to an early Veluwe
Beaker from Garderen,
Netherlands; 2. Copper
neck ring from Yarnton,
Oxfordshire. Photos:
National Museums
Scotland*

Beakers). The fact that lunulae were still in use (or were being made) after 2200 BC is indicated by the find from Harlyn Bay, Cornwall, with the clear association with a Migdale bronze axehead (Taylor 1980). Likewise, what was the overall currency for gold 'sun discs' and for copper halberds (cf. Needham 2004)? When were the continental-looking copper neck rings from Lumphanan and Yarnton made (Fig. 3.6, 2)? For how long did copper objects continue to be used after bronze started to be made? And when exactly did bronze use start in Britain and Ireland – was it the 22nd century, as many believe? What is the chronology (and scale) of copper artefact production between the 25th and 22nd centuries BC? And do the richest post-2300 BC Beaker grave assemblages actually date to the period after bronze began to be used – so that they belong to the 'get rich quick' society whose elite are so ostentatiously demarcated in funerary practices from the 22nd century onwards? While Bayesian modelling of existing dates can help address the last question, only new dates can help to address the others.

Similarly serious issues relate to the question of sourcing metal, especially gold. While recent research on the gold deposits in the Mourne Mountains of north-east Ireland appeared to confirm these as the source for many early gold objects (Warner *et al.* 2009), new research by Bristol University's Chris Standish, featuring lead isotope analysis of gold, has controversially suggested (in a lecture presented to the 2011 Bronze Age Forum, Cardiff) that Cornwall may be a potential source area for at least some Irish artefacts. As regards copper extraction, the possibility that Cornish sources were exploited at an early date needs to be investigated in the field, as does the possibility of early activity at Cwmystwyth, Ceredigion, where a gold 'sun disc' was found (Timberlake 2009).

Much more needs to be understood about the nature of settlement, subsistence activities, and domestic assemblages, especially to address the question of whether there is any read-across with Bell Beaker settlement, economy, and material culture on the continent (as may be hinted at by the boat-shaped houses of the Western Isles: Parker Pearson *et al.* 2004, 46–7). The record of the non-funerary Beaker ceramic repertoire has not been updated since Gibson's useful overview in 1982, and there is a pressing need for non-funerary and funerary Beaker pottery to be approached and dated as a unified

region in Europe – our understanding of the chronology of specific artefact types leaves much to be desired. Were gold lunulae in use before the 22nd century, when bronze began to be used? The traditional view (as expressed, for example, by Needham 2000) is that they developed around 2300 BC, as part of a flourishing, small-scale, innovating Irish gold-working 'industry'. This may well be correct, and yet the only direct dating evidence available to support this view remains the date of 3800±50 BP (GrA-13982, 2460–2050 cal BC) for a lunula box of alder from Crossdoney, Co. Cavan (Cahill 2006), plus the suite of dates for the jet spacer plate necklaces that copied them, which mostly span the 22nd–20th centuries BC (eg, 3635±35 BP, GrA-34345, 2130–1900 cal BC for an example from Inchmarnock. See also Curtis & Wilkin this volume on the dating of lunula motifs on

tradition. Allen and Maltby's contribution to this volume provides a vitally-important glimpse into the subsistence activities, as did Shepherd and Tuckwell's report on Beaker-period cultivation in the machair at Rosinish, Benbecula (1977); a Britain and Ireland-wide synthesis is long overdue.

Finally, there are many more specific questions to be answered, such as the nature and date of an enigmatic bone plate with Beaker-like decoration found at Jarlshof in Shetland (Fig. 3.7), and the chronological and stylistic relationship between Beaker and Grooved Ware – and indeed other – pottery. Overall, what is clearly needed is an approach to the 25th–22nd century BC that integrates all the diverse (and currently over-separated) current strands of investigation; takes a multi-scale view that ranges from the local to the international; and does not simply concentrate on Beaker pottery and associated material use to the exclusion of other contemporary developments.

Conclusions. So is this period worthy of its own label? And should that label be 'the Chalcolithic'?

Despite the plethora of uncertainties outlined above, it is this author's view that the period between the 25th century and the first appearance of bronze in Britain and Ireland is richly deserving of its own label. It is one of several instances throughout our prehistory where we can witness the widespread appearance of novel practices and ideologies from the continent (cf. the Mesolithic–Neolithic transition). While the full social and economic impact of this contact with the continent might not have been felt until the switch to bronze-using – when, as a form of power, control over the movement of resources seems to have become at least as important as control over beliefs – the 25th–22nd centuries BC paved the way for this transformation.

The choice of the term 'Chalcolithic' (or 'Copper Age') to describe this period is indeed fraught with potential problems, since many feel that it brings inappropriate socio-economic baggage. However, it is far preferable to the

Figure 3.7: A northern mystery: an enigmatic ?Beaker bone object from Jarlshof, Shetland. Photo: National Museums Scotland

ambiguous term 'Late Neolithic–Early Bronze Age', and to the downright wrong term 'Early Bronze Age', which are so often employed to describe the first few centuries of Beaker use in these islands. Others in this volume are indeed correct to point out that 'our Chalcolithic' is a very different beast from the Chalcolithics of north-west, central, or south-east Europe, not least because it is far shorter and started later and because, unlike in some parts of Europe, metal production does not appear to have been a major driver of behaviour (except perhaps in south-west Ireland). If one chooses to accrete specific, continental-derived models of social and economic organisation to the use of the term, then of course its use would be inappropriate here. However, if one chooses to loosen the conceptual shackles, and if one seeks to characterise this period on its own terms, tracing what actually transpired in Britain and Ireland, we shall all benefit.

Some sense of the scale of the task facing us has been presented above, and we should heed the immortal and eloquent words of our guru Donald Rumsfeld: 'Learn to say 'I don't know'. If used appropriately, it will be often'.

Acknowledgements
Warmest thanks are extended to Mike Allen and Julie Gardiner for their patience and hard work as editors. Copyright holders are thanked for their permission to reproduce images; Mary Cahill is thanked for alerting me to Robin Bendrey's research into domestic horses, and Robin Bendrey is thanked for promptly providing information. Thanks also to David Field, Jim Leary and Richard Strachan, Cormac Bourke and Tomás Ó Carragáin for their instant responses to my illustration requests.

Bibliography

Allen, M.J., Gardiner, J. & Sheridan, A. (eds), 2012. *Is there a British Chalcolithic? Place, people and polity in the later 3rd millennium.* Oxford: Prehistoric Society Research Paper 4

Abercromby, J. 1912. *A Study of the Bronze Age Pottery of Britain and Ireland and its associated Grave Goods.* Oxford: Oxford University Press

Bendrey, R. 2012. From wild horses to domestic horses: a European perspective. *World Archaeology* 44(1), 135–57

Bradley, R. 2000. *The Good Stones. A New Investigation of the Clava Cairns.* Edinburgh: Society of Antiquaries of Scotland

Bradley, R. 2005. *The Moon and the Bonfire. An Investigation of Three Stone Circles in North-east Scotland.* Edinburgh: Society of Antiquaries of Scotland

Bradley, R. 2011. *Stages and Screens. An Investigation of Four Henge Monuments in Northern and North-eastern Scotland.* Edinburgh: Society of Antiquaries of Scotland

Bray, P. this volume. Before $_{29}$Cu became copper: tracing the recognition and invention of metalleity in Britain and Ireland during the 3rd millennium BC. In Allen *et al.* (eds)

Brennan, J., Briggs, C.S. & ApSimon, A.M. 1978. A giant Beaker from Cluntyganny Townland, County Tyrone. *Ulster Journal of Archaeology* 41, 33–6

Brindley, A.L. & Lanting, J.N. 1992. Radiocarbon dates from wedge tombs. *Journal of Irish Archaeology* 6, 19–26

Broeke, P. van den, Fokkens, H. & Gijn, A. van. 2005. A prehistory of our time. In L.P. Louwe Kooijmans, P.W. van den Broeke, H. Fokkens & A.L. van Gijn (eds), *The Prehistory of the Netherlands*, 17–31. Amsterdam: Amsterdam University Press

Burgess, C. & Shennan, S.J. 1976. The Beaker phenomenon: some suggestions. In C. Burgess & R. Miket (eds), *Settlement and Economy in the Third and Second millennia BC*, 309–31. Oxford: British Archaeological Reports 33

Burrow, S. this volume. A review of radiocarbon dates from Wales for the period 2450–2100 cal BC. In Allen *et al.* (eds)

Butler, J. & Fokkens, H. 2005. From stone to bronze: technology and material culture. In L.P. Louwe Kooijmans, P.W. van den Broeke, H. Fokkens & A.L. van Gijn (eds), *The Prehistory of the Netherlands*, 371–99. Amsterdam: Amsterdam University Press

Cahill, M. 2006. John Windele's golden legacy–prehistoric and later gold ornaments from Co. Cork and Co. Waterford. *Proceedings of the Royal Irish Academy* 106C, 219–337

Card, N. 2010. Colour, cups and tiles – recent discoveries at the Ness of Brodgar. *PAST* 66, 1–3

Carlin, N. & Brück, J. This volume. Searching for the Chalcolithic: continuity and change in the Irish Final Neolithic/Early Bronze Age. In Allen *et al.* (eds)

Case, H. 2001. The Beaker culture in Britain and Ireland: groups, European contacts and chronology. In F. Nicolis (ed.), *Bell Beakers Today. Pottery, People, Culture, Symbols in Prehistoric Europe*, 361–77. Trento: Ufficio Beni Archeologici

Case, H.J. 1966. Were Beaker-people the first metallurgists in Ireland? *Palaeohistoria* 12, 141–77

Chenery, C.A. & Evans, J.A. 2011 A summary of the strontium and oxygen isotope evidence for the origins of Bell Beaker individuals found near Stonehenge. In Fitzpatrick 2011, 185–90

Clarke, D.L. 1970. *Beaker Pottery of Great Britain and Ireland.* Cambridge: Cambridge University Press

Cleal, R. & MacSween, A. (eds). 1999. *Grooved Ware in Britain and Ireland.* Oxford: Oxbow Books

Cleal, R. & Pollard, J. this volume. The Revenge of the Native: monuments, material culture, burial and other practices in the third quarter of the 3rd millennium BC in Wessex. In Allen *et al.* (eds)

Curtis, N. & Wilkin N. this volume. The Regionality of Beakers and Bodies in the Chalcolithic of North-East Scotland. In Allen *et al.* (eds)

Earwood, C. 1992. A radiocarbon date for Early Bronze Age wooden polypod bowls. *Journal of Irish Archaeology* 6, 27–8

Fitzpatrick, A.P. 2011. *The Amesbury Archer and the Boscombe Bowmen. Early Beaker burials at Boscombe Down, Amesbury, Wiltshire, Great Britain.* Salisbury: Wessex Archaeology Report 27

Fokkens, H. this volume. Dutchmen on the move? A discussion of the adoption of the beaker package. In In Allen *et al.* (eds)

Fokkens, H., Achterkamp, Y. & Kuijpers, M.H.G. 2008. Bracers or bracelets? About the functionality and meaning of Bell Beaker wrist-guards. *Proceedings of the Prehistoric Society* 74, 109–40

Gibson, A.M. 1982. *Beaker Domestic sites. A Study of the Domestic Pottery of the Late Third and Early Second Millennia B.C. in the British Isles.* Oxford: British Archaeological Report 107

Gibson, A. 1998. *Stonehenge and Timber Circles.* Stroud: Tempus

Gibson, A. 2007. A Beaker veneer? Some evidence from the burial record. In Larsson & Parker Pearson (eds) 2007, 47–64

Healy, F. This volume. Chronology, corpses, ceramics, copper and lithics. In Allen *et al.* (eds)

Henshall, A.S. 1972. *The Chambered Tombs of Scotland, Volume 2.* Edinburgh: Edimburgh University Press

Jay, M., Parker Pearson, M., Richards, M., Nehlich, O., Montgomery, J., Chamberlain, A. & Sheridan, A. this volume. The Beaker People Project: an interim report on the progress of the isotopic analysis of the organic skeletal material. In Allen *et al.* (eds)

Jones, A.M. & Quinnell, H. 2011. The Neolithic and Bronze Age in Cornwall, *c* 4000 cal BC to *c* 1000 cal BC: an overview of recent developments. *Cornish Archaeology* 50, 197–229

La Niece, S. 2011. Examination and analysis of the gold ornaments and comparative primary Beaker goldwork. In Fitzpatrick 2011, 138–40

Larsson, M. & Parker Pearson, M. (eds). *From Stonehenge to the Baltic: living with cultural diversity in the third millennium BC*, 41–6. Oxford: British Archaeological Report S1692

Leary, J. & Field. D. 2010. *The Story of Silbury Hill.* Swindon: English Heritage

Leary, J., Field, D. & Russell, M. 2010. Marvels at Marden henge. *PAST* 66, 14–16

Lelong, O. & MacGregor, G. 2007. *The Lands of Ancient Lothian. Interpreting the Archaeology of the A1.* Edinburgh: Society of Antiquaries of Scotland

Longworth, I.H. 1999. The Folkton drums unpicked. In Cleal & MacSween (eds) 1999, 83–8

Manby, T.G., Moorhouse, S. & Ottaway, P. 2003. *The Archaeology of Yorkshire: an Assessment at the Beginning of the 21st century*. Leeds: Yorkshire Archaeological Society

Needham, S.P. 2000. The development of embossed goldwork in Bronze Age Europe. *Antiquaries Journal* 80, 27–65

Needham, S.P. 2004. Migdale-Marnoch: sunburst of Scottish metallurgy. In I.A.G. Shepherd & G.J. Barclay (eds), *Scotland in Ancient Europe: the Neolithic and Early Bronze Age of Scotland in their European context*, 217–45. Edinburgh: Society of Antiquaries of Scotland

Needham, S.P. 2005. Transforming Beaker culture in north-west Europe; processes of fusion and fission. *Proceedings of the Prehistoric Society* 71, 171–217

Needham, S.P. 2007. Isotopic aliens: Beaker movement and cultural transmissions. In Larsson & Parker Pearson (eds) 2007, 41–6

Needham, S.P. 2011. Gold basket-shaped ornaments from Graves 1291 (Amesbury Archer) and 1236. In Fitzpatrick 2011, 129–38

Needham, S.P. this volume. Case and place for the British Chalcolithic. In Allen *et al.* (eds)

O'Brien, W. 2004. *Ross Island. Mining, Metal and Society in Early Ireland*. Galway: National University of Ireland, Galway. Bronze Age Studies 6

O'Brien, W. This volume. The Chalcolithic in Ireland: a chronological and cultural framework. In Allen *et al.* (eds)

Parker Pearson, M. 2007. The Stonehenge Riverside Project: excavations at the east entrance of Durrington Walls. In Larsson & Parker Pearson (eds) 2007, 125–44

Parker Pearson, M. & Cox Willis, C. 2011. Burials and builders of Stonehenge: social identities in Late Neolithic and Chalcolithic Britain. In M. Furholt, F. Lüth & J. Müller (eds), *Megaliths and Identities: early monuments and Neolithic societies from the Atlantic to the Baltic*, 285–93. Bonn: Habelt

Parker Pearson, M., Sharples, N. & Symonds, J. 2004. *South Uist: archaeology and history of a Hebridean island*. Stroud: Tempus

Piggott, S. 1963. Abercromby and after: the Beaker cultures of Britain re-examined. In I.Ll. Foster & L. Alcock (eds), *Culture and Environment. Essays in Honour of Sir Cyril Fox*, 53–92. London: Routledge & Kegan Paul

Piggott, S. 1971. Beaker bows: a suggestion. *Proceedings of the Prehistoric Society* 37, 80–94

Pitts, M. 2011. Proof that mound in college grounds is Silbury twin. *British Archaeology* 119, 6

Richards, C. 2005. *Dwelling Among the Monuments – the Neolithic Village of Barnhouse, Maeshowe Passage Grave and Surrounding Monuments at Stenness. Orkney*. Cambridge: McDonald Institute

Roberts, B. & Frieman, V. this volume. Drawing boundaries and building models: investigating the concept of the 'Chalcolithic Frontier' in north-west Europe. In Allen *et al.* (eds)

Roe, F. 1966. The battle-axe series in Britain. *Proceedings of the Prehistoric Society* 32, 199–245

Roe, F. 2011. Bracers. In Fitzpatrick 2011, 103–12

Salanova, L. 2000. *La question du Campaniforme en France et dans les îles anglo-normandes: productions, chronologie et roles d'un standard ceramique*. Paris: Editions du Comité des Travaux Historiques et Scientifiques /Société Préhistorique Française

Salanova L. 2007. Les sépultures campaniformes: lecture sociale. In J. Guilaine (ed), *Le Chalcolithique et la construction des inégalités, t. I: Le continent européen*, 213–28. Paris: Editions Errance

Shepherd, A.N. this volume. Stepping out together: men, women and their Beakers in time and space. In Allen *et al.* (eds)

Shepherd, I.A.G. 1986. *Powerful Pots: Beakers in north-east prehistory*. Aberdeen: Aberdeen Museum of Anthropology

Shepherd, I.A.G. 2009. The V-perforated buttons of Great Britain and Ireland. *Proceedings of the Prehistoric Society* 75, 335–69

Shepherd, I.A.G. & Tuckwell, A.N. 1977. Traces of beaker-period cultivation at Rosinish, Benbecula. *Proceedings of the Society of Antiquaries of Scotland* 108 (1976–7), 108–13

Sheridan, J.A. 2004. Going round in circles? Understanding the Irish Grooved Ware 'complex' in its wider context. In H. Roche, E. Grogan, J. Bradley, J. Coles & B. Raftery (eds), *From Megaliths to Metals: essays in honour of George Eogan*, 26–37. Oxford: Oxbow Books

Sheridan, J.A. 2007. Scottish Beaker dates: the good, the bad and the ugly. In Larsson & Parker Pearson (eds) 2007, 91–123

Sheridan, J.A. 2008. Upper Largie and Dutch-Scottish connections during the Beaker period. In H. Fokkens, B J Coles, A.L. van Gijn, J.P. Kleijne, H.W. Ponjee & C.J. Slappendel (eds), *Between foraging and farming. An extended broad spectrum of papers presented to Leendert Louwe Kooijmans*, 247–60. *Analecta Praehistorica Leidensia* 40

Sheridan, J.A. in press. The Neolithic (and Chalcolithic and Early Bronze Age) of Shetland: a view from the Mainland. In D. Mahler (ed.), *Farming on the edge: cultural landscapes of the North II*. Copenhagen: Nationalmuseet

Sheridan, J.A. & Davis, M. 2002. Investigating jet and jet-like artefacts from prehistoric Scotland: the National Museums of Scotland project. *Antiquity* 76, 812–25

Simpson, D.D.A., Murphy, E.M. & Gregory, R.A. 2006. *Excavations at Northton, Isle of Harris*. Oxford: British Archaeological Report 408

Taylor, J.J. 1980. *Bronze Age Goldwork of the British Isles*. Cambridge: Cambridge University Press

Timberlake, S. 2009. Copper mining and metal production at the beginning of the British Bronze Age. In P. Clark (ed), *Bronze Age Connections: cultural contact in prehistoric Europe*, 94–121. Oxford: Oxbow Books

Warner, R., Chapman, R., Cahill, M. and Moles, N. 2009. The gold-source found at last? *Archaeology Ireland* 23(2), 22–25

Woodward, A. & Hunter, J. 2011. *An Examination of Prehistoric Stone Bracers from Britain*. Oxford: Oxbow Books

4

Before $_{29}$Cu became Copper: tracing the recognition and invention of metalleity in Britain and Ireland during the 3rd millennium BC

Peter Bray

Through chemical and chronological analysis of the British and Irish metalwork, it should be relatively easy to assess whether there was a period when copper was in use but rarely alloyed with tin. This straightforward definition of a Chalcolithic appears to fit well with the mid-3rd millennium BC artefacts of Needham's Metalwork Assemblages 1 and 2. However, this paper argues that labelling this period a Chalcolithic, or any other similar name, is highly problematic from a number of perspectives. It is a restrictive term, which carries the implication that copper already had a complete, universal, and finished set of attributes. The concept and possibilities of metalleity in fact continued to develop and morph throughout the 3rd and 2nd millennia. Allied to this is evidence for very early tin-bronze objects being recycled into later objects, indicating that any period of using solely unalloyed copper may have been extremely brief. Through combining the complete scientific dataset with the latest archaeological and theoretical insights, this paper explores the material and conceptual traces of early British and Irish metallurgy. Rather than increasing the number of materials-based period labels, it is more important to explore the changing roles and compositions of metal, within a framework provided by absolute chronologies.

When considering the possible existence and nature of a Chalcolithic, archaeometallurgists may be said to have an easier time than other specialists. In a traditional formulation of the problem we merely have to identify whether there was a period where the dominant metal in use was unalloyed copper and then derive an absolute date for this section of the past. This paper attempts to go beyond this through focusing on the crucial difference between presence and understanding. It will investigate the local conception of metal during the first 500 years of metallurgy in Britain and Ireland. Put simply, the presence of copper in the archaeological record is a necessary condition for the defining of a Chalcolithic period, but is it a sufficient criterion? In a material world dominated by stone, timber, soil, ceramic, and textile, what elements of metalleity were actually recognised and exploited by 3rd millennium societies? Unfortunately including gold in this discussion was beyond the limits of the paper; however, can we begin to trace the process of creating a social and material identity for copper?

Metalleity is not a neologism, but is a rather forgotten and useful word for the collective properties and potential that come with metal (Huxham 1753, 859). I am using it here, rather than a word like 'metalness', to emphasise that what constitutes 'metal' is a *package* of attributes that are potentially available to human society. Copper contains many possibilities of expression, use and understanding. We must go beyond the identification of ₂₉Cu and attempt to understand the shifting flow of metalleity.

Characterising early metalwork: chemistry and typology

Through the painstaking application of chemical and typological analysis, a broad standard model has coalesced for the earliest indigenous metallurgy in Britain and Ireland. The best expression of this is clearly the Metalwork Assemblage (MA) system of Stuart Needham (1996) which, in turn, builds on substantial advances by Colin Burgess (1980) and others (Coles 1968; Gerloff 1975). Under Needham's MA system, metallurgy before *c*. 2200 BC, MAs 1 and 2, consists almost exclusively of copper and gold. The deposition of tin-bronze appears suddenly in the metallurgical sequence, and during MA 3 (*c*. 2200–2000 BC) becomes immediately ubiquitous across Britain and Ireland (Needham *et al.* 1989). It is not much of a jump to say that, *de facto*, MA 1 and 2 represent a Chalcolithic and should be studied as such.

If we consider the main classes of early metal artefacts – namely axes, daggers, and halberds – only 14 of those objects that were assigned an MA 1 and 2 date and had their composition tested were found to contain more than 2% tin. This represents 2.57% of all chemically analysed MA 1 or 2 objects. This paper collates the results of a number of analytical programmes, the principal ones being Gowland (1906), Case (1954), Coghlan and Case (1957), Britton (1961; 1963), Junghans *et al.* (1968), Allen *et al.* (1970), Coghlan (1979), Needham (1983), Rohl and Needham (1998),

Northover (1999), and unpublished data kindly provided by Peter Northover.

The number of MA 1/2 axes, daggers, and halberds with a known chemical composition is as follows:

Whole island of Ireland	407
Scotland	51
Wales	27
Central England	25
Eastern England	22
South-west England	13
(Non-Irish Total	138)

The corresponding figures for MA 3 axes, daggers and halberds are:

Whole island of Ireland	173
Scotland	126
Wales	38
Central England	35
Eastern England	16
South-west England	16
(Non-Irish Total	231)

Of these MA 3 artefacts only 19 contain *less* than 2% tin, which is 4.70% of the analysed total. Under the most straightforward definition, and within the criteria of Metalwork Assemblages, the existence of a Chalcolithic period in British and Irish metalworking seems clear.

It must be said at the outset that the main aim of this paper is to not critique in detail the MA system. Typology-based dating schemes must remain at the heart of Bronze Age metallurgy studies in order to allow further investigations. As Stuart Needham argues:

> 'Without that bedrock, virtually none of these more penetrating questions could be tackled, or even in some cases formulated. Those who decry the value of detailed typological schemes and the establishment of patterns of association as sterile and introspective need to heed the consequences of their abandonment or neglect.' (Needham 2007, 278)

For this reason, the MA system will be employed here as an organising tool in this investigation of the local uptake of metal use and metalworking in Britain and Ireland.

Changing theories of technology and material

The study of technology and material has always been central to archaeological thought. Beyond naming many of our archaeological periods, metal use has often implied to archaeologists the presence of modernity, science and cultural progress:

> 'Modern science and industry not only go back to the period when bronze was the dominant industrial metal, their beginnings were in a very real sense conditioned and inspired by the mere fact of the general employment of bronze and copper.' (Childe 1930, 2–3)

Similar thinking can be seen in Hawkes' (1954) famous ladder of inference where technology and the understanding of material are most straightforward to modern archaeologists. As the production of a material can be defined chemically and physically it is easy to see how a strong 'common sense' link can be made between modern experience and ancient practice. It used to be very common to see change in materials explained in terms of modern science and advancing operating temperatures:

> 'One can only speculate that, with the advent of smelting, feverish experimentation with ores, woods, and charcoals, and with furnace design, blowing devices and clays, was carried out.' (Wertime 1964, 1261)

Killick (2001, 487) characterises this type of metallurgy as armchair archaeology. Despite a significant amount of scholarship tackling its deficiencies it still underlies some current thinking about metals, such as this work from 2000:

> 'The evolution of metal and alloys preparation has been directed, *since the beginning of metallurgy*, towards (1) the research of better products – better properties, better reproducibility, larger production' (Le Coze 2000, 219, my emphasis)

This is clearly a 'presentist fallacy' (Budd & Taylor 1995; Killick 2001), wherein superficially similar materials are assumed to represent similar values to those expected today. If we assume that small amounts of metal dated to the mid-3rd millennium BC represent a new 'metal defined age', we are in danger of falling into a similar trap. This point also underlines why I avoided using 'metalness' in this argument, as it is too easy to imagine the discovery of *our* version of metal, rather than a shifting collage of potentially very different meanings.

A number of scholarship traditions over the last 60 years have proposed new ways of theorising about and investigating technology and materials. Common to all this work is an effort to break down the crude evolutionary model of earlier thinkers. Technological progress used to be seen as inevitable and founded upon humanity's 'alertness' to using their surroundings to solve their numerous problems (Levin 1976). A loose coalition of research projects have overturned this approach, each with slightly different aims and datasets; these include anthropological fieldwork (Herbert 1993), technological drama (Pfaffenberger 1992), agency theory (Dobres & Robb 2005), materiality (Jones 2004 and replies), Science and Technology Studies (Geselowitz 1993), and so forth. In the broadest terms all these scholars would agree that copper and other archaeological materials cannot be seen as passive objects to be exploited by human beings:

> 'To construct a technology is not merely to deploy materials and techniques; it is also to construct social and economic alliances, to invent new legal principles for social relations, and to provide powerful new vehicles for culturally-provided myths.' (Pfaffenberger 1988, 249).

The simple expression that technology is a socially embedded phenomenon is an extremely powerful idea. The realisation that technology and society are indivisibly symbiotic, and that influence flows both from people and things, inevitably led to a reassessment of the object in archaeological theory. Archaeologists are now very comfortable with using terms about 'things' that were formerly restricted to describing people, such as biography (Appadurai 1986) and social agency (Dobres & Hoffman 1994; Gosden 2005).

It is clearly important to apply these new theoretical ideas to the scientific archaeo-metallurgical dataset in order to reassess the earliest British and Irish metalwork. However, this would appear to be a major challenge due to the paucity of the archaeological dataset compared to, for example, anthropology or history. To assess the material itself we have to appreciate that 'metal technology' and 'copper' are, for this purpose, too broad as labels. Ingold (2007) recently focused on a conception of materials as the interplay of overlapping attributes, each with a socially embedded history of exploitation. This concept has clear links with existing archaeological research and may be of great practical use. There are substantial philosophical ties with David Clarke's (1968) view of artefact forms consisting of overlapping attributes. This mode of description is named polythetic entitation and had its most famous application in Clarke's (1970) typology of Beaker pottery.

A scale of analysis whereby we aim to look separately at various attributes of a material meshes neatly with our modern archaeometallurgical toolkit. Metallography (Scott 1991), use-wear analysis (Wall 1987), lead isotope analysis (Rohl & Needham 1998), chemical composition analysis (see above), site excavation (O'Brien 2004), laboratory-based experimental metallurgy (McKerrell & Tylecote 1972; Ottaway & Wang 2004), and typographical analysis (Gerloff 1975; Needham 1983) each have strengths in addressing particular aspects of copper. An attribute-based approach to material challenges our culturally-biased assumptions about what aspects of metal would have been important in the 3rd millennium. Rather than using models of technological change it is firmly grounded in archaeological data.

Metallurgical behaviour in the 3rd millennium BC: tracing the discovery and exploration of some attributes of metalleity

Metal has a wide range of intrinsic properties ranging from its colour, hardness, toughness, expansion upon heating, and ability to be melted and formed into new shapes, through to more modern concerns, such as its ability to conduct electricity and sometimes become magnetised. Each metal-using society throughout history has drawn out its own particular concept of metalleity from the potential repertoire that the substance provides. The metalleity of copper varies, grows, and shifts as its various attributes are recognised, adopted or discarded. Crucially a number of these attributes can be traced empirically using archaeological datasets (Bray 2009).

This paper highlights recently developed approaches to some of these attributes (*ibid.*). It will challenge the existence of a British and Irish Chalcolithic on two counts: first, and most importantly, that many of the characteristics of metal were clearly not fully appreciated until a later time; and secondly, that the subsequent recycling of metal has hidden very early tin-bronzes from archaeological view.

Extractive metallurgy in the mid-3rd millennium BC: Ross Island, Cornwall and the invention of ore

A metal-using society does not necessarily have to produce its own metal. It is possible to conceive of a situation where the connection between ore, heat and the resulting copper is not made. Evidence in Britain is very sparse and controversial for pre-Beaker metalwork. Two claimed examples are tin-bronze awls that were assigned Neolithic dates by their excavators. The first recovered was from Castell Bryn-Gwyn, Anglesey (Wainwright 1962) and a similar-sized awl from Tewksbury was found in a pit containing sherds of Peterborough Ware (Hannan 1993). Being made of tin-bronze makes these finds even more extraordinary and controversial and the evidence clearly needs to be revisited critically. However, the standards of excavation that were employed, and the unlikely association with Neolithic pottery, mean that these finds can probably be safely dismissed from the history of British metallurgy's origins. While the evidence for pre-Beaker metal in Britain and Ireland remains elusive, what is not disputed is that this contrasts with the situation in northern France, where there is clear evidence for pre-Beaker metallurgy (Blanchet 1984; Mohen 1977, 34 No. 1).

Generally cited as the earliest securely dated examples of metalwork in the south of England are the three copper wire or strip rings from the Beaker Grave 919 at Barrow Hills, Radley in Oxfordshire (Barclay & Halpin 1999). The associated calibrated radiocarbon date (OxA-1875, 3970±80 BP, 2850–2210 cal BC at 95.4%, OxCal 4.1 using IntCal 09) indicates that the metal was probably deposited much earlier than 2200 BC, although the calibrated date range is unfortunately rather wide. Attempts to locate the human remains to redate them have so far proved unsuccessful (A. Sheridan, pers. comm.). The chemical composition of the objects is distinctive and without clear parallels in slightly later MA 1/2 metalwork (Northover 1999). Overall the Barrow Hill rings are probably an import into an area with little or no concept of extractive metallurgy, and they underline the fact that that the concept of ore has to be invented and adopted.

Despite some early scepticism (Briggs 1983), archaeologists have provided definitive evidence for the mining of British and Irish copper ore in the mid-3rd millennium BC, falling slightly after the kind of contacts suggested by Barrow Hills (Ixer & Budd 1998; Timberlake 2002). O'Brien's (2004) excavations of the site of Ross Island, County Kerry in south-west Ireland show a clear link between tennantite ore deposits and a Beaker working camp. The radiocarbon evidence for exploitation of these ores from around 2400–2000 BC matches extremely well with a distinct chemical composition of early metal work with a high arsenic, antimony and silver pattern. Around 73% of all MA 1/2 British and Irish copper objects that have been analysed can be shown to be derived from Ross Island ore due to their chemical and isotopic composition (Bray 2009). The metal, commonly named 'A Metal' from Northover's (1980) classification system, was most probably smelted close to the mine itself (O'Brien 2004). This one mining site, initially worked by Beaker-using continental prospectors, was responsible for the vast majority of copper deposited in 3rd millennium Britain and Ireland.

Around 5% of the remaining MA 1/2 copper work is named Bell Beaker metal. It derives its name from Butler and Van der Waals' (1966) study where it was dubbed 'Dutch Bell Beaker metal'. Unfortunately this tripartite name contains two misleading sections, as this composition type is not exclusive either to just Dutch or just Bell Beaker contexts. Detailed analysis by Needham (2002) led him to conclude that the Bell Beaker metal group, defined by its high arsenic and high nickel chemical composition, actually represents a mixture of two separate sources, if not more. He argues that it is likely that a high nickel source is located on the European mainland, possibly northern Spain. It is increasingly clear that one source of the 'low nickel' Bell Beaker is the copper ores of Cornwall (Bray 2009). It should be noted that the Great Orme mine in north-west Wales added a copper of similar composition into circulation during the later Early Bronze Age and on into the Middle Bronze Age (Bray in prep.).

The key to making a case for early Cornish copper production is the lead isotope analysis of Rohl and Needham (1998), in particular the five MA 1/2 artefacts they dubbed 'IMP-LI group 2'. Four of these can be classed as Bell Beaker metal, with the other showing a very similar composition, classed as 'Arsenic Only' metal. These artefacts stand out from

the British lead isotope dataset as they possess uranogenic lead isotope ratios caused by the presence and decay of uranium in the ore source. As both ^{206}Pb and ^{207}Pb are derived from the decay of uranium isotopes, ^{238}U and ^{235}U respectively, they will be found in a fixed ratio in samples taken from a single uranogenic ore body. If the ratios ^{206}Pb/^{204}Pb versus ^{207}Pb/^{204}Pb are plotted, the gradient and intercept of the resulting straight line will reflect the age of mineralisation (Budd *et al.* 2000; Faure 1986). When this technique is applied to the IMP-LI 2 artefacts they lie on a Pb-Pb isochron with a model age of 205±72Ma, which is within the range of only a small number of ore bodies. However, the chemical composition of the artefacts is consistent with them being smelted using five metal association ores (Ag-Co-Ni-As-Bi ± U) which have a very restricted occurrence (Ixer 1990; Budd *et al.* 2000). Taken together, the artefact chemistry and lead isotope composition indicate:

> 'unambiguously that the five Copper Age IMP-LI 2 metal artefacts reported by Rohl (1995) were made from copper from a five metal association ore within a single source region in northwest Europe, namely Cornubia and perhaps, even within this region, the St. Austell and Bodmin Moor area.' (Budd *et al.* 2000, 3).

Therefore we have excellent evidence that Cornwall was producing low nickel Bell Beaker metal and also Arsenic Only metal at the start of the British and Irish Early Bronze Age. Moving beyond this, we can identify a sustained industry of Cornish copper extraction through tracing the presence of cobalt in Early Bronze Age metalwork that also contains arsenic and nickel (Bray 2009).

Up till now the lack of a Cornish copper industry has been a central problem to understanding early British archaeometallurgy (Ixer & Pattrick 2003, 17). The lack of confirmed Early Bronze Age metalworking activity in Cornwall, aside from the extraction of tin ores of course, has generally been met with amazement. Budd *et al.* (1997) saw it as extremely surprising how far the Cornish copper mineralisations seem to have been generally overlooked in antiquity. They ascribe this apparent absence to archaeometallurgy's over-emphasis on the importance of south-west Ireland and the loss of early mining evidence due to later work. Many archaeologists (Budd *et al.* 1997; Ixer & Pattrick 2003) have noted that

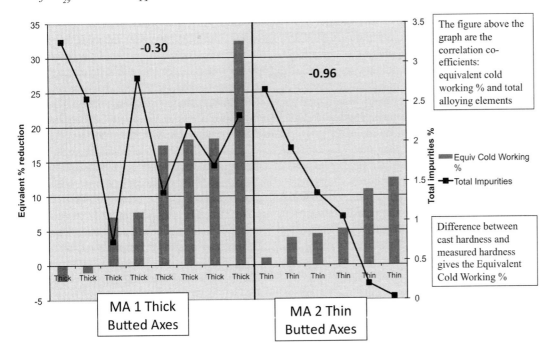

the arsenic-containing cupriferous orefields in Cornwall were probably the richest in Britain and Ireland. Cornwall is certainly not isolated from the rest of Britain and Ireland, since there had already been significant exchange between Cornwall and other regions in the period long before widescale tin use, as shown for example in the distribution of Neolithic axes of Cornish greenstone (Clough & Cummins 1988).

Perhaps the main impact of the establishment of early Cornish arsenical-copper metallurgy is that it helps to make the sequence of British and Irish metallurgy far more logical. It provides further insight into what *kind* of rocks were seen as being associated with copper at the beginning of metallurgy. With Cornwall producing copper objects in the mid-3rd millennium (ie, pre-MA 3), we now have an early counterpart to the highly productive mine at Ross Island. We also have a metallurgical predecessor to the tin ore industries of the south-west and to the mines of central and northern Wales, which begin to be exploited during the 2nd millennium BC (Timberlake 2002). The presence of people exploiting metal ores in the English south-west allows us to build a more realistic, organic model of technological knowledge spreading from continental Europe and on through Britain and Ireland. Phenomena such as the introduction of tin-bronze technology (Needham *et al.* 1989) can be seen as being

part of an established low level appreciation of metal use, rather than a dramatic shift within Cornish society.

Creating an association between metal objects and geological deposits in Britain and Ireland was a long process, which must be seen in the context of continental behaviour. The fact that the evidence points to the use of relatively complex primary sulphide ores, along with clear Beaker links, shows that the realisation that ore can be turned into metal was not an indigenous one. The addition of Cornwall to the picture of early copper metallurgy, while broadening out the base of continental influence, also (and counter-intuitively) implies that the recognition of metal sources was rather limited at this time.

The radiocarbon evidence for mining in Wales currently places it in the 2nd millennium, exploiting mostly chalcopyrite to produce a copper free from arsenic or nickel (Ixer & Budd 1998; Timberlake 2002). It is commonly assumed that all ore sources would have been recognised as such after the first appearance of metal, and so therefore the late exploitation of Welsh ores has often been seen as problematic. There are 13 objects found in Wales with known chemical composition from MA 1/2; 12 have 'impurity patterns' associated with the Ross Island mine (Bray 2009). O'Brien (1999, 234) raises one possibility that within the Welsh metalliferous regions the local interests who controlled the stone axe production centres such as Graig Lywd (Warren 1919) did not want to undergo the changes that metal extraction would require. This model is reminiscent of ideas of industrial efficiency and progress that many theoreticians have recently criticised. Chronologically this is also a difficult position to maintain, due to the large gap between the main period of stone extraction and later metal use (A. Sheridan, pers. comm.).

A simpler explanation is derived from the fact that the earliest interest in copper-bearing rocks clearly focuses on those containing arsenic. This focus on arsenical copper ores could be characterised as the search for copper from the *right* rocks, as opposed to the search for any kind of copper ores. The small group of people interested in smelting probably did not realise the range of minerals that could produce copper. Perhaps instead, they were looking for those stones that smelled of garlic when crushed, or those with the right grey lustre. O'Brien (2004) lists a number of continental parallels to the Ross Island workings, emphasising the prevalence of Beaker metalworking using arsenical copper types in Atlantic France. The north-west European picture as a whole, now including Cornwall, may indicate that during the initial spread of extractive metallurgical knowledge the Welsh ore fields may have not have been *recognised*, as opposed to being known about but ignored. It takes many centuries of contact with minerals, metal objects and new concepts before chalcopyrite use in Wales becomes commonplace.

This scenario highlights how distant the use of ores in the mid-3rd millennium was from modern metallurgy. It also leads us to conclude that the process of the invention of 'ore', as a useful concentration of the right rock, was a lengthy one, extending well into the 2nd millennium. The use of materials at this time is clearly not an experimental science with knowledge independent of time or place; rather it is steeped in local tradition and the repetition of accepted behaviour. The definition of ore continues to undergo radical changes, as we can see for example in the way in which the slag from Roman iron production later became the ideal raw material for blast furnaces (Stearns 1967, 129). Modern concepts of a potential ore are very specific and essentially relate to which mineralisations can be reasonably mined at a profit.

Tracing copper's shifting metalleity in Britain and Ireland
Artefact production: smithing techniques

The use of a material in a molten state is clearly a novel attribute and must have had an instant major impact on how metal was conceived of and understood. However the way that copper reacts to hammering and heating leads to radical changes in the material properties of the finished artefact. These intrinsic attributes of metal had to be recognised and adopted by early smiths at some point. Below it is argued that for people removed from the initial smelt, the ability to finish a copper axe in a 'metal' way was a slowly won skill. The use of heat and focused hammering to finish objects was not always part of society's conception of metalleity.

A tremendous amount of laboratory-based experimental archaeology has defined the relationship between the chemical composition of a metal sample, its hardness, the amount of mechanical work it has undergone (often recorded as the percentage of its original thickness the sample was reduced by hammering) and how much annealing has been applied – that is, the heating of the sample to relieve small stress fractures and increase malleability (Ottaway & Wang 2004). These chemical and physical connections are, of course, universal and can therefore be applied directly to investigating smithing practice during MA 1 and 2. Put simply, for a given composition, hammering will increase the hardness of the metal up to a point, but will cause brittleness. Annealing will alleviate this brittleness, but soften the metal.

The chemical behaviour of arsenic further complicates the 'smithing relationship' between composition, heat and hammering. McKerrell and Tylecote (1972) demonstrated that heating and hammering arsenic-copper alloys would cause arsenic to be lost under a normal air atmosphere. These losses are not caused by the sublimation of arsenic gas, but by the formation of arsenic oxides. During smithing early smiths would have noticed a distinctive garlic smell as arsenic oxide was given off from the artefact. This effect is crucial when we analyse the relationship between applied work and composition for MA 1 axes and MA 2 axes from Ireland.

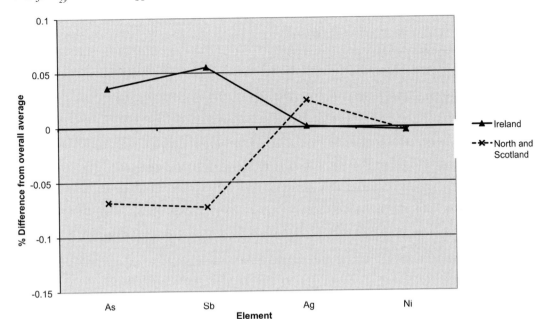

*Figure 4.2: A Metal:
percentage difference from
overall average for key
elements corrected for the
addition of tin over time*

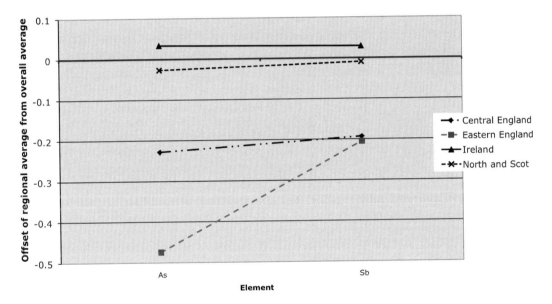

*Figure 4.3: A Metal
MA 3 axes: offset of
regional averages from
overall average for key
elements (adjusted for the
addition of tin)*

Throughout this paper the phrase 'MA 1/2' has tended to be used to cover pre-2200 BC metallurgy, largely for the sake of convenience and also due to the occasional overlap of artefact associations in British burial assemblages. Differences in the way in which metal objects were made and deposited in Ireland means that the earliest Irish material can be considered slightly differently from the British. Needham (1996, 126) argues that the MA 1 and MA 2 division really only works for Irish objects due to a clear differences in the deposition of thick- and thin-butted axes. Unlike the MA 1 contexts, Irish MA 2 hoards

also contain other objects such as daggers, awls and halberds (see table 1 in Needham 1996, 126). The Moel Arthur hoard (Forde-Johnston 1964) clearly shows that this division is blurred in the British assemblage as it contains Class 1 (MA 1) and Class 2 (MA 2) axes (Needham 1996, 126).

Figure 4.1 plots the 'Equivalent Cold Working %' versus the 'Total Impurities' in the chemical composition for MA 1 and MA 2 axes from Ireland. The Equivalent Cold Working percentage is the minimum amount of cold working that the artefact must have undergone to produce the final hardness that

Figure 4.4: MA 1/2 A metal axes: offset of regional averages from overall average for key elements (adjusted for the addition of tin)

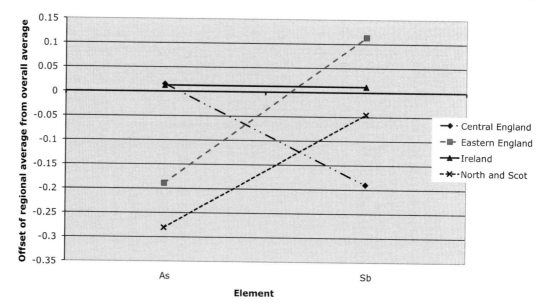

Figure 4:5: Percentage of each metal assemblage formed by recycled metal

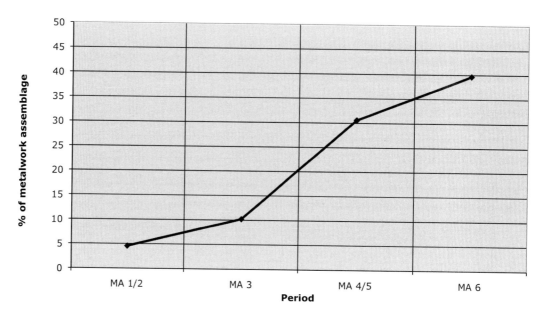

was measured by archaeometallurgists. This can be calculated as we know the hardness for that particular composition before smithing starts, thanks to experimental reconstruction (Bray 2009). 'Total Impurities' is essentially a short hand term for the level of arsenic and antimony in the chemical composition of the artefact. At this time the high arsenic and antimony composition pattern, named 'A Metal', was ubiquitous in Ireland, produced from Ross Island ores (see above).

What is important to note in Figure 4.1 is the very tight inverse correlation for MA 2, between the level of hammering needed to produce the final hardness and the final

composition of the artefact. The tightness of this relationship is due to the fact that the loss of arsenic upon heating and hammering is a constant chemical reaction; essentially this binds the two values together. Therefore we can deduce that in MA 2 smiths across Ireland had begun to use a relatively regular approach to applying heat and mechanical work to produce their axes. (The artefacts in question are from the Pitt-Rivers collection in Oxford (Allen *et al.* 1970), rather than from one site.) This relationship was obviously not present in MA 1 smithing as this displays a chaotic range of final hardness values, compositions and equivalent work percentages.

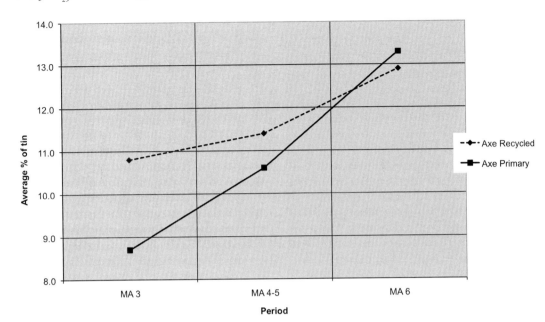

Figure 4.6: Average level of tin in axes made of primary and recycled metal

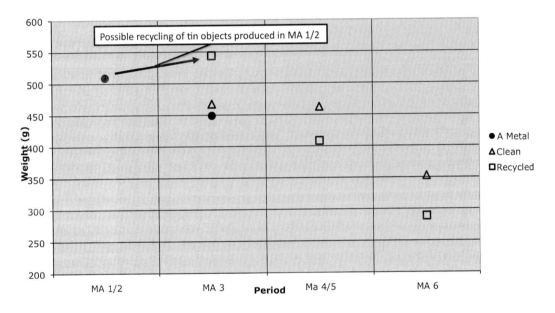

Figure 4.7: Average weight of axes by period and metal type. Weighed by Needham (1983) therefore mostly central and southern England artefacts

Overall, a slow shift in people's understanding of the mechanical attributes of copper can tentatively be proposed. During MA 1 and throughout the 3rd millennium the smelting undertaken in Ireland was relatively sophisticated as it was using primary sulphide ores. This relative sophistication was due to the plantation of continental, Beaker-related experience into County Kerry. The resulting copper was then being passed to people who were unfamiliar with the new material and unaware of how best to exploit it. If we go back to the beginning of this section, the axes –

though cast to shape – were not being finished in a way that exploited the metal's properties. Instead heat and hammering were applied in haphazard ways that quickly disappeared as any conceptual links with other materials, such as stone, diminished. By MA 2, we see a shift in the experience of using copper in Ireland, with smiths appreciating more of the intrinsic mechanical attributes of copper on a regular basis. The following section argues that this appreciation would not widely occur in Britain until MA 3, post-2200 BC.

Remodelling and recasting

The losses of some minor elements within a copper matrix during melting or simply heating is an invaluable marker for a range of metallurgical behaviours. Figure 4.2 demonstrates how this process can track the movement of Ross Island 'A Metal'-composition copper from its origin in Ireland to Scotland. This is because the Irish copper was remodelled into local forms and this, of course, required the application of heat. As would be expected the Scottish material is relatively depleted in both arsenic and antimony. The rise in the relative level of silver is explained if we remember that copper is also being lost through oxidation during the remodelling events. Silver is more noble than copper, less prone to oxidation (Ellingham 1944), and therefore remains in the new artefacts at a relatively enriched level.

The chemical composition dataset shows that by MA 3 people in Britain had begun to appreciate fully the potential of metal to be remelted, worked, and annealed, a phenomenon which, as previously argued, first became ubiquitous in Ireland during MA 2. Figure 4.3 shows a clear pattern of increasing losses of arsenic and antimony as the copper from Ross Island moves away from its source. This picture is caused by a new, more widespread appreciation of the attributes of copper. This is further supported by the proliferation of local artefact forms and also the discovery of moulds from MA 3 in areas away from ore sources (Hodges 1958 and 1960).

Figure 4.4 plots the data from MA 1/2 'A Metal' axes and shows a less straightforward pattern. The lack of a clear division between MA 1 and 2 objects in Britain causes some of this confusion. Overall, the chemical dataset supports the view that in the mid-3rd millennium (pre- MA 3) there are some incipient local metalworking traditions in Britain and there was also some deposition of unaltered axes imported from Ireland. It is not until later that more sophisticated appreciation of some of the mechanical attributes of copper spreads throughout Britain.

Recycling and alloying copper with tin

Archaeologists now possess a detailed understanding of early mining in Britain and Ireland thanks to a combination of archaeological

excavation, absolute dating and geology. This allows us to reconstruct the approximate composition of the primary copper that would have been produced by smelting these ores (Ixer & Pattrick 2003). Where the chemical composition of an Early Bronze Age artefact falls outside the range that could have been produced by the primary smelt, it can be inferred that that unit of metal must have undergone recycling. Rather than merely being remodelled by a smith, this definition of recycling indicates that the copper has undergone a series of melting events or has been mixed with copper from another source (Bray 2009).

Empirically determining the volume of recycling is a crucial step towards understanding the volumes of metal involved in early metallurgy. Alongside this, the appreciation that metal can be recycled is a major step in the way in which society conceived of metal. As Needham sums up:

> 'The primary/secondary metal distinction does also bear on an important conceptual matter: whether metal was treated just as any previously exploited material or recognised as having an essential distinguishing property. In other words, whether it was simply reworked and modified in the mode of lithics and other non-metals, or was appreciated to be capable of utter transformation. It might be suggested that this would be an important factor in separating a Neolithic metalworking idiom from a Bronze Age one' (Needham 1998, 288)

Figures 4.1, 4.3, and 4.4 already indicate the slow emergence of an appreciation of annealing and remodelling. Through plotting the amount of compositions that fall outside the range of primary metal (Fig. 4.5), we can see that it was well into the Early Bronze Age that the potential for 'utter transformation' became commonly exploited. By MA 6 around 40% of deposited bronze consisted of metal that had been mixed or had been recycled from an earlier form several times. It took around 1000 years for two parallel processes to occur: for a large population of old metal to build up and for taboos against melting and mixing old objects to break down. During MA 1 and 2 it was very uncommon for recycling to take place.

Through plotting the average level of tin in primary and recycled axes, an important indicator of people's motivation to recycle emerges. Figure 4.6 shows that earlier in the history of metal use, recycling is associated with adding more tin to *tin-bronze* objects, a process that can be called secondary alloying. Recycled objects have usually gone through two separate alloying events. By MA 6 this is no longer the case as the recycling signal is now caused by mixing old objects together, a process that appears taboo earlier in the Early Bronze Age (Bray 2009). The fact that early bronze smiths were seeking out low-tin bronzes as an easy source of tin, to which more tin could then be added, has important chronological and conceptual implications for the possible existence of a British and Irish Chalcolithic.

The traditional history of the beginning of tin use in Britain sees its introduction as very sudden and widespread. Needham (*et al.* 1989) proposed a new chronological scheme that shows a swift shift from a copper age (MA 1/2) towards a period where practically all copper-based artefacts were tin-bronze. This dramatic change is quite puzzling, as it seems to imply that the technology of alloying copper with tin was developed, adopted, and spread nationwide extremely quickly. Of course tin-bronze was in use earlier elsewhere, however Britain is seen as being the first country in Europe to completely change to sole use of tin-bronze (Pare 2000). Unfortunately as Needham himself admitted:

> 'Looking at the metalwork assemblages as a whole, there is a virtually exclusive association of MA II with copper (including arsenical copper) and MA III with tin bronze. This correlation is partly contrived in that the boundary between MA II/III was defined in the axe series to optimise this relationship' (Needham *et al.* 1989, 391)

This admission, coupled with the recognition of early extractive metallurgy in Cornwall and the importance of reusing the earliest low tin objects in later periods, can lead to a new model of early tin use. Tin-bronze in this conception is still ubiquitous in Britain from around 2100 BC; however, it can be argued that there is a far longer lead-time into this position. If we allow the creation of tin-bronzes in MA 1/2 the problem of an extremely rapid adoption of a radical new technology disappears.

It is possible that recycling, as well as design decisions, has obscured much of the early use of tin. Figure 4.7 shows the average weight of southern English axes for different copper composition patterns. Generally the weights trend downwards as the Early Bronze Age progresses, except for the recycled axes in MA 3. These axes have a very high level

of tin and a very large mass compared to their contemporaries; but not a high weight compared to the normal mass of MA 1/2 axes.

The simplest explanation for the chemistry and mass patterns is that the MA 3 recycled axes were often units of metal that were originally MA 1/2 tin-bronze axes. Artefacts that may contain tin that originated in the mid-3rd millennium include the flat axe from Parwich Moor, Derbyshire (British Museum collection, Needham 1983, code Dy 14. Note that this is not the axe from Parwich Moor in the Sheffield Museum, which is from MA 4, Needham 1983, code Dy 13/1) and the axe from Fritchley, Derbyshire (Sheffield Museum collection, Needham 1983, code Dy 5). MA 1/2 may not simply have consisted of copper and gold metallurgy; the Cornish interest in metal at this time may have extended to cassiterite. This obviously challenges the simple definition of a Chalcolithic period. Formerly anomalous objects such as the 2.57% of the MA1/2 assemblage that contain tin (see above), can now be recognised as key survivors of a technological practice that has been generally obscured due to recycling.

Conclusions

This paper has only touched on a limited number of the potential attributes of copper. Others that can clearly be investigated using similar tools include the changing acceptable uses for metal, colour, lustre, and as a surface for decoration. This paper is also limited in that it mostly consists only of the scientific analysis of the copper and bronze artefacts. Of course the gold work is crucial to a complete understanding of metalleity at this time, but is unfortunately beyond the scope of this paper. The possibilities raised above also have to be weighed up against the landscape, settlement, monumentality, ceramic evidence and so forth.

Overall, it appears possible that old, extant scientific datasets can be used to explore new theoretical models of materials. It is encouraging that the traditional tools of archaeometallurgy fit so neatly with the direction in which some theorists are heading. What emerges is a multifaceted, non-linear history of the concept of metalleity, which is not easy to fit into a neatly labelled box.

There is a fascinating blend of traits in mid-3rd millennium metallurgy. If we use the old-fashioned language of material analysis there are often mixtures of 'primitive' and 'advanced' technology. A clear case study for this is the smelting of complex primary ores at Ross Island; but then the smithing to produce the final objects in MA 1 often do not fully exploit the inherent 'metalness' of the material. In south-west England there is the possibility of very early tin-bronzes being produced before the commonly accepted MA 3 beginning. However, overall Britain appears to have a slightly later appreciation of remelting and recycling compared to Ireland. Cassiterite appears to be exploited before the copper ores in north and central Wales were recognised and mined.

Archaeologists often discuss the spread of technology in broad sweeps, usually with coloured circles or arrows on maps. A central aim of archaeometallurgy remains the identification of centres of innovation and neighbouring regions that inherited material slightly later. What this tends to overlook is that innovation and adoption is continuous and does not only occur at the first appearance of a material. Each new person who encountered metal will have had his or her personal reaction; each family unit, extended kinship group, society, tribe (however you subdivide and name groups of people) will have had a unique collective interaction with technology. The presence of the metallic chemical $_{29}Cu$ does not of itself imply a steady package of attributes, or links in conception between areas. There will have been a complex mix of a number of continua: novice to expert, eager adopter to stubborn holdout, outside influence to indigenous continuity. Some of the methods outlined above can contribute to analysing the changing personal and regional understanding of what constitutes 'metal'.

Rather than a problem, a mixed story is a reflection of how technology actually operates in any society. Rather than attempting to apply an overarching logical scheme of change, we should let the archaeological datasets reveal the patterns in their historical and geographical context. A term such as 'the Chalcolithic' may therefore be misleading in that it can be taken to imply a unified, coherent understanding of metal that simply does not exist. How metalleity is defined consists of a number of

regional stories, with a complex interplay of attributes; this is too subtle a phenomenon to be reduced to a single period name. Finally, further work on the form, composition and weight of MA 1, 2, and 3 artefacts may also indicate that the history of tin-bronze stretches surprisingly close to the first metal use in Britain and Ireland. There may have been little time where copper and gold were the only metals used by British and Irish society.

Acknowledgments

Thanks to Alison Sheridan for her advice on an earlier version of this paper. Tim Darvill, Cate Frieman, Ben Roberts, and Peter Northover also contributed data and useful comments. Sections of this paper are based upon a DPhil that was supervised by Mark Pollard at the University of Oxford, funded by the AHRC and Mitchells and Butlers.

Bibliography

Allen, I.M., Britton, D. & Coghlan, H.H. 1970. *Metallurgical Reports on British and Irish Bronze Age Implements and Weapons in the Pitt Rivers Museum*. Oxford: Pitt Rivers Occasional Paper 10

Appadurai, A. 1986. *The Social Life of Things*. Cambridge: Cambridge University Press

Barclay, A. & Halpin, C. 1999. *Barrow Hills, Radley, Oxfordshire. Volume 1. The Neolithic and Bronze Age Monument Complex*. Oxford: Oxford Archaeological Unit, Thames Valley Landscapes 11

Blanchet, J.-C. 1984. *Les Premiers Metallurgists en Picardies et dans le Nord de la France*. Memoires de la Societié Préhistorique Française 17

Bray, P.J. 2009. *Exploring the Social Basis of Technology: reanalysing regional archaeometric studies of the first copper and tin-bronze use in Great Britain and Ireland*. Unpubl. DPhil thesis, University of Oxford

Briggs, C.S. 1983. Copper mining at Mount Gabriel, County Cork: Bronze Age bonanza or post-famine fiasco? *Proceedings of the Prehistoric Society* 49, 317–35

Britton, D. 1961. A study of the composition of Wessex Culture bronzes. *Archaeometry* 4, 39–52

Britton, D. 1963. Traditions of metalworking in the later Neolithic and Early Bronze Age of Britain: Part 1. *Proceedings of the Prehistoric Society* 29, 258–325

Budd, P., Gale, D. & Thomas, R.G. 1997. Cornish copper and the origins of extractive metallurgy in the British Isles: some scientific considerations. In P. Budd & D. Gale (eds), *Prehistoric Extractive Metallurgy in Cornwall*, 15–17. Truro: Cornwall Archaeology Trust

Budd, P., Haggerty, R., Ixer, R.A., Scaife, B. & Thomas, R.G. 2000. Copper deposits in south-west England identified as a source of Copper Age metalwork. Website, http://goodprovenance.com/provenance.html. Accessed: 10/2/2006

Budd, P. & Taylor, T. 1995. The fairie smith meets the bronze industry: magic versus science in the interpretation of prehistoric metal-making. *World Archaeology* 27, 133–43

Burgess, C. 1980. *The Age of Stonehenge*. London: Phoenix Press

Butler, J.J. & Waals, J.D. van der. 1966. Bell Beakers and early metalworking in the Netherlands. *Palaeohistoria* 12, 41–139

Case, H.J. 1954. Studies of Irish and British early copper artefacts: Second series. Reports of the Ancient Mining and Metallurgy Committee of the Royal Anthropological Institute. *Man* 54, 18–27

Childe, V.G. 1930. *The Bronze Age*. Cambridge: Cambridge University Press

Clarke, D.L. 1968. *Analytical Archaeology*. London: Methuen

Clarke, D.L. 1970. *Beaker Pottery of Great Britain and Ireland*. Cambridge: Cambridge University Press

Clough, T.H. McK. & Cummins, W.A. 1988. *Stone Axe Studies Volume 2: The Petrology of Prehistoric Stone Implements from the British Isles*. London: Council for British Archaeology Research Report 67

Coghlan, H.H. 1979. Analyses of Bronze Age artefacts from Irish museums. *Historical Metallurgy* 13, 98–105

Coghlan, H.H. & Case, H.J. 1957. Early metallurgy of copper in Ireland and Britain. *Proceedings of the Prehistoric Society* 23, 91–123

Coles, J.M. 1968–9. Scottish Early Bronze Age metalwork. *Proceedings of the Society of Antiquaries of Scotland* 101, 1–110

Dobres, M.A. & Hoffman, C.R. 1994. Social agency and the dynamics of prehistoric technology. *Journal of Archaeological Method and Theory* 1, 211–58

Dobres, M.A. & Robb, J.E. 2005. 'Doing' agency: Introductory remarks on methodology. *Journal of Archaeological Method and Theory* 12, 159–66

Ellingham, H.J.T. 1944. Reducibility of oxides and sulphides in metallurgical processes. *Journal of the Society of Chemical Industry* 63, 125–33

Faure, G. 1986. *Principles of Isotope Geochemistry* (2nd edn). New York: John Wiley & Sons

Forde-Johnston, J. 1964. A hoard of flat axes from Moel Arthur, Flintshire. *Transactions of the Flintshire Historical Society* 21, 99–100

Gerloff, S.M. 1975. *The Early Bronze Age Daggers in Great Britain and a Reconsideration of the Wessex Culture*. Munich: Prähistorische Bronzefunde VI(2)

Geselowitz, M. N. 1993. Archaeology and the social study of technological innovation. *Science Technology and Human Values* 18, 231–46

Gosden, C. 2005. What do objects want? *Journal of Archaeological Method and Theory* 12, 193–211

Gowland, W. 1906. Presidential address: copper and its alloys in prehistoric times. *Journal of the Anthropological Institute of Great Britain and Ireland* 36, 11–38

Hannan, A. 1993. Excavations at Tewkesbury 1972–74. *Transactions of the Bristol and Gloucestershire Archaeological Society* 111, 21–75

Hawkes, C.F.C 1954. Archaeological theory and method: some suggestions from the Old World. *American Anthropologist* 56, 155–68

Herbert, E.W. 1993. *Iron, Gender and Power: rituals of transformation in African Societies*. Bloomington: Indiana University Press

Hodges, H.W.M. 1958–9. The Bronze Age moulds of the British Isles, Part 1: Scotland and Northern England

– moulds of stone and clay. *Sibrium* 4, 129–37

Hodges, H.W.M 1960. The Bronze Age moulds of the British Isles, Part 2: England and Wales – moulds of stone and bronze. *Sibrium* 5, 153–62

Huxham, J. 1753–4. Medical and chemical observations upon antimony. *Philosophical Transactions* 48, 832–69

Ingold, T. 2007. Materials against materiality. *Archaeological Dialogues* 14, 1–15

Ixer, R.A. 1990. *Atlas of Opaque and Ore Minerals in their Associations*. Milton Keynes: Open University Press

Ixer, R.A. & Budd, P. 1998. The mineralogy of Bronze Age copper ores from the British Isles: implications for the composition of early metalwork. *Oxford Journal of Archaeology* 17, 15–41

Ixer, R.A. & Pattrick, R.A.D 2003. Copper-arsenic ores and Bronze Age mining and metallurgy with special reference to the British Isles. In P.T. Craddock & J. Lang (eds), *Mining and Metal Production Through the Ages*, 9–20. London: British Museum Press

Jones A. 2004. Archaeometry and materiality: materials-based analysis in theory and practice. *Archaeometry* 46, 327–38

Junghans, S. Sangmeister, E. & Schröder, M. 1968. *Kupfer und Bronze in der frühen Metallzeit Europas*. Berlin: Studien zu den Anfängen der Metallurgie 2

Killick, D. 2001. Science, speculation and the origins of extractive metallurgy. In D.R. Brothwell & A.M. Pollard (eds), *Handbook of Archaeological Sciences*, 483–92. London: John Wiley

Le Coze, J. 2000. Purification of iron and steels a continuous effort from 2000 BC to AD 2000. *Materials Transactions JIM* 41, 219–32

Levin, M.E. 1976. On the ascription of functions to objects, with special reference to inference in archaeology. *Philosophy of Social Science* 6, 227–34

McKerrell, H. & Tylecote, R.F. 1972. Working of copper-arsenic alloys in the Early Bronze Age and the effect on the determination of provenance. *Proceedings of the Prehistoric Society* 38, 209–218

Mohen, J.-P. 1977. *L'Age du Bronze dans le Region de Paris*. Paris: Éditions des musées nationaux

Needham, S.P. 1983. *The Early Bronze Age Axeheads of Central and Southern England*. Unpubl. PhD Thesis, University College, Cardiff

Needham, S.P. 1996. Chronology and periodisation in the British Bronze Age. In K. Randsborg (ed.), *Absolute Chronology: archaeological Europe 2500–500 B.C*, 121–40. *Acta Archaeologica* 67

Needham, S.P. 1998. Modelling the flow of metal in the Bronze Age. In C. Mordant, M. Pernot & V. Rychner (eds), *L'Atelier du Bronzier en Europe du xxe au viiie siècle avant notre ère; III, Production, Circulation et Consommation du Bronze*, 285–307. Paris: CTHS

Needham, S.P. 2002. Analytical implications for Beaker metallurgy in North-west Europe In M. Bartelheim, E. Pernicka & R. Krause (eds), *Die Anfänge der Metallurgie in der alten Welt*, 99–133. Rahden: Forschungen zur Archäometrie und Altertumswissenschaft 1

Needham, S.P. 2007. Bronze makes a Bronze Age? Considering the systemics of Bronze Age metal use and the implications of selective deposition. In C. Burgess, P. Topping & F. Lynch (eds), *Beyond Stonehenge: essays on the Bronze Age in honour of Colin Burgess*, 278–87. Oxford: Oxbow Books

Needham, S.P., Leese, M.N., Hook, D.R. & Hughes,

M.J. 1989. Developments in the Early Bronze Age metallurgy of southern Britain. *World Archaeology* 20, 383–402

Northover, P. 1980. The analysis of Welsh Bronze Age metalwork. In H. Savory (ed.), *Guide Catalogue of the Bronze Age Collections*, 229–243 Cardiff: National Museum of Wales

Northover, P. 1999. The earliest metalworking in southern Britain. In A. Hauptmann, E. Pernicka, T. Rehren & U. Yalçin (eds), *The Beginnings of Metallurgy: proceedings of the international conference 'The Beginnings of Metallurgy', Bochum, 1995*, 211–26. Der Anschnitt, Beiheft 9

O'Brien, W. 1999. Resource availability and metal supply in the insular Bronze Age. In A. Hauptmann, E. Pernicka, T. Rehren & U. Yalçin (eds), *The Beginnings of Metallurgy: proceedings of the international conference 'The Beginnings of Metallurgy', Bochum*, 1995, 227–35. Der Anschnitt, Beiheft 9

O'Brien, W. 2004. *Ross Island. Mining, Metal and Society in Early Ireland.* Galway: National University of Ireland, Galway, Bronze Age Studies 6

Ottaway, B.S. & Wang, Q. 2004. *Casting Experiments and Microstructure of Archaeologically Relevant Bronzes.* Oxford: British Archaeological Report S1331

Pare, C.F.E. (2000) Bronze and the Bronze Age. In C. F. E. Pare (ed.), *Metals Make the World Go Round. The Supply and Circulation of Metals in Bronze Age Europe*, 1–38. Oxford: Oxbow Books

Pfaffenberger, B. 1988. Fetishised objects and humanised nature: towards an anthropology of technology. *Man* 23, 236–52

Pfaffenberger, B. 1992a. The social anthropology of technology. *Annual Review of Anthropology* 21, 491–516

Pfaffenberger, B. 1992b. Technological dramas. *Science, Technology and Human Values* 17(3), 282–312

Rohl, B. & Needham, S.P. 1998. *The Circulation of Metal in the British Bronze Age: the application of lead isotope analysis.* London: British Museum Occasional Paper 102

Scott, D.A. 1991. *Metallography and Microstructure of Ancient and Historic Metals.* Los Angeles: The Getty Conservation Institute, The J. Paul Getty Museum

Stearns, P.N. 1967. The revolutionary period of the Industrial Revolution: industrial innovation and population displacement in Belgium, 1830–1880. *Journal of Social History* 1, 119–48

Timberlake, S. 2002. Ancient prospection for metals and modern prospection for ancient mines – the evidence for Bronze Age mining within the British Isles. In M. Bartleheim, E. Pernicka & R. Krause (eds), *Die Anfänge der Metallurgie in der alten Welt*, 328–57. Rahden: Forschungen zur Archäometrie und Altertumswissenschaft 1

Wainwright, G.J. 1962. The excavation of an earthwork at Castell Bryn-Gwyn, Llanidan, Anglesey. *Archaeologia Cambrensis* 111, 25–58

Wall, J. 1987. The role of daggers in Early Bronze Age Britain: the evidence of wear analysis. *Oxford Journal of Archaeology* 6, 115–18

Warren, S.H. 1919. A stone-axe factory at Graig-Lwyd, Penmaenmawr. *Journal of the Royal Anthropological Institute of Great Britain and Ireland* 49, 342–65

Wertime, T.A. 1964. Man's first encounters with metallurgy. *Science* 146, 1257–67

The Importance of Being Insular: Britain and Ireland in their north-western European context during the 3rd millennium BC

Marc Vander Linden

This paper discusses the impact, if any, of copper on the cultural and social history of the British Isles in the second half of the 3rd millennium cal BC. After a brief review of the available evidence of both sides of the Channel (ie, western France, Belgium, and Netherlands on one hand, Britain and Ireland on the other) for the first and second half of the 3rd millennium cal BC, it appears that copper played only a very limited role in the re-establishment of cross-Channel contacts during the 'Bell Beaker Phenomenon'. In this sense, although there was definitely a period of exclusive use of copper during the later prehistory of the British Isles, there never was a British Chalcolithic in the sense that copper did not have any significant influence on the cultural and social changes that characterise this period.

Is there a British Chalcolithic?

As all too often with words, the answer lies in semantics. If we consider a minimal definition of 'Chalcolithic' as a period when copper artefacts are either produced or in use, at the exclusion of other metal such as bronze or iron, the answer is obviously positive and hardly controversial (see below). Yet, beyond the mere introduction of a new technique, 'Chalcolithic' has another, much wider and ambitious, meaning as a proper historical epoch primarily characterised by the development of new specific social structures causally related to copper metallurgy (eg, Lichardus & Echt 1991; Strahm 1994). It is the pertinence of this second, controversial, meaning for Britain that I would like to investigate here.

Rather than casting our eyes on the 'Chalcolithic' only, it is imperative to re-assess both terms of the equation, 'British' and 'Chalcolithic', in order to distinguish the local from the regional, the contingent from the evolutionary. Whatever the kind of Chalcolithic considered, the question of its potential British identity remains crucial: are the changes, if any, associated with the British Chalcolithic a local development, or the mere geographical extension of continental traits?

In the possibility of a true Chalcolithic epoch, was Britain ineluctably dragged by historical forces beyond human agency, or was there a definitive Britishness to this evolution? From this point of view, it must be remembered that continental Europe, Britain, and Ireland are separated from each other by stretches of seas of varying sizes and navigational quality. Besides the technicalities associated with sea travel (eg, Case 1969; Van de Noort 2006), the British and Irish insularity, so crucial to their inhabitants, implies that communication and interaction with external regions always depends of highly particular channels, the sea acting either as a connecting fluid or as a liquid frontier.

What is eventually at stake is not so much whether or not one should bother in referring to a British Chalcolithic, but the possibilities and gains of putting back prehistoric Britain in a wider geographic context (Vander Linden & Webley forthcoming). The tactics adopted here are therefore explicitly comparative, with the description and confrontation of the archaeological sequences on both sides of the Channel and North Sea all during the 3rd millennium cal BC, it is before and during the few centuries of use of copper in the area and before its eventual replacement by bronze (the Danish Bell Beaker group is not addressed here: Vandkilde 2001; Sarauw 2007). Such exercise, by definition, implies the use of potentially too broad a brush, hence the focus on copper and wider patterns of cultural variation in the archaeological record. Such sketchy exercise probably sounds old-fashioned, but it constitutes a necessary step in order to recognise long-term trends and historical processes otherwise too easily obscured by the minutia of detailed small-scale studies.

Fragmented units and connections

In order to identify copper production in the first half of the 3rd millennium, the geographical boundaries of the inquiry must be stretched in order to encompass the French Midi. Copper mining and metallurgy are indeed attested in the Languedoc area during the late 4th and the entire 3rd millennium (eg, Ambert & Carozza 1998; Carozza & Mille 2007). The oldest evidence comes from the district of Cabrières-Péret, where extensive ore mining

and associated metallurgical production is well-documented (Hérault: Ambert *et al.* 2002). Considering the required logistics, this copper-related activity must have been rather significant for the corresponding communities. Yet, compositional analysis shows that the diffusion of the resulting products (eg, ornaments) mostly operated at the local scale, with a few geographical outliers (eg, near absence of metal in Provence). This pattern hardly changes during the following centuries, marked by a relative multiplication of the units of regional production (Carozza & Mille 2007). All in all, the societal impact of this new technique on the local communities thus appears minimal. There is no direct relationship between the scale and organisation of copper mining and metallurgy on the production sites and the supposedly associated social structures predicted by various interpretive models (*ibid.*). Although the southern French Late Neolithic evidently presents a distinctive history marked by social fragmentation and competition (Vander Linden 2006a), copper is integrated, rather than initiates, this dynamics.

Further north, all regions are importing copper; for instance, in the French Centre-Ouest, copper artefacts in the Artenac culture are imports from the southerly copper-rich zones of the Grands Causses (Costantini 1984). This is not the place to detail here this particular archaeological culture (eg Burnez 1976; Roussot-Laroque 1998), and I will thus only briefly discuss its integration within the wider processes at play on this side of the Atlantic façade during the first centuries of the millennium.

First, this culture is partially associated with one of the most famous exchange networks of the western European Neolithic. Located in Touraine, the area of the Grand-Pressigny is renowned for the production and massive export of impressive flint daggers up to 200 mm in length. This production begins during the 4th millennium and reaches its peak during the first half of the 3rd millennium. Contrary to the large flint mines opened during the 5th and 4th millenna all across Europe, extraction is undertaken here in rather small workshops (eg, Millet-Richard 2000). Although six different *chaînes opératoires* can be recognised (Ihuel 2004), the complexity required for the realisation of the emblematic long, narrow blades (so-called *nucléi en livres de beurre*) implies that this production was in the hands of highly skilled, specialised flint knappers (Pèlegrin 2002). Comparatively, the literature on the distribution of the Grand-Pressigny daggers is much more extensive. The general absence of raw, non-retouched blades in their various distribution areas, notwithstanding subsequent resharpening and reuse, indicates that these daggers circulated as finished products. The geographical range of these exports is impressive, with finds in western, central, and eastern France (Mallet 1992; Ihuel 2004; Mallet *et al.* 2004), as well as further north in Belgium, the Netherlands, and western Germany (eg, Hurt 1988; Drenth 1989; van der Waals 1991; Delcourt-Vlaeminck 2004; see below). In the Paris Basin and in eastern France, their frequency decreases regularly with distance, with intermediary concentrations probably corresponding to redistribution areas (Mallet *et al.* 2004). The distribution pattern differs in Brittany, where finds in coastal areas account for up to 90% of the known assemblage, suggesting a preferential maritime diffusion (Ihuel 2004).

Secondly, recent research has brought to light the existence of a series of rather monumental long-houses of which length varies between 21 m and more than 100 m, their width being more constant at 10–18 m (Louboutin *et al.* 1997). The purpose of the 'houses' is unknown: the segmentation of the internal space of Pléchâtel (Ille-et-Villaine) has been interpreted as an indication of a real domestic use (*ibid.*; Cottiaux *et al.* 2005, 149), while Bradley identifies them, without much supporting evidence, as collective drinking halls (Bradley 2005). Whatever their exact – most probably changing – function, it is noteworthy that this architectural tradition of long-houses can also be identified to some extent further north on the French side of the Channel (see below).

Brittany presents a scatter of small-scaled archaeological cultures which all share the practice of collective burials in megaliths, often reused buildings from previous periods (L'Helgouach 1998). The production of battle-axes in local material indicates contacts of unknown nature with more northerly regions of the Corded Ware/Single Grave cultural sphere. The same cultural fragmentation applies for the Paris Basin as, for instance, recent re-evaluation of the ceramic typology

questions the material unity of the Seine-Oise-Marne culture (Brunet *et al.* 2004). Copper finds in the area are extremely scarce for the end of the 4th millennium and the first half of the 3rd millennium. Mille and Bouquet's recent inventory only lists about 20 copper finds for the last period, despite hundreds of sites known (Mille & Bouquet 2004). These are mostly beads imported from southern France.

Paradoxically, the Paris Basin has yielded the earliest occurrence of copper known so far. It consists of a necklace made of ten beads found in the small collective burial of Vignely, dated to 3300–3200 cal BC. The shape and technique of these beads proves that they were imported from central Europe, where this type is common (Mille & Bouquet 2004). The second half of the 3rd millennium corresponds to the development of the Gord and Deûle-Escaut groups, which cover the Paris Basin and parts of southern and western Belgium (Blanchet 1984; Brunet *et al.* 2004; Martial *et al.* 2004). These groups are closely related and present some influences from the Artenac, exemplified by ceramics, but also by the presence of roughly comparable long rectangular houses of varying dimensions (Bostyn & Praud 2000; Praud & Martial 2000; Martial *et al.* 2004; Elleboode *et al.* 2008; Joseph 2008; Julien & Leroy 2008; Waardamme, in the sandy part of Belgium: Demeyere *et al.* 2004). Several sites also present large enclosing palisades (Arleux: Julien & Leroy 2008; Houplin-Ancoisne *Marais de Santes* and *Rue Marx Dormoy*: Martial *et al.* 2004). Let us note that the suspected Late Neolithic enclosure observed in Ghislenghien (Belgium: Deramaix 1997) has been recently radiocarbon dated to the Late Bronze Age (Deramaix 2009).

Funerary practices are dominated by small collective burials, set in reused monuments (Chambon & Salanova 1996). There is a relative individualisation of the dead, as grave goods are explicitly associated with specific individuals, and no longer placed in a separate chamber (Polloni *et al.* 2004). The archaeological record for south-eastern Belgium mostly consists of a few megaliths and numerous collective burials in caves (Jadin *et al.* 1998; Cauwe 2004), while the period remains poorly known in the Belgian Flanders (Vanmontfort 2004). Anyway, copper remains conspicuously absent for the early 3rd millennium for the entire present-day

Belgium (Cauwe *et al.* 2001; Vanmontfort 2004; Warmenbol 2004).

Single graves, single ideas

The cultural sequence significantly differs in the Netherlands, with the Single Grave Culture (SGC), centered upon the northern half of this country (provinces of Drenthe, Groningen, and Friesland) and dated 2900–2500 cal BC (Drenth & Hogestijn 2001; Drenth 2005). Despite a slowly but steadily growing number of known settlements (Fokkens 2005, 407–9; Hogestijn 2005), the main source of information for this culture remains burial mounds covering individual graves. These graves are noteworthy for their stereotypy, especially the placing of the dead in the graves by reference to cosmological points (Drenth & Lohof 2005), and the recurrent deposition of a limited range of grave goods such as zone-decorated beakers (van der Waals & Glasbergen 1955), and weapons such as stone battle-axes and flint daggers. Grand-Pressigny daggers have been found in several graves (Drenth 1989; van der Waals 1991), as well as imitations made of tertiary flint, probably produced somewhere in northern France and of which distribution seems to be modelled on the Grand-Pressigny daggers (Delcourt-Vlaeminck 2004). Both Grand-Pressigny and tertiary flint daggers tend to be discovered in mounds of larger dimensions, suggesting the existence of different status amongst the dead (Drenth 1989). The SGC is also associated with the introduction of plough agriculture and the concomitant use of new lands, which is sometimes identified as the trigger for the corresponding cultural changes (Fokkens 1998). Copper is remarkably absent, proving that the cultural dynamics of the period are disconnected from the metallurgical novelty.

Pots and monuments across the landscape

On the other side of the Channel, Britain also exhibits large-scale interaction processes, as exemplified by both Grooved Ware traditions and the new favour for populating the landscape with various monuments. Without entering much into details, let us remind ourselves that the Grooved Ware tradition originates in northern Scotland and the Orkneys during the last centuries of the 4th millennium cal BC (Ashmore 1998) and then gradually diffuses to the south during the 3rd millennium (Garwood 1999). The extent of its geographical distribution parallels its relative stylistic homogeneity. For instance, Ann MacSween has suggested that the Scottish Grooved Ware decoration presents a limited number of compositional rules, which determines the geographical variation (MacSween 1995). For England, only three dominant variations are recognised, with the Durrington Walls, Clacton, and Woodland styles, the last two being sometimes indistinguishable (Barclay 1999; Cleal 1999). The new preference for building open, circular monuments (timber and stone circles, henges) presents a roughly comparable sequence, with early dates around 3000 cal BC in Scotland for both timber and stone circles (Gibson 1994; Ashmore 1998; Bradley 2007, 118–9). Both elements suggest that, all things being equal, the corresponding human communities share some common traits, or at least resort a common repertoire of material culture and practices.

Regionalisation remains, however, salient in other dimensions of the archaeological record, especially funerary practices. Megalithic tombs are still erected to shelter collective burial places around 3000 cal BC in both Scotland and Orkney. Further south, these practices seem to disappear altogether, as well as individual burials (Healy this volume) and the dead mostly feature in a few cremation cemeteries, sometimes placed in a monumental setting (eg, Stonehenge Phase 1: Parker Pearson *et al.* 2009).

Contacts across the Irish Sea are evident, with geographical clusters of both Grooved Ware and comparable monuments on the eastern coast (Brindley 1999; Grogan & Roche 2002). Further similarities between Ireland, northern Scotland and the Orkneys are noticeable in megalithic architecture and associated art (eg, Bradley 2007, 99–106, 117–8).

Divided we stand

We can now try to put together these various elements into a synthetic cultural geography (Fig. 5.1). On the continental side, Atlantic Europe appears fragmented, with several small-scale archaeological cultures linked together in many ways. The practice of building long, rectangular 'houses', whatever their function,

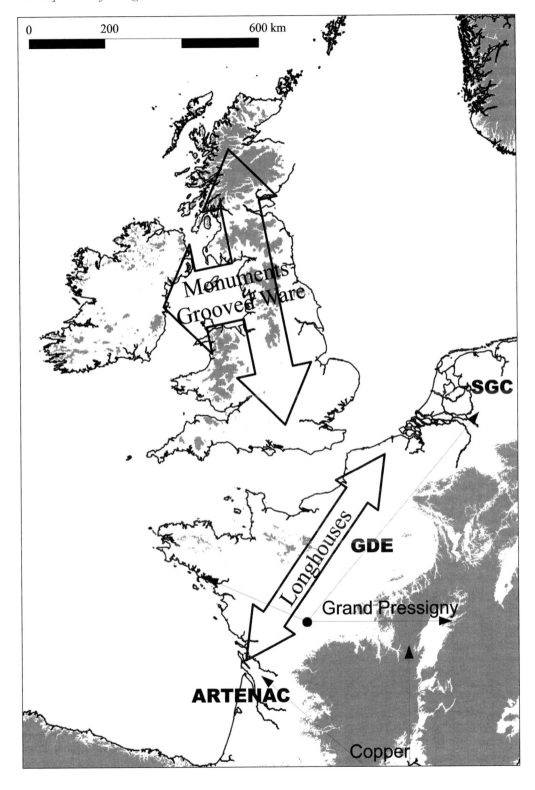

Figure 5.1: Cultural geography of north-western Europe during the first half of the 3rd millennium cal BC. Single lines indicate movements of goods, and double arrows correspond to cultural interaction

is shared over much of western and northern contemporary France, while the diffusion of Grand-Pressigny flint daggers reaches even further, with finds in the SGC which otherwise belongs to a clearly distinct cultural universe. Likewise, the production of battle-axes in local material in Brittany provides another example of these reciprocal north–south contacts. It is noteworthy that, in any of these regions, produced or imported copper appears to have a significant social role. On the insular side, interaction occurs across Britain and the Irish Sea, as evidenced by Grooved Ware and monuments. Beyond this general similitude, regions with a more marked cultural specificity are also noticeable, but perhaps on a less pronounced tone than on the continent (such as the general north–south divide put forward by Bradley (2007, 88–141)).

Yet, despite extensive evidence for interaction, the Channel and the North Sea seem to act as liquid frontiers, as none of the aforementioned traits bridges them. This archaeological invisibility of potential contacts does not, of course, prove their complete absence during the first centuries of the 3rd millennium cal BC. This point still needs to be taken into consideration, especially as it contrasts with the following period.

From the SGC, to the AOO and the BB?

The Dutch Late Neolithic sequence is renowned for showing a gradual, continuous development from the Single Grave Culture to the Bell Beaker (hereafter BB) Phenomenon, with an intermediary chronological horizon characterised by the co-occurrence of SGC and All-Over-Ornamented (hereafter AOO) ceramics. Recognised on typological grounds more than half a century ago (van der Waals & Glasbergen 1955), the local validity of this sequence has since became a pillar of Dutch Neolithic studies, as further research has proved its validity and extended it to every facet of the archaeological record (Lanting & van der Waals 1976; van der Beek & Fokkens 2001; Drenth & Hogestijn 2001; Vander Linden 1998; 2004; 2006, 31–42). There is, however, a long-lasting debate regarding the use of this sequence in other BB regions, and its role in the making of this archaeological culture (see recently the opposing opinions expressed in Guilaine 2004; Guilaine *et al.* 2004; Salanova 2004a; Vander Linden 2004). Before entering into these muddy waters, let us first recall the supporting data.

Although settlement evidence remains as limited as for the SGC (Fokkens 2005), it is generally considered that the Dutch BB settlement pattern does not introduce any

change from the previous period, excepted for a marked geographical expansion to most of the territory of present-day Netherlands (Drenth 2005). As already mentioned, continuity is evident in the ceramic typology, from both morphological and decorative points of view (van der Waals & Glasbergen 1955; Lanting & van der Waals 1976; Drenth & Hogestijn 2001). The only distinction between SGC and BB pottery lies in the extent of the decoration, limited to the upper part of the pots during the SGC, whilst covering their entire surface in both the eponymous AOO and BB pottery (a trait which lies at the core of van der Waals and Glasbergen's (1955) classification). Otherwise, throughout the centuries covered by the SGC–AOO–BB sequence, generations of potters resorted to the same restricted set of geometric rules, especially translation and simple symmetries, to elaborate the repeated horizontal bands of motifs which constitute the decoration of their pots (Vander Linden 1998). Lastly, BB funerary practices are in the direct continuity of the older SGC ones (Drenth & Lohof 2005). Individual graves are placed under mounds, sometimes with a surrounding palisade of evenly spaced posts (the so-called 'Gerritsen's law': van der Veen *et al.* 1989). Bodies are oriented in the graves according to cosmological points, although there seems to be a changing preference for these from one period to the other (Beuker *et al.* 2001). Likewise, the range of grave goods remains as restricted as before, with the eponymous beakers, while daggers, stone wristguards and arrowheads overtake battle-axes as material expressions of the ideal hunter/warrior identity of the male (Fokkens *et al.* 2008). Despite the identification of a couple of burials of smiths on basis of the deposition of metalworking tools, the presence of copper in the Dutch BB group remains incidental (Butler & van der Waals 1966; Butler & Fokkens 2005).

The local validity of the Dutch sequence cannot thus be questioned. And, with the exception of its ruthless application to the British data by Lanting and van der Waals in their review of Clarke's doctoral dissertation (Lanting & van der Waals 1972), it is noteworthy that only non-Dutch scholars used the 'Dutch model' (after Harrison 1980) to put some order in their own confusing data (eg, Guilaine 1967; Harrison 1980). Since then, renewed typologies and extensive radiocarbon programmes have demonstrated the complexity of each local sequence, generally leading to the abandon of the 'Dutch model' (eg, Kinnes *et al.* 1991). This local demise has also provided the justification for several scholars to reject claims of a Dutch BB 'homeland' (eg, Needham 2005), a position sometimes adopted by Dutch scholars themselves (van der Beek & Fokkens 2001). For instance, both Jean Guilaine and Laure Salanova have recently argued that the absence of a clear-cut, autonomous Maritime horizon in the Dutch sequence constitutes the last nail in the coffin of the Dutch origins of the BB Phenomenon (Guilaine 2004; Salanova 2004a). This position presents two major flaws: first, such a pure Maritime BB horizon does not exist anywhere in any BB regions (see the radiocarbon annex in Strahm 1995); secondly it can alternatively be argued that the seamless integration of the maritime beakers in the Dutch sequence demonstrates their local roots. Lastly, it must be reminded that the SGC beakers constitute the only plausible typological prototype for the Bell Beaker as, for instance, the sometimes invoked Portuguese *copos* are, in the opinion of advocates of a Portuguese origin themselves, unsatisfactory on typological grounds (Salanova 2004a).

The Atlantic façade

As for the preceding centuries, the situation in Belgium remains poorly known. The Flanders have witnessed a recent increase in the number of individual burials (Sergant 1997; Hoorne *et al.* 2008), which fit well with the sequence on the other side of the Dutch border, although on a different order of magnitude in terms of both quantity and density of findspots. To the south, the BB presence in Wallonnia remains limited to a few AOO Beaker potsherds in the megalithic tomb of Wéris (Huysecom 1981), a beaker pot found in secondary position in the cave of Trou de la Heide (Comblain-au-Pont: Toussaint & Becker 1992), and some sparse lithic surface finds (Cauwe 1988).

Likewise, the number of BB finds is relatively low in the Paris basin (Billard *et al.* 1998). This situation cannot be explained by the sole history of research, as the Paris basin is, for instance, one of the most intensively excavated regions in France by developer-led archaeology. Furthermore, this paucity of BB sites contrasts with the local abundance of Late Neolithic sites (Salanova 2004b) and the rich BB group in the neighbouring Moselle (eg, Lefebvre *et al.* 2008). Individual burials are known (such as Wallers: Félix & Hantute 1969), in particular the site of Jablines, which has yielded an AOO beaker which points to potential early connections with the Netherlands (Laporte *et al.* 1992). Copper finds are limited, with eight daggers and some ornaments (Mille & Bouquet 2004). Small-scale copper metallurgy is attested on the settlement of Les Florentins, along the Seine river (end of the 3rd millennium: Billard 1991).

Brittany has yielded numerous beakers in megalithic tombs, for which precise contexts of discovery are rarely available (L'Helgouach 2001). Several settlements have been recorded along the Atlantic coast, and are often badly damaged by sea erosion (Joussaume 1981). There are also a few beakers in megaliths, and even less rare individual burials, such as the recently discovered site of La Folie, near Poitiers, which presented a enclosing palisade and an AOC (All-Over-Corded) Beaker with strong Dutch reminiscences (Tcheremissinoff *et al.* 2000). Copper assemblage is dominated by daggers, flat axes, and Palmela points, the latter indicating links with Iberian Peninsula (Briard & Roussot-Laroque 2002).

The return of the dead

It is hardly original to say that cross-Channel contacts are re-instated with the introduction of the Bell Beaker Phenomenon in Britain and Ireland. But there is most probably more to say – and to discuss – about the extent and impact of this external influence on British communities during the second half of the 3rd millennium cal BC.

The return of individual burial and of their covering mounds is without doubt the most significant event of the period, be it only in terms of re-organisation of the landscape with the new, constant, visual reference to the dead (eg, Woodward & Woodward 1996). Comparisons of funerary practices point to Dutch origins, rather than the geographically closer Normandy or Brittany, for the British BB group. Funerary mounds for instance are rare in the BB Phenomenon outside of these two areas (Vander Linden 2006b, 160–2). The preference for stereotypical grave goods also recalls the Dutch situation, with the deposition alongside the remains of the dead of beakers, ornaments, and weapons such as daggers (Gerloff 1975), arrowheads (Edmonds 1995), and stone wristguards (Woodward *et al.* 2006). Among the latter, imported copper daggers and gold ornaments are key findings, as they assure the existence of a British Chalcolithic, in the minimal sense of the word noted in the introduction. The metallic fabric of these daggers however seems only to have been an additional, albeit most valuable, feature of these artefacts, as the primary emphasis appears to have been on the association of some dead with weapons, true or imaginary. Lastly, the cosmological placing of the dead also finds its clearest parallels in the Netherlands, although Britain exhibits a greater regional variability (Tuckwell 1975; Vander Linden 2006b, 160–2).

Other elements indicate a definitive British flavour to this regional BB group. If single grave is the apparent dominant rite, an extensive but overlooked amount of data suggests that other treatments of the dead body were existing in parallel (Petersen 1972; Brassil & Gibson 1999). Likewise, the expanding construction and use of monuments, theatres to complex practices of deposition often involving beakers, is deeply rooted in the local Late Neolithic and does not present any continental parallel, within or without the BB distribution area.

The advent of isotope studies has put human mobility back on the British (post-processual) radar again, so that, whether in terms of migration or individual human mobility, it is simply impossible today to think of the re-establishment of cross-Channel contacts, or the Bell Beaker Phenomenon in its entirety, without people moving across Europe in a structured manner (Fitzpatrick 2002; Price *et al.* 2004; Evans *et al.* 2006; Vander Linden 2007). In the case of Britain, the hypothetical identification of early migrants has been put forward for the Amesbury archer (Fitzpatrick 2002) and for the Scottish grave of Sorisdale (Sheridan 2008, with other potential early 'foreigners'). Such cases are generally interpreted as pioneer individuals, seeking power outside their existing communities, and/or embedded in wide ranging post-marital residential networks (Brodie 2001; Needham 2005; Vander Linden 2007).

No beakers please, we're metallurgists

Although we are still debating the British Chalcolithic, there is without doubt an Irish Chalcolithic. Copper mining and associated metallurgical production were carried out on the site of Ross Island during the second half of the 3rd and early 2nd millennia cal BC (O'Brien 2001). The extent of this activity is rather subsequent, as it supplied not only the vast majority of copper artefacts for Ireland, but for Britain as well.

However, if classic BB artefacts (such as beakers and wristguards) are routinely found in Ireland, their contexts of discovery drastically differ from mainland Britain. For instance, iconic individual graves with beakers and weapons are virtually non-existent in Ireland, despite the explosion of known sites under the realms of developer-led archaeology (Carlin & Brück this volume). Likewise, beakers are often found within wedge tombs, but rarely in association with other elements of the classical Beaker package (such as weapons: Harbison 1988, 89–92; Case 1998).

United we stand?

If we undertake a similar exercise of cultural geography as we did previously, we observe interesting patterns and obvious differences with the beginning of the 3rd millennium (Fig. 5.2). Contacts across the continent and across the Irish Sea still occur, while the Channel now acts as a connecting fluid between Britain and, in particular, the Netherlands. Yet, a closer inspection reveals more profound changes in this cultural geography than one could think at first glance.

On the continent, interaction still occurs along the Atlantic façade, with Palmela points pointing to southern connections, and, most noticeably, the influx of Bell Beakers, wherever their origins lie. Yet, the BB Phenomenon is not the cultural roller-coaster sometimes invoked, as clearly evidenced by the Paris basin and probably, though the deficient documentation does not allow us to be conclusive, in southern Belgium. There, despite some individual burials and very late settlements, the BB Phenomenon remains a secondary event of the local history. Be it in Brittany or in western France, the multiplicity of contexts for BB finds (coastal

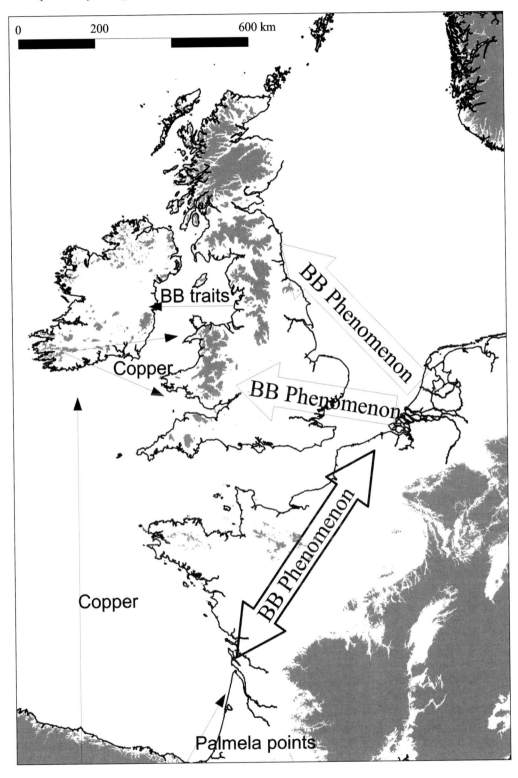

Figure 5.2: Cultural
geography of north-
western Europe during
the second half of the
3rd millennium cal BC.
Single lines indicate
movements of goods, and
double arrows correspond
to cultural interaction

settlements, rare individual burials, finds in megaliths) illustrates well the plasticity of the BB Phenomenon. By contrast, the Dutch long-lasting sequence shows the closest thing to a 'Beaker package', with the recurrent association of beakers, weapons, and other funerary practices (individual burial under mound, systematic rules of deposition of the dead). Let us also mention that in none of these regions does copper plays a leading role in the making of these cultural and social processes.

Surely the big novelty concerns the re-establishment of cross-Channel contacts. Comparison between the British and continental sequences points to a more-than-likely Dutch origin for the British BB group. More importantly, parallel to this privileged link, connections between Britain and the rest of the BB network are reinstated, as evidenced by the suggested central European origin of the Amesbury Archer. Two remarks must be made regarding the significance of this extraordinary discovery. Firstly, the Amesbury Archer is part of a wider set of both insular (eg, Sorisdale) and continental (Jablines, La Folie) individual burials exhibiting potentially very early contacts between the Netherlands and other BB areas, of which implications for the BB Phenomenon are hardly explored (for instance, the potential argument in favour of a Dutch ?'homeland'). Secondly, the mere fact that these individuals were buried following norms that allow us to label them as 'Bell Beaker' imply that they were not isolated in alien cultural milieus but part of a larger group responsible for conducting the proper funerals. In this sense, rather than focusing on 'extraordinary individuals', there is more to gain by considering, from the very beginning onwards, entire communities involved in the making of the BB network.

As on the continent, the cultural weight of copper in Britain appears to be minimal in these processes. Copper daggers were indeed placed in several burials, but it seems that their copper fabric mattered less that the fact that they were daggers, weapons instrumental in the making of the identity of some of the dead. In this sense, the coincidence between the introduction of the BB Phenomenon and the existence of a British Chalcolithic is, at best, serendipitous.

This validity of this last point is reinforced by the nature of the interactions across the Irish Sea. On one hand, copper production was undoubtedly a significant activity on a site such as Ross Island, and exports of copper to Britain constitute one of the key features of the interactions we observe at that time across the Irish Sea. In this sense, copper doubtlessly contributes to the feeling of extensive connectivity observed during the second half of the 3rd millennium. But, on the other hand, these dense economic relationships are not witnessed in the contemporary culture-history of Ireland, which has its own take on the BB Phenomenon, rather than a mere replication of the British situation. The Irish Sea thus acts, at the same time, as connecting fluid for goods as well as a liquid frontier for ideas. Such major disjunction between economic/technological and cultural/ideological networks can actually be observed in several areas of the Bell Beaker Phenomenon (Vander Linden 2007). In this sense, it seems more and more that any definition of the BB Phenomenon rests in the understanding of its variability rather than its few stable components (Vander Linden 2006b).

The importance of being insular

Reaching the end of this too brief exposé, it appears that it would be misleading to answer the question of a British Chalcolithic through the sole investigation of copper, as it is just one out of many potential traits to be analysed and which all contribute, in their own way, to the shaping of many changing networks. Obviously, such polythetic game could be extended and the networks refined, but the preliminary analysis undertaken here shows that, far from having any leading role, copper is embedded into wider processes which redraw the cultural geography of (north-western) Europe at the end of the 3rd millennium cal BC. To adapt Zvelebil and Rowley-Conwy's (1984) three-phase model of the neolithisation in north-western Europe to the case of metal, one could say that, to a long phase of availability where metal is produced and consumed in many parts of the European continent but not in Britain (see Roberts 2008 for a recent summary), succeeds a short phase of substitution, corresponding here to the BB Phenomenon, during which metal, in this case copper, is introduced alongside other elements. The third and last consolidation phase would be the Bronze Age, when metal will eventually be given more and more prominence.

Acknowledgements

This paper was written as a Research Fellow in the School of Archaeology and Ancient History, University of Leicester, as part of a research project funded by the Leverhulme Trust and co-directed by Profs Richard Bradley (University of Reading) and Colin Haselgrove (University of Leicester). I would also like to thank the organisers for inviting me to this conference. Special thanks to Alison Sheridan and Ben Roberts for their patience in teaching me a little bit of their knowledge of British prehistory. I remain, of course, sole responsible for any mistakes and interpretations made here.

Bibliography

Ambert, P. & Carozza, L. 1998. Origine(s) et développement de la première métallurgie française. Etat de la question. In B. Fritsch, M. Maute, I. Matuschik, J. Müller & C. Wolf (eds), *Tradition und Innovation. Prähistorische Archäologie als historische Wissenschaft. Festschrift für Christian Strahm*, 149–73. Rahden: Verlag Marie Leidorf

Ambert, P., Coularou, J., Cert, C., Guendon, J.-L., Bourgarit, D., Mille, B., Dainat, D., Houlès, N. & Baumes, B. 2002. Le plus vieil établissement de métallurgistes de France (IIIe millénaire av. J.-C.): Péret (Hérault). *Comptes-rendus Palevol* 1, 67–74

Ashmore, P. 1998. Radiocarbon dates for settlements, tombs and ceremonial sites with Grooved Ware in Scotland. In A. Gibson & D. Simpson (eds), *Prehistoric Ritual and Religion. Essays in Honour of Audrey Burl*, 139–47. Stroud: Sutton

Barclay, A. 1999. Grooved Ware from the Upper Thames region. In Cleal & MacSween (eds) 1999, 9–22

Beek, Z. van der & Fokkens, H. 2001. 24 years after Oberried: the 'Dutch Model' reconsidered. In Nicolis (ed.) 2001, 301–8

Beuker, J.R., Cuijpers, A.G.F.M., Drenth, E., Lanting, A.E. & Maat, G.J.R. 2001. Nogmaals de grafheuvel 'de ketenberg' te Eext: over de dodenhouding in graven van de klokbekercultuur in Nederland. *Nieuwe Drentse Volksalmanak* 118, 109–18

Billard, C. 1991. L'habitat des Florentins à Val-de-Reuil (Eure). *Gallia Préhistoire* 33, 140–71

Billard, C., Querré, G. & Salanova, L. 1998. Le phénomène campaniforme dans la basse vallée de la Seine: chronologie et relation habitats-sépultures. *Bulletin de la Société Préhistorique Française* 95, 348–63

Blanchet, J.-C. 1984. *Les premiers métallurgistes en Picardie et dans le nord de la France. Chalcolithique, âge du Bronze et début du premier âge du fer*. Paris: Société Préhistorique de France

Bostyn, F. & Praud, I. 2000. Le site néolithique de Raillencourt-Sainte-Olle 'Le Grand Camp' (Nord). *Internéo* 3, 119–29

Bradley, R. 2005. *Ritual and Domestic Life in Prehistoric Europe*. London: Routledge

Bradley, R. 2007. *The Prehistory of Britain and Ireland*. Cambridge: Cambridge University Press

Brassil, K. & Gibson, A. 1999. A Grooved Ware pit group and Bronze Age multiple inhumation at Hendre, Rhydymwyn, Flintshire. In Cleal & MacSween (eds) 1999, 89–97

Briard, J. & Roussot-Laroque, J. 2002. Les débuts de la métallurgie dans la France atlantique. In M. Bartelheim, E. Pernicka and R. Krause (eds), *Die Anfänge der Metallurgie in der Alten Welt*, 135–60. Rahden: Verlag Marie Leidorf

Brindley, A. 1999. Irish Grooved Ware. In Cleal & MacSween (eds) 1999, 23–35

Brodie, N. 2001. Technological frontiers and the emergence of the Beaker culture. In Nicolis (ed.) 2001, 487–96

Brunet, P., Cottiaux, R., Hamon, T., Langry-François, F., Magne, P. & Salanova, L. 2004. La céramique de la fin du 4e et du 3e millénaire dans le Centre-Nord de la France. Bilan documentaire. *Anthropologica et Praehistorica* 115, 155–78

Burnez, C. 1976. *Le Néolithique et le Chalcolithique dans le Centre-Ouest de la France*. Paris: Société Préhistorique Française

Butler, J.J. & Fokkens, H. 2005. From stone to bronze: technology and material culture. In Louwe Kooijmans *et al.* (eds) 2005, 371–400

Butler, J.J. & van der Waals, J.D. 1966. Bell Beakers and early metal-working in the Netherlands. *Palaeohistoria* 12, 41–140

Carlin, N. & Brück, J. this volume. Searching for the Chalcolithic: continuity and change in the Irish Neolithic/Early Bronze Age. In M.J. Allen, J. Gardiner & S. Sheridan (eds), *Is there a British Chalcolithic?: place, people and polity in the later 3rd millennium*. Oxford: Prehistoric Society Research Paper 4

Carozza, L. & Mille, B. 2007. Chalcolithique et complexification sociale: quelle place pour le métal dans la définition du processus de mutation des sociétés de la fin du Néolithique en France? In J. Guilaine (ed.), *Le Chalcolithique et la construction des inégalités sociales, tome I, le continent européen*, 195–232. Paris: Errance

Case, H. 1969. Neolithic explanations. *Antiquity* 43, 176–86

Case, H. 1998. Où en sont les Campaniformes de l'autre côté de la Manche? *Bulletin de la Société Préhistorique Française* 95, 403–11

Cauwe, N. 1988. *Le Néolithique final en Belgique. Analyse du matériel lithique*. Treignes: Editions du CEDARC

Cauwe, N. 2004. Les sépultures collectives néolithiques en grotte du Bassin mosan. Bilan documentaire. *Anthropologica et Praehistorica* 115, 217–24

Cauwe, N., Vander Linden, M. & Vanmontfort, B. 2001. The Middle and Late Neolithic. *Anthropologica et Praehistorica* 112, 77–89

Chambon, P. & Salanova, L. 1996. Chronologie des sépultures du IIIe millénaire dans le bassin de la Seine. *Bulletin de la Société Préhistorique Française* 93, 103–18

Cleal, R. 1999. Introduction: the what, where, when and why of Grooved Ware. In Cleal & MacSween (eds) 1999, 1–8

Cleal, R. & MacSween, A. (eds). 1999. *Grooved Ware in Britain and Ireland*. Oxford: Oxbow Books

Costantini, G. 1984. Le Néolithique et le Chalcolithique des Grands Causses. *Gallia Préhistoire* 27, 121–210

Cottiaux, R., Jallot, L. & Marchand, G. 2005. Les grands bouleversements du IIIe millénaire. In J.-P. Demoule (ed), *La révolution néolithique en France*, 140–59. Paris: La Découverte

Delcourt-Vlaeminck, M. 2004. Les exportations du silex du Grand-Pressigny et du matériau tertiaire dans le nord-ouest de l'Europe au Néolithique final/Chalcolithique. *Anthropologica et Praehistorica* 115, 139–54

Demeyere, F., Bourgeois, J. & Crombé, P. 2004. Plan d'une maison du groupe de Deûle-Escaut à Waardamme

(Oostkamp, Flandre occidentale). *Notae Praehistorica* 24, 167–73

Deramaix, I. 1997. Néolithique final dans la zone industrielle de Ghislenghien? *Notae Praehistoricae* 17, 221–3

Deramaix, I. 2009. Les occupations protohistoriques de la ZAE de Ghislenghien (province de Hainaut, Belgique). Bilan des recherches. *Lunula. Archaeologica protohistorica* 17, 41–6

Drenth, E. 1989. Een onderzoek naar aspecten van de symbolische betekenis van Grand-Pressigny en Pseudo-Grand-Pressigny dolken van de Enkelgraf-cultuur in Nederland In A.T.L. Niklewicz-Hokse & C.A.G. Lagerwerf (eds), *Bundel van de Steentijddag (Groningen, 1 April 1989)*, 100–21. Groningen: Biologisch-Archaeologisch Instituut

Drenth, E. 2005. Het Laat-Neolithicum in Nederland. *Archeologie* 11/12, 333–65

Drenth, E. & Hogestijn, W.J.H. 2001. The Bell Beaker culture in the Netherlands: the state of research in 1998. In Nicolis (ed.) 2001, 309–32

Drenth, E. & Lohof, E. 2005. Mounds for the dead. Funerary and burial ritual in Beaker period, Early and middle Bronze Age. In Louwe Kooijmans *et al.* (eds) 2005, 433–54

Edmonds, M. 1995. *Stone Tools and Society: working stone in Neolithic and Bronze Age Britain*. London: Batsford

Elleboode, E., Coubray, S. & Martial, E. 2008. Un batiment daté du IIIe millénaire av. J.-C. découvert à Arques (Pas-de-Calais). *Internéo* 7, 153–62

Evans, J., Chenery, C. & Fitzpatrick, A. 2006. Bronze Age childhood migration of individuals near Stonehenge, revealed by strontium and oxygen isotope tooth enamel analysis. *Archaeometry* 48, 309–21

Félix, R. & Hantute, G., 1969. La sépulture campaniforme d'Aremberg (commune de Wallers – Nord). *Bulletin de la Société Préhistorique Française* 66, 276–82

Fitzpatrick, A. 2002. 'The Amesbury Archer': a well-furnished Early Bronze Age burial in southern England. *Antiquity* 76, 629–30

Fokkens, H. 1998. From the collective to the individual: some thoughts about culture change in the third millenium BC. In M. Edmonds & C. Richards (eds), *Understanding the Neolithic of North-western Europe*, 481–91. Glasgow: Cruithne Press

Fokkens, H. 2005. Longhouses in unsettled settlements. Settlements in Beaker period and Bronze Age. In Louwe Kooijmans *et al.* (eds) 2005, 407–28

Fokkens, H. 2008, Achterkamp, Y. & Kuijpers, M. 2008. Bracers or bracelets? About the functionality and meaning of Bell Beaker wrist-guards. *Proceedings of the Prehistoric Society* 74, 109–40

Garwood, P. 1999. Grooved Ware in southern Britain: chronology and interpretation. In Cleal & MacSween (eds) 1999 145–76

Gerloff, S. 1975. *The Early Bronze Age Daggers of Great Britain, with a Reconsideration of the Wessex Culture*. Munich: Prähistorische Bronzefunde 6(2)

Gibson, A. 1994. Excavations at the Sarn-y-bryn-caled cursus complex, Welshpool, Powys, and the timber circles of Great Britain and Ireland. *Proceedings of the Prehistoric Society* 60, 143–23

Grogan, E. & Roche, H. 2002. Irish palisade enclosures

– a long story. In A. Gibson (ed.), *Behind Wooden Walls: Neolithic palisaded enclosures in Europe*, 24–7. Oxford: British Archaeological Report S1013

Guilaine, J. 1967. *La civilisation du vase campaniforme dans les Pyrénées françaises*. Carcassonne: C.N.R.S.

Guilaine, J. 2004. Les Campaniformes et la Méditerranée. *Bulletin de la Société Préhistorique Française* 101, 239–52

Guilaine J., Besse M., Lemercier O., Salanova C., Strahm C. & Vander Linden, M. 2004. Avant-propos: les Campaniformes aujourd'hui. *Bulletin de la Société Préhistorique Française* 101, 197–200

Harbison, P. 1988. *Pre-Christian Ireland. From the First Settlers to the Early Celts*. London: Thames & Hudson

Harrison, R. 1980. *The Beaker Folk*. London: Thames & Hudson

Healy, F. this volume. Chronology, corpses, ceramics, copper, and lithics. In M.J. Allen, J. Gardiner & S. Sheridan (eds), *Is there a British Chalcolithic?: place, people and polity in the later 3rd millennium*. Oxford: Prehistoric Society Research Paper 4

Hogestijn, W.J. 2005. Shell fishers and cattle herders. Settlements of the Single Grave Culture in Westfrisia. In Louwe Kooijmans *et al.* (eds) 2005, 429–32

Hoorne, J., Sergant, J., Bartholomieux, B., Boudin, M., De Mulder, G. & Strydonck, M. van. 2008. Een klokbekergraf te Sint-Denijs-Westrem – *Flanders Expo* (Gent, provincie Oost-Vlaanderen). *Notae Praehistoricae* 28, 99–108

Hurt, V. 1988. La problématique du Grand-Pressigny à travers une découverte à Bras. *Vie Archéologique. Bulletin de la Fédération des Archéologues de Wallonie* 31, 43–89

Huysecom, E. 1981. A propos des fragments de gobelets 'AOO' exhumés dans les allées couvertes de Wéris, Luxembourg. *Helinium* 21, 55–60

Ihuel, E. 2004. *La diffusion du silex du Grand-Pressigny dans le massif armoricain au Néolithique. Supplément n° 2 au Bulletin de l'Association des Amis du Musée du Grand-Pressigny*. Paris: C.T.H.S.

Jadin, I., Toussaint, M., Becker, A., Frébutte, C., Goffioul, C., Hubert, F. & Pirson, S. 1998. Le mégalithisme de Famenne. Approche pluridisciplinaire et perspectives. *Anthropologie et Préhistoire* 109, 95–119

Joseph, F. 2008. Le site d'habitat du IIIe millénaire av. J.-C. de la 'ZAC Jules Verne' à Glisy (Somme): présentation préliminaire. *Internéo* 7, 163–71

Joussaume, R. 1981. *Le Néolithique de l'Aunis et du Poitou occidental dans son cadre atlantique*. Rennes: Université de Rennes I

Julien, M. & Leroy, E. 2008. L'habitat du Néolithique finql dans la région dde Douai (Nord): résultats préliminaires. *Internéo* 7, 143–52

Kinnes, I., Gibson, A., Boast, R., Ambers, J., Leese, M. & Bowman, S. 1991. Radiocarbon dating and British Beakers. *Scottish Archaeological Review* 8, 35–68

Lanting, J.N. & Waals, J.D. van der. 1972. British beakers as seen from the continent. A review article. *Helinium* 12, 20–46

Lanting, J.N. & Waals, J.D. van der. 1976. Beaker culture relations in the Lower Rhine basin. In J.N. Lanting & J.D. van der Waals (eds). *Glockenbecher Symposion. Oberried 1974*, 2–80. Haarlem: Fibula-Van Dishoeck

Laporte, L., Guy, H. & Blaizot, F. 1992. La sépulture à mobilier campaniforme de Jablines Le Haut Château.

In F. Bostyn and Y. Lanchon (eds), *Jablines, Le Haut Château (Seine-et-Marne): une minière de silex au Néolithique*, 224–9. Paris: Maison des Sciences de l'Homme

Lefebvre, A., Gazenbeek, M. & Pernot, P. 2008. Les sépultures campaniformes du site de Montelange 'La Sente' (Moselle). Résultats préliminaires. *Internéo* 7, 187–201

L'Helgouach, J. 1998. L'ouest de la France. In J. Guilaine (ed.), *Atlas du Néolithique européen II. L'Europe occidentale*, 653–88. Liège: E.R.A.U.L. 46

L'Helgouach, J. 2001. Le cadre culturel du campaniforme armoricain. In Nicolis (ed.) 2001, 289–99

Lichardus, J. & Echt, R. (eds). 1991. *Die Kupferzeit als historische Epoche: Symposium Saarbrücken und Otzenhausen 6.13.11.1988*. Bonn: R. Habelt

Louboutin C., Burnez C., Constantin, C. & Sidéra, I. 1997. Beaumont-La Tricherie (Vienne) et Challignac (Charente): deux sites d'habitat de la fin du Néolithique. *Antiquités Nationales* 29, 49–64

Louwe Kooijmans, L., Broeke, P. van den, Fokkens, H. & Gijn, A. van (eds). 2005. *The Prehistory of the Netherlands*. Amsterdam: Amsterdam University Press

MacSween, A. 1995. Grooved Ware from Scotland: aspects of decoration. In I. Kinnes & G. Varndell (eds), *'Unbaked Urns of Rudely Shape'. Essays on British and Irish Pottery for Ian Longworth*, 41–8. Oxford: Oxbow Books

Mallet, N. 1992. *Le Grand-Pressigny. Ses Relations avec la Civilisation Saône-Rhône*. Argenton-sur-Creuse: Les Amis du Musée de Préhistoire du Grand-Pressigny

Mallet, N., Richard, G., Genty, P. & Verjux, C. 2004. La diffusion des silex du Grand-Pressigny dans le Bassin parisien. *Anthropologica et Praehistorica* 115, 123–38

Martial, E., Praud, I. & Bostyn, F. 2004. Recherches récentes sur le Néolithique final dans le nord de la France. *Anthropologica et Praehistorica* 115, 49–71

Mille, B. & Bouquet, L. 2004. Le métal au 3e millénaire avant notre ère dans le Centre-Nord de la France. *Anthropologica et Praehistorica* 115, 197–215

Millet-Richard, L.-A. 2000. Exploitation du silex dans la région pressignienne au Néolithique final. Problématique et évaluation d'un site. *Internéo* 3, 111–17

Needham, S. 2005. Transforming Beaker culture in North-West Europe; processes of fusion and fission. *Proceedings of the Prehistoric Society* 71, 171–218

Nicolis, F. (ed.). 2001, *Bell Beakers Today. Pottery, People, Culture, Symbols in Prehistoric Europe. Proceedings of the International Colloquium Riva del Garda (Trento, Italy) 11–16 May 1998*, 487–96. Trento: Ufficio Beni Archeologici

Noort, R. van der 2006. Argonauts of the North Sea: a social maritime archaeology for the 2nd millennium BC. *Proceedings of the Prehistoric Society* 72, 267–87.

O'Brien W., 2001. New light on Beaker metallurgy in Ireland. In Nicolis (ed.) 2001, 561–76

Parker Pearson, M., Chamberlain, A., Jay, M., Marshall, M., Pollard, J., Richards, C., Thomas, J., Tilley, C. & Welham, C. 2009. Who was buried at Stonehenge? *Antiquity* 83, 23–39

Pèlegrin, J., 2002. La production des grandes lames de silex du Grand-Pressigny. In J. Guilaine (ed.), *Matériaux, Productions, Circulations, du Néolithique à l'Âge du Bronze*, 125–41. Paris: Errance

Petersen, F. 1972. Traditions of multiple burial in later Neolithic and early Bronze Age England. *Archaeological Journal* 129, 22–55

Polloni, A., Sohn, M. & Sidéra, I. 2004. Structure du mobilier funéraire en os, bois de cerf, dents et coquillages à la fin du 4e et au 3e millénaire en Bassin parisien. *Anthropologica et Praehistorica* 115, 179–95

Praud, I. & Martial, E. 2000. Une nouvelle occupation du Néolithique final dans la vallée de la Deûle, à Annoeullin (Nord). *Internéo* 3, 131–41

Price, T.D., Knipper, C., Grupe, G. & Smrcka, V. 2004. Strontium isotopes and prehistoric human migration: the Bell Beaker period in central Europe. *European Journal of Archaeology* 7, 9–40

Roberts, B. 2008. Creating traditions and shaping technologies: understanding the earliest metal objects and metal production in Western Europe. *World Archaeology* 40, 354–72.

Roussot-Laroque, J. 1998. Le sud-ouest de la France. In J. Guilaine (ed.), *Atlas du Néolithique Européen II. L'Europe Occidentale*, 689–761. Liège: E.R.A.U.L. 46

Salanova, L. 2004a. Le rôle de la façade atlantique dans la genèse du Campaniforme en Europe. *Bulletin de la Société Préhistorique Française* 101, 223–6

Salanova, L. 2004b. The frontiers inside the western Bell Beaker block. In J. Czebreszuk (ed.), *Similar but Different. Bell Beakers in Europe*, 63–75. Poznań: Adam Mickiewicz University

Sarauw, T. 2007. Male symbols or warrior identities? The 'archery' burials of the Danish Bell Beaker culture. *Journal of Anthropological Archaeology* 26, 65–87

Sergant, J. 1997. Klokbekervondst te Teralfene. *Notae Praehistoricae* 17, 225–7

Sheridan, J.A. 2008. Upper Largie and Dutch-Scottish connections during the Beaker period. *Analecta Praehistorica Leidensia* 40, 240–60

Strahm, C. 1994. I grandi focolari dell'età del Rame. In J. Guilaine & S. Settis (eds), *Storia d'Europa. 2–1. Preistoria è antichità*, 311–31. Torino: Einaudi

Strahm, C. (ed.). 1995. *Das Glockenbecher-Phänomen. Ein Seminar*. Freiburg: Institut für Ur- und Frügeschichte der Universität Freiburg

Tcheremissinoff, M., Fouéré, P. & Salanova, L. 2000. La sépulture campaniforme de la Folie (Poitiers, Vienne): présentation préliminaire. *Internéo* 3, 161–7

Toussaint, M. & Becker, A. 1992. La sépulture Michelsberg du trou de la Heid à Comblain-au-Pont (province de Liège, Belgique). *Bulletin de la Société royale belge d'Études géologiques et archéologiques 'Les Chercheurs de la Wallonie'* 32, 7–30

Tuckwell, A. 1975. Patterns of burial orientation in the round barrows of East Yorkshire. *Bulletin of the Institute of Archaeology* 12, 95–123

Vander Linden, M. 1998. La révolution spatiale du Campaniforme : essai sur les structures spatiales du Campaniforme en Europe du Nord-Ouest. *Anthropologie et Préhistoire* 109, 277–92

Vander Linden, M. 2004. Elle tomba dans la bonne terre et elle donna du fruit qui monta (Marc 4, 8): la culture à Céramique cordée comme substrat du phénomène campaniforme. *Bulletin de la Société Préhistorique Française* 101, 207–14

Vander Linden, M. 2006a. For whom the bell tolls: social hierarchy vs social integration in the Bell Beaker

Culture of southern France (third millennium BC). *Cambridge Archaeological Journal* 16, 317–32

Vander Linden M., 2006b. *Le Phénomène Campaniforme dans l'Europe du 3ème Millénaire avant notre ère. Synthèses et Nouvelles Perspectives.* Oxford: British Archaeological Report S1470

Vander Linden, M. 2007. What linked the Bell Beakers in third millennium BC Europe? *Antiquity* 81, 343–52

Vander Linden M. & Webley L. forthcoming. Putting the British Bronze Age back on the map. In B. Roberts (ed.), *A Research Agenda for the Bronze Age in Britain (c. 2500-800 BC).* London: Trustees of the British Museum

Veen, M. van der, Lanting, J. & Gerritsen, J. 1989. A group of tumuli on the 'Hooghalen' estate near Hiken (municipality of Beilen, province of Drenthe, the Netherlands). *Palaeohistoria* 31, 191–234

Vandkilde, H. 2001. Beaker representation in the Danish Late Neolithic. In Nicolis (ed.) 2001, 333–60

Vanmontfort B., 2004. Les Flandres durant la fin du 4e et le début du 3e millénaire avant notre ère. Inhabitées ou invisibles pour l'archéologie? *Anthropologica et Praehistorica* 115, 9–25

Waals, J.D. van der. 1991. Silex du Grand-Pressigny aux Pays-Bas. In *Actes du 14e colloque interrégional sur le Néolithique, Blois, 16–17–18 octobre 1987*, 193–200. Blois: Société archéologique scientifique et littéraire du Vendômois

Waals, J.D. van der & Glasbergen, W. 1955. Beaker types and their distribution in the Netherlands. *Palaeohistoria* 4, 5–46

Warmenbol, E. 2004. Le début des âges des Métaux en Belgique. *Anthropologica et Praehistorica* 115, 27–48

Woodward, A., Hunter, J., Ixer, R., Roe, F., Potts, P.J., Webb, P.C., Watson, J.S. & Cones, M.C. 2006. Beaker age bracers in England: sources, function and use. *Antiquity* 80, 530–43

Woodward, A. & Woodward, P. 1996. The topography of some barrow cemeteries in Bronze Age Wessex. *Proceedings of the Prehistoric Society* 62, 275–91

Zvelebil, M. & Rowley-Conwy, P. 1984. Transition to farming in northern Europe: a hunter–gatherer perspective. *Norwegian Archaeological Review* 17, 104–28

6

Sense and Non-sense of the Term 'Chalcolithic'

Martin Bartelheim and Raiko Krauß

According to a widespread view, the introduction of metals denotes a crucial event in the history of mankind. In large areas of Europe they appeared within a period of rapid evolution of technology, economy, society, and settlement structures. It is believed that the production of metals, especially copper, was closely linked with the emergence of a complex economic and social organisation like the one which we begin to see during that period in some parts of Europe. The intense use of metals, especially for symbols of prestige, consequently became a defining factor for the Chalcolithic which was added to the traditional three period system as an intermediate step from the Stone Age to the full Metal Ages. In this paper the importance of metals for the developments of that epoch is analysed by looking across continental Europe and discussing the relevance of 'chalkos' as an eponymous element.

In view of the title of this book – the question whether there is a Chalcolithic in Britain – it seems appropriate to analyse the term and its use in other parts of prehistoric Europe. In the European archaeological research literature one can find synonyms of the term 'Chalcolithic', such as 'Eneolithic', 'Copper-Stone Age' and 'Copper Age' (Lichardus 1991a) in which the words 'copper' and 'stone' form the basis of the first three denominations. The term 'Copper Age' breaches the three-period system set up by Thomsen in 1831 and which forms the basis of the chronological order of European prehistory. In 1862 Wilde remarked in the catalogue of the Museum of the Royal Irish Academy in Dublin that copper objects had to be dated earlier than those of bronze. While categorising the rich prehistoric gold finds of Ireland, which appeared approximately as early as the first copper objects in Ireland, Wilde realised that objects of pure or arsenical copper were abundant before the appearance of tin-bronzes. Therefore, he postulated the existence of a 'Copper Age' that could be separated from the Bronze Age (Wilde 1862). For Scotland and England Sir Daniel Wilson and Sir John Evans also acknowledged the existence of a period when copper was used (O'Connor 2008, 119, 126). On the European continent Pulszky could show clearly, with the help of the Hungarian finds, the independence of the Copper Age in reference to earlier and later periods (Pulszky 1884). In the same year the term 'Copper Age' was introduced by Vilanova y Piera (1884) for the Iberian peninsula. This early use of the denomination 'Copper Age' in three regions of Europe as far apart as Ireland, the Carpathian Basin, and the Iberian peninsula seems remarkable. Whereas in Ireland it is now hardly used, it is well established in south-east Europe and on the Iberian peninsula.

In central Europe, the term is applied only scarcely. There, as in Scandinavia and the British Isles, the period of the 5th to the 3rd millennia BC, before the beginning of the Bronze Age, is considered by the vast majority of scholars to be the final part of the Neolithic (Fischer 1991; Lüning 1996). The term 'Copper Age', however, is applied only rarely (Lichardus 1991a; Nadler 2006). The denomination 'Eneolithic' is also in use, mainly in the Czech Republic and in Slovakia (Neustupný 1981). There is no consensus about the emergence and character of this period as well as the role that the eponymous new material played in its development. Černych stated that metallurgy had a major significance for the rise of the Copper Age in south-eastern Europe and that other factors were of secondary importance (Černych 1982, 39). According to Pleslová-Štiková the principal elements were knowledge about metals and animal traction in agriculture (Pleslová-Štiková 1977). Instead Lichardus (1991a, 19) argued that on the one hand the economy of the Eneolithic in central Europe was based on new technological processes in metallurgy. On the other hand he sees in accordance with Neustupný (1981) that not only copper but also the combination of several structural changes is the key element for the definition of the new civilisation. Strahm (1981, 82) adds that during the early phase of metal use in central Europe only those cultures should be called 'Chalcolithic' in which copper was worked and metal used to an extent that a local production can be assumed. In his view the first manufacture and use of the metal supposedly had hardly any socio-economic effects.

On the Iberian peninsula, the start of the Chalcolithic has long been associated with a colonisation by eastern Mediterranean copper prospectors – who on their search for that metal in order to compensate the demand in their area of origin built defensive settlements in some parts of the coast – and the following cultural transfer (Blance 1961; cf. also Chapman 1990). In recent years copper has ceased to be regarded as the principal element of the Iberian Chalcolithic, and especially in economic terms it plays a secondary role behind subsistence (eg, Nocete 2001). In view of this, it seems therefore important to discuss a) whether the Chalcolithic can be considered to have been a self-contained cultural epoch, b) which elements characterise it, and c) which role the eponymous copper played in it. For this the archaeological record in three different regions of Europe will be analysed in which questions about the existence and the character of a Copper Age have been discussed for a long time, where there was direct access to copper ore and also the exploitation of these resources as well as the use of the finished products have been proven for that period: south-eastern Europe, the north Alpine area, and the southern Iberian peninsula.

South-eastern Europe

Historical Background

In south-eastern Europe the Chalcolithic begins earlier than anywhere else on the continent due to its proximity to Anatolia (Table 6.1). Whereas in Anatolia metal finds were already abundant during the 6th millennium, to an extent that the beginning of the Chalcolithic defined at 6000 BC (cf. Schoop 2005, 14–17; Pernicka & Anthony 2010, 162–8) large parts of south-eastern Europe at that time only just experienced the spreading of the productive way of life. Metal artefacts appeared in large numbers in the southern Balkan region around the middle of the 5th millennium. In the Carpathian Basin only at the end of the 5th and during the 4th millennium can cultural and technological innovations be observed that justify the use of the denomination 'Copper Age' for cultures of that period (Hansen 2009, 25–9). Differences to the Neolithic are well visible due to a change of the settlement system by which cultural groups (Bodrogkeresztúr, Tiszapolgár, Baden) can be described almost exclusively by their burials. This period is also characterised by obvious innovations like the intensified use of animals for traction and for the production of milk and wool (Sherratt 1981).

In the southern and eastern part of the Balkans the term Chalcolithic is being applied

years BC	Anatolia	SE Europe (Bulgaria)	Carpathian Basin (Hungary)	Southern Germany	Iberian Peninsula
2000	Early Bronze Age III	Middle Bronze Age	Early Bronze Age	Early Bronze Age	Early Bronze Age
2500	Early Bronze Age II	Early Bronze Age		Final Neolithic	Chalcolithic
3000	Early Bronze Age I			Late Neolithic	Late Neolithic
3500	Chalcolithic	Transitional period	Chalcolithic	Young Neolithic	Middle Neolithic
4000					
4500		Chalcolithic	Late Neolithic	Middle Neolithic	
5000		Late Neolithic	Middle Neolithic	Early Neolithic	Early Neolithic
5500		Middle Neolithic	Early Neolithic		

Table 6.1: Chronological chart of the cultural development 6th–3rd millennia BC in Anatolia, south-eastern Europe, the Carpathian Basin, southern Germany, and the Iberian peninsula (after Harmankaya & Erdoğu 2002; Schoop 2005; Kalicz 1998; Bertemes & Heyd 2002; Link 2006; Lüning 1996; Castro et al. 1996 and Kunst 2001).

to cultures of the early 5th millennium which is not based on an increased use of metals. In Bulgaria, for example, the Marica culture is considered to represent the earliest Chalcolithic because of the early use of metal in that region next to Anatolia. Finds of heavy copper implements of the Early Chalcolithic are still very scarce. Two copper axes from the settlements in Slatino and Djakovo in the Struma valley can be regarded as the earliest massive copper tools (Pernicka *et al.* 1997, fig. 9.1, 9; Čochadžiev 1998, fig. 2.1, 3; Krauß 2001, fig. 32). According to Todorova, the beginning of the Copper Age in south-eastern Europe is characterised by a widespread abundance of copper ornaments and the first heavy copper implements, as well as the construction of planned fortified settlements (1981, 91). At least the criterion of the building of those settlements seems to be clearly fulfilled by

places like Poljanica (Todorova 1982, figs 159–74) which can be regarded as representative of many others of that period in north-eastern Bulgaria. However, even the Neolithic settlements of the region show some degree of organisation eg, Aşağı Pınar (Karul 2003), Gălăbnik (Bakamska 2007) and Karanovo (Hiller & Nikolov 1997, 19–92), and a therefore some kind social differentiation. Also metal ornaments can be occasionally detected within the Balkan Neolithic (Hansen 2009, 12–13). A small rolled copper sheet from the Late Neolithic settlement of Asparuhovo (Todorova & Vajsov 2001, 36, no. 14) is regarded as the oldest copper object. A real concentration of metal objects cannot be detected until the second half of the 5th millennium, so that Lichardus (1991a, 26) only then begins to speak of a Copper Age. This late date can be harmonised better with the beginning of the

Copper Age in the neighbouring regions to the north and to the west. During the Copper Age a considerable amplification of settlement areas can be observed that goes beyond those of the Neolithic (Krauß 2008, figs 20, 24, 29, 35). Also the available economic data show hardly any changes from the preceding Late Neolithic (Manhart 1998; Marinova 2006).

Technological innovations

Painting of pottery with graphite in the Chalcolithic marks an important difference from the decoration techniques in the preceding Late Neolithic. It has to be seen in context with a new highly specialised pottery technology which emerges from the Late Neolithic tradition and was apparently a product of centralised manufacture. Its origins were in the lower Strymon valley where this kind of decoration can be found as early as the Late Neolithic (Vajsov 2007). During the first half of the 5th millennium the use of graphite painting expanded as far as the southern Carpathians and subsequently replaced the Neolithic techniques of scoring and incrustation. Thus, for the identification of the beginning of the Copper Age in the Balkans, the appearance of copper and gold were not the decisive element, since copper metallurgy became important for the emerging cultural complexes Kodžadermen-Gumelniţa-Karanovo VI (KGK VI) and Krivodol-Sălcuţa-Bubanj Hum I (KSB I) only from the mid-5th millennium onwards. That was the time of the great tell settlements and the rich cemeteries, of which Varna, with its numerous metal finds, is definitely the most prominent. According to Häusler the social and sexual differentiation on these cemeteries seems to be the earliest in Europe (1992). The emergence of ritual installations outside residential buildings can already be assumed for the Neolithic, although proofs for the existence of mere cultic buildings are hard to find. A possible example might be the exceptional building in the settlement of Parţa (Lazarovici *et al.* 2001, fig. 181). Evidence for other innovations with enduring consequences for the economic development like the introduction of the wheel, chariots, and ploughs, the breeding of woolly sheep, and indications for an increased use of milk exists in south-eastern Europe only from a period after the decline of the prosperous tell cultures (Maran 2004; Benecke 1994, 121–61).

Metals and metallurgy

From the mid-5th millennium onwards metals were present in south-eastern European settlements and cemeteries to an extent that an intense metal production can be assumed (Vulpe 1970; Kuna 1981; Todorova 1981; Patay 1984; Klassen 2000; 2004; Pernicka & Anthony 2010, 168–73). The copper objects are standardised to a certain degree which points towards a strongly specialised, perhaps even industrial production. There is evidence for mining in the copper ore districts of Ai Bunar (Černych 1978, 58–71) in the eastern Balkans as well as in Majdanpek and Rudna Glava in the Serbian Ore Mountains (Jovanović 1978; Pernicka *et al.* 1993). Besides these there are still more ore deposits within the same mineralisation zone between the Balkan and the Rhodope Mountains. Next to the well-known copper ore deposit of Medni Rid in the northern Strandža Mountains (Pernicka *et al.* 1997, 83–8) a settlement site close to Černomorec revealed evidence for the whole metallurgical *chaîne opératoire* from the beneficiation of the ore to the final metal object.[1] Natural alloys were in use. As far as it is known the ores were mined in open-cast pits which like in Ai Bunar could have a large almost industrial extension. Several techniques like cold and warm forging, hammering, embossing and casting were known (Ryndina & Orlovskaja 1979; Echt *et al.* 1991; Mareş 2002, 65–92). Not only copper was used in this period but also gold. Besides the objects from the cemeteries from the Black Sea region gold has been found in settlements as well (Dumitrescu 1961; Todorova & Vajsov 2001). While the preservation of many gold finds in graves may be due to cultural circumstances, the settlement finds show clearly that this precious metal was constantly available in the Balkan-Carpathian region. Finds like the bossed idol from Moigrad (764 g) or the rectangular plate from 'grave 1' in Varna (189 g) constitute large quantities of the valuable metal in one single object (Ivanov 1991, 131; Draşovean 2008, cat. no. 88; Pernicka & Anthony 2010, 162 plate).

Non-metallurgical resources

H. Todorova brought *Spondylus* into discussion as an important resource of the Chalcolithic cultures in the western Black Sea region (Todorova & Vajsov 2001, 14–17). A finer chronological dissolution of the European *spondylus* finds reveals a dichotomy between an

Adriatic/western Balkan area with finds mostly of the end of the 6th millennium BC and an eastern Balkan area with *spondylus* finds only from the mid-5th millennium onwards (Müller 1997). Since a provenance of the shells from the Black Sea can obviously be excluded (Renfrew & Shackleton 1970; Shackleton & Elderfield 1990; *contra* Todorova & Vajsov 2001, 14–17) the many *spondylus* shells in the area of KGK VI have to be imported from the northern Aegean (Séfériadès 2010). The relatively long distance to the source of the shells may be a reason for their high esteem in the Balkan area and in the regions north of it, since *spondylus* shell ornaments, like gold and copper objects, belong to the equipment of the rich graves. In the eastern Mediterranean, *spondylus* was used mainly as an important source of proteins for nutrition for which reason their shells had no exotic value there. Only with the distance to the source and the corresponding restricted access did the added value for the shells emerge. In their area of origin they were actually a by-product of food production.

Another important element of the south-eastern European Chalcolithic is the production of very long flint blades which due to their size could have had no practical function. For their manufacture only selected and very homogeneous flint types could be used whose availability must have been as important as the control of gold and copper deposits. The enormous blades of the Varna graves have been made of a special kind of flint which can be mined in the region of Razgrad (Načev *et al.* 1981, fig. 1; Manolakakis 2005, 211). The production of those blades that are up to half a metre long and very thin requires a lot of experience. The ability to manufacture that kind of object alone reveals a great mastership and points towards a high degree of craft specialisation. These blades were made exclusively by pressure techniques and probably by the help of lever devices (Pelegrin 2007, 13). In recent years it has become increasingly obvious that salt was also an economic factor in the western Black Sea region. Apart from the potential availability of salt from the sea, the region around the Varna lake is very rich in mineral salt that also emerges at some places as salt springs. First evidence for a use of these resources as early as the Late Neolithic were found on tell Provadija *c.* 40 km west of Varna (Nikolov 2008).

Conclusions

In south-eastern Europe the use of copper and gold was a consequence of accelerated development in the 5th millennium BC. Its archaeological expression is pottery made with a new kind of technology, a complex settlement system, and rich burials. It is difficult to determine the delimitations of this new epoch at the beginning towards the Neolithic and at the end towards the Early Bronze Age which lead in different countries to varying temporal intervals (Table 6.1). The so-called 'Copper Age' on the Balkans emerged organically and seamlessly from the local Late Neolithic. Technological innovations and a more efficient economic strategy as well as an intensified use of natural resources favoured a constant growth of the population which agglomerated in the emerging settlement centres (tells and their immediate vicinity). This concentration of population in a small area in turn enhanced the development of technology. In this interdependent system of growing population and increasingly stratified societies, the use of metals was an important, but not the only, incentive. The exchange of *spondylus* shells over long distances and the technological possibility of long flint blades are further hints of cultural changes. The economic basis for the wealth displayed in the burials could have been the control of the copper and gold deposits as well as of the large resources in mineral salt that are very abundant in the western Pontic area. For south-eastern Europe, the use of metals has to be seen as a logical consequence of the cultural development which has definitely not been initiated by the advent of metal technology.

North Alpine region

Innovations in the Young Neolithic

As a distant echo of the 5th millennium developments in south-eastern Europe, during the Young Neolithic (*c.* 4400–3500 BC, Table 6.1) central Europe experienced a number of innovations linked mainly to A. Sherratt's (1981) so-called 'secondary products' (specialised animal husbandry, animal traction, carts, ploughs, production of milk and textiles), but encompassing also new crops and patterns of land-use. However, they were introduced only successively and remained embedded in a clear cultural and social continuity. The first appearance of metal (copper) also happened at that time already in considerable quantity with the material being imported most likely from south-eastern Europe. As yet no local metal production, only metal working, has been documented in several settlements along the foothills of the Alps.

Metallurgy and Metals

Late Neolithic

From the Late Neolithic (*c.* 3500–2800 BC) hardly any metals are present in the archaeological record of the north Alpine region, even though their number increased during the last years (Matuschik 1997; 1999, 80; Hafner & Suter 2000). Residues of the Late Neolithic (*c.* 3500–2800 BC) hardly any metals are present in the archaeological record of the north Alpine region, even though their number increased during the last years (Matuschik 1997; 1999, 80; Hafner & Suter 2000). Residues of metallurgy are as yet totally unknown. One can only assume that, at that time, metal objects were still objects of prestige by looking at the many depictions of, for instance, daggers on the contemporaneous stelae of the north Italian Remedello culture (de Marinis 1995). That region went through a metallurgical boom whose products can be found on a number of cemeteries (de Marinis 1997) and in the equipment of the 'Ice Man' from the Alpine Ötz valley (Egg & Spindler 2009). Therefore, it seems very likely that more metal was also present north of the Alps than we can deduce from the archaeological record, which is presumably mostly due to a continuing lack of graves.

Final Neolithic

The Final Neolithic in central Europe (*c.* 2800–2200 BC) is dominated by the two large cultural complexes of the Corded Ware culture and the Bell Beaker culture. In the Corded Ware culture metals still remain scarce, although burials become a common feature in the archaeological record. In the north Alpine region only 5% of the graves contain metals (copper), including also small pieces of ornaments, but no gold (Šumberová 1992; Strahm 1994; Heyd 2000, 35, 82–3). In the Bell Beaker culture in southern Germany and Austria metals are more abundant. From there we know 25 copper daggers, 12 copper awls, 3 copper and 6 gold ornaments (Kuna & Matoušek 1978; Heyd 2000, 269–73, 278,

296–8; Matuschik 2004, list 1), which derive mostly from graves. In total approximately 13% of the graves contain metals. In a few graves of well-equipped warrior burials, metal (mostly daggers) seems to underline the special status of the deceased; we can deduce this from the images on the impressive stelae in Sion-Petit Chasseur in the Swiss Valais (Favre *et al.* 1986; Harrison & Heyd 2007). Concerning Bell Beaker metallurgy there is still a total lack of finds with the exception of some of the so-called 'cushion stones' which have been proved to have been used for metalworking (Bertemes *et al.* 2000). The production of copper can only be demonstrated indirectly by comparing the impurity patterns of the finished objects with those of Alpine ores. There the Bell Beaker material in the north Alpine region shows a high degree of coincidence with the local ores (Matuschik 2004, 290–6). This could be a hint for the existence of mining and smelting at that time in the region which still remains to be detected in the archaeological record.

Conclusions

In general the low number of metal objects (mainly of copper, but also of precious metals) in the north Alpine area during the 5th–3rd millennia BC, and the rare evidence for metallurgical activities, do not speak for an important economic function of metal production in that period. There are many indications that metals became more and more significant as prestige objects, especially with high-quality objects as can be seen in the Bell Beaker culture. The economic background for their acquisition was provided by agriculture which according to pollen profiles boomed especially during the 3rd millennium (Haas *et al.* 2003). There are neither indications that the important innovations of the Young Neolithic had any causal links with the upsurge of metallurgy, nor do metals seem to have been a dominant element during the 5th–3rd millennia in the north Alpine area or anywhere else in central Europe. In spite of its innovative character, the Young Neolithic in the north Alpine area has to be seen in a clear tradition from the Middle Neolithic without any major social or economic changes. This tendency continued in a similar way during the Late and the Final Neolithic.

Metallurgy and metals in the southern Iberian Chalcolithic

The Chalcolithic on the Iberian peninsula

The metal bearing phase of the Iberian Stone Age is usually named Chalcolithic and represents its final development stage and the transition to the Bronze Age (Table 6.1). The course of the development and the absolute chronology are still much debated. At the beginning of the 20th century a division was made between a Bell Beaker and a pre-Bell Beaker phase according to the finds in the south Spanish settlement and necropolis of Los Millares (Molina & Cámara 2006, 26–30). By using settlement stratigraphies in Vila Nova de São Pedro and Zambujal (Portugal) and on the Cerro de la Virgen (Andalusia) (do Paço & Sangmeister 1956; Schüle 1980; Sangmeister & Schubart 1981) the chronology could be refined towards an Early, Full, and Final Chalcolithic (Chapman 1981). The Full Chalcolithic is represented by the Los Millares culture (or Los Millares I culture; Blance 1961) and the Late Chalcolithic by the appearance of Bell Beakers (Los Millares II). In terms of absolute chronology it can only be stated that the entire Los Millares culture covered the period from *c.* 3100/3000 BC until *c.* 2300/2200 BC (Castro *et al.* 1996, 79–82).

The transition from the Late Neolithic to the Chalcolithic has not yet been satisfactorily defined. In many regions the Late Neolithic is still poorly known. It is characterised by small open settlements and by the use of Megalithic tombs. In contrast to that, the Chalcolithic in the southern half of the Iberian peninsula is usually characterised by the appearance of several innovations: large fortified settlements, a greater difference in settlement sizes, new types of burials, and metals. The surface of the large complex settlements covers several hectares and like some of the smaller settlements, eg, Almizaraque, Terrera Ventura, El Malagón, Cerro de la Virgen (Nocete 2001), they are surrounded by defence systems. According to their size it seems very likely that the large settlements had the function of central places for the surrounding area. This is supported by the character of the complex fortifications. The position of settlements is mostly on hilltops or on the foothills of mountain ranges. With this they offer good accessibility either to agricultural or to mineral resources and traffic routes. The importance of traffic is reflected by finds that show trade in raw materials on a larger scale than in the Neolithic. Generally, it seems as if size and complexity of the fortified large settlements of the full Chalcolithic point towards a social and economic structure which differed significantly from that of the Neolithic.

Chalcolithic burials are usually in collective tombs, mostly within Megaliths (Leisner & Leisner 1943), but occur also in caves or in the new Tholos tombs. Only from the mid-3rd millennium onwards are individual burials also known, but they remain a minority until the beginning of the Bronze Age. The emergence of the large fortified settlements and the appearance of some monumental and wealthy tombs eg, Los Millares, Alcalar, Valencina de la Concepción (Ruiz & Martín 1995; Morán & Parreira 2004; Molina & Cámara 2006), make it necessary to think about the existence of a socially leading group. However, until now this is not reflected in the building structure of the settlements.

Early metallurgy on the Iberian peninsula

The Iberian peninsula bears a high potential for the early production of metals due to its almost ubiquitous wealth in ores (Bartelheim 2007, fig. ii.7). The appearance of metal comes at about the same time as the other innovations. However, our knowledge about Chalcolithic metallurgy and metals differs significantly from region to region. The best state of knowledge is in the southern half of the peninsula, especially in the Spanish region of Andalusia which will here, therefore, be the area of reference. The beginnings of the treatment of copper ores have been observed during the excavations in the Neolithic settlement of Cerro Virtud, prov. Almería (Andalusia). According to the excavators a pottery sherd with adherent copper slag was found in a secure stratigraphic context of the Middle Neolithic. The corresponding archaeological layer in which no metal objects were found has been dated by radiocarbon to the mid-5th millennium (4700–4350 cal BC; Beta-90844, 5660±80 BP; Montero & Ruiz 1996).

Metal objects have not been found in significant numbers on the Iberian peninsula until one and a half millennia later, in graves of the Full Chalcolithic – after an ill-defined Late

Neolithic/Early Chalcolithic with almost no metals (Montero 2004). Most of these metal finds come from Andalusia with the fortified settlement of Los Millares being the most prominent site. Indications for metallurgical activities are restricted almost entirely to mobile remains of copper production. They comprise pieces of ore, mortars, grinding stones, hammer stones, slags, and fragments of reduction vessels with adherent slags that were used to smelt ores. Residues of metalworking appear fairly frequently in settlements, mainly in the south of the peninsula, eg, Los Millares, Almizaraque, La Pijotilla, and Cabezo Juré (Montero 1994; Gómez 1999; Müller et al. 2004), and in the west sites such as Zambujal, Leceia, and Vila Nova de São Pedro (Gómez 1999, 54–5; Hunt 2003, 296–9, 377; Müller & Soares 2008). But some large fortified settlements with finds that date very early within the Chalcolithic did not reveal any metal, eg, Juromenha I, Águas Frias, Sagada, Carretas, Moinho de Valadares, and Mercador (Calado 2004). Until recently Chalcolithic copper mines were unknown on the Iberian peninsula. Only two years ago in Mocissos and Angerinha (southern Portugal) traces of copper mining were detected that could be dated by radiocarbon to the 3rd millennium. The ores in use were oxidic ones (mostly malachite, azurite, and ores of arsenical copper) of which fragments have been found frequently in Chalcolithic settlements on the Iberian peninsula (Montero 1994).

Cultural and socioeconomic context of early metallurgy on the Iberian peninsula

Only few of the sites with archaeological evidence for metallurgical activities have been investigated to an extent that allows substantiated statements to be made on the scale and the importance of metallurgy. Nevertheless, the distribution of residues of the production and the working of metals almost all over the Iberian peninsula shows that metal had rarely to be imported from afar. This is also valid for the raw materials – in the Chalcolithic mostly copper – as the distribution map of ore resources shows (Bartelheim 2007, fig. ii.7). On the sites which have been investigated sufficiently to make statements on the scale of metallurgical activities, such as Almizaraque (Montero 1994, 114–15) and Los Millares (Hook et al. 1987; Montero 1994,

143–6), it becomes obvious that metallurgy could have hardly been the economic basis of the settlements. Metallurgical residues were found only in small quantities and it seems as if production served only local needs. Apparently it was only an additional occupation besides other more important economic activities like agriculture and pastoralism.

Among the finds of the Iberian Chalcolithic metal plays a minor role. On the most sites metal objects were found only in small numbers. They are composed mainly of pure copper, but a significant number contains 1–10% arsenic (Rovira et al. 1998, figs 3–4). Gold is very rare. The range of object types is limited and consists of axes, daggers, awls, knives, saws, and projectile heads (Bartelheim 2007, fig. ii.19). Ornaments are hardly known. Presumably most of the weapons and tools were made of stone or organic materials. However, in view of the narrow range of types and the fairly low numbers of pieces in Chalcolithic finds contexts on the Iberian peninsula, it seems as if metallurgy was not the driving force of technological, cultural, and social change and it did also not have an important economic function (cf. Chapman 1990). Settlement concentrations as places of primary economic interest were oriented towards regions with good agricultural conditions. Therefore, it looks as if, due to their scarcity, metals were mostly status objects for elites whose power was economically based on agriculture (cf. also Nocete 2001, 45).

Synthesis

In none of the three surveyed regions does the archaeological record provide indications that either metals or metallurgy were the driving force behind the development of culture, economy or society during the later part of the local Neolithic (Table 6.2). Rather, they formed part of a package of innovations that led to significant changes in these regions during a stage of their cultural evolution that, in some areas, has been named 'Chalcolithic'. Nonetheless, in that period metal seems to have been a very important material and its production well reflects technical skills and interest in the improvement of technologies. The high esteem in which this material was held becomes obvious by its frequent appearance in connection with leading social groups.

	SE Europe	North Alpine Region	Southern Iberian Peninsula
Metals in the archaeological record	• Isolated finds from first half of 5th millennium • During second half 5th millennium metals are significant cultural feature	• Isolated finds from second half of 5th millennium • Higher frequency of objects from first half of 4th millennium; from second half only isolated finds • More frequent again in Bell Beaker culture of 3rd millennium	• Isolated finds with no secure context from 4th millennium • Higher frequency of objects from 3rd millennium
Continuity or discontinuity from preceding period	• Clear continuity from preceding Late Neolithic • Continuity of settlement area • Largely identical economic strategy • Appearance of gender-specific burial rites	• Clear continuity from preceding Middle Neolithic • Extension of settlement area • Largely identical economic strategy • Changes in house construction • Almost no burials	• Transition from Late Neolithic to Chalcolithic poorly known • Continuity of settlement area • Emergence of large settlements • More complex economic system
Socio-economic context	• Clear tendency towards social differentiation • Accumulation of prestige objects in settlements & graves • Complex settlement system	• Only in 3rd millennium weak indications of social inequality • Little diversity in settlement structure	• Clear tendency towards social differentiation • Monumental burials • Accumulation of prestige objects in graves • Complex settlement system

Table 6.2: Characteristic features of the Late Neolithic/Chalcolithic in south-eastern Europe, the north Alpine region and the southern Iberian peninsula

However, although metal is present in the archaeological record of the north Alpine area as well as on the Iberian peninsula and in those areas easily accessible ores provided good possibilities to produce metal, stone and bone remained by far the prevailing materials for tools, weapons, and ornaments. As in most of Europe metal was a scarce material for a long period after its introduction. Only in the south-east of Europe did metals become so abundant during the 5th millennium.

In south-eastern Europe a distinct metal technology evolved in the context of a strong tendency towards centralisation in settlements (tells and their immediate vicinity) and of an increasing social and gender differentiation in cemeteries. At the same time it becomes obvious that these changes were only part of a major techno-complex which is evidenced in a high floruit of pottery production as well as in the trade of *spondylus* shells and special types of flint. In comparison to these resources, fully developed metallurgy appeared rather late. Nevertheless, the agglomeration of heavy implements in settlements and graves in south-eastern Europe at that time makes it seem justifiable to talk about a 'Copper Age' there. In central Europe, especially in the north Alpine region at the end of the 5th millennium BC it is actually debatable whether to define a transition to a period which has to be separated from the Stone Age or to stress the continuity in the development of the Neolithic after having received strong cultural impulses from the south-east. Towards the north and the west those impulses become less noticeable. In the south of the Iberian peninsula it is mainly the new element of the large settlements in the south and southwest with their implicit social differentiation, but also changes in economy and burial practices that suggest defining the beginning of a new epoch around 3000 BC. However, the northern half of the peninsula hardly participated in that development.

Nevertheless, there are also remarkable similarities between some regions: In south-east Europe and on the Iberian Peninsula the beginning of the 'Chalcolithic' marks a period of centralisation and of social differentiation with outstanding burials. This goes along with significant economic changes in terms of trade in raw materials on a larger scale, a better use of the agricultural potential of landscapes, and an intensification of the use of mineral resources. This was then complemented by the introduction of metal production and use which, basically, had the character of a by-product of that development. In central Europe however, the innovations of the 5th–4th millennia apparently influenced modes of production and the supply of goods, but had hardly any noticeable effects on the economic, social, and settlement structure. Therefore, in south-east Europe and on the Iberian Peninsula it seems more justified to talk about a new epoch that started with a period of innovations than in central Europe, where more elements of continuity from the Neolithic can be spotted. By comparing the periods in question that have been called 'Chalcolithic' from south-east Europe to the Iberian Peninsula it becomes obvious that there are considerable variations which make it difficult to find a common definition for these phenomena. A view on the absolute chronology shows that there are significant chronological differences from region to region and the Chalcolithic starts subsequently later, if one moves west from south-east Europe (Table 6.2). Whereas in south-east Europe it covers almost the entire 5th millennium, in the Carpathian Basin it starts during the late 5th millennium, but covers mainly the 4th millennium. This is mostly contemporaneous with the north Alpine Young Neolithic. On the Iberian Peninsula however, the Chalcolithic is a feature of the 3rd millennium. Therefore, if the Chalcolithic is to be considered a common European cultural epoch as it has been successfully demonstrated for the Neolithic

and the Bronze Age, these phenomena should at least be partly contemporaneous.

After evaluating the archaeological record of these three distant European neighbours of Britain it becomes obvious that in most areas and during most of the time metals were not the dominant feature in the economy or in everyday life during the period in question. Therefore the term 'Chalcolithic' or 'Copper Age' seems hardly to be an appropriate name for it with the exception of a few regions, one of them being south-eastern Europe. Nonetheless, this is not meant to be an appeal to radically change the denomination of the period everywhere in Europe, which would cause too much confusion. Where it has been widely adopted, as on the Iberian Peninsula, to describe the 3rd millennium BC it should continue to be used as a technical term while we remain aware of its problematic character. Preferably the period in question should be rather defined structurally than by just stressing the appearance of one specific material.

Endnote

1 Ongoing excavations by Petăr Leštakov (Sofia) in Akladi Čeiri, south of Černomorec since 2007

Bibliography

Bakamska, A. 2007. Tell Gălăbnik. Architecture and Site Planning. In H. Todorova, M. Stefanovich, & G. Ivanov (eds), *The Struma/Strymon River Valley in Prehistory. In the Steps of James H. Gaul*, 175–80. Sofia & Düsseldorf: Gerda-Henkel-Stiftung

Bartelheim, M. 2007. *Die Rolle der Metallurgie in vorgeschichtlichen Gesellschaften. Sozioökonomische und kulturhistorische Aspekte der Ressourcennutzung. Ein Vergleich zwischen Andalusien, Zypern und dem Nordalpenraum*. Rahden: Forschungen zur Archäometrie und Altertumswissenschaft 2

Benecke, N. 1994. *Der Mensch und seine Haustiere. Die Geschichte einer jahrtausendealten Beziehung*. Stuttgart: Theiss

Bertemes, F. & Heyd, V. 2002. Der Übergang Kupferzeit/Frühbronzezeit am Nordwestrand des Karpatenbeckens. Kulturgeschichtliche und paläometallurgische Betrachtungen. In M. Bartelheim, E. Pernicka & R. Krauss (eds), *Die Anfänge der Metallurgie in der Alten Welt*, 185–228. Rahden: Forschungen zur Archäometrie und Altertumswissenschaft 1

Bertemes, F., Schmotz, K. & Thiele, W.-R. 2000. Das Metallurgengrab 9 des Gräberfeldes der Glockenbecherkultur von Künzing, Lkr. Deggendorf. In M. Chytráček, J. Michálek & K. Schmotz (eds), *9. Treffen Archäologische Arbeitsgemeinschaft Ostbayern/West- und Südböhmen*, 53–61. Rahden: Leidorf

Blance, B. 1961. Early Bronze Age colonists in Iberia. *Antiquity* 35, 192–202

Calado, M. 2004. *Menires do Alentejo Central*. Tese de

Doutoramento apresentada à la Faculdade de Letras de Lisboa (ed. policopiada). www.crookscape.org/tesemc/tese.html

Castro, P.V., Lull, V. & Micó, R. 1996. *Cronología de la Prehistoria Reciente de la Península Ibérica y Baleares (c. 2800–900 cal ANE)*. Oxford: British Archaeological Report S652

Černych, E.N. 1978. *Gornoje dělo i metallurgija v drevnejšej Bolgarii*. Sofia: Izdatstvo Bolgarskoj Akademii Nauk

Černych, E.N. 1982. Periodisierung der Frühmetallzeit: allgemein oder regional? In *Passagio dal Neolitico all'età del Bronzo*, 27–43. Verona: Museo Civico

Čochadžiev, S. 1998. Contribution to the research of the earliest copper extraction and processing in the Struma Basin. *Archaeologia Bulgarica* 2, 10–14

Chapman, R. 1981. Los Millares y la cronología relativa de la Edad del Cobre en el Sudeste de España. *Cuadernos de Prehistoria de la Universidad de Granada* 6, 75–87

Chapman, R. 1990. *Emerging Complexity: the later prehistory of south-east Spain, Iberia and the west Mediterranean*, London: Routledge

Drașovean, F. (ed.) 2008. *Neolithic Art in Romania*. Napoli: Arte-M

Dumitrescu, H. 1961. Connections between the Cucuteni-Tripolie Cultural Complex and the Neighbouring Eneolithic Cultures in the Light of the Utilisation of Golden Pendants. *Dacia N.S.* 5, 69–93

Echt, R., Thiele, W.-R. & Ivanov, I.S. 1991. *Varna – Untersuchungen zur kupferzeitlichen Goldverarbeitung*. In Lichardus (ed.) 1991b, 633–91

Egg, M. & Spindler, K. 2009. *Kleidung und Ausrüstung der kupferzeitlichen Gletschermumie aus den Ötztaler Alpen*. Regensburg: Monographien des Römisch-Germanischen Zentralmuseums Mainz 17

Fansa, M. & Burmeister, S. (eds). 2004. *Rad und Wagen. Der Ursprung einer Innovation im Vorderen Orient und Europa*. Mainz: Beiheft der Archäologischen Mitteilungen aus Nordwestdeutschland 40

Favre, S., Gallay, A., Farjon, K. & Peyer, K. de. 1986. *Stèles et Monuments du Petit-Chasseur: un site néolithique du Valais. Documentation*. Genève: Département d'Anthropologie

Fischer, U. 1991. Zur Terminologie der kupferführenden Kulturen in Mittel- und Süddeutschland. In Lichardus (ed.) 1991b, 735–45

Gómez Ramos, P. 1999. *Obtención de Metales en la Prehistoria de la Península Ibérica*. Oxford: British Archaeological Report S753

Haas, J.-N., Giesecke, T. & Karg, S. 2003. Die mittel-europäische Subsistenzwirtschaft des 3. und 2. Jahrtausends v. Chr. aus paläoökologischer Sicht. http://www.jungsteinsite.de

Häusler, A. 1992. Die Bestattungssitten des Neolithikums und Äneolithikums in Bulgarien und ihre Beziehungen zu Mitteleuropa. *Studia Praehistorica* 11/12, 131–50

Hafner, A. & Suter, P.J. 2000. *–3400 v. Chr. Die Entwicklung der Bauerngesellschaften im 4. Jahrtausend v. Chr. am Bielersee*, Bern: Berner Lehrmittel- und Medienverlag

Hansen, S. 2009. Kupfer, Gold und Silber im Schwarz-meerraum während des 5. und 4. Jahrtausends v. Chr. In J. Apakidze, B. Govedarica & B. Hänsel (eds), *Der Schwarzmeerraum vom Äneolithikum bis in die Früheisenzeit (5000–500 v. Chr.)*, 11–50. Rahden: Prähistorische Archäologie in Südosteuropa 25

Harmankaya, S. & Erdoğu, B. 2002. *Türkiye arkeolojik yerleşmeleri. Oğuz Tanındı 4, Ilk tunç*. Istanbul: TASK Vakfı yayınları 9

Harrison, R. & Heyd, V. 2007. Sion, Aosta and the Transformation of Europe in the 3rd millennium BC. *Prähistorische Zeitschrift* 82, 129–214

Heyd, V. 2000. *Die Spätkupferzeit in Süddeutschland*. Bonn: Saarbrücker Beiträge zur Altertumskunde 73

Hiller, S. & Nikolov, V. 1997. *Karanovo I,1. Die Aus-grabungen im Südsektor 1984–1992*. Salzburg & Sofia: Österreichisch-Bulgarische Ausgrabungen und Forschungen in Karanovo 1

Hook, D.R., Arribas, A., Craddock, P., Molina, F. & Rothenberg, B. 1987. Copper and silver in Bronze Age Spain, in W.H. Waldren & R.C. Keenard (eds), *Bell Beakers of the Western Mediterranean*, 147–72. Oxford: British Archaeological Report S331

Hunt, M. 2003. *Prehistoric Mining and Metallurgy in South West Iberian peninsula*, Oxford: British Archaeological Report S1188

Ivanov, I.S. 1991. Der Bestattungsritus in der chalk-olithischen Nekropole von Varna (mit einem Katalog der wichtigsten Gräber). In Lichardus (ed.) 1991b, 125–49

Jovanović, B. 1978. Rudna Glava – ein Kupferbergwerk des frühen Eneolithikums in Ostserbien. *Der Anschnitt* 28, 150–7

Kalicz, N. 1998. *Figürliche Kunst und bemalte Keramik aus dem Neolithikum Westungarns*. Budapest: Archaeolingua Series Minor 10

Karul, N. 2003. Die Architektur von Aşağı Pınar. In N. Karul, Z. Eres, M. Özdoğan & H. Parzinger, *Aşağı Pınar I. Einführung, Forschungsgeschichte, Stratigraphie und Architektur*. 42–125, Mainz: Archäologie in Eurasien 15

Klassen, L. 2000. *Frühes Kupfer im Norden. Untersuchungen zu Chronologie, Herkunft und Bedeutung der Kupferfunde der Nordgruppe der Trichterbecherkultur*. Højbjerg: Jutland Archaeological Society Publication 36

Klassen, L. 2004. *Jade und Kupfer. Untersuchungen zum Neolithisierungsprozess im westlichen Ostseeraum unter besonderer Berücksichtigung der Kulturentwicklung Europas 5500–3500 BC*. Aarhus: Jutland Archaeological Society publication 47

Krauß, R. 2001. Die prähistorische Siedlung beim Dorf Djakovo, Kr. Kjustendil (Bulgarien). Ein Beitrag zum Äneolithikum im Strumatal. *Prähistorische Zeitschrift* 76, 129–78

Krauß, R. 2008. Karanovo und das südosteuropäische Chronologiesystem aus heutiger Sicht. *Eurasia Antiqua* 14, 117–149

Kuna, M. 1981. Zur neolithischen und äneolithischen Kupferverarbeitung im Gebiet Jugoslawiens. *Godišnijak Sarajevo* 19/17, 13–81.

Kuna, M. & Matoušek, V. 1978. Měděná industrie kultury zvoncovitých pohárů ve střední Evropě, 65–89. Praha: *Varia Archaeologica* 1, *Praehistorica* 7

Lazarovici, Gh., Drașovean, F. & Maxim, Z. 2001. *Parța. Monografie archeologică I*. Timișoara: Bibliotheca historica et archaeologica banatica 13

Leisner, G. & Leisner, V. 1943. *Die Megalithgräber der Iberischen Halbinsel. Der Süden*. Berlin: Römisch-Germanische Forschungen 17, Madrider Forschungen 1, Tafelband

Lichardus, J. 1991a. Die Kupferzeit als historische Epoche. Eine forschungsgeschichtliche Einleitung. In Lichardus (ed.) 1991b, 13–34

Lichardus, J. 1991b. *Die Kupferzeit als historische Epoche.* Bonn: Saarbrücker Beiträge zur Altertumskunde 55

Link, T. 2006. *Das Ende der neolithischen Tellsiedlungen. Ein kulturgeschichtliches Phänomen des 5. Jahrtausends v.Chr. im Karpatenbecken.* Bonn: Universitätsforschungen zur prähistorischen Archäologie 134

Lüning, J. 1996. Erneute Gedanken zur Benennung der neolithischen Perioden. *Germania* 74, 233–7

Manhart, H. 1998. *Die vorgeschichtliche Tierwelt von Koprivec und Durankulak und anderen prähistorischen Fundplätzen in Bulgarien aufgrund von Knochenfunden aus archäologischen Ausgrabungen.* München: Documenta naturae 116

Manolakakis, L. 2005. *Les Industries Lithiques Énéolithiques de Bulgarie.* Rahden: Internationale Archäologie 88

Maran, J. 2004. Die Badener Kultur und ihre Räderfahrzeuge. In M. Fansa & S. Burmeister (eds), *Rad und Wagen. Der Ursprung einer Innovation. Wagen im Vorderen Orient und Europa,* 265–82. Mainz: Beiheft der Archäologischen Mitteilungen aus Nordwestdeutschland 40

Mareş, I. 2002. *Metalurgia aramei în Neo-Eneoliticul României.* Suceava: Bucovina Istorică

Marinis, R.C. de 1997. The eneolithic cemetery of Remedello Sotto (BS) and the relative and absolute chronology of the Copper Age in Northern Italy. *Notizie Archeologiche Bergomensi* 5, 33–51

Marinova, E. 2006. *Vergleichende paläoethnobotanische Untersuchungen zur Vegetationsgeschichte und zur Entwicklung der prähistorischen Landnutzung in Bulgarien.* Stuttgart: Dissertationes Botanicae 401

Matuschik, I. 1997. Eine donauländische Axt vom Typ Şiria aus Überlingen am Bodensee – Ein Beitrag zur Kenntnis des frühesten kupferführenden Horizontes im zentralen Nordalpengebiet. *Prähistorische Zeitschrift* 72, 81–105

Matuschik, I. 1998. Kupferfunde und Metallurgie-Belege, zugleich ein Beitrag zur Geschichte der kupferzeitlichen Dolche Mittel-, Ost- und Südosteuropas. In M. Mainberger (ed.), *Das Moordorf von Reute,* 207–61. Staufen: Terraqua

Matuschik, I. 1999. Riekofen und die Chamer Kultur Bayerns. In M. Strobel & H. Schlichtherle (eds), *Aktuelles zu Horgen-Cham-Goldberg III-Schnurkeramik in Süddeutschland. Rundgespräch Hemmenhofen 26. Juli 1998,* 69–95. Freiburg: Hemmenhofer Skripte 1

Matuschik, I. 2004. Kupfer der Glockenbecherkultur im Nordalpengebiet. Zur endneolithischen Kupfergewinnung in den nordöstlichen Alpen. In G. Weissgerber & G. Goldenberg (eds), *Alpenkupfer,* 285–303. Bochum: Der Anschnitt, Beiheft 17

Micó, R. 1993. *Pensamientos y prácticas en las arqueologías contemporáneas. Normatividad y exclusión en los grupos arqueológicos del III y II milenios cal ANE en el sudeste de la península Ibérica.* Barcelona: Universitat Autònoma

Molina, F. & Cámara, J.A. 2006. *Los Millares. Guía del yacimiento.* Sevilla: Junta de Andalucía

Montero, I. 1994. *El origen de la metalurgia en el sudeste de la Península Ibérica.* Almeria: Instituto de Estudios Almerienses

Montero, I. 2004. Der prähistorische Kupferbergbau in Spanien. Ein Überblick über den Forschungsstand. *Der Anschnitt* 56, 54–63

Montero, I. & Ruiz, A. 1996. Enterramiento colectivo y metalurgia en el yacimiento neolítico de Cerro Virtud (Cuevas del Almanzora, Almería). *Trabajos de Prehistoria* 53, 55–75

Morán, E. & Parreira, R. 2004. O povoado calcolítico de Alcalar (Portimâo) na paisagem cultural do Alvor no III milénio antes da nossa era. In S. Oliveira Jorge (ed.), *Recintos Murados da Pré-história Recente: técnicas construtivas e organizaçao do espaço: conservaçao, restauro e valorizaçao patrimonial de arquitecturas pré-históricas,* 307–27. Porto: Universidade do Porto

Müller, J. 1997. *Neolithische und chalkolithische Spondylus-Artefakte. Anmerkungen zu Verbreitung, Tauschgebiet und sozialer Funktion.* In: C. Becker, M.-L. Dunkelmann, C. Metzner-Nebelsick, H. Peter-Röcher, M. Roeder & B. Teržan (eds), Χρόνος, Beiträge zur Prähistorischen Archäologie zwischen Nord- und Südosteuropa. Festschrift für Bernhard Hänsel, 91–106. Espelkamp: Internationale Archäologie. Studia Honoraria 1

Müller, R. & Soares, A.M.M. 2008. Traces of early copper production at the Chalcolithic fortification of Vila Nova de São Pedro, Portugal. *Madrider Mitteilungen* 49, 94–114

Müller, R., Rehren, Th. & Rovira, S. 2004. Almizaraque and the early copper metallurgy of southeast Spain: new data. *Madrider Mitteilungen* 45, 33–56

Načev, I., Kovnurko, G. & Kănčev, K. 1981. Kremăčnite skali v Bălgarija i tjahnata eksploatacija. *Interdisciplinarni izsledvanija* 7/8, 41–59

Nadler, M. 2006. Der lange Weg in eine neue Gesellschaft – Die Kupferzeit. In S. Sommer (ed.), *Archäologie in Bayern,* 76. Regensburg: Friedrich Pustet

Neustupný, E. 1981. Das Äneolithikum Mitteleuropas. In H. Behrens (ed.), Tagung über die Walternienburg-Bernburger Kultur Halle 1977. *Jahresschrift für Mitteldeutsche Vorgeschichte* 63, 177–87

Nikolov, V. 2005. Părvi svidetelstva za naj-rannoto solodobivane v Evropa. *Arheologija Sofija* 46, 109–17

Nikolov, V. (ed.), 2008. *Praistoričeski solodobiven centăr Provadija-Solnicata. Razkopki 2005–2007g.* Sofija: Bălgarska Akademija na Naukite, Nacionalen Archeologičeski Institut i Muzej

Nocete, F. 2001. *Tercer Milenio antes de Nuestra era. Relaciones y Contradicciones Centro/Periferia en el Valle del Guadalquivir.* Barcelona: Bellaterra

O'Connor, B. 2008. 'Au silence et au travail': Evans and the Bronze Age. In A. MacGregor (ed.), *Sir John Evans 1823–1908,* 116–30. Oxford: Ashmolean Museum

Paço, A. do & Sangmeister, E. 1956. Vila Nova de São Pedro. Eine befestigte Siedlung der Kupferzeit in Portugal. *Germania* 34, 211–34

Patay, P. 1984. *Die kupferzeitlichen Meißel, Beile und Äxte in Ungarn.* München: Prähistorische Bronzefunde 9(15)

Pelegrin, J. 2007. Au Néolithique final – chalcolithique, un „paysage" européen complexe et diversifié. In J.-C. Marquet (ed.), *L'Europe, Déjà, à la Fin des Temps Préhistoriques. Des Grandes Lames en Silex dans Toute l'Europe. Catalogue de l'Exposition,* 11–13. Tours: Archéa

Pernicka, E. & Anthony, D.W. 2010. The invention of copper metallurgy and the Copper Age of Old Europe. In D.W. Anthony (ed.), *The Lost World of Old Europe. The Danube Valley, 5000–3500 BC* 162–77. Princeton: Princeton University Press

Pernicka, E., Begemann, F., Schmitt-Strecker, S. & Wagner,

G.A. 1993. Eneolithic and Early Bronze Age copper artefacts from the Balkans and their relation to Serbian copper ores. *Prähistorische Zeitschrift* 68, 1–54

Pernicka, E., Begemann, F., Schmitt-Strecker, S., Todorova, H. & Kuleff, I. 1997. Prehistoric copper in Bulgaria: Its composition and provenance. *Eurasia Antiqua* 3, 1–138

Pleslová-Štiková, E. 1977. Die Entstehung der Metallurgie auf dem Balkan, im Karpatenbecken und in Mitteleuropa unter besonderer Berücksichtigung der Kupferproduktion im ostalpenländischen Zentrum (kulturökonomische Interpretation). *Památky Archeologické* 78, 56–73

Pulszky, F. von 1884. *Die Kupferzeit in Ungarn*. Budapest: Kilian

Renfrew, C. 1969. The autonomy of the south-east European Copper Age. *Proceedings of the Prehistoric Society* 35, 12–47

Renfrew, C. & Shackleton, J.C. 1970. Neolithic trade routes realigned by oxygen isotope analyses. *Nature* 228, 1062–5

Rovira, S., Montero, I. & Gómez, P. 1998. The beginning of the use of metals in Spain. *Proceedings of the Fourth International Conference on the Beginning of the Use of Metals and Alloys (BUMA IV)*, 153–8, Sendai: Japan Institute of Metals

Ruiz, M.T. & Martín, A. 1995. Nuevos datos en torno al dolmen de la Pastora (Valencina de la Concepción, Sevilla). In V.M. Oliveira Jorge (ed.), *1. Congresso de Arqueologia Peninsular: (Porto, 12–18 de Outubro de 1993): actas* 5, 81–3. Porto: Sociedade Portuguesa de Antropologia e Etnologia

Ryndina, N.V. & Orlovskaja, L.B. 1979. Rezultaty metallografičeskogo issledovanija. In E.N. Černych, *Gornoje dělo i metallurgija v drevnejšej Bolgarii*, 286–321. Sofia: Izdatstvo Bolgarskoj Akademii Nauk

Sangmeister, E. & Schubart, H. 1981. *Zambujal. Die Grabungen 1964–1973*. Mainz: Madrider Beiträge 5, 1

Schoop, U. 2005. *Das anatolische Chalkolithikum*. Remshalden: Urgeschichtliche Studien 1

Schüle, W. 1980. *Orce und Galera*. Mainz: von Zabern

Séfériadès, M.L. 2010, Spondylus and long-distance trade in prehistoric Europe. In: D.W. Anthony (ed.), *The Lost World of Old Europe. The Danube Valley, 5000–3500 BC*, 179–90. Princeton: Princeton University Press

Shackleton, J. & Elderfield, H. 1990. Strontium isotope dating of the source of Neolithic European Spondylus shell artefacts. *Antiquity* 64, 312–15

Sherratt, A. 1981. Plough and pastoralism. Aspects of the Secondary Products Revolution. In I. Hodder, G.L. Isaac & N. Hammond (eds), *Pattern of the Past: Studies in honour of David Clarke*, 261–305. Cambridge: Cambridge University Press

Strahm, C. 1981. Die Bedeutung der Begriffe Kupferzeit und Bronzezeit. *Slovenská Archeologia* 29, 191–202

Strahm, C. 1994. Die Anfänge der Metallurgie in Mitteleuropa. *Helvetia Archaeologica* 25, 2–39

Šumberová, R. 1992. Typologie des Kupferschmucks und der Kupfergeräte in der schnurkeramischen Kultur Böhmens und Mährens. In M. Buchvaldek & C. Strahm (eds), *Die koninentaleuropäischen Gruppen der Kultur mit Schnurkeramik, Schnurkeramik-Symposium 1990*, 117–25. Praha: Praehistorica 19

Todorova, H. 1981. *Die kupferzeitlichen Äxte und Beile in Bulgarien*. München: Prähistorische Bronzefunde 9(14)

Todorova, H. 1982. *Kupferzeitliche Siedlungen in Nordostbulgarien*. München: Materialien zur Allgemeinen und Vergleichenden Archäologie 13

Todorova, H. & Vajsov, I. 2001, *Der kupferzeitliche Schmuck Bulgariens*. Stuttgart: Prähistorische Bronzefunde 20(6)

Vajsov, I. 2007. Promachon-Topolnica. A typology of painted decorations and its use as a chronological marker. In H. Todorova, M. Stefanovich, & G. Ivanov (eds), *The Struma/Strymon River Valley in Prehistory. In the Steps of James H. Gaul* 2, 79–120. Sofia & Düsseldorf: Gerda-Henkel-Stiftung

Vilanova y Piera, J. 1884. Du cuivre et du bronze en Espagne et de la periode qui les a précédés. *Congrès international d'anthropologie et d'archéologie préhistorique. Compte rendu de la neuvième session à Lisbonne 1880*, 352–5. Lisbon: Académie Royale des Sciences

Vulpe, A. 1970. *Die Äxte und Beile in Rumänien I*. München: Prähistorische Bronzefunde 9(2)

Wilde, W.R. 1862. *A Descriptive Catalogue of the Antiquities of Gold in the Museum of the Royal Irish Academy*. Dublin: Smith

7

Growth and Expansion: social, economic, and ideological structures in the European Chalcolithic

Volker Heyd

A long-term and ongoing evolutionary progress is attested for prehistoric Europe between the mid-5th and late 3rd millennium BC. Deep-reaching social and ritual changes transform the existing pattern as early as the first Chalcolithic horizon in south-east Europe. Similar changes occur in the western half of the continent though manifested in different ways and based on other materials. The period 3600–2500 BC sees then the revolution in terms of subsistence economy. Lines of interconnections in Europe and a new stage in the human–animal symbiosis are crucial for our understanding of the ideological changes that shatter the continent in these centuries. The Europe-wide Bell Beaker Phenomenon of the mid–later 3rd millennium is only the apex of this ideological domination. In such, it completes the process of the Chalcolithisation of Europe.

European prehistory is social, economic, and ideological evolution. In this paper, I outline some of the paradoxes involved when we talk of the European Chalcolithic, and try to move beyond the standard topics such as 'identity', 'autonomy', and 'social structure'.

The term 'Chalcolithic' throws into stark relief its origins in an evolutionary model, one however where we need to separate *causal processes* that lie behind social changes, from mere *correlations* of changes with artefacts. On the whole, prehistoric archaeologists fall too easily into the error of asserting correlations as causes. The matching of climatic changes with cultural ones is such an example; managerial models of social exchanges are another; emphasising determined technologies such as metallurgy is a third.

To move beyond narrative and correlation, and examine social, economic, and ideological evolution, three structures are needed. The first is an economic *infrastructure* featuring the progressive intensification of food production, leading to systematic surpluses. The second is the deployment of these surpluses for schemes of social promotion, which in turn stimulates the *superstructure* of hierarchies and cults, prestige goods, and metallurgies. The third, the over-arching *hyperstructure*, is finally the creation of the right environment for exchange, communication, and the spread of innovations and ideas, culminating in fashionable ideologies. All structures rest upon an empirical framework which can be tested; and by this I do not mean assembling more data of the same sort as we already have but, rather, introducing fundamentally new science to determine cause and discount correlation.

It was the genius of Andrew Sherratt to propose a model for understanding the Chalcolithic as a process of economic intensification, then of the creation of new social worlds, and finally of charismatic ideologies and cults that spread across the continent: thus was the Secondary Products Revolution created. In a complementary manner, Jan Lichardus has rightly confronted us with the early start of the causal process and the true European dimension of this transformation. He also guided us through its social and ritual implications, thus constituting the *Kupferzeit* as an historical epoch, after the Neolithic and before the Bronze Age.

My starting point for assessing this process of 'Chalcolithisation' is not the one that most scholars have taken when looking at its presumed beginnings. Instead, I will open the record at its end, just before the beginnings of the Early Bronze Age in Europe. And here it is the Bell Beaker Phenomenon, spreading over much of Europe, that grabs our attention.

The third quarter of the 3rd millennium BC: the pan-European Bell Beaker Phenomenon as a Chalcolithic network

The Bell Beaker Phenomenon pertains, over most of its distribution area, to the period between *c.* 2500 and 2200 BC. In a few regions, we see Beaker traditions continuing until the 21st century BC but by 2000 BC, by and large, even the very latest beakers have ceased to be made. As for its beginnings, it is only on the Iberian Peninsula that we have secure radiocarbon evidence for an early Bell Beaker emergence. This reaches back as early as *c.* 2700 BC (eg, Harrison & Heyd 2007).

This formation phase contains basic elements: characteristic Bell Beakers are the tall-narrow monotone comb-stamp decorated, so-called *Maritime* beakers. Additionally, the all-over-corded Beakers (AOC Beakers) also seem to have had an early start, perhaps even as early as the *Maritime* beakers. This early Iberian Bell Beaker tradition is apparently confined to the peninsula for over a century. At this early stage, the Bell Beaker 'package' (Burgess & Shennan 1976) is not yet fully developed, lacking, for example, two of its most prominent components: the tanged copper daggers and the wristguards. It was around 2600 BC when the phenomenon seemingly altered its ideas, imaginations, values, and world-view (ie, ideology), and an expansionistic drive – almost missionary in its appearance – became the dominant element. This is the moment when the first Bell Beaker vessels, and the people regarding them as their common symbol, were bypassing the Pyrenees along the Atlantic and Mediterranean coastline, reaching, for example, the mouth of the Rhône river or Brittany, during the 26th century BC. From now on, the Phenomenon accelerates dramatically, with more people being involved and taking the chance to promote themselves by adopting the, by now well-defined, package of novelties, and with the community of Beaker users growing. At the same time, around 2500 BC, Bell Beakers expand geographically to encompass more distant regions, and in transforming the traditions of an increasing number of local populations, the Phenomenon was itself being transformed, from being the driver of change to being a part of more established regional cultures with their own distinct flavour. This, in turn, shaped the course of developments over the succeeding centuries.

The Bell Beaker Phenomenon thus became pan-European in nature (Nicolis 2001), with its centre of gravity located firmly in the western half of the continent (Fig 7.1). The distribution of the expansion clearly follows the Atlantic and Mediterranean coasts and the main river systems, such as the Rhône, Rhine, and Danube, and their tributaries.

When trying to overview the distribution, four larger geographical entities can be discerned: an Atlantic domain, a Mediterranean one, the Central European or East Group, and a Beaker tradition in the western part of the great Northern European Plain, also including southern Scandinavia (Heyd 2007a). Within these entities, regional Beaker networks can be recognised. Here the British Beaker groups find their place, with their closest neighbours in the lower Rhine. In some entities, such as the East Group, different provinces can be

Figure 7.1: Distribution of the Bell Beaker Phenomenon in Europe; with regional groups, peripheries and some mentioned sites in the margins (map based on Heyd 2007a; 2007b; with modifications)

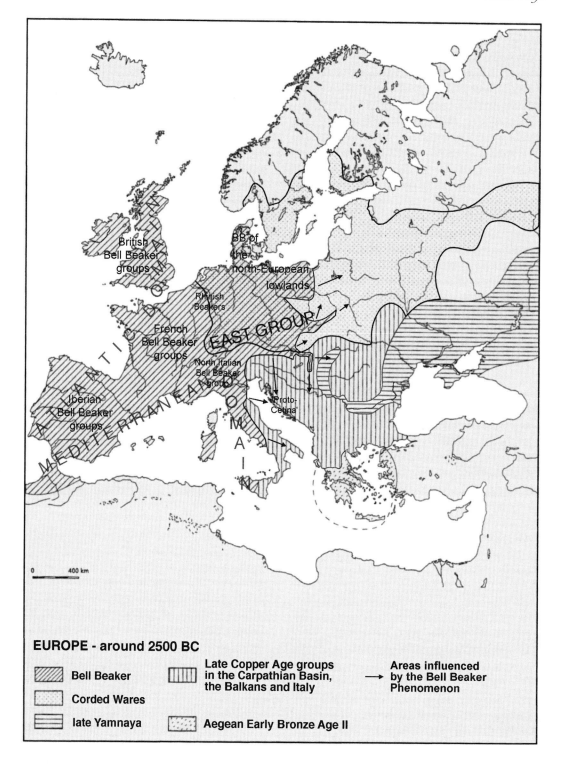

distinguished, and even within the provinces differences can be demonstrated, sometimes going down to the county level.

Beside these four domains, a kind of eastern periphery has recently come under our radar (Heyd 2007b). This is in the form

of syncretistic cultures: 'adopting different components of the Bell Beaker ideology and the package in its repertoire ..., transforming it together with parts of their own traditional inventory to build a new identity' (*ibid.*, 102) in a zone north to south roughly between 15°

and 20° eastern longitude. These syncretistic Beaker/local cultures start about 100–200 years after the more western regional Beaker cores but become very much the dominant regional players in the following Early Bronze Age. Representatives from north to south are the archaeological cultures of Iwno/Trzciniec in the western Baltic region; Chłopice-Veselé in Lesser Poland, western Slovakia and eastern Moravia; Pitvaros/Maros in the south-eastern Carpathian basin; Proto-Cetina/Cetina in the Adriatic basin; and the Grotta Cappuccini aspect of the Laterza-Cellino San Marco culture in south-east Italy. This eastern periphery and the adjacent margins (Rahmstorf 2008; Demchenko 2009) as more distant parts of the Bell Beaker idea are making it a truly European phenomenon. If one adds the structurally similar Corded Ware/Single Grave Culture/ Battle Axe cultures (Buchvaldek & Strahm 1992) as well as the Yamnaya of the steppes (Anthony 2007; Heyd 2011) then the continent is covered by three interrelated phenomena from the Urals to the Atlantic

Bell Beaker and metals

Copper and gold objects are found in Beaker contexts, but always in low numbers. For example in the Bell Beaker East Group metal has only been found in approximately 8% of all graves, and the figures seem similar in other parts of the Bell Beaker distribution area. Moreover, Bell Beaker metal objects are almost all rather small: all the gold objects ever found amount to not much more than 250 g, while the copper objects amount to just over 10 kg. Three categories of object are represented in Bell Beaker graves mostly, but are occasionally found in settlement contexts: weaponry, exclusively associated with males; tools, almost exclusively associated with female and craftsman's graves; and finally jewellery known to be used by both sexes.

Jewellery constitutes the largest group of Bell Beaker objects, in copper and gold, and occasionally silver. Surprisingly, there is not much variety as most objects only belong to three groups, namely: i) hair-rings in the form of simple rings or spirals; *Noppenringe* (fine wire rings or spirals having a U-turn in the twist); and the basket-shaped hair rings of Britain and Ireland; ii) simple rectangular or oval plates of gold and/or copper, sometimes decorated; and iii) beads of various forms (Carozza &

Mille 2007). Additional gold objects include strips, which are likely to be band-shaped head diadems; little *tutuli* (foil cones); and the small but massive V-perforated buttons from Nin-Privlaca in Dalmatia. Rather questionable, however, are the gold *lunulae* of the west and north-west, for which a Beaker relation has often been suggested (eg, Taylor 1980). The origins of lunulae, remain a matter for debate (O'Connor 2004).

There can be no doubt that the metallurgy that lies behind these objects is the result of a full metallurgical chain, from ores and their regular exploitation to the wider distribution and the consumer, including also a specific technical know-how and the rules for the final deposition. The copper mine at Ross Island in south-west Ireland finds its place here, as do some others in western Spain/eastern Portugal (Müller & Cardoso 2008), and surely there are others awaiting discovery soon in central Europe and northern Italy. These arguments make it apparent that the Bell Beaker Phenomenon of the period 2500–2200 BC represents a metal society: people understood its sources, valued it, desired it, exchanged it, and deposited it with care and by following distinct rules.

Social and economic achievements beyond metals

Social exchange networks and growing economic activity lie behind the expansion of the Bell Beaker West and East Groups. They include the beginning of social stratification, seen particularly when analysing cemeteries and assessing customs in grave good deposition, highlighting the unequal deposition of objects of special symbolism, prestige, and perhaps even status.

Here, the concept of over-equipment (Hansen 2002) finds its application, since lavishly equipped children's graves play a role, as indicators of inherited status: boys perhaps in the role as first-born sons and heirs of capital and wealth, and girls for exogamic marriages to peers (Heyd *et al.* 2005; Vander Linden 2007). At the same time, the practice of displaying the deceased's individual social role was progressing from the east to the west and became manifested in the grave context (Salanova & Heyd 2009); and – at least in central Europe – a core family social order is established, perhaps as a tradition stemming from Corded Ware society (Heyd 2007a; Haak *et al.* 2008; Müller *et al.* 2009).

The complexity of the subsistence economy deserves attention. Stock, and cattle in particular, seem to play the predominant role (Harrison & Mederos Martín 2001; Dörfler & Müller 2008). Other Beaker communities specialised in different livestock: the horse herders of the Beaker Csepel group in Hungary are famous for this, and in central Spain it also seems that there is a close link between the regional Bell Beaker development and the domestication of horses (Harrison 2007, 186ff). The same might account for sheep farmers and the early exploitation of wool, when more scientific data are available. Compared with stock, agriculture seems to play a reduced role. Emmer and barley were widely used, as well as spelt (*Triticum spelta*) as a newly emerging crop species, making it possible to bring marginal lands under cultivation (Jacomet 2008). Nevertheless more grassland for growing stock numbers is attested by pollen (Dörfler 2008).

The distribution and exchange of exotic and rare raw materials are reaching an unprecedented scale at this period from 2500 to 2200 BC, such as amber from the Baltic, Mediterranean shell, variscite gemstones from Catalonia, ostrich egg shells and elephant ivory from Africa and the Levant (Harrison & Gilman 1977; Schuhmacher *et al.* 2009), walrus tusk and sperm whale teeth from the north Atlantic, special stone varieties (porphyry; tuff) for wristguards in central Europe and Britain (Woodward *et al.* 2006), and also gold, copper (eg, Needham 2002; Matuschik 2004), and – last but not least – the first tin-bronzes (in central Europe: Krause 2003). Only a little jet however, perhaps from Yorkshire and other continental sources (Needham 2005; this volume), was in use in the 25th–23rd century BC. Nevertheless, it must be evident that this degree of communication and exchange, and the internationality of this period, can only be achieved through an increased human mobility as well.

It is in this context that the fortified sites in south-west Europe need to be mentioned. From smaller circular enclosures in the French Midi (Guilaine *et al.* 2001, 244–6), to middle-sized fortifications such as Leceia, Alcalar, and Zambujal in Portugal (Cardoso 2000; Kunst 2001), finally to the 'macro-villages'

of Spain (eg, Valencina de la Concepcion; Marroquíes Bajos; Los Millares: Díaz-del-Río 2004a; 2004b); Beaker users keep on occupying them. No doubt they act as central places in a landscape that operated to a settlement system that was at least two-fold in nature.

The same continuous occupation of monuments, with episodes of refurbishment and extension, is also well known for the Atlantic domain. This includes the many megalithic monuments from Galicia to Brittany (Salanova 2000; Prieto Martinéz & Salanova 2009), as well as the ritual sites of Britain and Ireland and their landscapes, of which Stonehenge and Avebury only representing the upper echelons (Sheridan 2008).

So, the European Bell Beaker Phenomenon is far from being a close-knit entity. Janusz Czebreszuk (2003) is surely right in saying that all is 'similar but different'. Also, much of it may be restricted to the *Zeitgeist* of the mid- and 3rd quarter of the 3rd millennium, but there are also Beaker achievements that need to be acknowledged, such as the establishment of the full metallurgical chain, the advanced social and economic system, the outstanding internationality and interchangeability of this period, and – not least – this expansionistic ideological drive behind the use of Beakers.

The first half of the 3rd and the second half of the 4th millennium BC: the 'Chalcolithic' aspects of Andrew Sherratt's 'Secondary Products Revolution'

By moving backwards into the first half of the 3rd millennium and roughly the second half of the 4th millennium BC, we are entering the arena where the late Andrew Sherratt's 'Secondary Products Revolution' finds its stage. No doubt, his brilliant concept from 1981 (1983; 1997a; see also 2004; 2006) still stands as the emblematic economic model of later European prehistory (Fig. 7.2). What we understand much better since the early 1980s, however, are the relative and absolute chronologies. Sherratt asserted correlations of his components rather than proving their contemporaneity, and generally did not go into much chronological detail (eg, Chapman 1982; Lichardus 1991a, 20). His chronological attribution derived mainly from his knowledge

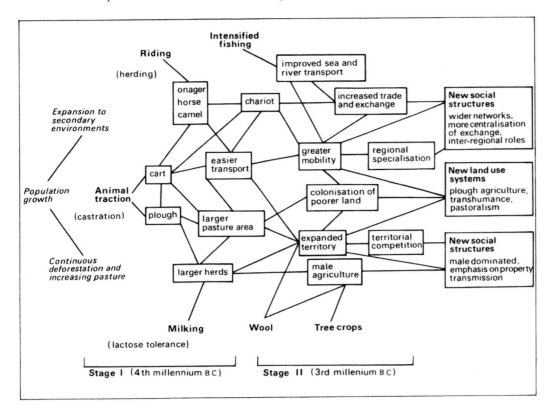

Figure 7.2: Andrew Sherratt's graph of the 'Interaction of the components of the secondary products complex through time' (Sherratt 1981, fig. 10.16)

of the absolute chronologies of Mesopotamia and the Near East, and his perspective that many of those innovations, if not all, originate ultimately in Mesopotamia. Indeed, the traction complex of wheel, cart, yoke, wagon, and plough as a key innovation/invention of his 'Secondary Products Revolution' has been proved empirically valid: it has a secure appearance in the record from *c.* 3600 BC (generally Fansa & Burmeister 2004 and Pétrequin *et al.* 2006). However, in contrast to his traction complex, his dairy complex seems invalid, since milking and the use of dairy products have now been confirmed to have taken place much earlier and over a wide geographical extent (Evershed *et al.* 2008).

Still controversial are the issues of horse riding and the domestication of the horse, as well as the introduction of the woolly sheep (eg, Anthony 2007). At least both innovations and their wider dissemination in Europe certainly fall into the period between around the mid-4th and the first half of the 3rd millennium. All over central Europe, woolly breeds of sheep must have been widely exploited by the last two centuries of the 3rd millennium at the latest, as shown by the many and diagnostic copper and bone pins from Early Bronze Age

(Reinecke A1) grave contexts. Their position in relation to the skeleton (and to the corpse thus represented) can only indicate the former existence of a woollen cloak or cape that must have become desirable for people of a certain social position. However, as for the chariot and the spoked wheel – further inventions in speed, flexibility, and warfare, as mentioned in Sherratt's graph (1981, fig. 10.16) – there is now sufficient evidence to date their appearance to a much later period, around or after 2000 BC (eg, Anthony 2007, 371ff.; Kristiansen 2007).

The 'Secondary Products Revolution' still describes very well an advanced stage that is different from the Neolithic (cf. Harrison 1985 for Iberia). In this, traction, dairy farming, horse riding, and wool production represent innovations. But Sherratt takes the argument further, setting the agenda for consecutive, more processional effects such as economic and social complexity, population growth and density pressure, expansion to secondary environments, deforestation and increasing pasture, as well as easier transport, greater mobility, regional specification, etc. We can arguably take his argument still further and even claim a major dependency on animals for subsistence and a much closer and more complex animal–human symbiosis than is suggested by secondary products and traction from the mid-4th millennium onwards. This would also include the attribution of a new esteem to the indirect and symbolic value of stock. If properly thought through, the consequences of this model would be even more dramatic than those proposed by Sherratt, since this new emphasis on stock, and subsequent changes in the economic foundations, would require a different lifestyle and settlement organisation, with enhanced mobility and communications. In turn this would trigger a complete change in all social systems, affecting ritual and spiritual beliefs and cult practices, including burial and hoard deposition. This would then lead to significant new paramount ideas, a different world-view and ideology, reflected not least in a new material culture and pottery. Nevertheless, what Sherratt is offering is a socio-economic definition of a mature stage of the Neolithic. Metals are not necessary for his concept of economic intensification, and play no primary role in it. No wonder, then, that he does not mention them.

Chalcolithisation: three stages of cultural change in Europe

For Sherratt his 'Secondary Products Revolution' is very much a counterbalance to, and European response to, V. Gordon Childe's famous 'Urban revolution' of the Near East (Childe 1934; 1936). However, despite many subsequent claims, Near Eastern connections with, and influence over, Europe during this period are virtually non-existent, except in the Caucasus region (Kohl 2007; Hansen 2009). So, the big cultural change and breakdown of the ancient 'Danubian' tradition, from *c.* 3600 BC, must have had another background. This background can only be the scenario, described above and materialised in the newly formed, rapidly expanding value and symbol systems that we name after pottery forms and two key sites where they occur: 'Cernavodă III' in Romania and 'Boleráz' in Slovakia (Roman & Diamandi 2001; Sherratt 2003; Furholt *et al.* 2008). It was probably the ever-increasing interaction between culturally different groups of herders of the Pontic Steppe belt and their advanced sedentary neighbours at the lower Danube and the eastern Carpathians that triggered fresh values and symbols of wealth, prestige and power. This was probably

also the routeway for the transmission of the domesticated horse, and potentially also of the woolly sheep.

The next stage is reached by the Baden-Coţofeni from *c.* 3350 BC as well as the contemporary emerging Globular Amphora culture. This super-regional system dominates half of the continent for half a millennium. Even in northern and Central Greece and in north-western Anatolia, we find typical Baden relations in the pottery assemblages (Maran 1998; Roodenberg & Thissen 2001; Nikolova 2008), also confirming that the observed cultural changes are European and not Asian in their origin. In the north-west, Globular Amphora culture pottery can be found as far as the river Rhine, forming here a kind of ideological periphery (Szmyt 2003; Salanova & Heyd 2009). In the French Midi, Spain, and Portugal, this period 3500–3250 BC is seen as the beginning of a Mediterranean Chalcolithic in established terminological tradition (eg, Gocchi Genick 1996; Díaz-del-Río 2004a; 2004b; Guilaine 2007). Arguments for its establishment are an increase in production, a change in herding practices, intensification in agriculture, population growth, trends towards a hierarchical society, nucleation of the settlement organisation, political centralisation, and, of course, copper extraction and its processing and distribution (Roberts 2008).

The third stage, immediately preceding the Beaker Phenomenon, is signalled by the infiltration of the Yamnaya population from the Pontic steppe into areas of south-east Europe in the early 3rd millennium (Anthony 2007; Heyd 2011), bringing with them a distinct package of innovations (Harrison & Heyd 2007). Next, we see neighbouring societies responding to this package. This is seen as the beginning of a Late Copper Age. The deepest social transformation occurs however, north of the Carpathians. Here societies gradually react against groups of Yamnaya people migrating up the rivers Prut, Dnestr, and Dnepr. The result is the emergence of a distinctive new lifestyle, economy, settlement and social organisation, called the Corded Ware Complex. This dominates the record 2900–2100 BC between the Volga river and the Rhine (cf. Buchvaldek & Strahm 1992).

Enclosures, central places, and copper

Hillforts, enclosures, and consequently the

question of central places and a hierarchical settlement organisation are terms well-attested for much of Europe in the later 4th and early 3rd millennia (Gibson 2002; Harding *et al.* 2006; Zápotocký & Zápotocká 2008). Key examples can be named in regions as far away from each other as the western Mediterranean (where they form the basis for the later Beaker occupation mentioned above), the southern Carpathian basin and Transylvania (as at the site of Vučedol, for instance), the Aegean, and several spots in southern Scandinavia of what is there termed the 'Late Early Neolithic' and the whole of the 'Middle Neolithic' (eg, Sarup on Fyn island, Stävie in Scania and Büdelsdorf in Schleswig-Holstein).

The period of the second half of the 4th millennium BC is said to show a break, or depression, in metal production and circulation. This certainly accounts for the south-east of Europe and the Carpathian basin, where this horizon coincides with the end of use of the heavy copper holed axes, having dominated the record for more than a millennium. Gold also disappears completely from the record here, as does most of the silver in the Aegean. However, flat axes continue to be used (eg, Dobeš 1989) and daggers even flourish in some regions in the east (Vajsov 1993). Jewellery continues as well, but is rarer. One reason for this 'metal depression' might be a change in depositional practices, since copper hoards and single deposits of axes disappear, and graves are no longer properly furnished.

Further to the east, in the Caucasus region, the pattern goes in the opposite direction: here we now see a variety of new metal forms appearing in the record in larger quantities. A peak is reached with the famous Majkop princely grave, and several other well-furnished tumulus graves (Sherratt 1991; Hansen 2009), displaying a variety of copper weapons and tools, as well as prestige objects and jewellery of gold, silver and copper. Some jewellery and metal vessels show distinct Mesopotamian connections. This led the Russian scholar Evgeni Chernikh to define his second metallurgical province, the 'Circum-Pontic Metallurgical Province' (*passim*, eg, Chernikh 1992; Chernikh *et al.* 2000) which finds its stage here in this environment. However this distinct metal package only occasionally leaves its Caucasus catchment zone towards the north and west. This situation changes only from 3000 BC onwards, when the Balkans and Carpathians see the reappearance of the single edged shaft-hole axes, along with the tanged dagger, distinctive awls, and hair-rings.

To the west, in central Europe, 'the metal depression' after 3600 BC did not have the same effect as in the south-east of Europe. One reason for this is the fact that metal had not been that prominent in this part of Europe: any comparison must take into account this disparity in scale. Also, some copper axes continue to be used, albeit in different forms. Even innovations appear in this period, as shown by the early flanged copper axe possessed by the 'Iceman'.

There is, surprisingly, another European region that sees a flourishing of metal circulation in this period between *c.* 3600 and 3300 BC: southern Scandinavia, with more than 50 copper objects, most of them flat axes as single finds, but several coming from TRB graves and hoards (Klassen 2000). This distinct hoarding tradition extends into Poland (Łęczycki 2004). All of the copper is imported from the south, probably mostly from the Eastern Alps and the Slovakian ore mountains, roughly 1000 km away. But metal is only consumed here and not produced.

What I have tried to demonstrate, in this review of the process of Chalcolithisation in the three time horizons prior to the Bell Beaker Phenomenon, is that metal is not the primary signal. Instead, it is the advanced socio-economic structure that really matters. In this, Andrew Sherratt has paved the way with his subsistence model and Jan Lichardus (see below) has broadened it by adding social arguments. Speaking in traditional terminology, Europe in the second half of the 4th and the first half of the 3rd millennium BC is now a tripartite continent: by that time, an advanced south-east and east-central Europe has already experienced a Chalcolithic for more than a millennium. South-central and south-west (Mediterranean) Europe are both rapidly transforming, and there is good reason to describe this period as an *Età del Rame/Chalcolithique/Calcolítico*. It is the west-central, north-west, and north regions, that are seen to contain societies that are more reluctant, or else are too far away from the then centres of innovation. But, as demonstrated above, this is only partly the case and Europe during this period is already sharing many common traits.

A. Society

1. Emergence of sharply organised settlement centres and fortifications along traffic roads.
2. Advance of a hierearchised social order. Existence of a regional and super-regional upper class, tied to distinct families. Inclusion of children in the hierarchical system.
3. Emergence of first status symbols and signs of power.
4. Erection of first monumental burial grounds through the accumulation of earthern mounds.
5. Segmentation of the society based on the specialisation of labour: prospectors, miners, craftsmen, traders, beside a population with an agro-pastoral life subsistence.
6. Pronunciation of the different role of both gender in society also through a gender differentiated burial custom.
7. Application of metric systems as well as an astronomical knowledge.

B. Economy

1. Specialising in stock elevation and creation of larger herds, indications of a new sheep race.
2. Begin of horse elevation and use of the horse as riding and traction animal.
3. Utilisation of animals for transport and use of their power for soil cultivation
4. Introduction of the ard (*Hakenpflug*) and through it the possibility of a more efficient soil cultivation.
5. Careful tillage with a systematic suppression of weed.
6. Cultivation of spices and herbs.
7. Increased salt production
8. Exploitation of flint, copper ores (and gold?) in mines.
9. Specialised craftsmanship, visible particularly in the highly developed gold and copper metallurgy, also by an altered flint technology
10. Sharp cutback of wood and production of charcoal as presupposition for a systematic metallurgy.
11. Organisation of transport and the dissemination of raw materials, emergence of trade, also with regions farer away.
12. First-time appearance of wheel models as a sign of knowledge about wagons.
13. Innovations in boat construction make possible secure transport also along the coastal shores.

C. Religion

1. First occurrence of cult places outside the settlement houses.
2. Construction of large ditch systems with cultic depositions in the ditch or in the enclosed area.
3. Orientation of other-world imaginations to the model of a strongly segmented societal order.
4. Changes in the burial cults, arise of partial burials, collective and multiple burials with funeral succession (*Totenfolge*).
5. Rise of new cult practices, connected with sun worship, with stock elevation and intensified with the male gender.
6. Introduction of new hoarding customs.

Table 7.1: Compilation and English translation of the 26 bullet points under the headings 'society, economy and religion' (from Lichardus 1991b, 787–8)

The first half of the 4th and the 5th millennium BC: the socio-economic 'Kupferzeit als Historische Epoche' of Jan Lichardus

The first third of the 4th and the 5th millennia BC form the period that the German scholar Jan Lichardus had in mind when he suggested his package of innovations, effects, and achievements, which he discussed in detail and then summarised under 26 bullet points (Lichardus 1991b, 787–8; see a primary definition in Lichardus *et al.* 1985; more recently, the ideas had been repeated, refined, and widened in an article by Marion Lichardus-Itten in 2007). Several of his points can already be found in Andrew Sherratt's arguments from the early 1980s. But Lichardus's list (Table 7.1) and argumentation goes beyond Sherratt, and

it is probably accurate to describe both concepts as complementary.

Lichardus's starting point lies in the southeast of Europe. Here, societies have already achieved an elevated degree of cultural complexity, obvious in the form of the tell settlements themselves and, as shown by recent fieldwork, their defences and contemporary outer settlement and satellite sites (eg, Hansen *et al.* 2007; 2008). Kodžadermen-Gumelniţa-Karanovo VI, Tripolye-Cucuteni, and the Tiszapolgár-Bodrogkeresztur-Hunjadi Halom sequence are the most important of these (Parzinger 1993; Whittle 1996; Bailey 2000; Chapman 2000). The famous cemetery of Varna and the Tripolye 'mega-villages' are the gemstones in the centre. Varna and the southeast of Europe, with their gold in abundance and a typical copper inventory of thousands of hammer-axes, mattocks, and different types of flat axes, also form the heartland of Colin Renfrew's 'Autonomous Southeast European Copper Age' (1969; 1978) and Chernikh's first metallurgical province, his 'Balkano-Carpathian-Metallurgical Complex'. However Lichardus's concept is intended to go beyond the south-east European Chalcolithic. He assembled many good arguments – in particular social ones – that fit a definition of the Chalcolithic that extends beyond metals and, geographically, beyond this traditional early Chalcolithic south-east/eastern-central Europe core area. He is also right in tracing these social achievements back not only into the 5th millennium but also in the western half of Europe where traditionally a Neolithic nomenclature system is applied. For example, settlement centres and fortifications are well-attested west and north-west of the Carpathian basin for the period between the later 5th millennium until *c.* 3600 BC, in the form of hillforts (eg, Zápotocký 2000), ditch systems, and enclosures, often causewayed (eg, Gojda 2006). The same is true for his 'Erection of first monumental burial grounds through the accumulation of earth mounds' (Lichardus 1991b, 770 *passim*) demonstrated by the long-barrows and related structures in a wide geographical zone of the north and north-west between north-central Poland, southern Scandinavia, Atlantic France, and Britain and Ireland.

Along with these monumental grave markers goes a change in the symbols and signs of prestige and power. The most striking examples are the polished stone axes. These are no doubt regarded as key components of the Neolithic package, irrespective of whether their users live in the Fertile Crescent, or later in south-east Europe, or later still in southern Scandinavia and in Britain and Ireland (Klassen 2004; Pailler & Sheridan 2009). The transformation, and a new period, starts when the axes are made of an exotic material with special colour and brilliance, and are acquiring a polish, form, and size that render them unsuitable for felling trees. From that moment on, the object has acquired a socially valorised function. The famous Alpine jadeitite axes and their wide European distribution network (eg, Pétrequin *et al.* 2003) are the key example for this process in the west. Roughly contemporaneously, a similar transformation happens in the south-east of Europe when flat axes here become

cast in the brilliant and shiny, but rather soft, copper of more than 99% purity (see also Klassen 2004).

Copper and gold

Metal objects peak in frequency from 4000 to 3700/3600 BC in the Carpathian basin (eg, Schubert 1965; Klassen 2000, fig. 115). This is why Hungarian tradition calls this period the 'high Copper Age'. It is also in these four centuries around and after 4000 BC that we see exports of this metallurgy to regions further to the west, triggering a dependent local Alpine metallurgy, one expression of this centred around the Austrian Mondsee and another with the Swiss Pfyn (Bartelheim 2007). The furthest exports of flat axes extend to eastern France (Klassen *et al.* 2007) and perhaps even as far as the Atlantic west (Briard & Roussot-Larroque 2002, 156–7, figs 10–12). The famous gold lozenge from a richly furnished grave at Pauilhac in Aquitaine, geographically in the Atlantic zone and dated to around 3800 BC (Roussot-Larroque 2008), seem to belong to the same trajectory (Fig. 7.3), and there can be no doubt that this piece is a far-away offspring from a cluster of such gold lozenges and plates in Hungary and Romania (Makkay 1989; Hansen 2007). The same Carpathian centre is simultaneously radiating towards the south-west and the first copper artefacts also enter the southern Alps and the Po valley (Gleirscher 2008), activating a first independent Italian metallurgy there soon after. The situation described here is similar for the north and the north-west when axes of this Carpathian manufacture reach the northern European plain (Müller 2001; Łęczycki 2005) and, in Klassen's phases 1 and 2, southern Scandinavia (Klassen 2000, figs 111–13), prior to or contemporary with the advent of the Neolithic package. The only difference is the lack of copper ore sources here. Therefore independent TRB metallurgy can hardly develop.

Sharing practices in hoarding and technology

Hoarding is also mentioned by Lichardus, and this period sees the first pure metal hoards as well as the beginnings of hoard deposition outside settlement sites (Lichardus-Itten 1991; 2007, 14). But it was Pierre Pétrequin who illuminated the geographical differences between hoarding stone objects and metal

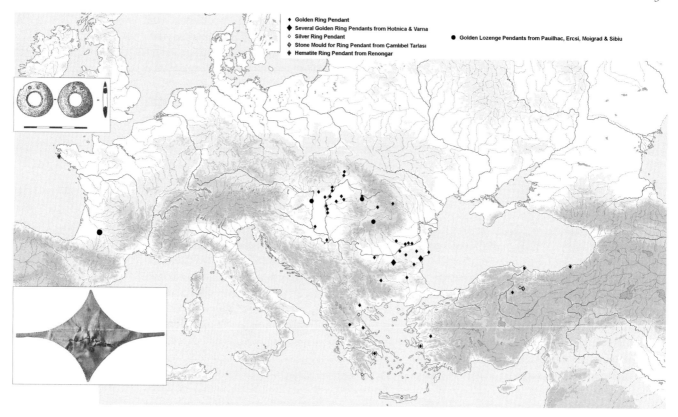

♦ Golden Ring Pendant
◆ Several Golden Ring Pendants from Hotnica & Varna
◇ Silver Ring Pendant
⬦ Stone Mould for Ring Pendant from Çamlıbel Tarlası
◆ Hematite Ring Pendant from Renongar

● Golden Lozenge Pendants from Pauilhac, Ercsi, Moigrad & Sibiu

Figure 7.3: Distribution of the gold, silver and copper ring-pendants and the golden lozenges of the Early Chalcolithic horizon (c. 4600–37/3600 BC); added is the haematite pendant from Renongar in Brittany (based on a map provided by Hansen 2007, fig. 175; and Zimmermann 2007, fig. 1; golden lozenges by information from Makkay 1976 (Acta Archaeologica Hungaricae 28, 251–300) and Bona 1986 (Veszprém megyei múzeumok közleményei 18, 21–81; all modified and with additions)

objects, thus creating a picture – somehow contrary to the one of interconnection presented here – of a western *Stone Age* Europe versus a eastern *Copper Age* Europe (Pétrequin *et al.* 2002). Interestingly the border between the two 'worlds' is approximately along the river Rhine, a frontier line of eastern and western influences already named in the previous chapters on several occasions for the later 4th and 3rd millennium BC periods. Pétrequin's map of the different areas of hoarding practice is indeed an impressive and powerful picture. Nevertheless it is one-dimensional because single metal axes go further west beyond the respective distribution zones, as noted above, just as single jadeitite axes reach as deep as into the heart of Chalcolithic south-east Europe. Indeed, a hoard consisting solely of Alpine jadeitite axes seems recently to have been identified in Bulgaria, along with further hoards of polished stone or flint (Pétrequin *et al.* in press) Despite these clarifications, it is clearly to the credit of Pierre Pétrequin, and Marion Lichardus-Itten, to have opened our eyes to a common hoarding practice, uniting the east and west of Europe in the 5th and early 4th millennium, irrespective of whether

the hoards contain metal, stone, or both. Indeed, the same situation can be seen with the flint mines of this period, and with salt exploitation (Lichardus-Itten 2007, 14–16).

One should, therefore, highlight the message that specialised stonework and simple metallurgy share technological similarities, rather than stressing that they are different materials, and that *skeuomorphism* between them is common. This is best demonstrated, again, by the tomb at Pauilhac in the French south-west. Here, it is not only the golden lozenge that is outstanding, but also the over-sized stone axes and flint blades, which can only be pure prestige objects. Both stone axes, made from Alpine jadeitite, have cutting edges imitating copper ones. Likewise, the outsize flint blades find their best parallels in the cemetery of Varna. Julia Roussot-Larroque (2008) concludes that copper also plays a role, because of the copper micro-traces left by a tipped flaking tool, used to shape the flint blades by controlled pressure flaking (Pelegrin 2006). Similar analogies exist for the haematite (another brilliant semi-precious stone) ring pendant from the long-barrow of Renongar (Plovan; Finistère) in the extreme west of Brittany (Cassen 2003; Pailler & Sheridan 2009).

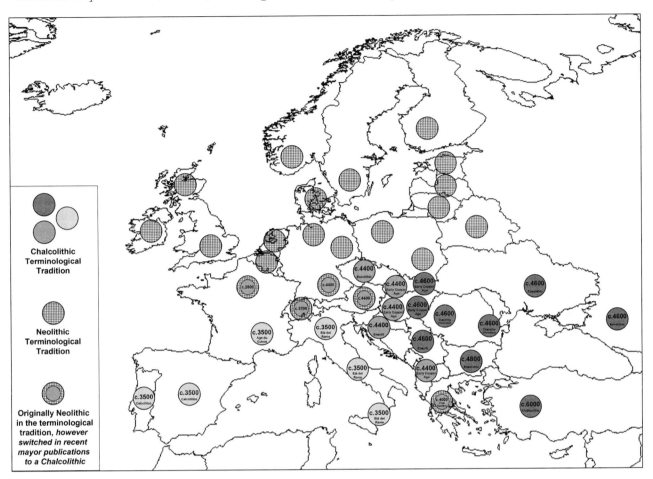

Without the golden pendants of the south-east European Chalcolithic (cf. Fig. 7.3), like those from the settlement hoard of Hotnica in Bulgaria, 2500 km away, its form could not be understood.

Yet this makes it clear that even as early as 4600 BC, prehistoric Europe was more closely interrelated than the technological differences between metal and stone imply. For all this Lichardus has set the agenda in synthesising these transformations in the social sphere, from lavishly equipped graves, structured tell settlements and mega-villages in the southeast to grave monumentality, hillforts, and causewayed enclosures in the centre and north-west, clamped together by a similar system of prestige and symbols of power, of practices and technologies. The only component which is not shared between the two 'worlds' is – as it seems – their preferred materials.

Defining progress in human culture: a final word

Clearly, then, we can trace a long-term and ongoing evolutionary progress. Traditionally, prehistoric archaeology has used materials – flint, stone, and different metals – and their sequence of appearance in order to define stages within this evolution. For a long time this was the easiest way to divide up the past, and one which was reflected in the material record. However, since then, the concept of progress has also made it into the archaeologist's way of looking at the past, of its definitions and methods. Crucial to this has been the application of various sciences, and their input in helping us to understand the past, not least as regards prehistoric economy and subsistence strategies. Consequently, it has been the Neolithic period that has been separated out from this material-based tradition, now being successfully defined by – primarily – its mode of subsistence, plus – secondarily – its set of cultural, social, and

Figure 7.4: Traditional terminology in the European countries with regard to a Neolithic and/or Chalcolithic nomenclature; for those countries using the term 'Chalcolithic', the absolute date of its approximate beginning is given

ritual novelties. Thus, polished stones and pottery have rightfully become third-class criteria for determining Neolithic societies. Similar efforts are also underway for defining the Bronze Age: we are now beginning to eschew the introduction of tin-bronze as the key driver, and to appreciate that its mode of use differs considerably from that of other aspects of material culture. This leaves us focusing more on the socio-economic sphere and on matters of cultural complexity.

For the Chalcolithic, the current situation in Europe and its *c.* 50 recognised countries (Fig. 7.4) seems to display a kind of geographically and chronologically staggered introduction: from the 5th millennium in south-east and central east Europe, followed in the mid-/later 4th millennium by central south and south-west Europe, while much of central Europe, the north and north-west of the continent and the Atlantic façade is still described as being 'Neolithic' at this time. Occasionally, as in Austria, Germany, Switzerland, and France, one accepts here the truly Chalcolithic nature at least for the 3rd millennium and the Bell Beaker Phenomenon.

As neat and convincing as this model might seem, built as it is on local traditions, this tripartite Europe does not actually reflect past reality. From as early as the mid-5th millennium onwards, prehistoric Europe is so interconnected and has reached such a level of social and economic complexity that it is a different world from the period of its Neolithisation and first expansion some 50–100 generations previously. Throughout the 1500 years, from the later 5th to the early 3rd millennium, societies in both the east and west experienced significant population growth, resulting in larger sites and denser and more structured settlement networks, and in inland colonisation and further outside expansion, as in the case of southern Scandinavia and Britain and Ireland. Key innovations are making it into everyday life and this period sees *the revolution* in economic and subsistence terms. Parallel to this goes the growing importance of animal husbandry, triggering a series of fundamental changes in general mobility pattern, in communication networks, and exchange of goods, genes, information, and ideas. Human beings must react in this system. Archaeologically, we see in it a new material culture and new rites and customs, culminating

in a complete social reorganisation and a new way of life, with implications and challenges for the whole system of ideas, imaginations, values, symbols, and terms. The end result of this, in Europe, is major ideological changes and the emergence of the novel, expansionistic, and thus super-regional phenomena of Boleráz-Cernavodă (with the Baden sequence), the Globular Amphora Complex and indeed the whole Corded Ware Complex.

The apex of this Chalcolithic Europe is then reached when the Bell Beaker Phenomenon extends, together with the structurally associated Corded Ware Complex, shortly after 2500 BC from the Urals to the Atlantic, from Norway to Africa. The ideological component is now the dominating factor. Communication, mobility, exchange, as well as a common material package and its super-regional recognition, become unprecedented in Europe. No matter whether you look into the record of southern Scandinavia, Britain and Ireland, the lower Rhine, or Atlantic France and Spain, Beaker Europe is – despite its existing regional flavours – basically interchangeable in its core programme and its achievements. At last, Europe as a whole has arrived in the Chalcolithic.

Acknowledgements

I wish to thank Richard J. Harrison, Professor emeritus from Bristol University, who has gratefully taken the task to read through an early draft of the text, condensed this much longer draft into a printable size, then polished my Germanic English, and finally commented on the content and helped me rewriting the introduction. I am also grateful to Marion Lichardus-Itten, Professor emerita from the Université Paris I-Sorbonne, who has kindly sent me a copy of her article in Guilaine (ed.) 2007 at an early stage of work on the article. Taking my long and intensive relationship to both, Marion and her late husband, I would like to dedicate this article to the memory of Professor Jan Lichardus (24 January 1939–8 March 2004).

Bibliography

Anthony, D.W. 2007. *The Horse, the Wheel and Language. How Bronze-Age Riders from the Eurasian Steppes Shaped the Modern World*. Princeton & Oxford: University Press

Bailey, D.W. 2000. *Balkan Prehistory: exclusion, incorporation and identity*. London: Routledge

Bartelheim, M. 2007. *Die Rolle der Metallurgie in vorgeschichtlichen Gesellschaften.* Rahden: Forschungen zur Archäometrie und Altertumskunde 2

Briard, J. & Roussot-Larroque, J. 2002. Les débuts de la métallurgie dans la France atlantique. In M. Bartelheim, R. Krause & E. Pernicka (Hrsg.), *Die Anfänge der Metallurgie in der Alten Welt,* 135–60. Rahden: Forschungen zur Archäometrie und Altertumswissenschaft 1

Buchvaldek, M. & Strahm, C. 1992. *Die kontinentaleuropäischen Gruppen der Kultur mit Schnurkeramik.* Praha: Praehistorica 19

Burgess, C. & Shennan, S.J. 1976. The Beaker Phenomenon: some suggestions. In C. Burgess & R. Miket (eds), *Settlement and Economy in the Third and Second Millennia BC,* 309–31. Oxford: British Archaeological Report 33

Cardoso, J.L. 2000. The fortified site of Leceia (Oeiras) in the context of the Chalcolithic in Portugese Estremadura. *Oxford Journal of Archaeology* 19, 37–55

Carozza, L. & Mille, B. 2007. Chalcolithique et complexification sociale: quelle place pour le métal dans la définition du processus de mutation des sociétés de la fin du Néolithique en France. In J. Guilaine, *Le Chalcolithique et la Construction des Inégalités: tome 1, le continent européen,* 195–232. Paris: Collection des Hesperides, Errance

Cassen, S. 2003. To import, to copy, to inspire? – Central-European object signs in the Armorican Neolithic Age. *L'Anthropologie* 107(2), 255–70

Chapman, J. 1982. The 'Secondary Products Revolution' and the Limitations of the Neolithic. *Bulletin of the Institute of Archaeology London* 19, 107–22

Chapman, J. 2000. *Fragmentation in Archaeology: people, places and broken objects in the prehistory of south eastern Europe.* London: Routledge

Chernykh, E.N. 1992. *Ancient Metallurgy in the USSR. The Early Metal Age.* Cambridge: Cambridge University Press

Chernykh, E.N., Avilova, L.I. & Orlovskaya, L.B. 2000. *Metallurgical Provinces and Radiocarbon Chronology.* Moskva: Institut Arkheologii Rossiiskaia Akademiia Nauk

Childe, V.G. 1934. *New Light on the Most Ancient East.* London: Keegan Paul

Childe, V.G. 1936. *Man Makes Himself.* London: Library Science and Culture 5

Czebreszuk, J. (ed.). 2003. *Similar but different. Bell Beakers in Europe.* Poznań: Adam Mickiewicz University

Demchenko, T. 2009. Памятники типа Коржеуць в контексте истории центральнои и восточнои Европы раннего бронзового века (Monuments of the Corjeuți type within the context of the Early Bronze Age History of Eastern and Central Europe). *Tyragetia* S.N. 3(18)/1, 9–30

Díaz-del-Río, P. 2004a. Copper Age ditched enclosures in central Iberia. *Oxford Journal of Archaeology* 23(2), 107–21

Díaz-del-Río, P. 2004b. Factionalism and collective labour in Copper Age Iberia. *Trabajos de Praistoria* 61(2), 85–98

Dörfler, W. 2008. Das 3. Jahrtausend v.Chr. in hoch auflösenden Pollendiagrammen aus Norddeutschland. In Dörfler & Müller (eds) 2008, 135–48

Dörfler, W. & Müller, J. (eds) 2008. *Umwelt – Wirtschaft –*

Siedlungen im dritten vorchristlichen Jahrtausend Mitteleuropas und Südskandinaviens. Neumünster: Offa-Bücher 84

Dobeš, M. 1989. Zu den äneolithischen Kupferflachbeilen in Mähren, Böhmen, Polen und in der DDR. In M. Buchvaldek & E. Pleslová-Štiková E. (eds), *Das Äneolithikum und die früheste Bronzezeit (C14 3000–2000 b.c.) in Mitteleuropa: kulturelle und chronologische Beziehungen,* 39–48. Praha: Praehistorica 15

Evershed, R.P., Payne, S., Sherratt, A.G., Copley, M.S., Coolidge, J., Urem-Kotsu, D., Kotsakis, K., Özdoğan, M., Özdoğan, A.E., Nieuwenhuyse, O., Akkermans, P.M.M.G., Bailey, D., Andeescu, R.-R., Campbell, S., Farid, S., Hodder, I. Yalman, N., Özbaşaran, M., Bıçakcı, E., Garfinkel, Y., Levy T. & Burton, M.M. 2008. Earliest date for milk use in the Near East and southeastern Europe linked to cattle herding. *Nature* 455, 528–31

Fansa, M. & Burmeister, S. 2004. *Rad und Wagen. Der Ursprung einer Innovation. Wagen im Vorderen Orient und Europa.* Mainz: von Zabern

Furholt, M., Szmyt, M. & Zastawny, A. (eds). 2008. *The Baden Complex and the Outside World.* Bonn: Studien zur Archäologie in Ostmitteleuropa/Studia nad Pradziejami Europy Środkowej 4

Gibson, A. (ed.). 2002. *Behind Wooden Walls. Neolithic Palisaded Enclosures in Europe.* Oxford: British Archaeological Report S1013

Gleirscher, P. 2008. Frühes Kupfer und früher Kupferbergbau im und um den Ostalpenraum. In M. Blečić, M. Črešnar, B. Hänsel, A. Hellmuth, E. Kaiser & C. Metzner Nebelsick (eds), *Scripta Praehistorica in Honorem Biba Teržan.* Situla 44, 93–110. Ljubljana: Narodni musej

Gocchi Genick, D. 1996. *Manuale di Preistoria. Vol. 3: L'età del rame.* Firenze: Octavo Franco Cantini

Gojda, M. 2006. Large prehistoric enclosures in Bohemia: the evidence from the air. In Harding *et al.* (eds) 2006, 5–19

Guilaine, J. 2007. *Le Chalcolithique et la construction des inégalités: tome 1, le continent européen.* Paris: Collection des Hesperides, Errance

Guilaine, J., Claustre, F., Lemercier, O. & Sabatier, P. 2001. Campaniforme et environnement culturel en France méditerranéenne. In Nicolis (ed.) 2001, 229–75

Haak, W., Brandt, G., De Jong, H.N., Meyer, C., Ganslmeier, R., Heyd, V., Hawkesworth, C., Pike, A.W.G., Meller, H. & Alt, K.W. 2008. Ancient DNA, Strontium isotopes, and osteological analyses shed light on social and kinship organization of the Later Stone Age. *Proceedings of the National Academy of Sciences* 47(105), 18226–31

Hansen, S. 2002. 'Überausstattungen' in Gräbern und Horten der Frühbronzezeit. In J. Müller, *Vom Endneolithikum zur Frühbronzezeit: Muster sozialen Wandels?,* 151–73. Bonn: Universitätsforschungen zur Prähistorischen Archäologie 90

Hansen, S. 2007. *Bilder vom Menschen der Steinzeit. Untersuchungen zur anthropomorphen Plastik der Jungsteinzeit und Kupferzeit in Südosteuropa.* Mainz: Archäologie Eurasiens 20

Hansen, S. 2009. Kupfer, Gold und Silber im Schwarzmeergebiet während des 5. und 4. Jahrtausends v. Chr. In J. Apakidze, B. Govedarica & B. Hänsel, *Der Schwarzmeerraum vom Äneolithikum bis in die Früh-*

bronzezeit, 11–50. Rahden: Prähistorische Archäologie in Südosteuropa 25

Hansen, S., Toderaş, M., Reingruber, A., Gatsov, I., Georgescu, C., Görsdorf, J., Hoppe, T., Nedelcheva, P., Prange, M., Wahl, J., Wunderlich, J. & Zidarov, P. 2007. Pietrele, Măgura Gorgana. Ergebnisse der Ausgrabungen im Sommer 2006. *Eurasia Antiqua* 13, 43–112

Hansen, S., Toderaş, M., Reingruber, A., Gatsov, I., Georgescu, C., Görsdorf, J., Hoppe, T., Nedelcheva, P., Prange, M., Wahl, J., Wunderlich, J. & Zidarov, P. 2008. Pietrele, Măgura Gorgana. Ergebnisse der Ausgrabungen im Sommer 2007. *Eurasia Antiqua* 14, 19–100

Harding, A., Sievers, S. & Venclová, N. (eds). 2006. *Enclosing the Past: inside and outside in prehistory*. Sheffield: Sheffield Archaeological Monograph 15

Harrison, R.J. 1985. The 'Policultivo Ganadero', or the Secondary Products Revolution in Spanish Agriculture, 5000–1000bc. *Proceedings of the Prehistoric Society* 51, 75–102

Harrison, R.J. 2007. *Majaladares. A Bronze Age Village of Farmers, Hunters and Herders*. Rahden: Internationale Archäologie 107

Harrison, R.J. & Gilman, A. 1977. Trade in the second and third millennia B.C. between the Maghreb and Iberia. In V. Markotic (ed.), *Ancient Europe and the Mediterranean. Studies in Honor of Hugh Hencken*, 90–104. Warminster: Aris & Phillips

Harrison, R.J. & Heyd, V. 2007. The transformation of Europe in the third millennium BC: the example of 'Le Petit Chasseur I+III' (Sion, Valais, Switzerland). *Praehistorische Zeitschrift* 82(2), 129–214

Harrison, R.J. & Mederos Martín, A. 2001. Bell Beakers and social complexity in central Spain. In Nicolis (ed.) 2001, 111–24

Heyd, V. 2007a. Families, prestige goods, warriors, and complex societies: Beaker groups and the third millennium cal BC along the Upper and Middle Danube. *Proceedings of the Prehistoric Society* 73, 321–70

Heyd, V. 2007b. When the west meets the east: the eastern periphery of the Bell Beaker Phenomenon and its relation with the Aegean Early Bronze Age. In I. Galanaki, I. Galanakis, H. Tomas & R. Laffineur (eds), *Between the Aegean and Baltic Seas: prehistory across borders*, 91–107. Liège: Aegaeum 27

Heyd, V. 2011. Yamnaya groups and tumuli west of the Black Sea. In S. Müller-Celka & E. Borgna (eds), *Ancestral Landscapes: burial mounds in the Copper and Bronze Ages (central and eastern Europe – Balkans – Adriatic – Aegean, 4th–2nd millennium BC)*, 529–49. Lyon: Travaux de la Maison de l'Orient et de la Méditerranée 61

Heyd, V., Winterholler, B., Böhm, K. & Pernicka, E. 2005. Mobilität, Strontiumisotopie und Subsistenz in der süddeutschen Glockenbecherkultur. *Berichte der Bayerischen Bodendenkmalpflege* 43/4, 2002/3, 109–35

Jacomet, S. 2008. Subsistenz und Landnutzung während des 3. Jahrtausends v.Chr. aufgrund von archäobotanischen Daten aus dem südwestlichen Mitteleuropa. In Dörfler & Müller (eds) 2008, 355–77

Klassen, L. 2000. *Frühes Kupfer im Norden*. Moesgard & Aarhus: Jutland Archaeological Society 36

Klassen, L. 2004. *Jade und Kupfer. Untersuchungen zum*

Neolithisierungsprozess im westlichen Ostseeraum unter besonderer Berücksichtigung der Kulturentwicklung Europas 5500–3500 BC. Moesgard & Aarhus: Jysk Arkæologisk Selskabs Skrifter 47

Klassen, L., Pétrequin, P. & Grut, H. 2007. Haches plates en cuivre dans le Jura français. Transferts à longue distance de biens socialisés valorisés pendant les IVe et IIIe millénaires. *Bulletin de la Société Préhistorique Française* 104(1), 101–24

Kohl, P.L. 2007. *The Making of Bronze Age Eurasia*. Cambridge: Cambridge University Press

Krause, R. 2003. *Studien zur kupfer und frühbronzezeitlichen Metallurgie zwischen Karpatenbecken und Ostsee*. Stuttgart: Vorgeschichtliche Forschungen 24

Kristiansen, K. 2007. Eurasian transformations: mobility, ecological change, and the transmission of social institutions in the third millennium and early second millennium B.C.E. In A. Hornborg & C. Crumley (eds), *The World System and the Earth System: global socioenvironmental change and sustainability since the Neolithic*, 149–62. Walnut Creek: Left Coast Press

Kunst, M. 2001. Invasion? Fashion? Social Rank? Considerations concerning the Bell Beaker phenomenon in Copper Age fortifications of the Iberian Peninsula. In Nicolis (ed.) 2001, 81–90

Łęczycki, S. 2004. Kietrz, Bytyn, Szczecin-Smierdnica. Einige Anmerkungen zur Kulturzugehörigkeit des Hortfundes von Bytyn. *Sprawozdania Archeologiczne* 56, 33–77

Łęczycki, S. 2005. Massive Kupferartefakte aus dem Äneolithikum im Gebiet des heutigen Mittelschlesiens. *Sprawozdania Archeologiczne* 57, 53–73

Lichardus, J. 1991a. Kupferzeit als historische Epoche. Eine forschungsgeschichtliche Einleitung. In Lichardus (ed.) 1991c, 13–32

Lichardus, J. 1991b. Kupferzeit als historische Epoche. Versuch einer Deutung. In Lichardus (ed.) 1991c, 763–800

Lichardus, J. (ed.). 1991c. *Die Kupferzeit als historische Epoche*. Bonn: Saarbrücker Beiträge zur Altertumskunde 55

Lichardus, J., Lichardus-Itten, M., Bailloud, G. & Cauvin, J. 1985. *La Protohistoire de l'Europe. Le Néolithique et le Chalcolithique entre la Méditerranée et la mer Baltique*. Paris: Nouvelle Clio

Lichardus-Itten, M. 1991. Hortfunde als Quellen zum Verständnis der frühen Kupferzeit. In Lichardus (ed.) 1991c, 735–62

Lichardus-Itten, M. 2007. Le Chalcolithique – une époque historique de l'Europe. In J. Guilaine, *Le Chalcolithique et la Construction des Inégalités: tome 1, le continent européen*, 11–22. Paris: Collection des Hesperides, Errance

Makkay, J. 1989. *The Tiszaszölös Treasure*. Budapest: Studia Archaeologica 10

Maran, J. 1998. Die Badener Kultur und der ägäisch-anatolische Bereich. Eine Neubewertung eines alten Forschungsproblems. *Germania* 76, 497–525

Matuschik, I. 2004. Kupfer der Glockenbecherkultur im Nordalpengebiet. Zur endneolithischen Kupfergewinnung in den nordöstlichen Alpen. In G. Weisgerber & G. Goldenberg, *Alpenkupfer – Rame delle Alpi*, 285–302. Bochum: Der Anschnitt, Beiheft 17

Müller, J. 2001. *Soziochronologische Studien zum Jung- und Spätneolithikum im Mittelelbe-Saale-Gebiet (4100–2700 v.Chr.)*. Rahden: Vorgeschichtliche Forschungen 21

Müller, J., Seregély, T., Becker, C., Christensen, A.-M.,

Fuchs, M., Kroll, H., Mischka, D. & Schüssler, U. 2009. A Revision of Corded Ware settlement pattern – new results from the central European low mountain range. *Proceedings of the Prehistoric Society* 75, 125–42

Müller, R. & Cardoso, J.L. 2008. The origin and use of copper at the Chalcolithic fortification of Leceia, Portugal. *Madrider Mitteilungen* 49, 64–93

Needham, S. 2002. Analytical implications for Beaker metallurgy in north-west Europe. In M. Bartelheim, R. Krause & E. Pernicka (eds), *Die Anfänge der Metallurgie in der Alten Welt*, 99–133. Rahden: Forschungen zur Archäometrie und Altertumswissenschaft 1

Needham, S.P. 2005. Transforming Beaker culture in north-west Europe: processes of fusion and fission. *Proceedings of the Prehistoric Society* 71, 171–217

Needham, S. this volume. Case and place for the British Chalcolithic. In M.J. Allen, J. Gardiner & A. Sheridan, *The British Chalcolithic: people, place and polity in the later 3rd millennium*. Oxford: Prehistoric Society Research Paper 4

Nicolis, F. (ed.), 2001. *Bell Beakers Today. Pottery, People, Culture and Symbols in Prehistoric Europe*. Trento: Ufficio Beni Culturali

Nikolova, L. 2008. Balkan-Anatolian cultural horizons from the fourth millennium BC and their Relations to the Baden Cultural Complex. In M. Furholt, M. Szmyt & A. Zastawny (eds), *The Baden Complex and the Outside World*, 157–166. Bonn: Studien zur Archäologie in Ostmitteleuropa/Studia nad Pradziejami Europy Środkowej 4

O'Connor, B.J. 2004. The earliest Scottish metalwork since Coles. In I.A.G. Shepherd & G.J. Barclay (eds), *Scotland in Ancient Europe. The Neolithic and Early Bronze Age of Scotland in their European Context*, 205–16. Edinburgh: Society of Antiquaries of Scotland

Pailler, Y. & Sheridan, J.A. 2009. Everything you always wanted to know about ... la néolithisation de la Grande-Bretagne et de l'Irlande. *Bulletin de la Société Préhistorique Française* 106(1), 25–56

Parzinger, H. 1993. *Studien zur Chronologie und Kulturgeschichte der Jungstein-, Kupfer- und Frühbronzezeit zwischen Karpaten und Mittlerem Taurus*. Mainz: Römisch-Germanische Forschungen 52

Pelegrin, J. 2006. Long blade technology in the Old World: an experimental approach and some archaeological results. In J. Apel & K. Knutsson (eds), *Skilled Production and Social Reproduction*, 37–68. Uppsala: SAU Stone Studies 2

Pétrequin, P., Cassen, S., Croutsch, C. & Errera, M. 2002. La valorisation sociale des longues haches dans l'Europe néolithique. In J. Guilaine (ed.), *Matériaux, Productions, Circulations du Néolithique à l'Age du Bronze*, 67–98. Paris: Errance

Pétrequin, P., Errera, M., Cassen, S. & Croutsch, C. 2003. De la pétrographie aux approches sociales: la circulation des grandes haches en roches alpines pendant le Néolithique. In F. Surmely (ed.), *Les Matières Premières Lithiques en Préhistoire*, 253–75. Préhistoire du Sud-Ouest, numéro spécial 5

Pétrequin, P., Arbogast, R.-M., Pétrequin, A.-M., van Willigen S. & Bailly M. 2006. *Premiers Chariots, Premiers Araires. La Diffusion de la Traction Animale en Europe pendant les IVe et IIIe millénaires avant notre ère*. Paris: CNRS éditions, CRA 29

Pétrequin, P., Cassen, S., Errera, M., Tsonev, T., Dimitrov, K., Klassen, L. & Mitkova, R. in press. Les haches en 'jades alpins' en Bulgarie (Axeheads of 'Alpine jade' in Bulgaria). In P. Pétrequin, S. Cassen, M. Errera, L. Klassen & J.A. Sheridan (eds), *JADE. Grandes haches alpines du Néolithique européen Ve et IVe millénaires av. J.-C.* Besançon & Gray: Presses Universitaires de Franche-Comté & CRAVA (Centre de Recherche Archéologique de la Vallée de l'Ain)

Prieto Martínez, M.P. & Salanova, L. 2009. Coquilles et Campaniforme en Galice et en Bretagne: mécanismes de circulation et stratégies identitaires. *Bulletin de la Société Préhistorique Française* 106(1), 73–94

Rahmstorf, L. 2008. The Bell Beaker Phenomenon and the interaction spheres of the Early Bronze Age East Mediterranean: similarities and differences. In A. Lehoërff (dir.), *Construire le Temps. Histoire et méthodes des chronologies et calendriers des derniers millénaires avant notre ère en Europe occidentale*, 149–70. Glux-en-Glenne: Bibracte 16

Renfrew, C. 1969. The autonomy of the south-east European copper age. *Proceedings of the Prehistoric Society* 35, 12–47

Renfrew, C. 1978. Varna and the social context of early metallurgy. *Antiquity* 52, 197–203

Roberts, B.W. 2008. Creating traditions and shaping technologies: understanding the emergence of metallurgy in Western Europe *c.* 3500–2000 BC. *World Archaeology* 40(3), 354–72

Roman, P. & Diamandi, S. 2001. Cernavodă III – Boleráz. Ein vorgeschichtliches Phänomen zwischen dem Oberrhein und der Unteren Donau. Bucureşti

Roodenberg, J. & Thissen, L. (eds). 2001. *The Ilipinar Excavations II*. Leiden: Nederlands Instituut voor het Nabije Oosten

Roussot-Larroque, J. 2008. La 'sépulture de chef' de Pauilhac (Gers). *Préhistoire du Sud-Ouest* 16(1), 91–142

Salanova, L. 2000. *La question du Campaniforme en France et dans les îles anglo-normandes. Productions, chronologie et rôles d'un standard céramique*. Paris: CTHS

Salanova, L. & Heyd, V. 2009. Du collectif à l'individu, de la région à l'Europe: le 3e millénaire avant J.-C. entre le Bassin parisien et la vallée rhénane. In F. Le Brun-Ricalens, F. Valotteau & A. Hauzeur (eds), *Relations Interrégionales au Néolithique entre Bassin Parisien et Bassin Rhénan*, 469–93. Luxembourg: Archaeologia Mosellana 7

Schubert, F. 1965. Zu den südosteuropäischen Kupferäxten. *Germania* 43, 274–95

Schuhmacher, Th.X., Cardoso, J.L & Banerjee, A. 2009. Sourcing African ivory in Chalcolithic Portugal. *Antiquity* 83, 983–97

Sheridan, A. 2008. Towards a fuller, more nuanced narrative of Chalcolithic and Early Bronze Age Britain 2500–1500 BC. *Bronze Age Review* 1, 57–78

Sherratt, A. 1981. Plough and pastoralism: aspects of the secondary products revolution. In N. Hammond, I. Hodder & G. Isaac (eds), *Pattern of the Past: studies in honour of David Clarke*, 261–305. Cambridge: Cambridge University Press

Sherratt, A. 1983. The secondary exploitation of animals in the Old World. *World Archaeology* 15(1), 90–104

Sherratt, A. 1991. Troy, Maikop, Altyn Depe: Early Bronze Age urbanism and its periphery. Reprint in: Sherratt 1997b, 457–70

Sherratt, A. 1997a. Plough and pastoralism: aspects of the

Secondary Products Revolution. Reprint in Sherratt 1997, 261–305

Sherratt, A. 1997b. *Economy and Society in Prehistoric Europe: changing perspectives.* Edinburgh: Edinburgh University Press

Sherratt, A. 2003. The Baden (Pécel) Culture and Anatolia: perspectives on a cultural transformation. In E. Jerem & P. Raczky (eds), *Morgenrot der Kulturen. Frühe Etappen der Menschheitsgeschichte in Mittel- und Südosteuropa. Festschrift für N. Kalicz zum 75. Geburtstag*, 415–29. Budapest: Archaeolingua

Sherratt, A. 2004. Wagen, Pflug, Rind: ihre Ausbreitung und Nutzung – Probleme der Quelleninterpretation. In M. Fansa & S. Burmeister, *Rad und Wagen. Der Urprung einer Innovation. Wagen im Vorderen Orient und Europa*, 409–28. Mainz: von Zabern

Sherratt, A. 2006. La traction animale et la transformation de l'Europe néolithique. In Pétrequin *et al.* (eds) 2006, 329–360

Szmyt, M. 2003. Verbreitung und Kontakte der Kugelamphorenkultur: Ein Blick auf die polykulturellen Peripherien. *Germania* 81(2), 401–42

Taylor, J.J. 1980. *Bronze Age Goldwork of the British Isles.* Cambridge: Cambridge University Press

Vajsov, I. 1993. Die frühesten Metalldolche Südost- und Mitteleuropas. *Praehistorische Zeitschrift* 68, 103–45

Vander Linden, M. 2007. What linked the Bell Beakers in third millennium BC Europe? *Antiquity* 81, 343–52

Whittle, A. 1996. *Europe in the Neolithic: the creation of new worlds.* Cambridge: Cambridge University Press

Woodward, A., Hunter, J., Ixer, R., Roe, F., Potts, P.J., Webb, P.C., Watson, J.S. & Jones, M.C. 2006. Beaker age bracers in England: sources, function and use. *Antiquity* 80, 530–43

Zápotocký, M. 2000. *Cimburk und die Höhensiedlungen des frühen und älteren Äneolithikums in Böhmen.* Praha: Památky archeologické, Supplementum 12

Zápotocký, M. & Zápotocká, M. 2008. *Kutná Hora – Denemark. Hradiště řivnáčské kultury (ca 3000–2800 př. Kr.).* Praha: Památky archeologické, Supplementum 18

Zimmermann, T. 2007. Anatolia and the Balkans, once again – ring-shaped idols from western Asia and a critical reassessment of some 'Early Bronze Age' items from Ikiztepe, Turkey, *Oxford Journal of Archaeology* 26, 25–33

8

Dutchmen on the Move? A discussion of the adoption of the Beaker package

Harry Fokkens

After having been abandoned in the 1960s, Beaker migrations are back as an explanation of the transmission of Beaker ideas and material culture. Though the present form of these theories is much better argued and well understandable, the present author still feels that we have arrived at these conclusions too quickly. Much is based on the idea that Beakers and associated artefacts were prestige items – valuables that everyone adopted as soon as they were within reach. That would explain how (im)migrants could be responsible for bringing about culture change in, for instance, Britain.

Instead the author argues that this theory does not explain why other aspects of material culture, especially burial rites, were also adopted. Instead it is argued that Beaker burial assemblages in general do not represent the burials of prestigious Beaker People, but are constructed ancestral identities.

In May 2009 a group of Leiden master students in Archaeology visited Scotland and, of course, went to Kilmartin Glen. This phenomenal monumental landscape with its cairns, standing stones, stone circles, and rock carvings, enclosed by high hills, easily rates as one of the most impressive prehistoric landscapes in Europe. Interestingly, in a recent article Alison Sheridan (2008) suggested that one of the graves in the Glen, now destroyed by quarrying of the gravel terrace at the northern end of the Glen, was of Dutch type and contained three international Beakers that could be Dutch. To quote Sheridan:

'The fact that early Beaker period graves described above represent such a striking novelty within mid-third millennium Scotland, and point so forcefully towards the Netherlands as place of origin for their occupants, raises the very real possibility that we are dealing with Dutch immigrants during or around the 25th century BC'. (Sheridan 2008, 258)

Standing in Kilmartin valley, having arrived freshly from the Dutch flat and wet lands with sand, clay, and peat soils, we wondered what on earth Dutchmen had being doing 4500 years earlier in a landscape that must have been even more alien to them then it is to us nowadays.[1] Which social processes might have led to these supposed migrations? One wonders what moved them. Why did they leave the Netherlands? Was there a drought, a war, were they prospectors for copper, or did they seek healing at sites like Stonehenge, as Darvill and Wainwright suggest (2009, 16)? Was the beginning of the Chalcolithic in Great Britain brought about by migrants, or are models for indigenous development equally feasible?

This paper aims to discuss the Bell Beaker period from the angle of these social questions, starting with a discussion of processes of migration and colonisation. The question is raised as to how innovations are adopted and how rapid culture change can be explained without referring to migrations. This leads to a discussion of what Beaker objects actually mean: were they desirable and prestigious objects and does that explain their rapid adoption? Or did Beakers, and especially Beaker type burials, bring about a more fundamental change of attitude towards the dead in Britain and on the continent?

The problems with migration as a mechanism for cultural transmission

Since Childe's migrationist ideas were abandoned in the 1970s, nowadays we can discern a new interest in migration theories, albeit in a moderate form (cf. Needham 2007). The Beaker package figures prominently in these new migration theories. In fact the Beaker package always has been resistant to processual explanations since it is so uniform and since it seems to have spread in such a short time. To explain such changes in terms of cultural diffusion processes is difficult. With respect to Beakers, therefore, migrations have never been abolished completely (cf. Thorpe & Richards 1984, 67), but now are being actively revived again. Isotope studies, which actually prove mobility (cf. Price *et al.* 1994; 1998; Budd *et al.* 2004), seem to support this interpretative shift, though cases in which long distance mobility is proposed are still rare.[2]

One of the reasons that migration is accepted as an explanation of rapid transmission of ideas is that typical Beaker artefacts, such as wristguards, golden objects, and (in particular) daggers of copper and of Grand-Pressigny flint are interpreted as scarce and therefore valuable (prestige) goods (cf. Burgess & Shennan 1976; Shennan 1982; Thorpe & Richards 1984). This would explain why local people readily wanted to adopt these new valuables. According to Needham a 'bow-wave' of adoption took place

in very short time (Needham 2007, 41) and is, in later stages, consolidated and spread further by well-aimed marriage alliances (Brodie 1997; Needham 2007, 43).

My problem with this interpretation is that it is based on implicit assumptions related to modern western ways of looking at valuables. One of those assumptions is that value is created predominantly by scarcity or exclusiveness: in other words, we are projecting our own values, which count as valuable and prestigious those objects that are made of precious metals, or are beautifully crafted, or that come from afar and/or are scarce (cf. Friedman & Rowlands 1977; Thorpe & Richards 1984; Helms 1988; 1993; Earle 2002, 294 ff.). According to this prestige goods model, daggers that have been made of precious shiny metal are, of course, preferred to old-fashioned flint tools, which are difficult to make and easy to break, and so everyone would want them.

From a modern perspective this sounds all very plausible and it is, in fact, a generally accepted scenario. The problem with this *colonial contact scenario* is that it does not explain why the Beaker package was adopted in its entirety including burial rites that, in most regions, seem fundamentally different from what was the prior tradition. Especially if the objects were acquired from immigrants or foreign settlers and, therefore, were alien to the receiving culture groups, one would expect to see appropriation and re-contextualisation in local rituals and contexts (cf. Thomas 1991, 83 ff.). Interestingly Thomas describes several colonial contact situations in the South Pacific where valued objects were exchanged between Europeans and locals but where, evidently, the islanders tried to avoid the social relations that were normally associated with exchange by making 'free, unsocial commodities out of precisely the things they would not have exchanged between themselves' (*ibid.*, 91). Neither Brodie (1997) nor Needham (2005; 2007) nor, in fact, anyone following the colonial contact scenario of adoption, has discussed such social processes. Instead, it is implicitly assumed that exchange of goods, and even of spouses, between Beaker groups and local people would have been unproblematic. Thomas's research, however, demonstrates that this assumption is too simplistic.

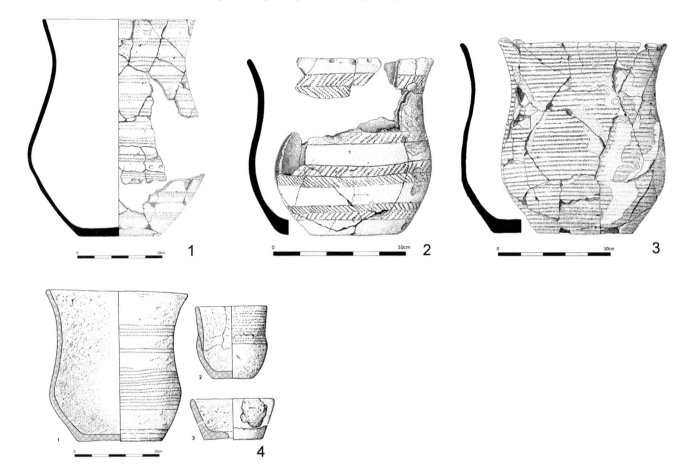

Considering the archaeological evidence for migration

What archaeological proof is actually present to suggest migration as a process of change? Several arguments are used to suggest a continental origin for British Beaker graves. Most prominent is the analyses of artefacts, especially of Beakers themselves. The Upper Largie grave in Kilmartin Glen, with its two maritime Bell Beakers and one All Over Corded Beaker, is a good example (Sheridan 2008). Sheridan is right that there are Dutch *comparanda* for these Beakers (*ibid.*, 252 ff). The problem, however, is that the comparisons are often made on the basis of style and decoration and much less on technological aspects (but see Gibson 1982, 66 for exceptions). Consequently, pottery form and decoration patterns are the most important elements in the analysis but these are relatively subjective arguments and discussions about them generally remain inconclusive.

If we take, for instance, Sheridan's other proposed examples of Dutch style Beakers, the ones from Biggar Common and Sorisdale, the likeness with Dutch examples is less clear than in the case of the Upper Largie Beakers. The largest Biggar Common Beaker has a design that, according to Sheridan, is clearly 'Maritime-influenced' (Fig. 8.1; 2008, 253). The smaller vessel is cord decorated, but only over the upper half. This is rare for British Beakers, but typical for early Protruding Foot Beakers as are found in the Netherlands (Fig. 8.2; type 1a: Lanting & van der Waals 1976; Sheridan 2008, 253). Those statements are true, but neither the decorative patterns of the larger Beaker, nor the style, have Dutch parallels. Protruding Foot Beakers are slender, S-shaped, have a small foot, and are thinner-walled than the smaller vessel of Biggar Common appears to be (Fig. 8.1). Type 1a Beakers are early (29th century cal BC) and, therefore, older than the Scottish Beakers. Moreover, the vessels at Bigger Common were deposited in a shallow pit lined with boulders. That too is an uncommon practice in the Netherlands.

Fig. 8.1. The pottery of Upper Largie (1–3) and Biggar Common (4) (after Sheridan 2008, fig. 21.3–5, 21.9)

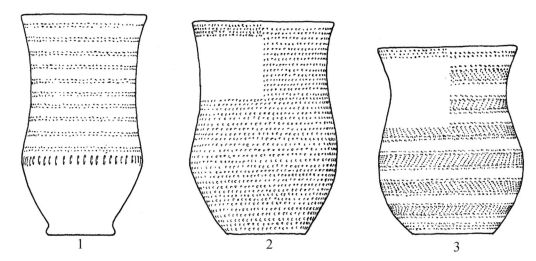

This shows us that arguments in favour of Dutch origin can be countered by arguments against it and, at best, the evidence demonstrates that contacts with Beaker-using people in the Low Countries should be considered likely, but the similarities could also be due to Scottish explorers visiting the Lowe Rhine basin and, back home, imitating the things they had seen on their travels.

A similar argument can be made for another issue of comparison: the Dutch style grave. Here too there are indeed many points of comparison, but – if one wants to make the point – just as many differences. For instance, a small cairn may have topped the Upper Largie grave (Sheridan 2008, 247), but the Dutch Beaker mound is a low earthen mound and generally stones are no part of it. The ditch around the grave with posts in it is also cited by Sheridan as a Dutch element. This is indeed a feature that also occurs underneath Dutch Beaker barrows, especially Single Grave Beaker burials and occasionally with AOO burials. But the size of the burial chamber in Upper Largie is more than twice the size of the normal Dutch chamber, the ditch is irregular, and the posts are standing on the outside of the ditch; in the Netherlands they would be standing in the middle of a narrow ditch. So, if the people who buried their dead here in the Kilmartin Glen were originally Dutchmen, they had already forgotten their homeland traditions. But if that is the case, there are no clear arguments why these Scottish burials were Dutch in origin, or whether this might

have been the result of local Late Neolithic Scotsmen imitating continental Beaker burial rites.

In fact, this type of argument is immaterial and a form of scientific bickering of which the outcome per definition remains inconclusive. Sheridan and I could both be right: it is just a matter of scientific taste. From a methodological point of view our arguments *pro* and *contra* are just different interpretations of the same material. All that we can say for sure is that that there is no solid evidence for migration: the new elements that Sheridan observes could just as well have been brought about by travellers from Scotland to the continent, as by continentals settling in Scotland. What remains as well is the need to explain the fast adoption of the innovations: within a few generations (2500–2400 cal BC; Needham 2005) Bell Beakers were adopted in Britain and also, in an equally short period, elsewhere. If migration was not instrumental, what then is a possible explanation?

The diffusion of innovations

For alternatives to migration as a mechanism for culture change, we might refer to theoretical approaches about the adoption of innovations. What conditions ought to prevail in order for rapid culture change to be possible? Rogers, in particular, who has devoted his career to research of the adoption of innovations, has described the process of adoption and diffusion of innovations in detail and suggested that a number of conditions need to be met if an innovation wants to be accepted. Innovation is defined here as:

> 'an idea, practice or object that is perceived as new by an individual or other unit of adoption. It matters little, so far as human behaviour is concerned, whether or not an idea is 'objectively' new. [...] The perceived newness of the idea for the individual determines his or her reaction to it. If an idea is new to the individual, it is an innovation'. (Rogers 2003, 12)

About 50% of the adoption rate is determined by the *perceived* attributes (*ibid.*, 222). 'Perceived' is emphasised here because it is not the precise physical qualities that are most important, but how they are perceived.

This perception is closely linked to the concept of compatibility, defined as 'the degree to which an innovation is persistent with existing values, past experiences and needs' (*ibid.*, 240). In other words, is the innovation socially acceptable, does it fit the cultural traditions? Furthermore the rate of innovation is influenced by how the community is structured, how the chains of command are organised, and how the communication networks function. Important also is the nature of the decision. Is it optional; is it a collective decision to adopt; or is adoption prompted by authority?

With regard to the rate of introduction, critical mass is an important concept (Fig. 8.3; Rogers 2003, 343). When an innovation becomes known, people generally start to experiment with it, a few adopt it but most people wait and watch first. But a point comes when so many people have adopted the innovation that others follow in an ever faster rate. That turn-over point is called the 'critical mass'. Elsewhere, I have suggested that, in the archaeological record, we generally do not see the trajectory of adoption before the critical mass is reached (Fokkens 2008, 20). After that point is reached, culture changes very fast as the innovation is adopted by many people in a relatively short period of time. The implication is that innovations are almost invisible to us in the initial phase and do not affect the whole society: they change nothing yet. This also implies that, if archaeologists want to investigate real culture change, it is useless to look for the oldest occurrence of an innovation: we have to find the turn-over point, which is the point where most dates appear to cluster (*ibid.*, 19).

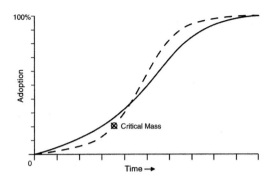

Fig. 8.3. *The concept of critical mass, showing how the rate of adoption of an innovation changes after the critical mass has been reached (from Rogers 2003, 344)*

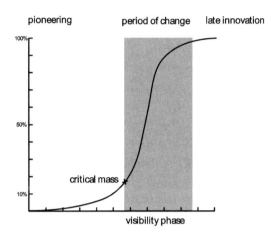

Fig. 8.4. *The period of change occurs when the critical mass is reached and innovation is accepted in fast rate. This is the period in which most innovations become visible archaeologically (from Fokkens 2008, fig. 2.6)*

With respect to the Bell Beaker package the diffusion of innovation theory enables us to determine a number of attributes of the process of change that we may not have realised before. For instance, innovation theory predicts a trajectory of adoption that involves an initial period of experimentation and slow acceptance, followed by a relatively short period of widespread acceptance (Fig. 8.4; Rogers 2003, 281). The rate of adoption of an innovation depends most on the perceived attributes, but it needs to be compatible with the existing values and needs, otherwise it is not adopted at all, or only very slowly. This last condition tells us that, given an enormously diverse cultural palette in the Late Neolithic, the rate of adoption ought to be different in most places, while in others it is not adopted at all. Indeed, if we look at the distribution maps for Continental Europe (Fig. 8.5), there are areas where Bell Beakers follow Corded Ware or are even contemporaneous with it; there are areas where Beakers are initially added to the existing cultural manifestations; and there are areas without any Beakers, where existing traditions continue in a different fashion. But

Fig. 8.5. Distribution of the Corded Ware (1) and Bell Beaker (3) cultural phenomena. (2) indicates areas where Corded Ware and Bell Beaker overlap (after Benz & Stadelbacher 1995, 14, and Vander Linden 2006, fig. 116)

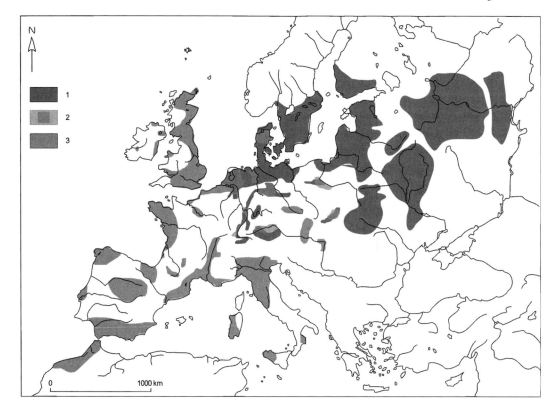

in the regions where the Beaker is adopted, it is – strangely enough – adopted as a package: Beakers, associated artefacts, and also the burial rites (cf. Shennan 1977).

The fact that the trajectory of adoption is everywhere short tells us that there was a critical mass effect. Apparently, at a certain point in time, so many local communities had adopted the innovation that communication between groups became difficult without its adoption. This observation may indicate several things. First, that the innovation was perceived as fitting somehow into the existing traditions or, at least, was easily adoptable. Secondly, innovation theory predicts that, after the critical mass was reached, adoption was necessary because *not* to adopt meant not to belong to a fast-growing majority of adopters. That could, of course, cause problems. If we accept that gift exchange was an important means of connecting people and communities (cf. Godelier 1999; Mauss 1990 (1923); Weiner 1992) one may assume that failing to adopt the innovation made exchanges fail because one was not considered a desirable exchange partner any more. Eventually, not adopting the innovation meant existence on the fringes of the community. Exchange in this respect

does not necessarily concern the Beakers or the associated objects proper, but could just as well be related to the idea or ideology of which the Beaker was an exponent (see Strahm 2004). Here one might use the Beaker as *pars pro toto* for a set of values: a particular ideology. Objects like that become fused with ideas and subjects: they not only represent them, but they *are* these ideas (cf. Barraud *et al.* 1994, 5). From such a perspective, *having* Beakers was equivalent to *being* Beaker.

Being Beaker: beyond prestige goods

In many regions, especially in Britain, the introduction of Beakers encompassed a whole new burial tradition as well. Though there was a lot of variability: burials frequently follow a distinct pattern: the dead was placed in a contracted position in a burial chamber, left arm folded under the chin, head to the north (men) or to the south (women), facing east, pottery placed behind the head or at the feet (Fig. 8.6). Bell Beaker burial ritual seems to have followed more or less strict rules, not only with respect to the position of the dead but also in terms of the classes of grave gifts. Since burial traditions are often an integral part of the way in which the living and the ancestors or the supernatural relate to each other, a change in burial ritual thus implies a change in that cosmology as well.

Realising this, we might need to develop a much more nuanced view on Beaker burial gifts and their meaning. So far, Beaker burials have always been interpreted as representing status positions of an individual. Following the prestige goods model, items like wrist-guards, copper or flint daggers, amber, jet, or gold objects were valuables and their owners wealthy and powerful persons within their communities – ie, elites (eg, Shennan 1977, 54, 55; Vandkilde 2001). However, the prestige goods approach ignores more nuanced theories about how value is created in pre-modern societies (cf. Barraud *et al.* 1994; Bazelmans 1999). It does not incorporate the role of exchange as a fundamental means of creating relations between people or between people and the supernatural.

Louis Dumont and his followers, in particular, have emphasised the importance of analysing societies as a whole. In their view, in non-modern societies, exchanges constitute a person and should be analysed in coherence to each other, as a whole (cf. Barraud *et al.* 1994; Bazelmans 1999; Dumont 1986; Fontijn 2002; Platenkamp 1988). With exchanges, they mean especially those exchanges that take place during life cycle rituals such as birth, initiation, marriage, and death. If we extend that view to the Early Bronze Age, the Beaker package – which is by definition a burial package – may be expected to be concerned with the complex exchange relations between people and the ancestors, exchanges that ought to be explained in relation to cosmology. From that point of view graves will contain a selection of objects that constitute persons as valuable members of a society – in other words, as persons who possess the qualities that are considered important for the existence and reproduction of the society as a whole. In other words, we may expect burial gifts to construct an idealised ancestral identity instead of being a representative mirror of real persons.

The question is, how do we know whether processes like this were indeed part of the archaeological record? In my view that becomes only visible when we consider not individual graves but the whole set of burial

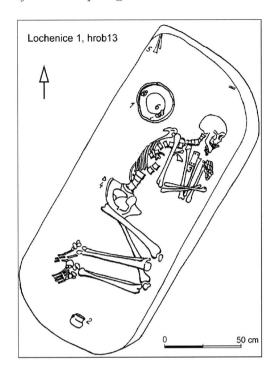

Fig. 8.6. *Typical Bell Beaker burial from the Czech Republic: Lochenice I, burial 13 (from Fokkens et al. 2008, fig. 15)*

gifts in the Bell Beaker world (not only in Britain), and when we categorise these items. I have distinguished four categories: pottery, weapons, tools, and ornaments (Table 8.1). This appears to represent almost all conceivable categories of artefacts. However, on closer scrutiny it becomes clear that, within those categories, a selection has been made for specific classes of artefacts. This selection, in my view, signifies values that were important in the Bell Beaker world. For instance, the Beakers that are present in burials are not just domestic wares. Even in the Netherlands, where there are clearly defined Beaker domestic assemblages consisting of Pot Beakers and Beaker fine ware (the 'true' Beakers; cf. Fokkens 1998, 117; Louwe Kooijmans 1974), only the latter are present in graves. Beaker fine ware consisted of containers for serving food and drink, the latter possibly of an alcoholic or intoxicating nature (cf. Sherratt 1987; 1995, 26). It is clear that stylistic aspects refer to a 'universally' understood notion of 'being' Bell Beaker. It was important not only that the ancestors had food and drink but, especially, that they had Beakers to consume it from. That classified them as members of a larger community of Beaker using people.

Considering weapons, it appears that archery equipment is especially emphasised in the

Table 8.1: A survey of Corded Ware and Bell Beaker burial gifts divided into four categories

Category	Numbers	Corded Ware	Bell Beaker
Pottery/Food-drink	1-3	Beaker fine ware	Beaker fine ware
Weapons/Martiality	1 or more	arrowheads	arrowheads
	1 or set of 2	arrow shaft smoother	arrow-shaft smoother
	1		wristguard
	1	flint dagger	copper (flint) dagger
	1	battle axe	
Tools/Craftmanship	1	flint knife	flint knife
	1	flint strike-a-light	flint strike-a-light
	1	stone axe	stone axe
	several		flint artefacts
	1		bone tools
	1		copper awl
	1 or more		cushion/hammer stone
Ornaments/Personal adornment	several	beads	beads
	1	pendants	pendant
	sets of 2		boars' tusks
	sets of 2		gold ornaments

grave. Arrowheads, wristguards, and arrow-shaft straighteners/polishers are frequently encountered objects. In my opinion they indicate that martiality, especially archery, was an important value in the Bell Beaker world (Fokkens *et al.* 2008). However, no two burials are the same: there are no clear patterns in the ways that classes of objects cluster. Arrowheads are often absent. Apparently it was not necessary to include the whole set of weapons in a burial: one of the objects related to that quality would suffice. This may indicate that these objects were not only seen as weapons, but really 'were' martiality, just like Beakers; similarly, perhaps even a Beaker sherd referenced the whole world of ideas behind it. Like the flint daggers in earlier Corded Ware burials and in late Beaker burials, the copper dagger probably addresses that value as well (cf. Shennan 1977, 55). The dagger might be interpreted as an integral part of the archer's gear, as the instrument that could be used to conduct a *coup de grâce*, no matter whether that concerned humans or animals (Fokkens 1999; Fontijn 2002, 221).

Occasionally battle axes are still also present in Beaker burials, at least in the lower Rhine group. They were already part of the earlier Corded Ware assemblage (Lanting and van der Waals 1976) and of Late TRB assemblages (Bakker 1979) and they appear in greater numbers in the Early Bronze Age assemblages with Barbed Wire Beakers (Lanting 1973). Notably absent, however, are copper halberds and contemporary copper axes. They only occur in hoards, so with respect to these categories of weapons too, selective deposition seems to have been practised (Needham 1989; Fontijn 2002, 71 ff).

Selective deposition also seems to have been practised in the category of tools. Tools that refer to normal subsistence activities are lacking: there are no farming tools such as sickles, no fishing gear, or other subsistence tools.[3] The classes of tools that are present are stone axes, flint tools (knives, scrapers, strike-a-lights), bone tools (awls), and, of course smiths' tools. The general impression is that these tools refer especially to crafting (cf. Brodie 1997; Turek 2004) which, of course, is most clearly visible in smiths' tools such as hammers and anvils (cushion stones).

Some of the artefacts that can be classified as personal adornments (beads of jet and amber, gold ornaments, boars' tusks) may have been referencing craftsmanship and martiality as well. An example of the latter are the bone pendants shaped in the form of a bow that are common in middle Europe (eg, Heyd 2000, 286 ff; Metzinger-Schmitz 2004, 120 ff). Golden ornaments (for the hair) also appear in sets, sometimes in combination with smiths' tools, which may indicate a relation with that particular craft (Fontijn 2002, 66; Fitzpatrick 2003).

To sum up, if we categorise Beaker burials, a specific selection of qualities appears to have been emphasised over and over again and in a consistent manner all over Europe. These qualities are represented by one or more artefacts in a particular category but, generally, just one item or in sets of two: there is no clear pattern of association between categories. That indicates that burials were not seen as an arena for the display of wealth but as being for the creation of ideal ancestors (Fokkens 2005). Ancestors were required to have certain qualities, represented by artefacts that addressed that quality in one way or another. Ancestral identities were constructed according to long lived collective traditions.

The longevity of these traditions can be demonstrated by the fact that the same elements had are already been present in Corded Ware burials on the continent (cf. Anthony 2007; Fokkens 1999; Heyd 2000; Shennan 1977) and are still present in Bronze Age burials (Fontijn 2002).

Beaker burials as constructed ancestral identities

Above I stated that the Beaker burials probably represent a constructed ancestral identity. This implies that Beaker burials, as the most noticeable expression of Beaker cultural manifestations, do not constitute a representative collection of possessions of a deceased individual. In my view the objects buried with the dead address only a few selected qualities of a person. For men, these seem to have been the qualities of martiality and craftsmanship. In this respect it is remarkable that – apart form the Beakers – the objects that are presented to the dead are often made from exotic materials, such as amber, jet, metal, or high quality stone. They were not 'run-of-the-mill' artefacts, but special, and their very remote origin or high craftsmanship may have been perceived as being 'of ancestral origin' (Helms 1988, 1993; Wentink 2006). Fontijn has drawn attention to this phenomenon as 'dressed in interregionality', a quality that is present both in male and female burials. In his view the ancestors were represented as members of 'imagined non-local communities' (Fontijn 2002, 229).

The European character of this collective image implies that there existed an intricate network of social relations over large distances. People knew their world and they knew their way around. Exchange with foreign partners may have been much more institutionalised than we realise. If Polynesian tribesmen and tradesmen kept contacts over hundreds of kilometres of rough sea, why not British or Dutch Beaker Persons and British Late Neolithic folk? If the Trobriand Islanders laid much of their being in overseas Kula exchanges, why should British Late Neolithic people not have done so? They had the knowledge, they even transported huge stones over seas (cf. Darvill & Wainwright 2009), so why should we deny them the intelligence and the ability to visit the continent? In my opinion, it is quite probable that Late Neolithic British people also knew what was happening on the continent; they too were part of that larger change in ideology and cosmology that transformed the Late Neolithic world between 2600 and 2400 cal BC. It came a bit later in Britain but when it came it followed the same swift trajectory as elsewhere. This indicates that Late Neolithic people were not ignorant of the outside. Their traditions were different but the new ideology fitted seamlessly and, therefore, could be adopted as quickly as anywhere else.

To return to Kilmartin Glen: just as Dutchmen may have travelled to Scotland, Scots may have travelled to the Low Countries and further. Local communities in both areas were part of larger communication and exchange networks and were aware of developments outside their regions. They may not have adopted innovations right away, but history proves that they eventually did so. When the Scots adopted Beakers and Beaker traditions, they *became* Beaker People, but they also stayed Islanders with their own traditions of building houses, monuments, and burial mounds.

Endnotes
1 If the Late Neolithic people had been as hospitable and helpful as their modern descendants one might also ask why not all Dutchmen came over to live in Scotland. I want to thank Nick Card, David Clarke (National Museums Scotland), Jane Downes, Julie Gibson, and last but absolutely not least, Alison Sheridan (National Museums Scotland) for guiding us, helping us out, for showing us great hospitality, and providing inspiration for this article. I also want to thank David Fontijn (Faculty of Archaeology, Leiden University) and Maikel Kuijpers (Department

of Archaeology, University of Cambridge) and Alison Sheridan for their constructive remarks on the different versions of the text.

2 The reputation of the Amesbury Archer as a wanderer from the Alps needs reassessment. The oxygen isotope data, as they are preliminary published in my view have been severely over-interpreted. The distribution map is very global and based on modern values, moreover the analysis does not take in account climatic changes, seasonal variability, or possible taphonomic processes. Any form of baseline research on the continent appears to be lacking. The suggestion that the Amesbury Archer possibly came from the Alpine region, in my opinion, is overstretching the resolution of the data. We need to be critical of scientific methods in their first stages of development: not necessarily sceptical, but cautious in using its first result to overthrow existing archaeological patterns of thought. The interpretative caution, source criticism and care for taphonomic processes that makes the analyses of strontium isotopes credible, so far seems to have been lacking in oxygen isotope analysis.

3 Interestingly the burials that were excavated by Louwe Kooijmans in the context of the settlement of Molenaarsgraaf did contain subsistence artefacts. One of the bodies had burial gifts of bone fish hooks and a tool that was considered a hook for picking up fish traps. This burial was possibly associated with a Barbed Wire Beaker (Louwe Kooijmans 1974, 250 ff). This may indicate that people buried in the vicinity of settlements were treated differently from people buried underneath barrows outside the settlement proper.

Bibliography

Anthony, D.W. 2007. *The Horse, the Wheel and Language. How Bronze-Age Riders from Eurasian Steppes Shaped the Modern World.* Princeton: University Press

Bakker, J.A. 1979. *The TRB West Group. Studies in the Chronology and Geography of the Makers of the Hunebeds and Tiefstich Pottery.* Amsterdam: Albert Egges van Giffen Instituut voor Prae- en Protohistorie. Cingula 5

Barraud, C., de Coppet, D., Iteanu, A. & Jamous, R. 1994. *Of Relations and the Dead. Four Societies Viewed from the Angle of their Exchanges.* Oxford: Berg

Bazelmans, J. 1999. *By Weapons made Worthy. Lords, Retainers and their Relationship in Beowulf.* Amsterdam: Amsterdam Archaeological Studies 5

Benz, M. & Stadelbacher, A. 1995. *Das Glockenbecherphänomen: Ein Seminar.* Freiburg: Institut fur Ur-und Fruhgeschichte der Universität Freiburg

Brodie, N. 1997. New perspectives on the Bell-Beaker Culture. *Oxford Journal of Archaeology* 16, 297–314

Budd, P., Millard, A, Chenery, C., Lucy, S. & Roberts, C. 2004. Investigating population movement by stable isotope analysis: a report from Britain. *Antiquity* 78, 127–41

Burgess, C.B. & Shennan, S.J. 1976. The beaker phenomenon: some suggestions. In C.B. Burgess & R.F. Miket (eds), *Settlement and Economy in the Late Third and Early Second Millennium B.C,* 309–31. Oxford: British Archaeological Report 33

Darvill, T. & Wainwright, G.J. 2009. Stonehenge excavations 2008. *Antiquaries Journal* 89, 1–20

Dumont, L. 1986. *Essays on Individualism. Modern Ideology in Anthropological Perspective.* Chicago: Chicago Press

Earle, T. 2002. *Bronze Age Economics. The Beginnings of Political Economies.* Boulder: Westview Press

Fitzpatrick, A.P. 2003. The Amesbury Archer. *Current Archaeology* 184, 146–52

Fokkens, H. 1998. *Drowned Landscape. The Occupation of the Western Part of the Frisian-Drenthian Plateau, 4400 BC–AD 500.* Assen: Van Gorcum

Fokkens, H. 1999. Cattle and martiality. Changing relations between man and landscape in the Late Neolithic and the Bronze Age. In C. Fabech & J. Ringtved (eds), *Settlement and Landscape,* 31–8. Århus: University Press/Jutland Archaeological Society

Fokkens, H. 2005. *Voorbeeldige voorouders: graven naar de ideeënwereld van prehistorische boerengemeenschappen. Rede uitgesproken door Prof. dr H. Fokkens bij de aanvaarding van het ambt van hoogleraar op het gebied van de Europese Prehistorie aan de Universiteit Leiden op 15 november 2005.* Leiden: Leiden University

Fokkens, H. 2008. The temporality of culture changes. In H. Fokkens, B. Coles, A.L. van Gijn, J.P. Kleijne, H.H. Ponjee & C.G. Slappendel (eds), *Between Foragining and Farming. An Extended Broad Spectrum of Papers Presented to Leendert Louwe Kooijmans,* 15–24. Leiden: *Analecta Praehistorica Leidensia* 50

Fokkens, H., Achterkamp, Y. & Kuijpers, M.H.G. 2008. Bracers or bracelets? About the functionality and meaning of Bell Beaker wrist-guards. *Proceedings of the Prehistoric Society* 74, 109–40

Fontijn, D.R. 2002. *Sacrificial Landscapes. Cultural Biographies of Persons, Objects and 'Natural' Places in the Bronze Age of the Southern Netherlands, c. 2300–600BC.* Leiden: *Analecta Praehistorica Leidensia* 33/4

Friedman, J. & Rowlands, M. 1977. Notes towards an epigenetic model of the evolution of 'civilisation'. In J. Friedman & M. Rowlands (eds), *The Evolution of Social Systems,* 201–78. London: Duckworth

Gibson, A.M. 1982. *Beaker Domestic Sites: a study of the domestic pottery of the late third and early second millennia B.C. in the British Isles.* Oxford: British Archaeological Report 102

Godelier, M 1999. *The Enigma of the Gift.* Cambridge/Oxford: Polity Press

Helms, M.W. 1988. *Ulysses' sail. An Ethnographic Odyssey of Power, Knowledge and Geographical Distance.* Princeton: University Press

Helms, M.W. 1993. *Craft and the Kingly Ideal. Art, Trade, and Power.* Austin: University of Texas Press

Heyd, V. 2000. *Die Spätkupferzeit in Süddeutschland.* Bonn: Saarbrücker Beiträge zur Altertumskunde, 73.

Lanting, J.N. 1973. Laat-Neolithicum en Vroege Bronstijd in Nederland en N.W.-Duitsland: continue ontwikkelingen. *Palaeohistoria* 15, 215–317

Lanting, J.N. & Waals, J.D. van der 1976. Beaker Culture relations in the Lower Rhine Basin. In J.N. Lanting & J.D. van der Waals (eds), *Glockenbecher Symposium Oberried 1974,* 1–80. Haarlem: Fibula-Van Dishoek

Louwe Kooijmans, L.P. 1974. *The Rhine/Meuse Delta; Four Studies on its Prehistoric Occupation and Holocene Geology.* Leiden: *Analecta Praehistorica Leidensia* 7

Mauss, M. 1923. *The Gift. The Form and Reason for Exchange in Archaic Societies.* London: Routledge (1990 reprint)

Metzinger-Schmitz, B. 2004. *Die Glockenbecherkulur in Mähren und Niederösterreich. Typologische und chronologische Studien auf dem Hintergrund der Kulturhistorischen Abläufe während der späten Kupferzeit im Untersuchungsgebiet. Mit einem paläometallurgischen Exkurs.* Saarbrücken: Uni-Saarbrücken

Needham, S.P. 1989. Selective deposition in the British Early Bronze Age. *World Archaeology* 20, 229–48

Needham, S.P. 2005. Transforming Beaker Culture in north-west Europe; processes of fusion and fission. *Proceedings of the Prehistoric Society* 71, 171–217

Needham, S.P. 2007. Isotopic aliens: Beaker movement and cultural transmissions. In M. Larsson & M. Parker Pearson (eds), *From Stonehenge to the Baltic. Living with Cultural Diversity in the Third Millennium BC*, 41–6. Oxford: British Archaeological Report S1692

Platenkamp, J.D.M. 1988. *Tobelo. Ideas and Values of a North Moluccan Society.* Leiden: Leiden University

Price, T. D., Grupe, G. & Schröter, P. 1994. Reconstruction of migration patterns in the Bell Beaker period by stable strontium isotope analysis. *Applied Geochemistry* 9, 413–7

Price, T. D., Grupe, G. & Schröter, P. 1998. Migration in the Bell Beaker period of central Europe. *Antiquity* 72, 405–11

Rogers, E.M. 2003. *Diffusion of Innovations.* New York: Free Press

Shennan, S. 1982. Ideology, change and the European Early Bronze Age. In I. Hodder (ed.), *Symbolic and Structural Archaeology*, 155–61. Cambridge: Cambridge University Press

Shennan, S.J. 1977. The appearance of the Bell Beaker assemblage in Central Europe. In R. Mercer (ed.), *Beakers in Britain and Europe: four studies*, 51–70. Oxford: British Archaeological Report S26

Sheridan, J.A. 2008. Upper Largie and Dutch-Scottish connections during the Beaker period. In H. Fokkens, B. Coles, A.L. van Gijn, J.P. Kleijne, H.H. Ponjee & C.G. Slappendel (eds), *Between Foraging and Farming. An Extended Broad Spectrum of Papers Presented to Leendert Louwe Kooijmans*, 247–60. Leiden: *Analecta Praehistorica Leidensia* 50

Sherratt, A.G. 1987. Cups that cheered. In W. Waldren & R. Kennard (eds), *Bell Beakers of the Western Mediterranean*, 81–114. Oxford: British Archaeological Report S331

Sherratt, A.G. 1995. Alcohol and its alternatives: symbol and substance in pre-industrial cultures. In J. Goodman, P.E. Lovejoy & A.G. Sherratt (eds), *Consuming Habits*, 11–46. London: Routledge

Strahm, Ch. 2004. Das Glockenbecher-Phänomen aus der Sicht der Komplementär-Keramik. In J. Czebreszuk (eds), *Similar but Different. Bell Beakers in Europe*, 101–26. Poznan: Adam Mickiewicz University

Thomas, N. 1991. *Entangled Objects. Exchange, Material Culture and Colonialism in the Pacific.* Cambridge, Massachusetts: Harvard University press

Thorpe, I.J. & Richards, C. 1984. The decline of ritual authority and the introduction of Beakers into Britain. In R. Bradley & J. Gardiner (eds), *Neolithic Studies: a review of some current research*, 67–84. Oxford: British Archaeological Report 133

Turek, J. 2004. Craft symbolism in the Bell Beaker burial customs: resources, production and social structure at the end of the Eneolithic period. In M. Besse & J. Desideri (eds), *Graves and Funerary Rituals During the Late Neolithic and the Early Bronze Age in Europe (2700–2000 BC)*, 147–56. Oxford: British Archaeological Report S1284

Vander Linden, M. 2006. *Le Phénomène Campaniforme dans l'Europe du 31eme Millénaire avant notre ère. Synthèse et Nouvelles Perspectives.* Oxford: British Archaeological Report S1470

Vandkilde, H. 2001. Beaker Representation in the Danish Late Neolithic. In F. Nicolis (ed.), *Bell Beakers Today. Pottery, People, Culture and Symbols in Prehistoric Europe*, 333–60. Trento: Provincia Autonome di Trento. Servizio Beni Culturali. Ufficio Beni Archeologici

Weiner, A.B. 1992. *Inalienable Posessions; the paradox of keeping-while-giving.* Berkeley: University of California Press

Wentink, K. 2006. *Ceci n'est pas une Hache: Neolithic depositions in the northern Netherlands.* Leiden: Sidestone Press

9

Working Copper in the Chalcolithic: a long-term perspective on the development of metallurgical knowledge in central Europe and the Carpathian Basin

Tobias L. Kienlin

In this contribution attention is drawn to some shortcomings of our conventional approach to early metalworking. It is argued that we employ notions of progress and evolution to account for long-term technological change that fall short of representing a more complex ancient reality. With the benefit of hindsight we see 'progress' and increasingly better solutions in terms of the working and properties of copper and copper alloys whereas, in fact, there were alternative trajectories, and change towards the 'better' (in modern terms) was far from immediately apparent. As a result our approaches are often reductionist. We fail to understand adequately the technological choices taken through time by the countless individuals who depended on their local cultural background as much as they did on the laws of nature involved in the production and working of copper. The examples drawn upon cover the development of early metallurgy in the Carpathian Basin and central Europe from what is locally termed the Late Neolithic, Chalcolithic, or Copper Age. Some aspects touched upon in this brief review of the development of metallurgical knowledge are specific to the time and area under consideration. But it is proposed that some of the points raised may be of wider relevance to the study of early metallurgy – in particular the need for a long-term perspective on the development of metallurgical knowledge that allows for contingency in technological choices and a context-specific approach to early metalworking beyond our own modern science-based understanding of technological progress.

The cultural setting

Our use of concepts such as Chalcolithic, Copper Age, or Bronze Age does not only carry chronological implications. It often entails assumptions about the socio-cultural implications of metallurgy which tend to go unstated. It also relies heavily upon the academic tradition in which we are working. Before reviewing the development of metallurgical knowledge in Chalcolithic central Europe and the Carpathian Basin it is appropriate, therefore, to turn to some of the discrepancies emerging from the different approaches to periodisation and to provide an outline of the cultural setting of early metallurgy (Table 9.1).

Generally speaking, the term 'Chalcolithic' or 'Copper Age' (which is widely used in Hungary, for example) and related terms such as 'Eneolithic' (which is the preferred term in the former Jugoslavia, for example) are more widely used in the Carpathian Basin and the Balkans than they are in central Europe. The obvious reason is the large number of copper artefacts known from south-east Europe, some of which are fairly massive. In this tradition, 'Copper Age' denotes a technological stage – not necessarily coeval throughout south-east Europe – which is to be added to the tripartite system of the Stone, Bronze, and Iron Ages (cf. Lichardus 1991a, 14–17; Eggert 2001, 33–5; Hansen 2001). By contrast, a structural definition of 'Copper Age' or 'Eneolithic' seeks to correlate technological change with perceived progress in the wider economic and cultural domains (see, for example, Lichardus 1991b). Problems with this approach arise because the nature of changes in economy, society, and ideology – if any – are subject to debate and, across the vast area from the Black Sea to central Europe, may not occur at the same time and can take different forms. These two strategies – technological and structural – for defining the 'Copper Age' are not easily combined since a causal relationship between metals and society is hard to demonstrate.

The well-known Vinča sequence (named after the tell site of Vinča-Belo Brdo in Serbia), which is widely used to correlate culture groups of the Balkans and the Carpathian Basin, provides an excellent example of such problems (cf. Schier 1997; Link 2006, 15–28). In its early stages the Vinča culture is clearly Neolithic (Vinča-Tordos/Turdaş after Garašanin 1993; 1997; roughly Vinča A and B after Milojčić 1949, 70–5). But does it qualify as Eneolithic during its later phases (Vinča-Gradac and -Pločnik after Garašanin 1993; Vinča C and D after Milojčić 1949) because of the appearance of copper and copper mining (eg, Jovanović 1996; Garašanin 1997, 18)? Or should we refer to this period as Late Neolithic (eg, Tasić 1994, 20–1) because it is only with the end of Vinča (-Pločnik/Vinča D) that there is evidence of profound culture change in burial customs, and (Late) Neolithic tell settlement comes to an end (cf. Link 2006, 15; Parkinson 2006, 40–63)?

Following the latter definition the Late Neolithic of the north-central Balkans and the Carpathian Basin comprises the late Vinča (-Pločnik/Vinča C–D) in northern Serbia and in the Vojvodina and the Banat regions, and the Tisza culture north of the Danube, extending along the floodplain of the eponymous river Tisza with the somewhat later but closely related Herpály and Csőszhalom groups. Defined and further subdivided mainly by their distinctive pottery styles, these groups nonetheless share some distinctive traits, in particular burials in settlements and a complex settlement system with firmly integrated communities drawing their cultural identity from elaborate ritual and tell sites that were permanent foci in the landscape (Meier-Arendt 1990; Parzinger 1993, 260–3, horizon 6 and 7; Gogâltan 2003; Parkinson 2006, 43–51; Link 2006, 18–41).

In contrast, the subsequent Early Copper Age (in Hungarian terminology) Tiszapolgár culture is noticeable for its homogeneous pottery which is distributed over larger parts of the Great Hungarian Plain. The earlier tell sites were abandoned and Tiszapolgár is characterised by a dispersal of settlement and the appearance of extramural cemeteries (Bognár-Kutzián 1972; Parzinger 1993, 263–5, horizon 8; Lichter 2001, 267–93; Parkinson 2006, 51–5; Link 2006, 33–5). This pattern continues into the Middle Copper Age (in Hungarian terminology), the Bodrogkeresztúr culture, with some changes to pottery form and decoration as well as an extension of this culture's area to the west with new sites occurring in the interfluvial zone between the Tisza and the Danube rivers (Patay 1974; Parzinger 1993, 265–7, horizon 9; Lichter 2001, 311–53; Parkinson 2006, 55–63). In Transdanubia it is only at this stage (ie, later than the Tiszapolgár culture) that the late Lengyel (IIIb) evolves into the Copper Age/Eneolithic Balaton-Lasinja and Ludanice cultures north of the Danube. In the northern and central Balkans, late Vinča (-Pločnik/Vinča D) is replaced by Eneolithic Bubanj-Hum Ia/Sălcuţa II (Kalicz 1995; Link 2006, 37–41; Schreiner 2007, 70–8). The Bodrogkeresztúr horizon is followed by the Hunyadi-halom and *Furchenstichkeramik* groups further west. The end of the Copper Age sequence is marked

Year BC (Calibrated)	Serbie	Transdanubia	Great Hungarian Plain			Transylvania	Bulgaria	Period
			Middle and Lower Tisza	Upper Tisza	Eastern Plain			
3500	Bubanj-Hum	Balaton-Lasinja	B Bodrogkeresztúr A	B Bodrogkeresztúr A	B Bodrogkeresztúr A	Pécska Bodrogkeresztúr A	?	**Middle Copper Age**
4000	Vinča D2	Lengyel III	B Tiszapolgár A	B Tiszapolgár A	B Tiszapolgár A	B Tiszapolgár A	Karanovo VI (Gumelnița)	**Early Copper Age**
4500	Vinča D2	Lengyel III	Proto-Tiszapolgár	Proto-Tiszapolgár	Proto-Tiszapolgár	Proto-Tiszapolgár Petreşti, Erösd	Karanovo VI	**Final Neolithic**
5000	Vinča D1 Vinča C	Lengyel II Lengyel I Sopot-Bicske II	Tisza III Tisza II Tisza I/II	Csőszhalom (Oborin) Tisza I/II	Herpály III Herpály I–II Tisza I/II	Petreşti Lumea Noua	Karanovo V (Marica)	**Late Neolithic**
5500	Vinča B2 Vinča B1 Vinča A	Sopot-Bicske Zseliz-Notenkopf DVK	Tisza I Szakálhát AVK Körös IV	Szakálhát Bükk – Szmileg AVK	Esztár AVK	Precucteni I–II Criş IV	Karanovo IV Karanovo III	**Middle Neolithic**
6000	Starčevo III – IV Starčevo II Starčevo I	Starčevo III Starčevo II Starčevo I?	Körös III Körös II Körös I	Körös-Szatmár	Körös-Szatmár	Criş III Criş Ii Criş I1	Karanovo II Karanovo I	**Early Neolithic**

Table 9.1 Chronology of the Neolithic and Early–Middle Eneolithic/Copper Age of the Carpathian Basin and south-eastern Europe (after Parkinson 2006, 57 fig. 4.4)

by the (early Baden-) Boleráz horizon and by the Baden culture (Patay 1984, 7 fig. 1; Kalicz 1991; Parzinger 1993, 267–9, horizon 10 and 11; Roman & Diamandi 2001; Schreiner 2007, 78–85). A significant culture change is marked by the Boleráz and Baden, Cernavodă III and Coțofeni horizons since it is at this time that the earlier copper industry came to an end over much of the western Carpathian Basin and adjacent areas. No more heavy copper implements were produced and there is very little evidence of metallurgy during this period (Parzinger 1993, 348–51; Schreiner 2007, 82–5).

In absolute terms the Neolithic Vinča sequence in the northern Balkans starts *c.* 5400/5300 BC, and the Late Neolithic Vinča (-Pločnik/Vinča C–D) phase is dated to *c.* 5000–4500/4400 BC (Link 2006, 41; cf. Borić 2009, 234–7, who proposes a somewhat earlier end around 4650/4600 BC. The Late Neolithic Tisza culture of the Carpathian Basin starts *c.* 5200/5100 BC and comes to an end in its main area around 4700/4600 BC. It is followed by the intermediate proto-Tiszapolgár phase and the Early Copper Age Tiszapolgár culture proper, dating *c.* 4400–3800 BC at the latest. The Middle Copper Age Bodrogkeresztúr culture is dated *c.* 4000–3700 BC. After a transitional period (featuring the Hunyadi-halom group, etc), the Bodrogkeresztúr culture is replaced *c.* 3700/3600 BC by the Boleráz culture, with the Baden sequence ending around 3000/2800 BC with Baden-Kostolac. The succeeding Vučedol sequence is dated *c.* 3000–2500 BC when Early Bronze Age groups (in Hungarian terminology) – such as Makó make their appearance (Forenbaher 1993; Raczky 1995; Hertelendi *et al.* 1995; Maran 1998, 347–51, 354, table 82; Stadler *et al.* 2001; Link 2006, 41).

In central Europe during the 5th and 4th millennia, the massive copper implements that are so widely distributed throughout south-east Europe (for example in Tiszapolgár and Bodrogkeresztúr contexts: Patay 1984), and the rich grave furnishings with weapons and ornaments of copper and gold that are found there (as at Varna: Ivanov & Avramova 2000; Chapman *et al.* 2006) are unknown except for occasional imports. The earliest evidence for metallurgy (as seen for example in the Pfyn, Altheim, and Mondsee groups) is small in scale. These make their appearance around 3800 BC,

around the same time as the Hunyadi-halom and proto-Boleráz groups, etc, and continue their development after 3600 BC and well into the second half of the 4th millennium, in parallel with the Boleráz culture (Matuschik 1996, 10–11; Matuschik 1997, 98–9; Maran 1998, 348–9). Neolithic traditions persist in society and economy and this is why the term Copper Age (or Eneolithic/Chalcolithic) is not generally used in this part of Europe despite attempts to redefine the central and western European Late Neolithic as a 'Copper Age' and to link the cultures in question to contemporaneous south-east Europe, on the basis of supposedly widespread changes in society and economy (Lichardus 1991b, 770–88; Klassen 2000, 17–22, 295–301; 2004, 325–39). This approach has not won general acceptance, not only because it tends to neglect the apparent regional differences at that time but also because of its underlying assumptions about Copper Age society. Instead, the period in question is referred to as the (Late) Neolithic, and is divided, according to Lüning's widely used scheme (1996), into the *Jungneolithikum* (*c.* 4400–3500 BC), which comprises the Michelsberg culture and more local groups such as Pfyn, Altheim, and Mondsee, and the *Spätneolithikum* (*c.* 3500–2800 BC), encompassing groups such as Horgen, Cham, and Wartberg. These are, in turn, followed by the final Neolithic Beaker cultures (*Endneolithikum*, *c.* 2800–2200 BC).

The early use of copper and copper minerals

In the Carpathian Basin and the Balkans the earliest artefacts made of copper and copper minerals, such as beads, fish-hooks, and awls, are known from Early to Middle Neolithic contexts such as the Starčevo/Criș settlements of Iernunț and Balomir in Transsylvania, the Starčevo site of Obre I in Bosnia, the Early Neolithic levels of Ovcharova I in Bulgaria and the Middle Neolithic (phase III) site at Lepenski Vir in the Danube Gorges (cf. Pernicka 1990, 31–2; Parzinger 1993, 344–5; Thornton 2001, 24–5, table 2; Borić 2009, 191–2). These finds pre-date metallurgy proper which, in addition to the working of native copper and copper minerals, involves the mining of ores for the deliberate production of copper metal, together with the smelting and casting of the metal. Instead, the earliest interest in native copper and copper minerals falls into the wider field of Neolithic communities' involvement with their natural surroundings and their attempts at the manipulation of matter. It must not be seen as purposive experimentation in a modern sense, leading to the science of metallurgy, but may rather reflect symbolic concerns expressed and negotiated through material culture.

A significant increase in the number of such finds occurred during the early 5th millennium BC in the Late Neolithic (Eneolithic) Vinča culture on the north-central Balkans (during the Vinča-Gradac and -Pločnik phases) and in the neighbouring Late Neolithic groups of the Carpathian Basin such as Sopot, Lengyel, Tisza, and Herpály. In addition to the beads and awls that had already been known from previous periods and the abundant finds of copper minerals from the Vinča settlement of Belovode, this phase saw an expansion of the copper artefact types in use. Although they were still mostly ornaments, the occasional chisel is also known, eg, from the Vinča tell sites of Pločnik, Divostin and Gomolava, from Marica, Präcucuteni and Petreşti sites further east, and from Tisza/Herpály contexts such as Berettyóujfalu-Herpály (Bognár-Kutzián 1976; Chapman 1981, 125–30; Parzinger 1993, 260–3, 345, horizon 6 and 7; Thornton 2001, 24–25 table 2).

From Vinča culture sites there may also be evidence of smelting, and recent radiocarbon dates show that the mining site of Rudna Glava in Serbia was most likely exploited from at least 5400 BC, the beginning of Vinča, until its end around 4600 BC (Borić 2009, 194–207, 234–5). It is apparent that during the Late Neolithic – in the Vinča culture and adjacent groups – the potential for the emergence of a proper metallurgy was gradually building up in southeast Europe. Vinča evidence also provides important insights into the background against which this process must be seen: the early use of copper and copper minerals as ornaments and pigments reflects a concern with colour and with the aesthetic values of matter that pertains both to the domestic and to the burial domains (see also Borić 2002; Chapman 2002). Driven by cultural and social needs the earliest mining may have been directed towards copper minerals that were desirable for their colour; people were also still working native copper into ornaments.

However, it is unlikely that some small 'tools' initially affected practical activities to the same extent that pigments and ornaments did in the symbolic domain. Invention as opposed to innovation is typically beyond the reach of archaeology, and we will probably never know in detail how and why this system evolved into metallurgy proper. However, we can propose that, to these people who were working in an essentially lithic tradition and thinking in terms of the symbolic potential of colour, the transformation of matter's outward appearance by the application of heat (smelting) might have been more significant than the metal's mechanical properties. Later on, when casting was developed, this technique came to dominate the symbolic potential of copper by the increase in size and variety of shapes it allowed.

It is during this stage that we encounter the large number of sometimes massive copper implements which initially gave rise to the definition of a Copper Age period in southeast Europe (Fig. 9.1). Starting in the southeast – in Romania and Bulgaria (Gumelniţa culture/KGK VI) and Serbia and Transylvania (late Vinča and Tiszapolgár; Parzinger 1993, 263–5, horizon 8) – the centre of metallurgical activity then moved west into the Carpathian Basin during the Bodrogkeresztúr horizon (Parzinger 1993, 265–7, horizon 9) and a variety of different types of shaft-hole hammer axe (eg, the Pločnik and Vidra types; horizon 8) and axe-adze (eg, the Jászladány type; horizon 9), flat axes and chisels (Schubert 1965; Vulpe 1975; Todorova 1981; Patay 1984; Parzinger 1993, 345–8) were made.

In the north Alpine region of central Europe there was only a weak reflection of the early development of metallurgy seen in the Carpathian Basin and the Balkans. From Neolithic contexts of the late 5th and the early 4th millennia no more than around 10–20 copper objects are known. These include the well-known disc from the lakeside settlement of Hornstaad-Hörnle IA on Lake Constance, two shaft-hole axes and one flat axe from Linz-St Peter, Austria and from Überlingen on Lake Constance, awls such as the one from Schernau, and some small copper beads and rings (cf. Matuschik 1997, 97–104 list 3; Bartelheim *et al.* 2002, 60–3, 71 list 1).

It is only somewhat later, after about 3800 BC, with the Late Neolithic (*Jungneolithikum*) Cortaillod, Pfyn, Altheim, and Mondsee

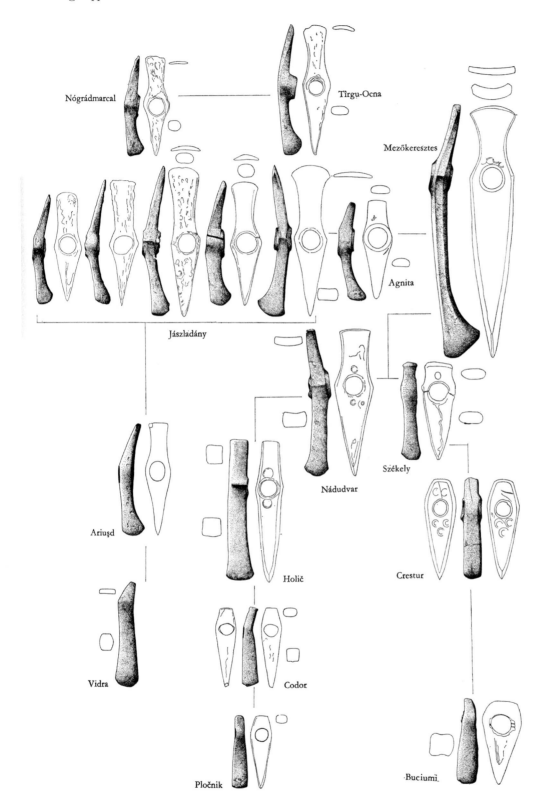

Figure 9.1: Typology and supposed development of Eneolithic/Copper Age shaft-hole axes in Romania (after Vulpe 1975, 15 fig. 1)

groups, that the number of copper artefacts increases, with numerous flat axes, daggers, awls, and ornaments such as spirals and beads being found, mainly at the wetland sites along the Alpine foothills (cf. Ottaway 1982; Bartelheim *et al.* 2002, 63–5, 72–5 list 2; Krause 2003, 237–41). In this context there is also good evidence for metalworking, in the form of numerous crucibles and copper prills relating to the casting process (Schlichtherle & Rottländer 1982; Matuschik 1998, 209–12; Bartelheim *et al.* 2002, 75–6 list 3). It has been suggested that extractive metallurgy was taking place at this time, but this has not been proven. Hence the copper is thought either to have been derived from nearby Alpine ore deposits or/and to have been imported from south-east Europe (eg, Ottaway 1982, 181–5; Fasnacht 1995, 184–5; Strahm 1994, 10–12; Matuschik 1998, 239–44). In particular, the east Alpine mining district is thought to have been exploited at this time by the population of the Mondsee group, although related evidence of extractive metallurgy (smelting) from the Götschenberg settlement in the Alpine Salzach valley is disputed (Moesta 1992, 147–55, *contra* Bartelheim *et al.* 2002, 55, 65). The composition of the copper may instead point towards ongoing exchange with the Carpathian Basin and indicate the exploitation of ore deposits in the western Carpathians/Slovakian ore mountains (cf. Schreiner 2007).

Approaches to early metalworking

This early metalworking from the 5th to the 2nd millennium BC took place in groups that varied widely in their cultural and organisational complexity. This raises two questions: first, what strategies were used to incorporate copper and bronze into existing cultural schemes? and secondly (and conversely): what was the impact of metalworking and metal objects on the societies in question? Typically, however, attempts to answer these questions still take the form of evolutionist grand narratives linking perceived technological progress to the emergence of hierarchical society (eg, Strahm 1994). Similarly, a number of recent syntheses have tried to integrate the evidence at hand into a coherent culture-historical picture involving the spread of metallurgy from south-east to central and northern Europe (eg, Parzinger 1993; Klassen 2000; Krause 2003; Roberts *et al.* 2009). In fact it is obvious that Late Neolithic or Eneolithic/Copper Age metallurgy in south-east Europe pre-dates, and was more advanced than, contemporary Neolithic metallurgy in central Europe. But concepts of 'spread', 'influence', 'diffusion', or 'drift' do not significantly add

to our knowledge of early metallurgy in the respective regions.

The field of craft specialisation and social complexity is an area which might profit from a true integration of a science-based reconstruction of technological processes and choices with an anthropologically informed discussion of its social and ideological context. The application of scientific methods has already played an important role in the study of early metalworking in prehistoric Europe. A number of important syntheses sum up much of this scientific work (eg, Pernicka 1990; Ottaway 1994; Krause 2003; Ottaway & Roberts 2008). Large-scale projects have been carried out with thousands of analyses typically focusing on composition as a guide to provenance. Less attention has been paid to the knowledge gained by prehistoric metalworkers of the properties of the different types of copper and copper alloys they were working and the development of methods of casting and forging (eg, Northover 1996). Science, however, is not dissimilar to archaeology in that data (from the compositional and metallurgical analyses) require interpretation and contextualising within a model of society and beliefs (cf. Budd & Taylor 1995; Thornton 2009). This tends to be concealed by the application of ever more sophisticated analytical methods, which is also why specialist studies focusing on technological aspects tend to dominate the field to the detriment of integrating this 'functional' perspective with wider culture-historical concerns.

In particular, there are interpretative problems with the notion of technological 'progress' and people's increasing control over nature. The early evidence for copper mining and smelting is discussed in terms of evolution, and the succession in use of different types of copper and copper alloys is interpreted as an improvement in operational and functional terms. In the following sections some aspects of this broad picture are taken up in order to deconstruct and challenge these underlying evolutionist assumptions and commonly held perceptions of early metallurgy.

It will become clear that previously clear-cut technological stages tend to become blurred by new discoveries, and we cannot rely any more on evolutionist assumptions and/or geological conditions as a guide to the development and 'progress' of metallurgy. Instead, the introduction of metallurgy and its subsequent development – from pure copper via arsenical copper to *fahlore* copper and tin-bronze – was the result of technological choices drawing upon and embedded within the respective groups' cultural and social fabric. These decisions were taken over time by countless individuals who were firmly integrated in networks of information exchange and whose decision-taking was determined neither by the laws of chemistry or physics alone nor by any 'political' authority manipulating the production and circulation of prestigious copper objects.

Smelting: geology-derived 'stages' and prehistoric reality

At the beginning of south-east and central European metallurgy high-purity copper, derived either from native copper or from the smelting of oxide copper ores (copper carbonate minerals), was used. Later on this *Reinkupfer* was increasingly replaced by arsenical copper (Sangmeister 1971; Schubert 1981; Pernicka 1990, 49–52) which is thought to be easier to work and to offer superior mechanical properties (eg, improved casting properties and ductility, higher hardness after cold-work; for discussion see below). With typically rather low arsenic contents up to about 2%, arsenical copper is not an alloy but derives from the smelting of copper ores associated with arsenic-bearing minerals (cf. Northover 1989; Lechtman 1996; Ottaway & Roberts 2008, 208–9; Kienlin 2008a, 251–80). There is evidence from various Late Neolithic/ Eneolithic groups that high-arsenic copper produced in this way was deliberately chosen for the production of daggers, while axes were cast from copper with lower arsenic contents. This choice points towards the importance of colour for the production of weapons in contrast to the mechanical properties that were important for tools and implements – in other words, what mattered was the silvery appearance of daggers produced by arsenic, whereas the higher hardness for the axes was less important (cf. Budd & Ottaway 1995; Matuschik 1998; Müller *et al.* 2007). It was only much later, during the Early Bronze Age, that arsenical copper was replaced by *fahlore* copper and other copper varieties derived from sulphide ores (cf. Kienlin 2008a; see below).

This sequence is conventionally interpreted in terms of geology and technological progress, since the earliest miners and smelters are thought to have worked the upper, oxidised regions of their mines with relatively simple technology while the exploitation of the deeper, sulphide ore bodies required advances both in mining and smelting techniques (eg, Hauptmann & Weisgerber 1985; Strahm 1994, 33–4; Ottaway 1994, 16–18).

This standard model is derived from a simplified geological view of the ore bodies in question and early modern sources such as Agricola's description of the smelting of sulphide copper ores in a multi-stage process involving the roasting of the ore prior to smelting (Fig. 9.2; eg, Bachmann 2003). It is this process that we encounter in the Late Bronze Age eastern Alps (eg, Cierny *et al.* 2004; Giumlia-Mair 2005, 287–8). But the model itself is simplistic and evolutionist (cf. Shennan 1995, 298–300; Moesta 2004, 270–1; Hauptmann 2007, 130–3; 2008, 128–30), and there is increasing evidence for a much more nuanced picture with the earliest working of sulphide ores reaching back far into the Eneolithic/Copper Age. Until recently sulphur had not been detected in analytical programmes and trace elements are of limited value as a guide to the ore type used. Early Bronze Age *fahlore* copper typically has high impurity levels indicating the use of this specific type of sulphide ore (eg, EBA Salez type axes; Krause 1988, 214–45), and compositional data may be taken to imply the early use of such copper prior to the Early Bronze Age in some parts of central Europe (eg, the 'diluted' *fahlore* copper in the Late/Final Neolithic of east-central Germany: Krause 2003, 153–7, 235–7). But there is also high-purity copper from the Early Bronze Age which only metallography can relate to sulphide ores by demonstrating the presence of copper sulphide inclusions (eg, EBA Neyruz type axes; Kienlin *et al.* 2006; Kienlin 2008a, 187–215). Similarly, it is by metallography that Eneolithic/Copper Age objects can be shown on occasion to contain sulphide inclusions pointing towards the early use of (mixed oxide and) sulphide ores (eg, Preßlinger 1997). In western Europe the early pre-Bronze Age use of sulphide ore deposits is well-attested (at Ross Island, south-west Ireland: O'Brien 2004, 451–77; and at Cabrières in southern France: Bourgarit 2007). In the earliest metalworking

Der Röstftadel A. Die Höltzer B. Das Ertz C. Kegelförmiger Haufe D. Das Waffergerinne E.

horizon of central and south-eastern Europe the evidence for smelting is more ambiguous and often disputed, but even so there is some information to be gained from the (potential) mines themselves and from the scientific analysis of installations and residues related to the smelting process.

From the 5th millennium Vinča sites of Belovode, Divostin, Pločnik and Selevac in Serbia there is evidence of thermally altered copper carbonate minerals or 'slags', thought to relate to smelting activities (cf. Šljivar *et al.* 2006, 252–7; Borić 2009, 234–8). Typically these are small pieces of slag whose interpretation as residues of smelting rather than as slags from casting copper and forging activities is difficult (eg, Bartelheim *et al.* 2002, 62 on the Selevac evidence). If they do indeed indicate smelting, this was apparently done in ephemeral installations such as small pots – an approach to early smelting found throughout the Old World that relies on highly concentrated, self-fluxing ores to produce small copper prills embedded in a matrix of partially smelted ore and slag (cf. Hauptmann 2007, 125–130; 2008, 131–135). Using a combination of metallography (copper sulphide inclusions in artefacts) and the scientific analysis of refractory ceramics, this crucible-type smelting technique can be shown to have worked equally well on sulphide copper ores as early as the second half of the 5th millennium in the Bulgarian Gumelniţa and Varna groups (Ryndina *et al.* 1999). At about the same time in the Münchhöfen culture (*c.* 4500–3900 BC) from the site of

Brixlegg-Mariahilfberg, Tyrol, what is thought to be the earliest evidence of smelting in the north Alpine region is recorded (Bartelheim *et al.* 2002; Höppner *et al.* 2005). This would indicate a rapid spread of smelting from south-east to central Europe (and/or roughly contemporaneous local experimentation); and at Brixlegg it is also clear that sulphide copper ore from nearby *fahlore* deposits was already in use at this early stage (Bartelheim *et al.* 2002, 54–6). There is a problem, however, with the dating of the metallurgical remains in question since these could also belong to the later phase of the Pfyn, Altheim, and Mondsee horizon at Brixlegg (*c.* 3900–3600 BC). However, the previously accepted evidence of Mondsee period oxide ore smelting at the Alpine Götschenberg site (Moesta 1992; cf. Ottaway & Roberts 2008, 206) is now disputed by the authors of the Brixlegg study (Bartelheim *et al.* 2002, 55, 65), so the overall situation is not yet clear. Smelting evidence from the (late) 5th and 4th millennium tends to be problematic because of the poor archaeological visibility of the processes and installations involved. But early experimentation with both oxide and sulphide ores clearly has to be taken into consideration, and it is not the case that the smelting of these two types of ore belong to discrete, clear cut technological stages. Hardly any mine follows the ideal model of bearing oxide ores on top and sulphide ores underneath. This is why early miners found different types of copper minerals which typically, but by no means universally, could have been distinguished and sorted by colour and/or other properties. Experimental work shows why this did not pose fundamental problems for subsequent smelting: it is exactly the 'primitive' nature of early oxide ore smelting under oxidising conditions that allowed for sulphide ores to be incorporated as well without causing the entire process to fail (eg, Timberlake 2007, 33–4; Hauptmann 2007, 132). Knowledge of advanced medieval and modern smelting techniques alone is a poor guide to the earliest stages of the development of this process.

Casting, working, and compositional 'determinism'

The earliest copper artefacts were hammered to shape and annealed to restore their deformability. Somewhat later casting was introduced, and

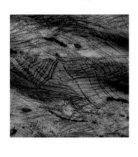

recrystallized, cold-worked

recrystallized, annealed

as-cast, cold-worked

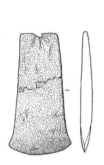

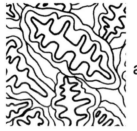

as-cast

Figure. 9.3: Chaîne opératoire *for the production of Late Neolithic/Eneolithic Altheim type flat axes and Early Bronze Age Saxon type flanged axes*

there is circumstantial evidence that from an early stage heavy shaft-hole implements were cast in closed moulds (Kienlin 2008b, 94–5). Some centuries later, with the Late Neolithic Altheim type flat axes of the north Alpine region, there is unequivocal evidence for this casting method: a shrinkhole in the neck of one of these axes clearly shows that casting took place in a closed mould that had stood upright (see also the Iceman Ötzi's axe: Sperl 1992, 454–5 fig. 1). More information on the development of methods of casting and forging can be obtained from metallographic analyses, and meaningful patterning was found in case studies that compared microstructural evidence from earlier and later Copper Age horizons (Kienlin 2008b).

In general terms one would expect the production of copper-based weapons or tools to involve the following steps: casting – cold-working the as-cast object – annealing – final cold-hammering (cf. Northover 1989; Scott 1991). This procedure has a twofold aim: to achieve the requisite degree of deformation in order to finish the as-cast object, and to achieve a smooth surface, free of feeders or casting seams, through hammering and subsequent grinding and polishing. If a stronger deformation is required, such as for shaping an axe's body or blade, this may require more than one annealing process. By contrast, final cold-working increases hardness and adds to the strength and durability of a weapon or tool. Late Neolithic flat axes of Altheim and related types clearly follow this procedure and their microstructures show traces of cold-working of the as-cast object, followed by annealing and final cold-hammering (Fig. 9.3).

Figure 9.4: Chaîne
opératoire *for the
production of Copper
Age/Eneolithic
Jászladány type
axe-adzes and
contemporaneous flat axes*

**recrystallized,
hot-worked**

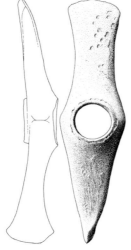
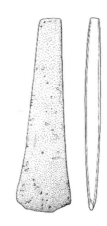

hot-work

as-cast

Figure 9.4: Chaîne opératoire *for the production of Copper Age/Eneolithic Jászladány type axe-adzes and contemporaneous flat axes*

Their producers fell short of recognising the differential work hardening of pure copper and arsenical copper (cf. Budd 1991). But for their most part they clearly operated on the basis of an empirically gained knowledge of a *point of diminishing returns* for the cold-working of copper with low trace element contents. They certainly were interested in the hardness of their axes (Kienlin *et al.* 2006, 455–457). The tradition they established can be traced right down to the Early Bronze Age, when a two-step working of flanged axes was the rule (Fig. 9.3; cf. Kienlin 2008a). Profiting from the new *fahlore* type copper and tin-bronze, a considerable increase in hardness was achieved by a vigorous final cold-working (see below).

In contrast, Jászladány type axe-adzes, dating to the late 5th and early 4th millennium Tiszapolgár and Bodrogkeresztúr horizon, and contemporaneous flat axes (eg, of Szakálhát or Stollhof type) have a recrystallised microstructures without any trace of deliberate cold-working having taken place in the final step (Fig. 9.4; cf. Kienlin 2008b). They were hot-worked and, unlike in the case of the later axes, no attempt was made to improve the

mechanical properties by cold-working. This finding can be explained by the presence of a specific type of oxide inclusion, the so-called $(Cu+Cu_2O)$-eutectic, which is typically found in the earlier axes but rarely in the later ones. The presence of this kind of oxide inclusion, which is hard and brittle, increases the hardness of the whole object to values well above what can be expected from a microstructure with little or no signs of final cold-work. Forging was carried out at high temperatures to make up for reduced deformability. But for the same reason – the additional hardness the eutectic provided – the durability of the axes was felt to be sufficient.

From a modern perspective, much of the eutectic is regarded as a 'deficiency' in casting, as it is thought to embrittle the material. But in our prehistoric example its presence provided an alternative mechanism to improve performance by benefiting – unconsciously – from 'shortcomings' in the casting technique. This point about modernist conceptions in our judgement of prehistoric metalworking can be taken further to encompass what might be called 'compositional' determinism. The earlier axes are mostly of relatively pure copper while the later ones saw the introduction of arsenical copper. This compositional change is thought to have had a beneficial effect on casting quality – in particular by the supposed de-oxidising effect of arsenic (Charles 1967, 21; cf. Ottaway 1994, 130). Instead, however, it can be shown that both an overall decline in oxide frequency and the replacement of the eutectic oxide type in the later axes does not directly correlate with arsenic content (cf. Kienlin 2008b). It is indicative of changes in casting technique, such as different ways of handling the molten copper prior to and during casting, or the use of a charcoal layer to cover the crucible.

The cognitive aspects of early metallurgy – that is, the knowledge gained by prehistoric metalworkers of the raw materials they were working, the exercise of choice beyond mere functional improvement, and the subtle ways in which traditional practice changed over time – must not be neglected in favour of an approach that focuses on composition and straightforward 'progress'. Even as early as our earlier horizon, we find different groups of implements, with oxide content that varies systematically, occurring alongside each other. Oxygen absorption during casting Jászladány type axe-adzes was different from that experienced by contemporary flat axes, and since there is no correlation with trace element (arsenic) content, handling must have been the decisive factor (cf. Kienlin & Pernicka 2009). Obviously, in casting Jászladány type axe-adzes, a method was used which reduced oxygen absorption in comparison with contemporaneous flat axes. There may have been a deliberate attempt to control oxygen absorption and strategies might have been developed to manipulate the casting atmosphere. However, what we are seeing is probably the cumulative effect of minor modifications to various aspects of the casting process, with attention paid to details of handling otherwise thought unimportant, and with greater care being taken in casting more complex forms such as Jászladány type shaft-hole tools. This may have been a technical necessity in order to achieve such forms. However, it might also be a reflection of wider social and ideological concerns in the field of metallurgy.

The 'evolution' of material properties? Casting

Turning back to the first step in metalworking, namely casting, it has been argued that along the sequence from pure copper via arsenical copper to *fahlore* copper and tin-bronze the presence of trace elements, and the addition of tin, permit the casting temperature to be lowered (eg, Spindler 1971, 199; Hauptmann & Weisgerber 1985, 30; Pernicka 1998, 135; Northover 1998, 117; O'Brien 1999, 34, 40; Junk 2003, 20; Krause 2003, 207; Schwenzer 2004, 203). This is the first in a series of modernist assumptions about the properties of different types of copper and copper alloys used in prehistory (cf. Kienlin 2008a, 251–80) and it is easily refuted by a look at the actual evidence: copper containing 'impurities' such as arsenic or tin solidifies over a wider temperature range between the so-called 'liquidus' and 'solidus' lines of the phase diagram. But for this interval to drop significantly below the melting point of pure copper (1084°C) impurity contents exceeding 10% are required (for arsenic and tin see phase diagrams in Scott 1991). Such concentrations are rarely found in Neolithic/Copper Age arsenical copper, and most of the earliest bronzes in our area (as opposed to Britain and Ireland) remain well below 10% in tin content, so that during the early stages of metallurgy composition would have had little effect on casting temperature in the way suggested by many reviews of early metalworking (cf. Pernicka 1990, 48; Ottaway 1994, 130, 138–40). Moreover, metallographic data show that, even with higher trace-element contents in Early Bronze Age *fahlore* copper (with its combination of arsenic, antimony, silver, and nickel), and with the advent of high-tin bronze in the second half of the Early Bronze Age, the casting temperature did not drop. Many of the axes that have been examined contain copper sulphide inclusions which solidified at around 1100°C; these show that casting still took place at high temperatures (cf. Kienlin 2008a) – which at this stage meant superheating the molten copper with beneficial effects on the success of the casting process. Clearly, then, our own interest in lower casting temperatures does not adequately reflect the concerns of prehistoric metalworkers.

A related point concerns the supposed effect of impurities such as arsenic, and the alloying element tin, on porosity and oxide content (eg, Charles 1967, 21; Spindler 1971, 199; Sangmeister 1971, 109, 123; McKerrell & Tylecote 1972, 209; Coghlan 1975, 81; Schubert 1981, 447–8; Hauptmann & Weisgerber 1985, 30; Penhallurick 1986, 4–5; Strahm 1994, 12; Northover 1998, 117–8; O'Brien 1999, 33–4; Junk 2003, 21–2; Krause 2003, 207; Schwenzer 2004, 207). It is possible that the wider solidification interval of impure or alloyed copper facilitated the casting of more complex objects because part of the molten copper remained liquid somewhat longer, thereby facilitating a complete fill of the casting mould. This may apply, for example, to some Early Bronze Age pins and solid-hilted daggers (Schwenzer 2004), and it requires a differentiated approach to the production of different kinds of ornaments and weapons or tools. It is not, however an argument in favour of tin-bronze alone, since much Early Bronze Age _fahlore_ copper would have offered the same advantage. However, complex objects made from relatively pure copper are also known, and from a metallographic examination of Copper and Early Bronze Age weapons and tools it is quite obvious that not only comparatively simple Early Bronze Age flanged axes, but also complex shapes such as Copper Age shaft-hole axes, could be cast to a high standard using pure copper. There was certainly porosity after casting, but this was reduced by subsequent forging and it did not necessarily result in frequent breakage. On a related issue, it was shown above that there is no clear correlation between composition (arsenic content) and oxide frequency or type. Initially, 'poor' casting quality in terms of the $(Cu+Cu_2O)$-eutectic present in earlier Copper Age axes provided additional strength and improved hardness. Later on, there was still a high amount (in modern terms) of mixed copper-arsenic oxides. But these were plastically deformed, and at no stage do oxides appear to have caused problems due to brittleness and breakage. Of course, we do not know the relative numbers of spoilt casts in relation to composition, and slightly better casting properties may have mattered in the production of more complex shapes as outlined above. But from a wider perspective it appears that the success of casting was not dependant on composition alone, but also upon the care taken and the expertise acquired

in various steps of the casting process (cf. Kienlin 2008a, 251–80; 2008b).

The 'evolution' of material properties? Workability and hardness

As far as weapons and tools are concerned, during the Copper and Bronze Ages it is likely that the advantages of new types of copper and copper alloy, in terms of their superior mechanical properties, would have been obvious and it is logical to suppose that they were readily adopted for this reason. But again, we must be wary of projecting our own knowledge, derived from a reading of modern materials science, onto traditional prehistoric metalworking. We have to differentiate carefully between the various mechanisms involved and consider the actual composition of the prehistoric artefacts in question.

Solid solution hardening and work hardening are examples of different properties that are often conflated when a new alloy such as tin-bronze is claimed to be superior to (ie, harder than) its forerunner. Solid solution hardening occurs whenever atoms of a trace or alloying element are present in the copper matrix. It confers additional hardness and strength in the as-cast or recrystallised state. By contrast, work hardening requires a deformation below the recrystallisation temperature (ie, cold-work) and, depending on composition, it may result in a considerable increase in hardness compared to the as-cast state. Both processes have been claimed as an advantage of arsenical copper and tin-bronze over pure copper, and they tend to be discussed together (eg, Charles 1967, 24; Spindler 1971, 199; Sangmeister 1971, 109, 123; McKerrell & Tylecote 1972, 209; Coghlan 1975, 80; Schubert 1981, 447–8; Hauptmann & Weisgerber 1985, 30–1; Northover 1989, 113–4; Budd & Ottaway 1991, 138–9; Strahm 1994, 12; Lechtman 1996, 502–6; Pernicka 1998, 135; O'Brien 1999, 33; Krause 2003, 207; Schwenzer 2004, 203–4).

The presence of arsenic and (somewhat more so) of tin does indeed increase the as-cast hardness of the resulting (natural or artificial) copper alloy. However, with arsenic contents up to around 3–4% this effect is limited (~60–70 HV), and even for tin, contents of around 10% are required for an increase in hardness to twice the value of pure copper at 50 HV (cf.

Lechtman 1996). A minor increase in hardness and strength at lower concentrations may or may not have been noticed. It may have been relevant in the production of copper objects such as ornaments, which could not be cold-worked, or whenever mechanical properties were of little interest. In the case of ornaments (or prestigious weaponry, etc) colour also has to be taken into consideration to account for the presence of trace and alloying elements. But for all weapons proper and tools it is a modernist misconception to suppose that prehistoric metalworkers relied on manipulating as-cast hardness via composition: the application of heat (annealing) to restore deformability, and hence the knowledge of work-hardening, goes back to the Early Neolithic working of native copper (cf. Pernicka 1990, 28–31). In our Copper Age horizon 1 a different mechanism was involved, with hardness provided by the $(Cu+Cu_2O)$-eutectic, but metallographic data clearly show that thereafter – at least well into the Bronze Age – hardness was a function of cold-working (which in some cases could be substantial), along with composition (Figs 9.3 & 9.4; Kienlin 2008a, 251–80; 2008b). As-cast hardness (ie, solid solution hardening) was certainly a concept familiar to the metalworkers themselves in this period. But whenever an object such as an axe entered the sphere of exchange and use its mechanical properties had been determined by previous cold-working and would have been attributed to the effort involved in forging and to the expertise of the smith.

Here, too, composition is thought to play an important role. Different types of copper and copper alloy are discussed together in terms of progress and improvement because of (assumed) differences in their deformability and work-hardening; this is particularly the case as regards arsenical copper and tin-bronze (see above for references.) Recent experimental work has shown, however, that these differences are relatively slight (eg, Lechtman 1996). They often occur under circumstances not directly relevant to prehistoric metalworking: arsenical copper, for example, is clearly more ductile than pure copper and can be worked to a very high reduction in thickness and a considerable increase in hardness. Bronze may achieve even higher hardness values, but this requires tin concentrations in excess of 10%, which were not reached in a majority of early tin-bronzes

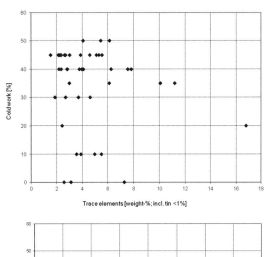

Figure 9.5: Comparison between the strength of final cold-work (in terms of reduction in thickness) of Early Bronze Age Saxon type axes made of fahlore copper (top) and tin-bronze (bottom).

in our area. In addition, unrealistically high deformation rates are involved from a Copper or Bronze Age perspective: metallographic analyses show that cold-work was typically in the 20–50% range of reduction in thickness, and the act of alloying, i.e. the manipulation of the mechanical properties through composition, was obviously seen as an opportunity to reduce the required effort in forging, as can clearly be seen, for example, in the case of the Early Bronze Age Saxon type axes (Fig. 9.5). From this it is clear that working was not undertaken with the highest possible hardness of the respective copper or copper alloy in mind (cf. Kienlin 2008a; 2008b). Rather, it was carried out to profit from the strong initial increase in hardness that occurs at lower deformation and which, for different concentrations of arsenic and tin, is very similar (Lechtman 1996). Because of this initial closeness and parallelism in their cold-working behaviour arsenical copper and tin-bronzes reached comparable hardness values under prehistoric conditions. For the same reason the alleged brittleness of copper in comparison with that of arsenical copper or tin-bronze may not have been as relevant as modern expectations have us believe. Irrespective of the composition of the object, its working was simply not strong enough to cause intolerable embrittlement. Annealing took place relatively early to restore deformability and facilitate final shaping. Subsequent forging aimed to improve mechanical properties, but it relied to a considerable degree on the initial increase in hardness during the early stages of deformation involved.

Conclusions: deconstructing technological determinism

From the perspective advocated here, we can abandon many of the various functional reasons that have previously been advanced to support claims for the inherent superiority of successive novel kinds of copper and, finally, of tin-bronze – including arguments regarding their lower casting temperature, their better casting properties and their greater hardness, both in the as-cast state and after working. Often such arguments fall short of the actual compositions used or the approach to forging taken. There are strong evolutionist notions involved in our conception of technological progress and the interpretation of changing compositional patterns. Thus, early low-tin bronzes in the 2–6% range tend to be seen as a result of poor initial control over the alloying process or of problems with access to tin, but the overall direction is thought to be obvious and directed towards achieving the superior alloy – high-tin bronze. This is certainly true in retrospect, and eventually tin-bronze became the standard alloy of the European Bronze Age. But in many parts of the Old World bronze did not replace copper for a considerable period of time, indicating that its adoption was 'a cultural choice, not a product of technological determinism' (Pare 2000, 25). In particular this is true wherever arsenical or *fahlore* copper was in widespread use, offering a serious alternative to tin-bronze. We see this, for example, in parts of central Europe (see above), and also in the Aegean and Iran, where arsenical copper and bronze coexisted for a long time (cf. Pigott 1999). Britain and Ireland, where tin-bronze replaced arsenical copper rather quickly, provide an example to the contrary (cf. Needham *et al.* 1989; Pare 2000, 20–2). These are technological choices that are informed by the rapid spread of metallurgical

knowledge among metalworkers in a wider area (cf. Kienlin 2007) and which depend on the availability of different sorts of copper and tin. But they were taken against a local or regional background which needs to be understood in cultural terms and must not be subsumed within our modern knowledge of long-term trends in Copper to Bronze Age metallurgy.

Bibliography

Bachmann, H.-G. 2003. Bunt- und Edelmetalle aus mitteleuropäischen Komplexerz-Lagerstätten: Fahlerz-Verhüttung von der Bronzezeit bis zur Renaissance. In Th. Stöllner, G. Körlin, G. Steffens & J. Cierny (eds), *Man and Mining – Mensch und Bergbau. Studies in Honour of Gerd Weisgerber on Occasion of his 65th Birthday*, 25–35. Bochum: Deutsches Bergbau-Museum

Bartelheim, M., Eckstein, K., Huijsmans, M., Krauß, R. & Pernicka, E. 2002. Kupferzeitliche Metallgewinnung in Brixlegg, Österreich. In M. Bartelheim, E. Pernicka & R. Krause (eds), *Die Anfänge der Metallurgie in der Alten Welt*, 33–82. Rahden: Forschungen zur Archäometrie und Altertumswissenschaft 1

Bognár-Kutzián, I. 1972. *The Early Copper Age Tiszapolgár Culture in the Carpathian Basin*. Budapest: Archaeologia Hungarica Series Nova 48

Bognár-Kutzián, I. 1976. On the origins of early copper-processing in Europe. In J.V.S. Megaw (ed.), *To Illustrate the Monuments. Essays on Archaeology Presented to Stuart Piggott*, 69–76. London: Thames & Hudson

Borić, D. 2002. Apotropaism and the temporality of colours: clourful Mesolithic–Neolithic seasons in the Danube gorges. In A. Jones & G. MacGregor (eds), *Colouring the Past. The Significance of Colour in Archaeological Research*, 23–43. Oxford: Berg

Borić, D. 2009. Absolute dating of metallurgical innovations in the Vinča Culture of the Balkans. In Kienlin & Roberts (eds) 2009, 191–245

Bourgarit, D. 2007. Chalcolithic copper smelting. In La Niece *et al.* (eds) 2007, 3–14

Budd, P. 1991. A metallographic investigation of Eneolithic arsenical copper artefacts from Mondsee, Austria. *Journal of the Historical Metallurgy Society* 25, 99–108

Budd, P. & Ottaway, B.S. 1991. The properties of arsenical copper alloys: implications for the development of Eneolithic metallurgy. In P. Budd, B. Chapman, C. Jackson, R. Janaway & B.S. Ottaway (eds), *Archaeological Sciences 1989*, 132–42. Oxford: Oxbow Books

Budd, P. & Ottaway, B S. 1995. Eneolithic arsenical copper: chance or choice? In B. Jovanović (ed.), *Ancient Mining and Metallurgy in Southeast Europe*, 95–102. Belgrade: Archaeological Institute

Budd, P. & Taylor, T. 1995. The Faerie smith meets the bronze industry: magic versus science in the interpretation of prehistoric metal-making. *World Archaeology* 27, 133–43

Chapman, J. 1981. *The Vinča Culture of South-East Europe. Studies in Chronology, Economy and Society*. Oxford: British Archaeological Report S117

Chapman, J. 2002. Colourful prehistories: the problem with the Berlin and Kay colour paradigm. In A.

Jones & G. MacGregor (eds), *Colouring the Past. The Significance of Colour in Archaeological Research*, 45–72. Oxford: Berg

Chapman, J., Higham, T., Slavchev, V., Gaydarska, B. & Honch, N. 2006. The social context of the emergence, development and abandonment of the Varna cemetery, Bulgaria. *European Journal of Archaeology* 9, 159–83

Charles, J. A. 1967. Early arsenical bronzes – a metallurgical view. *American Journal of Archaeology* 71, 21–6

Cierny, J., Marzatico, F., Perini, R. & Weisgerber, G. 2004. Der spätbronzezeitliche Verhüttungsplatz Acqua Fredda am Passo Redebus (Trentino). Ergebnisse der Grabungen am Redebus-Pass. In G. Weisgerber & G. Goldenberg (eds), *Alpenkupfer – Rame delle Alpi*, 155–64. Bochum: Deutsches Bergbau-Museum

Coghlan, H.H. 1975. *Notes on the Prehistoric Metallurgy of Copper and Bronze in the Old World*. Oxford: Oxford University Press

Eggert, M.K.H. 2001. *Prähistorische Archäologie: Konzepte und Methoden*. Tübingen: A. Francke

Fasnacht, W. 1995. Metallurgie. In W.E. Stöckli, U. Niffeler & E. Gross-Klee (eds), *Die Schweiz vom Paläolithikum bis zum frühen Mittelalter II. Neolithikum*, 183–7. Basel: Verlag Schweizerische Gesellschaft für Ur- und Frühgeschichte

Forenbaher, S. 1993. radiocarbon dates and absolute chronology of the Central European Early Bronze Age. *Antiquity* 67, 218–20, 235–56

Garašanin, M. 1993. Zu den Problemen der Vinča-Gruppe in Rumänien. *Balcanica* 24, 7–20

Garašanin, M. 1997. Der späte balkanisch-anatolische Komplex – Ein Rückblick nach vier Jahrzehnten. *Starinar* 48, 15–31

Giumlia-Mair, A. 2005. Copper and copper alloys in the southeastern Alps: an overview. *Archaeometry* 47, 275–92

Gogâltan, F. 2003. Die neolithischen Tellsiedlungen im Karpatenbecken. Ein Überblick. In E. Jerem & P. Raczky (eds), *Morgenrot der Kulturen. Frühe Etappen der Menschheitsgeschichte in Mittel- und Südosteuropa. Festschrift für Nándor Kalicz zum 75. Geburtstag*, 223–62. Budapest: Archaeolingua

Hansen S. 2001. Von den Anfängen der prähistorischen Archäologie: Christian Jürgensen Thomsen und das Dreiperiodensystem. *Prähistorische Zeitschrift* 76, 10–23

Hauptmann, A. 2007. Alten Berg- und Hüttenleuten auf die Finger geschaut: Zur Entschlüsselung berg- und hüttenmännischer Techniken. In G.A. Wagner (ed.), *Einführung in die Archäometrie* 115–37. Berlin: Springer

Hauptmann, A. 2008. Vom Erz zum Metall – naturwissenschaftliche Untersuchungen innerhalb der Metallurgiekette. In A. Hauptmann & V. Pingel (eds), *Archäometrie. Methoden und Anwendungsbeispiele naturwissenschaftlicher Verfahren in der Archäologie* 125–40. Stuttgart: E. Schweizerbart'sche Verlagsbuchhandlung

Hauptmann, A. & Weisgerber, G. 1985. Vom Kupfer zur Bronze: Beiträge zum frühesten Berg- und Hüttenwesen. In H. Born (ed.), *Archäologische Bronzen, antike Kunst, moderne Technik*, 16–36. Berlin: Dietrich Reimer

Hertelendi, E., Kalicz, N., Raczky, P., Horváth, F., Veres, M., Svingor, E., Futó, I. & Bartosiewicz, L. 1995. Re-evaluation of the Neolithic in Eastern Hungary based on calibrated radiocarbon dates. *Radiocarbon* 37, 239–44

Höppner, B., Bartelheim, M., Huijsmans, M., Krauss, R., Martinek, K.-P., Pernicka, E. & Schwab, R. 2005. Prehistoric copper production in the Inn Valley (Austria), and the earliest copper in Central Europe. *Archaeometry* 47, 293–315

Ivanov, I. & Avramova, M. (eds). 2000. *Varna Necropolis. The Dawn of European Civilization*. Sofia: Agató

Jovanović, B. 1996. First use of metals in the Balkans. In B. Bagolini & F. LoSchiavo (eds), *The Copper Age in the Near East and Europe*, 57–64. Forli: Abaco

Junk, M. 2003. *Material Properties of Copper Alloys containing Arsenic, Antimony, and Bismuth. The Material of Early Bronze Age Ingot Torques*. Dissertation Bergakademie Freiberg

Kalicz, N. 1991. Beiträge zur Kenntnis der Kupferzeit im ungarischen Transdanubien. In Lichardus (ed.) 1991c, 347–87

Kalicz, N. 1995. Die Balaton-Lasinja-Kultur in der Kupferzeit Südost- und Mitteleuropas. In T. Kovács (ed.), *Neuere Daten zur Siedlungsgeschichte und Chronologie der Kupferzeit des Karpatenbeckens*, 37–49. Budapest: Magyar Nemzeti Múzeum

Kienlin, T.L. 2007. Von den Schmieden der Beile: Zu Verbreitung und Angleichung metallurgischen Wissens im Verlauf der Frühbronzezeit. *Prähistorische Zeitschrift* 82, 1–22

Kienlin, T.L. 2008a. *Frühes Metall im nordalpinen Raum. Eine Untersuchung zu technologischen und kognitiven Aspekten früher Metallurgie anhand der Gefüge frühbronzezeitlicher Beile*. Bonn: Habelt

Kienlin, T.L. 2008b. Tradition and Innovation in Copper Age metallurgy: results of a metallographic examination of flat axes from eastern central Europe and the Carpathian Basin. *Proceedings of the Prehistoric Society* 74, 79–107

Kienlin, T.L., Bischoff, E. & Opielka, H. 2006. Copper and Bronze during the Eneolithic and Early Bronze Age: a metallographic examination of axes from the northalpine region. *Archaeometry* 48, 453–68

Kienlin, T.L. & Pernicka, E. 2009. Aspects of the production of Copper Age Jászladány type axes. In Kienlin & Roberts (eds) 2009, 258–76

Kienlin, T.L. & Roberts, B. (eds). 2009. *Metals and Societies. Studies in Honour of Barbara S. Ottaway*. Bonn: Habelt

Klassen, L. 2000. *Frühes Kupfer im Norden. Untersuchungen zu Chronologie Herkunft und Bedeutung der Kupferfunde der Nordgruppe der Trichterbecherkultur*. Århus: Århus University Press

Klassen, L. 2004. *Jade und Kupfer. Untersuchungen zum Neolithisierungsprozess im westlichen Ostseeraum unter besonderer Berücksichtigung der Kulturentwicklung Europas 5500–3500 BC*. Hojbjerg: Jutland Archaeological Society

Krause, R. 1988. *Die endneolithischen und frühbronzezeitlichen Grabfunde auf der Nordstadtterrasse von Singen am Hohentwiel*. Stuttgart: Forschungen und Berichte zur Vor- und Frühgeschichte in Baden-Württemberg 32

Krause, R. 1996. Zur Chronologie der frühen und mittleren Bronzezeit Süddeutschlands, der Schweiz und Österreichs, Acta Archaeologica Supplementum 1. *Acta Archaeologica* 67, 73–86

Krause, R. 2003. *Studien zur kupfer- und frühbronzezeitlichen Metallurgie zwischen Karpatenbecken und Ostsee.* Rahden: VML

Krause, R. & Pernicka, E. 1998. The function of ingot torques and their relation with Early Bronze Age copper trade. In C. Mordant, M. Pernot & V. Rychner (eds), *L'Atelier du bronzier en Europe du XXᵉ au VIIIᵉ siècle avant notre ère. Band 2. Du minerai au métal, du métal à l'objet*, 219–26. Paris: CTHS

La Niece, S.,Hook, D.& Craddock, P. (eds). 2007. *Metals and Mines. Studies in Archaeometallurgy.* London: Archetype

Lechtman, H. 1996. Arsenic bronze: dirty copper or chosen alloy? A view from the Americas. *Journal of Field Archaeology* 23, 477–514

Lichardus, J. 1991a. Die Kupferzeit als historische Epoche. Versuch einer Deutung. In Lichardus (ed.) 1991c, 763–800

Lichardus, J. 1991b. Kupferzeit als historische Epoche. Eine forschungsgeschichtliche Einleitung. InLichardus (ed.) 1991c, 13–32

Lichardus, J. (ed.). 1991c. *Die Kupferzeit als historische Epoche.* Bonn: Habelt

Lichter, C. 2001. *Untersuchungen zu den Bestattungssitten des südosteuropäischen Neolithikums und Chalkolithikums.* Mainz: Zabern

Link, Th. 2006. *Das Ende der neolithischen Tellsiedlungen. Ein kulturgeschichtliches Phänomen des 5. Jahrtausends v. Chr. im Karpatenbecken.* Bonn: Habelt

Lüning, J. 1996. Erneute Gedanken zur Benennung der neolithischen Perioden. *Germania* 74, 233–7

Maran, J. 1998. *Kulturwandel auf dem griechischen Festland und den Kykladen im späten 3. Jahrtausend v. Chr. Studien zu den kulturellen Verhältnissen in Südosteuropa und dem zentralen sowie östlichen Mittelmeerraum in der späten Kupfer- und frühen Bronzezeit.* Bonn: Habelt

Matuschik, I. 1996. Brillen- und Hakenspiralen der frühen Metallzeit Europas. *Germania* 74, 1–43

Matuschik, I. 1997. Eine donauländische Axt vom Typ Siria aus Überlingen am Bodensee – Ein Beitrag zur Kenntnis des frühesten kupferführenden Horizontes im zentralen Nordalpengebiet. *Prähistorische Zeitschrift* 72, 81–105

Matuschik, I. 1998. Kupferfunde und Metallurgie-Belege, zugleich ein Beitrag zur Geschichte der kupferzeitlichen Dolche Mittel-, Ost- und Südosteuropas. In M. Mainberger, *Das Moordorf von Reute. Archäologische Untersuchungen in der jungneolithischen Siedlung Reute-Schorrenried*, 207–61. Staufen i. Br.: Teraqua

McKerrell, H. & Tylecote, R.F. 1972. The working of copper-arsenic alloys in the Early Bronze Age and the effect on the determination of provenance. *Proceedings of the Prehistoric Society* 38, 209–18

Meier-Arendt, W. (ed.). 1990. *Alltag und Religion: Jungsteinzeit in Ost-Ungarn.* Frankfurt a.M.: Museum für Vor- und Frühgeschichte

Milojčić, V. 1949. *Chronologie der jüngeren Steinzeit Mittel- und Südosteuropas.* Berlin: Gebr. Mann

Moesta, H. 1992. Bericht über die Untersuchungen einiger Fundstücke vom Götschenberg (Grabung Lippert). In A. Lippert, *Der Götschenberg bei Bischofshofen. Eine ur- und frühgeschichtliche Höhensiedlung im Salzachpongau*, 143–55. Wien: Österreichische Akademie der Wissenschaften

Moesta, H. 2004. Bemerkungen zu bronzezeitlichen Metallen mit hohem Gehalt an Arsen und/oder Antimon, den sog. Fahlerzmetallen. In G. Weisgerber & G. Goldenberg (eds), *Alpenkupfer – Rame delle Alpi*, 269–72. Bochum: Deutsches Bergbau-Museum

Müller, R., Goldenberg, G., Bartelheim, M., Kunst, M. & Pernicka, E. 2007. Zambujal and the beginnings of metallurgy in southern Portugal. In La Niece *et al.* (eds) 2007, 15–26

Needham, S P., Leese, M.N., Hook, D.R. & Hughes, M.J. 1989. Developments in the Early Bronze Age metallurgy of southern Britain. *World Archaeology* 20, 383–402

Northover, J.P. 1989. Properties and use of arsenic-copper alloys. In A. Hauptmann, E. Pernicka & G.A. Wagner, *Archäometallurgie der Alten Welt*, 111–8. Bochum: Deutsches Bergbau-Museum

Northover, J.P. 1996. Metal analysis and metallography of early metal objects from Denmark. In H. Vandkilde, *From Stone to Bronze: the metalwork of the Late Neolithic and earliest Bronze Age in Denmark*, 321–58. Aarhus: Aarhus University Press

Northover, J.P. 1998. Exotic alloys in antiquity. In: T. Rehren, A. Hauptmann & J.D. Muhly (eds), *Metallurgica Antiqua. In Honour of Hans-Gert Bachmann and Robert Maddin*, 113–21. Bochum: Deutsches Bergbau-Museum

O'Brien, W. 1999. Arsenical copper in early Irish metallurgy. In: S.M.M. Young, A.M. Pollard, P. Budd & R.A. Ixer (eds), *Metals in Antiquity*, 33–42. Oxford: Archaeopress

O'Brien, W. 2004. *Ross Island. Mining, Metal and Society in Early Ireland.* Galway: National University of Ireland

Ottaway B.S. 1982. *Earliest Copper Artifacts of the Northalpine Region: Their Analysis and Evaluation.* Bern: Seminar für Urgeschichte

Ottaway B.S. 1994. *Prähistorische Archäometallurgie.* Espelkamp: VML

Ottaway B.S. & Roberts, B. 2008. The emergence of metalworking. In A. Jones (ed.), *Prehistoric Europe: theory and practice*, 193–225. London: Blackwell

Pare, C.F.E. 2000. Bronze and the Bronze Age. In C.F.E. Pare, *Metals Make the World Go Round. The Supply and Circulation of Metals in Bronze Age Europe*, 1–38. Oxford: Oxbow Books

Parkinson, W.A. 2006. *The Social Organization of Early Copper Age Tribes on the Great Hungarian Plain.* Oxford: British Archaeological Report S1573

Parzinger, H. 1993. *Studien zur Chronologie und Kulturgeschichte der Jungstein-, Kupfer- und Frühbronzezeit zwischen Karpaten und Mittlerem Taurus.* Mainz: v. Zabern

Patay, P. 1974. Die hochkupferzeitliche Bodrogkeresztúr-Kultur. *Bericht der Römisch-Germanischen Kommission* 55, 1–71

Patay, P. 1984. *Kupferzeitliche Meißel, Beile und Äxte in Ungarn.* München: Beck

Penhallurick, R. D. 1986. *Tin in Antiquity: its mining and trade throughout the ancient world with particular reference to Cornwall.* London: Institute of Metals

Pernicka, E. 1990. Gewinnung und Verbreitung der Metalle in prähistorischer Zeit. *Jahrbuch des Römisch-Germanischen Zentralmuseums Mainz* 37, 21–129

Pernicka, E. 1998. Die Ausbreitung der Zinnbronze im 3. Jahrtausend. In B. Hänsel (ed.), *Mensch und Umwelt in der Bronzezeit Europas*, 135–47. Kiel: Oetker-Voges

Pigott, V.C. 1999. The development of metal production on the Iranian Plateau: an archaeometallurgical perspective. In V.C. Pigott (ed.), *The Archaeometallurgy of the Asian Old World*, 73–106. Philadelphia: University Museum

Preßlinger, H. 1997. Metallkundliche Bewertung des kupferzeitlichen Flachbeiles. *Kunst-Jahrbuch der Stadt Linz* 1996/7, 163–8

Raczky, P. 1995. New data on the absolute chronology of the Copper Age in the Carpathian Basin. In T. Kovács (ed.), *Neuere Daten zur Siedlungsgeschichte und Chronologie der Kupferzeit des Karpatenbeckens*, 51–60. Budapest: Magyar Nemzeti Múzeum

Roberts, B.W., Thornton, C.P. & Pigott V.C. 2009. Development of metallurgy in Eurasia. *Antiquity* 83, 1012–1022

Roman, P. & Diamandi, S. (eds). 2001. *Cernavodă III – Boleráz. Ein vorgeschichtliches Phänomen zwischen dem Oberrhein und der unteren Donau*. Bucureşti: Vavila Edinf

Ryndina, N., Indenbaum, G. & Kolosova, V. 1999. Copper production from polymetallic sulphide ores in the northeastern Balkan Eneolithic Culture. *Journal of Archaeological Science* 26, 1059–68

Sangmeister, E. 1971. Aufkommen der Arsenbronze in SO-Europa. In *Actes du VIIIe Congrès International des Sciences Préhistoriques et Protohistoriques, Béograd 9–15 Septembre 1971. Band 1*, 109–29. Belgrad

Schier, W. 1997. Vinča-Studien. Tradition und Innovation im Spätneolithikum des zentralen Balkanraumes am Beispiel der Gefässkeramik aus Vinča-Belo Brdo. *Archäologisches Nachrichtenblatt* 2(1), 37–46

Schlichtherle, H. & Rottländer, R. 1982. Gusstiegel der Pfyner Kultur in Südwestdeutschland. *Fundberichte aus Baden-Württemberg* 7, 59–71

Schreiner, M. 2007. *Erzlagerstätten im Hrontal, Slowakei. Genese und prähistorische Nutzung*. Rahden: VML

Schubert, F. 1965. Zu den südosteuropäischen Kupferäxten. *Germania 43*, 274–95

Schubert, E. 1981. Zur Frage der Arsenlegierungen in der Kupfer- und Frühbronzezeit Südosteuropas. In H. Lorenz (ed.), *Studien zur Bronzezeit. Festschrift für Wilhelm Albert v. Brunn*, 447–59. Mainz: v. Zabern

Schwenzer, S. 2004. *Frühbronzezeitliche Vollgriffdolche. Typologische, chronologische und technische Studien auf der Grundlage einer Materialaufnahme von Hans-Jürgen Hundt*. Mainz: Verlag des Römisch-Germanischen Zentralmuseums

Scott, D.A. 1991. *Metallography and Microstructure of Ancient and Historic Metals*. Marina del Rey: Getty Conservation Institute

Shennan, S.J. 1995. *Bronze Age Copper Producers of the Eastern Alps: Excavations at St. Veit-Klinglberg*. Bonn: Rudolf Habelt

Šljivar, D., Kuzmanović-Cvetković, J. & Jacanović, D. 2006. Belovode-Pločnik XX. New contributions regarding the copper metallurgy in the Vinča Culture. In N. Tasić & C. Grozdanov (eds), *Homage to Milutin Garašanin*, 251–66. Belgrade: Serbian Academy of Sciences & Arts & Macedonian Academy of Sciences & Arts

Sperl, G. 1992. Das Beil vom Hauslabjoch. In F. Höpfel, W. Platzer & K. Spindler (eds), *Der Mann im Eis. Band 1*, 454–61. Innsbruck: Universität Innsbruck

Spindler, K. 1971. Zur Herstellung der Zinnbronze in der frühen Metallurgie Europas. *Acta Praehistorica et Archaeologica* 2, 199–253

Stadler, P., Draxler, S., Friesinger, H., Kutschera, W., Priller, A., Rom, W., Steirer, P. & Wild, E.M. 2001. Absolute chronology for early civilizations in Austria and central Europe using ^{14}C dating with Accelerator Mass Spectrometry with special results for the absolute chronology of the Baden Culture. In P. Roman & S. Diamandi (eds), *Cernavodă III – Boleráz. Ein vorgeschichtliches Phänomen zwischen dem Oberrhein und der unteren Donau*, 541–62. Bucureşti: Vavila Edinf

Strahm, Ch. 1994. Die Anfänge der Metallurgie in Mitteleuropa. *Helvetia Archaeologica* 25, 2–39

Tasić, N. 1994. Das archäologisch-historische Bild der Entwicklung der Kulturen des Äneolithikums im südlichen Banat. *Balcanica* 25, 19–37

Thornton, Ch. P. 2001. *The Domestication of Metal: A Reassessment of the Early Use of Copper Minerals and Metal in Anatolia and Southeastern Europe*. M.Phil. Thesis. University of Cambridge

Thornton, Ch. P. 2009. Archaeometallurgy: evidence of a paradigm shift? In Kienlin & Roberts (eds) 2009, 25–33

Timberlake, S. 2007. The use of experimental archaeology/archaeometallurgy for the understanding and reconstruction of early bronze age mining and smelting technologies. In La Niece *et al.* (eds) 2007, 27–36

Todorova, H. 1981. *Die kupferzeitlichen Äxte und Beile in Bulgarien*. München: Beck

Vulpe, A. 1975. *Die Äxte und Beile in Rumänien II*. München: C. H. Beck

10

Chronology, Corpses, Ceramics, Copper, and Lithics

Frances Healy

Bayesian modelling of radiocarbon dates for articulated inhumations of the 4th, 3rd, and 2nd millennia cal BC in England indicates a pronounced lull in the practice in the earlier 3rd millennium. The Beaker burials of the later 3rd millennium thus seem to reflect a newly introduced continental tradition, rather than the revival of a long-lived insular one, a conclusion reinforced by differences in demographic composition and burial context between Beaker and earlier articulated burials. Modelling of the chronology of Beaker pottery in Britain suggests that the tradition may have persisted longest in southern England and highlights an imbalance between many dates for burials and few for settlements. Although the working of the Grime's Graves flint mines overlapped substantially with the currency of British pottery, which is abundant in the surrounding area, the tradition is virtually absent from the site. It is suggested that the continued working of the mines, if not their inception, may have been something of an assertion of old ways in the face of perhaps threatening innovations.

This paper considers three questions, all of them provisionally, not least because of major dating programmes forming part of the *Beaker People Project* and the *Stonehenge Riverside Project* and a further programme which aims to date the Grime's Graves flint mines more precisely:

1. The chronology of articulated inhumations before during and after the adoption of Beaker pottery
2. The chronology of Beaker pottery itself
3. The chronology of flint mining and working at Grime's Graves in Norfolk, and its relation to the uptake of metalworking and Beaker pottery

The radiocarbon calibration curve for the 3rd and early 2nd millennia cal BC is unfriendly (Fig. 10.1). It is nonetheless possible to analyse the existing stock of radiocarbon measurements by Bayesian modelling of the results. Summary results of models based on numerous dates are produced in text (Figs 10.3a, 10.3e, 10.5a, 10.5j, 10.5k, and 10.6; Tables 10.1–10.3) while the full models and the dates themselves are presented on the accompanying CD☺ (Figs 10.3b–d, 10.5b–i; Table 10.4).

Bayesian modelling

The Bayesian approach to the interpretation of archaeological chronologies has been described by Buck *et al.* (1996). It proceeds from the principle that, although the calibrated age of radiocarbon measurements accurately estimates the calendar ages of the samples themselves, it is the dates of archaeological events associated with those samples that are important. Its basis is Bayes' theorem (Bayes 1763). This means that new data collected about a problem (the 'standardised likelihoods') are analysed in the context of existing experience and knowledge about that problem (the 'prior beliefs'), leading to a new understanding of the problem which incorporates both (the 'posterior belief'). A posterior belief can in turn become a prior belief, informing the collection of new data and their interpretation as the cycle repeats. In terms of dating an archaeological site (Bayliss & Bronk Ramsey 2004), radiocarbon or other scientific dates are the 'standardised likelihoods' component of the chronological model. These dates are interpreted within the framework of understanding of the site, the taphonomy of the dated samples, and the stratigraphic relationships of the deposits from which they were recovered. This additional information forms the 'prior beliefs' component of the model. Together, these strands of evidence make it possible to suggest dates for when the site was in use. These are the 'posterior beliefs' that are the outputs of the model. In practice the most commonly employed prior information consists of stratigraphic relationships: if sample B was stratified above sample A and if both were contemporary with their contexts then B must be later than A. The second most commonly employed prior information is the assumption that the events concerned occurred within a bounded phase, in other words that they started, continued uniformly, and ended, and that the samples are randomly distributed throughout that phase. The boundaries of such a phase counteract the scatter derived from the errors attached to radiocarbon dates, an effect of which is that, within any group of dates relating to a period of activity, a proportion of the probability distributions will fall earlier or later than its actual span, making it appear to start earlier and finish later than it actually did (Steier &

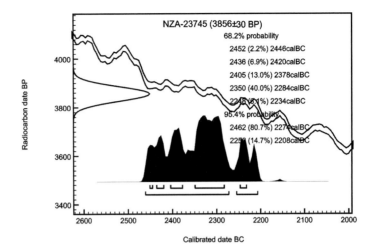

Rom 2000; Bronk Ramsey 2000). In practice, the uniform assumption is elastic, applicable to sites continuously used, used for a week once a year or used once by each generation. A quantified illustration of just how wrong this assumption has to be before the outputs of a model are misleading is provided by Bayliss *et al.* (2007d). Because this paper examines many dates from contexts unrelated to each other this form of constraint is particularly significant here.

A Bayesian model specifies the known or assumed relative ages of the radiocarbon samples. The program calculates the probability distributions of the individual calibrated radiocarbon results, then attempts to reconcile these distributions with the relative ages of the samples, by repeatedly sampling each distribution to build up the set of solutions consistent with the structure of the model. This process produces a posterior density estimate of each sample's calendar age, which occupies only part of the calibrated probability distribution (the prior distribution of the sample's calendar age). The technique used is a form of Markov Chain Monte Carlo sampling, and has been applied using the program OxCal v4.1.1 (http://c14.arch.ox.ac.uk/). Details of the algorithms employed by this program are available from the on-line manual or in Bronk Ramsey (1995; 1998; 2001; 2009). The posterior distribution is then compared to the prior distribution and an index of agreement is calculated that reflects the consistency of the two distributions. This is shown after the distribution name (eg, Fig. 10.3b☉: *Wk-17196 [A: 88]*). If the posterior distribution

Figure 10.1: A radiocarbon measurement with a range of 120 radiocarbon years at 95% confidence stretches to a fragmented overall range of more than 250 calendar years when calibrated because of the shape of the radiocarbon calibration curve for the 3rd quarter of the 3rd millennium cal BC

is situated in a high-probability region of the prior distribution, the index of agreement is high (sometimes 100% or more). If the index of agreement falls below 60% (a threshold value analogous to the 0.05 significance level in a χ^2 test) the radiocarbon result is regarded as inconsistent with the sample's calendar age, if the latter is consistent with the sample's age relative to the other dated samples. Sometimes this merely indicates that the radiocarbon result is a statistical outlier (more than two standard deviations from the sample's true radiocarbon age), but a very low index of agreement may mean that the sample is redeposited or intrusive (ie, that its calendar age is different to that implied by its stratigraphic position). An overall index of agreement ($A_{overall}$) calculated from the individual agreement indices, provides a measure of the consistency between the archaeological phasing and the radiocarbon results. A further index of agreement (A_{model}) indicates whether the model as a whole is likely, given the data. Both of these have a threshold value of 60.

It is possible to calculate distributions for events that have not been dated directly, such as the beginning and end of a continuous phase of activity (which is represented by several radiocarbon results; eg, Fig. 10.5c⊕: *Boundary start Scottish low-carinated*), and for the durations of phases of activity or intervals between them (Tables 10.2–3). Where there is reason to believe that a sample was older than the event which it is sought to date, the relevant measurement is modelled as a *terminus post quem*, constraining only the start of the probability distribution for the event in question and denoted by 'After' (eg, Fig. 10.5c⊕: *After Dalladies*); a date modelled as a *terminus ante quem*, constraining only the end of the probability distribution of the event in question, is similarly denoted by 'Before' (eg, Fig. 10.5h⊕: *Before Feltwell Anchor*). Where there are replicate measurements on the same sample and a χ^2 test shows those measurements to be statistically consistent, a weighted mean (Ward & Wilson 1978) has been taken of the results before calibration so that the same event does not contribute disproportionately to the overall model (eg, Fig. 10.3d⊕: *R_Combine Little Duke Farm 46*). The resulting combined measurement is more precise and has a smaller standard deviation

than the individual measurements: *R_Combine Little Duke Farm 46*, for example, is 3456±52 BP, while the two meaned measurements are 3440±60 BP and 3500±100 BP (Table 10.4⊕: GU-5342, -5343). The results of χ^2 tests are expressed in the form 'T'=x; T'(5%)=y; ν=z', where T' is the χ^2 value calculated, T'(5%) is the figure above which T' should not rise if the values examined are statistically consistent at 95% confidence, and ν is the degrees of freedom. The First function is used to estimate the earliest event in a series represented by the dates in a section of the model, eg, Figure 10.5c⊕: *First Scottish low-carinated*; the Last function to estimate the latest, eg, Fig. 10.5g⊕: *Last English long-necked*.

The structure of the models is defined by the square brackets at the left hand margins of the graphs. Posterior density estimates are cited in the text in italics, eg, '*UB-3306*' or '*2350–2200 cal BC (95% probability)*', to distinguish them from dates based on independent scientific information alone, which are shown in regular type. In the figures posterior density estimates are shown solid, with the unmodelled probability distributions shown in outline. The bar beneath a distribution represents 95% probability. A question mark following the name of a distribution shows that it has been excluded from the model and hence does not contribute to the overall results, although it is still shown on the figure (eg, Fig. 10.5c⊕: 'SUERC-2866?'). In these cases no posterior density estimates are calculated, and the entire probability distribution is shown solid. The ways in which individual dates have been treated in the models, including reasons for exclusion, are stated in the 'comments' column of Table 10.4⊕, except for articulated inhumations which are treated *ipso facto* as contemporary with their contexts. Cross-referencing, denoted by '=', is employed in the Beaker models to incorporate modelled distributions generated in one section of the model into another, such as a posterior density estimate for a single radiocarbon date which applies to more than one ceramic lineage (Fig. 10.5h⊕: '=OxA-13624'). Cross-referencing ensures that only one independent parameter is created for a given distribution, although it may figure at more than one place in the model. In Figures 10.5h–k and 10.6 parameters generated in other models are used as prior information (eg, Fig. 10.5j: *Prior/end_English_long_necked_1.*)

Samples and their contexts

Accurate assessment of the taphonomy of each sample, and hence its relation to the context it is intended to date, is essential. Articulated bone, which constitutes all of the burials in the first model and most of those in the second, provides ideal samples, because it must still have been connected by soft tissue and hence not long dead when it reached its context (Mant 1987). Objects of short-lived material in direct functional relation to their contexts are also valuable, a classic example being antler picks from the bases of earthwork ditches which they had been used to dig. Other potential samples are single charred grains or nuts or single fragments of charcoal from short-lived taxa, since they represent a year or a few years' growth. The risk of redepostion or intrusion is reduced by selecting them from coherent, single-event, deposits like hearths or dumps of charred material, and by dating multiple single-entity sample from a single context: the single fragments eliminate the risk of combining material of different ages in the same sample (Ashmore 1999), and the dating of more than one sample from the same context makes it possible to check against the inclusion of stray fragments of older and/or younger material using a χ^2 test (Ward & Wilson 1978).

Many of the dates in the Beaker models were, on the contrary, measured on bulk samples, in which the several charcoal fragments or several disarticulated bone fragments may have been of different ages, making the result potentially a mean of all and the age of none. Such results are treated as *termini post quos* for their contexts unless there are solid grounds for believing otherwise. Other obvious *termini post quos* are mature timbers, as in charred coffins (since, for example, only the outermost sapwood ring of an oak tree will be contemporary with its felling).

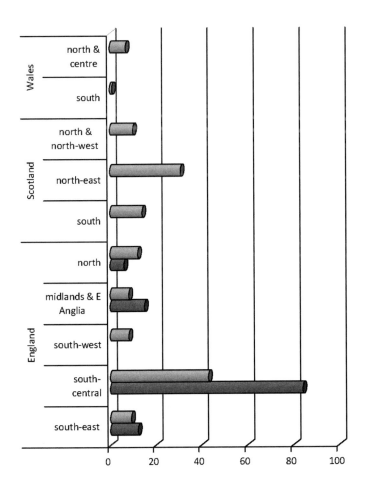

dates used in British Beaker pottery model

dates used in English articulated inhumation model

Figure 10.2: The composition of the radiocarbon dates used in the two main models by broad geographical area, showing how they are biased towards south-central England (Berkshire, Dorset, Gloucestershire, Hampshire, Oxfordshire, and Wiltshire) and north-east Scotland (Aberdeenshire, Angus, and Moray). Dates shown in figures but excluded from the models and dates listed in Table 10.4⊕ but otherwise not used are not included in these totals

The measurements

The measurements in Table 10.4⊕, most of which are modelled in Figures 10.3b–3d⊕ and/or Figures 10.5b–i⊕, vary in vintage, accuracy, and precision, ranging from some determined in the early years of radiocarbon dating to others recently measured by laboratories maintaining continual programmes of quality assurance procedures in addition to participation in international inter-comparisons. Those in the Beaker models are particularly diverse. The numerous different methods of pretreatment and measurement are described for the older determinations in datelists in the journal *Radiocarbon* and for those obtained more recently in the publications, printed and web-based, of the laboratories. Some dates which are not *termini post quos* are excluded from the Beaker model because they are in poor agreement with it or with replicate dates on the same individual. Some of these have already been considered too recent by Needham (2005) and/or Sheridan (2007), for example Table 10.4⊕: BM-2517, -2519; GU-1121; N-1240.

Figure 10.2 shows how uneven the geographical distribution of the measurements is. To some extent this reflects the varying frequency of relevant finds across the island. It also, however, reflects an uneven history of dating. Both articulated Neolithic inhumations and Beakers are frequent, though little dated, in Yorkshire and Derbyshire, and two further Beaker concentrations, one in East Anglia and the other extending from south-east Scotland into Northumberland, are also under-dated compared with those of south-central England and north-east Scotland. The imbalance will be improved in the north of England and in Scotland by the full results of the *Beaker People Project* and by ongoing work by Dominic Powlesland at West Heslerton in North Yorkshire.

The results listed in Table 10.4⊕ are conventional radiocarbon ages (Stuiver & Polach 1977), quoted according to the standards established by the Trondheim convention (Stuiver & Kra 1986). The calibrated date ranges (95% confidence intervals) were calculated by the maximum intercept method (Stuiver & Reimer 1986) and rounded outwards to the nearest 10 years, following Mook (1986). The probability distributions of the calibrated dates shown in the graphs were calculated by the probability method (Stuiver & Reimer 1993). Calibration and modelling were undertaken using OxCal v4.1.6 (Bronk Ramsey 1995; 1998; 2001; 2009) and the IntCal04 dataset (Reimer *et al.* 2004).

Articulated inhumations

Furnished articulated burials, generally in single graves and often under small round barrows, are characteristically associated with Beaker pottery. There have, however, been periodic assertions that 'Beaker' burials in Britain reflect the absorption of newly introduced practices and artefacts into an existing insular tradition of the individual burial of complete, fleshed corpses, sometimes furnished and sometimes in round barrows and ring ditches, as in the case of the predominantly northern English series of burials analysed by Kinnes (1979). Loveday *et al.* have pointed out (2007, 389–90) that radiocarbon dates for an antler macehead from Duggleby Howe and for an articulated skeleton from Whitegrounds, both in North Yorkshire, combine with the associated artefacts in these burials to place many of the series in the later 4th millennium cal BC, well before the advent of 'Beaker' burials.

A longer perspective is provided by a sample of 135 dated articulated inhumations from the 4th, 3rd, and 2nd millennia in England. They were chosen on the criterion that the skeleton should have been completely or very nearly articulated when the final funerary acts were complete. In long barrows, for example, where originally articulated skeletons were progressively rearranged leaving some in a partly articulated state, only fully articulated examples, often the most recent insertions, have been included. The measurements are listed in Table 10.4⊕. To ensure comparison of like with like and contemporaneity of dates and burials, only measurements made on the articulated skeletons are employed.

Figures 10.3a to 10.3d⊕ show a model in which the measurements are placed in four groups on grounds of context and associations (A_{model}=80.9; $A_{overall}$=75.5). The Early Neolithic group comprises burials made in classic monuments of the period such as long barrows and cairns and causewayed enclosures and/or associated with Early Neolithic artefacts. The non-classic Neolithic group comprises

Group	Start cal BC	End cal BC
Early Neolithic articulated	*3740–3630 (85% probability), 3620–3550 (10% probability); 3700–3640 (68% probability)*	*3500–3310 (95% probability); 3480–3340 (68% probability)*
Non-classic Neolithic articulated	*3670–3380 (95% probability); 3540–3390 (68% probability)*	*2900–2620 (95% probability); 2890–2750 (68% probability)*
Beaker and related articulated	*2510–2350 (95% probability); 2480–2390 (68% probability)*	*1810–1780 (3% probability), 1770–1610 (92% probability); 1840–1640 (68% probability)*
Other articulated	*2220–2040 (95% probability), 2170–2080 (68% probability)*	Continuing beyond arbitrary cut-off at end of 2nd millennium

Table 10.1: Results of English articulated inhumation model

burials from other kinds of monument and/or associated with Middle Neolithic artefacts, together with Neolithic burials without distinctive associations, typically un- or minimally furnished single burials in flat graves like those outside the Abingdon causewayed enclosure in Oxfordshire (Barclay & Halpin 1999, 31–34). The Beaker and related group comprises burials with Beaker pottery and/or cognate artefacts such as bracers or 'basket' ornaments. The remaining group comprises late third or second millennium cal BC burials, often in Early Bronze Age monuments, with artefacts of other traditions, such as Food Vessel pottery, with undistinctive artefacts, or with none at all.

The four groups are all modelled in the same way, as independent, potentially overlapping phases with no assumption of sequence between them. An interval nonetheless emerges between the non-classic Neolithic articulated inhumations and the Beaker and related ones (Fig. 10.3e), an interval that could have lasted *170–510 years (95% probability)*, probably *300–460 years (68% probability)*, between *2900–2620* and *2510–2350 cal BC (95% probability*; Fig. 10.3e: *end non-classic Neolithic articulated inhumations*; *start Beaker and related articulated inhumations)*, probably between *2890–2750* and *2480–2390 cal BC (68% probability)*. This does not exclude the possibility of some articulated inhumations in the interval so defined, but it does indicate that they were rare. The child dated by *OxA-2321* and the subadult dated by *AA-40353* could, for example, have died during this time (Fig. 10.3b☺).

If this result is valid, then there was virtually no surviving insular tradition of individual inhumation which might have contributed to the character of British Beaker burials, confirming Ian Kinnes' conclusion of more than 30 years ago:

> 'The specific native contributions to Bronze Age burial practices have yet to be properly assessed, but it is worth noting that on the scheme of the present work there are great chronological difficulties over specific affiliations. Single burial with personal grave-goods had been supplanted by cremation cemeteries before any identifiable Beaker presence is manifest' (1979, 75).

Crude profiling of the four groups of inhumations (Fig. 10.4) reinforces the impression of discontinuity in the 3rd millennium, since the Beaker group is distinguished from the non-classic Neolithic group not only by its grave goods but by its preponderance of males, its frequency of barrows and ring-ditches, and its infrequency of burial in other monuments, a combination suggestive of the introduction of new beliefs and practices. A scarcity of early 3rd millennium inhumations may also be reflected in the possible associations of the cave burials listed by Barnatt and Edmonds (2002, 118–9), which are predominantly Middle Neolithic and Beaker or Bronze Age, with very few Late Neolithic artefacts.

This impression is reinforced by a lag between the appearance of Beaker burials and that of other articulated Early Bronze Age inhumations lacking characteristic Beaker accoutrements (Fig. 10.3e), as if these developed from the introduced mode of burial rather than from any indigenous tradition. This interval can be estimated as *200–420 years (95% probability)*,

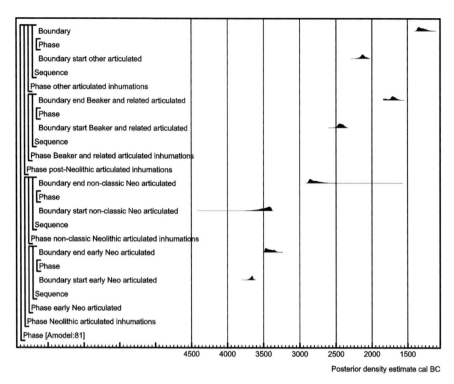

Figure 10.3a: Overall structure of a model in which 135 dates for articulated inhumations from England in the 4th–2nd millennium cal BC are treated as four groups, based on their contexts and associations. The model is defined by the square brackets down the left-hand side and by the OxCal keywords

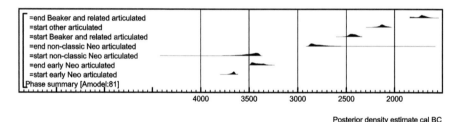

Figure 10.3e: Summary of the results of the model shown in Figures 10.3a to 10.3d⊕, see Table 10.1

probably *260–370 years (68% probability), falling between 2510–2350 cal BC and 2220–2040 cal BC (95% probability;* Fig. 10.3e: *start Beaker and related articulated inhumations; start other articulated inhumations),* probably between *2480–2390 cal BC and 2170–2080 cal BC (68% probability)*. It is easy to see this as an aspect of Needham's transition from Beaker values as intrusive and interstitial within the indigenous Late Neolithic to Beaker values as the prevailing cultural ethos (2005, 209). The extension of individual inhumation to a larger slice of the population could be reflected in a less skewed demographic balance among the other late 3rd

and 2nd millennium inhumations than among the Beaker ones (Fig. 10.4; cf. Garwood 2007a, table 4.1; Harding & Healy 2007, table 4.4).

The scarcity of inhumations in the earlier part of the 3rd millennium, effectively the Late Neolithic, corresponds to the exiguous contemporary Irish burial record described by Carlin and Brück (this volume). In Britain, Parker Pearson *et al.* (2009) emphasise the significance of cremation in this period, although the cemeteries which they cite (*ibid.*, fig. 9) would account for only a minute fraction of the population. There are rare examples of other treatments of the body in this period.

On the site of the Eton Rowing Course, parts of the skeleton of a probable male, dated to 2890–2570 cal BC (95% confidence; 4155±45 BP; OxA-8817) were dug from below the water-table in a palaeochannel of the Thames during contractors' excavations, the number of bones recovered suggesting that that he entered the river entire (T. Allen, pers. comm.), whether by drowning or by other agency. On dry land, the essentially complete disarticulated skeleton of a young adult male dated to 2860–2400 cal BC (95% confidence; 4020±60 BP; BM-2711) was placed in one of a cluster of intercutting pits at Barrow Hills, Oxfordshire (Barclay & Halpin 1999, 87–93). Complete disarticulation, with only the odd bone from any individual seeing eventual burial, seems to have been more common, whether at Raunds in Northamptonshire, where two worn and rolled human femurs from different individuals were caught up with much cattle bone in a wooden riverside structure for which a sequence of three radiocarbon measurements gives an estimated construction date of *2870–2800 cal BC at 13% probability* or *2760–2470 cal BC at 82% probability* (Harding & Healy 2007, 113–5) or in henges, exemplified by disarticulated fragments at Stonehenge (Cleal *et al.* 1995, table 57), two of which are now directly dated to the earlier 3rd millennium (Parker Pearson *et al.* 2009, 35). Unburnt, disarticulated human bone also occurs in some other henge monuments (Harding 2003, 113–5). If any funerary tradition persisted continuously from the 4th into the 2nd millennium it was the disarticulation of human bodies and the eventual burial of only some of their bones (cf. Gibson 2007, 56–59; Harding & Healy 2007, 228–30). The burials listed in Table 10.4⊕ include several examples of disarticulated burials from the later 3rd and early 2nd millennium cal BC (BM-2520, -2711, -2703, -2833, -2923; GU-1409; HAR-3880, -6630; OxA-1072, -4357, -5550, -13542, -13543, -13598, -13599, -13681; SUERC-4079; UB-3304, -3305).

The scarce articulated inhumations dated to the first half of the 3rd millennium, or just before, include a high proportion of children (Fig. 10.3b⊕). Children, in fact, form the largest single category in the non-classic Neolithic group, although they make up only 11% of the total sample (Fig. 10.4). Of the children in this group, only two were in simple flat graves (Fig. 10.3b⊕: OxA-1882,

BM-3170). Most were placed in monuments: one was in an ill-understood enclosure at Gatehampton Farm, Goring, Oxfordshire (Fig. 10.3b⊕: *BM-2835*); and two were in the Flagstones enclosure in Dorset (Fig. 10.3b⊕: *HAR-9158, OxA-2321*), where a third, undated burial of a 6–12-month-old was in a similar primary context to the 2–3-year-old dated by HAR-9158, and must have been coeval (Healy 1997, 37). Other child burials must be of similar age, notably three children buried in the Monkton-up-Wimborne 'temple' with a woman dated by *OxA-8035* (French *et al.* 2007, 114–21). It is noteworthy too that the partly articulated remains of six infants were placed in the West Kennet long barrow during its secondary infilling, modelled as having taken place between *3620–3240 and 2545–2065 cal BC (95% probability*; Bayliss *et al.* 2007c, 91–93). This suggests that the occasional burial of small children in monuments continued through a time when adult inhumations were very rare.

In this context, the fact that one early Beaker burial, including copper trinkets (Fig. 10.3c⊕: *OxA-1874, -1875*), was of a neonate and a 4–5-year-old, at a time when infant or child burials were scarce (Garwood 2007b, fig. 7.2) and Beaker burials were overwhelmingly adult and male, could suggest a link to older traditions, especially as the grave was dug at Barrow Hills in an area marked by hengiforms and Grooved Ware pits (Barclay & Halpin 1999, 35–87). The accompaniment of the neonate by a small amount of cremated bone from a 2–3-year-old could also echo older traditions. Two infant burials dug into the main enclosure ditch at Mount Pleasant after the formation of a stable horizon above layers that already contained Beaker pottery (Wainwright 1979, 44–5, 81) may reflect a similar continuity. The relation of the burial of a small child near the centre of Woodhenge (Cunnington 1929, 13) to the history of the monument remains uncertain. Distinctive funerary treatment for some children is not unusual. Two obvious examples are the Romano-British burial of infants in settlements while others were buried in extra-mural cemeteries (eg, Watts 1989) and the historical Irish practice of interring unbaptised infants outside consecrated ground. The interpretation of the 3rd millennium case is problematic. Garwood's review of changing and diverse child burial practices through the late 3rd and early 2nd millennia emphasises

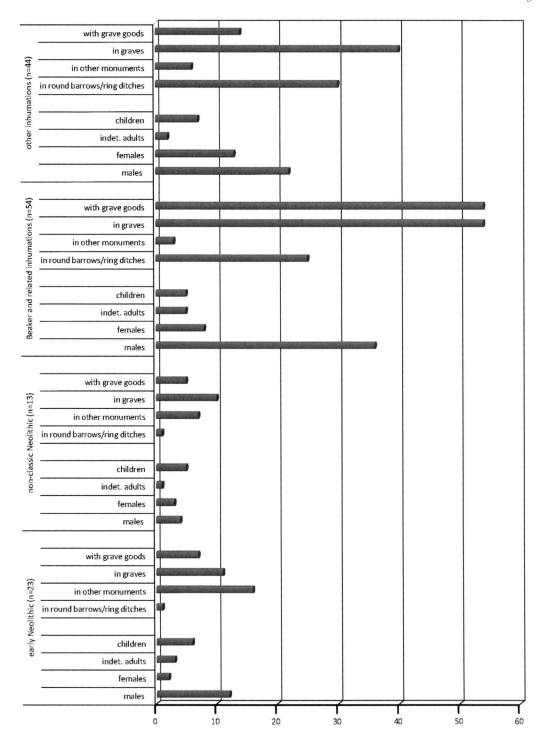

Beaker pottery

the effectively infinite range of processes of symbolic transformation, and ritual actions during which children and their remains were reconstituted and endowed with new qualities and significance (2007b, 79).

The model shown in Figures 10.5a to 10.5h☉ examines the chronology of Beaker pottery in Britain using the dates employed by Needham (2005) and Sheridan (2007) supplemented by others (A_{model}=78.3; $A_{overall}$=81.7). All the dates are listed in Table 10.4☉. The Beaker model

Source	Start Beakers cal BC	Fission horizon cal BC	End Beakers cal BC	Duration	
Kinnes *et al.* 1991 (Britain)	*c.* 2600		*c.* 1800	*c.* 800 years	*Table 10.2: Outline results from Beaker pottery models, compared with other estimates*
Needham 2005 (Britain)	*c.* 2500	*c.* 2250–2150	*c.* 1750	*c.* 750 years	
Bayliss *et al.* 2007b (England)	*2475–2315 (95% probability)* *2425–2350 (68% probability)*				
This paper Beaker model 1 (England)	*2490–2370 (95% probability)* *2450–2370 (68% probability)*		*1800–1620 (95% probability)* *1740–1670 (68% probability)*	*580–800 years (95% probability)* *640–740 years (68% probability)*	
This paper Beaker model 2 (England)	*2490–2340 (95% probability)* *2450–2360 (68% probability)*		*1880–1740 (95% probability)* *1870–1800 (68% probability)*	*480–670 years (95% probability)* *510–610 years (68% probability)*	
Sheridan 2007 (Scotland)	*c.* 2500	*c.* 2350	*c.* 1800	*c.* 700 years	
Bayliss *et al.* 2007b (Scotland)	*2385–2235 (95% probability)* *2345–2270 (68% probability)*				
This paper Beaker model 1 (Scotland)	*2350–2230 (95% probability)* *2320–2260 (68% probability)*		*2130–2010 (95% probability)* *2120–2050 (68% probability)*	*up to 300 years (95% probability)* *150–250 years (68% probability)*	
This paper Beaker model 2 (Scotland)	*2350–2240 (95% probability)* *2320–2260 (68% probability)*		*2130–2030 (95% probability)* *2130–2080 (68% probability)*	*120–290 years (95% probability)* *140–230 years (68% probability)*	

incorporates the ceramic lineages defined by Needham (2005 and this volume) without any assumption as to their chronological relation to each other. Those originally classed by him as 'weak-carinated' and 'tall mid-carinated' are grouped together as 'mid-carinated', following his paper in this volume. The large 'remainder' group consists of vessels of uncertain attribution and of Beaker material so fragmentary as to be unclassifiable in Needham's scheme — often the case with settlement assemblages.

At the time of writing, published measurements definitely associated with Beaker pottery in Wales (Fig. 10.5b☻) amounted to nine *termini post quos* on bulk charcoal samples and OxA-3814, a date measured on a female skeleton found in a stone cist with a long-necked Beaker, a flint flake and a bronze awl at Riversdale, Cardiff (see also Burrow, this volume). It is excluded from the Beaker models pending confirmation of its accuracy because it shows poor agreement (A=42) when modelled with other dates for long-necked Beakers and because, if OxA-3814 genuinely dates the burial, the awl is the earliest bronze, as distinct from copper, artefact in Britain. Interpretation must await the ongoing development of the corpus of Welsh dates.

The results for Scotland and England are shown in Figures 10.5c–h☻. They are modelled separately because they differ in significant respects. The location of the two major concentrations of dates close to the extremes of the island, in south-central England and north-east Scotland (Fig. 10.2) would by itself carry a strong possibility of different histories in each. That possibility is reinforced by the distinct characters of the archaeology of the period, including burial mode and Beaker

Figure 10.5a: Overall structure of the model for British Beaker pottery shown in Figures 10.5b–10.5i⊕. The model is defined by the square brackets down the left-hand side and by the OxCal keywords. Start and end dates (and durations) are estimated only for those lineages which are substantially represented in the relevant sections

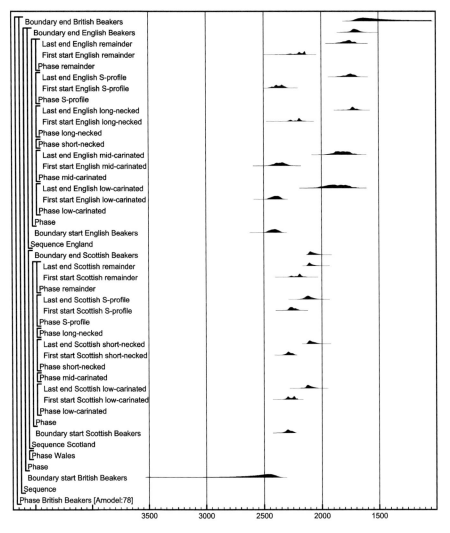

typology, in the two areas. A difference between estimated start dates for English Beakers here *(2490–2340 cal BC at 95% probability)* and for English Beaker and related articulated inhumations in the first model *(2510–2350 cal BC at 95% probability)* reflects the differing structures of the models and the differing numbers of dates. Figure 10.5a already makes it clear that the Scottish and English results are very different, with overall Beaker currencies of *2490–2340 to 1800–1620 cal BC (95% probability), probably 2450–2370 to 1740–1670 cal BC (68% probability)* for England and of *2350–2230 to 2130–2010 cal BC (95% probability), probably of 2320–2260 to 2120–2050 cal BC (68% probability)* for Scotland (Fig. 10.5j, Table 10.2).

It is necessary to consider why there are

such great differences between the English and Scottish estimates, especially between the end dates. Most obviously, a much higher proportion of the Scottish dates than of the English ones has been obtained in recent years (largely due to initiatives by Alison Sheridan of the National Museums of Scotland and Neil Curtis of the Marischal Museum, University of Aberdeen). These are probably more precise and more accurate than the high proportion of the English dates which was obtained in previous decades. The English results could be stretched by more frequent large standard deviations and inaccurate measurements, despite equal scrutiny of taphonomy and sample character for each series in the course of modelling. To examine this possibility, a second, pared-down, model was constructed,

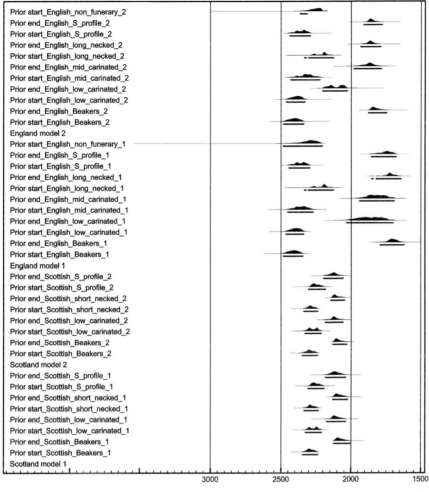

Posterior density estimate cal BC

Figure 10.5j: Summary of the results of the models shown in Figures 5a–5h (model 1)⊙ and Figure 10.5i⊙, as well as for an alternative models (model 2, equivalent to the model shown in Figure 10.5i⊙) with the same structure but excluding dates listed by Kinnes et al. (1991) and other dates measured in the same period, except for those which are statistically consistent with replicates subsequently measured on the same samples. The first set of results is suffixed '_1', the second '_2'. The horizontal lines below the distributions represent 95% probability. See Tables 10.2 and 10.3

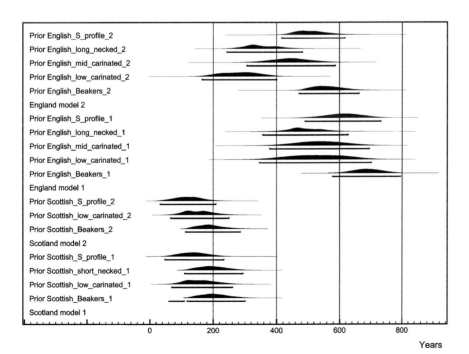

Years

Figure 10.5k: Estimated durations derived from the models shown in Figures 10.5a–10.5h (model 1)⊙ and Figure 10.5i⊙, as well as for an alternative model (model 2), equivalent to the model shown in Figure 10.5i⊙) with the same structure but excluding dates listed by Kinnes et al. (1991) and other dates measured in the same period, except for those which are statistically consistent with replicates subsequently measured on the same samples. The first set of results is suffixed '_1', the second '_2'. The horizontal lines below the distributions represent 95% probability. See Tables 10.2 and 10.3

taking as a baseline the Beaker dating paper of Kinnes *et al.* (1991). Model 2 has the same structure as model 1 (Fig. 10.3a), but does not use dates listed in the 1991 paper or a small number of others which, on the evidence of their laboratory numbers, were measured in the same period. The only exceptions are dates which are statistically consistent with others subsequently measured on the same samples. Weighted means have been taken of each set of replicates results before calibration, as described above. This reduces the dates employed (counting each set of replicates as 1 and not counting dates shown on the graphs but excluded from the models) from 54 to 43 for Scotland (a reduction of 20%) and from 101 to 58 for England (a reduction of 43%). The dates used in model 2 are indicated in the last column of Table 10.4⊕. This model too shows good overall agreement (A_{model}=81.1; $A_{overall}$=79.6). Its results are summarised with those of model 1 in Figures 10.5j–k and Tables 10.2–3. The Scottish results are effectively unchanged. The English results differ most from those of model 1 in the end date and overall span for English Beakers, the end date going from *1800–1620 cal BC* to *1880–1740 cal BC (95% probability*, a difference of *10–220 years (95% probability)*, the overall span going from *580–800 years* to *480–670 years (95% probability)*. The start date, however, is little changed.

The asymmetry of these differences is significant. If they were simply the result of greater precision in the smaller English series, achieved by removing dates with large standard deviations, it would have affected the start and end dates equally. Other factors must be involved, a strong candidate being that some of the dates removed were inaccurately recent. Three of them (BM-2704; HAR-2998, -5124) have already been considered too recent by Needham (2005, 185, 195). BM-2517, also considered too recent by Needham, is excluded from both models because it is statistically inconsistent with and later than a replicate obtained in the course of the *Beaker People Project* (M. Jay, pers. comm.). The removal of BM-2704 and HAR-5124 has a marked effect on the end date and duration of English low carinated Beakers, which go from *2040–1700 cal BC* and *350–710 years* to *2210–2030 cal BC* and *170–400 years* (95% probability; Figs 10.5j–k, Table 10.3). If some

dates measured in the mid- to late 20th century are indeed inaccurately recent, this should not invalidate the early 3rd millennium cal BC lull in English articulated inhumations suggested above, although the removal of such dates might make its start earlier.

Even in model 2 there remain substantial differences in the currencies of English and Scottish Beaker pottery (Figs 10.5j–k, Table 10.2). These match with aspects of the archaeology. One obvious consideration is that the Scottish dates are dominated by those for short-necked Beakers, which make up more than half the total. Clarke's (1970) illustrations indicate that their frequency among the dated examples is a fair reflection of their frequency among Scottish Beakers as a whole. The English dates, and the entire corpus of English Beakers, on the other hand, are more evenly distributed among the lineages. The dominance of a single lineage in Scotland could reflect a concentration of Beaker use in a shorter period, allowing less time for the development of diverse potting traditions. Some of the later Scottish Beaker dates are in poor agreement with model 1, and where they are employed in it, with model 2 (Fig. 10.5c⊕: *SUERC-2866*; Fig. 10.5d⊕: N-1240, OxA-V-2172-27; Fig. 10.5e⊕: GU-1121, *OxA-13215*). While these may be inaccurate, some or all of them could evidence rare, late survivals of a declining practice. The form of the vessel associated with SUERC-2866 (Shepherd 1982, fig. 17:163), seen by Sheridan (2007) as a Beaker/Food Vessel hybrid, would accord with this.

Food Vessels are significant here. An earlier fall-off in Beaker use in Scotland could relate to the greater frequency of Food Vessels there and in the north of England than farther south (Manby 2004, 217–19), especially as dates on associated inhumations and cremations now show that Food Vessels were current in Britain by the last quarter of the 3rd millennium cal BC, if not earlier (Manby 2004, 219–20; Sheridan 2004), as they were in Ireland (Brindley 2007). The national scale of the English section of the models used here is almost certainly inappropriate. What if Food Vessels began frequently to be placed with burials in Scotland and northern England while Beakers remained the norm farther south? There are too few Beaker dates from the north of England to indicate when the tradition declined there (Fig. 10.2): model 1 includes only 12 and model 2 only seven, counting each set of replicates as one. Practice in Scotland and the north of England was closer to that of Ireland, where inhumations with Food Vessels were frequent (Waddell 1990), than to that of southern England. The counterpart to this is the greater frequency in southern England of long-necked Beakers (Clarke 1970, maps 7–8), the latest-starting and one of the later-persisting lineages in both models (Fig. 10.5j, Table 10.3). What if Needham's phase of Beaker as past reference, persisting in funerary use within a complex mix of pottery styles and 'rich' burial rites (2005, 209–10), was a mainly southern English survival?

At the other end of the currency, the question of whether Beaker pottery was in use in Britain before it began to be placed in graves remains unanswered. Parker Pearson *et al.* point out that two Beaker sherds from a fill of Q-hole 5 (context 3167) at Stonehenge should date from before the construction of the sarsen circle, in the 26th or early 25th century cal BC (2007, 634). It is important to remember, however, that the two sherds in question have a combined weight of 2 g, the larger having a maximum dimension of 18 mm (Cleal *et al.* 1995, 352, 364). Their small size alone suggests that they could have been intrusive and, although no traces of disturbance were noted in Q-hole 5, the potential for intrusion into stone-holes at Stonehenge has been demonstrated by radiocarbon dates on samples from the 2008 excavation inside the circle (Darvill & Wainwright 2009). As Parker Pearson *et al.* point out (2007, 634–5), fragments of one rusticated vessel among the Beaker pottery in the secondary infilling of the West Kennet long barrow came from deposits underlying the early 3rd millennium infant skeletons cited above, but the looseness of the chalk rubble fills means that the sherds could have percolated from a higher level. A further possibly early occurrence is suggested by Needham's description of a burial at Sorisdale on the island of Coll as cutting an occupation layer already containing Beaker domestic ware (2005, 182). If so, the burial would provide a *terminus ante quem* for the occupation of *2270 cal BC (36% probability)* or *2260–2200 cal BC (59% probability*; Fig. 10.5c⊕: *R_Combine Sorisdale*). The three incomplete, plain, coarse pots from the midden layer (Ritchie & Crawford 1978, 78, fig. 3:2–4), however, may or may not be

Beaker. Sheridan has described them as 'a later style of pottery, of a kind seen in early Bronze Age settlements elsewhere in the Hebrides' (2008, 253–4), although this view goes against their context having been cut by the late 3rd millennium burial.

Even if this living site is dismissed, others should hold the answer to whether there was a pre-funerary phase of Beaker use. There are, however, far fewer dates from non-funerary contexts than from funerary ones, and most of them can be treated only as *termini post quos* and/ or are in uncertain association with the pottery. Seven are from Wales (Fig. 10.5b⊕: *Birm-85, -1113*; *BM-2837*; *CAR-572, -810*; *HAR-803*; *SWAN-17*). Five are from Scotland (Fig. 5c⊕: *SRR-687, SUERC-5299*; Fig. 10.5d⊕: *AA-53171*; 10. 5e⊕: *GU-7204, SUERC-5316*). The 36 from England which are used in model 1 (modelled independently in Fig. 10.5i⊕) drop to only 14 in model 2. Their low number is due to partly to a long-standing focus of interest on burials and their accoutrements, partly to the nature of contemporary settlement. The deposition of occupation material in pits became less frequent in the later 3rd millennium (cf. Garrow 2006, 138), thus reducing potential sources of securely associated artefacts and samples, especially in arable landscapes. Beaker settlements tend to survive as artefact scatters where surfaces have been covered and protected, whether beneath later earthworks, in coastal and estuarine dunes, beneath colluvium or alluvium, or beneath peat. A palaeosol remains an open context until it is sealed and may remain so for an extended period, as exemplified by the disparate radiocarbon dates from unit 8a at Brean Down, Somerset (Bell 1990, 108).

It is indeed possible to date non-funerary Beaker assemblages, given the appropriate strategy and resources. It has simply not been done often enough. The most notable success is a burnt mound at Northwold in the Norfolk Fens, in the midst of an area where Beaker settlement is recurrently preserved under peat (Bayliss *et al.* 2004). Here, stratigraphic sequence, multiple short-lived samples and Bayesian modelling have determined a use-life of *35 to 165 years*, between *2265–2165* and *2140–2065 cal BC (95% probability)*. This corresponds to the stylistically late Beaker pottery and possibly Food Vessel Urn pottery from contexts relating to the mound (Percival

2004). Figure 10.5i⊕, using the relevant dates from model 1, estimates a start date for Beaker in non-funerary contexts in England of *2490–2200 cal BC (95% probability)*, probably of *2350–2230 cal BC (68% probability)*. Like a comparable estimate from the dates used in model 2, it lies within the overall span of English Beakers (Fig. 10.5j). The jury is still out on whether there was a pre-funerary use of Beaker pottery in this country. It is noteworthy that many of the southern English non-funerary assemblages include stylistically late decorative motifs, such as infilled lozenges and triangles surrounded by reserve bands, such as are most often found on long-necked Beakers, suggesting that they were generated fairly late in the sequence.

The case is not advanced by two large, non-funerary assemblages from the henge monuments of Mount Pleasant in Dorset and Gorsey Bigbury in Somerset. In both cases, the assemblages can be described as domestic, in that they comprise sherds, lithics, animal bone, and burnt material. The problem is their genesis. Woodward (2002) argues that the typological heterogeneity of the Mount Pleasant Beaker (Longworth 1979), coupled with both varying states of preservation and purposeful, patterned deposition showing strong contrasts between different parts of the site (Thomas 1996, 205–22) point to circulation through other contexts, possibly over extended periods, before burial. In the face of these complications, the Mount Pleasant dates are not employed in the model. The much smaller henge monument at Gorsey Bigbury, Somerset, seems to reflect a simpler story. Six samples dated in the 1970s from various specific locations in the 'occupation layer' (Table 10.4⊕: BM-1086 to -1091), yielded statistically consistent results (T'=7.8; T'(5%)=11.1; ν=5), the total of over 120 fine and rusticated vessels represented by the sherds seems to be a typologically homogeneous long-necked Beaker assemblage (ApSimon *et al.* 1976), and there is reason to agree with Lewis' argument (2005, 82–3) that the material was dumped in a single event into the already partly silted monument ditch. The dates are therefore included in the overall Beaker model. Since they were measured on bulk charcoal and disarticulated bone samples, however, they provide no more than a *terminus post quem* for a typologically late assemblage.

There is a need to investigate chronological variation in the currency of Beaker pottery across Britain. This entails redressing the geographical imbalance of dates shown in Figure 10.2. The *Beaker People Project* has an important contribution to make here. It also entails the systematic, rigorous dating of contexts which do not yield such obviously suitable samples as articulated skeletons, whether these are settlements or burials in areas where bone does not survive.

Grime's Graves

The Grime's Graves flint mines lie about 12 km, say a 3–4 hour walk, east of the zone of at least formerly preserved Beaker settlement on the south-east edge of the Fenland Basin, a zone in which the Northwold burnt mound and another dated example at Feltwell Anchor (Bates & Wiltshire 2000) lay. The living sites were typically located on chalk or sandhills. Plantation Farm (Clark 1933) and Peacock's Farm (Clark & Godwin 1962), in the Cambridgeshire Fens a little to the south, are classic examples. Like the Northwold mound, these sites tend to yield stylistically late Beaker pottery, often mixed with Food Vessel Urn. While vessel form can rarely be reconstructed, decoration consistently includes reserve geometric motifs of Clarke's groups 4 and 5 (1970, 427–8), commonest on short- and long-necked Beakers (Bamford 1982). Some of the collections do, however, include a minority element which could indicate an earlier Beaker presence (eg, Healy 1996, fig. 8: P199, fig. 99: P332, fig. 100: P336).

Grime's Graves has been the subject of an extended dating programme, as part of the British Museum's research there (Ambers 1998; 2011) and is currently the subject of another, funded by English Heritage (Healy 2007). Provisional modelling of the dates available so far for over 100 antler implements and 15 bone ones from mining contexts indicates that flint was quarried and worked there between *2770–2650* and *1500–1420 cal BC (95% probability)*, probably between *2730–2670* and *1480–1440 cal BC (68% probability*, starting 100–410 *years (95% probability)*, probably 240–340 *years (68% probability)*, before Beaker pottery became current in England according to model 1 and continuing well after it had gone out of use (Fig. 10. 6). The material culture of the mines at Grime's Graves is, however, predominantly

	Model 1			Model 2		
	Start cal BC	**End cal BC**	**Duration in years**	**Start cal BC**	**End cal BC**	**Duration in years**
England						
Low-carinated	2470–2340 (95%) 2430–2360 (68%)	2040–1700 (95%) 1960–1770 (68%)	350–710 (95%) 440–630 (68%)	2470–2330 (95%) 2430–2350 (68%)	2210–2030 (95%) 2180–2120 (32%) or 2090–2040 (36%)	170–400 (95%) 220–350 (68%)
Mid-carinated	2460–2270 (95%) 2410–2300 (68%)	1950–1690 (95%) 1890–1750 (68%)	380–700 (95%) 460–620 (68%)	2440–2220 (95%) 2400–23270 (8%) or 2360–2270 (60%)	1990–1780 (95%) 1920–1830 (68%)	310–590 (95%) 380–520 (68%)
Long-necked	2340–2320 (1%) or 2310–2120 (94%) 2290–2250 (19%) or 2230–2220 (2%) or 2210–2120 (47%)	1860–1840 (1%) or 1830–1640 (94%) 1750–1680 (68%)	360–630 (95%) 440–550 (68%)	2340–2320 (1%) or 2310–2120 (94%) 2280–2250 (19%) or 2230–2220 (2%) or 2210–2160 (47%)	1940–1790 (95%) 1900–1830 (68%)	250–490 (95%) 300–410 (68%)
S-profile	2450–2290 (95%) 2410–2320 (68%)	1860–1680 (95%) 1790–1690 (68%)	490–730 (95%) 560–680 (68%)	2440–2290 (95%) 2410–2310 (68%)	1920–1770 (95%) 1890–1830 (68%)	420–620 (95%) 450–560 (68%)
Scotland						
Low-carinated	2330–2210 (95%) 2310–2230 (68%)	2180–2040 (95%) 2140–2080 (68%)	70–260 (95%) 110–210 (68%)	2330–2210 (95%) 2320–2230 (68%)	2190–2060 (95%0 2150–2090 (68%)	70–250 (95%) 110–200 (68%
Short-necked	2340–2230 (95%) 2310–2250 (68%)	2140–2020 (95%) 2130–2060 (68%)	110–300 (95%) 150–240 (68%)	2340–2230 (95%) 2320–2250 (68%)	2150–2040 (95%) 2140–2090 (68%)	110–270 (95%) 130–220 (68%)
S-profile	2310–2190 (95%) 2290–2230 968%)	2190–2040 (95%) 2160–2080 (68%)	50–240 (95%) 90–190 (68%)	2340–2240 (95%) 2320–2250 (68%)	2200–2060 (95%) 2160–2090 (68%)	40–210 (95%), 80–170 (68%)

Table 10.3: summary of results for the more frequently dated lineages

that of the insular Late Neolithic. The pottery of the deep mines, worked in the earlier part of the span, is in the Grooved Ware tradition, although in a distinctive substyle. More than a century of excavation there has yielded only two Beaker sherds, both from superficial contexts (Longworth *et al.* 1988, 15–22). Artefacts made there included discoidal knives (Saville 1981; Lech & Longworth 2000; Longworth *et al.* 2011), which are not habitually found in Beaker associations. The surrounding area and, especially, the relatively well preserved settlements of the fen edge to the west have yielded abundant Beaker pottery as well as barbed and tanged arrowheads and flint daggers, for both of which the flint mined at the site would have been an admirable raw material, but the mining area has yielded few barbed and tanged arrowheads, all from superficial contexts, and no daggers. Where there is evidence for continued use of the site in the early 2nd millennium (a prelude to extensive late 2nd millennium occupation which does not seem to have been related to mining), the associated pottery is Collared

Urn, not Beaker (Longworth *et al.* 1988, 23–4). A possible interpretation of the Beaker-free character of the site is that it continued to be worked and used in the accustomed manner by a population who asserted traditional ways and values against innovations, including the manufacture of fine objects in metal rather than flint.

This does not account for why Grime's Graves was initiated. In practical terms it was unnecessary. The surface flint of the surrounding Breckland is large, abundant, and of high quality. Local industries were predominantly made of this material, from the Palaeolithic onwards (Healy 1998). Flint mining in deep shafts runs counter to the usual pattern of later Neolithic flint procurement, which tended to take the form of an 'industrial' facies to occupation in the areas of more readily accessible deposits, whether in the Breckland itself, on the Clay-with-Flints of Cranborne Chase or the South Downs (Gardiner 1990; 1991), the dry valleys of Salisbury Plain (Richards 1990a, 158–71), or the tills of Flamborough Head (Durden 1995). The minutiae of the methods by which

Figure 10.6: The dating of mining implements from Grime's Graves in relation to two modelled currencies for Beaker pottery in England. The horizontal lines below the distributions represent 95% probability

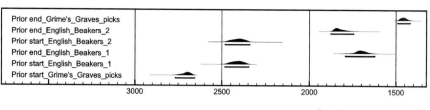

Posterior density estimate cal BC

the deep shafts were worked (Longworth & Varndell 1996) matched those practised on the South Downs 1000 years before (Barber *et al.* 1999, 38–40), and those standardised methods seem to have been introduced to the site fully developed, since, on currently available dates, the deep shafts of the east and centre, which display them, began to be worked no later than the shallower, less standardised, pits of the west and north. The recurrent symbolic aspects of mining and quarrying have been well-rehearsed (eg, Edmonds 1995, 59–66; Topping 2005). What if the inception of the complex, as well as its continuation, was a reaction to innovation? The recyclability of metals means that copper metallurgy could have been introduced into Britain before it crossed the archaeological visibility threshold. Parker Pearson has suggested that the scarcity at Durrington Walls of flint and stone axeheads and of the debitage resulting from flint axehead manufacture and maintenance, despite the massive scale of woodworking needed to build the structures, means that metal axeheads were already in use there (M. Parker Pearson, pers. comm.), perhaps in the second quarter of the 3rd millennium cal BC (although the dating programme there is in its initial stages). The suggestion is speculative; doubts may be entertained as to the efficacy of copper rather than bronze axeheads as woodworking tools; and there is the possibility of the zonation of different activities in the area of the monument. It does, however, raise the possibility that Grime's Graves, with all its anachronisms, might have not merely persisted but begun as an assertion of traditional ways and values in the face of innovations that may have been unwelcome and threatening.

Acknowledgements

Thanks are extended to the organisers of the original conference; Mike Allen for taking on the burden of editorship; Alex Bayliss for initiation into and mentoring during modelling; Peter Marshall and Stuart Needham for comment on a draft of the paper; Mike Parker Pearson, Mandy Jay and Neil Curtis for a sight of Beaker People Project results prior to publication and for permission to use selected dates; Gill Varndell, Janet Ambers and Richard Sabin for access to the Grime's Graves collections in the British and Natural History Museums; Tim Allen of Oxford Archaeology for information about results from the Eton Rowing Course; Steve Burrow for access to his compilation of radiocarbon dates from Wales and, with Ken Brassil, for information about Riversdale and permission to use the date; Seren Griffiths for information about Whitegrounds; Matt Leivers of Wessex Archaeology for permission to use the date from a grave north of Wilsford G1; David Mullin of Oxford Archaeology for permission to use two dates from Kings Hill North, Cirencester; and an anonymous referee for improvements to the end product.

Bibliography

Ambers, J.C. 1998. Dating Grime's Graves. *Radiocarbon* 40(2), 591–600

Ambers, J. 2011. The absolute chronology. In I. Longworth, G. Varndell & J. Lech, *Excavations at Grimes Graves, Norfolk, 1972–1976. Fascicule 6: Exploration and Exploration beyond the Deep Mines*. London: British Museum Press.

ApSimon, A.M., Musgrave, J.H., Sheldon, J., Tratman, E.K. & van Wijngaarden-Bakker, L.H. 1976. Gorsey Bigbury, Cheddar, Somerset: radiocarbon dating, human and animal bones, charcoals, archaeological reassessment. *Proceedings of the University of Bristol Spelaeological Society* 14, 155–83

Ashmore, P. 1999. Radiocarbon dating: avoiding errors by avoiding mixed samples. *Antiquity* 73, 124–30

Bamford, H.M. 1982. *Beaker Domestic Sites in the Fen Edge and East Anglia*. Gressenhall: East Anglian Archaeology 18

Barber, M., Field, D. & Topping, P. 1999. *The Neolithic Flint Mines of England*. Swindon: RCHME/English Heritage

Barclay, A. & Halpin, C. 1999. *Excavations at Barrow Hills, Radley, Oxfordshire. Volume I. The Neolithic and Bronze*

Age Monument Complex. Oxford: Oxford University Committee for Archaeology/Oxford Archaeological Unit

Barnatt, J. & Edmonds, M. 2002. Places apart? Caves and monuments in Neolithic and earlier Bronze Age Britain. *Cambridge Archaeological Journal* 12(1), 113–29

Bates, S. & Wiltshire, P.E.J. 2000. Excavation of a burnt mound at Feltwell Anchor, Norfolk, 1992. *Norfolk Archaeology* 43(3), 389–414

Bayes, T.R. 1763. An essay towards solving a problem in the doctrine of chances. *Philosophical Transactions of the Royal Society* 53, 370–418

Bayliss, A. & Bronk Ramsey, C. 2004. Pragmatic Bayesians: a decade integrating radiocarbon dates into chronological models. In C.E. Buck & A.R. Millard (eds), *Tools for Constructing Chronologies: Tools for Crossing Disciplinary Boundaries*, 25–41. London: Springer

Bayliss, A., Bronk Ramsey, C., Crowson, A. & McCormac, F.G. 2004. Interpreting chronology. In A. Crowson, *Hot Rocks in the Norfolk Fens: the excavation of a burnt flint mound at Northwold, 1994*–5, 28–32. Gressenhall: East Anglian Archaeology Occasional Paper 16

Bayliss, A., McAvoy, F. & Whittle, A. 2007b. The world recreated: redating Silbury Hill in its monumental landscape. *Antiquity* 81, 26–53

Bayliss, A., Whittle, A. & Wysocki, M. 2007c. Talking about my generation: the date of the West Kennet long barrow. *Cambridge Archaeological Journal* 17(1) supplement, 85–101

Bayliss, A., Bronk Ramsey, C., Plicht, J. van der & Whittle, A. 2007d. Bradshaw and Bayes: towards a timetable for the Neolithic. *Cambridge Archaeological Journal* 17(1) supplement, 1–28

Bell, M. 1990. *Brean Down. Excavations 1983–1987.* London: English Heritage Archaeological Report 15

Brindley, A.L. 2007. *The Dating of Food Vessels and Urns in Ireland. Bronze Age Studies 7.* Galway: Department of Archaeology, National University of Ireland, Galway

Bronk Ramsey, C. 1995. Radiocarbon calibration and analysis of stratigraphy: the OxCal program. *Radiocarbon*, 37(2), 425–30

Bronk Ramsey, C. 1998. Probability and dating. *Radiocarbon*, 40, 461–74

Bronk Ramsey, C, 2000. Comment on 'The Use of Bayesian Statistics for 14C dates of chronologically ordered samples: a critical analysis'. *Radiocarbon*, 42 (2) 199-202.

Bronk Ramsey, C. 2001. Development of the radiocarbon calibration program Oxcal. *Radiocarbon* 43, 355–63

Bronk Ramsey, C. 2009. Bayesian analysis of radiocarbon dates. *Radiocarbon* 51, 337–60

Buck, C.E., Cavanagh, W.G. & Litton, C.D., 1996. *Bayesian Approach to Interpreting Archaeological Data.* Chichester: Wiley

Burrow, S. this volume. A date with the Chalcolithic in Wales: a review of radiocarbon measurements for 2450–2100 cal BC. In M.J. Allen, J. Gardiner & A. Sheridan, *Is there a British Chalcolithic?: people, place and polity in the later 3rd millennium.* Oxford: Prehistoric Society Research Paper 4

Carlin, N & Brück, J. this volume. Searching for the Chalcolithic: continuity and change in the Irish Final Neolithic/Early Bronze Age. In M.J. Allen, J. Gardiner & A. Sheridan, *The British Chalcolithic: people, place and polity in the later 3rd millennium.* Oxford: Prehistoric Society Research Paper 4

Clark, J.G.D. 1933. Report on an early Bronze Age site in the south-eastern Fens. *Antiquaries Journal* 13, 266–96

Clark, J.G.D. & Godwin, H. 1962. The Neolithic in the Cambridgeshire Fens. *Antiquity* 36, 10–23

Clarke, D.L. 1970. *Beaker Pottery of Great Britain and Ireland.* Cambridge: Cambridge University Press

Cleal, R.M.J. & Walker, K.E. with Montague, R. 1995. *Stonehenge in its Landscape. Twentieth-century Excavations.* London: English Heritage Archaeological Report 10

Cunnington, M.E. 1929. *Woodhenge. A Description of the Site as Revealed by Excavations Carried out there by Mr and Mrs B.H. Cunnington, 1926–7–8. Also of Four Circles and an Earthwork Enclosure South of Woodhenge.* Devizes: George Simpson & Co.

Darvill, T. & Wainwright, G. 2009. Stonehenge excavations 2008. *Antiquaries Journal,* 89, 1–19

Durden, T. 1995. The production of specialised flintwork in the later Neolithic: a case study form the Yorkshire Wolds. *Proceeding of the Prehistoric Society* 61, 409–32

Edmonds, M. 1995. *Stone Tools and Society: working stone in Neolithic and Bronze Age Britain.* London: Batsford

Evans, C. 2009. *Fengate Revisited. Further Fen-edge Excavations, Bronze Age Fieldsystems and Settlement and the Wyman Abbott/Leeds Archives.* Cambridge: Cambridge Archaeological Unit Landscape Archives Series Historiography & Fieldwork 1

French, C., Lewis, H., Allen, M.J., Green, M., Scaife, R. & Gardiner, J. 2007. *Prehistoric Landscape Development and Human Impact in the Upper Allen Valley, Cranborne Chase, Dorset.* Cambridge: McDonald Institute for Archaeological Research

Gardiner, J., 1990. Flint procurement and Neolithic axe production on the South Downs: a re-assessment. *Oxford Journal of Archaeology* 9(2), 119–40

Gardiner, J.P. 1991. The [later Neolithic] flint industries of the study area. In J.C. Barrett, R. Bradley & M. Green, *Landscape, Monuments and Society. The Prehistory of Cranborne Chase*, 59–69, Cambridge: Cambridge University Press

Garrow, D. 2006. *Pits, Settlement and Deposition during the Neolithic and Early Bronze Age in East Anglia.* Oxford: British Archaeological Report 414

Garwood, P. 2007a. Before the hills in order stood: chronology, time and history in the interpretation of early Bronze age round barrows. In J. Last (ed.), *Beyond the Grave. New Perspectives on Barrows*, 30–52. Oxford: Oxbow Books

Garwood, P. 2007b. Vital resources, ideal images and virtual lives: children in Early Bronze Age funerary ritual. In S. Crawford & G. Shepherd (eds), *Children, Childhood and Society*, 63–82. Oxford: British Archaeological Report S1696/IAA Multidisciplinary Seminar Series 1

Gibson, A. 2007. A Beaker veneer? Some evidence from the burial record. In M. Larsson & M. Parker Pearson (eds), *From Stonehenge to the Baltic. Living with Cultural Diversity in the Third Millennium BC*, 47–64. Oxford: British Archaeological Report S1692

Harding, J. 2003. *The Henge Monuments of the British Isles.* Stroud: Tempus

Harding, J. & Healy, F. 2007. *The Raunds Area Project: a Neolithic and Bronze Age Landscape in Northamptonshire.* Swindon: English Heritage

Healy, F. 1996. *The Fenland Project Number 11: The Wissey Embayment: evidence for pre-Iron Age settlement accumulated prior to the Fenland Project*. Gressenhall: East Anglian Archaeology 78

Healy, F. 1997. Site 3. Flagstones. In R.J.C. Smith, F. Healy, M.J. Allen, E.L. Morris, I. Barnes, & P.J. Woodward, *Excavations along the Route of the Dorchester By-pass, Dorset, 1986–8*, 27–48. Salisbury: Wessex Archaeology Report 11

Healy, F. 1998. The surface of the Breckland. In N. Ashton, F. Healy & P. Pettitt (eds), *Stone Age Archaeology. Essays in Honour of John Wymer*, 225–35. Oxford: Oxbow Monograph 102

Healy, F. 2007. *Dating Grime's Graves Project Proposal*. Project Design approved by English Heritage

Kinnes, I. 1979. *Round Barrows and Ring-ditches in the British Neolithic*. London: British Museum Occasional Paper 7

Kinnes, I., Gibson, A., Ambers, J., Bowman, S., Leese, M. & Boast, R. 1991. Radiocarbon dating and British Beakers: the British Museum programme. *Scottish Archaeological Review* 8, 35–68

Lech, J. & Longworth, I. 2000. Kopalnia krzemienia Grimes Graves w świetle nowych badań [The Grimes Graves flint mine site in the light of new research]. *Przegląd Archeologiczny* 40, 19–73 [In Polish with English summary and captions]

Lewis, J. 2005. *Monuments, Ritual and Regionality: the Neolithic of Northern Somerset*. Oxford: British Archaeological Report 401

Longworth, I.H. 1979. The Neolithic and Bronze Age pottery. In Wainwright 1979, 75–124

Longworth, I., Ellison, A. & Rigby, V. 1988. *Excavations at Grimes Graves Norfolk 1972–1976. Fascicule 2. The Neolithic, Bronze Age and Later Pottery*. London: British Museum Press

Longworth, I. & Varndell, G. 1996. *Excavations at Grimes Graves Norfolk 1972–1976. Fascicule 5. Mining in the Deeper Mines*. London: British Museum Press

Longworth, I., Varndell, G. & Lech, J. 2011. *Excavations at Grimes Graves, Norfolk, 1972–1976. Fascicule 6: Exploration and Exploration beyond the Deep Mines*. London: British Museum Press

Loveday, R., Gibson, A., Marshall, P.D., Bayliss, A., Bronk Ramsey, C. & Plicht, J. van der 2007. The antler maceheads dating project. *Proceedings of the Prehistoric Society* 73, 381–92

Manby, T.G. 2004. Food Vessels with handles. In A. Gibson & A. Sheridan (eds), *From Sickles to Circles. Britain and Ireland at the Time of Stonehenge*, 215–42. Stroud: Tempus

Manby, T.G., Moorhouse, S. & Ottaway, P. 2003. *The Archaeology of Yorkshire: an assessment at the beginning of the 21st century*. Leeds: Yorkshire Archaeological Society

Mant, A.K. 1987. Knowledge acquired from post-War exhumations. In A. Boddington, A.N. Garland & R.C. Janaway (eds), *Death, Decay, and Reconstruction. Approaches to Archaeology and Forensic Science*, 65–80. Manchester: Manchester University Press

Mook, W.G. 1986. Business Meeting: recommendations/resolutions adopted by the twelfth international radiocarbon conference. *Radiocarbon* 28, 799

Needham, S. 2005. Transforming Beaker culture in north-west Europe; processes of fusion and fission. *Proceedings of the Prehistoric Society* 71, 171–217

Needham, S. this volume. Case and place for the British Chalcolithic. In M.J. Allen, J. Gardiner & A. Sheridan, *Is There a British Chalcolithic?: people, place and polity in the later 3rd millennium*. Oxford: Prehistoric Society Research Paper 4

Needham, S. Parker Pearson, M., Tyler, A., Richards, M. & Jay, M. 2010. A first 'Wessex 1' date from Wessex. *Antiquity* 84(324), 363–73

Parker Pearson, M., Cleal, R., Marshall, P., Needham, S., Pollard, J., Richards, C., Ruggles, C., Sheridan, A., Thomas, J., Tilley, C., Welham, K., Chamberlain, A., Chenery, C., Evans, J., Knüsel, C., Linford, N., Martin, L., Montgomery, J., Payne, A. & Richards, M. 2007. The age of Stonehenge. *Antiquity* 81(313), 617–39

Parker Pearson, M., Chamberlain, A., Jay, M., Marshall, P., Pollard, J., Richards, C., Thomas, J., Tilley, C. & Welham, K. 2009. Who was buried at Stonehenge? *Antiquity* 83, 23–39

Percival, S., 2004. Pottery. In A. Crowson, *Hot Rocks in the Norfolk Fens: the Excavation of a Burnt Flint mound at Northwold, 1994–5*, 18–22. Gressenhall: East Anglian Archaeology Occaional Paper 16

Reimer P.J., Baillie M.G.L., Bard, E., Bayliss, A., Beck, J.W., Bertrand, C., Blackwell, P.G., Buck, C.E., Burr, G., Cutler, K.B, Damon, P.E., Edwards, R.L., Fairbanks, R.G., Friedrich, M., Guilderson, T.P., Hughen, K.A., Kromer, B., McCormac, F.G., Manning, S., Bronk Ramsey, C., Reimer, R.W., Remmele, S., Southon, J.R., Stuiver, M., Talamo, S., Taylor, F.W., Plicht, J. van der & Weyhenmeyer C.E. 2004. Intcal04 terrestrial radiocarbon age calibration, 0–26 cal. kyr BP. *Radiocarbon* 46, 1029–58

Richards, J.C. 1990a. *The Stonehenge Environs Project*. London: English Heritage Archaeological Report 16

Ritchie, J.N.G. & Crawford, J. 1978. Excavations at Sorisdale and Killunaig, Coll. *Proceedings of the Society of Antiquaries of Scotland* 109, 75–84.

Saville, A., 1981. *Grimes Graves, Norfolk, Excavations 1971–72, Volume 2: The Flint Assemblage*. London: Department of the Environment Archaeological Report 11

Shepherd, I.A.G. 1982. The artefacts, 99–113. In T. Watkins, The excavation of an early Bronze Age cemetery at Barns Farm, Dalgety, Fife. *Proceedings of the Society of Antiquaries of Scotland* 112, 48–141

Sheridan, A. 2004. Scottish Food Vessels chronology revisited. In A. Gibson & A. Sheridan (eds), *From Sickles to Circles. Britain and Ireland at the Time of Stonehenge*, 243–67. Stroud: Tempus

Sheridan, A. 2007. Scottish Beaker dates: the good, the bad and the ugly. In M. Larsson & M. Parker Pearson (eds), *From Stonehenge to the Baltic. Living with Cultural Diversity in the Third Millennium BC*, 91–123. Oxford: British Archaeological Report S1692

Sheridan, A. 2008. Upper Largie and Dutch-Scottish connections during the Beaker period. In H. Fokkens, B.J. Coles, A.L. van Gijn, J.P. Kleijne, H.H. Ponjee & C.G. Slappendel (eds), *Between Foraging and Farming: an extended broad spectrum, of papers presented to Leendert Louwe Kooijmans*, 247–60. Leiden: *Analecta Praehistorica Leidensia* 40

Steier, P. & Rom, W. 2000. The use of Bayesian statistics for 14C dates of chronologically ordered samples: a critical analysis. *Radiocarbon* 42(2), 183–98

Stuiver, M. & Kra, R.S. 1986. Editorial comment. *Radiocarbon* 28(2B), ii

Stuiver, M. & Polach, H.A. 1977. Reporting of ^{14}C data. *Radiocarbon* 19, 355–63

Stuiver, M. & Reimer, P.J. 1986. A computer program for radiocarbon age calculation. *Radiocarbon* 28, 1022–30

Stuiver, M. & Reimer, P.J. 1993. Extended ^{14}C data base and revised CALIB 3.0 ^{14}C age calibration program. *Radiocarbon* 35, 215–30

Thomas, J. 1996. *Time, Culture and Identity. An Interpretive Archaeology.* London & New York: Routledge

Topping, P. 2005. Shaft 27 revisited: an ethnography of Neolithic flint extraction. In P. Topping & M. Lynott (eds), *The Cultural Landscape of Prehistoric Mines*, 63–93. Oxford: Oxbow Books

Waddell, J. 1990. *The Bronze Age Burials of Ireland.* Galway: Galway University Press

Wainwright, G. J. 1979. *Mount Pleasant, Dorset: Excavations 1970–1971.* London: Report of the Research Committee of the Society of Antiquaries of London 37

Ward, G.K. & Wilson, S.R. 1978. Procedures for comparing and combining radiocarbon age determinations: a critique. *Archaeometry* 20, 19–31

Watts, D.J. 1989. Infant burials and Romano-British Christianity. *Archaeological Journal* 146, 372–83

Woodward, A. 2002. Beads and Beakers: heirlooms and relics in the British Early Bronze Age. *Antiquity* 76(294), 1040–7

Wymer, J.J. 1966. Excavations of the Lambourn long barrow. *Berkshire Archaeological Journal* 62, 1–16

11

Is there a Scottish Chalcolithic?

Ian Shepherd†[1]

This brief contribution discusses the concept of a Scottish Chalcolithic in terms of the available evidence from metalwork and early Beaker graves. It is argued that a Chalcolithic phase can be demonstrated to have existed in Scotland; it is characterised as/subsumed within an 'Early Beaker' identity.

Colin Burgess, in introducing the second edition of his *Age of Stonehenge*, argued: '… just about everyone else has one [a Copper Age], and we should too' (Burgess 2001). This author shares that view and will argue here that, although Scotland cannot be said to possess the spectacular or obvious characteristics of the mainland European Chalcolithic (as discussed elsewhere in this volume), there *was* a Scottish Chalcolithic, however different and strange it may appear by comparison with its continental counterparts. It is most clearly expressed in terms of the two principal novelties of the third quarter of the 3rd millennium BC in Scotland (as elsewhere in Britain), namely metalwork and early Beaker graves (with non-funerary Beakers adding to the picture). As will be argued below, these novelties are linked and they relate to the introduction of objects, ideas, practices, and people from the continent just after the middle of the 3rd millennium. Connections with the Lower Rhine appear to be strong, although links with Ireland – with its own connections

with the Atlantic copper- and Beaker-using world – also form an important element in defining the Scottish Chalcolithic.

Metalwork

For any consideration of the metalwork that serves to define a Chalcolithic in Scotland we need look no further than Brendan O'Connor's magisterial contribution to the volume dedicated to Stuart Piggott (O'Connor 2004), while also acknowledging the debt we owe to Stuart Piggott himself in his 'Abercromby and after' paper (Piggott 1963), to John Coles for his synthesis of the evidence available in the 1960s (Coles 1969), and to Stuart Needham for his discussion of Scottish copper axeheads and halberds (Needham 2004; see also Needham 2011a and 2011b for recent relevant discussion of tanged blades and gold basket-shaped ornaments).

In reviewing the evidence for the earliest Scottish metalwork and the advances made in understanding it since Coles's publication,

O'Connor emphasised that there is a strong (albeit numerically small) representation of copper objects that can be ascribed to the period between the 25th century BC, when metal use started in Britain, and the 22nd century, when the Migdale-Marnoch bronzeworking tradition emerged in north-east Scotland (*ibid.*; cf. Needham 2004). These copper objects (Figs 11.1–11.3) comprise blades, broad-butted flat axeheads, halberds, awls, and a remarkable pair of neck rings from Lumphanan (but see below regarding neck rings). The copper rivets in the wristguards from Culduthel, Highland, and Borrowstone cist 6, Aberdeenshire, may also be noted. There are also some sheet gold objects (Fig. 11.4) – namely basket-shaped ornaments, lunulae, and wristguard rivet caps – although these are rarer than the copper objects. These objects will not all have appeared at the same time: the halberds, lunulae, large basket-shaped ornament from Orbliston, and gold rivet caps probably appeared some time after the earliest blades, for example. Furthermore, not all of the copper and gold items necessarily belong to the pre-22nd century period, as it is clear from Needham's discussion of halberds (Needham 2004, 231; cf. O'Flaherty 2007, where a brief currency for these objects within the time bracket 2300–2100 BC is proposed). This is also clear from the radiocarbon date associated with the copper awl from Doons Law, Scottish Borders (namely 3645±65 BP, AA-29066, 2200–1780 cal BC at 2σ, using OxCal 4.1: Sheridan 2007, 114), and the radiocarbon dates associated with the aforementioned copper wristguard rivets both have calibrated ranges that extend past 2200 BC at the 95% probability level (see Curtis & Wilkin this volume for details).

It is not proposed to discuss all the artefact types in detail here, since most have been admirably dealt with by O'Connor and Needham in their 2004 publications (with the latter including distribution maps of the axeheads and halberds). Rather, the main point to be emphasised is that these copper and gold objects suggest mixed origins and influences for the Scottish Chalcolithic, and these can be traced both in the design of the objects and (regarding the copper objects, at least) in the likely source areas for the metal. Thus, the absolute dominance of Ross Island copper among the analysed examples of copper artefacts reflects the strong links with

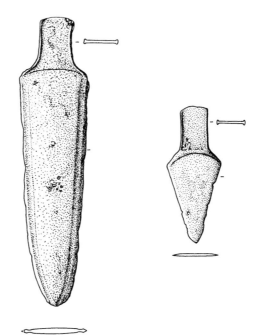

Figure 11.1 Tanged copper blades. Left: East Pitdoulsie, Auchterless, length 227 mm; Right: Inverurie, length 108 mm, both Aberdeenshire. Reproduced by kind permission of Sabine Gerloff

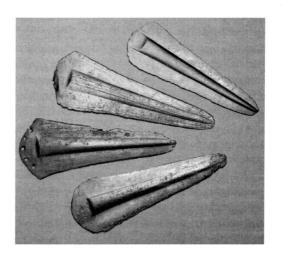

Figure 11.2: Hoard of copper halberds, Mains of Achingoul, Aberdeenshire, lengths 256–293 mm. Photo: National Museums Scotland

Ireland, as does the use of broad-butted flat axeheads and halberds, which numerically predominate in Ireland. (The ultimate origin for the halberds may well have lain further south in Atlantic Europe, but the proximate area of origin/inspiration for the Scottish examples was probably Ireland.) Similarly, given the distribution pattern of gold lunulae (Taylor 1980, map 1), it seems very likely that their use was adopted from Ireland, whether or not the lunulae themselves had been made there. (The Scottish examples, like most of the others found outside of Ireland, are of Taylor's 'Provincial' style, slightly less skilfully executed than the 'Classical' examples found in Ireland; see Wallace 1987.)

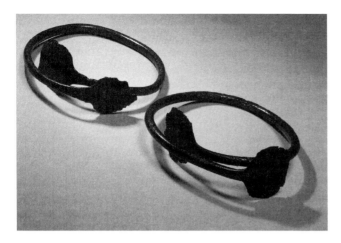

Figure 11.3: Pair of copper neck rings from Lumphanan, Aberdeenshire. Photo: National Museums Scotland

Some objects and metal types, however, suggest other areas of origin and inspiration and this is true of the copper blades found in Scotland, some of which are likely to have been among the earliest metal objects used here, to judge from dated *comparanda* in England (including those found with the Amesbury Archer: Needham 2011a; see also Needham this volume). Just seven blades are known from Scotland, all definitely or probably tanged; a possible eighth example may be represented at Brownhill, Aberdeenshire, where the remains of 'a short bronze [*sic*] knife-dagger' are reported to have been found in a cist, along with sherds of cord-decorated pottery (Shepherd 1986, 8), but the whereabouts of these finds are unknown. The examples from East Pitdoulsie, Auchterless, Aberdeenshire (Fig. 11.1, left), from Glenluce, Dumfries & Galloway (Gerloff 1975, pl. 1.8), and from 'Scotland' (*ibid.*, pl. 2.17A) had been over 150 mm long while those from Inverurie, Aberdeenshire (Fig. 11.1, right), and Glenforsa, Mull (*ibid.*, pl. 2.14), had been shorter than that. A second example from Mull, from Salen (Duns 1883), and another from Tavelty, Aberdeenshire (Ralston 1996, illus. 13), are both fragmentary and their original length cannot be estimated. Two of the blades had had riveted tangs. While Sabine Gerloff has described both the large and small blades as daggers (Gerloff 1975), the latter are more likely to have been knives and, as Humphrey Case has pointed out (Case 2004), the thinness and lingulate blade shape of the former rules out their use as stabbing daggers, suggesting instead their use as slashing knives, perhaps for delivering the *coup de grâce* to a hunted animal

or a human combatant. The find circumstances of four of the blades are unknown, but both the Mull examples and the fragment from Tavelty come from cists, with the Salen example associated with an All Over Cord (AOC) Beaker (Clarke 1970, 514), the Glenforsa example with one short-necked Beaker and one long-necked Beaker (plus a wristguard: *ibid.*, 362), and the Tavelty example with a short-necked Beaker (Ralston 1996). Some time depth in the use of these blades is suggested by the date for the skeleton associated with the Tavelty blade (3710±70 BP, GU-2169, 2330–1900 cal BC: Sheridan 2007, 114). However, it should be noted that the geographical distribution of some of these blades corresponds closely with areas of early Beaker use, especially in the Hebrides and in north-east Scotland (eg, around Auchterless: Shepherd 1986, 8).

In his recent discussion of tanged copper blades, Needham has underlined the international uniformity of Bell Beaker tanged copper blades across the western European area of Bell Beaker use, and the fact that they are most common in Iberia (Needham 2011a, 124). Furthermore, in an earlier publication, he had pointed out that the Auchterless and Inverurie blades are of Bell Beaker metal (like three Scottish halberds and one flat axehead: Needham 2002, 128). The question of the sources of the copper is also discussed in that paper, with Spain being the suggested origin for the high-nickel variant of Bell Beaker metal; the idea that south-west England could be the (or a) source for the low-nickel variant is taken up in Peter Bray's contribution to this volume. Clearly, Bell Beaker metal and the objects made from it travelled around over considerable distances; for present purposes it should be pointed out that one of the candidate areas whence the Auchterless and Inverurie blades could have come is the Netherlands, where clear parallels for the former are known from Exloo and Ginkelse Heide, Ede (Lanting & van der Waals 1976, fig. 25; Cowie 1988; Needham 2011a, 124).

As has been argued previously (Shepherd 1986, 9), a strong link with the Netherlands is also suggested by the pair of copper neck rings (or diadems) with spade-shaped terminals from Lumphanan, Aberdeenshire (Fig. 11.3), which find an echo in the spatulate-ended gold object from Bennekom (Clarke *et al.* 1985, fig. 7.33). The latter was found with a Veluwe type beaker, a style of Beaker which is believed to have emerged in the Netherlands around 2200 BC (Butler & Fokkens 2005, 372) and whose early examples are comparable with some short-necked Beakers in north-east Scotland. It may therefore be that the Lumphanan rings (and perhaps also the similar example from Yarnton, Oxfordshire: Clarke *et al.* 1985, fig. 7.24) were not used before bronze had started to be used. While not all the *comparanda* are from the Netherlands – other examples of gold, suspected to be unfinished lunulae, are known from Arlon in Luxemburg (*ibid.*, 307) and Kerivoa, Brittany (in this case, along with lunulae: Taylor 1980, pl. 16) – nevertheless it is this author's opinion that there had been strong links between Scotland and the Netherlands, both at the beginning of the Chalcolithic and during subsequent centuries, extending into the Early Bronze Age. The nature of these links will be explored below.

Early Beaker graves

A Dutch connection for the users of (at least some) early Beaker graves in Scotland has long been claimed, with particularly strong evidence emerging from the Dutch-style grave with Dutch-style Beaker (and other grave goods) at Newmill, Perth and Kinross (Fig. 11.5; Watkins & Shepherd 1980). This suggestion has been taken up by Sheridan in her report on the recently-discovered early Beaker grave at Upper Largie and its *comparanda* (Sheridan 2008; Cook *et al.* 2010), and is discussed further by Harry Fokkens in this volume. It is therefore not intended to discuss the evidence in detail here, or to enter into debate about the closeness of the Dutch parallels. Suffice it to note that these earliest Beaker graves do not feature stone cists, but rather pits, with

the deceased probably or definitely being interred in a wooden coffin or chamber that constitutes the forerunner of the stone cist. (The example from Upper Largie may well have been rectangular and plank-built; that from Newmill seems to have been U-sectioned). The alien nature of these graves within a Late

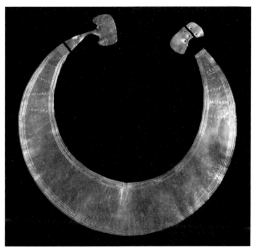
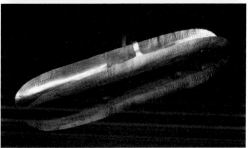

Figure 11.4: Gold lunula (top) and one of a pair of large (and typologically late) basket-shaped gold ornaments (bottom), from a possible grave at Orbliston, Moray. Photo: National Museums Scotland

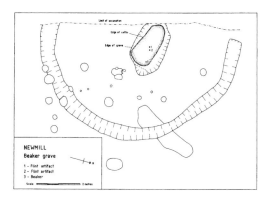

Figure 11.5: Dutch-style grave (left) and grave goods (right) from Newmill, Perth & Kinross. Plan from Watkins & Shepherd 1980, reproduced by courtesy of the Society of Antiquaries of Scotland; photo: National Museums Scotland

Figure 11.6:
Distribution of definite
and possible early Beaker
graves, excluding those
featuring stone cists. Key:
1. Beechwood Park,
Inverness, Highland;
2. Barflat, Rhynie,
Aberdeenshire;
3. Balnahanaid, Perth
& Kinross; 4. Newmill,
Perth & Kinross;
5. Bathgate (× 2), West
Lothian;
6. Biggar Common,
South Lanarkshire;
7. Upper Largie, Argyll
& Bute; 8. Sorisdale,
Coll. 9. Broadford, Skye,
Inverness Map prepared
by Georgina Brown

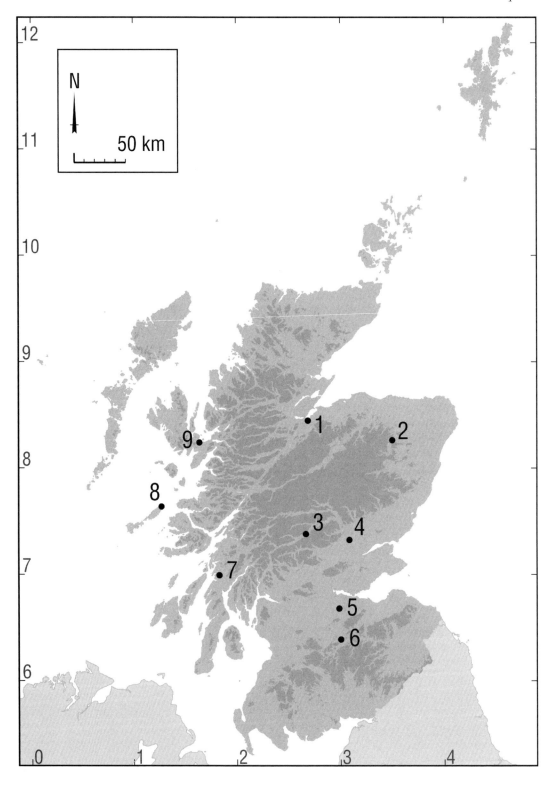

Neolithic Scottish milieu is clear, and the isotopic analysis of the skeletal remains from the Sorisdale individual (Sheridan 2008, 254) has suggested that we are indeed dealing with an 'isotopic alien', with the Netherlands being one possible area of origin on geochemical grounds.

The geographical spread of these few graves across Scotland is fairly wide (Fig. 11.6), with examples from north-east Scotland (at Beechwood Park, Inverness, Highland: Suddaby & Sheridan 2006, and Barflat, Rhynie, Aberdeenshire: Sheridan 2008, 256–7); from southern Scotland (at Biggar Common, South Lanarkshire: Johnston 1997; Sheridan 2008, fig. 21.9.2) and from west Scotland (Upper Largie) and the Hebrides (Sorisdale: Ritchie & Crawford 1978; Sheridan 2008, fig. 21.9.3). A possible new example has recently been excavated at Broadford on Skye (inf. Steven Birch and Alison Sheridan). Further probable and possible examples include the two low-carinated AOC Beakers found in a sand quarry at Bathgate, West Lothian (Mann 1906, 369–71; Sheridan 2008, fig. 21.10.3), and the small, low-carinated, All Over comb-impressed Beaker found at Balnahanaid below Ben Lawers, near the northern shore of Loch Tay (Turner 1999 and inf. Alison Sheridan). That a switch to using stone cists occurred early in the Chalcolithic is suggested by the aforementioned find of a small AOC Beaker along with fragments of a copper blade at Salen, Mull (Duns 1883, 84), and by Beaker cists that have produced radiocarbon dates between 3900 and 3800 BP, including one with a low-carinated AOC Beaker and early-style wristguard from Dornoch Nursery, Highland (Ashmore 1989; Sheridan 2007, appx 1 and see Curtis & Wilkin this volume).

Discussion

Thirty-five years ago, Graham Ritchie and this author began a paper discussing south-west Scottish Beakers (Ritchie & Shepherd 1973) with the following quotation from Margaret Crichton Mitchell (Mitchell 1934, 161):

> 'The beaker ceramic on the west owes its provenance to maritime enterprise. The small number of the examples and their sporadic distribution over a relatively wide area are additional proof of the character of this movement. On the west the beaker folk were explorers. They did not come to colonise or settle, they came in a spirit of curiosity which, though it meant no cultural supremacy, is a notable commentary upon a type of migratory spread which is almost unique in prehistory'.

Such a view, of immigration from the continent being responsible for the appearance of Beaker pottery and associated novelties (including metal-using) to Britain and Ireland, was to fall out of favour for many years (eg, Burgess & Shennan 1976). However, with the relatively recent application of isotopic analysis and the discovery that the 'Amesbury Archer' in Wiltshire is an indubitable example of a continental immigrant (Fitzpatrick 2011), the debate about Beaker immigration has been re-ignited. Given the broad spread of the early Beaker graves and metalwork (and indeed of early Beakers in general in Scotland: Clarke 1970, maps 1–3), the Scottish evidence does indeed support the idea of some immigration from the continent, albeit small in scale. The strong indications of a lower Rhine link – which includes the sharing of orientation patterns in graves (A. Sheperd this volume) – suggest to this author that many or most of Scotland's earliest users of Beakers, metal, and Beaker-style funerary practices may well have originated in or around the Netherlands. Furthermore, if this is correct, then the route of their spread around Scotland could have included a westwards, Perthshire–Argyll axis. The use of Strathearn as one route westwards is suggested by the Newmill grave mentioned above, and also by finds of low-carinated AOC Beaker pottery at Forteviot, a few kilometres along the Strath (Brophy & Noble 2011). An alternative or additional route, along Loch Tay, is suggested by the Balnahanaid find mentioned above. However, as Humphrey Case has pointed out (Case 2001), as far as western Scotland is concerned we also have to bear in mind the possibility of an additional, northwards movement, along the Atlantic façade.

Why did these people come to Scotland? One obvious possible reason is that they were seeking sources of copper (as are known to exist in Kilmartin Glen, where Upper Largie is located), and this would make sense if we are dealing with Dutch metalworkers, since there were no indigenous sources of metal in the Lower Rhine even though metal was being worked there. However, there is no evidence that any of the Scottish copper sources were actually exploited at this time, in contrast to south-west Ireland where the opening of the Ross Island copper mine by Beaker users is beyond question (O'Brien 2004). If the individuals in the early Beaker graves had not been metal prospectors, then an alternative possibility is that they might have been undertaking the kind of heroic, long-distance journey that Laure Salanova has proposed to account for some Bell Beaker graves on the continent (Salanova 2007). Whatever the reasons for the initial arrival of our putative immigrants from the Lower Rhine, the Scottish evidence suggests that they and their descendants (who will, no doubt, have included members of the indigenous population) established links with early metal users in Ireland, perhaps using pre-existing channels of contact that had existed throughout the Neolithic. Furthermore, the connections with the Lower Rhine seem to have continued, or been renewed, over several centuries – at least as far as north-east Scotland was concerned (and probably also elsewhere in northern Britain, if the adoption of battle axeheads as a prestige object can be attributed to such a link). This is suggested by the Lumphanan rings, and by the stylistic similarities between some short-necked Beakers in north-east Scotland with early Veluwe Beakers in the Netherlands (as discussed in Shepherd 1986). Indeed, if the nature of the initial and subsequent link was connected with Dutch metalworkers' interest in Scotland, then might the concentration of early metal finds in north-east Scotland be linked with the subsequent emergence of the Migdale-Marnoch bronzeworking 'industry' (cf. Needham 2004)? This is indeed a possibility.

To conclude, it does indeed seem that Scotland had 'a Chalcolithic', if we define that period primarily in terms of the use of metal other than bronze. The evidence for pre-'fission horizon' activity (to use Needham's 2005 term to describe the widespread uptake of, and diversification in, the use of Beaker pottery and other novelties) may be sparse, but it is growing, and the task for the future will be to explore further its nature and external connections. One avenue for fruitful collaboration will be a more systematic examination of the evidence for links with the Netherlands, and it is hoped that the warm relations with Dutch colleagues that have been enjoyed in the past will continue, with new generations of scholars.

Endnote

1   This paper has been produced from the notes made by Ian to accompany his Powerpoint presentation at the Bournemouth Chalcolithic conference. He had begun to develop those notes into this paper and, after his untimely death in May 2009, the task was completed by his wife, Lekky Shepherd, and by Alison Sheridan. Some relevant information obtained since 2009 has been included, since this accords with Ian's practice of staying abreast of recent developments.

Acknowledgements

Thanks are expressed to the copyright holders for permission to reproduce the images here, to Jeff Sanders for his assistance, and to Georgina Brown for creating the map in Fig. 11.6.

Bibliography

Allen, M.J., Gardiner, J. & Sheridan, A. (eds), 2012. *Is There a British Chalcolithic? Place, people and polity in the later 3rd millennium*. Oxford: Prehistoric Society Research Paper 4

Ashmore, P.J. 1989. Excavation of a beaker cist at Dornoch Nursery, Sutherland. *Proceedings of the Society of Antiquaries of Scotland* 119, 63–71

Bray, P. this volume. Before $_{29}$Cu became copper: tracing the recognition and invention of metalleity in Britain and Ireland during the 3rd millennium BC. In Allen *et al.* (eds)

Brophy, K. & Noble, G. 2011. From Beakers to daggers: Bronze Age funeral practice at Forteviot. *PAST* 67, 1–3

Burgess, C. 2001 *The Age of Stonehenge* (2nd edn). London: Phoenix Press

Burgess, C. & Shennan, S.J. 1976. The Beaker phenomenon: some suggestions. In C. Burgess & R. Miket (eds), *Settlement and Economy in the Third and Second Millennia BC*, 309–31. Oxford: British Archaeological Report 33

Butler, J. & Fokkens, H. 2005. From stone to bronze: technology and material culture. In L.P. Louwe Kooijmans, P.W. van den Broeke, H. Fokkens & A.L. van Gijn (eds), *The Prehistory of the Netherlands*, 371–99. Amsterdam: Amsterdam University Press

Case, H.J. 2001. The Beaker culture in Britain and Ireland: groups, European contacts and chronology. In F. Nicolis (ed.), *Bell Beakers Today. Pottery, People, Culture, Symbols in Prehistoric Europe*, 361–77. Trento: Ufficio Beni Archeologici

Case, H.J. 2004. Bell Beaker and Corded Ware culture burial associations: a bottom-up rather than top-down approach. In A.M. Gibson & J.A. Sheridan (eds), *From Sickles to Circles: Britain and Ireland at the time of Stonehenge*, 201–14. Stroud: Tempus

Clarke, D.L. 1970. *Beaker Pottery of Great Britain and Ireland*. Cambridge: Cambridge University Press

Clarke, D.V., Cowie, T.G. & Foxon, A. 1985. *Symbols of Power at the Time of Stonehenge*. Edinburgh: Her Majesty's Stationery Office

Coles, J.M. 1969. Scottish Early Bronze Age metalwork. *Proceedings of the Society of Antiquaries of Scotland* 101, 1–110

Cook, M., Ellis, C. & Sheridan, J.A. 2010. Excavations at Upper Largie Quarry, Argyll & Bute, Scotland: new light on the prehistoric ritual landscape of the Kilmartin Glen. *Proceedings of the Prehistoric Society* 76, 165–212

Cowie, T.G. 1988. *Magic Metal: early metalworkers in the north-east*. Aberdeen: Anthropological Museum, University of Aberdeen

Curtis, N. & Wilkin N. this volume. The regionality of

Beakers and bodies in north-east Scotland: creating a Chalcolithic. In Allen *et al.* (eds)

Duns, J. 1883. Notes on North Mull. *Proceedings of the Society of Antiquaries of Scotland* 17, 79–89

Fitzpatrick, A.P. 2011. *The Amesbury Archer and the Boscombe Bowmen. Early Beaker Burials at Boscombe Down, Amesbury, Wiltshire, Great Britain.* Salisbury: Wessex Archaeology Report 27

Fokkens, H. this volume. Dutchmen on the move? A discussion of the adoption of the beaker package. In Allen *et al.* (eds)

Gerloff, S. 1975. *The Early Bronze Age Daggers in Great Britain and a reconsideration of the Wessex Culture.* Munich: Prähistorische Bronzefunde 6(2)

Johnston, D.A. 1997. Biggar Common 1987–93: an early prehistoric funerary and domestic landscape in Clydesdale, South Lanarkshire. *Proceedings of the Society of Antiquaries of Scotland* 127, 185–253

Lanting, J.N. & Waals, J.D. van der 1976. Beaker culture relations in the Lower Rhine basin. In J.N. Lanting & J.D. van der Waals (eds), *Glockenbechersymposion Oberried 1974,* 1–80. Bussum/Haarlem: Fibula-van Dishoeck

Mann, L. McL. 1906. Notes on (1) A drinking-cup urn found at Bathgate… *Proceedings of the Society of Antiquaries of Scotland* 40, 369–402

Mitchell. M.C. 1934. A new analysis of the Early Bronze Age beaker pottery of Scotland. *Proceedings of the Society of Antiquaries of Scotland* 68, 132–89

Needham, S.P. 2002. Analytical implications for Beaker metallurgy in north-west Europe. In M. Bartelheim, E. Pernicka & R. Krause (eds), *Die Anfänge der Metallurgie im den alten Welt,* 99–133. Rahden: Verlag Marie Leidorf GmbH

Needham, S.P. 2004. Migdale-Marnoch: sunburst of Scottish metallurgy. In I.A.G. Shepherd & G.J. Barclay (eds), *Scotland in Ancient Europe: the Neolithic and Early Bronze Age of Scotland in their European context,* 217–45. Edinburgh: Society of Antiquaries of Scotland

Needham, S.P. 2005. Transforming Beaker culture in north-west Europe; processes of fusion and fission. *Proceedings of the Prehistoric Society* 71, 171–217

Needham, S.P. 2011a. Copper dagger and knives. In Fitzpatrick 2011, 120–7

Needham, S.P. 2011b. Gold basket-shaped ornaments from Graves 1291 (Amesbury Archer) and 1236. In Fitzpatrick 2011, 129–38

Needham, S.P. this volume. Case and place for the British Chalcolithic. In Allen *et al.* (eds)

O'Brien, W. 2004. *Ross Island. Mining, Metal and Society in Early Ireland.* Galway: National University of Ireland, Galway. Bronze Age Studies 6

O'Connor, B.J. 2004. The earliest Scottish metalwork since Coles. In I.A.G. Shepherd & G.J. Barclay (eds), *Scotland in Ancient Europe: the Neolithic and Early Bronze Age of Scotland in their European context,* 205–16. Edinburgh: Society of Antiquaries of Scotland

O'Flaherty, B. 2007. A weapon of choice – experiments with a replica Early Bronze Age Irish halberd. *Antiquity* 81, 423–34

Piggott, S. 1963. Abercromby and after: the Beaker cultures of Britain re-examined. In I.Ll. Foster & L. Alcock (eds), *Culture and Environment. Essays in Honour of Sir Cyril Fox,* 53–92. London: Routledge & Kegan Paul

Ralston, I. 1996. Four short cists from north-east Scotland and Easter Ross. *Proceedings of the Society of Antiquaries of Scotland,* 126, 121–55

Ritchie, J.N.G. & Crawford, J. 1978. Recent work on Coll and Skye: (i) Excavations at Sorisdale and Killunaig, Coll … *Proceedings of the Society of Antiquaries of Scotland* 109, 75–84

Ritchie, J.N.G. & Shepherd, I.A.G. 1973. Beaker pottery and associated artifacts in south-west Scotland. *Transactions of the Dumfriesshire & Galloway Natural History & Antiquarian Society* 50, 18–36

Salanova L. 2007. Les sépultures campaniformes: lecture sociale. In J. Guilaine (ed), *Le Chalcolithique et la construction des inégalités, t. I: Le continent européen,* 213–28. Paris: Editions Errance

Shepherd, I.A.G. 1986. *Powerful Pots: Beakers in North-East prehistory.* Aberdeen: Anthropological Museum, University of Aberdeen

Shepherd, A.N. this volume. Stepping out together: men, women and their Beakers in time and space, in M.J. Allen, J. Gardiner & A. Sheridan (eds) *Is there a British Chalcolithic?* Oxford: Oxbow Books

Sheridan, J.A. 2007. Scottish Beaker dates: the good, the bad and the ugly. In M. Larsson & M. Parker Pearson (eds), *From Stonehenge to the Baltic: living with cultural diversity in the third millennium BC,* 91–123. Oxford: British Archaeological Report S1692

Sheridan, J.A. 2008. Upper Largie and Dutch-Scottish connections during the Beaker period. In H. Fokkens, B J Coles, A.L. van Gijn, J.P. Kleijne, H.W. Ponjee & C.J. Slappendel (eds), *Between Foraging and Farming. An Extended Broad Spectrum of Papers Presented to Leendert Louwe Kooijmans,* 247–60. *Analecta Praehistorica Leidensia* 40

Suddaby, I. & Sheridan, J.A. 2006. A pit containing an undecorated Beaker and associated artefacts from Beechwood Park, Raigmore, Inverness. *Proceedings of the Society of Antiquaries of Scotland* 136, 77–88

Taylor, J.J. 1980. *Bronze Age goldwork of the British Isles.* Cambridge: Cambridge University Press.

Turner, R. 1999. Grave discoveries. *National Trust for Scotland Archaeology Bulletin* 12, 1

Wallace, C. 1986. A note on two gold lunulae. *Proceedings of the Society of Antiquaries of Scotland* 116, 566–7

Watkins, T. & Shepherd, I.A.G. 1980. A Beaker burial at Newmill, near Bankfoot, Perthshire. *Proceedings of the Society of Antiquaries of Scotland* 110, 32–41

A Date with the Chalcolithic in Wales: a review of radiocarbon measurements for 2450–2100 cal BC

Steve Burrow

Wales has not featured prominently in discussions about the transition from the Neolithic to the Early Bronze Age despite its pivotal position between Ireland and other hotspots of late 3rd millennium BC archaeology. This paper addresses this lacuna with a review of the chronological foundations upon which the story of Wales in this period must be based. Eighty-nine determinations are selected as being of particular relevance to the subject of Wales's 'Chalcolithic', and these are considered with reference to themes including the introduction of copper mining to Wales, monumentality in the region, the role of Beakers and the evidence for domestic occupation. The paper ends with discussion of whether a definable Chalcolithic period can be identified from the evidence available in Wales alone.

The transition from the Late Neolithic to the Early Bronze Age in Britain has attracted the attention of researchers for decades. The differences between the archaeology of the two periods can be easily characterised – large ritual monuments in one, small burial mounds in the other; stone tools replaced by bronze tools; Grooved Ware by urns; and the embellishment of utilitarian items by adornment with exotic materials (compare Whittle 1999 and Parker Pearson 1999). How this change came about is less clear, although the appearance of continental innovations such as Beakers (and any associated cultural ideals) and metallurgy (copper and gold working) presumably provided something of a cultural catalyst. Much effort has been invested in dating the appearance of these external influences, and

it now seems that the years after 2450 cal BC were pivotal (Needham 2002, fig. 2; 2005, fig. 13). The relatively rapid adoption of bronze around 2100 cal BC (Needham *et al.* 1989, 399), and the loosely contemporary appearance of urn pottery and burial mounds provide an end date by which the transition from Neolithic to Early Bronze Age had been achieved (Brindley 2007; Garwood 2007, table 4.1).

In characterising this span of time as a named archaeological period, the Chalcolithic, it is reasonable to expect it to contain distinctive material culture and this is certainly the case, for example, the use of copper appears to stop soon after bronze is adopted, and some decorative schemes on Beakers are also restricted to this period. But whether such date-specific phenomena hold true in all parts of Britain remains to be tested in the face of the ever-growing body of radiocarbon determinations from all regions. This paper reviews the radiocarbon-dated evidence from Wales – a largely mountainous peninsula comprising 10% of Britain's land mass, and set at the geographic centre of several of those regions which are more normally considered in reviews of this period: Scotland, Ireland, Wessex and Yorkshire. On the grounds of its pivotal position alone it is hoped that an overview of Wales's radiocarbon evidence will be thought useful.

The dataset

This paper draws on a database of 5500 published radiocarbon measurements from Wales and the Borders which is freely available online (Burrow & Williams 2008), enhanced by unpublished results generously made available by researchers for the purposes of this study (see acknowledgements). The first step in the analysis was the establishment of clear criteria for the selection of measurements relevant to the study period. Over 400 radiocarbon measurements from Wales have calibrated ranges which overlap the period 2450–2100 cal BC at 2 standard deviations, however, in many cases this overlap is very small. For example, OxA-7656 3995±45 BP, which dates a human skull found at Alexandra Docks (Bell *et al.* 2000, 69), has a calibrated range of 2620–2410 cal BC at 2 standard deviations, but when calibrated by the probability method (see below), it can be seen that only 8.2% of that range falls in the period 2450–2100 cal BC. To focus attention on those dates most likely to be relevant to this review, the calibrated range of each one was assessed in detail using the raw output function of Oxcal 4.1.3, with resolution set to one year. Only those determinations which have more than 10% of their calibrated ranges overlapping the period 2450–2100 cal BC, were used. (The exact degree of overlap is given beside each date in the accompanying tables: see Appendix). To give structure to this research, only those radiocarbon measurements were reviewed which were relevant to specific archaeological themes: metallurgy, Beakers, monuments, burials without Beakers, and occupation sites. A total of 89 nine determinations met all these criteria (relevant sites shown on Fig. 12.1). These, and

all the other results excluded from this review, can be found in the online database.

Although these criteria aid the selection of measured samples which were formed during the period 2450–2100 cal BC this does not mean that the contexts in which they were found, or the material culture with which they are associated also belongs to this period. Dated samples may incorporate an age-at-death offset, or may be either residual or intrusive to their findspot, artefacts may also be incorporated from earlier contexts. Problems caused by the use of samples which are possibly residual or intrusive to their context, or which are not relevant to the event which it is hoped to date are noted in the sections given below.

Problems associated with the dating of long-life materials (eg, oak charcoal or wood) are also widely acknowledged (Ambers *et al.* 1999, 331), the result being that the determination over-estimates the age of the event which it was intended to date. Of the determinations referenced in the tables, 14 are based on oak – without the qualification that outer-rings were used. More problematic still are those radiocarbon measurements for which the only published identification of the sample material is 'charcoal', or similarly ill-defined descriptors. It is parsimonious to consider that these may also have been affected by age-at-death offsets, and as such should be treated as only providing *termini post quos* for the contexts in which they are found. The remaining 44 determinations are based on short-life materials such as bone, short-lived woods or twigs.

Throughout this paper, all calibrated dates have been produced using the IntCal 04 calibration curve (Reimer *et al.* 2004) and OxCal v4.1.3 (Bronk Ramsey 1995; 1998; 2001; 2009), and are presented at 95% confidence. They are quoted as recommended by Mook (1986), with end points rounded out to 10 years (for error ranges equal or greater than 25 years). The ranges quoted in the text and tables have been calculated using the maximum intercept method (Stuiver & Reimer 1986), those in the figures are derived from the probability method (Stuiver & Reimer 1993).

Metallurgy

The use of copper axes and halberds in Wales has been clearly demonstrated since the pioneering work of C.H. Desch (Wheeler

Figure 12.1: Location of sites listed in tables. 1 Afon Wen, Gwynedd; 2 Blaen y Cae, Gwynedd; 3 Breiddin, Powys; 4 Bryn Bachau, Gwynedd; 5 Cae Gronw, Denbighshire; 6 Capel Eithin, Anglesey; 7 Carne, Pembrokeshire; 8 Cefn Bryn, Swansea; 9 Cleifiog Uchaf, Anglesey; 10 Coed-y-Dinas, Powys; 11 Collfryn, Powys; 12 Copa Hill, Ceredigion; 13 Crawcwellt West, Gwynedd; 14 Dyffryn Lane, Powys; 15 Erglodd Mine, Ceredigion; 16 Felin Fulbrook, Ceredigion; 17 Figin Fawr, Anglesey; 18 Four Crosses, Powys; 19 Graeanog, Gwynedd; 20 Gwalchmai, Anglesey; 21 Hendre, Flintshire; 22 Hindwell, Powys; 23 Llandegai, Anglesey; 24 Llyn Morwynion, Gwynedd; 25 Meusydd, Powys; 26 Moel y Gaer, Flintshire; 27 Moel y Gerddi, Gwynedd; 28 Mynydd Parys, Anglesey; 29 Parc Bryn Cegin, Anglesey; 30 Parc le Breos Cwm, Swansea; 31 Parry's Castle Farm, Carmarthenshire; 32 Peterstone Great Wharf, Newport; 33 Plasgwyn Farm, Carmarthenshire; 34 Redberth, Pembrokeshire; 35 Riversdale, Cardiff; 36 Sarn-y-bryn-caled, Powys; 37 South Hook, Pembrokeshire; 38 Tandderwen, Denbighshire; 39 Thornwell Farm, Monmouthshire; 40 Trelystan, Powys; 41 Twll Carw Coch, Rhondda Cynon Taf; 42 Yr Allor, Pembrokeshire.

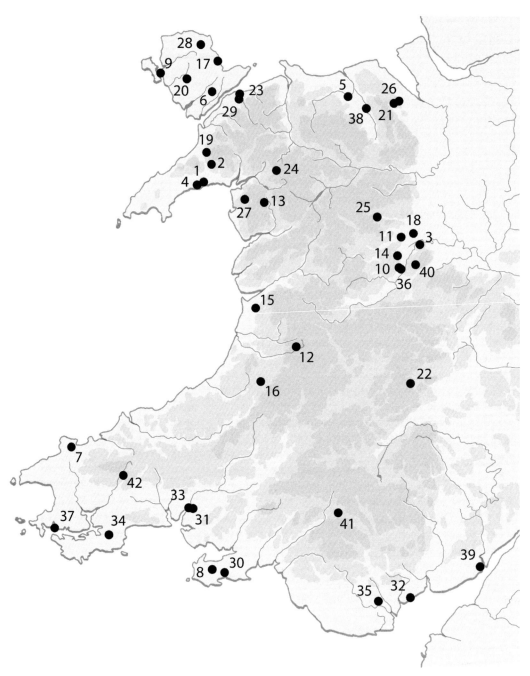

1925) and through subsequent large scale studies carried out by Northover (1980) and Rohl and Needham (1998). These have shown that people in this region were able to obtain tools made from copper mined in south-west Ireland in the years after 2450 cal BC (O'Brien 2004), but a lack of radiocarbon measurements from contexts containing copper artefacts prevents direct dating of the advent and duration of copper tool-use in Wales specifically. However, while there are

no determinations from which to date directly copper tool-use in Wales, over 60 are available with which to date the start of copper mining in this region. This is in large part thanks to more than 20 years work undertaken by Simon Timberlake and other members of the Early Mines Research Group.

Seven of these measurements have calibrated ranges which overlap with the period 2450–2100 cal BC (see Table 12.1; Fig. 12.2), although since there is only a very low probability

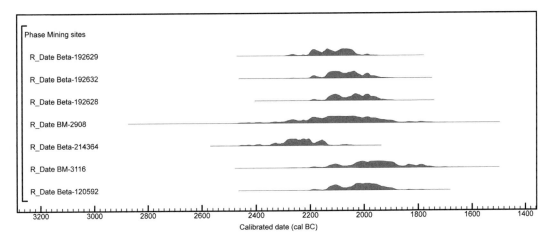

that the determinations from Mynydd Parys (Ambers & Bowman 1999, 189) and Tyn y fron (Timberlake 1998, 80) overlap with this period they are not considered further. The date of 2430–2130 cal BC (Beta-214364) found in an ore crushing floor at Erglodd mine (Timberlake 2006, 83) is of greater interest, but since it is the only one from this site, and is from a context which may not have been rapidly sealed, it presents a tantalising hint that mining occurred before 2100 cal BC, rather than clear proof.

More secure evidence is available from the Copa Hill mine site where 29 results have been produced on a range of materials (including antler, moss, and leaf matter) from within the 12 m deep mine, from surface spoil tips, and from nearby peat bogs. These show that the mine was in use until around 1600 cal BC, by which time near-surface deposits approached exhaustion and flooding was becoming a serious obstacle to further work (Timberlake 2003, i). The earliest dates from Copa Hill comes from oak charcoal found at the base of a lateral tip formed to the south-east of the mine (OxA-10026, 6745±45 BP; Wk-9544, 4136±58 BP). Assuming that this charcoal is not the product of natural forest fires, these demonstrate that the area was visited in the Mesolithic and Neolithic periods. More relevant here is a group of five measurements recovered from a sequence of mine spoil layers and soil horizons signalling hiatuses in activities (Timberlake 2004). There is a good probability that the lower three of these (Beta-192632, Beta-192628, Beta-192629) originated in the period of interest here (2190–1940 cal BC, 2190–1920 cal BC, and 2270–1980 cal

BC respectively), but since these dates are derived from charcoal found in layers which may have had complex histories, they can only be considered as *TPQs* for mining activity. Avoiding the problems of dating layers, an alder launder found within the mine, which had presumably been purpose-made to aid drainage of the site, returned a date of 2340–1820 cal BC (BM-2908), although the broad spread of this calibrated range makes it an imprecise tool from which to make detailed arguments. Viewed as a whole, the radiocarbon measurements from Copa Hill suggest that mining began a few decades before or after 2100 cal BC, meaning that at present the radiocarbon-backed case for mining in Wales pre-2100 cal BC rests on the insecure foundations offered by the single date from Erglodd.

Beakers

The appearance of Beaker pottery in Britain has long been viewed as a pivotal moment, and in Ireland, the link between early metalworking and Beaker use is of particular interest (O'Brien 2004). In other regions, the case has been made that the introduction of Beakers coincided with the spread of new cult practices (Burgess & Shennan 1976), or of a prestige good economy (Thorpe & Richards 1984). Whether early Beakers in Wales are linked to the appearance of metallurgy or of ideological change is unproven, but the possibility that this is the case increases the importance of producing regionally-specific chronologies for Beaker introductions – especially in regions where copper ores can be found.

A lack of well-preserved human bone in Wales

Figure 12.3: Context associated with Beakers; calibrated dates which have a >10% unmodelled probability of an overlap with the period 2450–2100 cal BC

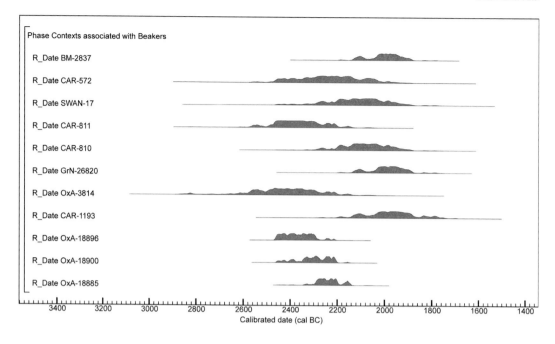

Figure 12.3: Context associated with Beakers; calibrated dates which have a >10% unmodelled probability of an overlap with the period 2450–2100 cal BC

has meant that UK-wide Beaker radiocarbon dating programmes have generally focused on material from other areas. Nonetheless, a total of 11 radiocarbon determinations from eight Beaker contexts in Wales have calibrated ranges overlapping with the period 2450–2100 cal BC (see Table 12.2; Fig. 12.3). Of these, two, from a pit containing Beaker sherds found at Four Crosses, site 2 (Warrilow *et al.* 1986), are excluded since their contradictory results make it impossible to be certain which is accurate: CAR-810 calibrates to 2280–1890 cal BC and CAR-811 to 2560–2140 cal BC, the combined results fail a chi-squared test at 5%.

A determination on human bone from an inhumation burial at Riversdale (K. Brassil, pers. comm.) dated to 2830–2140 cal BC (OxA-3814) also seems anomalously early given that this body was accompanied by a bronze awl, although there is no other obvious reason for rejecting this date. At the other extreme, there is a small chance that a charcoal date (2190–1750 cal BC, CAR-1193) associated with a Beaker burial at Tandderwen (Brassil *et al.* 1991) may belong to this period, but it is much more likely to be more recent.

No other burials of individuals with Beakers have been dated to the period 2450–2100 cal BC in Wales. But, radiocarbon measurements from Thornwell Farm, a Neolithic megalithic tomb which has produced All-Over-Decorated Beaker pottery (Maylan 1991), demonstrates that not all Beaker burials were afforded

this individual rite. Seventeen determinations are available from this site from a total tomb population containing a minimum of eighteen individuals (R. Schulting, pers. comm.). Results from three separate individuals overlap with the period presented here: OxA-18896 (2460–2210 cal BC); OxA-18900 (2450–2200 cal BC) and OxA-18885 (2330–2140 cal BC). The reuse of megalithic tombs by Beaker-using communities is relatively common in Wales, with a similar situation represented at Tinkinswood megalithic tomb, 40 km to the west. Here a large number of inhumed bones were found, with sherds from a single AOC Beaker mixed among them (Ward 1916). Unfortunately, in this instance only four individuals have been radiocarbon dated and only Neolithic dates have been returned (A. Whittle, pers. comm.), although it is likely that more recent human bone is also present in the surviving assemblage. Beaker sherds have also been recovered from several other megalithic tombs in Wales (Dyffryn Ardudwy in Gwynedd; Capel Garmon in Conwy, Penywyrlod near Llanigon, Pant-y-Saer on Anglesey, and Ty-Isaf in Powys), although no radiocarbon dates are available from these sites.

Moving on from burial evidence, two pits containing Beaker sherds have produced calibrated dates which overlap this period: from Collfryn (CAR-572, 2470–1950 cal BC; Britnell 1989) and Crawcwellt West (SWAN-17, 2340–1890 cal BC; Crew 1998). The former

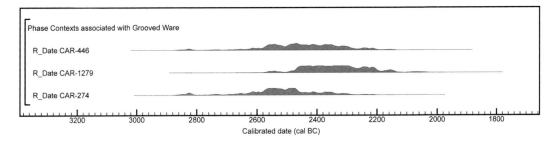

Figure 12.4: Contexts associated with Grooved Ware; calibrated dates which have a >10% unmodelled probability of an overlap with the period 2450–2100 cal BC

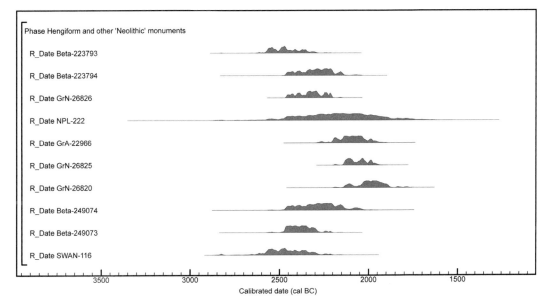

Figure 12.5: Hengiform and other 'Neolithic' monuments; calibrated dates which have a >10% unmodelled probability of an overlap with the period 2450–2100 cal BC

is derived from a mixed oak/hazel sample, the sampled material is not listed in the latter case; the possibility therefore exists that both only provide *TPQ*s for their contexts. The degree of association between samples and sherds is also unclear in both cases. Yet despite these difficulties the tentative dating of these non-funerary pit deposits to this period is of interest since pits containing ceramics are an important site type of the preceding Neolithic and are relatively rare in Wales's Early Bronze Age (see also Thomas 1999, fig. 4.4).

The possibility of a Neolithic cultural tradition being perpetuated with Beakers is of particular interest since there is some evidence for the continuation of Grooved Ware pits post-2450 cal BC. Three potentially relevant determinations come from Capel Eithin (CAR-446; White & Smith 1999), Trelystan (CAR-274; Britnell 1982) and Hendre (CAR-1279; Brassil & Gibson 1999) (see Table 12.3; Fig. 12.4). The sample material upon which the Capel Eithin date (2830–2200 cal BC) was based is not known, raising the possibility again that it only provides a *TPQ* for its

findspot. The material used for the Trelystan (2830–2290 cal BC) and Hendre (2560–2130 cal BC) measurements were hazelnut shells and alder, decreasing the possibility of an age-at-death offset, and increasing the possibility that they relate to Grooved Ware activity during this period.

Monuments

While metallurgy and Beakers are innovations relevant to Britain as a whole, the apparent cessation of large scale monumental construction projects by 2100 cal BC is only of interest in those regions which obviously took part in such projects before this date. In their paper on peer-polity interactions, Bradley and Chapman (1986) singled out north-west Wales – with its later Neolithic passage tombs and henges – as the only part of Wales which was relevant to this subject. Since this time, Alex Gibson's work has made clear the importance of Late Neolithic monumental traditions in central Wales (Gibson 1999), while the role of south-west Wales in the Stonehenge building project is well-established (Atkinson 1956; Darvill & Wainwright 2009). It is not clear that all communities in Wales built monuments, but there is sufficient evidence to make it worth exploring the theme of monumentality for the region as a whole (see Table 12.4; Fig. 12.5).

Best known of Wales's henges is Llandegai B in Gwynedd (Lynch & Musson 2001). Here, no radiocarbon determinations date the construction of the monument, but a number of features inside it have been dated. Of these, two dates come from a pit (FB151) immediately inside the ditch (4210±50 BP, GrN-26827, and 4140±50 BP, GrA-20014). The former is based on mixed charcoal, including oak (2900–2630 cal BC), the latter on an acorn (2880–2500 cal BC). A similar sample from a pit (FB147) immediately outside the probable position of the ploughed-out bank was dated to 2870–2480 cal BC (4100±50 BP, GrA-20013). Assuming that these were positioned with reference to the bank and ditch, it can be argued that the henge was built before 2600 cal BC; however, this assumption is unproven.

Nonetheless, there is evidence for the continued use of the area it occupied throughout the period of interest here. A sample from an oak plank found in internal pit FB130 has produced a date of 2460–2200 cal BC (GrN-26826), and use of the site continued in subsequent centuries. For example GrA-22966 dates cremated human bone found in a pit to 2270–1940 cal BC. This is interesting since the pit was dug at the very centre of the henge, suggesting that the monument's form continued to have a direct bearing on people's behaviour long after it was constructed. A Beaker was also deposited in a pit within the henge around the same time, 2130–1880 cal BC (GrN-26820) although, in this instance, the dated sample was oak, raising the possibility of an age-at-death offset and eliminating the probability of this determination's, already slight, chance of being relevant here. This aside, the evidence makes clear that there was no rejection of the Llandegai henge in the period 2450–2100 cal BC, although whether the henge continued to be used as its builders had intended is a more difficult question.

Evidence for the use of henges around the time that Beakers appeared in Wales can also be seen at Dyffryn Lane, a complex monument consisting of a henge built around a ruined stone circle and subsequently, or perhaps at the same time, infilled with a mound (Gibson 2010b). Bayesian modelling of the dates from this site suggest the construction of the henge took place in the third quarter of the 3rd millennium cal BC (Gibson 2010b, fig. 22).

Although use of henges post-2450 cal BC is well-established across Britain – and indeed there is evidence for continued use of the Llandegai henge post-2100 cal BC – by this latter date it is likely that most had been abandoned, with new monumental forms becoming common instead, for example ring cairns, stone circles, and embanked stone circles.

Few high quality samples have been used to date the construction of ring cairns in Wales, with the best available sequences being those from Moel Goedog, circle 1 (Lynch 1984) and Brenig 44 (Lynch 1993). Seven radiocarbon measurements on unidentified charcoal are available from the former site, and 11 on identified charcoal fragments and one on cremated human bone, are available from the latter. In both cases, dates from the earliest features suggest that construction post-dated the period of interest here. At Moel Goedog, circle 1, the two determinations stratigraphically linked to the first phase of monument use are: 3500±70 BP, CAR-160 (from a pit dug at the same time as the ring cairn was built) which provides a date of 2020–1630 cal BC; and 3450±70 BP, CAR-161 (from a central feature) which provides a date of 1940–1600 cal BC, both are likely to be *TPQ*s for these contexts. At Brenig 44, HAR-501 3630±100 BP (2280–1740 cal BC) and 3500±80 BP, HAR-1133 (2030–1620 cal BC) are both from charcoal (twigs and branches) found in pits undercutting the ring-cairn, and sealed by later bank building. A review of the entire sequences from these sites provides no reason to believe that ring cairns were in use in Wales much prior to 2100 cal BC, if at all.

Radiocarbon measurements for stone circles are very rare, although given the blending morphological categories of cairns, ring-cairns, embanked stone circles, and stone circles proper (Burrow 2011; Grimes 1963; Lynch 1972), it seems likely that these last two would have appeared at broadly the same time as those monuments described above. The dating of timber and pit circles is less period-specific, with Neolithic and Early Bronze Age

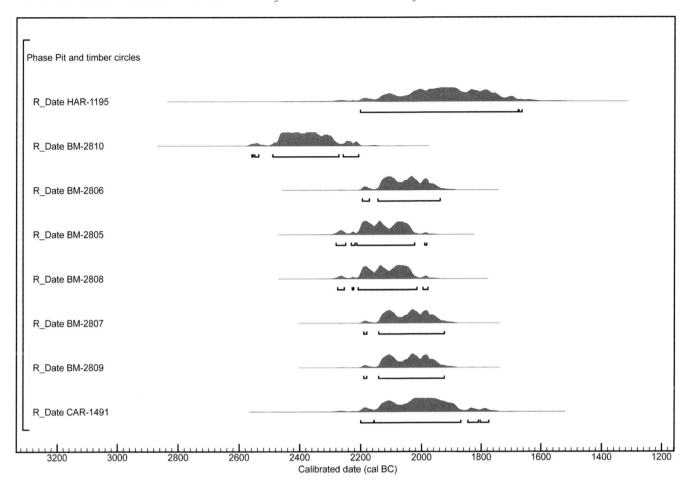

examples being known across Britain as a whole (see Gibson 1998). Three Welsh sites have produced results which might pre-date 2100 cal BC (see Table 12.5; Fig 12.6). Those from a pit circle at Yr Allor (CAR-1491; Kirk & Williams 2000) and a possible timber circle at Moel y Gaer (HAR-1195; Guilbert 1975, 33; Gibson 1994, 202) only have a relatively small chance of overlap with this period. The timber circle at Sarn-y-bryn-caled (Gibson 1994) is more securely dated with measurements on charcoal from the outer-rings of oak posts and on cremated human and animal bone allowing the production of a Bayesian model (Gibson 2010a, fig. 1). This suggests that the construction of the circle began at the end of the period of interest here – or more likely shortly after – with the burials and ritual activity at the site dating to the decades around 2000 cal BC.

The period 2450–2100 cal BC is therefore of considerable interest for an exploration of the decline of Late Neolithic monument traditions in Wales, but available radiocarbon-based evidence suggests that Early Bronze Age communal monuments in Wales were not widely adopted until around 2100 cal BC or after.

One unusual monument which dates to this period, but which has few contemporary parallels is the 100 m diameter ring-ditch at Walton Court in Powys (SO2523 5995) (Jones 2009a). Morphologically this monument is similar to the formative henges of Llandegai A and Stonehenge (Burrow 2010), but a date of 2570–2340 cal BC (SUERC-26430 (GU-20134) 3945±35 BP). The calibrated range of this date has a 50.0% chance of overlap with the period of interest here, broadening the range of monument types which are likely to have been built in Wales's Chalcolithic and hinting that the period may contain monument types peculiar to itself.

Burials without Beakers

A focus on metallurgy, Beakers, and monumentality plays to international themes

Figure 12.6: Pit and timber circles ; calibrated dates which have a >10% unmodelled probability of an overlap with the period 2450– 2100 cal BC

*Figure 12.7: Burials
(other than those
associated with Beakers);
calibrated dates
which have a >10%
unmodelled probability of
an overlap with the period
2450–2100 cal BC*

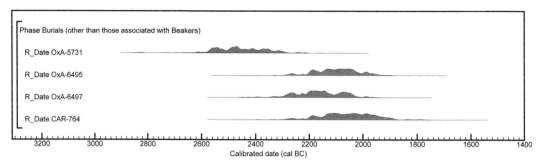

which were no doubt important in this period, but radiocarbon measurements make clear that these do not represent the totality of human interest in Wales over this period. For example, the reuse of megalithic tombs by those who had adopted Beaker rites has been noted above. But these Beakers 'tomb' burials may have been just a subset of a wider tradition of reuse of these sites which did not include the use of Beakers, as suggested by human bone at Parc le Breos Cwm on Gower, dated to 2330–1980 cal BC (OxA-6497) and 2280–1940 cal BC (OxA-6495; Whittle & Wysocki 1998) (see Table 12.6; Fig 12.7). Without dating all individuals in all tombs it is impossible to be certain how widespread this Beaker-free burial rite was, but it can be noted that radiocarbon determinations show that some earlier Neolithic tombs were used in the pre-2450 cal BC later Neolithic, for example at Ty-Isaf (A. Whittle, pers. comm.) and at Thornwell. It is possible therefore that the reuse of megalithic tombs 2450–2100 cal BC may have been a continuation of an existing tradition to which Beakers were added in some cases, rather than a new departure prompted by the arrival of Beakers.

Another possible continuation of Neolithic burial practices can be proposed for some human remains found in caves. Most notably remains from Cae Gronw dated to 2610–2280 cal BC (OxA-5731; Aldhouse Green *et al.* 1996) and Twll Carw Coch dated to 2270–1880 cal BC (CAR-764; Aldhouse Green *et al.* 1996). If caves served as ready-made surrogate tombs during the Neolithic, and if tombs continued to be used 2450–2100 cal BC, there seems every reason to expect caves to also have continued in use as burial places in this latter period. However, it should be noted that there are other reasons why human remains may have found their way into caves: carnivore kills and accidental death among them.

While burials in this period centred around the disposal of bones, in the centuries after 2100 cal BC cremation burial becomes the dominant funerary rite at newly flourishing types of burial monuments in Wales: round barrows, cairns, and cremation cemeteries. Around 120 radiocarbon measurements have been returned from these monuments, sometimes from contexts of varying relevance and based on samples of dubious quality. Many of these were produced some years ago and, even where multiple dates exist for a single site, it can be difficult to reconcile stratigraphy and radiocarbon measurements. Nonetheless, an initial review of the evidence suggests that some sites may have been begun pre-2100 cal BC, although detailed Bayesian modelling would be required to test whether this is actually the case.

Bearing this caveat in mind, sites where sequences of dates are already available which might repay more detailed analysis include:

- Brenig 45 burial mound (Lynch 1993). Five results available, of which 3570±100 BP (HAR-657) and 3620±100 BP (HAR-1027) have calibrated ranges of 2190–1680 cal BC and 2280–1690 cal BC respectively.
- Trelystan 1 round barrow (Britnell 1982). Six results available of which 3650±70 BP (CAR-280) and 3700±70 BP (CAR-281), calibrate to 2200–1780 cal BC and 2290–1890 cal BC respectively.
- Capel Eithin flat cemetery (White & Smith 1999), where four of 13 unidentified charcoal determinations associated with cremations suggest an early start for this burial rite: 3610±70 BP, CAR-488 (2190–1750 cal BC); 3670±70 BP, CAR-451 (2270–1880 cal BC); 3760±70 BP, CAR-452 (2450–1970 cal BC), and 3760±60 BP, CAR-453 (2420–1980 cal BC).

The potential to refine these and other sequences

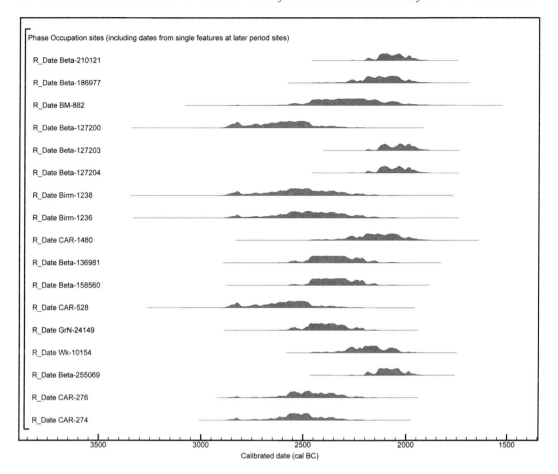

by dating cremated bone rather than associated charcoal are obvious and ongoing projects have already begun to capitalise on this (see Brindley 2007, 361–7; Hughes 2003; and Needham & Woodward 2008 for examples). But at present the evidence for cremation before 2100 cal BC remains weak, the earliest dated example coming from a pit at the Llandegai henge (3700±50 BP, GrA-22966) which was probably interred between 2270 and 1940 cal BC (Lynch & Musson 2001).

One site which provides a strong indication that ring-ditches were adopted as burial places during this period is Meusydd, a 19 m diameter ring-ditch in Powys (Jones 2009b). Here a date of 2470–2030 cal BC was returned from charcoal in an initial stabilisation layer in the 1.15 m deep ditch (3820±70 BP, Beta-249074). This provides a *TAQ* for the site's construction, while charcoal from a post-pipe set in a palisade trench inside the ditch, was dated to 2470–2210 cal BC (3900±40 BP, Beta-249073). Near the centre of the ring-ditch

was an elongated pit containing Beaker pottery, presumably a grave.

Occupation sites and other evidence of activity

The characterisation of settlement during this period is as problematic as it is for the Neolithic and Early Bronze Age more generally. A number of radiocarbon results have been recovered from sites in Wales which can be broadly described as containing 'occupation' evidence, but structural remains are rare and the evidence is often ambiguous (see Table 12.7; Fig 12.8). For example, at Redberth a number of post-hole alignments and stake-hole circles indicate occupation in the earlier Neolithic, with one date (Wk-10154) from one of three aligned post-holes suggesting that this continued in the period 2380–2020 cal BC. But, no artefactual evidence was recovered from these, or any other features, across the 1379 m² of excavated area, to aid in the characterisation

Figure 12.9: Burnt mounds; calibrated dates which have a >10% unmodelled probability of an overlap with the period 2450–2100 cal BC

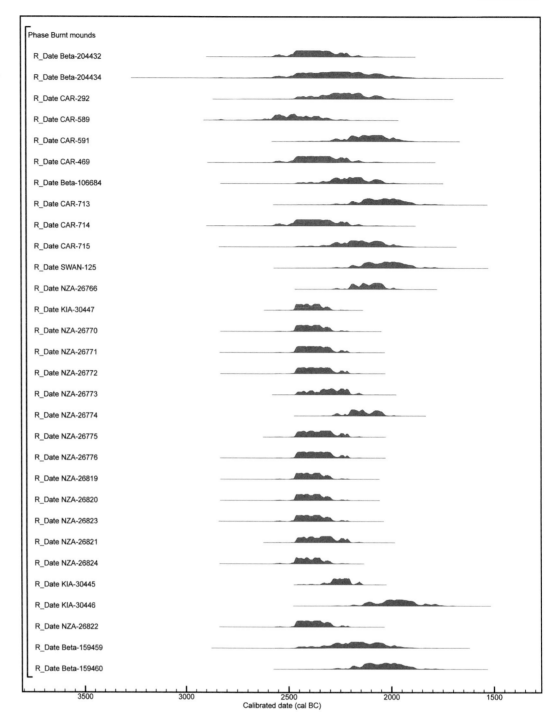

of the activities behind this post-row (Page, nd). Similarly ambiguous evidence has been returned from the excavation of a 536 m² area at Cleifiog Uchaf on Anglesey (Davidson forthcoming). Here a scatter of pits and post-holes was found, one of which contained Beaker pottery, with later funerary activity on the site in the form of a cist. Unspecified charcoal from two pits a few metres apart returned dates of 2190–1920 cal BC (Beta-127203) and 2190–1930 cal BC (Beta-127204). But, although a stratigraphic sequence was discernible in each pit – documenting their reuse as post-holes, the removal of their posts, and finally their infilling – these activities could not be closely linked to other features on the site. Other determinations listed on Table 12.7, from Afon Wen, Blaen y Cae, Breiddin,

Hindwell Ash and Moel y Gerddi, take this difficulty to extremes, reflecting the dating of isolated features, without the ability to contextualise them at a broader level.

Perhaps the best preserved structural evidence which can be dated to this period are a line of six posts found in a palaeochannel at Peterstone Great Wharf, an example of which, complete with axe marks, was dated to 2560–2200 cal BC (GrN-24149; Bell & Brown 2005, 93). In other instances where sufficient evidence exists from which to interpret ground plans, the dates which suggest construction during this period appear as outliers to a broader range, as at Trelystan, or are contradicted by associated artefacts, as at Cefn Bryn (see Table 12.7; Fig 12.8).

The most easily interpretable structural evidence for settlement likely to belong to this period comes from Llyn Morwynion, an upland valley containing two hut circles and wandering walls of similar design. The start of peat formation above one of the huts dating to 2560–2130 cal BC (Beta-136981), provides a *TAQ* for its occupation. Caseldine *et al.* (2001, 24) note morphological similarities between these and other undated round-houses from north-west Wales, suggesting that structures from this period may be more common than has been appreciated to date. The round form of these huts is foreshadowed by sites like the Late Neolithic Trelystan houses mentioned above, and foreshadows in turn the Early Bronze Age house on Stackpole Warren, the construction, or demolition, of which is dated to 1870–1460 cal BC (3350±70 BP, CAR-100; Benson *et al.* 1990) on the basis of hazel charcoal found in its destruction layer, but possibly derived from its wattle walls. Such evidence, limited as it is, hints that round-houses may have been current across this period.

While the identification of houses remains an important goal of Late Neolithic and Early Bronze Age studies, they are not the only ?domestic structures known to date to this period. Thirty radiocarbon measurements from Wales from 17 separate burnt mounds indicate the use of this site type in this period (see Table 12.8; Fig. 12.9). Unfortunately, context and sample details are incomplete in several cases, but groups of dates from Bryn Bachau, Carne, site B and Graeanog provide tantalising, albeit imperfect, evidence that this is the case (Berks *et al.* 2007; James 1986; Kelly

1992). Fortunately, recent excavation across a 23 ha area at Parc Bryn Cegin has produced a series of 30 measurements from 16 burnt mounds, the great majority based on short life charcoal and including repeated dating of key contexts (Kenny 2008). The earliest dated use of a burnt mound comes from site 6094 and dates to the Middle Neolithic. Excluding one anomalous date from site 1097, there follows a hiatus in activity until shortly after 2500 cal BC, when determinations indicate burning at seven mounds. Of these, only single radiocarbon measurements are available for sites 4199 and 4200, but two consistent determinations from site 6016 date the site to this period, and even more positively, eight out of nine dates from five contexts at site 2176 have produced a similar outcome.

Present evidence suggests, therefore, that the character of occupation in Wales 2450–2100 cal BC has much in common with that of the preceding period – isolated and hard to interpret pits and pit clusters, and occasional, archaeologically fragile, round structures. The same themes are in evidence in the Early Bronze Age, perhaps with a decreasing emphasis on pit digging. But the dating of burnt mounds to this period presents an opportunity to broaden the characterisation of activities at this time, although it is an opportunity which is hampered by continuing problems in the interpretation of these features (see Barfield & Hodder 1987 and ó Drisceoil 1988).

Conclusion

This review of the available radiocarbon evidence might give grounds for frustration – for instance, Wales currently has little to offer ongoing debates about Beaker chronology – but it also highlights specific areas where evidence from this region can inform broader debates. For example, the majority of radiocarbon measurements relevant to prehistoric mining in Britain come from Wales, and researchers in Wales have also produced important series of results through which the chronology of burnt mound use can be understood.

Are there then sufficient grounds to define a Chalcolithic in Wales? This inevitably depends on the basis of the definition and the purpose for which it is intended. If one defined the Chalcolithic as the period during which Wales began to use Beakers, copper, and gold then yes, there was a Chalcolithic in the period 2450–2100 cal BC. This seems a hollow definition though, based as it is on typological comparisons with dated evidence from other regions, rather than on chronological evidence found in Wales itself. It does not allow us to address questions such as: were AOC beakers in use over the same period in Wales as they were in Wessex? Did the use of copper axes begin earlier or last longer than elsewhere in Britain? Can distinctive burial rites be demonstrated for this period in Wales, or are they simply extensions of practices current in the later Neolithic? Was there anything peculiarly 'Welsh' about life in this region? Wales has yet to produce sufficient radiocarbon dated evidence of its own to answer these questions, and how long it will take to rectify this deficiency depends almost entirely on the pace of chance discoveries and their skilful exploitation with multiple short-life single entity samples. Until such determinations are produced the definition of a regionally-specific Chalcolithic for Wales, as opposed to a general Chalcolithic for Britain, seems a little premature.

More can be said about the progress that has been made in dating the start of the Early Bronze Age in Wales (the end of the Chalcolithic, or the end of the Neolithic, depending on your perspective). Enormous strides have been made in the development of a mining chronology for Wales, and many more sites await study on the scale pursued at Copa Hill (Timberlake 2003), the Great Orme (Lewis 1996), and Mynydd Parys (Jenkins 2003). Similarly, a great number of round barrows, cairns, and other cremation sites have already been dug over the course of the last century and many have produced cremated bone, now amenable to radiocarbon dating. Reanalysis of these would tell us much about how Wales's Chalcolithic ended, even if it may take longer to define how the period began, and whether it changed its character over its history.

Clearly much remains to be done, but it is worth noting that there is another important type of dated information, already available, which remains to be exploited for the period 2450–2100 cal BC: radiocarbon measurements relating to the environment, and specifically of human impact on the environment. In total more than 90 radiocarbon dates from environmental sites in Wales have calibrated ranges which overlap with this period. An inexpert review of this dataset shows a probability that dated clearances at Barland's Farm (Bell 2000, 76), Cefn Gwernffrwrd site B (Chambers 1983, 310, 313), Hill Farm Pond (Goldcliff) (Bell *et al.* 2000, 337), and Moel y Gerddi (Chambers & Price 1988, 96; Dresser 1985, 340), belong to the period 2450–2100 cal BC, while species indicative of farming probably reappeared at Goldcliff East site 1 (Smith & Morgan 1989, 154), during this time. They provide a rich resource with which the archaeological evidence presented in this paper could be contextualised.

Acknowledgements
The database upon which this article draws was produced by the author and Sian Williams, with funding provided by a Research Grant from the Research Requirements Board and Friends of Amgueddfa Cymru – National Museum Wales. Dating of Thornwell Farm was undertaken in partnership with Rick Schulting, Oxford University. Additional unpublished dates and context information was made available through the generosity of: Ken Brassil, Amgueddfa Cymru – National Museum Wales (Riversdale); Peter Crane and Ken Murphy, Dyfed Archaeological Trust (Fan Foel and South Hook); Andrew Davidson and Jane Kenney, Gwynedd Archaeological Trust (Cleifiog Uchaf and Parc Bryn Cegin); Alex Gibson (Bradford University); David Jenkins (Mynydd Parys); Nigel Jones, Clwyd-Powys Archaeological Trust (Meusydd); and Alasdair Whittle, Cardiff University (Ty-Isaf). A draft of this article was read by Frances Healy, Stuart Needham, John Ll Williams and Peter Marshall, and by my colleagues Mary Davis and Jody Deacon. It has also benefited from the comments of anonymous referees. I am grateful to them all for the improvements they suggested.

Bibliography

Aldhouse-Green, S.H.R., Pettitt, P. & Stringer, C. 1996. Holocene humans at Pontnewydd and Cae Gronw caves. *Antiquity* 70, 444–7

Ambers, J. & Bowman, S. 1999. British Museum Natural Radiocarbon Measurements 25. *Archaeometry* 41(1), 185–95

Ambers, J., Bowman, S., Garwood, P., Hedges, R. & Housley, R. 1999. Appendix 1: radiocarbon dating.

In A. Barclay & C. Halpin (eds), *Excavations at Barrow Hills, Radley, Oxfordshire. Volume 1: the Neolithic and Bronze Age monument complex*, 330–6. Oxford: Oxford University Committee for Archaeology

Ashmore, P., Cook, G.T. & Harkness, D.D. 2000. A radiocarbon database for Scottish archaeological samples. *Radiocarbon* 42(1), 41–8

Atkinson, R.J.C. 1956. *Stonehenge*. London: Thomas Hamilton.

Barfield, L. & Hodder, M. 1987. Burnt mounds as saunas, and the prehistory of bathing. *Antiquity* 61, 370–9

Bell, M. 2000. Environmental archaeology in the Severn Estuary: progress and prospects. *Archaeology in the Severn Estuary* 11, 69–103

Bell, M. & Brown, A.D. 2005. Prehistoric activity in Peterstone Great Wharf palaeochannels: field survey 2005–6. *Archaeology in the Severn Estuary* 16, 85–97

Bell, M., Caseldine, A.E. & Neumann, H. 2000. *Prehistoric Intertidal Archaeology in the Welsh Severn Estuary*. York: Council for British Archaeology Research Report 120

Benson, D., Evans, J.G., Williams, G.H., Darvill, T.C. & David, A.E.U. 1990. Excavations at Stackpole Warren, Dyfed. *Proceedings of the Prehistoric Society* 56, 179–245

Berks, T., Davidson, A., Kenney, J., Roberts, J.A. & Smith, G. 2007. A497 improvement: prehistoric sites in the vicinity of Abererch and Chwilog. *Archaeology in the Wales* 47, 3–17

Bradley, R.J. & Chapman, R. 1986. The nature and development of long distance relations in later Neolithic Britain and Ireland. In C. Renfrew & J. Cherry (eds), *Peer Polity Interaction and Socio-political Change*, 127–36. Cambridge: Cambridge University Press

Brassil, K.S. & Gibson, A. 1999. A Grooved Ware pit group and Bronze Age multiple inhumation at Hendre, Flintshire. In R. Cleal & A. MacSween (eds), *Grooved Ware in Britain and Ireland*, 89–97. Oxford: Oxbow Books

Brassil, K. S., Owen, W.G. & Britnell, W.J. 1991. Prehistoric and early medieval cemeteries at Tandderwen, near Denbigh, Clwyd. *Archaeology Journal* 148, 46–97

Brindley, A.L. 2007. *The Dating of Food Vessels and Urns in Ireland*. Galway: National University of Ireland

Britnell, W.J. 1982. The excavation of two round barrows at Trelystan, Powys. *Proceedings of the Prehistoric Society* 48, 133–201

Britnell, W.J. 1989. The Collfryn hillslope enclosure, Llansantffraid Deuddwr, Powys: excavations 1980–1982. *Proceedings of the Prehistoric Society* 55, 89–134

Bronk Ramsey, C. 1995. Radiocarbon calibration and analysis of stratigraphy: the OxCal program. *Radiocarbon* 37, 425–30

Bronk Ramsey, C. 1998. Probability and dating. *Radiocarbon* 40, 461–74

Bronk Ramsey, C. 2001. Development of the radiocarbon program. *Radiocarbon* 43(2A), 355–63

Bronk Ramsey, C. 2009. Bayesian analysis of radiocarbon dates. *Radiocarbon* 51, 337–60

Burgess, C. & Shennan, S. 1976. The Beaker phenomenon: some suggestions. In C. Burgess & R. Miket (eds), *Settlement and Economy in the Third and Second millennia BC*, 309–31. Oxford: British Archaeological Report 33

Burrow, S. 2010 The formative henge: speculations drawn from the circular traditions of Wales and adjacent counties. In J. Leary, T. Darvill & D. Field (eds), *Round Mounds and Monumentality in the British Neolithic and Beyond*, 182–196. Oxford: Oxbow Books

Burrow, S. 2011. *Shadowland: Wales 3000 – 1500 BC*. Oxford: Oxbow Books/Amgueddfa Cymru – National Museum Wales

Burrow, S. & Williams, S., 2008 The Wales and Borders radiocarbon database, Amgueddfa Cymru – National Museum Wales. [http://www.museumwales.ac.uk/en/1151. Last accessed 13/05/09]

Caseldine, A.E., Smith, G. & Griffiths, C.J. 2001. Vegetation history and upland settlement at Llyn Morwynion, Ffestiniog, Meirionnydd. *Archaeology in Wales* 41, 21–33

Chambers, F.M. 1983. The palaeoecological setting of Cefn Gwernffrwd – a prehistoric complex in mid-Wales. *Proceedings of the Prehistoric Society* 49, 303–16

Chambers, F. M. & Price, S.-M. 1988. The environmental setting of Erw-wen and Moel y Gerddi: prehistoric enclosures in Upland Ardudwy, North Wales. *Proceedings of the Prehistoric Society* 54, 93–100

Crew, P. 1998. Excavations at Crawcwellt West, Merioneth, 1986–1990: a late prehistoric upland iron-working settlement. *Archaeology in Wales* 29, 11–6

Darvill, T.C. & Wainwright, G. 2009. Stonehenge excavations 2008. *The Antiquaries Journal* 89, 1–19

Davidson, A. forthcoming. Excavations at Cleifiog Uchaf in May 1998 (G1550). *Transactions of the Anglesey Antiquarian Society and Field*

Dresser, P.Q. 1985. University College Cardiff radiocarbon dates I. *Radiocarbon* 27(2B), 338–85

Garwood, P. 2007. Before the hills in order stood: chronology, time and history. In J. Last (ed.), *Beyond the Grave: new perspectives on barrows*, 30–52. Oxford: Oxbow Books

Gibson, A. 1994. Excavations at the Sarn-y-bryn-caled cursus complex, Welshpool, Powys, and the timber circles of Great Britain and Ireland. *Proceedings of the Prehistoric Society* 60, 142–223

Gibson, A. 1998. *Stonehenge and Timber Circles*. Stroud: Tempus

Gibson, A. 1999. *The Walton Basin, Powys, Wales: survey at the Hindwell Neolithic enclosure*. Welshpool: Clwyd-Powys Archaeological Trust

Gibson, A. 2010a. New dates for Sarn-y-bryn-caled, Powys, Wales. *Proceedings of the Prehistoric Society*, 76, 213–48

Gibson, A. 2010b. *Excavation and survey at Dyffryn Lane henge complex, Powys, and a reconsideration of the dating of henges*. *Proceedings of the Prehistoric Society*, 76, 213–48

Green, H. S. 1987. The Disgwylfa Fawr round barrow, Ceredigion, Dyfed. *Archaeologia Cambrensis* 136, 43–50.

Grimes, W.F. 1963. The stone circles and related monuments of Wales. In I. L. Foster & L. Alcock (eds), *Culture and Environment: essays in honour of Sir Cyril Fox*, 93–152. London: Routledge & Kegan Paul

Guilbert, G.C. 1975. Moel y Gaer (SJ211691). *Archaeology in Wales* 1975, 33

Hughes, G. 2003. Fan Foel, Llanddeusant (SN 8215 2234). *Archaeology in Wales* 43, 92

James, H.J. 1986. Excavations of burnt mounds at Carne, nr Fishguard, 1979 and 1981. *Bulletin of the Board of Celtic Studies* 33, 245–65

Jenkins, D.G. 2003. Mynydd Parys copper mines, Amlwch (SH 441 904). *Archaeology in Wales* 43, 106

Jones, N.W. 2008. *Excavation and survey at Meusydd henge and timber circles, Llanrhaeadr-ym-Mochnant, Powys, 2007.* Welshpool: Clwyd Powys Archaeological Trust (unpublished typescript report)

Jones, N.W. 2009a. Walton Court Farm ring ditch, Walton. SO 2523 5995. *Archaeology in Wales* 49, 104–6

Jones, N.W. 2009b Meusydd timber circles and ring-ditch, Llanrhaeadr-ym-Mochnant, Powys: excavation and survey 2007. *Archaeologia Cambrensis* 158, 43–68

Kelly, R.S. 1988. Two late prehistoric circular enclosures near Harlech, Gwynedd. *Proceedings of the Prehistoric Society* 54, 101–51

Kelly, R.S. 1992. The excavation of a burnt mound at Graeanog, Clynnog, Gwynedd in 1983. *Archaeologia Cambrensis* 141, 74–96

Kenney, J. 2008. Recent excavations at Parc Bryn Cegin, Llandygai, near Bangor, North Wales. *Archaeologia Cambrensis* 157, 9–142

Kirk, T. & Williams, G. 2000. Glandy Cross: a later prehistoric monumental complex in Carmarthenshire, Wales. *Proceedings of the Prehistoric Society* 66, 257–95

Lewis, C.A. 1996. *Prehistoric mining at the Great Orme.* Bangor: University of Wales. Unpublished MPhil thesis. [Available at: http://www.greatormemines.info/MPhil.htm]

Lynch, F.M. 1971. Report on the re-excavation of two Bronze Age cairns in Anglesey: Bedd Branwen and Treiorwerth. *Archaeologia Cambrensis* 120, 11–83

Lynch, F.M. 1972. Ring cairns and related monuments in Wales. *Scottish Archaeological Forum* 4, 61–80

Lynch, F. M. 1984. Moel Goedog Circle I, a complex ring cairn near Harlech. *Archaeologia Cambrensis* 133, 8–50

Lynch, F.M. 1993. *Excavations in the Brenig valley: a Mesolithic and Bronze Age landscape in North Wales.* Cardiff: Cambrian Archaeological Association

Lynch, F.M. & Musson, C. 2001. A prehistoric and early medieval complex at Llandegai, near Bangor, North Wales. *Archaeologia Cambrensis* 150, 17–142

Martin, C. & Phipps, R., 2003 A research framework for the archaeology of Wales: southwest Wales – radiocarbon dates from archaeological sites. Welshpool: Clwyd-Powys Archaeological Trust [http://www.cpat.org.uk/research/swrada.htm. Last accessed 13/05/09]

Maylan, N. 1991. Thornwell Farm, Chepstow. *Archaeology in Wales* 31, 22

Mook, W.G. 1986. Business meeting: recommendations/ resolutions adopted by the twelfth international radiocarbon conference. *Radiocarbon* 28, 799

Musson, C.R. 1991. *The Breiddin Hillfort: a later prehistoric settlement in the Welsh Marches.* York: Council for British Archaeology Research Report 76

Needham, S P., Leese, M.N., Hook, D.R. & Hughes, M J. 1989. Developments in the Early Bronze Age metallurgy of southern Britain. *World Archaeology* 20(3), 383–402

Needham, S. 2002. Analytical implications for Beaker metallurgy in north–west Europe. In M. Bartelheim, E. Pernicka & R. Krause (eds), *Die Anfänge der Metallurgie in der Alten Welt*, 99–133. Freiberg: Forschungen zur Archäometrie und Altertumswissenschaf 1

Needham, S. 2005. Transforming Beaker culture in

north-west Europe; processes of fusion and fission. *Proceedings of the Prehistoric Society* 71, 171–217

Needham, S. & Woodward, A. 2008. Clandon Barrow finery: synopsis of success in an Early Bronze Age world. *Proceedings of the Prehistoric Society* 74, 1–52

Northover, J.P. 1980. The analysis of Welsh Bronze Age metalwork. In H.N. Savory (ed.), *Guide Catalogue of the Bronze Age Bollections*, 229–36. Cardiff: National Museum of Wales

O'Brien, W. 200. *Ross Island: mining, metal and society in early Ireland.* Galway: National University of Ireland.

ó Drisceoil, D.A. 1988. Burnt mounds: cooking or bathing? *Antiquity* 62, 671–80

Page, N. nd. *A477(T) Sageston-Redberth Bypass: excavation of a Neolithic occupation site, 2001.* Llandeilo: Dyfed Archaeological Trust (unpublished typescript report)

Parker Pearson, M. 1999. The earlier Bronze Age. In J. Hunter & I. Ralston (eds), *The Archaeology of Britain: an introduction from the Upper Palaeolithic to the Industrial Revolution*, 77–94. London: Routledge

Reimer, P.J., Baillie, M.G.L., Bard, E., Bayliss, A., Beck, J.W., Bertrand, C.J.H., Blackwell, P.G., Buck, C.E., Burr, G.S., Cutler, K.B., Damon, P.E., Edwards, R.L., Fairbanks, R.G., Freidrich, M., Guilderson, T.P., Hogg, A.G., Hughen, K.A., Kromer, B., McCormac, G., Manning, S., Ramsey, C.B., Reimer, R.W., Remmele, S., Southon, J.R., Stuiver, M., Talamo, S., Taylor, F.W., van der Plicht, J. & Weyhenmeyer, C.E. 2004. IntCal04 terrestrial radiocarbon age calibration, 0–26 cal KYR BP. *Radiocarbon* 46, 1029–58

Rohl, B. & Needham, S. 1998. *The Circulation of Metal in the British Bronze Age: the application of lead isotope analysis.* London: British Museum Press

Sheridan, A. 2004. Scottish Food Vessel chronology revisited. In A. Gibson & A. Sheridan (eds), *From Sickles to Circles: Britain and Ireland at the time of Stonehenge*, 243–70. Stroud: Tempus

Smith, A.G. & Morgan, L.A. 1989. A succession to ombrotrophic bog in the Gwent Levels, and its demise: a Welsh parallel to the peats of the Somerset Levels. *New Phytologist* 112, 145–67

Smith, G. 1997. Moelfre to Benllech Sewage pumping main (SH512863 to SH522827). *Archaeology in Wales* 37, 57

Smith, G.H. 2006. An Early Bronze Age cremation cemetery at Blaen y Cae, Bryncir, Garndolbenmaen, Gwynedd. *Archaeology in Wales* 46, 11–20

Stuiver, M. & Reimer, P.J. 1986. A computer program for radiocarbon age calculation. *Radiocarbon* 28, 1022–30

Stuiver, M. & Reimer, P.J. 1993. Extended 14C data base and revised CALIB 3.0 14C age calibration program. *Radiocarbon* 35, 215–30

Thomas, J. 1999. *Understanding the Neolithic.* London: Routledge

Thorpe, I.J. & Richards, C. 1984. The decline of ritual authority and the introduction of Beakers into Britain. In R. J. Bradley & J. Gardiner (eds), *Neolithic Studies: a review of some current research*, 67–86. Oxford: British Archaeological Report 133

Timberlake, S. 1998. Survey of early metal mines within the Welsh uplands. *Archaeology in Wales* 38, 79–81

Timberlake, S. 2003. *Excavations on Copa Hill, Cwmystwyth (1986–1999): an Early Bronze Age copper mine within the uplands of central Wales.* Oxford: Archaeopress

Timberlake, S. 2004. Comet Lode opencast, Copa Hill,

Cwmystwyth (SN 8116 7523). *Archaeology in Wales* 44, 139–41

Timberlake, S. 2006. Excavations at early mine workings at Twll y Mwyn (Cwm Darren) and Erglodd, Ceredigion. *Archaeology in Wales* 46, 79–86

Ward, A.H. 1987. Cefn Bryn, Gower. *Archaeology in Wales* 27, 39–40

Ward, J. 1916. The St Nicholas chambered tumulus, Glamorgan. *Archaeologia Cambrensis* ns 6(16), 239–66

Warrilow, W., Owen, G. & Britnell, W.J. 1986. Eight ring-ditches at Four Crosses, Llandysilio, Powys. *Proceedings of the Prehistoric Society* 52, 53–87

Wheeler, R.E.M. 1925. *Prehistoric and Roman Wales.* Oxford: Clarendon Press

White, S.I. & Smith, G. 1999. A funerary and ceremonial centre at Capel Eithin, Gaerwen, Anglesey. *Transactions of the Anglesey Antiquarian Society*

Whittle, A.W.R. 1999. The Neolithic period. In J. Hunter & I. Ralston (eds), *The Archaeology of Britain: an introduction from the Upper Palaeolithic to the Industrial Revolution*, 58–76. London: Routledge

Whittle, A.W.R. & Wysocki, M. 1998. Parc le Breos Cwm transepted long cairn, Gower, West Glamorgan: date, contents, context. *Proceedings of the Prehistoric Society* 64, 139–82

Appendix

Tables of radiocarbon measurements from Wales which have at least 10% of their calibrated ranges overlapping the period 2450–2100 cal BC

Site	Date BP, δ¹³C (where available)	Sample	Context	Calibrated BC (95% confidence)	Unmodelled probability sample dates to 2450–2100 cal BC
Copa Hill (lateral tip) SN811752	Beta-192629: 3720±40	Charcoal	Soil horizon (014) formed during hiatus in mining activity, above layer 018 (Timberlake 2004, 141)	2270–1980	54.1%
	Beta-192632: 3680±40	Charcoal	Basal layer of spoil tip (019) containing ore mineral frags (Timberlake 2004, 141)	2190–1940	32.2%
	Beta-192628: 3660±40	Charcoal	Layer containing hammer spalls (018), above layer 019 (Timberlake 2004, 141)	2190–1920	22.9%
Copa Hill (mine)	BM-2908: 3690±90, -18.2 ‰	Wood (alder)	Launder, found *c.* 8 m below mine surface (Timberlake 2003, 38)	2340–1820	44.7%
Erglodd mine SN657903	Beta-214364: 3800±40	Charcoal	Basal layer (011) of mine spoil (Timberlake 2006, 83)	2430–2130	96.3%
Mynydd Parys SH441904	BM-3116: 3600±70, -26.0 ‰	Charcoal (?birch, branch-wood)	Prehistoric spoil exposed by 19th century workings *c.* 20 m deep (Ambers & Bowman 1999, 189)	2200–1750	10.7%
Tyn y fron	Beta-120592: 3640±50	Charcoal	Buried mine spoil (Timberlake 1998, 80).	2200–1880	16.9%

Table 12.1. Mining sites

Site	Date BP, δ¹³C (where available)	Sample	Context	Calibrated BC (95% confidence)	Unmodelled probability of overlap with 2450–2100 cal BC
Coed-y-Dinas ring-ditch 1 SJ221053	BM-2837: 3630±45, -24.6 ‰	Charcoal (poplar, rowan, thorn, oak, hazel, field maple)	Charcoal patch containing Beaker sherds in secondary ditch fills (Gibson 1994, 163, 164)	2140–1880	12.2%
Collfryn SJ222173	CAR-572: 3790±90	Charcoal (oak, hazel)	Pit containing Beaker sherds & lithics (Britnell 1989, 104)	2470–1950	77.1%
Crawcwellt West SH688303	SWAN-17: 3710±80	Charcoal	Pit containing Beaker sherds & lithics (Crew 1998, 28)	2340–1890	52.1%
Four Crosses 2 SJ270188	CAR-811: 3890±70	Charcoal	Pit (1) containing Beaker sherds, lithics, & seeds, below later mound (Warrilow *et al.* 1986, 60)	2560–2140	81.7%
	CAR-810: 3690±70	Charcoal	As above	2280–1890	42.2%
Llandegai, henge B SH593711	GrN-26820: 3620±50	Wood (oak)	Pit (FB27) inside henge containing Beaker set inside wooden framework (Lynch & Musson 2001, 67, 121)	2140–1880	10.6%
Riversdale ST145789	OxA-3814: 3929±90	Bone (human, <30 yr old, female)	Cist burial accompanied by Beaker, flint flake, bronze awl (K. Brassil, pers. comm.)	2830–2140	60.5%
Tandderwen SJ081661	CAR-1193: 3610±70	Charcoal (plank)	Beaker inhumation (2) inside larger ring-ditch (Brassil *et al.* 1991, 92).	2190–1750	13.0%
Thornwell Farm megalithic tomb ST539916	OxA-18896: 3876±28, -21.1 ‰	Bone (human, adolescent?, r. humerus)	Chamber	2460–2210	94.4%
	OxA-18900 3838±29, -21.3 ‰	Bone (human, child, l. radius)	Chamber	2450–2200	98.5%
	OxA-18885 3802±28, -20.8 ‰	Bone (human, adult, r. humerus)	Chamber	2330–2140	99.4%

Table 12.2. Contexts associated with Beakers

Site	Date BP, δ^{13}C (where available)	Sample	Context	Calibrated BC (95% confidence)	Unmodelled probability of overlap with 2450–2100 cal BC
Capel Eithin SH489727	CAR-446: 3950±80	Charcoal	Pit 17 containing Grooved Ware, lithics, utilised pebble (White & Smith 1999, 34)	2830–2200	51.4%
Hendre SJ194683	CAR-1279: 3870±70	Charcoal (alder)	Pit containing Grooved Ware & lithics (Brassil & Gibson 1999, 91, 96)	2560–2130	86.5%
Trelystan SJ277070	CAR-274: 3990±70, -25.1 ‰	Hazelnut shells	Soil containing Grooved Ware & lithics, overlying hearth within round-house (Britnell 1982, 141)	2830–2290	25.3%

Table 12.3. Contexts associated with Grooved Ware

Site	Date BP, δ^{13}C (where available)	Sample	Context	Calibrated BC (95% confidence)	Unmodelled probability of overlap with 2450–2100 cal BC
Dyffryn Henge SJ204104	Beta-223793: 3960±50	Charcoal (hazel, birch)	Turfline (41) formed above stone circle & buried by turf mound (Gibson & Jones 2006, 109)	2570–2290	39.3%
	Beta-223794: 3830±50	Charcoal	Immediately below turfline (41) (Gibson & Jones 2006, 109)	2470–2130	95.7%
Llandegai, henge B SH593711	GrN-26826: 3850±30	Charcoal (oak, ?plank)	Pit (FB130) containing lithics (Lynch & Musson 2001, 56, 64)	2460–2200	97.4%
	NPL-222: 3740±145	Charcoal (oak, mature)	Pit (FB2) containing cremation in ?shored wooden box, outside SW henge entrance (Lynch & Musson 2001, 61, 121). Date produced over 40 years ago; militates against continued use	2580–1740	53.9%
	GrA-22966: 3700±50	Cremated bone (1 individual)	Central pit (FB138) containing cremation (Lynch & Musson 2001, 64, 121)	2270–1940	44.0%
	GrN-26825: 3670±30	Charcoal (oak, plank)	Pit (FB131) containing pebbles & charred ?tray (Lynch & Musson 2001, 56, 64)	2140–1950	27.5%
	GrN-26820: 3620±50	Wood (oak)	Pit (FB27) containing Beaker set inside wooden framework (Lynch & Musson 2001, 67, 121)	2130–1880	10.6%
Hindwell palisaded enclosure SO257618	SWAN-116: 3960±70	Charcoal (oak, outer rings)	Post in perimeter of palisaded enclosure (Gibson 1999, 17). Other determinations suggest that date is late outlier (SWAN-231 4130±80BP; SWAN-230 4040±80BP and SWAN-117 4070±70BP)	2840–2210	44.9%

Table 12.4. Hengiform and other 'Neolithic' monuments

Site	Date BP, δ^{13}C (where available)	Sample	Context	Calibrated BC (95% confidence)	Unmodelled probability of overlap with 2450–2100 cal BC
Moel y Gaer ?timber circle SJ211690	HAR-1195: 3570±100, -26.7	Charcoal (hazel)	Packing in 1 of 7 post-holes encircling pit, set within IA hillfort (Guilbert 1975, 33)	2200–1680	11.5%
Sarn-y-bryn-caled timber circle SJ219048	BM-2810: 3900±50, -23.9 ‰	Charcoal (oak, outer rings)	Primary cremation in central pit (Gibson 1994, 155). Date anomalous since it comes from context post-dating timber circle (see BM-2805–9 below)	2670–2200	84.7%
	BM-2806: 3670±40, -23.2 ‰	Charcoal (oak, outer rings)	Post (E) in inner circle (Gibson 1994, 150, 155)	2190–1930	27.5%
	BM-2805: 3730±40, -24.8 ‰	Charcoal (oak, outer rings)	Post (F) in inner circle (Gibson 1994, 150, 155)	2280–2020	60.7%
	BM-2808: 3720±40, -23.2 ‰	Charcoal (oak, outer rings)	Post (11) in outer circle (Gibson 1994, 150)	2270–1980	54.0%
	BM-2807: 3660±40, -25.0 ‰	Charcoal (oak, outer rings)	Post (12) in outer circle (Gibson 1994, 150)	2190–1920	22.9%
	BM-2809: 3660±40, -23.4 ‰	Charcoal (oak, outer rings)	Secondary cremation associated with Food Vessel in central pit (Gibson 1994, 155)	2190–1920	22.9%
	SUERC-27590: 3640±45, -22.5 ‰	Cremated bone (pig)	Secondary cremation associated with Food Vessel in central pit (Gibson 1994, 155; 2010a)	2140–1900	13.1%
Yr Allor pit circle SN139266	CAR-1491 3630±70	Charcoal (oak, hazel)	Recut of central pit (Kirk & Williams 2000, 265, 271). Other dates from site suggest later date more likely (CAR-1490 3550±70BP; CAR-1464 3460±70BP)	2200–1770	18.7%

Table 12.5. Pit and timber circles

Site	Date BP, δ^{13}C (where available)	Sample	Context	Calibrated BC (95% confidence)	Unmodelled probability of overlap with 2450–2100 cal BC
Cae Gronw Cave SJ014711	OxA-5731: 3955±60, -22.1 ‰	Bone (human, radius)	Aldhouse Green *et al.* (1996)	2610–2280	47.2%
Parc le Breos Cwm megalithic tomb SS537898	OxA-6495: 3705±55, -21.4 ‰	Bone (human, subadult, skull)	Passage (Whittle & Wysocki 1998, 148)	2280–1940	47.4%
	OxA-6497: 3750±55, -21.6 ‰	Bone (human, adult, occipital)	Passage (Whittle & Wysocki 1998, 148)	2330–1980	72.0%
Twll Carw Coch swallow hole SN977123	CAR-764: 3670±70	Bone (human, skull)	11 m deep (Aldhouse-Green *et al.* 1996, 446)	2270–1880	33.5%

Table 12.6. Burials (other than those associated with Beakers)

Site	Date BP, δ¹³C (where available)	Sample	Context	Calibrated BC (95% confidence)	Unmodelled probability of overlap with 2450–2100 cal BC
Afon Wen H449377	Beta-210121: 3680±40	Charcoal (hazel)	Primary fill of pit adjacent to ring-ditch (Berks *et al.* 2007, 4). Another date from oak stake in base of ring-ditch returned Beta-210122: 3670±70BP	2200–1940	32.2%
Blaen y Cae SH482452	Beta-186977: 3720±60	Charcoal	Charcoal-filled feature (Smith 2006, 18). Although site had funerary role in EBA, this feature had no clear link to this activity	2300–1940	55.8%
Breiddin SJ294143	BM-882: 3826±106	Charcoal (hazel)	Firepit/bowl-hearth in interior of hillfort (Musson 1991, microfiche 188)	2580–1960	74.9%
Cleifiog Uchaf SH282796	Beta-127200: 4040±90	Charcoal	Burnt area above pits (Davidson forthcoming)	2890–2300	12.0%
	Beta-127203: 3660±40	Charcoal	Pit (132), later reused as post-hole (Davidson forthcoming)	2190–1920	22.9%
	Beta-127204: 3670±40	Charcoal	Pit (118), later reused as post-hole (Davidson forthcoming)	2190–1930	27.5%
Great Carn, Cefn Bryn SS490905	Birm-1238: 3990±100	Burnt hazelnut shell	Post-hole sealed by OLS & later cairn. Context assoc. with Peterborough pottery, suggesting earlier use (Ward 1987, 40)	2880–2200	32.4%
	Birm-1236: 3960±100	Charcoal	Hearth sealed by OLS & later cairn. Context assoc. with Peterborough pottery, suggesting earlier use (Ward 1987, 40)	2870–2140	45.4%
Hindwell Ash SO257611	CAR-1480: 3730±70	Charcoal (oak)	Posthole, poss. part of rectilinear group below later mound (Gibson 1999, 20)	2350–1940	60.9%
Llyn Morwynion SH738425	Beta-136981: 3880±70 -28.7 ‰	Peat	Base of peat above hut circle. Sample point 75.5–77.5 cm deep in peat column (1) (Caseldine *et al.* 2001, 26, 29)	2560–2130	84.4%
	Beta-158560: 3870±60 -27.6 ‰	Peat	73.5–74.5 cm deep in peat column (1) (Caseldine *et al.* 2001, 26, 29)	2550–2140	89.8%
Moel y Gerddi SH616317	CAR-528: 4030±80, -25.9 ‰	Charcoal (wood)	Pit containing lithics & seeds inside later prehistoric enclosure (Kelly 1988b, 107)	2880–2340	11.6%
Peterstone Great Wharf ST262791	GrN-24149: 3910±60	Wood (oak)	Axe-marked post in line of 6 set in palaeochannel (Bell & Brown 2005, 93)	2560–2200	77.3%
Redberth SN082038	Wk-10154: 3761±56	Charcoal	1 of 3 aligned post-holes (Page unpublished)	2390–2020	77.3%
South Hook SM8605	Beta-255069: 3690±40	Charcoal	Feature (Crane, pers. comm.)	2200–1950	37.1%
Trelystan, house A SJ277070	CAR-276: 3960±70, -26.2 ‰	Wood (hazel)	Slot beside hearth (Britnell 1982, 139)	2830–2210	44.9%
Trelystan, house B SJ277070	CAR-274: 3990±70, -25.1 ‰	Hazelnut shells	Soil containing Grooved Ware & lithics, above hearth (Britnell 1982, 141)	2840 – 2290	25.3%

Table 12.7. Occupation sites (including measurements from single features at later period sites)

Site	Date BP, δ¹³C (where available)	Sample	Context	Calibrated BC (95% confidence)	Unmodelled probability of overlap with 2450–2100 cal BC
Bryn Bachau SH432371	Beta-204432: 3890±70	Charcoal (hazel, oak)	From discrete stone deposit on top of mound (Berks *et al.* 2007, 10)	2570–2140	81.7%
	Beta-204434: 3810±120	Charcoal (hazel, oak)	From primary fill of pit beside S edge of mound (Berks *et al.* 2007, 10)	2580–1920	68.9%
Carne, site A SM929371	CAR-292: 3790±70	Charcoal	Pit below central mound (James 1986, 245, 253)	2470–2020	83.7%
Carne, site B SM930371	CAR-589: 3960±65	Charcoal	Pit (77) below stone dumps (James 1986, 259). 3 other dates indicate later use of site	2630–2280	44.2%
	CAR-591: 3710±65	Charcoal	Pit (76) below stone dumps (James 1986, 259)	2300–1920	51.1%
Felin Fulbrook SN670625	CAR-469: 3875±70	Charcoal	Spread of charcoal & burnt stone (Benson & Williams 1981, 22)	2570–2140	85.5%
Figin Fawr SH5184	Beta-106684: 3770±60	Charcoal	Mound (Smith 1997, 57)	2460–2020	80.2%
Graeanog SH461494	CAR-713: 3660±70	Charcoal (inc. hazel, birch)	Lower fills of pit (M 14) sealed by mound (Kelly 1992, 84, 85)	2280–1880	29.4%
	CAR-714: 3890±70	Charcoal (inc. hazel, birch)	Lower fills of pit (M 14) sealed by mound (Kelly 1992, 84, 85)	2570–2140	81.7%
	CAR-715: 3740±70	Charcoal (oak & others)	Layer near base of mound (Kelly 1992, 85)	2410–1940	65.5%
Gwalchmai SH389777	SWAN-125: 3650±70	Charcoal		2210–1820	25.6%
Parc Bryn Cegin, site 2031 SH5970	NZA-26766: 3716±40	Charcoal (hazel)	Fill (2145) of trough (2149) (Kenney 2008, 126)	2280–1980	51.5%
Parc Bryn Cegin, site 2176 SH5970	KIA-30447: 3904±30	Charcoal (?hazel)	Main fill (2200) of trough (2197) (Kenney 2008, 126)	2480–2290	88.0%
	NZA-26770: 3899±35	Charcoal (hazel)	Fill of trough (2186) (Kenney 2008, 126)	2480–2240	88.9%
	NZA-26771: 3886±40	Charcoal (hazel)	Fill of trough (2186) (Kenney 2008, 126)	2480–2200	91.3%
	NZA-26772: 3878±40	Charcoal (hazel)	Fill (2208) of trough (2197) (Kenney 2008, 126)	2480–2200	92.8%
	NZA-26773: 3839±40	Charcoal (hazel)	Fill (2203) of trough (2202) (Kenney 2008, 126)	2470–2140	97.3%
	NZA-26774: 3738±40	Charcoal (hazel)	As above	2290–2020	66.3%
	NZA-26775: 3869±40	Charcoal (hazel)	Fill (2209) of hearth (2212) (Kenney 2008, 127)	2480–2200	94.2%
	NZA-26776: 3879±40	Charcoal (hazel)	As above	2480–2200	92.7%
Parc Bryn Cegin, site 4199 SH5970	NZA-26819: 3904±35	Charcoal (hazel)	Fill (4222) of trough (4208) (Kenney 2008, 127)	2480–2280	87.2%
Parc Bryn Cegin, site 4200 SH5970	NZA-26820: 3903±35	Charcoal (hazel)	As above	2480–2280	87.6%
Parc Bryn Cegin, site 6016 SH5970	NZA-26823: 3903±40	Charcoal (hazel)	Fill (6037) of pit (6018) (Kenney 2008, 127)	2490–2210	86.4%
	NZA-26821: 3863±40	Charcoal (hazel)	As above	2470–2200	95.0%
Parc Bryn Cegin, site 6019 SH5970	NZA-26824: 3913±35	Charcoal (hazel)	Fill (6020) of pit (6023) (Kenney 2008, 127). Same context also dated NZA-26825 2872±35BP	2490–2290	83.3%
Parc Bryn Cegin, site 7035 SH5970	KIA-30445: 3811±28	Charcoal (?oak)	Upper fill (7049) of pit (7045) (Kenney 2008, 128)	2350–2140	99.6%
	KIA-30446: 3612±68	Charcoal (?oak)	Middle fill (7048) of pit (7045) (Kenney 2008, 128)	2200–1770	13.1%
Parc Bryn Cegin, site 7039 SH5970	NZA-26822: 3898±40	Charcoal (hazel)	Fill (7044) of pit (7043) (Kenney 2008, 128). Same context also dated as NZA-26828 2829±35BP	2480–2210	88.2%
Parry's Castle Farm SN4114	Beta-159459: 3750±80	Charcoal	Mound (Martin & Phipps 2003)	2470–1940	68.4%
Plasgwyn Farm SN4014	Beta-159460: 3660±70	Charcoal	Pit associated with mound (Martin & Phipps 2003)	2280–1880	29.4%

Table 12.8. Burnt mounds

13

Searching for the Chalcolithic: continuity and change in the Irish Final Neolithic/Early Bronze Age

Neil Carlin and Joanna Brück

It is widely acknowledged that the Irish Early Bronze Age was significantly different in character to that of its neighbour, Britain. For example, Beaker burials of the type found elsewhere in north-west Europe are absent, yet as a major source of early copper, Ireland was far from marginal or insular. This paper will examine settlement and ceremonial sites, as well as mortuary and depositional practices in Ireland over the period 2900–1700 BC to consider whether there was a distinct 'Chalcolithic'. The strong evidence for continuity between the Late Neolithic and Early Bronze Age will be highlighted and it will be argued that metal had a very limited role in initiating and creating social change.

This paper will explore aspects of continuity and change in social practice in Ireland over the period 2900–1700 BC. Copper was introduced *c.* 2500 BC and was replaced by bronze *c.* 2200 BC. However, the broader chronological context within which this occurred will form the focus of discussion here so that the existence of a distinct Irish 'Copper Age' may be considered. The evidence for settlement, burial, depositional practices, ritual activities, special purpose artefacts, and international links will each be examined. Aspects of the archaeology of this period are very well-known (for example the Early Bronze Age burial record: eg, Waddell 1990; Mount 1997a; Brindley 2007), yet the transition from the Neolithic to the Bronze Age has rarely formed a detailed focus of discussion. Although the occasional presence of Grooved Ware has long

been recognised in Ireland (eg, Ó Ríordáin 1951; Liversage 1968), only recently has this ceramic begun to be widely identified (Cleary 1983; Roche 1995; Sheridan 1995; Brindley 1999). Prior to this, there was relatively little recognisable evidence for a distinct post-passage tomb Late Neolithic. O'Kelly (1989), for example, argues for a considerable degree of continuity between elements of the passage tomb complex (which we would now date to the Middle Neolithic) and Early Bronze Age monuments such as wedge tombs, and he employs the phrase 'Late Neolithic/Beaker' to describe the period of transition. Since the recognition of a Grooved Ware associated Late Neolithic (Cooney & Grogan 1999, 75–94; Cooney 2000; Roche & Eogan 2001), most studies have continued to argue for a considerable degree of continuity between the two periods. For example, Cooney and Grogan (1999, 75) identify what they characterise as a 'Final Neolithic' from 2800–2300 BC during which monuments such as timber circles were erected, the earliest Beaker ceramics were deposited at wedge tombs, and the first copper artefacts were introduced. In addition, Cooney (2000, 18) argues that wedge tombs (radiocarbon dated to a post-2400 BC horizon) can be seen as a final *floruit* of an essentially Neolithic tradition of megalithic tomb construction.

In this paper, we will examine evidence for diachronic change in different elements of the archaeological record, drawing on both published and unpublished material. We will examine in turn sites from which Grooved Ware (in an Irish context, dated *c.* 3000–2500/2400 BC: Brindley 1999; Sheridan 2004, 31), Beaker (*c.* 2500/2400–1900 BC: Brindley 2007, 321) and classic Early Bronze Age ceramics (Bowls 2160–1920 BC; Vases 2020/1990–1740 BC; Vase Urns 2000–1700 BC; Encrusted Urns 2000/1980–1700 BC; Collared Urns 1900–1650 BC; Cordoned Urns 1730–1500 BC: Brindley 2007) have been recovered. However, rather than attempting to construct a precise radiocarbon chronology for the period, this paper will identify broad trends in social practice and assess their significance. Aspects of the archaeological record that have been examined elsewhere, for example the development of mining and metallurgy in south-west Ireland (O'Brien 2004), will not be addressed; likewise, Irish rock art is now largely considered to be a Neolithic phenomenon (O'Connor 2006) and will not be considered here. In addition, subjects with which the authors cannot claim to be sufficiently familiar – such as evidence for palaeo-environmental change – will not be considered, such as possible indications of climatic deterioration identified by Baillie (1995). In parts of the country such as North Mayo, blanket bog was developing during this period, and there is some evidence for an increase in agricultural activity (O'Connell & Molloy 2001), although there was doubtless considerable regional variation. However, the relationship between these factors and contemporary social and technological change remains unclear and is unfortunately beyond the scope of the current paper.

Settlement

We will begin with the settlement record. Here, we will provide an overview of the types of structures, features and finds from possible 'domestic' sites of the period. For reasons of space, and because they have not been the focus of recent detailed study, Late Neolithic and Early Bronze Age settlement patterns and landscape organisation will not be considered here. Notwithstanding the difficulty of distinguishing houses from ceremonial structures (Brück 1999), there are few if any examples of domestic sites or buildings associated with Grooved Ware. One such is Slieve Breagh, Co. Meath, where the remains of two circular wooden structures have been interpreted as houses (de Paor & Ó h-Eochaidhe 1956; Grogan 2004, 111). Elsewhere, Grooved Ware has often been recovered from pits, either in isolation or clustered, for example at Low Park, Co. Mayo (Gillespie 2007). Spreads are also relatively common, for example at Dundrum, Co. Down (Collins 1952; 1959); and similar spreads are known from monumental contexts such as Knowth (Eogan & Roche 1997, 197, 202–11). At all of these sites, the range of artefact associations is similar, and includes animal bone and lithics, often of high quality Antrim flint, particularly end-scrapers made from long blades, discoidal knives, and oblique arrowheads (Roche & Eogan 2001, 127; Sheridan 2004, 27). Clearly, the question of whether any of these types of site can be identified as 'domestic' is a problematic issue and we will return to this later.

After 2500 BC, the number of possible domestic sites increases, although these are still very few. For example, at Graigueshoneen, Co. Waterford (Fig. 13.1), a sub-oval structure composed of stake-holes produced Beaker ceramics, a hearth, and a radiocarbon date of 2860–2490 cal BC (Johnston *et al.* 2008, fig. 1). In general, Beaker-associated buildings are not substantial, and a distinct architectural form cannot be recognised. Clusters of Beaker pits have been identified at many sites (Carlin 2011). These have produced pottery along with burnt and unburnt animal bone, the charred remains of cereals (especially barley) and wild plant resources such as sloes, apples, and hazelnuts. Flint artefacts include thumb-nail scrapers, barbed-and-tanged, and hollow-based arrowheads. There is good evidence for flint tool

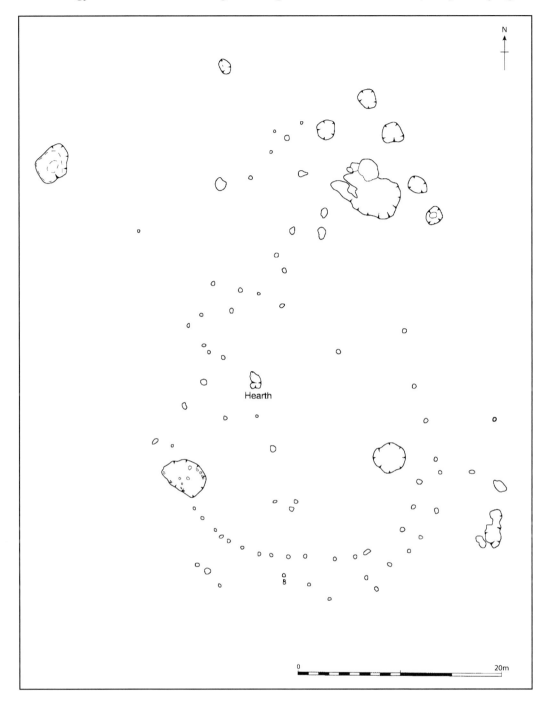

Figure 13.1: The Beaker associated oval structure at Graigueshoneen, Co. Waterford, excavated by John Tierney of Eachtra Archaeological Projects (after Johnston et al. 2008)

Hearth

0   20m

production usually from local sources. Polished stone axes, both complete and fragmentary, are also found. For example, at Cloghers, Co. Kerry, one of the pits produced Beaker pottery along with a kit for the production of stone axes comprising a complete polished sandstone axe, a hammer stone, and a grinding stone (Kiely & Dunne 2005).

Both Beaker and Grooved Ware pits range from examples containing 'formalised'

or structured deposits of large numbers of artefacts, some of them 'special' – for example the polypod bowl from Newtownbalregan 2, Co. Louth (Bayley 2008) – to those containing only a few sherds of ceramics. It is therefore difficult to distinguish a purely 'domestic' component to either Grooved Ware or Beaker pit deposition. Although there have been attempts to distinguish Beaker domestic from Beaker fineware ceramics in an Irish context (eg, Cleary 1983), in fact pit groups and ceremonial sites produce both of these classes, often from the same features. The same can be said for fine and coarse Grooved Ware (Roche 1995; Carlin *et al.* forthcoming). Nonetheless, it seems likely that some pit groups are the only surviving component of longer term forms of occupation.

Both Grooved Ware and Beaker occupation spreads have been identified, but Beaker spreads are far more common. Examples of the latter include an extensive occupation spread, some 26 m long by 9 m wide, at Kilgobbin, County Dublin (Ines Hagen pers. comm.), which produced pottery and lithics. It seems likely that some of these represent the eroded remains of middens, suggesting a significant change to depositional practices after 2500 BC and perhaps providing evidence for longer-term attachment to place.

After 2100 BC, both pit groups and occupation spreads associated with Food Vessels – predominantly Vases – are known. For example, at False Bay, Co. Galway, a midden that produced chert scrapers and ceramics of Vase form was discovered in sand dunes (McCormick 1995). However, the range and quantity of other artefact types from these sites is more restricted than for Beaker and Grooved Ware associated sites; for example, although scrapers, projectile points, and flint debitage are found, other types of artefact are seldom recovered. Domestic structures are also extremely rare. Some of the few known examples were identified at Omey Island, Co. Galway, where two circular and one rectangular structure were associated with Bowl ceramics (O'Keeffe 1993). Vase urns are also occasionally found in possible domestic contexts, notably pit groups. However, it is only after 1700 BC in association with Cordoned Urns that recognisable evidence for houses becomes more widespread.

Burial

The burial evidence shows some interesting patterns. A very small number of Grooved Ware associated burials are known. At Lyrath, Co. Kilkenny, a pit cluster produced two complete Grooved Ware pots filled with cremated human bone (E. Devine, pers. comm.). Significantly, this is one of the few examples of plausible burials known from the

many Grooved Ware associated sites discovered in recent developer-funded excavations.

There is more evidence for Beaker associated burial activities, mostly cremations. For example, at Monadreela, Co. Tipperary, cremated human bone was recovered from a pit containing 110 sherds from at least 10 Beakers (including fine and coarsewares), a large quantity of hazelnuts and acorns, and a small polished stone axe (R. O'Brien and J. Hughes, pers. comm.). What is interesting about this, and similar finds, is that they are often found in association with evidence for possible domestic activities. There are also a small number of possible Beaker inhumations. These include a prone inhumation within a partially stone lined grave at Mell, Co. Louth (McQuade 2005). The body was that of adult female and was east–west oriented; her head lay to the west and she was accompanied by animal bone and two convex scrapers. This burial, which bears strong resemblances to Beaker burials in northern Britain, has been radiocarbon dated to 2490–2200 cal BC. Although it was not accompanied by Beaker ceramics, a Beaker associated occupation spread, metalled surface, and possible structure were found on the same site.

Possible Beaker burials have also been identified in monumental contexts. The majority of sub-megalithic cists may date to the Late Neolithic/Early Bronze Age transition (Cooney & Grogan 1999, 86) and more specifically, perhaps, to the centuries 2500–2300 BC. For example at Furness, County Kildare, a sub-megalithic cist located next to a standing stone contained a cremation deposit, a fragment of a bracer, and one sherd of possible domestic Beaker (Macalister *et al.* 1913). Beaker-related human remains have also been found in many kerbed cairns. At Gortcobies, Co. Derry, for example, fragments of cremated human bone were recovered from the rectangular stone chamber at the centre of an oval cairn (May 1947; Fig. 13.2). These were accompanied by a flint blade and flake, Beaker ceramics, and a pymgy bowl.

We suggest that there is continuity between these funerary practices and the wedge tomb tradition. The latter comprises chambers of wedge-shape or trapezoidal plan predominantly found in the west of Ireland (Walsh 1995; O'Brien 1999). Their construction and main period of use has been firmly dated to the period 2400–2050 BC, although deposition continued after this date (Brindley & Lanting 1991). The chambers of most wedge tombs contained more than one individual, predominantly cremations (Cooney & Grogan 1999, 86). Obvious grave goods are rare: examples include the flint scrapers associated with two of the cremations from Island, Co. Cork (O'Kelly 1958). Beakers and Bowls associated with human bone are found in primary contexts within the chambers themselves (Brindley 2007, 51), for instance at Aughrim, Co. Cavan (Channing 1993). Vases and urns, however, form part of the evidence for secondary re-use of the tombs and are often found in cists and pits cut into the primary deposits or located outside of the monuments themselves. Although cremations are the predominant mortuary rite in wedge tombs, this does not appear to be the case for burials associated with Beaker ceramics. These include 12 inhumations and only four cremations. Hence, although there are significant elements of continuity in use and depositional practice at these sites over the course of the Early Bronze Age, there may also have been important changes perhaps reflecting wider transformations in funerary traditions.

The relationship between wedge tombs and preceding traditions of megalithic tomb construction in the Neolithic merits further comment. Although, as we will discuss later, ceremonial activities dating to the Late Neolithic can be identified at many passage tombs, these and other classes of megalithic tomb were predominantly constructed during the 4th millennium BC. We would therefore argue that the practice of building wedge tombs should be seen not as evidence for continuity but as the reinvention of a megalithic tradition.

This interest in earlier megalithic monument traditions is indicated by the reuse of a variety of Early and Middle Neolithic tombs for funerary purposes between 2900 and 1700 BC, and especially after 2200 BC.

Grooved Ware burials have occasionally been found in passage graves. For example, at Knowth, a cremation from the right-hand recess of passage tomb 6 was partly surrounded by the fragments of an incomplete Grooved Ware vessel (Eogan 1984, 312, fig 116; Roche & Eogan 2001, 127). Beaker burials have not been found in passage graves although a complete Beaker pot was placed next to an earlier cremation burial in Tomb 15 at Knowth (Figure 13.3). A longbone fragment from this burial has recently yielded a date of 2912–2877 cal BC (UBA-12683, 4265±24 BP) (Schulting *et al.* forthcoming).

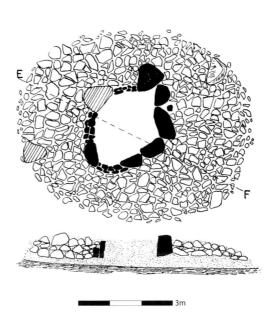

Figure 13.2: The Beaker associated cairn and chamber at Gortcobies, Co. Derry (after May 1947, fig. 5)

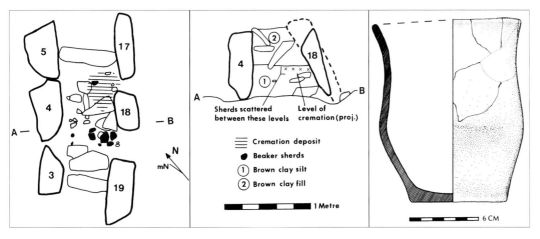

Figure 13.3: The cremation burial and associated Beaker from Tomb 15 at Knowth, Co. Meath (after Eogan 1984, fig. 117)

*Figure 13.4: Grave 6
at Keenoge, Co. Meath:
a cist containing an
east–west orientated
crouched inhumation
(adult female), a Bowl of
the Food Vessel tradition
placed beside the head
(after Mount 1997b,
fig. 11)*

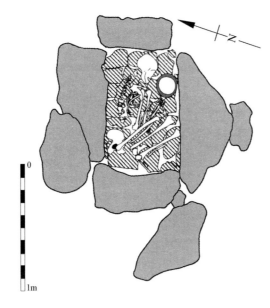

No Grooved Ware has been found either at court or portal tombs, but Beaker sherds have been found in secondary contexts in at least 11 court tombs (Carlin 2011). In most cases, these have been found in disturbed deposits that include artefacts ranging from the Early Neolithic to the Late Bronze Age, so it is usually impossible to identify reliable associations between the human bone recovered and particular finds. At Ballyglass, Co. Mayo, Beaker pottery was found in the front chamber of the eastern gallery within a layer that included human bone, Middle Neolithic pottery, and Late Bronze Age pottery (Ó Nualláin *et al.* forthcoming). Elsewhere, Beaker burials were inserted into the cairns that overlay court tombs. For example, a stone-lined pit dug into the cairn at Ballybriest, Co. Derry, contained the cremated remains of an adult male and sherds from a Beaker pot (Evans 1939). Finds of this date from portal tombs are less common and their identification as funerary deposits is problematic. For example, the portal tomb at Poulnabrone produced two Beaker sherds (E. Grogan, pers. comm.) and a hollow-based arrowhead, although the association between these finds and the human remains from the site remains unclear (Lynch & Ó Donnabháin 1994).

Later forms of Early Bronze Age pottery, notably Bowls and Vases, but also Collared and Cordoned Urns, occur with secondary burials in a number of Early and Middle Neolithic tombs. In contrast to the Beaker examples, these are more common and their depositional context and associations are often clearer: the presence of complete inhumations accompanied by Bowls or cremations in Urns means that these deposits can be readily identified as formal burials. For example, inhumation and cremation burials accompanied by Bowls, Vases, Encrusted, and Collared Urns were deposited inside the chamber and inserted into the mound itself at the Mound of the Hostages, Tara, Co. Meath (O'Sullivan 2005).

The increase in formal burials accompanied by Food Vessels and Urns in Neolithic monuments suggests that although there was continued interest in pre-existing monuments throughout the period, the nature of depositional practices at these sites changed after *c.* 2200 BC. This reflects the situation outside of megalithic contexts. With the emergence of Bowls and Vases, we see a dramatic increase in the number of single burials with grave goods (Waddell 1990). These form part of the coherent and distinctive mortuary traditions that developed after 2200 BC, often comprising small groups of 10–15 burials in cists or pits, either in flat cemeteries (Mount 1997a) or placed under round barrows and cairns (Eogan, J. 2004). Both inhumations and cremations are present, with a marked shift towards the latter over time (Cooney & Grogan 1999, 105). With the exception of pottery, grave goods are relatively rare.

The earliest of these traditions of single burial deserves special comment. Between 2200 and 1900 BC, inhumation burials appear accompanied by Bowls and other grave goods (Brindley 2007, 249). Marked similarities between Irish Bowl burials and Scottish Beaker burials can be observed (Waddell 1974, 35). These traditions share the common practice of east–west oriented inhumation, often placed within a cist, with the pot deposited by the head (Case 2004, 195–7; Fig. 13.4). Similarities can also be noted in accompanying grave goods which include boars' tusks, bronze knives, awls and bangles, and beads and buttons of jet-like materials. We therefore argue that Bowl burials formed the Irish equivalent of the Beaker mortuary tradition. This development can be seen as part of Needham's (2005, 205) fission horizon, *c.* 2250–1950 BC, which saw marked diversification and regionalisation in funerary practices in Britain. Interestingly, Bowls are rarely found in domestic contexts or

Figure 13.5: The Grooved Ware associated timber circle at Kilbride, Co. Mayo, excavated by Eamon Cotter for Archaeological Consultancy Services Ltd (after Cotter 2006)

2 metres

in association with other contemporary pottery types (Brindley 2007, 52). Vases, on the other hand, occur more regularly on domestic sites where they are sometimes found together with Beaker ceramics. This suggests that Bowls – unlike Irish Beakers – were considered special purpose funerary vessels whose use was restricted outside of the mortuary context. We might, therefore, suggest that Bowls were a completely new ceramic form designed specifically to function as the Irish version of British funerary Beakers while Vases and Beakers performed both domestic and funerary roles in an Irish context.

Ceremonial monuments

Open-air, communal ceremonial monuments

may have remained in use over the Late Neolithic–Early Bronze Age transition. However, the dating of embanked enclosures – the possible Irish version of British henge monuments – remains controversial and very few have been excavated. At Balregan, Co. Louth (Ó Donnchadha & Grogan 2007), a circular enclosure *c.* 60 m in diameter was defined by two ditches and an intervening stone bank. Grooved Ware pottery was discovered in the upper fills of the outer ditch. The embanked enclosure at Monknewtown, Co. Meath (Sweetman 1976), is generally dated to the Late Neolithic (Stout 1991; Condit & Simpson 1998; Cooney & Grogan 1999, 87–91), yet the dating evidence is extremely problematic. Finds of Middle Neolithic, Beaker, and Middle Bronze Age date were recovered from features in the interior (Roche & Eogan 2001, 135) but their relationship with the monument is unclear. The complexity of the issue is underlined by Roche's (2004) recent and convincing redating of the Grange embanked enclosure at Lough Gur, Co. Limerick, to the Late Bronze Age.

An increasing number of Grooved Ware and Beaker related pit- and post-circles have been identified in recent years. The excavation of a timber circle at Kilbride, County Mayo, radiocarbon dated to 2900–2670 cal BC, revealed a pit in front of the entrance that contained Grooved Ware, cremated bone, and flint debitage (Cotter 2006; Fig. 13.5). The three timber circles at Paulstown, Co. Kilkenny, produced only Beaker ceramics (Elliott 2009). In many cases, the Grooved Ware and Beaker pottery was deposited in pits cut into the top of the original post-holes as part of ritualised acts of abandonment or commemoration.

Perhaps the clearest evidence of continuity in ceremonial practice across the centuries on either side of 2500 BC comes from Newgrange. The large pit-circle immediately south-east of the main passage tomb was 70 m in external diameter and consisted of a series of concentric rows of pits and post-holes enclosing a small passage tomb, Site Z (O'Kelly *et al.* 1983, 16–21; Sweetman 1985). The investigations produced 13 radiocarbon dates covering the period 2865–2145 cal BC (Grogan 1991). Grooved Ware was found in at least three of the pits (O'Kelly *et al.* 1983, 18, 21), as well as within the interior of the circle in stake-holes and spreads of habitation debris (Roche & Eogan 2001, 129). Two further almost concentric arcs of large pits were discovered 30 m west of the main mound and may form a second circle with a diameter of *c.* 20 m (Sweetman 1987, 283–98). Finds retrieved from the pits included Beaker pottery, flint scrapers, *petit tranchet* derivative arrowheads, and a portion of a decorated stone bowl, as well as burnt cattle and pig bone. Radiocarbon dates from the pits of 2650–2320 cal BC combine with the ceramic evidence to suggest that this may post-date the use of Grooved Ware at the site. Other Beaker activity at Newgrange includes evidence for metalworking, a number of hearths, spreads of occupation debris, and up to 18 possible structures (O'Kelly *et al.* 1983; Cooney & Grogan 1999, 80). This is usually interpreted as domestic or industrial in character (eg, Stout & Stout 2008, 91), but it is in fact extremely difficult to identify distinct domestic and ritual spheres during this period (Brück 1999), and we argue that the majority of Beaker associated activity at Newgrange was produced in the context of ongoing ceremonial activities at the site. Indeed, as a magical and dangerous transformative activity, an ancestral site of ongoing ritual significance provided an entirely appropriate location for early metalworking.

The key point here is that there is significant evidence for continuity over the period of use of Grooved Ware and Beaker ceramics at Newgrange: the Middle Neolithic monument continued to be a focus of interest throughout this period and the forms of ceremonial practice that took place, such as the digging of pit-circles, did not change dramatically. However, here, as elsewhere, post- and pit-circles appear to fall out of use after 2200 BC. We can perhaps see this as indicating the demise of interest in large-scale, open-air external enclosures (at least until the Later Bronze Age), as concepts of community became increasingly focused on the local.

The deposition of special purpose objects

We have already discussed a variety of different forms of deposition. However, we would like to turn now to the deposition of special purpose items, many of which appeared for the first time during the Early Bronze Age.

The production and deposition of metalwork

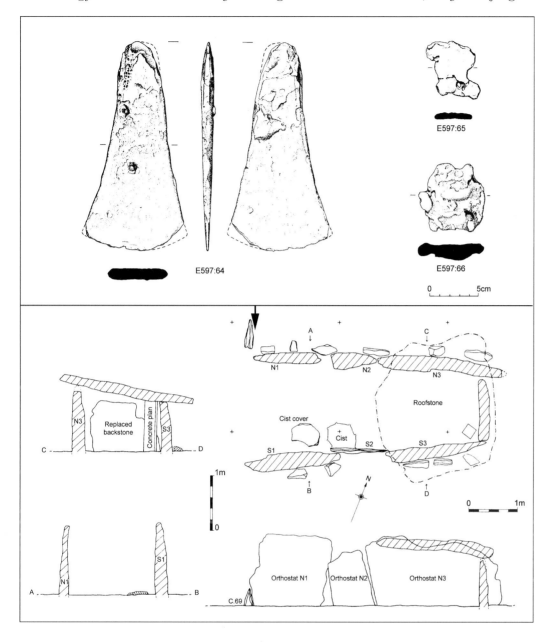

Figure 13.6: The wedge tomb at Toormore, Co. Cork; the hoard (location indicated by arrow) was deposited immediately beside of one of the upright stones that formed part of the entrance (after O'Brien 1999, figs 75 & 83)

is of course one of the key characteristics that archaeologists have traditionally employed to differentiate the Neolithic from the Bronze Age. Copper axes (78%) dominate the period 2500–2100 BC, followed by halberds (15%) and daggers (5%) (Becker 2006, 80). These were mostly deposited as single finds, and usually in wet places (81%), especially bogs (*ibid.*, 83). There is a much smaller number of hoards of copper objects; more of these – some 59% – were deposited in dryland contexts than the single finds. Gold ornaments – mostly lunulae and discs – were also deposited. Roughly half of these were recovered from dryland contexts (*ibid.*).

Some changes in depositional practice occurred around 2100 BC. The deposition of gold decreased, while larger numbers of bronze objects were deposited (Becker 2006, 93). Again, axes dominate the bronze finds (88%), while halberds disappear from the archaeological record. The number of hoards decreases, with 92% of bronzes deposited as single finds (*ibid.*, 94). More metal was deposited in graves (4%), but the overall amount is still extremely small. There is an increase in deposition in rivers in this period (*ibid.*, 95). Throughout the period 2500–1500 BC extremely few metal objects are known from possible settlement contexts. Likewise, metalwork is rarely found in monumental contexts. The deliberate deposition of a bronze flat axe and two copper cakes at the entrance to the wedge tomb at Toormore, Co. Cork, is one of the few known examples (O'Brien 1999, 169–71; Fig. 13.6).

Given the clear significance of metal axes in the Early Bronze Age, it may be useful to consider the deposition of polished stone axes. Stone axes were made and used throughout the Neolithic and into the Early Bronze Age. There is evidence for the production of stone axes associated with Beaker ceramics, but the occasional occurrence of stone axes in later contexts probably indicates the retention of heirlooms rather than the production of new artefacts. Unfortunately, it is difficult to distinguish those of different date on typological grounds alone so that changes over time may be masked. 45% of all polished stone axes from known contexts come from rivers, with a further 12% from bogs, and a small number from other wet contexts, for example lakes (Cooney & Mandal 1998, 34).

Alongside these, however, polished stone axes have been discovered in a wide variety of others locations (*ibid.*, 34–8) and it seems that there is greater diversity in their depositional context than was the case for their metal cousins. Stone axes have been recovered from pit groups and possible domestic contexts of both Late Neolithic and Early Bronze Age date. Neolithic ceremonial monuments such as timber circles have also produced stone axes. At Knowth, a porcellanite polished stone axe and two small axe fragments were recovered from the post-pits of the timber circle (Eogan & Roche 1997, 105). Axes have also been found in court tombs, passage tombs, and portal tombs (Cooney & Mandal 1998). In addition, they have been documented in Early Bronze Age funerary contexts including wedge tombs, Food Vessel, and Urn burials. For example, an axe fragment was discovered in the chamber of the wedge tomb at Lough Gur, Co. Limerick (Ó Ríordáin & O h-Iceadha 1955), while a cremation burial in a Cordoned Urn at Monasterboice, Co. Louth, was accompanied by a polished stone axe (Kavanagh 1976, 368–9).

Battle axes, maceheads, and bracers were generally deposited as single finds in the Early Bronze Age (Simpson 1996; Becker 2006, 100). Unlike the small number of contexted Late Neolithic maceheads, which predominantly come from lakes and bogs, those of Early Bronze Age date tend to come from rivers (Simpson 1996, 70). Battle-axes too were mainly deposited in rivers (Becker 2006, 100). Small numbers of battle-axes and maceheads are also known from funerary contexts: for example a battle-axe accompanied a cremation burial in a Cordoned Urn from the Mound of the Hostages, Tara, Co. Meath (O'Sullivan 2005, 191–5; E. Grogan, pers. comm.). Almost all Irish bracers are unprovenanced single finds without any associations (Harbison 1976, 7). However, a few examples are known from mortuary and ceremonial contexts. A bracer was found in the court tomb at Ballywholan, Co. Tyrone, although its context is unknown (Kelly 1985, 162). A further bracer was found with jet beads and two possible gold discs in a wooden box at Corran Bog, Co. Armagh (Case 1977, 21), and an occupation deposit at Rathmullan site 10, County Meath, produced 250 beaker sherds and a bracer (Bolger 2001); however, this is the only example known from a possible domestic context.

Turning now to v-perforated buttons, these occur in mortuary contexts, particularly megalithic tombs, and in 'natural' places such as bogs (Harbison 1976; Carlin 2011). Two anthracite buttons from the chamber of the passage tomb at the Mound of the Hostages appear to have accompanied Early Bronze Age inhumation burials (O'Sullivan 2005, 104–9). Two button hoards from wet contexts are also known: for instance, at Skeagh, Co. Cavan, ten bone buttons were deposited 'on a flagstone pavement' in a bog (Harbison 1976, 15). Only one v-perforated button has been found in a single burial in a non-megalithic context. This example, from Kinkit, Co. Tyrone, was made of bone and accompanied a cremation with a bone pin (Glover 1975). After 2100 BC, the number and variety of ornaments increases, with beads of bone, stone, faience, and amber known, predominantly from burials; however, the number remains very small – of the order of a few tens of ornaments from the whole of Ireland (Waddell 1990, 21–2, 26–7).

Overall, then, axes continue to play a particularly significant role over both the Neolithic and Early Bronze Age, although the material from which they were made changed. Importantly, however, metal axes were deposited in a much more restricted range of contexts than stone examples. The deposition of other types of metal artefact, including gold ornaments, also appears to have followed particular rules. This is the case for Early Bronze Age maceheads and battle-axes too. Other special-purpose artefacts, such as v-perforated buttons and bracers, appear to have been deposited in a slightly wider variety of contexts. However, other than the maceheads, there are few special purpose objects or personal ornaments of Late Neolithic date with which these can be compared. After 2100 BC, deposition in 'natural' places such as bogs continues, but there is greater emphasis on the deposition of grave goods in burials in tandem with the increased evidence for funerary activity. As the Early Bronze Age progresses, then, the contexts in which particular categories of artefact are found become more circumscribed (see also Becker 2006, 103–4). However, a detailed study of the deposition of different categories of artefact in the Irish Late Neolithic is required before diachronic trends can be identified with any certainty.

International links

The strong links between Ireland and Scotland during the early part of the Late Neolithic have been widely discussed, with the appearance of Grooved Ware and related artefact types (Roche 1995; Brindley 1999; Sheridan 2004, 32). North-eastern Ireland, south-west Scotland, and north-west England were also linked through the exchange of porcellanite and tuff axes during the Neolithic (Cooney 2000, 204). By the end of the Late Neolithic, however, attention had shifted towards Wessex, with links expressed in monuments such as timber circles (Sheridan 2004, 33).

Between 2500 and 2200 BC, however, the range of links both increases and diversifies. Beaker ceramics show influences from Wessex as well as from other areas of the Atlantic façade including France and Iberia (Case 1995, 20; 2001, 375). Contacts along the Atlantic façade appear to form part of a pre-existing tradition, as shared traditions of megalithic architecture and art (mostly of Middle Neolithic date) suggest (Shee Twohig 1993). Beaker polypod bowls are known from sites such as Mell, Co. Louth; these have parallels in central Europe (Harrison 1980, 26,

30, 39, 45) and southern France (Besse 2003; 2004). Irish bracers include both two-holed varieties, characteristic of the Atlantic tradition, and a small number of four-holed examples, indicative of northern European influences (Harbison 1976; Woodward *et al.* 2006, 534; Fokkens *et al.* 2008, 112). Both thick-butted and thin-butted copper axes are widely known, the former characteristic of the Atlantic tradition, the latter characteristic of northern European metalworking (Burgess 1979, 213). Gold items, such as the well-known sun-discs, have predominantly Atlantic affinities (Case 2001, 375). Traditions of collective burial in megalithic monuments, as identified in wedge tombs, are well known from other Beaker-using regions along the Atlantic façade, including Iberia and northern France; in these areas, older Neolithic tombs were also reused during this period (Vander Linden 2006, 319; Salanova 2007). Throughout the Atlantic region, as in Ireland, metal tended to be deposited in hoards and as single finds rather than in burials (Burgess 1979, 213). On the other hand, the presence of halberds in both Ireland and central Europe indicates ongoing links between these regions in terms of metal technology and use (Schuhmacher 2002, 282–4; O'Flaherty 2003). Networks of exchange with Britain are evident in the prevalence of A-Metal, probably from Ross Island, Co. Kerry, in the earliest British metalwork. Indeed, Ross Island metal is known from some southern British Beaker burials (Northover *et al.* 2001, 28; Needham 2004, 235).

After 2200 BC, the range of links decreases and the emphasis is again primarily on Britain. For example, the emergence of Food Vessels and Cordoned Urns, and the appearance of battle-axes, faience, and jet ornaments indicates that relationships with northern Britain were again strong. However, the discovery of bronze axes of Ballyvalley type, dating to *c.* 1900 BC and confirmed as Irish exports by metal analysis, in the Netherlands, Germany, France, Denmark, and Sweden indicates ongoing exchange with these regions (Mount 2000, 70). Overall, however, the evidence suggests an increase in interaction with Europe *c.* 2500–2300 BC and a willingness to display certain forms of European identity through the use of material culture. This contrasts with the situation in the Late Neolithic when exchange and interaction seems to focus almost exclusively on Britain.

After 2200 BC, the intensity of international links again decreased.

Summary: continuity or change?

What we see, then, is evidence for gradual and incremental change in social practice from 2900 to 1700 BC. There is a slight increase in the archaeological visibility of settlement sites, but the form and character of these do not change dramatically. Importantly, the ubiquity of both Grooved Ware and Beaker ceramics outside of ceremonial and mortuary contexts suggests that these were not restricted to an elite group, even from the earliest appearance of these pottery types. There is an increase in the evidence for burial with the appearance of Beaker ceramics. However, this does not take the same form as it does in Britain and central Europe. Instead, we see marked diversity in mortuary practice, with both cremations and inhumations, the construction of wedge tombs, the reuse of earlier Neolithic chambered tombs, and the deposition of burials in possible domestic contexts. In particular, the construction of wedge tombs differentiates the Late Neolithic from the earliest Bronze Age; megalithic monuments were not built in the Late Neolithic and we have suggested that wedge tombs represent the reinvention of a tradition. This reflects the heightened interest in Neolithic tombs amongst Beaker-using communities, as evidenced by increasing depositional activities at court, portal and passage tombs.

After 2200 BC, the number of burials again increases. Coherent traditions of mortuary practice now appear, notably Bowl burial, which we have suggested formed the Irish equivalent of British Beaker burials. The numbers of grave goods are still very small in comparison with Britain, however, and it is difficult to argue for either an institutionalised elite or a prestige goods economy during this period. There are also important elements of continuity with the preceding Neolithic: Irish Neolithic burials are predominantly cremations, and despite the brief florescence of inhumation between 2200 and 1900 BC, this long-standing cultural tradition re-emerges to dominate the funerary record of the later part of the Early Bronze Age and beyond.

Ceremonial monuments provide significant evidence for continuity between 2900 and

2200 BC. Both Grooved Ware and Beaker ceramics were employed in similar forms of depositional practice, and pit- and post-circles appear to have been constructed and used throughout this period. This is interesting, given that the production of Grooved Ware in Ireland ceased very suddenly and it was rapidly replaced by Beakers; certainly, there is nothing to suggest the level of overlap that is argued for southern Britain (eg, Needham 2005). Although the deposition of single finds of bronze in wet places increases after 2200 BC, pit- and post-circles fall out of use. The number of hoards, which can be interpreted as evidence for communal ritual activity, also decreased (Becker 2006, 106).

Axes retained their special role across the Late Neolithic–Early Bronze Age transition, with a focus on deposition in wet places. However, the range of locations in which Early Bronze Age metal axes were deposited was more limited, suggesting that their treatment was more rule-bound than that of their stone counterparts. This may suggest restricted access to this class of objects, or that the symbolism and social significance of axes may have changed. After 2500 BC, the variety of special purpose items in circulation increases; there is a further increase after 2200 BC at which point some were deposited in graves, although many – for example most bracers and battle-axes – were not.

Finally, as we have already noted, the scale and diversity of international links was noticeably greater at 2500–2200 BC. Both prior to and after this, relations with Britain dominate the archaeological record. In the light of such extensive but shifting international contacts, it is therefore all the more significant that the Irish evidence remains so different to that from other regions, particularly Britain. Throughout the period 2900–1700 BC, although British and continental European forms of material culture were adopted, these were employed in regional- and contextually-specific ways.

We therefore agree with Roche and Eogan (2001, 139) who argue that the most dramatic social changes of the 3rd millennium BC can be linked to the adoption of Grooved Ware and the decline of the passage tomb complex. These transformations appear to represent a breakdown in the centralised authority systems associated with the passage tombs and the emergence of local communities who began to develop their own unique identities by interacting with other local groups across the Irish Sea, adopting and adapting new ideas which they employed in idiosyncratic ways. If so, then it may be suggested that this provides the context for all subsequent developments over the course of the next millennium. The engagement of local communities with the international Beaker complex was simply the next step in this trajectory. The increasing interest in Neolithic monuments indicates a concern to define and underpin local identity in the context of wider inter-regional links. Developments after 2200 BC continue emerging trends towards regionalisation and diversification in social practice. For example, the decline in the use of timber circles and the greater emphasis on burial in small cemeteries is part of this increasing focus on the local community. Anthropological studies, for example of kingship, suggest that the human body often symbolises the body politic (eg, Douglas 1966). The dominance of single burial after 2200 BC many therefore indicate an increasing concern to maintain the symbolic boundaries of the corporate group, however that was defined.

Conclusion: Ireland and the Chalcolithic

This combination of elements of continuity and change makes the use in the Irish literature of terminology such as 'Final Neolithic' or 'Late Neolithic/Early Bronze Age' entirely understandable. But what of the term 'Chalcolithic'? Is this an appropriate label to describe the period 2500–2200 BC in Ireland? We argue that this term should not be employed in an Irish context as there is little evidence that the introduction of copper resulted in rapid or dramatic social change at this time. In Britain and on the continent, the introduction of metals is often thought to indicate the emergence of a hierarchical society in which individual status was attained by the competitive exchange and display of exotic goods (eg, Renfew 1974; Thorpe & Richards 1984; Clarke *et al.* 1985; Needham 2004; Heyd 2007; Sheridan 2008). However, there is little evidence for this in an Irish context. As we have seen above, copper artefacts were rarely deposited in mortuary contexts and, where they do occur, they should not be interpreted

solely in terms of the display of wealth or prestige (Brück 2004; Fokkens *et al.* 2008).

It is certainly true that large quantities of metal objects were deposited as single finds, particularly in wet places. However, the majority of these were axes and, as we shall discuss below, their use and deposition can only be understood in relation to pre-existing depositional practices. In a similar way, there is little to suggest that items such as gold lunulae should be interpreted simply as badges of status; it seems more likely that these were objects of ritual significance repeatedly hidden and retrieved because of their particular potency (Cahill 2005; Becker 2008; cf. Dickins 1996) and whose sacred power may have drawn on by more than one person during their lifespan. In addition, recent studies suggest that, in most other metal-using societies, political power was not based on control over metal production or exchange until many centuries (or even millennia) after the first appearance of metal objects (Thornton & Roberts 2009, 182) and we would argue that this was the case in Ireland too.

Indeed, the general emphasis on important individuals in the development of metallurgy is quite flawed. Roberts (2008a, 36) has demonstrated that metalworking was a community-based enterprise. It was necessary for communities to desire and support metal production by investing themselves in the laborious processes associated with the production of copper and by providing the various resources required. Roberts (2008b, 365–6) has also accentuated the strong influence of each community's worldview in determining the distinctive ways in which metallurgy was adopted and adapted to fit within pre-existing social practices. As such, although metallurgy may have been introduced by skilled – and possibly 'foreign' – individuals, it required both the practical and ideological support of the community to be accepted.

Of course, the introduction of metalworking could only have occurred through the movement of people with the requisite level of expertise (Roberts 2008a, 35), yet metallurgical knowledge spread very slowly across north-west Europe. In most areas, metal objects were very rare for the first few centuries after they appeared and neither metallurgical production nor consumption represented major changes in social practices (Roberts 2009). Although a large number of copper finds are known in Ireland, metal does not seem to have changed many (if any) aspects of everyday life (O'Brien 2004, 515) or offered many advantages over existing materials (Roberts 2008b, 365).

It is important to point out that the development of copper use in Ireland was strongly influenced by older traditions, particularly those associated with polished stone axes. For example, the dominance of flat axes within the restricted copper repertoire can be attributed to the importance of stone axes in the Mesolithic and Neolithic (Cooney 2004, 39). The exploitation of a single copper source for several centuries by communities in the south-west (O'Brien 2004, 563) and the wide distribution of the products from this quarry throughout the country and across the Irish Sea along pre-existing networks mirrors earlier traditions of polished stone axe manufacture (Cooney & Mandal 1998). As discussed above, the deposition of copper axes respects the custom of predominantly depositing stone axes in wet places. The discovery of a cache of polished stone axes in an Early Bronze Age copper mine at Ballyrisode, near Goleen, Co. Cork (O'Brien 2003, 53–4), illustrates the strong role played by existing crafts in the acceptance of the new technology. In terms of both exchange and deposition, then, the introduction of copper provides significant evidence for continuity, suggesting that stone and metal axes were involved in similar social practices and forms of identity production.

The transmission of metallurgical expertise to Ireland occurs at the same time as the adoption of aspects of Beaker associated social practices, as was the case across north-western Europe (Brodie 2001; Vander Linden 2007, 348). This can be attributed to the desire of communities to participate in wider networks of socio-cultural interaction which involved the circulation of people, ideas, beliefs, expertise, and objects including Beaker pottery and copper (Roberts 2008a, 36; see Vander Linden 2007). Participation in this inter-regional social network appears to have been part of a strategy chosen by local groups in the negotiation of their world-view that enabled the creation and maintenance of particular forms of social identity both within and beyond the local community (Barrett 1994, 97–107; Thomas 1999, 122; Vander Linden 2007, 350; Vander Linden *et al.* 2009, 77). At

the same time as the introduction of Beaker pottery to Ireland, we see a clear increase in the amount and diversity of inter-regional interaction. As past boundaries faded and older networks were reopened, enhanced interaction also resulted in the spread of metallurgical expertise. However, the Irish evidence suggests that Beakers and metals were not introduced as part of a unified cultural 'package'. The relatedness of these phenomena may have been greatly exaggerated because of their appearance during the same period and their co-occurrence as grave goods in other regions.

Instead, metal should be viewed as one of a variety of novel materials and objects that were circulating in inter-regional exchange networks from 2500–2200 BC. Early Irish metallurgy represents only one element in a range of new practices involving the creation, use, and deposition of both special and everyday objects. Like the production of Beaker pots, faience, and fine flintwork, early metallurgy was a transferable transformative technology that was employed in the construction of social identities and that helped communities mark and mediate the shifting social boundaries that defined their world. Craftsmanship and technical expertise appear to have been particularly valued during this period and it seems likely that such skills would have been central to the creation of age, gender, and ethnic identities (eg, Shell 2000; Butler & Fokkens 2005, 396; Fitzpatrick 2009). The possession of technical know-how would have given certain people special significance; as such, social status was undoubtedly interwoven with other aspects of identity in the performance of craft activities and the use and deposition of the objects produced, but should not be considered the sole or even the most noteworthy element. Most importantly, through the investment of time, energy and expertise in the creation and distribution of copper objects and other special items, people imbued these with social value and demonstrated connections with other communities. However, although copper was a novel material, its role in identity construction parallels – in certain important respects – previous traditions such as the distribution of jadeite axes from the western edge of the Alps as far west as Ireland during the late 6th to early 4th millennium BC (see Pétrequin *et al.* 2008; 2009).

We would, therefore, argue that the term

Chalcolithic is not appropriate in an Irish context, with metallurgy representing only one aspect of a broader series of gradual social and economic transformations. Indeed, too great a focus on terminology inevitably impoverishes our engagement with and understanding of the complexities of social change over the period 2900–1700 BC. Currently, there is too great a divide between specialists working on the Neolithic and the Bronze Age, despite the striking evidence of continuity discussed in this paper. With ongoing refinements in radiocarbon dating techniques, it should increasingly be possible to create finer chronologies that come closer to the human experience of change. These will inform a more nuanced understanding of the trajectory of change over this period. Ultimately, this may allow us to begin to ask why it was that the social and economic transformations we have outlined in this paper occurred.

Acknowledgements

Many thanks to Muiris O'Sullivan, Eoin Grogan, Helen Roche, and our anonymous referees for detailed and constructive comments on an earlier version of this paper. We are also grateful to Conor McDermott for assistance with the illustrations. Thanks to Rick Schulting and Kerri Cleary for permission to refer to the radiocarbon date from Knowth in advance of publication

Bibliography

Baillie, M. 1995. *A Slice Through Time: dendrochronology and precision dating.* London: Routledge

Barrett, J.C. 1994. *Fragments from Antiquity. An Archaeology of Social Life in Britain, 2900–1200 BC.* Oxford: Blackwell

Bayley, D. 2008. *Final Report on the Excavations at Newtownbalregan 2, Site 113, Co. Louth.* Unpubl. report, Irish Archaeological Consultancy Ltd on behalf of Louth Co. Council & the National Roads Authority

Becker, K. 2006. *Hoards and Deposition in Bronze Age Ireland.* Dublin: Unpubl. PhD thesis, University College Dublin

Becker, K. 2008. Left but not lost. *Archaeology Ireland* 22(1), 12–15

Besse, M. 2003. Les ceramiques communes des Campaniformes europ'eens. *Gallia Prehistoire* 45, 205–58

Besse, M. 2004. Bell Beaker common ware during the third millennium BC in Europe. In J. Czebreszuk (ed.), *Similar but Different. Bell Beakers in Europe*, 127–48. Poznan: Adam Mickiewicz University

Bolger, T. 2001. Three sites on the northern motorway at Rathmullan, Co. Meath. *Riocht na Midhe* 7, 8–17

Brindley, A. 1999. Irish Grooved Ware. In R. Cleal & A. MacSween (eds), *Grooved Ware in Britain and Ireland*, 23–35. Oxford: Oxbow Books, Neolithic Studies Group Seminar Papers 3

Brindley, A. 2007. *The Dating of Food Vessels and Urns in Ireland.* Galway: Galway University Press

Brindley, A. & Lanting, J.N. 1991. Radiocarbon dates from wedge tombs. *Journal of Irish Archaeology* 6, 19–26

Brodie, N. 2001. Technological frontiers and the emergence of the Beaker culture. In F. Nicolis (ed.), *Bell Beakers Today. Pottery, People, Culture, Symbols in Prehistoric Europe*, 487–96. Trento: Servizio Beni Culturali, Ufficio Beni Archeologici

Brück, J. 1999. What's in a settlement? Domestic practice and residential mobility in Early Bronze Age southern England. In J. Brück & M. Goodman (eds), *Making Places in the Prehistoric World: themes in settlement archaeology*, 53–75. London: UCL Press

Brück, J. 2004. Material metaphors: the relational construction of identity in Early Bronze Age burials in Ireland and Britain. *Journal of Social Archaeology* 4(3), 307–33

Burgess, C. 1979. The background of early metalworking in Ireland and Britain. In M. Ryan (ed.), *The Origins of Metallurgy in Atlantic Europe*, 207–47. Dublin: Stationery Office

Butler, J. & Fokkens, H. 2005. From stone to bronze. Technology and material culture. In L.P. Louwe Kooijmans, P.W. van den Broeke, H. Fokkens & A.L. van Gijn (eds), *The Prehistory of the Netherlands, Volume 1*, 371–99. Amsterdam: Amsterdam University Press

Cahill, M. 2005. Roll your own lunula. In T. Condit & C. Corlett (eds), *Above and Beyond: essays in memory of Leo Swan*, 53–62. Dublin: Wordwell

Carlin, N. 2011. Into the West: placing Beakers within their Irish contexts. In A. M. Jones & G. Kirkham (eds), *Beyond the Core: Reflections on Regionality in Prehistory*, 87–100. Oxford: Oxbow Books

Carlin, N., Smyth, J., Grogan, E. & Roche, H. forthcoming. *Squaring the Circle/Circling the Square – the Grooved Ware Phenomenon in Ireland*

Case, H. 1977. An early accession to the Ashmolean Museum. In V. Markotic (ed.), *Ancient Europe and the Mediterranean*, 18–34. Warminster: Aris & Phillips

Case, H. 1995. Irish Beakers in their European Context. In J. Waddell & E. Shee Twohig (eds), *Ireland in the Bronze Age*, 14–29. Dublin: Stationery Office

Case, H. 2001. The Beaker culture in Britain and Ireland: groups, European contacts and chronology. In F. Nicolis (ed.), *Bell Beakers Today. Pottery, People, Culture, Symbols in Prehistoric Europe*, 361–77. Trento: Servizio Beni Culturali, Ufficio Beni Archeologici

Case, H. 2004. Beaker burial in Britain and Ireland. A role for the dead. In M. Besse & J. Desideri (eds), *Graves and Funerary Rituals during the Late Neolithic and the Early Bronze Age in Europe*, 195–201. Oxford: British Archaeological Report S1284

Channing, J. 1993. Aughrim. In I. Bennett (ed.), *Excavations 1992*, 4. Wicklow: Wordwell

Clarke, D.V., Cowie, T.G. Foxon, A. 1985. *Symbols of Power at the Time of Stonehenge.* Edinburgh: HMSO

Cleary, R. 1983. The ceramic assemblage. In M.J. O'Kelly, R. Cleary & D. Lehane, *Newgrange, Co. Meath, Ireland: the Late Neolithic–Beaker period settlement*, 58–108. Oxford: British Archaeological Report S190

Collins, A.E.P. 1952. Excavations in the Sandhills at Dundrum, Co. Down, 1950–51. *Ulster Journal of Archaeology* 15, 2–26

Collins, A.E.P. 1959. Further investigations in the Dundrum Sandhills. *Ulster Journal of Archaeology* 22, 5–20

Condit, T. & Simpson, D. 1998. Irish hengiform enclosures and related monuments: a review. In A. Gibson & D. Simpson (eds), *Prehistoric Ritual and Religion*, 45–61. Sutton: Stroud.

Cooney, G. 2000. *Landscapes of Neolithic Ireland*. London: Routledge

Cooney, G. 2004. Performance and place: the hoarding of axeheads in Irish prehistory. In Roche *et al.* (eds) 2004, 38–44

Cooney, G. & Grogan, E. 1999. *Irish Prehistory: a social perspective*. Dublin: Wordwell.

Cooney, G. & Mandal, S. 1998. *The Irish Stone Axe Project. Monograph 1*. Bray: Wordwell

Cotter, E. 2006. *Excavations at Kilbride, Co. Mayo*. Unpublished report, Archaeological Consultancy Services Ltd

de Paor, L. & Ó h-Eochaidhe, M. 1956. Unusual group of earthworks at Slieve Breagh, Co. Meath. *Journal of the Royal Society of Antiquaries of Ireland* 86, 97–101

Dickins, J. 1996. A remote analogy?: from Central Australian tjuranga to Irish Early Bronze Age axes. *Antiquity* 70, 161–167

Douglas, M. 1966. *Purity and Danger: an analysis of the concepts of pollution and taboo*. London: Routledge & Kegan Paul

Elliott, R. 2009. *Excavations at Paulstown, Co. Kilkenny*. Unpublished report by Irish Archaeological Consultancy Ltd on behalf of Kilkenny Co. Council & the National Roads Authority

Eogan, G. 1984. *Excavations at Knowth, 1*. Dublin: Royal Irish Academy Monograph in Archaeology 1

Eogan, G. & Roche, H. 1997. *Excavations at Knowth, 2*. Dublin: Royal Irish Academy Monograph in Archaeology 3

Eogan, J. 2004. The construction of funerary monuments in the Irish Early Bronze Age: a review of the evidence. In Roche *et al.* (eds) 2004, 56–60

Evans, E.E. 1939. Excavations at Carnanbane, Co. Londonderry: a double horned cairn. *Proceedings of the Royal Irish Academy* 45C, 1–12

Fitzpatrick, A. 2009. In his hands and in his head: the Amesbury Archer as a metalworker. In P. Clarke (ed.), *Bronze Age Connections: cultural contact in prehistoric Europe*, 177–189. Oxford: Oxbow Books

Fokkens, H., Achterkamp, Y. & Kuijpers, M. 2008. Bracers or bracelets? About the functionality and meaning of Bell Beaker wrist-guards. *Proceedings of the Prehistoric Society* 74, 109–40

Gillespie, R. 2007. Prehistory and history on the N5 Charlestown Bypass in counties Mayo and Roscommon. In J. O'Sullivan & M. Stanley (eds), *New Routes to the Past*, 11–25. Dublin: Archaeology and the National Roads Authority Monograph 4

Glover, W. 1975. Segmented cist grave in Kinkit Townland, County Tyrone. *Journal of the Royal Society of Antiquaries of Ireland* 105, 141–4 & 150–5

Grogan, E. 1991. Radiocarbon dates from Brúgh na Bóinne, 126–32 in G. Eogan, Prehistoric and Early

Historic culture change at Brú na Bóinne. *Proceedings of the Royal Irish Academy* 91C, 105–32

Grogan, E. 2004. The implications of Irish Neolithic Houses. In I.A.G. Shepherd & G.J. Barclay (eds), *Scotland in Ancient Europe: the Neolithic and Early Bronze Age of Scotland in their European context*, 103–14. Edinburgh: Society of Antiquaries of Scotland

Harbison, P. 1976. *Bracers and V-perforated Buttons in the Beaker and Food Vessel Cultures of Ireland*. Archaeologica Atlantica Research Report 1. Bad Bramstedt: Moreland

Harrison, R.J. 1980. *The Beaker Folk. Copper Age Archaeology in Western Europe*. London: Thames & Hudson

Heyd, V. 2007. Families, prestige goods, warriors and complex societies: Beaker groups of the third millennium cal BC along the Upper and Middle Danube. *Proceedings of the Prehistoric Society* 73, 321–370

Johnston, P., Kiely, J. & Tierney, J. 2008. *Near the Bend in the River: the Archaeology of the N25 Kilmacthomas Re-alignment*. Bray: National Roads Authority Monograph/ Wordwell

Kavanagh, R. 1976. Collared and Cordoned Urns in Ireland. *Proceedings of the Royal Irish Academy* 76C, 293–403

Keeley, V. 1989. Taylorsgrange portal tomb. In C. Manning & D. Hurl (eds), Excavation bulletin 1980–4. *Journal of Irish Archaeology* 5, 74

Kelly, D. 1985. A possible wrist-bracer from County Tyrone. *Journal of the Royal Society of Antiquaries of Ireland* 115, 162

Kiely, J. & Dunne, L. 2005. Recent archaeological excavations in the Tralee area. In M. Connolly (ed.), *Past Kingdoms: recent archaeological research, survey and excavation in County Kerry*, 39–64. Tralee: Heritage Council/ Kerry Co. Council

Liversage, G.D. 1968. Excavations at Dalkey Island, Co. Dublin, 1956–1959, *Proceedings of the Royal Irish Academy* 66C, 53–233

Lynch, A. & Ó Donnabháin, B. 1994. Poulnabrone portal tomb. *The Other Clare* 18, 5–7

Lynch, R. 1998. *Excavations at Taylorsgrange, Dublin*. Unpublished report by Magaret Gowen & Co. Ltd

MacAllister, R.A.S. 1928. *The Archaeology of Ireland*. London: Methuen

MacAllister, R.A.S., Armstrong, E.C.R, & Praeger, R. 1913. A Bronze Age interment near Naas. *Proceedings of the Royal Irish Academy* 30C, 351–60

May, A. McL. 1947. Burial mound, circles and cairn, Gortcorbies, Co. Londonderry. *Journal of the Royal Society of Antiquaries of Ireland* 77, 5–22

McCormick, F. 1995. False Bay, Co. Galway, in the Bronze Age. *Archaeology Ireland* 9(1), 12–13

McQuade, M. 2005. Archaeological excavation of a multi-period prehistoric settlement at Waterunder, Mell, Co. Louth. *County Louth Archaeological and Historical Journal* 26, 31–66

Mount, C. 1997a. Early Bronze Age burial in south-east Ireland in the light of recent research, *Proceedings of the Royal Irish Academy* 97C, 101–93

Mount, C. 2000. Exchange and communication: the relationship between Early and Middle Bronze Age Ireland and Atlantic Europe. In J.C Henderson (ed.), *The Prehistory and Early History of Atlantic Europe*, 57–72. Oxford: British Archaeological Report S861

Needham, S.P. 2004. Migdale-Marnoch: sunburst of Scottish metallurgy. In I.A.G. Shepherd & G.J. Barclay (eds), *Scotland in Ancient Europe: the Neolithic and Early Bronze Age of Scotland in their European context*, 217–45. Edinburgh: Society of Antiquaries of Scotland

Needham S.P. 2005. Transforming Beaker culture in north-west Europe: processes of fusion and fission. *Proceedings of the Prehistoric Society* 71, 171–217

Northover, P., O'Brien, W. & Stos, S. 2001. Lead isotopes and metal circulation in Beaker/Early Bronze Age Ireland. *Journal of Irish Archaeology* 10, 25–48

Ó Donnchadha, B. & Grogan, E. 2007. *Excavation Report for Balregan 1 and 2, Site 116, Co. Louth.* Unpublished report by Irish Archaeological Consultancy Ltd on behalf of Louth Co. Council & the National Roads Authority

Ó Nualláin, S., Greene, S. & Rice, K. forthcoming. *Excavation of a Centre Court Tomb and Underlying House Site at Ballyglass, Co. Mayo.* Dublin: UCD School of Archaeology/Wordwell

Ó Ríordáin, S.P. 1951 Lough Gur excavations: the great stone circle (B) in Grange townland. *Proceedings of the Royal Irish Academy* 54C, 37–74

Ó Ríordáin, S.P. & O h-Iceadha, G.1955. Lough Gur excavations: the megalithic tomb. *Journal of the Royal Society of Antiquaries of Ireland* 85, 34–50

O'Brien, W. 1999. *Sacred Ground: Megalithic Tombs in Coastal South-West Ireland. Bronze Age Studies* 4. Galway: Dept of Archaeology, NUI Galway

O'Brien, W. 2003. The Bronze Age copper mines of the Goleen area, County Cork. *Proceedings of the Royal Irish Academy* 103C, 13–59

O'Brien, W. 2004. *Ross Island. Mining, Metal and Society in Early Ireland. Bronze Age Studies* 6. Galway: Dept. of Archaeology, NUI Galway

O'Connell, M. & Molloy, K. 2001. Farming and woodland dynamics in Ireland during the Neolithic. *Proceedings of the Royal Irish Academy* 101B, 99–128

O'Connor, B. 2006. *Inscribed Landscapes: Contextualising Prehistoric Rock Art in Ireland.* Dublin: Unpublished PhD thesis, University College Dublin

O'Flaherty, R. 2003. *A Consideration of the Early Bronze Age Halberd in Ireland.* Dublin: Unpublished PhD thesis, University College Dublin

O'Keeffe, T. 1993. Omey Island, Goreen and Sturakeen. In I. Bennet (ed.), *Excavations 1992*, 30–1. Bray: Wordwell

O'Kelly, M.J. 1958. A wedge-shaped gallery-grave at Island, Co. Cork. *Journal of the Royal Society of Antiquaries of Ireland* 88, 1–23

O'Kelly, M.J. 1989. *Early Ireland: an Introduction to Irish prehistory.* Cambridge: Cambridge University Press

O'Kelly M.J., Cleary, R. & Lehane, D. 1983. *Newgrange, Co. Meath, Ireland: the Late Neolithic–Beaker Period Settlement.* Oxford: British Archaeological Report S190

O'Sullivan, M. 2005. *Duma na nGiall. The Mound of the Hostages, Tara.* Dublin: UCD School of Archaeology/Wordwell

Pétrequin, P., Cassen, S., Errera, M, Gauthier E., Klassen, L., Pailler, Y., Pétrequin, A-M. & Sheridan, A. 2009. L'unique, la paire, les multiples. À propos des dépôts de haches polies en roches alpines en Europe occidentale pendant les cinquième et quatrième millénaires. In S. Bonnardin, C. Hamon, M. Lauwers & B. Quilliec, *Du Matériel au Spirituel. Réalités Archéologiques et Historiques des 'Dépôts' de la Préhistoire à nos Jours. XXIXe rencontres Rencontres Internationales d'Archéologie et d'Histoire d'Antibes*, 417–27. Antibes: Éditions APDCA

Pétrequin, P., Sheridan, A., Cassen, S., Errera, M., Gauthier E., Klassen, L., Le Maux, N. & Pailler, Y. 2008. Neolithic Alpine axeheads from the Continent to Great Britain, the Isle of Man and Ireland. In H. Fokkens, B.J. Coles, A.L. van Gijn, J.P. Kleijne, H.H. Ponjee & C.G. Slappendel (eds), *Between Foraging and Farming: an Extended Broad Spectrum of Papers Presented to Leendert Louwe Kooijmans*, 261–81. Leiden: *Analecta Praehistorica Leidensia* 40

Renfrew, A.C. 1974. Beyond a subsistence economy: the evolution of prehistoric Europe. In C.B. Moore (ed.), *Reconstructing Complex Societies*, 69–95. *Bulletin of the American Schools of Oriental Research* 20

Roberts, B.W. 2008a. Migration, craft expertise and metallurgy: analysing the 'spread' of metal in Europe. *Archaeological Review from Cambridge* 23(2), 27–45

Roberts, B.W. 2008b. Creating traditions and shaping technologies: understanding the emergence of metallurgy in Western Europe, *c.* 3500–2000 BC. *World Archaeology* 40(3), 354–72

Roberts, B.W. 2009. Production Networks and Consumer Choice in the Earliest Metal of Western Europe. *Journal of World Prehistory* 22, 461–81

Roche, H. 1995. *Style and Context for Grooved Ware in Ireland with Special Reference to the Assemblage at Knowth, Co. Meath.* Dublin: Unpublished MA thesis, University College Dublin

Roche, H. 2004. The dating of the embanked stone circle at Grange, Co. Limerick. In Roche *et al.* (eds), 2004, 109–16

Roche, H. & Eogan, G. 2001. Late Neolithic activity in the Boyne Valley, Co. Meath. In C.T.L. Roux (ed.), *Du Monde des Chasseurs à celui des Métallurgistes: Hommage Scientifique à la Mémoire de Jean L'Helgouach et Mélanges Offerts à Jacques Briard*, 125–40. Rennes: Revue Archéologiques de l'Ouest, Supplement 9

Roche, H., Grogan, E., Bradley, J., Coles, J. & Raftery, B. (eds). 2004. *From Megaliths to Metals: Essays in Honour of George Eogan.* Oxford: Oxbow Books

Salanova, L. 2007. Les sépultures campaniformes: lecture sociale. In J. Guilaine (ed.), *Le Chalcolithique et la Construction des Inégalités*, 213–28. Paris: Éditions Errance.

Schuhmacher, T.X. 2002. Some remarks on the origin and chronology of halberds in Europe. *Oxford Journal of Archaeology* 21, 263–88

Schulting, R., Bronk Ramsey, C., Reimer, P., Eogan, G., Cleary, K., Cooney, G. & Sheridan, A. forthcoming. Dating Knowth. In G. Eogan & K. Cleary, *The Archaeology of the Large Mound at Knowth, Volume 6.* Dublin: Royal Irish Academy

Shee Twohig, E. 1993. Megalithic tombs and megalithic art in Atlantic Europe. In C. Scarre & F. Healy (eds), *Trade and Exchange in Prehistoric Europe*, 87–99. Oxford: Oxbow Books

Shell, C. 2000. Metalworker or shaman: Early Bronze Age Upton Lovell G2a burial. *Antiquity* 74, 271–2

Sheridan, J.A. 1995. Irish Neolithic pottery: the story in 1995. In I. Kinnes & G. Varndell (eds), *Unbaked Urns of Rudely Shape. Essays on British and Irish Pottery for Ian Longworth*, 3–21. Oxford: Oxbow Books

Sheridan, J.A. 2004. Going round in circles? Understanding the Irish Grooved Ware 'complex' in its wider context. In Roche *et al.* (eds) 2004, 26–37

Sheridan, J.A. 2008. Towards a fuller, more nuanced narrative of Chalcolithic and Early Bronze Age Britain 2500–1500 BC. *Bronze Age Review* 1, 57–78

Simpson, D.D.A. 1996. Irish perforated stone implements in context. *Journal of Irish Archaeology* 7, 65–76

Stout, G. 1991. Embanked enclosures of the Boyne region. *Proceedings of the Royal Irish Academy* 91C, 245–84

Stout, G. & Stout, M. 2008. *Newgrange*. Cork: Cork University Press

Sweetman, P.D. 1976. An earthen enclosure at Monknewtown, Slane, Co. Meath. *Proceedings of the Royal Irish Academy* 76C, 25–72

Sweetman, P.D. 1985. A Late Neolithic/Early Bronze Age pit circle at Newgrange, Co. Meath. *Proceedings of the Royal Irish Academy* 85C, 195–221

Sweetman, P.D. 1987. Excavation of a Late Neolithic/Early Bronze Age Site at Newgrange, Co. Meath. *Proceedings of the Royal Irish Academy* 87c, 238–98.

Thomas, J. 1999. *Understanding the Neolithic*. London: Routledge

Thornton, P. & Roberts, B.W. 2009. Introduction: the beginnings of metallurgy in global perspective. *Journal of World Prehistory* 22, 181–4

Thorpe, I.J. & Richards, C. 1984. The decline of ritual

authority and the introduction of Beakers into Britain. In R. Bradley & J. Gardiner (eds), *Neolithic Studies: a review of some current research*, 67–84. Oxford: British Archaeological Report 133

Vander Linden, M. 2006. For whom the bell tolls: social hierarchy vs social integration in the Bell Beaker culture of southern France. *Cambridge Archaeological Journal* 16, 317–32

Vander Linden, M. 2007 What linked the Bell Beakers in third millennium BC Europe? *Antiquity* 81, 343–52

Vander Linden, M., Vandkilde, H., Makarowicz, P., Czebreszuk, J., Østmo, E., Prescott, C., Melheim, L., & Prieto-Martínez, M.P. 2009. Comments on M. Pilar Prieto Martínez, 'Bell Beaker communities in Thy: the first Bronze Age society in Denmark', *Norwegian Archaeological Review* 42(1), 71–100

Waddell, J. 1974. On some aspects of the Late Neolithic and Early Bronze Age in Ireland. *Irish Archaeological Research Forum* 1, 32–8

Waddell, J. 1990. *The Bronze Age Burials of Ireland*. Galway: Galway University Press

Walsh, P. 1995. Structure and deposition in Irish wedge tombs: an open and shut case. In J. Waddell & E. Shee Twohig (eds), *Ireland in the Bronze Age*, 113–27. Dublin: Stationery Office

Woodward, A., Hunter, J., Ixer, R., Roe, F., Potts, P.J., Webb, P.C., Watson, J.S. & Jones, M.C. 2006. Beaker Age bracers in England: sources, function and use. *Antiquity* 80, 530–43

14

The Chalcolithic in Ireland: a chronological and cultural framework

William O'Brien

This paper considers a distinct period of metal production and use in Ireland at the end of the Neolithic, spanning the second half of the 3rd millennium BC. This 'Chalcolithic' or 'Copper Age' was marked by a widespread adoption of copper and gold prior to the introduction of tin-bronze metallurgy c. 2000 BC. Metallurgy and other material innovations were introduced to Ireland at this time through contacts with the Beaker network of exchanges. The rapid spread of metal use was facilitated by the discovery of important sources of copper and gold. Yet, the Irish Chalcolithic was much more than a technological phase, but was also a time of ideological change, social transformation and possibly language development. A new society emerged out of the older Neolithic culture, heavily influenced by indigenous contacts with Britain and Atlantic Europe. The cultural relations and chronology of this period are examined. The paper affirms how the concept of a 'Chalcolithic' remains relevant to any understanding of what was a highly formative period in Irish prehistory.

It is broadly accepted that there was an important transition period at the end of the Neolithic in Ireland that spanned the second half of the 3rd millennium BC. This was marked by the introduction of an already developed copper metallurgy around 2500 BC, coincident with the first use of Beaker pottery, a new monument tradition, and changed funerary practices. In the centuries that followed there was widespread production of copper objects and, to a lesser extent, goldwork, on a technological par with contemporary metalworking in Europe. This transition period ended around 2150–2000 BC, with a slow introduction of tin-bronze metallurgy and the declining use of Beaker pottery in favour of new ceramic traditions that marked the developed Bronze Age.

The idea of an Irish Chalcolithic has been considered at different times, mostly through a narrow technological definition that emphasised the distinctive metalwork of that period. The recognition of a horizon of copper artefacts preceding the use of tin-bronze goes back to Wilde's (1857) catalogue of the Royal Irish Academy collections. Influenced by the writings of scholars such as Much (1893) and Montelius (1900; 1908), Coffey (1901; 1913) proposed a 'transitional copper period' in Ireland, equivalent to Montelius Period 1, commencing in the mid-3rd millennium and ending *c.* 2000–1800 BC. Macalister (1921) subsequently revised this date range to 2500–1900 BC, which is remarkably close to current estimates. Unlike their continental counterparts Irish researchers did not adopt the terms 'Chalcolithic' or 'Copper Age' for this transition period, regarding it instead as either of little significance (eg, Raftery 1951, 137), or else as representing the introductory phase of the Bronze Age (eg, Mahr 1937; Harbison 1969a; Brindley 1995), interchangeable with such labels as 'Beaker Period' (eg, Herity & Eogan 1977) and 'Final Neolithic' (eg, O'Brien 1999). This is more than semantics, as the loose terminology has undoubtedly obscured consideration of the early metal-using period in Ireland as an important transitional phase between the Neolithic and the Bronze Age.

This paper outlines the principal characteristics of the Chalcolithic in Ireland, a highly formative period lasting from *c.* 2500/2400–2100/2000 BC. It presents a chronological and developmental framework, while also addressing the regionality of this period and the cultural context of early metal circulation.

The Irish Chalcolithic *c.* 2500–2000 BC

Though the use of metal is often taken as the defining characteristic of Chalcolithic societies in Europe, there are examples where this occurred in fully Neolithic societies (eg, copper circulation in Denmark during the 4th millennium). The production of primary metal could, instead, be taken as the key indicator, in which case Ireland does have a distinct Chalcolithic, while Britain arguably may not. Ireland was a significant metal-producing region during the second half of the 3rd millennium, with copper and gold production exceeding that in many other parts of western Europe. This has led to a widespread belief that Ireland was some type of early *El Dorado*, a view that continues to influence research on the Chalcolithic and Bronze Age.

The concept of an Irish Chalcolithic has a broader significance than simply representing a short period when unalloyed copper was used and produced prior to tin-bronze. The process of 'becoming Chalcolithic' should be considered in terms of long-term culture change, in which metal was only one element, albeit a significant one. Any meaningful definition must consider broader structural changes in society, in such areas as settlement and economy, power relations and identity, religious belief and cosmology.

The following are some of the principal features of the Irish Chalcolithic:

1. Metal
Copper metallurgy was introduced to Ireland as an established technology *c.* 2500–2400 BC. The next four centuries witnessed the production and use of unalloyed copper on a significant scale, prior to the adoption of tin-bronze after 2000 BC (Fig. 14.1). The extensive use of metal over this period was made possible by the discovery of a major source of copper at Ross Island, Co. Kerry.

2. Craft specialisation
As elsewhere in Europe the Chalcolithic is marked by specialised craftworking and material innovation. This is most obvious in metal (copper and gold) and pottery, with intensive exploitation of raw materials, pyrotechnological expertise and fabrication skills, product uniformity and organised exchange systems. The introduction of goldworking *c.* 2300 BC was part of an increasing use of other exotic materials, such as jet. There is also continued specialisation in lithic production, as demonstrated by the flintwork and battle-axes of this period.

3. Beaker culture
There was exclusive use of Beaker pottery in Ireland *c.* 2450–2150 BC (Fig. 14.1), possibly overlapping with the final use of Grooved Ware *c.* 2500–2400 BC, and also with Bowl Food Vessels *c.* 2150–2400 BC. Other artefact types of the Beaker 'international assemblage' are also present, including bracers, new flint arrowhead types, v-perforated buttons, and gold sheetwork.

4. Exchange systems and mobility
Beaker material culture signifies extensive mobility within and outside of Ireland. This involved the movement of raw materials and finished artefacts through exchange networks established at local, regional, and supra-regional level. The circulation of copper was especially complex, involving both down-the-line and secondary redistribution of primary metal, as well as complex recycling systems.

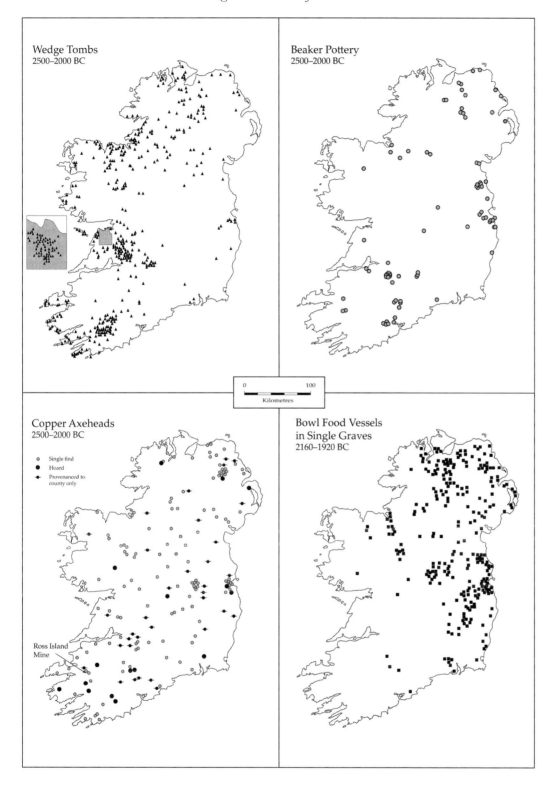

Figure 14.1:
Distribution of wedge
tombs (after De Valera,
R & Ó Nualláin
1982), Beaker pottery
(various sources);
Bowl pottery in single
graves (Brindley 2007)
and copper axeheads
(Harbison 1969a with
additions) in Ireland

5. Religion and cosmology

Wedge tombs are a distinct monument type of the Chalcolithic in Ireland, and reflect important changes in religious belief during this period (Fig. 14.1). Ritual activity continued at older Neolithic monuments such as passage tombs, with the continued construction of henge monuments in some areas. There was a diversity of funerary traditions with the use of chambered (wedge) tombs existing alongside the practice of single burial. It is notable that the classic Beaker single grave found in Britain and the continent is entirely absent in Ireland.

6. Settlement and population

There was a general expansion of settlement in existing Neolithic areas, spreading into parts of Ireland that were not previously occupied to any extent. The residential sites have a low archaeological visibility, with no distinctive house types or domestic layout, and almost no evidence of enclosure or fortification. There was no significant use of marginal environments, such as uplands or wetlands, though wooden trackways are recorded in some midland bogs. Coastal settlements with Beaker pottery have been recorded, but are not numerous.

7. Agricultural development

Pollen evidence indicates a possible intensification of farming in many parts of Ireland. The archaeological record points to a continuation of older Neolithic farming patterns (cattle/pig pastoralism; wheat/barley cultivation), with no obvious use of secondary products or innovations in farming methods. There is evidence for managed farmland in the form of field patterns and enclosures. Finally, there was a limited introduction of the horse in this period.

8. Social structure

Population growth may be inferred from an increased incidence of settlements, monuments, and artefacts. Their distribution indicates considerable variability in social structures across different territorial identities. Increased status and role differentiation is likely, but is not clearly evident until after 2150 BC when single burial customs were widely adopted (Fig. 14.1). Consumption of prestige artefacts (copper and gold) suggests an increasing hierarchisation of society and the emergence of new power structures during this period.

Continuity and change

While some features of the Irish Chalcolithic represent continuity from the Late Neolithic, the degree of change across many areas of society imparts a distinctiveness to this period. The former is evident in the continued occupation of Neolithic settlement zones, for example the Lough Gur area of Co. Limerick; Ballynagilly, Co. Tyrone; Lyles Hill, Co. Antrim, and Dalkey Island, Co. Dublin (see Waddell 2000, 117–8). There is further evidence in the ceremonial sphere, though whether continued ritual activity at Neolithic sites should be equated with continuity of belief is often uncertain. Continuity is evident in diverse expressions of funerary ritual, such as the burial sequence at Cahirguillamore, Co. Limerick (Hunt 1967) and Beaker deposits in court tombs (Herity 1987). It may also be inferred from the high regard that Beaker pottery-using groups had for older Neolithic monuments, in particular the passage tombs at Knowth and Newgrange in the Boyne valley, which were a focus of ceremonial activity, as were henge monuments in many areas. In southern England the building of monuments during this period was one of the ways by which an elite might distinguish itself from other members of society (Bradley 2007, 142). This process is not as obvious for Ireland in relation to either the continued use of henges or the construction of wedge tombs.

The discovery of Beaker pottery and Grooved Ware at a number of sites in Ireland finds parallels in Britain. This indicates some continuation of settlement and tradition, or as Needham (this volume) observes, an accommodation of one set of cultural values with another. In Ireland the relationship between these ceramic types and the cultural traditions they represent is poorly understood. Beaker and Grooved Ware have been found on the same settlement and ritual sites in Ireland, however it is questionable whether their use overlapped to any significant extent.

Regional identities

The Irish Chalcolithic had a strongly regional character, most evident in the distributions of wedge tombs, Beaker pottery, Bowl Food Vessels in single graves, and copper metalwork (Fig. 14.1). These point to strong territorial identities with their own 'tribal' structures and belief systems. Beaker pottery was once thought to be confined to the north and east of Ireland (cf. Harbison 1979), however its distribution has been greatly extended as a result of recent discoveries by commercial archaeology projects. While this ceramic may have been used throughout Ireland, the possibility of a Beaker and a non-Beaker Chalcolithic must be considered, the latter incorporating strong elements of the Late Neolithic substrate. This is relevant to the discovery of Beaker pottery at Moneen cemetery cairn, Co. Cork, '... and its mixing with an indigenous but otherwise unknown [funerary] tradition' (Brindley *et al.* 1988, 20).

The complementary distribution of wedge tombs and of single burials containing Bowl and Vase Food Vessels has previously given rise to suggestions of eastern and western Beaker provinces in Ireland (Herity and Eogan 1977, 117–32). While this is no longer accepted, the distribution of these ritual sites, as well as Beaker pottery and copper metalwork, does indicate widely held religious beliefs and common economic values across different parts of Ireland. This masks considerable variability at a local and regional level, in the same way that the spread of early Christianity in Ireland three millennia later cross-cut socio-political boundaries.

The Irish Chalcolithic differs from that in other parts of Europe in a number of respects, including the absence of structured settlement (proto-urban) and formal house types, fortifications, agricultural innovation (secondary products), and expansion into marginal areas such as uplands. Ireland does have many typical Chalcolithic features such as the production and use of copper and gold, craft specialisation, and participation in long-distance exchange networks. Metal could play a greater or lesser role in Chalcolithic societies depending on local circumstances. For example, the development of large fortified settlements in the Millaran and Vila Nova cultures of Spain and Portugal was closely linked to agricultural intensification and broader economic expansion, and not just to the development of metallurgy. The control of metal supply is likely to have been a significant agent of social change in Chalcolithic Ireland, however this must be set against other developments during this period.

Chronology and development of the Irish Chalcolithic

There are three discernible phases in the Irish Chalcolithic (Fig. 14.2):

- Early Chalcolithic: *c.* 2500–2400 BC (introduction of copper objects and metallurgical knowledge; earliest Beaker pottery, possibly overlapping with final use of Grooved Ware; first wedge tombs; continued use of henges)
- Middle Chalcolithic: *c.* 2400–2150 BC (Beaker pottery; copper and gold production; wedge tombs; continued use of henges and older Neolithic sites)
- Late Chalcolithic: *c.* 2150–2000 BC (earliest tin-bronze; Bowl Food Vessels and single burial customs; final construction of wedge tombs).

The Bronze Age commenced in Ireland around 2000 BC with the adoption of tin-bronze as the standard metal type, at a time when the use of Beaker pottery and the building of wedge tombs was coming to an end, replaced by increased emphasis on single graves and new types of funerary pottery.

Early Chalcolithic c. 2500–2400 BC

The beginning of the Chalcolithic is marked by increased mobility, most evident in the exchange of material culture within and outside of Ireland. During the Late Neolithic (*c.* 3000–2500 BC) most external contacts were directed across the Irish Sea, with Grooved Ware and henge connections probably extending from Scotland to the Wessex area. The circulation of Beaker material culture, including metal objects, from 2500 BC indicates new contacts with the continent, as well as the maintenance of established British connections.

Many important innovations in the Irish Chalcolithic have previously been linked to a colonisation of south-west Ireland in the mid-3rd millennium BC, driven by a search for metal (De Valera and Ó Nualláin 1982). Beaker prospectors from north-west France supposedly brought the knowledge of metallurgy and the idea of building gallery tombs to Ireland, with the wedge tomb emerging as an insular variant of *allées couvertes*. While such migration theories are regarded as out-dated explanations of culture change, it is worth revisiting the 'Breton colonists' model to consider alternative explanations to why Beaker Pottery, wedge tombs, and metallurgy were introduced to Ireland around the same time.

Beaker pottery in Ireland was part of a wider spread of this material culture across north-

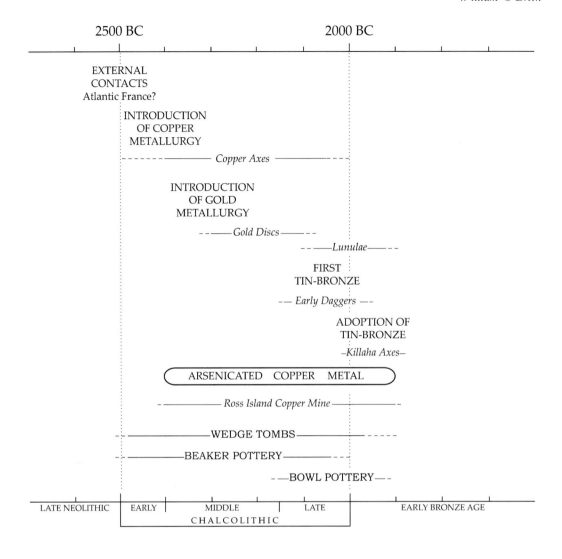

western Europe in the mid-3rd millennium. The development of the Irish pottery is poorly understood due to an absence of complete vessel forms and secure associations. According to Brindley (2007, 301), Beaker was the only ceramic used in Ireland *c.* 2450–2150 BC, overlapping with the introduction of Bowl Food Vessels and the first tin-bronze *c.* 2150–2000 BC (Fig. 14.1). The differences between Irish and British Beaker traditions are well known and are usually explained in terms of different origins. Both Case (1966; 1995) and Burgess (1979) argued for an important Atlantic influence on Irish Beaker traditions, followed later by assimiliation of Beaker elements from Britain. Irish Beakers are commonly found in settlement sites and in older monument types such as megalithic tombs, in what appears to be an Atlantic tradition stretching from Iberia to northern

France. British Beakers, on the other hand, fall into a north-west European pattern of use with an emphasis on funerary display in single grave contexts.

Needham (2005; this volume) has considered the massive social change that followed the arrival of Beakers in Britain, *c.* 2450–2150 BC. This involved the co-existence and then partial fusion of two different cultures with their radically different outlooks on the world. Was this also the case in Ireland? Whereas the British record suggests a major cultural intrusion with migrant populations, the evidence from Ireland points more to absorption of external influences through small-scale contacts involving trade and other social exchanges. Beaker contexts in Ireland are sufficiently different to indicate a strong indigenous background to the use of this pottery. It is also likely that the Beaker 'culture' received varying degrees of acceptance within

Ireland, though this is less true of its material innovations, in particular metallurgy which was enthusiastically adopted.

While British contacts were significant in the spread of Beaker culture to Ireland, important contacts were also established with metal-using Beaker groups in Atlantic France. Brittany is the most likely springboard, building on older connections between the two regions dating back to the Atlantic passage tomb tradition. This French connection is likely to be the most significant in terms of a Beaker-hosted introduction of metallurgy to Ireland, and may also have influenced the development of the wedge tomb.

The latter is a distinct monument type of the Chalcolithic in Ireland, with some 450 recorded examples in regional groupings of mostly western distribution (Fig. 14.1). Beaker pottery is commonly found in wedge tombs, especially those examples dated 2500–2200 BC (Brindley and Lanting 1992; Schulting *et al.* 2008). The absence of Beakers from later examples, such as those excavated at Altar and Toormore in Co. Cork (O'Brien 1993; 1999), may be explained by the decline of this ceramic tradition across Ireland *c.* 2200–1900 BC, or by regional variability in its use.

These monuments are interesting as the megalithic tomb tradition had died out in almost every part of Europe by the mid-3rd millennium. The wedge tomb may be seen as a re-invention of the megalithic tomb idea, referencing the past to maintain an older social order in the face of external pressures for change. While most wedge tombs in Ireland were expressions of group identity in small segmentary societies (O'Brien 1999; 2000), the restricted burial record from excavated examples could be linked to new social formations based on individual leadership and ruling lineages.

The origins of the wedge tomb remain controversial. The 'Breton colonists' model is not supported by the material record from these tombs, nor by the fact that there are significant copper, tin, and gold resources in Armorica. More convincing is a combination of indigenous development with external influences, where native populations adopted the idea of wedge tombs as part of the same cultural package involving Beakers and the appearance of metallurgy. The building of gallery tombs, including the *allée couvertes* series,

had largely ceased in north-west France by the time wedge tombs were first constructed in Ireland (after Patton 1993, 138). Though no longer built, the former clearly had a special significance for Beaker culture groups in Brittany and surrounding areas. The idea of the wedge tomb in Ireland may have been heavily influenced by this Beaker culture respect for older megalithic tombs, in particular the *allée couvertes* of the Brittany 'springboard' region.

The latter occurred at around the same time in Ireland as the introduction of metal. This technology was not invented in Ireland, as there is no evidence of incipient metallurgy, such as that based on the use of native copper or oxidised ores. Metal first appears *c.* 2500–2400 BC as an already developed technology with clear external origins. Within a century there is evidence of large-scale production of copper axeheads, which circulated over the entire island with some exchange into western Britain. The rapid adoption of metallurgy was made possible through the discovery of Ross Island mine, Co. Kerry, which supplied probably all of the arsenicated copper used in Ireland during the Chalcolithic (O'Brien 1995; 2004).

The origins of Irish metallurgy have long been contentious, with most discussion focusing on the significance of Beaker culture connections. It was Crawford (1912) who initially suggested that metal was introduced to Britain and Ireland by Beaker people. The idea of Beaker prospectors took hold in subsequent publications, including Case (1966), who proposed that metallurgy was brought to Ireland by Beaker Folk coming from southern Britain, though ultimately with a west-central European background. Others, such as Bremer (1928), Childe (1937), Raftery (1951), and Harbison (1979), argued for an introduction of metallurgy through Iberian connections separate from the Beaker culture.

Sheridan (1983) was the first to propose a significant indigenous contribution to the introduction of metallurgy to Ireland, involving different types of social exchange with metal-using groups on the continent. Metal may have been desirable for native Neolithic groups who had a growing interest in prestige goods and exotic materials, encouraged by extensive contacts along the Atlantic fringe of Europe (Bradley & Chapman 1986). They may have taken the initiative to introduce metallurgy once exposed to the idea of metal and its technology in the course of exchanges conducted through the Beaker network.

An alternative is an introduction of metallurgy to Ireland through external forces, involving the migration of metal-using groups from the continent. The circulation of Beaker material culture was certainly linked to an expanding use of metal in Atlantic Europe in the 3rd millennium, however, there is considerable debate as to the mechanisms involved. While a close Beaker association with early metallurgy in Ireland is conclusive, what this means in cultural terms is unclear. At issue is the social significance of Beaker material culture and whether innovations like metallurgy should be linked to the migration of ethnic groups or the small-scale movement of people, ideas, and objects through trade and other social exchanges.

Whereas it is possible to identify an early import horizon in southern Britain (Northover 1999), there are no such imported metal objects in Ireland. The beginning of Irish metallurgy is usually linked to a hypothetical 'Castletownroche stage', when trapeze-shaped copper axeheads of continental type provided a prototype for the production of insular equivalents (type Lough Ravel) *c.* 2400 BC (Harbison 1969a; Burgess 1979). The large-scale producton of those axeheads in the centuries that followed was based on the discovery of a major source of arsenicated copper at Ross Island, Co. Kerry. The ability to smelt fahlore must lie in mainland Europe, as there was no expertise in the production of arsenicated copper in Britain at this time.

Mining at Ross Island, therefore, was part of a wider Beaker metallurgical tradition that existed across Atlantic Europe in the mid-3rd millennium (cf. Ambert 1998). This is significant in that it allowed metal production to begin in Ireland at the same technological level as was established on the continent. It is tempting to see the origins of Irish metallurgy as being connected to contacts with metal-using Beaker groups in Atlantic France, *c.* 2500–2400 BC. These contacts may have taken place over only a generation or so, and may have commenced with a limited exchange of copper axes. In time, this led to a transfer of metallurgical knowledge, not necessarily through large-scale migration or prospecting expeditions, but involving a limited movement of specialists. The presence of even a few

foreign specialists might have been sufficient to initiate metalworking activity in Ireland and would explain why the early expertise in mining and metal production was concentrated at one location.

Copper metallurgy was an important part of the expanding Beaker network of contacts across Atlantic Europe in the mid-3rd millennium. From earlier Iberian origins, Beaker metallurgy was well established in Spain, Portugal, and south-east France by 2800–2600 BC, spreading west along the Garonne/Gironde corridor to reach Atlantic France by 2500 BC. Ambert *et al.* (1996) draw attention to the prevalence of Beaker metalwork using arsenicated copper in Atlantic France, from Normandy and Brittany to the Saintonge region. Numerous flat copper axeheads are known from Beaker and pre-Beaker contexts in this region, while finds of copper daggers, Palmella points, and other objects can be directly connected with Beaker metalworking. The earliest metallurgy in Ireland was thus established against a background of sustained contact within this Atlantic zone of Beaker metallurgy, and involved the same networks used in the exchange of Beaker pottery and associated culture. The insularity that is a feature of the first Irish metalworking suggests that the initiative may have come from indigenous Neolithic groups, reaching out to an Atlantic world through established maritime contacts.

Middle Chalcolithic period c. 2400–2160 BC

There is still a tendency to regard Beaker culture as a single homogeneous entity in those regions of Europe where it occurs. This was certainly not the case in Britain, where Beaker culture had at least three phases of different character and with different relations to indigenous society (Needham 2005). The first stage, *c.* 2500–2250 BC, involved the arrival of a north-west European Beaker culture, thinly distributed and interstitial within British Grooved Ware society. The second stage, *c.* 2250–1950 BC, occurred when Beaker culture became the prevailing cultural ethos, after what Needham calls a 'meeting of minds' took place with native groups (*ibid.*, 207).

The presence of Beaker pottery and its associated culture also had a major impact on indigenous societies in Ireland, though probably not the same as in Britain. Irish Beaker pottery is commonly found in older

Neolithic settlement and ritual contexts. This is generally taken to indicate the acculturation of indigenous peoples rather than the appearance of an intrusive culture. Metal may have been a key element of the Beaker-acculturation process, especially when it was discovered that Ireland had significant sources of copper and gold. The desirability of metal and other material innovations of the Beaker culture may have paved the way for more fundamental changes in society.

The question of what constituted Beaker society in Ireland is a complex one, as there were probably many different social formations during this period, each having its own version of Beaker culture. Heyd (this volume) suggests that Beaker society in western Europe was marked by an established individualism, core family social order, the beginnings of social stratification, functional differential (eg, craftsmens graves), and indications of inherited status. Some of these characteristics may also be identified in Beaker contexts in Ireland, though the evidence is open to varying interpretations. The majority of British Beakers form part of stereotyped funerary assemblages. This was not the case in Ireland where there is no evidence of ostentatious funerary display or the visible acknowledgement of powerful individuals in single grave contexts (though whether this was the case in wedge tombs is uncertain). This raises the question of whether Beaker pottery and its associated material culture in Ireland should be interpreted solely in terms of group status or personal prestige, or whether different meanings (religious, economic, etc) are appropriate.

The Lough Gur area of Co. Limerick is one of those Neolithic centres where Beaker pottery was introduced into an indigenous context. The continuity of settlement in that area is significant, extending from the 4th into the 2nd millennia, with a sequence of ceramic use from local Neolithic to Grooved Ware to Beaker pottery. It had been suggested that settlement enclosures at Knockadoon are indicative of a new element of social hierarchy in the organisation of Beaker settlement at Lough Gur (Grogan & Eogan 1987, 489; Cooney & Grogan 1999, 76). This can be dismissed in light of new dating evidence that points to a later Bronze Age date for those sites (cf. Cleary 2003, 144–7).

Staying with Lough Gur, the presence of both Grooved Ware and Beaker pottery at Grange stone circle is part of a continued use of henges during this period (*contra* Roche 2004). This is also evident at a number of sites in the Boyne valley (see Waddell 2000, 109–13). The great timber pit circle adjacent to Newgrange must rate as one of the great monuments of the Chalcolithic in Ireland (Sweetman 1985). A large Beaker settlement was also discovered in front of Newgrange (O'Kelly *et al.* 1983), with concentrations of Beaker pottery and occupation material at the nearby passage tomb of Knowth (Eogan & Roche 1997). The continued importance of Newgrange and Knowth as ritual centres and feasting locations contrasts with the low regard in which these sites were apparently held during the Early Bronze Age. This respect for the sacred places of the Neolithic does point to a strong indigenous background to the Irish Chalcolithic, however an analogy might be also made with the Christianisation of Ireland three millennia later, with Beaker groups legitimising their position through the take-over of older ritual centres.

As well as the production of copper (see below), gold was first introduced to Ireland during the Middle Chalcolithic. Small items of Beaker-inspired sheetwork appeared *c.* 2300 BC, beginning with basket-shaped ornaments and 'sun-discs', and followed by lunulae in the Late Chalcolithic. There was a lot of gold in Ireland during this period, certainly in comparison with many other parts of Europe, including Britain. Recent research has identified the western Mourne Mountains in Co. Down as one of several possible source regions for this gold (Warner *et al.* 2009).

The large number and wide distribution of monuments, settlements, and artefacts from the Middle Chalcolithic suggests a general rise in population across Ireland (Fig. 14.1). There is an obvious expansion of settlement within core Neolithic territories, as well as a spread to areas not previously settled to any great extent. The former include the Boyne valley, Lough Gur, and the north-east region, with a new settlement focus in counties Clare, Cork, and Kerry. A general decline in agriculture during the Late Neolithic was reversed after 2500 BC, with pollen records indicating increased farming in many parts of Ireland (eg, Smith 1975; Molloy & O'Connell 1991; 1995; Lynch 1981; Mitchell & Cooney 2004; Dodson 1990).

The animal bone and cereal records from Newgrange (Van Wijngaarden-Bakker 1986; Monk 1986, 32) indicate a well-established agricultural economy in that area. The same is true for Lough Gur and Killarney (Van Wijngaarden-Bakker 2004), and for the Burren, Co. Clare, where a Beaker culture farmscape is recorded at Roughan Hill (Jones 1998).

While there are more Beaker settlement contexts in Ireland than in Britain, no distinctive house form or settlement layout can be identified for this period. The majority of new discoveries of Beaker pottery sites in Ireland, from road schemes and other infrastructure projects, mostly comprise scattered pits, stake-hole concentrations, and occupation spreads. Some house structures are known, however their paucity in comparison to the Bronze Age is striking. This suggests that Beaker settlement in Ireland may have been marked by a significant degree of mobility, though this view must be set against the discovery of permanent farmsteads and field patterns (*ibid.*). This period is also marked by the growing use of hot stone/water-boiling methods in domestic cooking, and possibly for ceremonial feasting. A significant number of recently excavated burnt mound sites, called *fulachtaí fia* in Ireland, are dated to the second half of the 3rd millennium.

Finally, environmental records for the late 3rd millennium do not indicate any deterioration or amelioration of climate that would have significantly influenced Chalcolithic settlement in Ireland. Baillie (1995, 32) identified an environmental event dating to 2354 BC, which he argued was possibly connected to an eruption of the Hekla 4 volcano in Iceland. Though registering in the tree-ring record, there is no evidence that such an event had significant social and economic implications within Ireland (see Buckland *et al.* 1997).

Late Chalcolithic c. 2160–2000 BC

This period is marked by the adoption of new funerary practices in eastern Ireland, which are significantly different from the continued use of wedge tombs in western regions. While Beaker burials in wedge tombs have personal status significance, the earliest indication of overt social ranking comes after 2150 BC with a strong tradition of single burial, comprising individual or cemetery clusters of cist and pit graves that contain the burnt or unburnt burials of important men and women, accompanied by funerary ceramic (Bowl Food Vessels) and small personal items of bronze and other materials. This new funerary tradition in Ireland possibly emerged through prolonged contact with Britain in the late 3rd millennium. It is notable that those eastern and northern parts of Ireland that first adopted this Beaker-influenced funerary custom also had a large number of Beaker pottery sites (Fig. 14.1). While both ceramic types have been found on settlement sites and in wedge tombs, Beaker pottery has never been found with Bowl or Vase Food Vessels in single graves in Ireland, which might suggest that there was no significant overlap in their use.

The late Chalcolithic in Ireland is also marked by the earliest examples of tin-bronze. There is currently some discussion as to when this occurred. Lanting and van der Plicht (2001/2; translation in Brindley 2007, 375) have revised Needham's (1996) chronology, proposing that the early copper metalwork (Burgess 1979: Knocknagur/Needham MA I and II phases) continued down to 2000 BC, after which there is a widespread adoption of tin-bronze (Killaha/MA III phase, *c.* 2000–1900 BC; Ballyvalley/MA IV and V, *c.* 1900–1700 BC). This suggests that a transition to the Bronze Age in technological terms in Ireland may have occurred *c.* 2000 BC.

The earliest tin-bronze in Ireland consists of small daggers of type Corkey found in single grave contexts containing Bowl Food Vessels dating *c.* 2100–2000 BC (Brindley 2007, 372, table 74). These daggers are few in comparison with the production of type Killaha bronze axeheads, contemporary with British Migdale metalworking. The Killaha axeheads may be dated 2000–1900 BC, through associations in the Killaha East hoard, Co. Kerry, with type Breaghwy halberds, dated separately in the Moylough cremation burial, Co. Sligo (*ibid.*, 372), while a dagger in the hoard has parallels to Breton Type Quimperle examples (Needham 2000).

The introduction of bronze is important in terms of long-distance connections, as Ireland has no significant natural sources of tin. The alluvial tin deposits of south-west England were probably a major source for the Irish Early Bronze Age. This is supported by the discovery of Irish-type metalwork in Cornwall, including two lunulae at Harlyn Bay, as well as developed bronze axeheads found in stream tin workings at Trenovissick and in the Carnon valley (Penhallurick 1983). The discovery of Irish lunulae in north-west France (Taylor 1980) is relevant as that region has significant sources of alluvial tin. This suggests that contacts in the southern Irish Sea zone established by Beaker networks during the Chalcolithic continued into the Early Bronze Age, with the exchange of copper, tin, and gold between Ireland, Cornwall and Brittany.

Metal supply and social interactions in the Irish Chalcolithic

The single burial tradition adopted in Ireland during the Late Chalcolithic was part of a wider phenomenon across Europe *c.* 2500–1900 BC. These burials reflect increased social differentiation and the emergence of hierarchies in this period. Metalwork had an important role in this process, as a new medium of wealth that reinforced social inequality and as an important signifier of social standing. This is often explained in terms of the emergence of elites who were interested in prestige goods as signifiers of rank and power and were prepared to exploit the demand for new material innovations though control of production and exchange networks. These elites owed their position not just to control over the circulation of metal objects but also to the cosmic references with which these artefacts came to be associated (Bradley 1990, 75). One widely held view is that metallurgy spread because changing social conditions made the exchange of prestige goods, including metalwork, desirable in terms of elite aggrandisement and peer polity interactions.

It is clear from their wide occurrence that copper and gold had an intense appeal in Ireland during the Chalcolithic. The rapid adoption of metal was not based on a search for more efficient tool-kits but, rather, in the social contexts of its use. The early copper axeheads had the same dual symbolism as stone axeheads during the Neolithic, used for work purposes (and weapons?), as well as having powerful symbolism and exchange value. The circulation and life-cycle of these copper axeheads are poorly understood, largely

because they are rarely found in settlement contexts. The fact that neither copper axeheads nor gold discs and lunulae are found in graves is also interesting, as it suggests that such objects may not have had the same type of personal status associations that they had in other parts of Europe at this time.

The Irish Chalcolithic is known for the large numbers of copper objects in circulation, principally axeheads and daggers, the metal for which was sourced at Ross Island mine. The operation of this mine has recently been examined in relation to settlement in the Killarney area. The discovery of copper axeheads in that area may be linked to extensive Beaker culture settlement, *c.* 2400–1900 BC. Copper was exchanged from this local settlement zone into the Munster region, to other parts of Ireland and into western Britain. Some of the copper ingots and finished axeheads produced at Ross Island were exchanged across the north Kerry and Limerick areas, with Lough Gur one of several settlement zone generating a demand for this metal.

Therefore, the circulation of Ross Island metal crossed different social territories, which were Beaker acculturated to varying degrees (Fig. 14.3). Control over this resource almost certainly had long-term consequences for the groups in question. Metallurgy required a network of commodity exchange, the control of which gave certain individuals and groups an opportunity to establish positions of wealth and power. This may be especially relevant to control of critical resources such as the copper mine at Ross Island.

Ross Island and the 'Lunula Chiefs'
Chalcolithic settlement in Ireland was not a homogeneous entity, but was instead marked by regional diversity and fixed social territories with a definite sense of resource ownership. These regional geographies had a significant influence on contemporary metal circulation. For example, there appears to be a strong separation between Beaker/henge groups in north-central Munster, and the wedge tomb territories of the south-west peninsulas and mid-Cork region (Fig. 14.3). Metal production in the latter during the Early Bronze Age involved small local communities, who developed an approach to copper mining that suited the segmentary organisation of their society (O'Brien 1999; 2000). In contrast, the mining

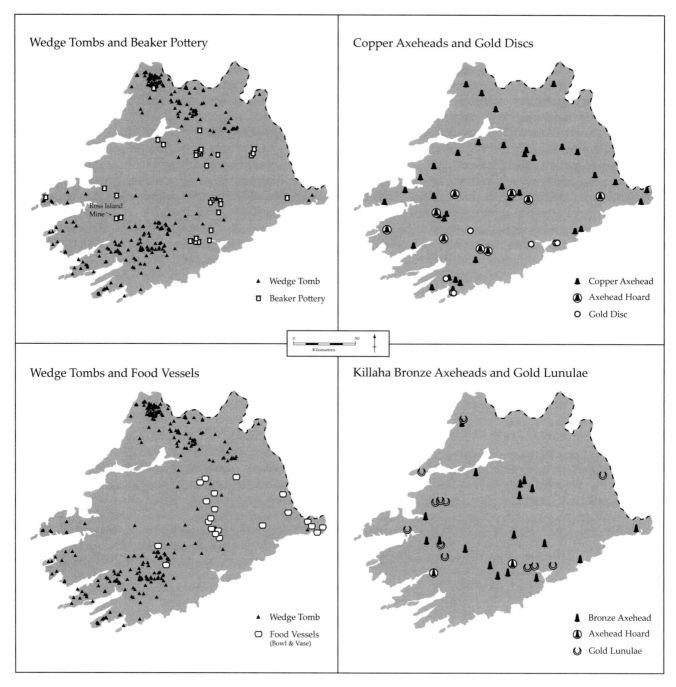

Figure 14.3: The Chalcolithic in Munster: distributions of Beaker pottery, wedge tombs, Food Vessel graves, copper axeheads, earliest bronze axeheads, gold discs and lunulae

at Ross Island represents a different type of social formation, associated with the presence of Beaker pottery, henge monuments, and gold lunulae in the central/north Kerry region.

Such divisions are reflected in the distribution of contemporary goldwork, notably discs and lunulae. Twenty decorated discs of sheet gold dating *c.* 2300–2000 BC have been discovered in Ireland, including six examples in Co. Cork (Fig. 14.3; Case 1977; Cahill 2006). Often referred to as 'sun-discs', their shape and colour

suggest solar imagery and a possible connection with wedge tomb rituals (O'Brien 1999, 284). Lunulae are magnificent collars of gold sheet, bearing Beaker-inspired ornament, and are an Irish innovation probably dating *c.* 2200–1900 BC (Taylor 1970; 1980). Some 85 examples are recorded in Ireland, with a wider distribution extending into western Britain and north-west France. A total of eight lunulae are recorded in the Cork/Kerry region, outside the main concentrations of wedge tombs (Fig. 14.3).

Apart from their aesthetic appeal, these discs and lunulae were highly symbolic objects, linked to the expression of power in different social settings. For wedge tomb communities, gold discs may have signified a wider tribal identity, created by loyalty to a leadership structure that combined secular and religious power. The significance of lunulae is unclear, but may be taken as evidence of personal or group aggrandisement during the Late Chalcolithic. Lunulae are never found in graves, suggesting that they were passed down through generations of hereditary leaders in powerful lineages.

The rise of the 'lunula chiefs', whatever that precisely means, was a wider phenomenon across Ireland. It occurred against a background of economic growth, which in most areas was based on agriculture and possibly trade. For some of these groups, particularly those in the Killarney and north Kerry areas, control over the supply of copper may have been significant, with growing demand for metal adding significantly to their economic power. There are indications of strong leadership structures behind the mining at Ross Island, though whether this was a powerful individual or group is unclear. Most probably, the production and circulation of metal was controlled by particular lineage groups who established exchange networks across Ireland, connecting into western Britain and north-west France.

Conclusions: Is there an Irish Chalcolithic?

This paper has considered the different elements that comprise the Irish Chalcolithic, focusing on Beaker material culture, metalwork, and wedge tombs. The circulation of metal continues to be the most striking feature, having considerable potential to affect social relations at a local, regional, and supra-regional level. The Irish Chalcolithic was, however, more than a technological phase. This period was marked by innovation, ideological change, and the emergence of new social formations shaped by the merging of indigenous Neolithic society with Beaker 'culture'. Chalcolithic Ireland also retained elements of an older Neolithic culture, expressed in the regard shown to older monuments on the landscape.

External influence and migration have previously been regarded as the main drivers of change during this period. It is certainly true that important connections existed between Ireland, Britain, and north-west France in the late 3rd millennium BC. It is also the case that a narrow emphasis on origins and external influences has limited consideration of contemporary developments within Ireland. With its international connections, the 'Beaker culture' continues to define the insular Chalcolithic, blinding us to the significant contribution made by indigenous peoples.

Finally, while many would question the relevance of Three-Age terminology in the radiocarbon dating era, there is still a need for chronological frameworks that have broader cultural meaning and emphasise parallel developments in western Europe in the later 3rd millennium. The value of a Chalcolithic is that it focuses our attention on what was an important transition period between two very different worlds. The concept helps us to better understand the complexities of that period and its diverse traditions, not only in terms of what went before or was to follow, but as distinct societies in their own right.

Bibliography

Ambert, P. 1998. Importance de la métallurgie campaniforme en France. In *L'Enigmatique Civilisation Campaniforme*, *Archéologia* 9, 36–41

Ambert, P., Carozza, L., Lecholon & Houles, N. 1996. De la mine au metal au sud du Massif Central au Chalcolithique. *Archéologie en Languedoc*. Revue de la Fédération Archéologique de L'Hérault, 35–42

Baillie, M. 1995. Dendrochronology and the chronology of the Irish Bronze Age. In Waddell & Shee Twohig (eds) 1995, 30–7

Bradley, R. 1990. *The Passage of Arms: an archaeological analysis of prehistoric hoards and votive deposits*. Cambridge: Cambridge University Press

Bradley, R. 2007. *The Prehistory of Britain and Ireland*. Cambridge: Cambridge University Press

Bradley, R. & Chapman, R. 1986. The nature and development of long-distance relations in later Neolithic Britain and Ireland. In C. Renfrew & J. Cherry (eds), *Peer Polity Interaction and Socio-Political Change*, 127–36. Cambridge: Cambridge University Press

Bremer, W. 1928. *Ireland's Place in Prehistoric and Early Historic Europe*. Dublin: Hodges Figgis

Brindley, A.L. 1995. Radiocarbon, chronology and the Bronze Age. In Waddell & Shee Twohig (eds) 1995, 4–13

Brindley, A.L. 2007. *The Dating of Food Vessels and Urns in Ireland. Bronze Age Studies 7*. Galway: National University of Ireland

Brindley, A.L. & Lanting, J.N. 1992. Radiocarbon dates

from wedge tombs. *Journal of Irish Archaeology* 6, 19–26

Brindley, A.L., Lanting, J.N. & Mook, W.G. 1988. Radiocarbon dates from Moneen and Labbacallee, Co. Cork. *Journal of Irish Archaeology* 4, 13–20

Buckland, P., Dugmore, A. & Edwards, K. 1997. Bronze Age myths? Volcanic activity and human response in the Mediterranean and North Atlantic regions. *Antiquity* 71, 581–93

Burgess, C. 1979. The background of early metalworking in Ireland and Britain. In M. Ryan (ed.), *The Origins of Metallurgy in Atlantic Europe*, 207–47. Dublin: Stationery Office

Cahill, M. 2006. John Windele's golden legacy: prehistoric and later gold ornaments from Co. Cork and Co. Waterford. *Proceedings of the Royal Irish Academy* 106C, 219–337

Case, H.J. 1966. Were Beaker-people the first metallurgists in Ireland? *Palaeohistoria* 12, 141–77

Case, H.J. 1977. An early accession to the Ashmolean Museum. In V. Markotic (ed.), *Ancient Europe and the Mediterranean*, 18–34. Warminster: Aris & Phillips

Case, H.J. 1995. Irish Beakers in their European context. In Waddell & Shee Twohig (eds) 1995, 14–29

Childe, V.G. 1937. The antiquity of the British Bronze Age. *American Anthropologist* 39, 1–22

Cleary, R. 2003. Enclosed Late Bronze Age habitation site and boundary wall at Lough Gur, Co. Limerick. *Proceedings of the Royal Irish Academy* 103C, 97–189

Coffey, G. 1901. Irish copper celts. *Journal of the Anthropological Institute of Great Britain and Ireland* 31, 265–79

Coffey, G. 1913. *The Bronze Age in Ireland*. Dublin: Hodges Figgis

Cooney, G. & Grogan, E. 1999. *Irish Prehistory: a social perspective*. Dublin: Wordwell

Crawford, 1912. The distribution of Early Bronze Age settlements in Britain. *Geographical Journal* 40, 1–184

De Valera, R. & Ó Nualláin, S. 1982. *Survey of the Megalithic Tombs of Ireland. Vol. IV. Counties Cork, Kerry, Limerick, Tipperary*. Dublin: Stationery Office

Dodson, J. R. 1990. The Holocene vegetation of a prehistorically inhabited valley, Dingle peninsula, Co. Kerry. *Proceedings of the Royal Irish Academy* 90B, 151–74

Eogan, G & Roche, H. 1997. *Excavations at Knowth* 2. Dublin: Royal Irish Academy

Grogan E. & Eogan G. 1987. Lough Gur excavations by Sean P. Ó Ríordáin: further neolithic and Beaker habitations on Knockadoon. *Proceedings of the Royal Irish Academy* 87C, 300–506

Harbison, P. 1969. *The Axes of the Early Bronze Age in Ireland*. Munich: Prahistorische Bronzefunde 9(1)

Harbison, P. 1979. Who were Ireland's first metallurgists? In M. Ryan (ed.), *The Origins of Metallurgy in Atlantic Europe*, 97–105. Dublin: Stationery Office

Herity, M. 1987. The finds from Irish court tombs. *Proceedings of the Royal Irish Academy* 87C, 5–281

Herity, M. & Eogan, G. 1977. *Ireland in Prehistory*. London: Routledge & Kegan Paul

Hunt, J. 1967. Prehistoric burials at Cahirguillamore, Co. Limerick. In E. Rynne (ed.) *North Munster Studies*, 20–42. Limerick: Thomond Archaeological Society

Jones, C. 1998. The discovery and dating of the prehistoric landscape of Roughan Hill in Co. Clare. *Journal of Irish Archaeology* 9, 27–44

Lanting, J.N. & Plicht, J. van der. 2001/2. Radiocarbon chronologie: bronstijd en vroege ijzertijd. *Palaeohistoria* 43/4, 117–262

Lynch, A. 1981. *Man and Environment in South-west Ireland, 4000 BC–AD 800*. Oxford: British Archaeological Report 85

Macalister, R.A.M. 1921. *Ireland in Pre-Celtic Times*. Dublin: Munsell & Roberts

Mahr, A. 1937. New aspects and problems in Irish prehistory: Presidential address for 1937. *Proceedings of the Prehistoric Society* 3, 261–436

Mitchell, F. & Cooney, T. 2004. Vegetation history in the Killarney valley. In O'Brien 2004, 481–93

Molloy, K. & O'Connell, M. 1991. Palaeoecological investigations towards the reconstruction of woodland and land-use history at Lough Sheeauns, Connemara, western Ireland, *Review of Palaeobotany and Palynology* 67, 75–113

Molloy, K. & O'Connell, M. 1995. Palaeoecological investigations towards the reconstruction of environment and land-use changes during prehistory at Céide Fields, western Ireland, *Probleme der Küstenforschung im südlichen Nordseegebiet* 23, 187–225

Monk, M. 1986. Evidence from macroscopic plant remains for crop husbandry in prehistoric and early Ireland. *Journal of Irish Archaeology* 3, 31–6

Montelius, O. 1900. *Die Chronologie der ältersen Bronzezeit in Nortdeutschland und Skandinavien*. Braunschweig: F. Vieweg und Sohn

Montelius, O. 1908. Chronology of the British Bronze Age. *Archaeologia* 61, 97–162

Much 1892. *Die Kupferzeit in Europa*. Jena

Needham, S. 1996. Chronology and periodisation in the British Bronze Age. *Acta Archaeologica* 67, 121–40

Needham, S. 2000. The gold and copper work. In G. Hughes, *The Lockington Gold Hoard. An Early Bronze Age Cemetery at Lockington, Leicestershire*, 38–47. Oxford: Oxbow Books

Needham, S. 2005. Transforming Beaker culture in north-west Europe: processes of fusion and fission. *Proceedings of the Prehistoric Society* 71, 171–217

Northover, P. 1999. The earliest metalwork in southern Britain. In A. Hauptmann (ed.), *The Beginnings of Metallurgy*. Proceedings of the International Symposium, April, 1995, 211–26. Der Anschitt, Beiheft 9. Bochum

O'Brien, W. 1993. Aspects of wedge tomb chronology. In E. Shee-Twohig & M. Ronayne (eds), *Past Perceptions: the prehistoric archaeology of south-west Ireland*, 63–74. Cork: Cork University Press

O'Brien, W. 1995. Ross Island and the origins of Irish-British metallurgy. In Waddell & Shee Twohig (eds), 1995, 38–48

O'Brien, W. 1999. *Sacred Ground. Megalithic Tombs in Coastal South-west Ireland. Bronze Age Studies 4*. Galway: Galway University Press

O'Brien, W. 2000. Megalithic tombs, metal resources and territory in prehistoric south-west Ireland. In A. Desmond, G. Johnson, M. McCarthy & E. Shee-Twohig (eds), *New Adventures in Irish Prehistory: papers in Commemoration of Liz Anderson*, 161–76. Bray: Wordwell

O'Brien, W. 2004. *Ross Island: mining, metal and society in early Ireland. Bronze Age Studies 6*. Galway: National University of Ireland

O'Kelly, M.J., Cleary, R.M. & Lehane, D. 1983. *Newgrange, Co. Meath, Ireland: The Late Neolithic/Beaker Period Settlement*. Oxford: British Archaeological Report S190

Patton, M. 1993. *Monuments and Society in Neolithic Brittany*. London: Routledge

Penhallurick, R. 1983. *Tin in Antiquity*. London: Institute of Metals

Raftery, J. 1951. *Prehistoric Ireland*. London: Batsford

Roche, H. 2004. The dating of the embanked stone circle at Grange, Co. Limerick. In H. Roche, E. Grogan, J. Bradley, J. Coles and B. Raftery (eds), *From Megaliths to Metal: essays in honour of George Eogan*, 106–16. Oxford: Oxbow Books

Schulting, R., Sheridan, A., Clarke, S. & Bronk Ramsey, C. 2008. Largantea and the dating of Irish wedge tombs. *Journal of Irish Archaeology* 17, 1–17

Sheridan, A. 1983. A reconsideration of the origins of Irish metallurgy. *Journal of Irish Archaeology* 1, 11–19

Smith, A.G. 1975. Neolithic and Bronze Age landscape change in Northern Ireland. In J. Evans, S. Limbrey & H. Cleere (eds), *The Effect of Man on the Landscape: the Highland Zone*, 64–74. London: Council for British Archaeology Research Report 11

Sweetman, D. 1985. A Late Neolithic/Early Bronze Age pit circle at Newgrange, Co. Meath. *Proceedings of the Royal Irish Academy* 85C, 195–221

Taylor, J. 1970. Lunulae reconsidered. *Proceedings of the Prehistoric Society* 36, 38–81

Taylor, J. 1980. *Bronze Age Goldwork of the British Isles*. Cambridge: Cambridge University Press

Van Wijngaarden-Bakker, L.H. 1986. The animal remains from the Beaker settlement at Newgrange, Co. Meath: final report. *Proceedings of the Royal Irish Academy* 86C, 17–111

Van Wijngaarden Bakker, L.H. 2004. The animal remains. In O'Brien 2004, 367–86

Waddell, J. 2000. *The Prehistoric Archaeology of Ireland*. Bray: Wordwell

Waddell, J. & Shee Twohig, E. (eds). 1995. *Ireland in the Bronze Age*. Dublin: Stationery Office

Warner, R., Chapman, R., Cahill, M. & Moles, N. 2009. The gold source found at last? *Archaeology Ireland* 23(2), 22–5

Wilde, W. 1857. *Catalogue of the Antiquities of Stone, Earthen, Vegetable and Metallic Materials in the Museum of the Royal Irish Academy*. Dublin

15

The Beaker People Project: an interim report on the progress of the isotope analysis of the organic skeletal material

Mandy Jay, Mike Parker Pearson, Mike Richards, Olaf Nehlich, Janet Montgomery, Andrew Chamberlain and Alison Sheridan

This paper is intended as an interim update for the Beaker People Project. The project aims to investigate mobility, diet, environment, and subsistence for the Late Neolithic, Chalcolithic, and Early Bronze Age population of Britain using a number of research tools, but particularly isotopic analysis of bones and teeth. This paper concentrates on the organic analyses yielding carbon, nitrogen, and sulphur isotope ratio data, but also discusses the project remit and the use of strontium and oxygen ratio values to track mobility. The project is discussed in general terms, an overview of the collagen analysis results is provided, general diet at this time is discussed, and interesting facets of the carbon and sulphur data are covered. Over 250 individuals from the north of Scotland down to southern England have been investigated for this project and a site list is included. This is a major five year project, so the discussion here is necessarily limited to the situation at the date of writing (June 2009) rather than to the publication date of this volume.

This overview summarises the progress made to date on the isotopic analysis of the skeletal material for the Beaker People Project. The project was designed to investigate mobility, migration, diet, health, environment, and subsistence strategies in the British Late Neolithic, Chalcolithic, and Early Bronze Age using isotope techniques (strontium and oxygen from tooth enamel, and carbon, nitrogen, and sulphur from bone and tooth dentine collagen) from around 250 individuals, and it is now a significant part of the way through the five year AHRC funded period.

A multi-disciplinary core team of researchers from a number of institutions is working on the archaeology, dating, osteology, and dental microwear in order to aid, complement, and support the interpretations of the isotope data. Whilst these features of the research are of critical importance to the project, they are not discussed in any detail in this paper, which is intended as a progress report on the isotopic analysis generally, with particular reference to the results from the organic material (collagen from bone and dentine).

We start with a brief outline of the project,

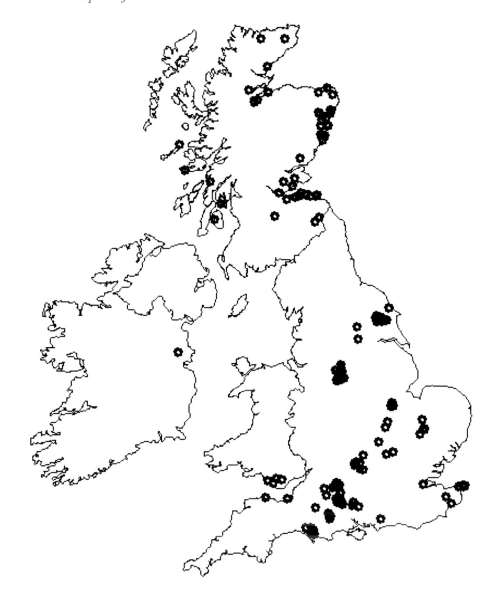

Figure 15.1. Map showing the distribution of sites at which isotopic analysis has been undertaken on skeletal remains for the Beaker People Project. All locations from Table 15.1☉ are included. The symbol for each site is an open circle, but where sites are located closely together the symbols merge to a more solid representation (eg for the Yorkshire Wolds there are c. 60 sites very closely grouped, and for the Peak District around 30)

move on to discuss the basic theory involved in the techniques employed, then discuss the progress within the project of the isotopic analysis generally. Finally, we provide some comments on the interpretation of the data obtained so far from the organic collagen analysis. Detailed isotope data are not presented here, since the work is not complete and the interpretation section must be considered as a work-in-progress, but sampling on the project is now closed and a list of sites and a distribution map can be provided at this stage (Table 15.1☉ and Fig. 15.1). Table 15.1☉ is currently the definitive site list for the isotopic work on this project, although it does not include a small number of sites on which other work, such as dental microwear,

has been done without isotopic analysis and it also does not include Scottish sites from the separate Leverhulme Trust funded Beakers and Bodies Project from which some collagen data are available for comparison, courtesy of Neil Curtis at the University of Aberdeen. The list published here will provide a reference tool until the final monograph is available following completion of the analyses during 2010, when full details of isotopic data and radiocarbon dates will be published alongside integrated discussion of the work undertaken.

The Beaker People Project

The question of whether long distance mobility is relevant to the population of Britain at this time (second half of the 3rd millennium BC) has been a matter of debate for generations of archaeologists. Were the 'Beaker people' immigrants or indigenous to prehistoric Britain? The differentiation, by cranial metrics, between skulls from Beaker associated individuals in graves (wide-headed, or brachycephalic) and those from Neolithic long barrows (narrow-headed, or dolichocephalic) goes back to the 19th century when it was noted by antiquarian barrow diggers, and interest in this distinction continues today (Davis & Thurnam 1865; Thurnam 1865; Parsons 1924; Hooke & Morant 1926; Brodie 1994). Thurnam attributed these individuals with different shaped skulls to different populations, giving rise to theories of a migrant 'Beaker folk' bringing their distinctive Beaker pottery and associated material culture into Britain from the European mainland (eg, Childe 1930, 153–4). Since then, theories involving the large-scale and long-distance physical movement of large numbers of such migrants have been challenged. Alternative explanations for the presence of the 'Beaker package' in Britain involve the adoption of a cultural pattern by local communities, with the transfer of ideas from outside, the evolution of material culture within Britain, and the possibility of some movement of materials and artefacts to the fore, and the movement of people themselves suggested to be at a much more limited scale (eg, Burgess & Shennan 1976; Vander Linden 2007). This debate has been revitalised since the discovery that the 'Amesbury Archer' and the 'Boscombe Bowmen' from Wessex have isotopic signatures which may indicate long-distance movement, with the suggestion having been made, on the basis of oxygen data, that this may have been from as far away as the Alps region of central Europe in the case of the 'Archer' (Fitzpatrick 2003; Evans *et al.* 2006). Strontium isotope studies of Bell Beaker inhumations from central Europe also indicate that people on the continental mainland during this period were probably quite mobile (Grupe *et al.* 1997; Price *et al.* 1998; Price *et al.* 2004).

Whilst the 'big' research question around the issue of population migration may be the most enticing for a project such as this, there are other issues to be addressed with isotope techniques which may, at least superficially, appear to be more mundane. What kinds of diets did these people have – were they concentrating on animal products or plants? Did they consume significant quantities of marine resources when living in coastal areas? What can we say about the local environments from which their foods were being obtained, and can this reveal anything about short distance, life-history movements which tie into subsistence strategies such as transhumance? Is it possible to say anything about the ways in which domesticated animals were being managed and foddered within the isotope data available? Were people living their lives and consuming their foods within strictly local areas involving habitation on long-term settlement sites, or were they moving around a lot in the landscape, taking their animals with them and consuming foods over a more regional or even national geographic range? Such questions may appear at first sight to be of lesser consequence than the issue of long-distance migration, but are in fact very significant to archaeologists studying this period. Whilst hard and fast answers to some of the more complicated of these questions may be difficult to obtain from the data being made available from this project, early results suggest that we can certainly answer some of them clearly, whilst for others we can begin to make headway which can be built on with future research. Thus, for example, we can say that they were not eating significant levels of marine resources, even when buried very close to the coast. In some locations at least, these people are unlikely to have spent the whole of their lives in one place, but had a significant level of at least regional movement, and this is something that can be explored further in the future by building on the existing research. It suggests that, for these people, habitation on long-term, year-long settlement sites may not have been the usual subsistence method.

The skeletal samples selected for analysis as part of the Beaker People Project have been taken from sites located across mainland Britain, from Scotland down to Wessex, in order to address the research questions for a population sample which was widely distributed geographically. Table 15.1⊕ provides a list of the individuals which have been included in the project and Figure 15.1 is a distribution map. The sampling focused on four regions, three of which were concentrated upon specific museum collections. These were Scotland (National Museums Scotland and Marischal

Museum), East Yorkshire (Hull and East Riding Museum, Mortimer collection) and the Peak District (Weston Park Museum in Sheffield, Bateman and Marsden collections). Outside of these, samples were taken from a number of other museums and commercial excavation units to expand the distribution and to include sites from across the south and midlands of England, Wales and one individual from Ireland, with particular emphasis on the collection held by the Duckworth Laboratory at the Leverhulme Centre for Evolutionary Studies in Cambridge.

For each individual, a bone sample (preferably mandible) and a tooth (preferably a 2nd molar) have been taken, with the intention of analysing the collagen from both the bone and the tooth root dentine for carbon, nitrogen, and sulphur isotope ratios, and the tooth enamel for strontium and oxygen isotope ratios. Only permanent dentitions were sampled and juveniles have not been included in the analysis. Individuals ranging from those with 'rich' grave goods to those with none at all, differing forms of grave (cist burials, barrow burials, flat graves), and a range of different Beaker forms have all been included, together with a range of dates, from later Neolithic through to the inclusion of some burials with Food Vessels. Where radiocarbon dates were not previously available, the project has dated many of the burials on the bone collagen extractions obtained as part of the isotopic analysis (Sheridan 2007; Sheridan *et al.* 2006; 2007).

In order to provide an archive record of the teeth taken, they have been CT scanned and a life-size, three-dimensional model has been 'printed' from the scan data using a form of plaster. The museums which have contributed samples to the project have been provided with these physical models for display and archive purposes, alongside digital models employing rotatable three-dimensional pdf files and compressed CT scan files which can be accessed using freely available software. The much larger raw CT scan data have been stored centrally, for access by future researchers.

Work on this project is being undertaken at a number of different institutions. Dental microwear and human osteology have been carried out at Sheffield University, the tooth modelling and laboratory work involving the organics (collagen from bone and dentine) and

the processing of the enamel for oxygen analysis have been based at the Max Planck Institute for Evolutionary Anthropology in Leipzig, whilst the other enamel-based work has been undertaken at the University of Bradford and at the NERC Isotope Geosciences Laboratory (NIGL) in Nottingham. (For an interim overview, see contributions in Larsson and Parker Pearson 2007).

Isotopic analysis: the basic theory

The theory behind the isotopic analysis of skeletal material is based on the fact that the constituents of biological tissues are formed from elements taken from the foods and liquids consumed by an individual. The old cliché 'you are what you eat' (and drink) is true for the chemical components which make up bones and teeth. These trace back to plants at the base of the food chain and these, in turn, will reflect local growing environments in terms of factors such as atmosphere, soil, geology, and water source (Bentley 2006; Hedges *et al.* 2006; Lee-Thorp 2008). Direct consumption of water will also reflect some aspects of local environment. It is these connections with the sources of food and water that can allow interpretations to be made about human (and animal) mobility. If the isotopic signals expected for the burial location do not match the data obtained from the skeletal material, then either the individual moved around, consuming food from other locations at certain points in their life history, or the foods themselves were moved (such as is the case for foodstuffs that were exchanged between communities, or where migrating wild animals are a dietary resource).

In addition to reflecting environments, isotope data can provide information about the general types of food being consumed. In particular, carbon data can differentiate between plants with different photosynthetic pathways (C_4 and C_3 plant groups), whilst nitrogen data can be used to interpret trophic level (herbivore *v.* carnivore), and a combination of carbon, nitrogen, and sulphur can be used to identify the consumption of marine and other aquatic resources. The component of the foods which is being reflected in the collagen isotope signals is largely protein (in diets where protein is not in restricted supply) and the dietary reconstruction undertaken therefore relates to protein consumption, rather than to carbohydrate or lipid ingestion (Ambrose & Norr 1993). The distinction between C_4 and C_3 plant groups mentioned above is not important in the context of this paper, since C_4 plants were not available in prehistoric Britain, these generally being adapted to more tropical environments, with plants using the C_3 photosynthetic pathway being those available in temperate Europe at this time. There is a possibility of millet (a C_4 plant) being available on the continental mainland from the Late Neolithic (Robinson 2003; Jacob *et al.* 2008; Kohler-Schneider & Caneppele 2009), but there is no record of it appearing in British prehistoric contexts, probably due to the unsuitable climate.

Isotopes are atoms of the same chemical element which have slightly different masses, so that, for instance, ^{13}C is slightly heavier than ^{12}C. In the techniques discussed here, two isotopes are measured for each element, a ratio is calculated and this is compared to the ratio for an international standard. The resulting difference between the two rates is shown as a delta (δ) value (except for strontium), for which the unit of measurement is per mil (‰) (eg, $\delta^{13}C$). The isotopes investigated are 'stable' (again, except for strontium) in the sense that they do not decay radioactively (as, for instance, ^{14}C does) and this means that, if contamination and diagenesis issues are dealt with effectively, the ratio of these stable isotopes in the archaeological skeletal material will be equivalent to that seen in the individual at the time of death. These ratios will then bear a direct relationship to those seen in the foods and water consumed during life, although the exact relationship involved will be slightly different according to the element considered, since issues such as fractionation during metabolic processes must be addressed individually.

Changes in the bone chemistry during burial are an important consideration and it is for this reason that the oxygen and strontium analyses for this project have been undertaken only on tooth enamel, which is considered to be a much more stable material in this respect than, for instance, bone mineral (Hoppe *et al.* 2003; Lee-Thorp & Sponheimer 2003). Collagen from bone and dentine is also a well-preserved component, particularly in temperate burial environments, which tends to produce data that are not significantly affected

by diagenesis or contamination, particularly when ultrafiltration methods are used during extraction as they have been for this project (Brown *et al.* 1988; Bronk Ramsey *et al.* 2004), and quality indicators are available for the collagen extract which allow the discard of suspect data (DeNiro 1985; van Klinken 1999; Nehlich & Richards 2009).

The formation timings of the various skeletal tissues being analysed vary. Dental tissues form during childhood and early adolescence, so that the signatures from the enamel and dentine will provide information about an early period in life. These fractions do not turn over during an individual's lifetime, unlike bone, for which the cells are replaced and remodelled over time. Although the isotopic signals from the enamel and the primary dentine of the tooth root will not change from those laid down at this early formation point, there is some formation of secondary dentine in the pulp cavity and root canal during life (Kvaal *et al.* 1995; Hillson 2005, 185) which is likely to contribute slightly to the overall primary dentine signal, this providing the bulk of the material being analysed. Bone turns over during life, which means that the signal from a mature adult will reflect an average of a lifetime's diet, but for cortical bone this is likely to show a much larger contribution from adolescence than from later life stages (Libby *et al.* 1964; Stenhouse & Baxter 1979; Wild *et al.* 2000; Hedges *et al.* 2007). Overall, this means that enamel, dentine, and bone isotopic signals reflect different periods of an individual's life and comparisons of the data between tissues can add information when interpreting the data.

Isotope analysis: project progress to date

Analysis of both bone and teeth, using the isotope ratios of five different chemical elements, from over 250 inhumations from a large number of individual burial sites from across Britain, is quite a complicated process administratively. A number of different researchers and laboratory facilities are involved for the different phases of the work and a 'rolling schedule' has been employed involving a number of stages following sampling. As each batch of samples was taken, the sequence of processing, involving different laboratories for each phase, has been instigated, so that the point in the progression that a group of samples has reached will depend upon the stage at which sampling was achieved and the schedule of availability of analytical equipment for final data production. At the time of writing, sampling is closed and the CT scanning is fully complete. Many of the other stages are either complete (eg, all enamel samples have now been removed from the teeth and all collagen has been extracted from the bone samples), or nearing that point. No oxygen data are yet available, but the majority of the carbon, nitrogen, sulphur, and strontium data for the Scottish and East Yorkshire groups are now on hand, with carbon, nitrogen, and some sulphur data available from the bone collagen of most of the rest of the sampled material.

Whilst early consideration of the data for groups and individuals is underway, a full set of isotopic ratio results is required for final conclusions to be reached, so it should be borne in mind that this paper discusses a work-in-progress in this respect and discussion here is based on tentative early interpretations.

Overview of organic analysis results

The currently available results for carbon, nitrogen, and sulphur from the organic collagen content of the bone and dentine will now be commented on in more detail. Three issues of interest to come out of these particular data are specifically considered here, the first concerning general dietary patterns, the second involving a chronological shift in the carbon signal which may be connected to the ways in which domesticated animals were managed and/or foddered and, lastly, the sulphur data-set which will form the largest group of such isotope ratios to be available from any group of archaeological skeletal material when the project is finished and which will contribute to the discussion of mobility amongst these people.

General diet

Overall, the carbon and nitrogen data show that the general diet was very similar for all individuals sampled. They were eating a high level of animal protein, without any indication of the consumption of significant levels of marine resources. The latter is true even where the burial sites were on the coast or very close

to it, as they were, for instance, in many cases in the Scottish group. It was not unexpected to find that foods from marine contexts, such as fish or sea birds, were not being consumed at levels visible in the isotope data. Although such resources were included in the diet during the Mesolithic, they are generally not traced at significant levels isotopically in British later prehistoric material from the Neolithic through to the Iron Age, only appearing again when Roman dietary influences start to take hold (Richards *et al.* 1998; 2003b;. 2006; Jay & Richards 2007b). When early analyses of the Scottish group revealed two individuals consuming high levels of marine foods (SK 21 and 44, see Table 15.1⊕), this was a surprise, but subsequent radiocarbon dating of both revealed that they were actually medieval, having been included in the project on the basis of the short cist burial form, but without grave goods (Jay & Richards 2007a).

Carbon chronological shift

The $\delta^{13}C$ values form an interesting pattern when compared to other later prehistoric British material, particularly a group of Middle Iron Age samples which provide a good geographical spread across England and southern Scotland and match some of the locations from which Beaker period samples have been taken, particularly East Yorkshire and East Lothian (Jay & Richards 2006; 2007b). In general, the Beaker People Project human carbon isotope ratios from bone collagen are more negative than those from the Middle Iron Age. There is a significant overlap between the chronological groups and the difference of the means for the chronological groups is only 0.6‰, but the difference is statistically

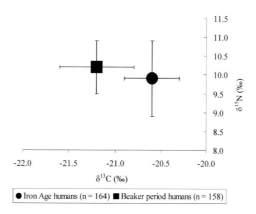

Figure 15.2. Comparison of the averages for Middle Iron Age and Beaker period humans from across Britain, showing the statistically significant shift in the $\delta^{13}C$ values from bone collagen between these two periods. The error bars are one standard deviation

clear ($t(320) = 15.13$; $p < 0.01$) (see Fig. 15.2). This distinction is not only apparent across the entire geographic range being considered, but is also present at individual sites and regions where data are available for both periods (eg, Wetwang in East Yorkshire, Ferry Fryston in West Yorkshire, the Glastonbury area in Somerset, and East Lothian in southern Scotland – see Jay *et al.* 2007; Jay & Richards 2007b; Jay 2008 for some of the Iron Age data).

Although the Beaker People Project itself does not include the analysis of animals, some groups of Early Bronze Age herbivore samples have been analysed in order to see whether this shift in $\delta^{13}C$ values can be seen in these as well as the humans. These data can be used to help consider whether the shift might be related to changes in the local environments at the base of the food chain, to the diets of the domesticated animals consumed by the humans, or specifically to a shift in the kinds of foods being eaten by the humans. A clear supporting shift has been seen in cattle at a number of sites (eg, Durrington Walls (Wiltshire), Gayhurst (Buckinghamshire), Irthlingborough (Northamptonshire), and material from the Yorkshire Wolds), but two sites have been found where it does not occur in these animals; Fir Tree Field pit at Down Farm (Dorset) and Barrow Hills, Radley (Oxfordshire).

At the time of writing, consideration of the reasons for this shift has involved factors such as climate change, deforestation, and the question of whether there was a subtle change in human foods. The $\delta^{13}C$ values of plants at the base of the food chain will reflect their environments because their carbon is taken up from the atmosphere during photosynthesis. Environmental controls such as light, water availability, temperature, and atmospheric carbon dioxide concentrations can affect this process and cause changes in the isotopic ratios, and these in turn will be reflected in animals and humans through the food chain. Two of the main drivers which have been looked at in archaeological material are climate change and the effects of deforestation (eg, van der Merwe & Medina 1991; Hedges *et al.* 2004; Stevens & Hedges 2004). The $\delta^{13}C$ values of plants grown in wetter and colder conditions would be expected to be more negative, as would those of plants growing under forest canopy. For the transition period between the Early Bronze Age and Middle Iron Age, climate change is known to have occurred towards a wetter and cooler environment, alongside extensive deforestation (eg, Turner 1970; Dark 2006; Amesbury *et al.* 2008).

Although the matter is still being investigated and much more work needs to be done, the current tentative interpretation is that the shift relates to a change in the way that domesticated herbivores were managed and/or foddered between the two periods, with the herbivore diet for the Late Neolithic, Chalcolithic, and Early Bronze Age appearing to have an unusually negative $\delta^{13}C$ signal when compared to most British prehistoric material, and the Iron Age comparative material in particular. Although climate change affecting the plants at the base of the food chain might be intuitively the first hypothesis to consider, given the known changes between the two periods being compared, early considerations of the herbivore bone would suggest that this is not the main explanation. Such a climate change effect ought to be visible in herbivores at *all* sites, which is not the case, and early results from herbivores from the later Bronze Age also do not appear to reflect the shift. The effects of deforestation may well come into play, since this will affect carbon isotope values where vegetation from under forest cover is being consumed by herbivores, but this can be included within an interpretation which relates to animal management strategies involving human decisions about what animals are consuming and where they are feeding.

Whatever the reason for this shift, it must apply to the whole of the area being investigated for this project, from Scotland down to southern England, since the shift in the humans is universal and not region-specific. If animal management is involved, then the specifics of this might need to be addressed when considering a way of life which spread across the communities of the British mainland during this period, although the lack of a shift in two of the herbivore groups investigated suggests that there may have been differences in the ways in which particular herds were being managed which were not necessarily regional. Consumption patterns in the humans which mixed protein input from such differing herds within regions (and also may have included animals such as pigs) may explain why the $\delta^{13}C$ distinction is much greater in many of the herbivores than it is in the humans, where the shift is statistically clear, but also involves significant overlap with the Iron Age.

Sulphur data-set

Sulphur isotope ratio data (δ^{34}S values) have been very difficult to obtain in any quantity from archaeological skeletal material until relatively recently for technical reasons, largely relating to the fact that there is very little sulphur in collagen (Richards *et al.* 2003). Only one of the 20 amino acids which form the collagen molecule contains sulphur. As the problems are overcome, small data-sets have started to appear in the literature, although interpretation of these continues to be difficult without extensive empirical baselines to work with from such material (eg, Craig *et al.* 2006; Privat *et al.* 2007; Fornander *et al.* 2008). A further issue to be dealt with relates to the development of quality indicators for the data which will help with discarding δ^{34}S values which appear to relate to diagenesis or contamination within the burial environment. Research being undertaken by the Leipzig group addresses this problem (Nehlich & Richards 2009).

The extensive sulphur isotope data-set from the project will not only provide us with information about people from the British Late Neolithic, Chalolithic, and Early Bronze Age, but will also provide a basis for future interpretation of sulphur data from other British archaeological contexts. As indicators of mobility, the data are valuable in combination with strontium and oxygen isotope ratios when interpreting an overall data-set. At the time of writing, the majority of the available sulphur data are from the Scottish and East Yorkshire samples, and they are significantly different for each of these groups, with the Scottish δ^{34}S average for bone at 14.7±1.5‰ (n = 43) and that for East Yorkshire at 11.2±2.5‰ (n = 47). The data from East Yorkshire are more variable within the group, with a range for the Scottish bone of 6.1‰ and for Yorkshire of 12.2‰. Dentine data are also available, with more variation seen between the bone/dentine pairs for Yorkshire than is seen in Scotland (see Fig. 15.3).

Sulphur isotope ratios will reflect local geology, as well as other factors such as proximity to the coast ('the sea spray effect') and consumption of aquatic resources (Richards *et al.* 2001; 2003). The data here are suggestive of mobility across the group, in terms of movement into and out of the Yorkshire Wolds chalk area, with the consumption of foods

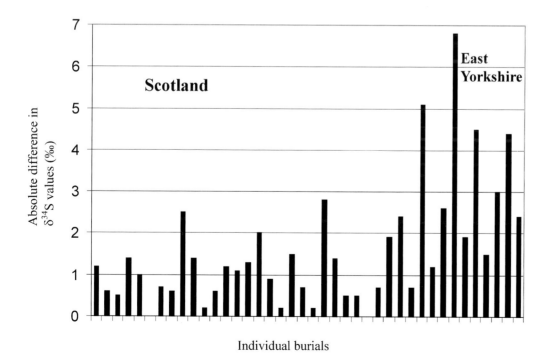

Figure 15.3. Absolute differences in δ^{34}S values between bone and dentine collagen pairs from the same individual compared between the Scottish and the East Yorkshire groups. The variation seen in East Yorkshire is noticeably greater than that seen for Scotland

which have been sourced at these different places being reflected in the different tissues at different formation times. When $\delta^{34}S$ values for herbivore animal bone are considered for the Yorkshire region, it is the higher values which appear to reflect the local geology, with the values at the lower end of the data range apparently reflecting movement between areas. The sulphur data do not reflect the consumption of significant levels of aquatic resources, since the carbon and nitrogen data do not support such an interpretation. Neither has a significant effect been found in these data-sets which would relate the $\delta^{34}S$ values to coastal proximity of the burial site. The variation seen is likely, therefore, to largely reflect the geology of the food source region at the appropriate tissue formation time. The suggested mobility may well be local or regional movement, or involve more long-distance travel for specific individuals, but the variation in the sulphur data is supported by the strontium data when discussing an overall level of mobility which is not seen later on in the Iron Age for this location (Jay & Richards 2006; Montgomery *et al.* 2007; Jay & Montgomery, unpublished data).

Part of the reason that this mobility appears to be so visible here is that the East Yorkshire group of burials have all come from the Yorkshire Wolds, which are formed from the Cretaceous Chalk, an extremely homogeneous rock. This means that movement into and out of that relatively small region is likely to be more perceptible than in, for instance, the Scottish group, where the burials are very widely distributed and the geology is relatively complex.

Conclusions

The project is a work-in-progress at this stage and a full set of isotope data, involving all five chemical elements from both bone and tooth, is not yet available for any one of the individuals being investigated. However, much has already been done and we have a good picture of the situation for the Scottish and East Yorkshire groups in particular. Mobility at various levels appears to be indicated for both groups and individuals. This is of particular interest for the East Yorkshire group, where at least local and regional movement on a regular basis appears to be indicated. This may

well reflect a very significant difference in the ways in which subsistence strategies were being applied by the Late Neolithic, Chalcolithic, and Early Bronze Age people being buried on the Yorkshire Wolds, as compared to the Middle Iron Age groups for whom such mobility is not in evidence at any significant level, except in isolated individuals.

A chronological shift in the carbon values is apparent and tentative interpretations of this are that it may well relate to animal management strategies during this period. This might involve factors such as herd movements, grazing under forest cover, or provision of winter fodder such as leafy browse material. Whatever the cause of the shift, it must be associated with communities from across the British mainland, so that if it does relate to animal management issues, then it may well form a standard way of feeding some herds of domesticated herbivores for all of the Beaker period people from Scotland down to southern England which differs from the ways in which Middle Iron Age people were keeping their animals.

The general diet of these people excludes significant levels of marine and other aquatic resources, regardless of the proximity of the site to the coast, and animal protein consumption (meat or dairy) is at relatively high levels. This does not mean that they were not also eating significant levels of plant foods, since the collagen isotope signatures reflect protein consumption and this is available at much higher levels in animal products than in many plant foods, so that a diet high in meat or dairy protein will tend to reflect the latter disproportionately. Given the range of carbon and nitrogen values which might be expected for one period across a large number of British sites from Scotland down to southern England (eg, Jay & Richards 2007b), the diet for these people appears to have been relatively homogeneous and the subsistence strategies would certainly have had commonalities across the entire geographical range being investigated.

Acknowledgements

The project has been funded by the Arts & Humanities Research Council (AHRC). The core team members, in addition to the authors on this paper, are Stuart Needham, Mike Hamilton, Patrick Mahoney, Alex Gibson, Jane Evans, Carolyn Chenery, Neil Curtis, Neil Wilkin, and Maura Pellegrini. Tom Higham and

Diane Baker from the Oxford Radiocarbon Accelerator Unit are thanked for their help with the dating programme. Those involved in allowing access to the samples must also be thanked. The list is extensive and space does not allow for them all to be listed here. However, Table 15.1⊕ reflects the institutions involved and all those individuals who have facilitated the work are thanked for their time and help, and in most cases for their enthusiasm for having the material included in this project.

Bibliography

Ambrose, S.H. & Norr, L. 1993. Experimental evidence for the relationship of the carbon isotope ratios of whole diet and dietary protein to those of bone collagen and carbonate. In J.B. Lambert & G. Grupe (eds), *Prehistoric Human Bone: archaeology at the molecular level*, 1–37. Berlin: Springer-Verlag

Amesbury, M.J., Charman, D.J., Fyfe, R.M., Langdon, P.G. & West, S. 2008. Bronze Age upland settlement decline in southwest England: testing the climate change hypothesis. *Journal of Archaeological Science* 35, 87–98

Bentley, R.A. 2006. Strontium isotopes from the earth to the archaeological skeleton: a review. *Journal of Archaeological Method and Theory* 13(3), 135–87

Brodie, N. 1994. *The Neolithic–Bronze Age Transition in Britain: a critical review of some archaeological and craniological concepts*. Oxford: British Archaeological Report 238

Bronk Ramsey, C., Higham, T., Bowles, A. & Hedges, R. 2004. Improvements to the pretreatment of bone at Oxford. *Radiocarbon* 46(1), 155–63

Brown, T.A., Nelson, D.E., Vogel, J.S. & Southon, J.R. 1988. Improved collagen extraction by modified Longin method. *Radiocarbon* 30 (2), 171–177

Burgess, C. & Shennan, S. 1976. The Beaker phenomenon: some suggestions. In C. Burgess & R. Miket (eds), *Settlement and Economy in the Third and Second Millennia BC*, 309–331. Oxford: British Archaeological Report 33

Childe, V. G. 1930. *The Bronze Age*. Cambridge: Cambridge University Press

Craig, O.E., Ross, R., Andersen, S.H., Milner, N. & Bailey, G.N. 2006. Focus: sulphur isotope variation in archaeological marine fauna from northern Europe. *Journal of Archaeological Science* 33, 1642–6

Dark, P. 2006. Climate deterioration and land-use change in the first millennium BC: perspectives from the British palynological record. *Journal of Archaeological Science* 33, 1381–95

Davis, J.B. & Thurnam, J. 1865. *Crania Britannica: Delineations and descriptions of the skulls of the aboriginal and early inhabitants of the British islands: with notices of their other remains*. London: Private publication

DeNiro, M.J. 1985. Postmortem preservation and alteration of *in vivo* bone collagen isotope ratios in relation to palaeodietary reconstruction. *Nature* 317, 806–9

Evans, J.A., Chenery, C.A. & Fitzpatrick, A.P. 2006. Bronze Age childhood migration of individuals near Stonehenge, revealed by strontium and oxygen isotope tooth enamel analysis. *Archaeometry* 48(2), 309–21

Fitzpatrick, A.P. 2003. The Amesbury Archer. *Current Archaeology* 16, 146–52

Fornander, E., Eriksson, G. & Lidén, K. 2008. Wild at heart: approaching Pitted Ware identity, economy and cosmology through stable isotopes in skeletal material from the Neolithic site Korsnäs in Eastern Central Sweden. *Journal of Anthropological Archaeology* 27, 281–97

Grupe, G., Price, T. D., Schröter, P., Söllner, F., Johnson, C.M. & Beard, B.L. 1997. Mobility of Bell Beaker people revealed by strontium isotope ratios of tooth and bone: a study of southern Bavarian skeletal remains. *Applied Geochemistry* 12, 517–25

Hedges, R.E.M., Stevens, R.E. & Richards, M.P. 2004. Bone as a stable isotope archive for local climatic information. *Quaternary Science Reviews* 23, 959–65

Hedges, R.E.M., Clement, J G., Thomas, C.D.L. & O'Connell, T.C. 2007. Collagen turnover in the adult femoral mid-shaft: modelled from anthropogenic radiocarbon tracer measurements. *American Journal of Physical Anthropology* 133, 808–16

Hedges, R.E.M., Stevens, R.E. & Koch, P.L. 2006. Isotopes in bones and teeth. In M.J. Leng (ed.), *Isotopes in Palaeoenvironmental Research*, 117–45. Dordrecht: Springer

Hillson, S. 2005. *Teeth*. Cambridge: Cambridge University Press

Hooke, G.E. & Morant, G M. 1926. The present state of our knowledge of British craniology in late prehistoric and historic times. *Biometrika* 18, 99–104

Hoppe, K.A., Koch, P.L. & Furutani, T.T. 2003. Assessing the preservation of biogenic strontium in fossil bones and tooth enamel. *International Journal of Osteoarchaeology* 13(1–2), 20–8

Jacob, J., Disnar, J.-R., Arnaud, F., Chapron, E., Debret, M., Lallier-Vergès, E., Desmet, M. & Revel-Rolland, M. 2008. Millet cultivation history in the French Alps as evidenced by a sedimentary molecule. *Journal of Archaeological Science* 35, 814–20

Jay, M. 2008. Iron Age diet at Glastonbury Lake Village: the isotopic evidence for negligible aquatic resource consumption. *Oxford Journal of Archaeology* 27(2), 201–16

Jay, M., Grimes, V., Montgomery, J., Lakin, K. & Evans, J. 2007. Multi-isotope analysis of humans and cattle from Ferry Fryston, West Yorkshire. In F. Brown, C. Howard-Davis, M. Brennand, A. Boyle, T. Evans, S. O'Connor, A. Spence, R. Heawood & A. Lupton (eds), *The Archaeology of the A1 (M) Darrington*, 351–54. Oxford: Oxford Archaeology

Jay, M. & Richards, M.P. 2006. Diet in the Iron Age cemetery population at Wetwang Slack, East Yorkshire, UK: carbon and nitrogen stable isotope evidence. *Journal of Archaeological Science* 33, 653–62

Jay, M. & Richards, M.P. 2007a. The Beaker People Project: progress and prospects for the carbon, nitrogen and sulphur isotopic analysis of collagen. In Larsson & Parker Pearson (eds) 2007, 77–82

Jay, M. & Richards, M.P. 2007b. British Iron Age diet: stable isotopes and other evidence. *Proceedings of the Prehistoric Society* 73, 171–92

Klinken, G.J. van. 1999. Bone collagen quality indicators for palaeodietary and radiocarbon measurements. *Journal of Archaeological Science* 26, 687–95

Kohler-Schneider, M. & Caneppele, A. 2009. Late Neolithic agriculture in eastern Austria: archaeobotanical results from sites of the Baden and Jevišovice cultures (3600–2800 BC). *Vegetation History and Archaeobotany* 18, 61–74

Kvaal, S.I., Kolltveit, K.M., Thomsen, I.O. & Solheim, T. 1995. Age estimation of adults from dental radiographs. *Forensic Science International* 74, 175–85

Larsson, M. & Parker Pearson, M. (eds). 2007. *From Stonehenge to the Baltic: living with cultural diversity in the third millennium BC*. Oxford: British Archaeological Report S1692

Lee-Thorp, J.A. 2008. On isotopes and old bones. *Archaeometry* 50(6), 925–50

Lee-Thorp, J. & Sponheimer, M. 2003. Three case studies used to reassess the reliability of fossil bone and enamel isotope signals for paleodietary studies. *Journal of Anthropological Archaeology* 22, 208–16

Libby, W.F., Berger, R., Mead, J.F., Alexander, G.V. & Ross, J.F. 1964. Replacement rates for human tissue from atmospheric radiocarbon. *Science* 146, 1170–3

Merwe, N.J. van der & Medina, E. 1991. The canopy effect, carbon isotope ratios and foodwebs in Amazonia. *Journal of Archaeological Science* 18, 249–59

Montgomery, J., Evans, J.A. & Cooper, R.E. 2007. Resolving archaeological populations with Sr-isotope mixing models. *Applied Geochemistry* 22, 1502–14

Nehlich, O. & Richards, M.P. 2009. Establishing collagen quality criteria for sulphur isotope analysis of archaeological bone collagen. *Archaeological & Anthropological Sciences* 1(1), 59–75

Parsons, F.G. 1924. The brachycephalic skull. *Journal of the Royal Anthropological Institute of Great Britain and Ireland* 54, 166–82

Price, T.D., Grupe, G. & Schröter, P. 1998. Migration in the Bell Beaker period of central Europe. *Antiquity* 72, 405–11

Price, T.D., Knipper, C., Grupe, G. & Smrcka, V. 2004. Strontium isotopes and prehistoric human migration: the Bell Beaker period in central Europe. *European Journal of Archaeology* 7(1), 9–40

Privat, K.L., O'Connell, T.C. & Hedges, R.E.M. 2007. The distinction between freshwater- and terrestrial-based diets: methodological concerns and archaeological applications of sulphur stable isotope analysis. *Journal of Archaeological Science* 34, 1197–1204

Richards, M.P., Fuller, B.T. & Molleson, T.I. 2006. Stable isotope palaeodietary study of humans and fauna from the multi-period (Iron Age, Viking and Late Medieval) site of Newark Bay, Orkney. *Journal of Archaeological Science* 33, 122–31

Richards, M.P., Fuller, B.T., Sponheimer, M., Robinson, T. & Ayliffe, L. 2003a. Sulphur isotopes in palaeodietary studies: a review and results from a controlled feeding experiment. *International Journal of Osteoarchaeology* 13(1–2), 37–45

Richards, M.P., Schulting, R.J. & Hedges, R.E.M. 2003b. Sharp shift in diet at onset of Neolithic. *Nature* 425, 366

Richards, M.P., Fuller, B.T. & Hedges, R.E.M. 2001. Sulphur isotopic variation in ancient bone collagen from Europe: implications for human palaeodiet, residence mobility, and modern pollutant studies. *Earth and Planetary Science Letters* 191(3–4), 185–90

Richards, M.P., Hedges, R.E.M., Molleson, T.I. & Vogel, J.C. 1998. Stable isotope analysis reveals variations in human diet at the Poundbury Camp cemetery site. *Journal of Archaeological Science* 25, 1247–52

Robinson, D.E. 2003. Neolithic and Bronze Age agriculture in southern Scandinavia – recent archaeobotanical evidence from Denmark. *Environmental Archaeology* 8, 145–65

Sheridan, A. 2007. Scottish Beaker dates: the good, the bad and the ugly. In Larsson & Parker Pearson (eds) 2007, 91–123

Sheridan, J.A., Parker Pearson, M., Jay, M., Richards, M. & Curtis, N. 2006. Radiocarbon dating results from the *Beaker People Project*: Scottish samples. *Discovery and Excavation in Scotland* 7, 198–201

Sheridan, A., Parker Pearson, M., Jay, M., Richards, M. & Curtis, N. 2007. Radiocarbon dating results from the Beaker People Project, 2007: Scottish Samples. *Discovery and Excavation in Scotland* 8, 222

Stenhouse, M.J. & Baxter, M. S. 1979. The uptake of bomb ^{14}C in humans. In R. Berger & H. E. Suess (eds), *Radiocarbon Dating: proceedings of the ninth international conference Los Angeles and La Jolla, 1976*, 324–41. Berkeley: University of California Press

Stevens, R.E. & Hedges, R.E.M. 2004. Carbon and nitrogen stable isotope analysis of northwest European horse bone and tooth collagen, 40,000 BP–present: palaeoclimatic interpretations. *Quaternary Science Reviews* 23, 977–91

Thurnam, J. 1865. *On the Two Principal Forms of Ancient British and Gaulish Skulls*. London: reprinted by T. Richards, from the *Memoirs of the Anthropological Society of London* 1

Turner, J. 1970. Post-Neolithic disturbance of British vegetation. In D. Walker & R.G. West (eds), *Studies in the Vegetational History of the British Isles: essays in honour of Harry Godwin*, 97–116. Cambridge: Cambridge University Press

Vander Linden, M. 2007. What linked the Bell Beakers in third millennium BC Europe? *Antiquity* 81, 343–52

Wild, E.M., Arlamovsky, K.A., Golser, R., Kutschera, W., Priller, A., Puchegger, S., Rom, W., Steier, P. & Vycudilik, W. 2000. [14]C dating with the bomb peak: an application to forensic medicine. *Nuclear Instruments & Methods in Physics Research, Section B – Beam interactions with materials and atoms* 172, 944–50

16

The Regionality of Beakers and Bodies in the Chalcolithic of North-East Scotland

Neil G.W. Curtis and Neil C.A. Wilkin

This paper discusses regional socio-cultural identities, changes and networks of interaction during the Chalcolithic (c. 2500/2400–2200/2150 cal BC) in north-east Scotland and the immediately adjacent regions of east-central Scotland and the Moray Firth area. Drawing on the findings of the Leverhulme Trust-funded Beakers and Bodies Project (Marischal Museum, University of Aberdeen), including an enlarged pool of radiocarbon dates, Bayesian modelling and a contextual approach to a range of material culture and traditions of funerary practice, it proposes several regional narratives/models in order to outline and explain the significance of chronological sequences and 'historical' events in north-east Scotland and beyond.

During the past 25 years, the rich evidence for Beakers and early metalwork in north-east Scotland has been productively surveyed and studied (*inter alia*. Shepherd 1986; Cowie 1988; Needham 2004; Gannon *et al.* 2007), indicating the distinctiveness of this region during the mid-/late 3rd millennium cal BC. While several recent dating projects and interpretative syntheses with a wide geographical scope have included a consideration of the north-east in this period (eg, Bradley 2007; Jones 2008; Parker Pearson 2006; Sheridan 2007), the Leverhulme Trust-funded *Beakers and Bodies Project* was established in the University of Aberdeen's Marischal Museum to undertake in-depth analysis and interpretation of this particular region. The project focused on all Beaker associated burials (and related funerary

traditions) in the north-east, including archival research, osteological analysis, a critical appraisal of existing dates, evaluation of burial assemblages, 40 new radiocarbon dates, and stable isotope analyses of human bones, accompanied by summary work in adjacent areas (the Moray Firth region and east-central Scotland). This paper will argue that such studies, sensitive to regional variations and detailed chronological sequences, are essential for the identification and understanding of the diverse forms of the 'Chalcolithic' in western Europe.

This paper considers three aspects. First, the now extensive pool of AMS radiocarbon dates for the period (Sheridan 2006; 2007; Curtis *et al.* 2008; Wilkin *et al.* forthcoming) is used to identify the material culture and practices that can be seen as relevant to a discussion of the Chalcolithic in north-east Scotland. Second, regional variation is discussed and set in the broader context of practices in adjacent areas. Finally, issues of the reception and adoption of particular funerary and non-funerary practices and material culture are considered. What influences did specific histories and the unique physical geography of eastern Scotland have on traditions of funerary practice and related material culture?

The development and chronology of the Scottish Chalcolithic

Most archaeological research investigating this period of Scottish prehistory may be characterised as either having a focus on artefacts or on monuments, in which artefact related studies have continued to be heavily influenced by culture-historical and positivist approaches, while studies of monuments have increasingly adopted a landscape focus and post-processual approaches. Although there have been useful recent attempts to draw together the different strands of evidence within a post-processual framework (eg, Brück 2004; Jones 2003), the thematic and selective nature of such work has meant that a detailed consideration of the chronology of developments within and between particular regions has often been lacking (but see MacGregor 2008).

While for considerable periods of the mid-/late 3rd millennium various classes of monuments, material culture, and single burial were common to large swathes of Britain, many of our explanations derive from southern England and it is possible that these may not be supported in other regions, such as eastern Scotland. While the character of cultural change during the 'British Chalcolithic' (*c.* 2500/2400–2200 BC) as a whole may be broadly explained with reference to the impact of copper artefacts and Beaker pottery (cf. Needham 2007), there has been little detailed consideration of how this situation varied across Britain and through the centuries in question. Indeed, if the idea of the Chalcolithic is to be useful in a consideration of this period, it should be built from a consideration and comparison of a series of regional studies in which shared or differing traditions and practices are proved rather

than assumed. Such investigations should also include a thorough study of issues of geography and regionality as physically experienced by many generations of communities. As Neal Ascherson has argued, from a perspective that shares more with recent phenomenological and landscape theory than with environmental determinism or processual-functionalism: 'human experience in ... northern place[s] has been built so intimately into the geology and the post-glacial ecology of Scotland that a people and its stone form a single cultural landscape' (Ascherson 2002, viii). Detailed studies of regional similarities and differences are therefore an essential aspect in researching the reception and adoption of technologies and practices, such as those characterising the Chalcolithic, thus avoiding the misleading impression that shared histories are necessarily implicit in shared material culture.

This period in Scottish prehistory has traditionally been defined by the appearance of copper artefacts, principally axes, daggers, halberds, and arm or neck-rings, goldwork, Low-Carinated Beakers, and a small number of burials in a continental, European style (Shepherd 1986, 7–10; Needham 2004, 236–8, fig. 19.17; 2005, 183–8; Sheridan 2008). While the end of this period is defined by the introduction of tin-bronze *c.* 2200 cal BC (Needham 2004; Gerloff 2006, 128–31, 140–1, table 13.1), the absolute chronology of the period is more difficult to define, largely due to the few datable associations of metalwork (Appendix 1, Table 16.2) and other artefacts that result from biases of preservation and collection.

In an attempt to address this problem, a substantially increased number of radiocarbon dates were studied using Bayesian analysis to refine the chronology of Beaker burials, metalwork and the broadly contemporary recumbent stone circles (RSCs) and henge enclosures. Bayesian statistical analysis of radiocarbon dates is becoming increasingly used in British archaeology as 'a way of combining archaeological knowledge – of context, stratigraphy and sample character – with explicit probabilistic modelling of date estimates, which, other things being equal, can result in much finer chronologies' (Whittle *et al.* 2008, 66). This methodology has been particularly effective in the study of individual sites in which multiple dates are associated with well-established relative stratigraphic positions of the dated material (eg, Whittle *et al.* 2007). The study of Beakers and accompanying burials, however, uses dates relating to a series of single events – the burial of a corpse with accompanying grave-goods in a stone cist – rather than sequences of events.

Whereas research into the stratigraphy of individual sites is based on assumptions relating to the relationships between different stratigraphic contexts, the use of grave groups that are not stratigraphically related depends on typology. As a technique, this is most robust when an artefact type can be defined very clearly or when a number of different features can be combined to identify groups for analysis (cf. Higham *et al.* 2007, 650). It is important to recognise the specificity of the questions considered through such Bayesian analysis, such as the comment by Bayliss *et al.* (2007) that the dates of Beakers 'may refer principally to the placement of Beakers in graves, and it remains an open question whether Beakers were in use in other contexts slightly before these dates' (Bayliss *et al.* 2007, 50). Figures 16.1–16.4 show the sums of modelled dates resulting from Bayesian analysis, each of which is based on the selection of a group of artefacts with significant typological relationships. Appendix 2☉ provides the data from which these figures are derived, including modelled boundary start and end dates.

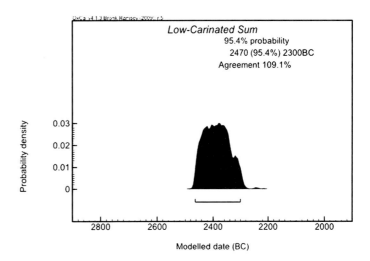

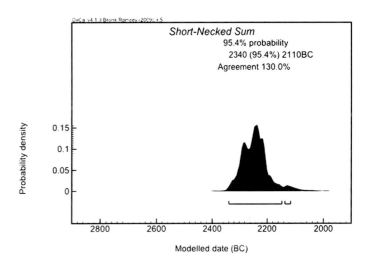

Figure 16.1: Sums of modelled dates for Low-Carinated ('continental-style') Beakers and the earliest Short-Necked Beakers in eastern Scotland

The earliest Beaker burials in Scotland

A number of Beaker burials from Scotland exhibit characteristics of continental European practices, principally the presence of Low-Carinated vessels and the use of earth-cut graves and ring-ditches, rather than the stone-lined short-cists which are a defining feature of Beaker burials in northern Britain. The former have, therefore, been interpreted as relating to an initial phase of pioneers from the continent (Sheridan 2007, 104–5; 2008). Several Beaker short-cist burials have dates, however, which overlap at the 95% probability level with these 'early' continental-style burials (Appendix 2, Fig. 16.9☉). While this may be due to the small number of examples of 'continental' Beaker burials and difficulties with radiocarbon calibration in the period *c.* 2500–2200 cal BC, it is worth considering more complex models for the introduction of Beakers and continental influences. For example, the appearance of

regionally-specific features such as short-cist burials in northern Britain could be seen as an indigenous approach to the adoption of single burial, raising the possibility that the adoption of Beaker practices in north-east Scotland was stimulated and enabled by internal social relations and links between different regions in Britain (eg, northern England; see Tuckwell 1975; A. Shepherd, this volume), as well as the impact of direct continental influences.

The earliest metalwork in eastern Scotland

The appearance of metalworking is generally considered to have played an important role in driving social change at this time (Needham 2007). There are, however, relatively few finds of non-alloyed metalwork of copper and gold in eastern Scotland, such as copper arm- or neck-rings and broad-tanged daggers (I. Shepherd 1986, 7–9), and even fewer radiocarbon dates,

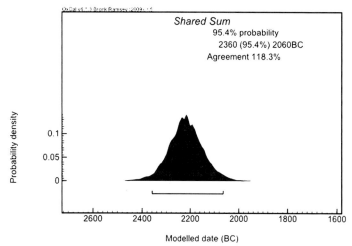

Figure 16.2: Sum of modelled dates for burials associated with Beakers from eastern Scotland sharing motifs with gold lunulae

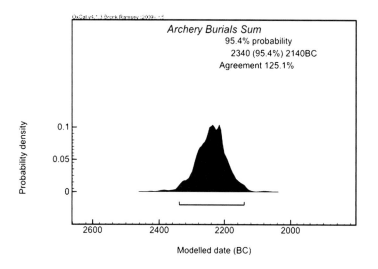

Figure 16.3: Sum of modelled dates for 'Archery' burials

having notably early dates. Although Gerloff (2006, 128) has suggested that motifs were curated from Beaker pottery and transferred onto goldwork after connections between eastern Scotland and Ireland were established through the Migdale-Marnoch tradition (*c.* 2200 cal BC) (cf. Taylor 1970, 59–64), it is suggested here that the very close parallels between motifs and techniques of composition shared by lunulae and Beakers (*ibid.*, 56) may equally indicate an earlier ('Chalcolithic') connection between copper-rich Ireland and eastern Scotland prior to the Migdale-Marnoch metalwork tradition. These initial links are also suggested by the apparent South-West Irish ('A-Metal') source of Auchingoul-type halberds (Needham 2004; 2006, 282) found in the study area. Thus, a small but significant number of Beaker short-cist burials may be identified as relating, culturally as well as chronologically, to the use of copper and gold at this time.

'Archery' graves

The complexity of the adoption of Beaker burials and metalwork in eastern Scotland is also shown in a small but important group of 'archery' graves. These are defined primarily the presence of 'wristguards', while there are often also bone belt-rings and, in several cases, Beakers that feature distinctive raised 'ribs' or cordons decorating the neck (Shepherd 1996, 145). A particularly fine example was found at Culduthel Mains, cist 2, Inverness (2280–2030 cal BC), which included a Short-Necked Beaker, bone belt-ring, and a C1 group (four-holed crescent-shaped cross-section) wristguard with copper rivets capped with sheet gold (Wedderburn 1975; Clarke *et al.* 1985, fig. 4.16, no. 74; Roe & Woodward 2007, 201–2, table 33).

A Bayesian model of dated 'archery' burials from Scotland and England has placed them during the period 2350–2150 cal BC (Appendix 2, Fig. 16.11☉), and therefore amongst the earlier Beaker burials from this region, possibly representing a relatively coherent phenomenon with connections to several other regions. As well as Culduthel Mains cist 2, there are two other Beaker assemblages from the study area with C1 wristguards: Fyrish, Evanton, Ross-shire (2440–2140 cal BC) and Borrowstone cist 6, Aberdeen (2470–2150 cal BC), the latter also with copper rivets and associated with a bone belt-ring. All are made from Langdale tuff-type

though depositional practices are likely to be a major factor limiting the identification of the earliest use of metal.

This may be partly offset by the consideration of a considerable number of Beakers from north-east Scotland that share motifs, and a compositional tendency towards symmetry, with gold lunulae (Taylor 1970, table B, *in passim*). There are now 25 such Beakers, suggesting a currency of this style of Beaker decoration *c.* 2360–*c.* 2070 cal BC (Appendix 2, Fig. 16.10☉; Appendix 1, Table 16.5). It is notable that the weight of the probability distribution lies before the proposed start of tin-bronze technology *c.* 2200 cal BC, with some Beakers that share motifs with lunulae

rocks (Roe & Woodward 2007), the Group VI rock used for Neolithic axeheads (Keiller *et al.* 1941). The three dates are statistically consistent, suggesting that they may have been included in funerary practices over a short period of time, which may accord with the suggestion that they derive from particular workshops or craftsmen (Roe & Woodward 2007, 302), although the potential for later curation clearly remains.

The presence of items such as wristguards and bone belt-rings may have been components of special dress that expressed bonds among particular Beaker-using communities. This apparel would have had symbolic meanings, such as references to archery (Woodward *et al.* 2006), while the use of Great Langdale rock may also have symbolised links with pre-existing exchange networks. It is therefore possible that the appearance and consolidation of Beaker practices in north-east Scotland involved at least two phases, with the 'archery' graves reflecting well-connected and/or travelled individuals buried in a distinctive style to highlight their status and social and geographical connections, albeit within as much as beyond British shores, perhaps even overlapping with the direct continental 'pioneers' buried in earth-cut graves discussed by Sheridan (2008).

It appears likely, however, that the 'archery' burial tradition continued in eastern Scotland after the introduction of bronze, given the date for the burial from Newlands, cist 2, Aberdeenshire (2290–2040 cal BC). It was accompanied by two wristguards that are morphologically and materially different from other examples (Roe & Woodward 2007, 301–2, tables 33–4) and a Beaker with 'cupped' neck and relatively squat profile that appears to represent a later sub-grouping of Needham's Short-Necked form (Needham 2005, 191–5; cf. dates in Sheridan 2007).

Bronze metalwork

With the addition of two dates for bronze flat-riveted daggers from Bught Park, Inverness and Carrick Drive, Fife as a consequence of the *Beakers and Bodies Project*, there are now five radiocarbon dates for bronze flat-riveted daggers and two for knife-daggers from eastern Scotland. The dates for all types of bronze daggers are statistically indistinguishable (P. Marshall pers. comm.), while a Bayesian

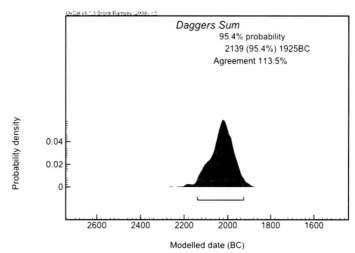

Figure 16.4: *Sum of modelled dates for burials associated with bronze daggers in eastern Scotland*

model for all early daggers from eastern Scotland (Appendix 2, Fig. 16.12⊙) provides a date range that is consistent with, if slightly shorter than, Needham's (1996: 130) range of *c.* 2300–1900 cal BC for the deposition of bronze flat-riveted daggers associated with the Migdale-Marnoch metalwork tradition and Reinecke's Bronze A1 period (Gerloff 2006, 128–31). The relatively narrow range of the available dates suggests that this type of dagger was not subject to long periods of curation (but see Bradley 2002a, 55–6) and that they date to a coherent cultural phenomenon involving the burial of adult males with bronze blades as part of the wider Migdale-Marnoch tradition that can be considered as marking the end of the Chalcolithic in north-east Scotland. The stimulus for the introduction of these funerary practices and the production of tin-bronze in the north-east that is suggested by the deposition of Burreldale axe moulds (Needham 2004) may be considered part of a wider, European, technological development (Gerloff 2006; Pare 2000), but the elaborate connections that were presumably involved in bringing tin and copper to north-east Scotland and the logistical and social mechanisms by which they were adopted do, however, also require a more detailed regional explanation.

Recumbent stone circles and henge monuments

The several hundred recumbent stone circles in north-east Scotland are distinguished by the south-western setting of a large recumbent

Figure 16.5. Comparison of models for the dating of Tomnaverie recumbent stone circle

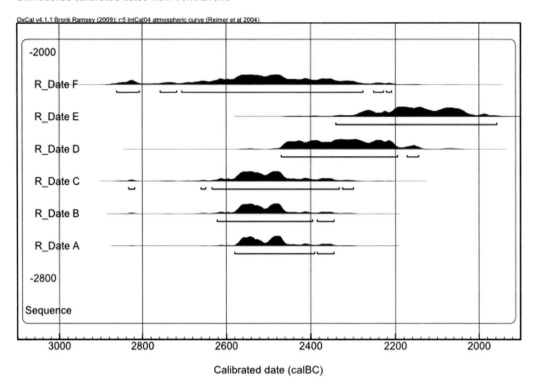

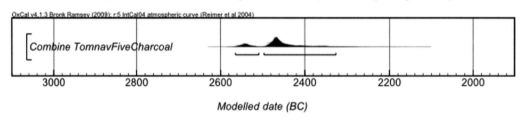

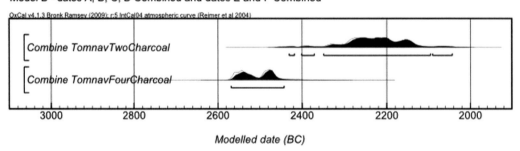

stone with upright 'flankers' on each side (Burl 1970; Bradley 2005, RCAHMS 2007). The chronology of this monument type has been a point of some contention (Shepherd 1987; Bradley 2005; Welfare 2011), with possible dates covering the later Neolithic and Early Bronze Age. Richard Bradley's (2002b; 2005) excavations at Tomnaverie resulted in

six radiocarbon determinations on charcoal. In Bradley's model (2005: 47), the latest determination was rejected as an 'outlier', with the remaining five combined to offer a date for its construction in te 25th century cal BC. The alternative statistical analysis proposed here (Fig. 16.5) suggests that the most recent two of the original six determinations can be

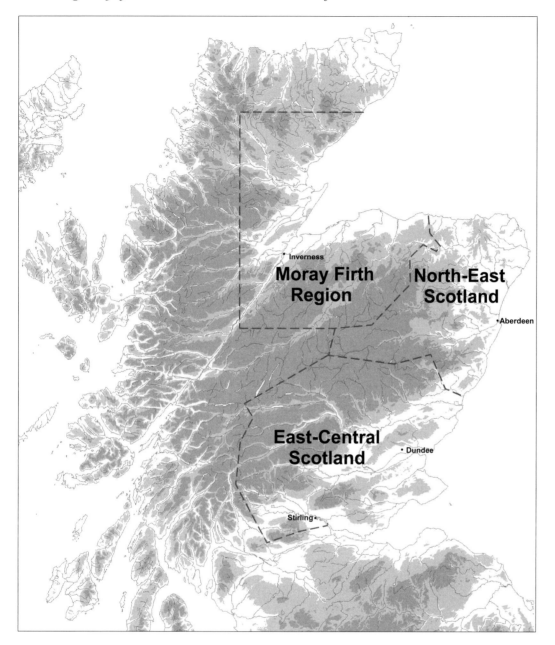

Figure 16.6. Map of Beakers and Bodies Project study areas

combined separately from the earlier four to offer a *terminus post quem* for construction in the 23rd/22nd centuries cal BC. While Bradley's model places the construction of Tomnaverie around a century (some four or five generations) before the practice of Beaker burials had become relatively common, and possibly even before the appearance of copper metalwork and the earliest Beakers (Sheridan 2008), the alternative model places this RSC at a time when Beaker burials, as well as the manufacture of tin-bronze, were routinely practiced. The cultural affinity of Beakers and RSCs in north-east Scotland is supported by the similarity of their distribution, the presence of Beaker sherds at numerous RSCs (Burl 1970) and the suggestion they shared certain cosmological principles, such as the importance of orientation (cf. A. Shepherd this volume). However, there is clearly a need for more radiocarbon dates before chronologies and relationships between RSCs, Beakers and other strands of evidence can be more fully understood.

Henge enclosures and timber circles share a distribution in eastern Scotland which is

*Table 16.1: Table
showing the regional
distribution of
funerary traditions in
eastern Scotland in the
Chalcolithic and Early
Bronze Age*

Table 16.1: Table showing the regional distribution of funerary traditions in eastern Scotland in the Chalcolithic and Early Bronze Age

Funerary item Region	Beakers	Food Vessels	Daggers	'Jet' Ornaments	TOTALS
North-east Scotland	107	6	2	4	119
East-central Scotland	54	160	23	32	269
Moray Firth region	49	32	5	14	100
Totals	210	198	30	50	488

mutually exclusive to that of RSCs (Barclay 2005, 84, 86, fig. 8.4, 8.7) and thus to the major concentrations of Beaker burials. Several of these sites have been successfully dated (Barclay 2005), placing the initial construction of henge enclosures and expansive ceremonial landscapes such as Balfarg, Fife and North Mains, Perth and Kinross in the later Neolithic, though their use continued after this date with single burials (bodies buried as articulated, coherent entities) becoming important features at these sites, primarily more recently than the 22nd century cal BC. Examples include the integration of Early Bronze Age single burials into the henge enclosures at North Mains, Perth and Kinross (Barclay 1983), Cairnpapple, West Lothian (Barclay 1999), and most recently at Forteviot, Perth and Kinross (Brophy & Noble 2009). It is argued here that pre-existing monument traditions, and the social and ritual implications of their construction, use and scale, may be related to different regional chronologies and tempos in the appearance of Beaker cultural traits, and single burial practices more generally.

Regional narratives of the Chalcolithic in eastern Scotland

While the preceding accounts have offered outlines of some of the key features and sequences of a Chalcolithic in eastern Scotland, there are significant regional variations within the area. The *Beakers and Bodies Project* identified three major regions for analysis that are not dissimilar to those proposed by Kirk in 1957 (discussed in Barclay 2004) (Fig. 16.6). While these areas reflect physical features and local government boundaries, they do not reflect neatly bounded prehistoric polities or timeless areas of regionally-specific ritual practices; rather they represent units of analysis with which to identify and contextualise major

episodes of socio-cultural similarity, difference and change. Such explanations need to take into account the differential survival – and discovery – of evidence that is itself a product of regional differences. For example, it is likely that fewer of the potentially earliest earth-cut graves with Beakers will have been recorded than stone-lined short-cists, while antiquarian practices and recent developer-led archaeology will have created other biases. Other traditions of practice (eg, lithics) that could further develop our knowledge of regional and chronological socio-cultural continuities and discontinuities also remain to be studied, as does a consideration of the environmental or settlement evidence which is currently very scanty. Nonetheless, it is possible to identify – however cautiously – some regional characteristics of cultural reception and change during the later 3rd millennium BC.

North-East Scotland

There are some 107 Beakers from burials in this region, representing 46% of the Beakers in the study area (Table 16.1). As well as reflecting the region's large area of fertile land, the distribution also shows a concentration of such burials near the coast and along the river-valleys of the Don/Urie and lesser concentrations near other rivers, such as the Dee and the Deveron, but not the Ythan. (Fig. 16.7). The regional prominence of Beakers is matched by the rare occurrence of traditions common elsewhere in eastern Scotland from the 22nd century cal BC. For example, there are records of only six Food Vessels burials in the study area, equivalent to only 3% of those found in the study area as a whole. In a further contrast, the vast majority (92%) of Beaker burials in the region were 'flat' graves, with no recorded covering monuments, whereas in other areas burials are more frequently associated with monuments after the 22nd century cal BC. As

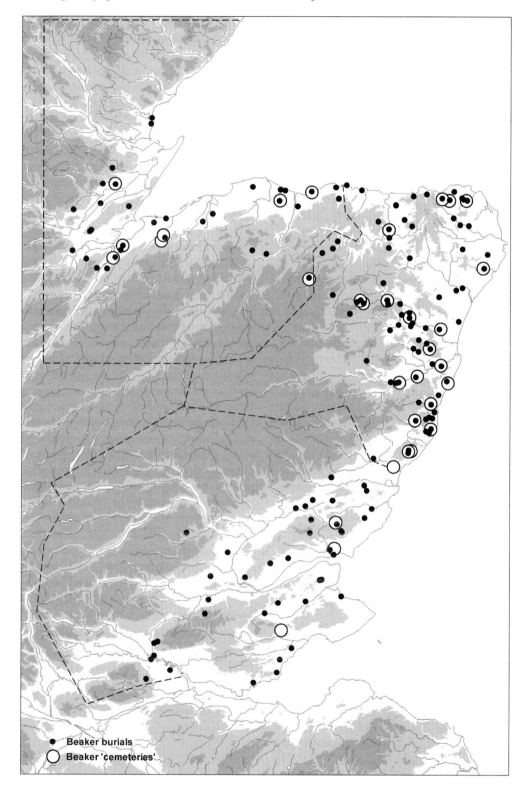

Beaker burials
Beaker 'cemeteries'

discussed above, this region is also notable for the coincidence of distinctive traditions of material culture, such as recumbent stone circles and bronze metalwork, while carved stone balls are a distinctive regional feature during the Neolithic. These traditions of monuments, portable objects and burials are notable for the way in which their creation resulted from repeatedly following detailed rules or prescriptions rather than an open 'bricolage' of varied alternatives (cf. Jones 2003). The learning of these rules might have been analogous to the way that the Blackfoot and other Native American societies transfer sacred bundles and knowledge by way of a formal ceremony, such that it is known only by those properly initiated (Conaty 2008).

East-central Scotland

Single burial practices only occurred in significant numbers in east-central Scotland from the 22nd century cal BC onwards, after the adoption of tin-bronze, accounting for 81% of all Food Vessels from the study area compared with only 26% of the Beakers (Table 16.1). There was also a relatively wide variety of grave-goods including 'late' (Handled and Weak-Carinated) Beakers, 'jet' ornaments, bronze daggers and many Food Vessels, while cremation was also practiced. Many burials have been found in barrow and cairn cemeteries, some with cists arranged in symmetrical patterns comparable with Irish funerary practices (Savory 1972, 120–24, 134–5; Wilkin 2009). Indeed, burials from this period in east-central Scotland are far more likely to be associated with monuments than those with Short-Necked or 'S'-Profile Beakers. For example, just under half of the bronze dagger and knife-dagger burials from eastern Scotland are associated with monuments. These details suggest that single burial practices were not adopted in significant numbers until the start of the Early Bronze Age proper, and were regionally specific when they did appear.

The apparent contrasts between east-central and north-east Scotland arguably occurred because of differences in the pre-existing beliefs and social organisation of both regions and the different contacts each region had with other areas. For example, the adoption of single burial practices on a significant scale in east-central Scotland coincided with the Migdale-Marnoch metalwork tradition in north-east Scotland (*c.* 2200 BC) rather than the appearance of Beakers and copper metalworking. Needham (2005) has identified a relationship between the diversification of funerary practices and the Migdale-Marnoch tradition at a British scale. As bronze-working involved the importation of resources from distant places (especially Ireland and southern England) (Needham 2004), it is probably significant that the areas of eastern Scotland in which funerary practices associated with bronze working are richest and where variability is most pronounced (principally east-central Scotland and the Moray Firth region) were the areas best located for contact with western Scotland and from there to Ireland and south-west England.

Moray Firth region

As in north-east Scotland, there is a considerable concentration of Beaker burials in the Moray Firth region (Fig. 16.7), though there is strong evidence that funerary practices also flourished later (ie, post-22nd century cal BC), with the inclusion of bronze daggers, jet-like substances and Food Vessels, resembling the patterns identified in east-central Scotland (Table 16.1). Indeed, Needham (2004) has argued that the appearance of 'rich' burials in the Moray Firth region (ie, with bronze daggers, armlets and jet-like substances) was related to similar burials in east-central Scotland, the product of individuals controlling the movement of tin and copper from the West into the bronze metalworking centre in north-east Scotland from the 22nd century cal BC.

A further important feature of this region is the re-use of Neolithic tombs in the mid-/late 3rd millennium for a variety of funerary and depositional practices (Henshall & Wallace 1964; Burl 1984; Woodham & Woodham 1957). Bradley (2000) has also suggested that the architectural forms of the distinctive Clava Cairns near Inverness represent a mixture of influences, including the Orkney-Cromarty-type tombs of the earlier Neolithic that are common in the western part of the Moray Firth region and areas to its north, the RSCs of north-east Scotland and traditions from western Scotland and Ireland. This combination of influences also appears in funerary pottery (both Beakers and Food Vessels), which also exhibits influences from Ireland (Cressey & Sheridan 2003, 80). The geographical location of the Moray Firth region, at the northern end of the Great Glen with its links to the Atlantic and lying intervisibly on both sides of the Moray Firth, therefore appears to have been both held together by the sea and linked by it to the wider world.

Geographical factors in cultural reception and change

Devine (2003, 14–15) has identified the 'harsh limitation' of Scotland's 'geology, marginal agriculture and uncertain weather' on mobility in the 17th century even in the most fertile eastern regions. Although there must have been similar limitations in prehistory, the influence of geography on the character of funerary practices during the mid-/late 3rd millennium has not been a subject of recent discussion. This may be partly due to a justified wariness of explanations that rely upon environmental determinism and large-scale migrations of people (Crichton Mitchell 1934; Walker 1966). It is important to recognise, however, that the distribution patterns themselves, if not such simplistic interpretations, are valid and require new explanations

It is striking that a cluster of Beaker burials in East Lothian shares much in common with those of the north-east, including their typology (Crichton Mitchell 1934) and position near the mouth of the Firth of Forth which would have provided access to the North Sea and thus with other Beaker using communities of eastern Britain with whom they appear to have maintained close social contacts (Brodie 2001; Vander Linden 2003). Other natural routeways such as the Firth of Lorn–Great Glen–Moray Firth axis, enabled people and influences to travel considerable distances across northern Scotland. Furthermore, the physical boundaries of the north-east may have led to it sometimes being bypassed by people travelling between east-central Scotland and the Moray Firth region. It may be that this contributed to the north-east having a lesser participation in the Neolithic traditions of henge enclosures and large ceremonial landscapes which appear to demonstrate a centralising 'pull' of people, material culture and funerary practices (cf. Thomas 1999, 60–1; Bradley 2007, 142).

Migdale-Marnoch and the end of the Chalcolithic in eastern Scotland

The introduction of the tin-bronze Migdale-Marnoch tradition can be considered as marking the end of the Chalcolithic in north-east Scotland. It also emphasises the importance of considering journeys and distant contacts alongside more local geographies. While Needham (2004, 241) has argued that 'knowledge of tin alloying arrived via the Short-Necked Beaker complex', it has not been possible to identify any effects on the frequency or the major characteristics of Beaker short-cist burials at this horizon in eastern Scotland. While the Beaker network may have offered a foundation for the adoption of bronze by establishing the connections with Ireland that are seen in the motifs shared between Beakers of the north-east and gold lunulae, it is not possible to identify the Beaker network as the reason why bronze-working was adopted. Likewise, while the suggestion that 'the Migdale-Marnoch tradition superseded the copper-using regime on the strength of being a divinely ordained new power in the Buchan heartland' (*ibid.*, 243) may be a possible ideological explanation, it does not explain the practicalities of how this 'ordainment' came to be respected and maintained over hundreds of kilometres for several centuries.

The series of 'rich' (eg, dagger and 'jet') burials dating to this period may instead offer insights into the introduction of bronze working. Cowie (1988, 18–19) has suggested that bronze dagger burials represent a form of 'elite' burial comparable to those associated with the Beaker 'archery' assemblage, while Needham (2004) suggests that dagger- and 'jet'-endowed graves represent individuals who profited from the transport and trade of copper and tin to the bronze-working 'hotspot' of north-east Scotland. The landscape placing of the dagger burials in eastern Scotland is noteworthy, with graves frequently overlooking passes and monumentalised to be obvious to people travelling by along rivers basins and firths. For example, in Fife bronze-dagger burials form a remarkably prominent 'string' of burials along the shores and crossing Fife between the Firths of Forth and Tay (Wilkin 2009, 73–8), rather than being arranged within dynastic, centralised cemeteries or only at key control zones (eg, key fording points) (Fig. 16.8; Tables 16.3 & 16.4). It can therefore be argued that the status and identity of the dead was bound up with the very route-ways themselves and the construction and maintenance of interactions between communities (cf. Johansen *et al.* 2004). Furthermore, the grave goods from rich burials, such as at Rameldry Farm, Fife and

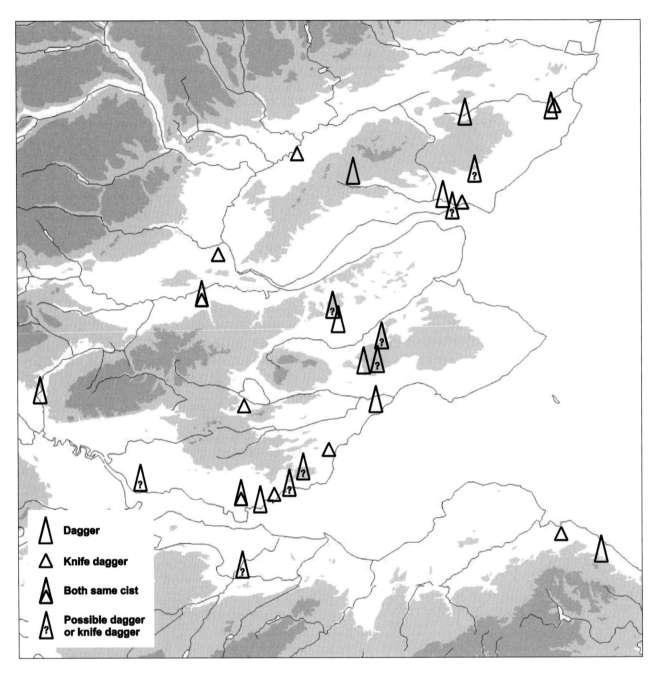

Figure 16.8. Map of dagger and knife-dagger burials in east-central Scotland

Seafield West, Inverness, appear to emphasise distant contacts by incorporating exotica such as Irish 'Bowl' Food Vessels, Cornish tin, Irish copper and bronze. The Seafield West burial was even made within a probable log-boat coffin (Cressey & Sheridan 2003). In these ways, 'rich' burials expressed access to, and control over, resources and distant places.

To consider these burials as merely the trace of a trade route, however, does not capture their full significance. Just as the occurrence of Beaker 'archery' burials can be seen to

have marked the introduction of new ideas and technologies during the Chalcolithic in eastern Scotland, so too do the 'rich' burials of the 22nd century cal BC mark the beginning of the Bronze Age in other regions of eastern Scotland. Perhaps in both cases the adoption of new practices and beliefs was aided by a heightened emphasis on ritual paraphernalia and costume in the funerary context. Thus, rather than being passive by-products of the Migdale-Marnoch 'system' in which transported goods met a divinely ordained demand, daggers and 'jet' ornaments may have provided a way of expressing and constraining identities and social relations at a time when trade, routeways, and travel were intensifying. It is therefore possible to reverse the conventional explanation of the relationship and suggest that it was the willingness of communities in east-central Scotland and the Moray Firth region to interact with others in Ireland, southern England, and north-east Scotland, not least through shared ritual and funerary practices, that helped to uphold or even to bring about the Migdale-Marnoch metalwork tradition and thus the end of the Chalcolithic.

Conclusions

This paper has considered the Chalcolithic of eastern Scotland to lie between the appearance of Beakers and copper metalwork in the 25th century cal BC and the appearance of 'rich' graves and bronze working in the 22nd century cal BC. Rather than interpreting these as horizons marking both ends of an archaeological period across the entire region, it has argued for particular processes and histories occurring in specific geographical settings.

While we should be cautious of general simplistic models, regional variation is clearly apparent from the available evidence, even accepting biases of preservation and survival. In the north-east, the Beaker tradition can be characterised by being highly formalised. Needham (2005, 191–5) has commented on the consistency of style of Short-Necked Beakers in Northern Britain, while Alexandra Shepherd (this volume) has discussed the regularity of patterns of position of bodies in Beaker burials. This regularity may have built on existing traditions that emphasised *normative reproduction*, such as the formal orientation and recurrent architectural features of recumbent stone circles. It may also have continued in the later formality of the stages in bronze working, which included the careful control of materials, temperatures and timing. As Needham (2007, 284) has argued, 'the technology involved in a given tradition can ... easily become locked within a belief system that respects the repeated generation of the accepted normative types' and that the 'components of the Migdale-Marnoch tradition of northern Britain are suggestive of this kind of circular reinforcement'. Perhaps the early adoption of both highly-formalised Beaker burials and later of bronze working in the north-east reflected a long-standing cultural attitude.

In east-central Scotland the continued ritual and ceremonial relevance of monument complexes appears to have prevented the widespread adoption of Beaker burial in this region by serving as reminders of older practices. When single burial funerary practices did appear in significant numbers in this region, from the 22nd century cal BC, they were associated with a greater range of funerary traditions: namely Food Vessels, bronze (flat-riveted and knife) daggers, jet-like ornaments, Food Vessel Urns, as well as the adoption of cremation burial and a greater number of funerary monuments and much older monuments re-used for burial, including henge monuments. In the same way, the Clava Cairns of the Moray Firth region display a variety of geographical and 'historical' references (Bradley 2000). This does not mean that such varied funerary practices lacked carefully prescribed rituals; rather it appears that it was the diversity of contacts that was being projected. In contrast to the reproduction of well-connected but normative traditions of material culture in north-east Scotland, practices in these regions are characterised by *hybridity* and bricolage, perhaps related to a continued acceptance of the centralising influences that bound communities to make journeys and pilgrimages to monument complexes during the Late Neolithic (cf. Noble 2007). The funerary practices and social organisation of the 'Chalcolithic' were inextricably related to earlier and later periods as well as to geography and long-lasting dimensions of social and cultural life. In the case of north-east Scotland, connections with Ireland and southern England established through the well-connected Beaker 'network' laid the foundations for the Migdale-Marnoch metalworking tradition. It may be that these intensifying communications also provided the conditions in which communities in the lands to either side of north-east Scotland adopted single burial practices that fitted with their own long-established ritual and cosmological principles. It was arguably the re-alignment of these existing structures that made the Migdale-Marnoch system operate and brought the 'Chalcolithic' to a close.

Acknowledgments
This paper is dedicated to the memory of Ian Shepherd for his great support and kindness before and throughout the project, including sight of his archive and Bournemouth conference paper.

The two-year *Beakers and Bodies Project* was funded by the Leverhulme Trust, grant F/00 152/S. The project was led by Neil Curtis, with Neil Wilkin as Research Assistant. Other team members were Dr Margaret Hutchison, Dr Mandy Jay, Ray Kidd, Alexandra Shepherd, Ian Shepherd, Dr Alison Sheridan, and Margot Wright. Dr Peter Marshall provided advice on Bayesian statistical analysis. Bill Risk is thanked for the production of maps for this paper. Neil Wilkin would like to acknowledge the support of the Arts and Humanities Research Council for funding his related M.Phil research at the University of Birmingham, and Paul Garwood for his generous supervision. All interpretations and errors are, of course, the responsibility of the authors.

Bibliography

Anderson, J. 1878. Notes on the character and contents of a large sepulchral cairn of the Bronze Age at Collessie. *Proceedings of the Society of Antiquaries of Scotland* 21, 439–61

Anderson, J. 1901. Notice of a hoard of bronze implements and ornaments, and buttons of jet, found at Migdale, on the estate of Skibo, Sutherland. *Proceedings of the Society of Antiquaries of Scotland* 35, 266–75

Ascherson, N. 2002. *Stone Voices: the search for Scotland*. London: Granta Books

Baker, L., Sheridan, A. & Cowie, T. 2003. An Early Bronze Age 'dagger grave' from Rameldry Farm, near Kingskettle, Fife. *Proceedings of the Society of Antiquaries of Scotland* 133, 85–123

Barclay, G. J. 1983. Sites of the third millennium bc to the first millennium ad at North Mains, Strathallan, Perthshire. *Proceedings of the Society of Antiquaries of Scotland* 113, 122–282

Barclay, G. J. 1999. Cairnpapple revisited: 1948–1988. *Proceedings of the Society of Antiquaries of Scotland* 65, 17–46

Barclay, G.J. 2004. '... Scotland cannot have been an inviting country for agricultural settlement': a history of the Neolithic in Scotland. In Shepherd & Barclay (eds) 2004, 31–44

Barclay, G.L. 2005. The 'henge' and 'hengiform' in Scotland. In V. Cummings & A. Pannett (eds), *Set in Stone. New Approaches to Neolithic Monuments in Scotland*, 81–94. Oxford: Oxbow Books

Bayliss, A., Bronk Ramsey, C., Plicht, J. van der & Whittle, A. 2007. Bradshaw and Bayes: towards a timetable for the Neolithic. *Cambridge Archaeological Journal* 17(1), supplement, 1–28

Bradley, R. 2000. *The Good Stones: A New Investigation of the Clava Cairns*. Edinburgh: Society of Antiquaries of Scotland

Bradley, R. 2002a. *The Past in Prehistoric Societies*. London: Routledge

Bradley, R. 2002b. The stone circles of northeast Scotland in the light of excavation. *Antiquity* 76, 840–8

Bradley, R. 2005. *The Moon and the Bonfire. An Investigation of Three Stone Circles in North-east Scotland*. Edinburgh: Society of Antiquaries of Scotland

Bradley, R. 2007. *The Prehistory of Britain and Ireland*. Cambridge: Cambridge University Press

Brodie, N. 2001. Technological frontiers and the emergence of the Beaker culture. In F. Nicolis (ed.), *Bell Beakers Today: pottery, people, culture, symbols in prehistoric Europe*, 487–96. Trento: Officio Beni Archeologici

Brophy, K. & Noble, G. 2009. *Forteviot, Pethshire, 2009 season: excavation of a henge and cist burial*. Unpublished Interim report and data structure report

Brück, J. 2004. Early Bronze Age burial practices in Scotland and beyond: differences and similarities. In Shepherd & Barclay (eds) 2004, 179–86

Burgess, C., Topping, P. & Lynch, F.M. (eds). 2006, *Beyond Stonehenge: essays on the Bronze Age in honour of Colin Burgess*. Oxford: Oxbow Books

Burl, H.A.W. 1970. The recumbent stone circles of north-east Scotland. *Proceedings of the Society of Antiquaries of Scotland* 102, 56–81

Burl, H.A.W. 1984. Report on the excavation of a Neolithic mound at Boghead, Speymouth Forest, Fochabers, Moray, 1972 and 1974. *Proceedings of the Society of Antiquaries of Scotland* 114, 35–73

Clarke, D.V., Cowie, T.G., & Foxon, A. 1985. *Symbols of Power at the Time of Stonehenge*. Edinburgh: National Museum of Antiquities of Scotland

Conaty, G.T. 2008. The effects of repatriation on the relationship between the Glenbow Museum and the Blackfoot people. *Museum Management and Curatorship* 23(3), 245–59

Cowie, T. 1988. *Magic Metal: early metalworkers in the North-east*. Aberdeen: Anthropological Museum, University of Aberdeen

Cressey, M. & Sheridan, A. 2003. The excavation of a Bronze Age cemetery at Seafield West, near Inverness, Highland. *Proceedings of the Society of Antiquaries of Scotland* 133, 47–84

Crichton Mitchell, M.E. 1934. A new analysis of the early Bronze Age beaker pottery of Scotland. *Proceedings of the Society of Antiquaries of Scotland* 68, 132–89

Curtis, N., Wilkin, N., Hutchison, M., Jay, M., Sheridan, A. & Wright, M. 2008. Radiocarbon dating results from the *Beakers and Bodies Project*. Discovery and Excavation in Scotland 2007, 198–201

Devine, T.M. 2003. *Clearance and Improvement: land, power and people in Scotland, 1700–1900*. Edinburgh: John Donald

Gannon, A., Halliday, S., Sherriff, H. & Welfare, A. 2007. The Neolithic and Bronze Age Landscape. In RCAHMS 2007, 45–78

Garwood, P. 1999. Grooved Ware in Southern Britain: chronology and interpretation. In R. Cleal & A. MacSween (eds), *Grooved Ware in Britain and Ireland*, 145–75. Oxford: Oxbow Books/Neolithic Studies Group

Gerloff, S. 1975. *The Early Bronze Age Daggers in Great

Britain and a Reconsideration of the Wessex Culture. München: Prähistorisches Bronzefunde 6(2)

Gerloff, S. 2006. Reinecke's ABC and the Chronology of the British Bronze Age. In Burgess *et al.* (eds) 2006, 117–61

Henshall, A.S. & Wallace, J.C. 1964. The excavation of a chambered cairn at Embo, Sutherland. *Proceedings of the Society of Antiquaries of Scotland* 96, 9–36

Higham, T., Chapman, J., Slavchev, V., Gaysarska, B., Honch, N., Yordanov, Y. & Dimitrova, B. 2007. New perspectives on the Varna cemetery (Bulgaria) – AMS dates and social implications. *Antiquity* 81, 640–54

Hutcheson, A. 1887. Notice of a burial place of the Bronze Age at Barnhill, near Broughty Ferry. *Proceedings of the Society of Antiquaries of Scotland* 21, 316–24

Hutcheson, A. 1898. Notice of the discovery of a burial of the Bronze Age on the hill of West Mains of Auchterhouse, the property of D.S. Cowans, Esq. *Proceedings of the Society of Antiquaries of Scotland* 32, 205–20

Johansen, K.L., Laursen, S.T., & Holst, M.K. 2004. Spatial patterns of social organization in the Early Bronze Age of South Scandinavia. *Journal of Anthropological Archaeology* 23, 33–55

Jones, A. 2003. Technologies of remembrance: memory, materiality and identity in Early Bronze Age Scotland. In H. Williams (ed.), *Archaeologies of Remembrance: death and memory in past societies*, 65–88. New York: Kluwer Academic/Plenum

Jones, A. 2008. How the dead live: mortuary practices, memory and the ancestors in Neolithic and Early Bronze Age Britain and Ireland. In J. Pollard (ed.), *Prehistoric Britain*, 177–201. London: Blackwell

Keiller, A., Piggott, S. & Wallis, F.S. 1941. First report of the Sub-Committee of the South-Western Group of Museums and Art Galleries on the petrological identification of stone axes. *Proceedings of the Prehistoric Society* 7, 50–72

Kirk, W. & McKenzie, J. 1955. Three Bronze Age cist burials in NE Scotland. *Proceedings of the Society of Antiquaries of Scotland*, 88, 1–14

MacGregor, G. 2008. Chapter 9: Changes in dwelling, people and place, *c.* 3500–1000 BC. In O. Lelong & G. MacGregor (eds), *The Lands of Ancient Lothian. Interpreting the Archaeology of the A1*, 221–37. Edinburgh: Society of Antiquaries of Scotland

Needham, S. 1996. Chronology and periodisation in the British Bronze Age. *Acta Archaeologica* 67, 121–40

Needham, S. 2004. Migdale-Marnoch: sunburst of Scottish metallurgy. In Shepherd & Barclay (eds) 2004, 217–45

Needham, S. 2005. Transforming Beaker Culture in north-west Europe: processes of fusion and fission. *Proceedings of the Prehistoric Society* 71, 171–217

Needham, S. 2006. Bronze makes a Bronze Age? Considering the systemics of Bronze Age metal use and the implications of selective deposition. In Burgess *et al.* (eds) 2006, 278–87

Needham, S. 2007. Isotopic aliens: Beaker movement and cultural transmissions. In M. Larsson & M. Parker Pearson (eds), *From Stonehenge to the Baltic: living with cultural diversity in the third millennium BC*, 42–6. Oxford: British Archaeological Report S1692

Noble, G. 2007. Monumental journeys: Neolithic monument complexes and routeways across Scotland. In V. Cummings & R. Johnston (eds), *Prehistoric Journeys*, 64–74. Oxford: Oxbow Books

Pare, C.F.E. 2000. Bronze and the Bronze Age. In C.F.E. Pare (ed.), *Metals Make The World Go Round. The Supply and Circulation of Metals in Bronze Age Europe*, 1–38. Oxford: Oxbow Books

Parker Pearson, M. 2006. The Beaker people project: mobility and diet in the British Early Bronze Age. *Archaeologist* 61, 14–15

Proudfoot, E. 1997. Short-cist burials from Fife. Upper Kenly Farm, Belliston Farm and Dalgety Bay. *Tayside & Fife Archaeological Journal* 3, 1–21

RCAHMS (Royal Commission on the Ancient and Historic Monuments of Scotland) 2007 *In the Shadow of Bennachie. A Field Archaeology of Donside, Aberdeenshire.* Edinburgh: RCAHMS/Society of Antiquaries of Scotland

Ralston, I.B.M. 1996. Four short cists from north-east Scotland and Easter Ross. *Proceedings of the Society of Antiquaries of Scotland* 126, 121–55

Reimer, P.J., Baillie, M.G.L., Bard, E., Bayliss, A., Beck, J.W., Bertrand, C.J.H., Blackwell, P.G. Buck, C.E., Burr, G.S., Cutler, K.B., Damon, P.E., Edwards, R.L., Fairbanks, R.G., Friedrich, M., Guilderson, T.P., Hogg, A.G., Hughen, K.A., Kromer, B., McCormac, G., Manning, S., Bronk Ramsey, C., Reimer, R.W., Remmele, S., Southon, J.R., Stuiver, M., Talamo, S., Taylor, F.W., Plicht, J. van der & Weyhenmeyer, C.E. 2004. IntCal04 terrestrial radiocarbon age calibration, 0–26 cal kyr BP. *Radiocarbon* 46(3), 1029–58

Roe, F. & Woodward, A. 2007. The wristguard from Burial 2245. In F. Brown, C. Howard-Davis, C., M. Brennand, A. Boyle, T. Evans, S. O'Connor, A. Spence, R. Heawood, & A. Lupton (eds), *The Archaeology of the A1 (M) Darrington to Dishforth DBFO Road Scheme*, 298–304. Lancaster: Oxford Archaeology North

Savory, H.N. 1972. Copper Age cists and cist-cairns in Wales: with special reference to Newton, Swansea, and other 'multiple-cist' cairns. In F. Lynch & C. Burgess (eds) *Prehistoric Man in Wales and the West*, 117–39. Bath: Adams & Dart

Shepherd, A. this volume. Stepping out together: men women and Beakers in time and space. In M.J. Allen, J. Gardiner & S. Sheridan (eds), *Is there a British Chalcolithic: place, people and polity in the later 3rd millennium*. Oxford: Prehistoric Society Research Paper 4

Shepherd, I.A.G. 1986. *Powerful Pots: Beakers in north–east prehistory*. Aberdeen: Anthropological Museum, University of Aberdeen

Shepherd, I.A.G. 1987. The early people. In D. Ormand (ed.), *The Grampian Book*, 119–30. Golspie: Northern Times

Shepherd, I.A.G. 1996. The Beaker (ABDUA 14261). In Ralston 1996, 143–5

Shepherd, I.A.G. & Barclay, G.J. (eds). 2004. *Scotland in Ancient Europe: the Neolithic and Early Bronze Age of Scotland in their European context*. Edinburgh: Society of Antiquaries of Scotland

Shepherd, I.A.G. & Bruce, M. F. 1987. Two beaker cists at Keabog, Pitdrichie, near Drumlithie, Kincardine and Deeside. *Proceedings of the Society of Antiquaries of Scotland* 117, 33–40

Sheridan, J.A. 2006. Dating the Scottish Bronze Age: 'There is clearly much that the material can still tell us'. In Burgess *et al.* (eds) 2006, 162–85

Sheridan, J.A. 2007. Scottish Beaker dates: the good, the bad and the ugly. In M. Larsson & M. Parker Pearson (eds), *From Stonehenge to the Baltic: living with cultural diversity in the third millennium BC*, 91–123. Oxford: British Archaeological Report S1692

Sheridan, J.A. 2008. Upper Largie and Dutch-Scottish connections during the Beaker period. In H. Fokkens, B.Y. Coles, A.L. van Gijn, J.P. Kleijne, H.H. Ponjee & C.G. Slappendel (eds), *Between Foraging and Farming. An extended broad spectrum of papers presented to Leendert Louwe Kooijmans*, 247–60. *Analectra Prehistorica Leidensia* 40

Stevenson, S. 1995. The excavation of a kerbed cairn at Beech Hill House, Coupar Angus, Perthshire. *Proceedings of the Society of Antiquaries of Scotland* 125, 197–235

Taylor, J.J. 1970. Lunulae reconsidered. *Proceedings of the Prehistoric Society* 36, 38–81

Thomas, J. 1999. *Understanding the Neolithic*. London: Routledge

Tuckwell, A.N. 1975. Patterns of burial orientation in the round barrows of East Yorkshire. *Bulletin of the Institute of Archaeology London* 12, 95–123

Vander Linden, M. 2003. Competing cosmos. On the relationships between Corded Ware and Bell Beaker mortuary practice. In J. Czebreszuk, & M. Szmyt (eds), *The Northeast Frontier of Bell Beakers*, 155–81. Oxford; British Archaeological Report S1155

Walker, I.C. 1966. The Counties of Nairnshire, Moray, and Banffshire in the Bronze Age – Part 1. *Proceedings of the Society of Antiquaries of Scotland* 98, 76–125

Ward, G. K., & Wilson, S. R. 1978. Procedures for comparing and combining radiocarbon age-determinations – critique. *Archaeometry* 20, 19–31

Wedderburn, L.M. 1975. *A short cist burial at Culduthel Mains, Inverness*. Unpublished report in Inverness Museum

Welfare, A. 2011. *Great Crowns of Stone. The Recumbent Stone Circles of Scotland*. Edinburgh: Royal Commission on the Ancient and Historicsl Monuments of Scotland

Whittle, A., Bayliss, A. & Healy, F. 2008. The timing and tempo of change: examples form the fourth millennium cal BC in Southern England. *Cambridge Archaeological Journal* 18(1), 65–70

Whittle, A., Bayliss, A & Wysocki, M. 2007. Once in a lifetime: the date of the Wayland's Smithy long barrow. *Cambridge Archaeological Journal* 17(1), supplement, 103–21

Wilkin, N.C.A. 2009. *Regional Narratives of the Early Bronze Age. A contextual and evidence-led approach to the funerary practices of east-central Scotland*. Institute of Archaeology and Antiquity, University of Birmingham: unpublished M.Phil thesis

Wilkin, N., Curtis, N., Hutchison, M., & Wright, M. forthcoming. 'Further radiocarbon dating results from the Beakers and Bodies Project' *Discovery and Excavation in Scotland* 2008

Woodham, A.A. & Woodham, M.F. 1957. The excavation of a chambered cairn at Kilcoy, Ross-shire. *Proceedings of the Society of Antiquaries of Scotland* 90, 102–15

Woodward, A., Hunter, J., Ixer, R., Roe, F., Potts, P.J., Webb, P.C., Watson, J.S. & Jones, M.C. 2006. Beaker age bracers in England: sources, function and use. *Antiquity* 80, 530–43

Appendix 1

Dates from eastern Scotland for early metal artefacts (Tables 16.2–16.4) and for dated burials for Beakers which share motifs with gold lunulae (Table 16.5).

Note: All dates are calibrated using OxCal v.4.1b3, with IntCal04 atmospheric curve (Reimer *et al.* 2004), with end points rounded outwards to 10 years. See Garwood (1999, 164) for criteria for assessment of date's value/integrity. For National Monument Record of Scotland (NMRS) numbers see the Royal Commission on the Ancient and Historical Monuments of Scotland 'Canmore' database (http://canmore.rcahms.gov.uk/).

Site name NGR; *References (inc. NMRS nos)*	Details	Date Lab code; date (BP); calibrated date; sample (i. dated material; ii. sample type; iii. sponsor; iv. assessment of value/integrity)
1. Borrowstone, cist 6, Kingswells, Aberdeenshire (NJ 852 081) Shepherd (1984, 13–14; 1986, 13–15, Illus. 12); Roe & Woodward (2007) I. Shepherd pers. comm.; NMRS: NJ80NE 73	Short-cist burial, inhumation adult male: C1 group wristguard, Langdale tuff, 4 copper rivets; Beaker (Short-Necked); bone belt-ring; sinew (poss. bowstring); charcoal & *in situ* burning; 3 pebbles	**1.** GrA-29082; 3820±40 BP *Cal. date*: 68% probability: 2350–2150 cal BC; 95% probability: **2460–2140 cal BC;** *Sample*: i. Collagen; ii. Human bone (femur); iii. Aberdeenshire Archaeology; iv. High value date **2.** GrA-29083; 3835±40 BP *Calibrated date*: 68% probability: 2400–2200 cal BC; 95% probability: **2470–2150 cal BC;** *Sample*: i. Collagen; ii. Human bone (femur); iii. Aberdeenshire Archaeology; iv. High value date **3.** Combined date (Ward and Wilson 1978) 3828±29 BP *Calibrated date*: 68% probability: 2400–2200 cal BC; 95% probability: **2470–2150 cal BC**
2. Mains of Scotstown, Old Machar, City of Aberdeen (NJ 935 107) Ralston (1996, 121–30); Sheridan (2007, appx 1); Curtis *et al.* (2007); NMRS: NJ91SW 13	Short-cist burial, inhumation adult male: trace copper on floor of cist – poss. from awl or similarly sized artefact; Beaker (Short-Necked); flints	**1.** UB-2097; 3140±70 BP *Calibrated date*: 68% probability: 1500–1310 cal BC; 95% probability: **1610–1210 cal BC;** *Sample*: i. Charcoal, unspecified 'carbonised material' from pebble floor; ii. Not known; iii. Ralston 1996; iv. Low value date due to contextual & physical integrity of sampled material **2.** OxA-V-2246-39; 3813±27 BP *Calibrated date*: 68% probability: 2290–2200 cal BC; 95% probability: **2400–2140 cal BC;** *Sample*: i. Collagen; ii. Human bone (femur); iii. *Beakers and Bodies Project*; iv. High value date
3. Culduthel (1975), Inverness & Bona, Highland (NH 6662 4224) Wedderburn (1975); *et al.* 1985, fig. 4.16, no. 74; Roe & Woodward 2007, 201–2, table 33 NMRS: NH64SE 36	Short-cist burial, inhumation adult male: C1 group wristguard, Langdale tuff, 4 copper rivets capped with gold sheet; Beaker (Short-Necked); bone belt-ring; 8 barbed&tanged arrowheads; amber bead; flint	SUERC-26462 (GU-20165); 3735±35 BP *Calibrated date*: 68% probability: 2200–2040 cal BC; 95% probability: **2280–2030 cal BC;** *Sample:* i. Collagen; ii. Human bone (femur); iii. *Beakers and Bodies Project* (hitherto unpublished); iv. High value date
4. Tavelty Farm, Kintore, Aberdeenshire (NJ 7867 1721l) Ralston (1996, 141–51); Shepherd (1986, 38); Needham (2005, 191–4); NMRS: NJ71NE072	Short-cist burial, inhumation adult male: copper-alloy knife-dagger frag.; Beaker (Short-Necked); barbed&tanged arrowhead; additional flints	GU-2169; 3710±70 BP *Calibrated date*: 68% probability: 2210–1980 cal BC; 95% probability: **2340–1900 cal BC;** *Sample*: i. Collagen; ii. Human bone; iii. Ralston (1996); iv. High value date (SD increased by P. Ashmore)

Table 16.2 Copper artefacts. Dagger typology following Gerloff (1975); Beaker typology following Needham (2005)

Site name NGR; *References (inc. NMRS nos)*	Details	Date Lab code; date (BP); calibrated date; sample (i. dated material; ii. sample type; iii. sponsor; iv. assessment of value/integrity)
1. Barnhill, City of Dundee, Angus (Alternative name: Broughty Ferry) (NO 4816 3181) Hutcheson (1887); NMRS: NO43SE 28	Short-cist, inhumation: bronze knife-dagger; 2 sheet gold discs	OxA-11025; 3607±39 BP *Calibrated dates*: 68% probability: 2030–1910 cal BC; 95% probability: **2130–1880 cal BC**; *Sample*: i. Cremated bone; ii. Human bone; iii. National Museums Scotland; iv. High value date
2. Beech Hill House, cist 1, Auchterhouse, Angus (NO 220 404) Stevenson (1995); NMRS: NT57SW 75.00	Cremation burial in short-cist within kerbed-cairn: ?knife-dagger; burnt bone toggle; flint.	GrA-19426; 3665±45 BP *Calibrated dates*: 68% probability: 2140–1970 cal BC; 95% probability: **2200–1920 cal BC**; *Sample*: i. Cremated bone; ii. Human bone; iii. National Museums Scotland; iv. High value date
3. Bught Park, Inverness & Bona, Highland (NH 656 437) Kirk & McKenzie (1955, 7–10); Gerloff (1975, 59, no. 75); NMRS: NH64SE 9	Short-cist, inhumation, adult male (late 30s): Masterton type dagger	OxA-V-2247-48; 3695±31BP *Calibrated date*: 68% probability: 2140–2030 cal BC; 95% probability: **2200–1970 cal BC**; *Sample*: i. Collagen; ii. Human bone; iii. *Beakers and Bodies Project* (hitherto unpublished); iv. High value date
4. Carrick Drive, cist 2, Dalgety, Fife (NT 1545 8341) Proudfoot (1997, 10–20); NMRS: NT18SE 21	Short-cist, inhumation, adult male (*c.* 30 yrs): Masterton type dagger; shaft of limb bone from unident. immature animal; high conc. meadowsweet (*filipendula sp.*) suggesting floral tribute	OxA-V-2247-46; 3610±30 BP; *Calibrated date*: 68% probability: 2030–1930 cal BC; 95% probability: **2120–1880 cal BC**; *Sample*: i. Collagen; ii. Human bone; iii. *Beakers and Bodies Project* (hitherto unpublished); iv. High value date
5. Collessie Cairn, Collessie, cremation deposit, Fife (*Alternative name*: Gask Hill) (NO 2884 1309) Anderson (1878); Gerloff (1975, 60, no. 84); Henshall (1986, 186, no. 8); Sheridan (2006, appendix); NMRS: NO21SE 14	Cremation burial, adult beneath cairn: Masterton type dagger	**1.** GrA-19054; 3695±45 BP; *Calibrated dates*: 68% probability: 2200–2020 cal BC; 95% probability: **2210–1950 cal BC**; *Sample*: i. Cremated bone; ii. Human bone; iii. National Museums Scotland *Dating Cremated Bones Project*; iv. High value date **2.** OxA-4510; 3610±80 BP; *Calibrated dates*: 68% probability: 2140–1880 cal BC; 95% probability: **2200–1750 cal BC**; *Sample*: i. Scabbard (hide); ii. Scabbard (hide); iii. *NMS*; iv. High value date
6. Hill of West Mains, Auchterhouse, Angus (NO 315 376) Hutcheson (1898); Henshall (1968, 180–1, no. 3); Gerloff (1975, 67, no. 100); NMRS: NO33NW 2	Cremation burial from 2-compartment short-cist beneath cairn: Ridgeway (Auchterhouse-Barrasford variant) dagger	GrA-19990; 3610±50 BP; *Calibrated dates*: 68% probability: 2030–1900 cal BC; 95% probability: **2140–1780 cal BC**; *Sample*: i. Cremated bone; ii. Human bone; iii. National Museums Scotland *Dating Cremated Bones Project*; iv. High value date
7. Rameldry Farm, by Kingskettle, Kettle, Fife (NO 3316 0630) Baker *et al.* (2003); NMRS: NO30NW 173	Short-cist burial, inhumation, adult male; Butterworth type dagger; 6 v-perforated buttons (5 Whitby jet, 1 lizardite)	GU-9754; 3725±40 BP; *Calibrated dates*: 68% probability: 2200–2040 cal BC; 95% probability: **2280–1980 cal BC**; *Sample*: i. Collagen; ii. Human bone; iii. Baker *et al.* (2003); iv. High value date
8. Seafield West, Inverness & Bona, Highland (NH 6946 4582) Cressey & Sheridan (2003); NMRS: NH64NE 40	Log-coffin burial within ring-ditch, inhumation; Butterwick type dagger; flint flakes	**1.** AA-29064; 3385 ±45 BP; *Calibrated dates*: 68% probability: 1740–1620 cal BC; 95% probability: **1870–1530 cal BC**; *Sample*: i. Scabbard (cattle skin); ii. Scabbard (cattle skin); iii. Cressey & Sheridan (2003); iv. Low value date: questionably late **2.** GrA-27037/27039 (av); 3600±30 BP; *Calibrated dates*: 68% probability: 2020–1910 cal BC; 95% probability: **2040–1880 cal BC**; *Sample*: i. Scabbard (hide and wood); ii. Scabbard (hide and wood); iii. Sheridan 2007; iv. High value date

Table 16.3 Bronze daggers and knife-daggers from funerary contexts. Dagger typology following Gerloff (1975)

Site name NGR; *References (inc. NMRS nos)*	Details	Date Lab code; date (BP); calibrated date; sample (i. dated material; ii. sample type; iii. sponsor; iv. assessment of value/integrity)
1. Migdale hoard, Creich, **Highland** (NH 6336 9214) Anderson 1901; Clarke *et al.* 1985, no. 147, fig. 4.33–7; NMRS: NH69SW 22	Bronze hoard, inc.: axe; tubular beads; cones sheet bronze; frags sheet bronze; frags basket earring; bar armlets; 6 'jet' buttons (see Clarke *et al.* 1985 for details)	OxA-4659; 3655±75 BP; *Calibrated dates*: 68% probability: 2140–1930 cal BC; 95% probability: **2290–1770 cal BC**; *Sample*: i. wood ; ii. wood from tubular bronze bead; iii. Cressey & Sheridan (2003); iv. High value date

Table 16.4: Bronze Artefacts (other contexts)

Site name *NGR; NMRS no.*	Date Lab code; date (BP); Calibrated date	Relevant references Illustration of vessel; *publication of dating evidence*
Keabog Quarry, Pitdrichie farm, nr Drumlithnie, Glenbervie, Aberdeenshire, cist 2 NO 7987 8195; NMRS: NO78SE0 18	OxA-V-2172-22; 3910±33 BP; *Calibrated dates*: 68% probability: 2470–2340 cal BC; 95% probability: **2480–2290 cal BC**	Shepherd & Bruce (1987*); Sheridan (2007, appx 1)*
Borrowstone, Kingswells, City of Aberdeen, cist 1 NJ 8532 0805; NMRS: NJ80NE 28	GrA-29077; 3865±40 BP; *Calibrated dates*: 68% probability: 2460–2280 cal BC; 95% probability: **2470–2200 cal BC**	I. Shepherd (1986, 13–15, illus. 12); *Shepherd (2005, 184)*
Broomend of Crichie, Kintore, Aberdeenshire, cist 2 NJ 7789 1923; NMRS: NJ71NE011	**1.** OxA-15056; 3856±29 BP; *Calibrated dates*: 68% probability: 2460–2230 cal BC; 95% probability: **2470–2200 cal BC** **2.** OxA-11243; 3932±35 BP; *published Sheridan (2002), now deleted (Sheridan 2007, 109, 122)*	Clarke (1970, nos 1435–6, figs 542–4); *Sheridan (2007, appx 1)*
Garmouth, Corbiewells, Urquhart, Moray NJ 3112 6497; NMRS: NJ36NW 54	**1.** OxA-V-2247-50; 3806±31 BP; *Calibrated dates*: 68% probability: 2300–2200 cal BC; 95% probability: **2400–2130 cal BC** **2.** SUERC-14947; 3850±40 BP; *Calibrated dates*: 68% probability: 2450–2200 cal BC; 95% probability: **2470–2200 cal BC**	c/o AOC Archaeology Group; *Beakers and Bodies Project*
Sandhole, Fetterangus, Aberdeenshire NJ 9981 5211; NMRS: NJ95SE 25	**1.** GU-2100; 3650±50 BP; *Date from mid-1980s, questioned by Sheridan (2007)* **2.** OxA-V-2172-23; 3845±32 BP; *Calibrated dates*: 68% probability: 2430–2200 cal BC; 95% probability: **2460–2200 cal BC**	Ralston (1996, 134-40); *Sheridan (2007, appx 1)*
Broomend of Crichie, Kintore, Aberdeenshire, cist 1 (adult male 1 & 2) NJ 7789 1923; NMRS: NJ71NE011	**1.** OxA-V-2166-34; 3835±33 BP; *Calibrated dates*: 68% probability: 2350–2230 cal BC; 95% probability: **2460–2150 cal BC** **2.** OxA-13214; 3720±35 BP; *Calibrated dates*: 68% probability: 2200–2030 cal BC; 95% probability: **2280–1980 cal BC**	Clarke (1970, nos 1433–4, figs 659–60); *Sheridan (2004, 174–5; 2007, appx 1)* (not clear which Beaker associated with this male)
Keabog Quarry, Pitdrichie farm, near Drumlithnie, Glenbervie, Aberdeenshire, cist 1 NO 7987 8195; NMRS: NO78SE0 18	**1.** OxA-V-2243-42; 3831±28 BP; *Calibrated dates*: 68% probability: 2340–2200 cal BC; 95% probability: **2460–2150 cal BC** **2.** OxA-V-2243-43; 3816±29 BP; *Calibrated dates*: 68% probability: 2300–2200 cal BC; 95% probability: **2400–2130 cal BC** *Dates combined*: (Ward & Wilson 1978) 3824±21 BP *Calibrated dates*: 68% probability: 2300–2200 cal BC; 95% probability: **2400–2150 cal BC**; *(X2-Test: df=1 T=0.1(5% 3.8))*	Shepherd & Bruce (1987); *Beakers and Bodies Project*

Table 16.5: (this page and overleaf) Dated Beaker burials for Beakers which share motifs with gold lunulae (after Taylor 1970, with additions)

Site name *NGR; NMRS no.*	Date Lab code; date (BP); Calibrated date	Relevant references Illustration of vessel; *publication of dating evidence*
Mains of Scotstown, Old Machar, City of Aberdeen NJ 935 107; NMRS: NJ91SW13	**1.** UB-2097; 3140±70 BP, date rejected (Sheridan 2007, 123) **2.** OxA-V-2246-39; 3813±27 BP; *Calibrated dates*: 68% probability: 2290–2200 cal BC; 95% probability: **2400–2140 cal BC**	*Ralston (1996, 121–30); Sheridan (2007, 123, appx 1); Beakers and Bodies Project*
Clinterty, Newhills, Kinellar, City of Aberdeen NJ 84 10; NJ81SW22	OxA- V-2243-41; 3813±30 BP; *Calibrated dates*: 68% probability: 2300–2200 cal BC; 95% probability: **2430–2140 cal BC**	Clarke (1970, No. 1443, fig. 661); *Beakers and Bodies Project*
Cookston, Airlie, Angus NO 336 492; NMRS: NO34NW 14	BM-2523; 3800±50 BP; *Calibrated dates*: 68% probability: 2340–2140 cal BC; 95% probability: **2460–2040 cal BC**	Coutts (1971, 46-8); *Sheridan (2007, appx 1)*
Roadside of Catterline, Kinneff, Aberdeenshire ('Harveston Cottage') NO 8579 7886; NMRS NO87NE 10	OxA-V-2243-57; 3819±27 BP; *Calibrated dates*: 68% probability: 2300–2200 cal BC; 95% probability: **2410–2140 cal BC**	Small *et al.* (1988); *Beakers and Bodies Project*
Uppermains of Catterline, Kinneff, Aberdeenshire, cist 1 NO 8577 7904; NMRS: NO87NE002	OxA-V-2166-44; 3770±31 BP; *Calibrated dates*: 68% probability: 2280–2130 cal BC; 95% probability: **2300–2040 cal BC**	Clarke (1970, 518, no. 1692, fig. 718); *Sheridan (2007, appx 1)*
Newlands, Oyne, Aberdeenshire, cist 2 NJ 6949 2533; NMRS: NJ62NE 24	OxA-V-2243-46; 3757±29 BP; *Calibrated dates*: 68% probability: 2280–2060 cal BC; 95% probability: **2290–2040 cal BC**	Clarke (1970, 512, no. 1478, fig. 721); *Beakers and Bodies Project*
Borrowstone, Kingswells, City of Aberdeen, cist 3NJ 8520 0787; NMRS: NJ80NE 72	GrA-29079; 3750±45 BP; 68% probability: 2280–2040 cal BC; 95% probability: **2300–2020 cal BC**	I. Shepherd (1984, 13–14; 1986, 13–15, illus. 12); *Beakers and Bodies Project*
Nether Criggie, Dunnottar, Aberdeenshire NO 8378 8238; NMRS: NO88SW006	OxA-V-2166-46; 3741±32 BP; *Calibrated dates*: 68% probability: 2210–2050 cal BC; 95% probability: **2280–2030 cal BC**	Clarke (1970, nos 1683–5; figs 322–4); *Sheridan (2007, 123, appx 1)*
Manar, Inverurie, Aberdeenshire NJ 7489 2012; NMRS: NJ72SW 50	GrA-29084; 3760±45 BP; *Calibrated dates*: 68% probability: 2280–2050 cal BC; 95% probability: **2340–2030 cal BC**	Sheridan (2007); *Sheridan (2007, appx 1)*
Keir, Belhelvie, Aberdeenshire NJ *c*. 961 177; NMRS: NJ91NE003	3715±32 BP (OxA-V-2172-18); *Calibrated dates*: 68% probability: 2200–2030 cal BC; 95% probability: **2210–2020 cal BC**	Clarke (1970, nos 1459–61, figs 715–7); *Sheridan (2007, appx 1)*
Tavelty Farm, Kintore, City of Aberdeen NJ 7867 17211 ; NMRS: NJ71NE072	GU-2169; 3710±70 BP; *Calibrated dates*: 68% probability: 2210–1980 cal BC; 95% probability: **2340–1900 cal BC**	Ralston (1996, 141–51); *Sheridan (2007, appx 1)*
Persley Quarry, Old Machar, City of Aberdeen NJ 909 100; NMRS: NJ91SW 7	OxA-V-2243-44; 3647±29 BP; *Calibrated dates*: 68% probability: 2120–1960 cal BC; 95% probability: **2140–1930 cal BC**	Clarke (1970, no. 1486, fig. 522); *Beakers and Bodies Project*

Stepping Out Together: men, women, and their Beakers in time and space

Alexandra Shepherd

This paper presents the evidence for patterns of arrangement amongst the crouched inhumations of the British Chalcolithic–Early Bronze Age, principally in the two core areas of Beaker-using people in north-east Scotland and east Yorkshire. It demonstrates the predominant gender-defined burial pattern in these areas, of males on their left orientated east and females on their right orientated west, all facing south (LESM/RWSF). It subsequently looks in detail at the Beakers accompanying each burial and investigates the possibility of discernible gender-specific indicators in their style and decoration. Case studies of paired inhumations identify both conformities and variations in the observance of burial formalities and choice in the provision of accompanying pots. The paper reviews the mechanisms by which the embedded traditions of burial arrangement and Beaker styles were transmitted and maintained in a period of flux in the wider Chalcolithic sphere. The contribution seeks to highlight the existence of cohesive ideologies manifested in strict adherence to burial formalities over a wide area from the British northern east coast to central Europe; it stresses the human dimension discernible within the otherwise technologically-defined period.

Patterns within Beaker burial positioning

The fundamental source which provides the structure for the Chalcolithic period in Britain (*c.* 2500/2400–2200/2150 BC) is the proliferation of crouched inhumation burials accompanied by Beakers, the pot form which dominates the later 3rd millennium, and whose use extended into the Early Bronze Age. These offer a rich assemblage of fully-contexted human and artefactual material, not just supplying the core dating and evidence of technological development which help define the period but also one of the clearest indicators of organised funereal activity over a substantial area. Crouched inhumations afford more than the single orientation factor of supine inhumations, giving the three major variables of side on which the body is placed, orientation (ie, direction of the top of head and spine) and line of sight (ie, direction in which the head was facing). The multivariate quality of these data provides a crucial means of assessing complex patterns of human activity.

The Beakers themselves have been the subject of major study and continuous reassessment for Britain and the continental Beaker heartlands (principally Clarke 1970; Lanting & van der Waals 1972; Shennan 1976; subsequently *inter alia* Case 1977; Needham 2005). The pattern of arrangement of the burials has been referred to generally in these wider studies (in particular Lanting & van der Waals 1972, 37–41) but rarely have the Beakers and their bodies been viewed together as units. This paper concentrates on data obtained from two detailed studies by the author of discrete concentrations of Beaker burials in the Wolds of east Yorkshire (Tuckwell 1970; 1975) and the north-east corner of Scotland, principally Aberdeenshire (A.N. Shepherd 1989). The two databases differ in origin. The Yorkshire material is drawn from the 19th century reports of J.R. Mortimer (1905) and Canon Greenwell (1877; 1890) (Table 17.1). Amongst the many crouched inhumations excavated

subsequently (Haughton & Powlesland 1999, 53–4; Roberts 2005, 44–48; Brown *et al.* 2007, 29–32) five have provided additional Beaker orientation and gender data which reinforce the previous conclusions; these have also provided comparative date brackets for the Yorkshire assemblage (see below). The north-east Scottish material derives principally from 20th and early 21st century excavations, and has formed the basis for a recent exhaustive study and dating program (the *Beakers and Bodies Project*: see Curtis & Wilkin this volume). This, along with another Beaker-centred research project, the *Beaker People Project* (see Jay *et al.* this volume) and other dating initiatives (summarised in Sheridan 2007), has provided a comprehensive dating suite (Table 17.2). This anchors the earliest phases of Beaker use within Chalcolithic brackets (2500/400–2200/2150 BC), continuing through a core or *instituted* (Needham 2005) Beaker phase, of 2250–1950 BC.

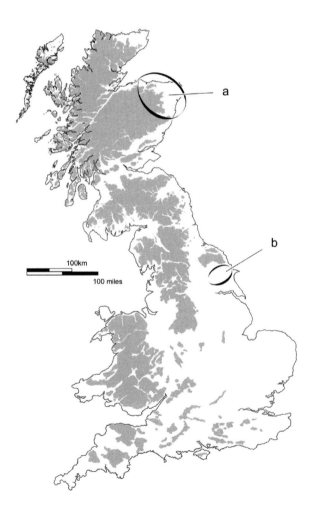

Figure 17.1: Map indicating areas covered by the two core Beaker-using areas discussed in the text: a) north-east Scotland; b) the East Yorkshire Wolds

Barrow group name	Barrow no	Side	Orien-tation	Line of sight	Sex (as stated)	Original reference	Orig. Fig. ref	Clarke illus no	Clarke Corpus no	Clarke classif-ication	L&v de W Step
Aldro	116	R	SW	SE	–	*40 Years*, 54	95	807	1217	S2(W)	5
Ganton	28 (XXVIII)	R	–	–	F	*B B*, 175	[cf 83]	–	–	–	[4]
Garrowby Wold	143 (C43)	R	W	S	F	*40 Years*, 147	–	–	–	–	–
Garton Slack	81	R	W	S	–	*40 Years*, 241	608	288	1300	N/NR	4
Garton Slack	81	R	W	S	F	*40 Years*, 240	–	–	1301F	–	–
Garton Slack	163 (C63)	R	W	S	F	*40 Years*, 215	543	666	1306	NR	4
Goodmanham	99 (XCIX)	R	NW	SW	–	*B B*, 308	134	675	1309	N3	4
Goodmanham	99 (XCIX)	R	NW	SW	F	*B B*, 308	133	302	1310	N/NR	3
Hanging Grimston	55	L	W	N	?F	*40 Years*, 101	243	873	1323	S2(E)	6
Hanging Grimston	56	R	SW	SE	F	*40 Years*, 99	–	–	–	–	–
Huggate and Warter Wold	254	R	W	S	–	*40 Years*, 320	955	531	1334	N2	4
Huggate and Warter Wold	254	R	W	S	–	*40 Years*, 320	–	508	1335	N2	4
Huggate Wold	216	R	W	S	–	*40 Years*, 310	927	515	1332	S1	5
Hunmanby	250 (CCL)	R	W	S	–	*Arch.*, 18	–	–	–	–	–
Painsthorpe Wold	4	R	W	S	F	*40 Years*, 115	271	789	1352	S1	5
Rudston	66 (LXVI)	R	W	S		*B B*, 255		526	1375	N2	4
Rudston	61 (LXI)	R	W	S	F	*B B*, 230	–	511	1366	N2	4
Rudston	62 (LXII)	L	E	S	F	*B B*, 237	82	705	1370	N3(L)	5
Rudston	66 (LXVI)	R	W	S	F	*B B*, 254	122	865	1374	S2(E)	5
Rudston	67 (LXVII)	R	NW	SW	F	*B B*, 258	–	10	1376	AOC	1/2
Sherbum	7 (VII)	R	–	–	–	*B B*, 146	–	–	1384	N2	4
Towthorpe	21	R	–	–	F	*40 Years*, 11	27	828	1400	S2(W)	5
Towthorpe	211 ½	R	W	S	F }	*40 Years*, 19	41	533	1402	N2	4
Acklam Wold	124	B/L	NE	SE	M	*40 Years*, 91	217	780	1210	S1	5
Aldro	54	L	E	S	–	*40 Years*, 64	131	284	1213	N/NR	4
Aldro	116	L	NE	SE	–	*40 Years*, 54	99	888	1218	S2(W)	6
Aldro	116	L	NE	SE	–	*40 Years*, 55	101–3	1065	1219	SH3(C)	7
Driffield	138 (C38)	L	E	S	M	*40 Years*, 274	745	553	1265	N2(L)	4
Folkton	242 (CCXLII)	L	E	S	–	*Arch.*, 10	3	979	1280	S4	7
Ganton	21 (XXI)	L	E	S	M	*B B*, 162	101	811	1283	S2(W)	6
Ganton	21 (XXI)	L	E	S	–	*B B*, 166	83	927	1284	S3(E)	6
Garrowby Wold	104	R	S	E	M	*40 Years*, 135	347	817	1293	S2(W)	6
Garton Slack	37	B/L	E	S	M	*40 Years*, 209	510	778	1296	S1	6
Garton Slack	80	L	E	S	M	*40 Years*, 236	597	290	1299	N/NR	3
Garton Slack	161 (C61)	B/L	N	E	M	*40 Years*, 211	527	555	1303	N2(L)	5
Garton Slack	163 (C63)	L	E	S	M	*40 Years*; 215	540	667	1305	N3(L)	5
Garton Slack	75	R	W	S	M	*40 Years*, 223	576	763	1298	S1	5
Garton Slack	163 (C63)	L	SE	SW	–	*40 Years*, 214	538	665	1304	N3	4
Goodmanham	113 (CXIII)	L	NE	SE	M	*B B*, 321	86	1071	1314	SH4(B)	7
Hanging Grimston	55	L	W	N	Y	*40 Years*, 101	246	507	1322	N2	4
Hanging Grimston	55	L	E	S	–	*40 Years*, 100	241	835	1324	S2(W)	5
Hanging Grimston	56	L	E	S	– }	*40 Years*, 99	238	863	1320	S2(E)	6
Hanging Grimston	56	L	E	S	– }	*40 Years*, 99					
Hunmanby	251 (CCLI)	L	SE	SW	–	*Arch.*, 21	–	–	1339F	–	–
Middleton-on-the-Wolds		L	E	S	M	*E.R.A.S.*, 103	pl. II	876	1347	S2	6
Painsthorpe Wold	4	L	SW	NW	M	*40 Years*, 115	270	810	1351	S2(W)	6
Painsthorpe Wold	4	L	SE	SW	–	*40 Years*, 117	282	790	1353	FP	6
Painsthorpe Wold	83	L	E	S	– }	*40 Years*, 119	–	963	1355F	S3	5
Painsthorpe Wold	83	L	E	S	– }	*40 Years*, 119					
Rudston	62 (LXII)	L	SE	SW	M	*B B*, 237	?85	386	1371	E Ang?	4
Rudston	62 (LXII)	L	S	W	M	*B B*, 240	[cf 120]	530	1367	N2	4
Rudston	66 (LXVI)	-	E	–	–						
Thwing	60 (LX)	L	E	S	–	*B B*, 227	–	–	1398F;		
Thwing	60 (LX)	L	E	S	–	*B B*, 227	871	871	1397	S2(E)	6

Table 17.1: (continued over the next page) Data from burials with Beakers from east Yorkshire: orientation, side positioning, and sexed skeletal information. List ordered alphabetically by sex and orientation/side

Notes: BB = *Greenwell 1877; Arch = Greenwell, W.G. 1890; 40 Years = Mortimer 1905*

Barrow group name	Barrow no	Side	Orien-tation	Line of sight	Sex (as stated)	Original reference	Orig Fig. ref	Clarke illus no	Clarke Corpus no	Clarke classif-ication	L&v de W Step
Towthorpe	211 ½	L	E	S	M }	*40 Years*, 19	41	533	1402	N2	4
Weaverthorpe	42 (XLII)	L	E	S	M	*B B*, 193	640	640	1403	N3	5
Willerby	32 (XXXII)	L	SE	SW	–	*B B*, 180	–	–	–	–	–
Acklam Wold	204	R	N	W	–	*40 Years*, 86	196	988	1211	S4	7
Aldro	116	R	NE	NW	–	*40 Years*, 55	100	28	1215	AOC	1/2
Aldro	116	R	N	W	–	*40 Years*, 55	104	755	1216	S1	4
Garrowby Wold	143 (C43)	R	E	N	–	*40 Years*, 147	–	–	–	–	–
Rudston	LXIII	R	S	E		*B B*, 247	–		1011	S4	7

Table 17.1 (continued)

Site	Side	Orient-ation	Line of sight	Sex	C14 BP	Reference	Illus ref	Clarke illus. no.	Clarke corpus no.	Clarke classifi-cation	L&v derW Step
Borrowstone, Newhills 4	R	W	S	–	–	Shepherd 1986	ANS	–	–		5
Borrowstone, Newhills 1	R?*	W	S?	F	3865 ±40	Shepherd 1986	ANS	–	–	[N3]	5
Boysack	R	W	S	F	3460±50	Murray & Ralston 1997	21	–	–		5
Broomend of Crichie 2	–	–	–	F?	[3856±29]	Davidson 1867		544	1436	N2	4
Donside Field, Manar Estate	R	W	S	F?	3725 ±33	Unpublished	ANS	–	–		5
Fallaws Farm, Monikie	?	E	–	F	3785 ±26	Coutts 1966	3	445	1516	N1/D	5
Keir, Belhelvie	L [ex]	–	–	F	3715 ±32	Aberdeen Mus. Coll.		715–6	1459–60	N4, N3(L)	5 5
Kemnay, Paradise Road	R	W*	S	F	3833 ±28	Woodham 1974	ANS	–	–	[N3(L)]	5
Ladymire, Logie Buchan	R?	W	S?	F	–	Woodham 1973	ANS	–	–	[N3]	5
Lesmurdie A	R?	SW	SE?	–	–	Robertson 1851–4		702	1587	N3(L)	
Mains of Balnagowan	R	WSW	SSE	F?	3700 ±35	Shepherd *et al.* 1984	4	–	–	[N/NR]	4
Mains of Leslie, Premnay 1	R	W*	S	F	3829 ±29	Callander 1907	1	602	1470	N3	4
Nether Criggie, Dunnottar	R	W	S	F	3741 ±32	Kirk & McKenzie 1955		322–4	1683–5	N3/L; N3/L	5 5
Stoneywood 1	R [ex]	–	–	F	3686 ±32	Low 1902–4		486	1497	N2	5
Auchrynie	–	NE	–	M?	–	Shepherd 1986		722	1429	N4	5
Borrowstone, Newhills 2	L	E	S	M	3845 ±40	Shepherd 1986	ANS	–	–	[N2]	4
Borrowstone, Newhills 3	L	E	S	M	3750 ±45	Shepherd 1986	ANS	–	–	[N2]	4
Borrowstone, Newhills 5	L [ex]	E	–	M?	3834±29	Shepherd 1986	ANS	–	–	[N2(L)]	4
Borrowstone, Newhills 6	L	E	S	M?	3820±40 3835±40	Shepherd 1986	ANS	–	–	[N2(L)]	4
Broomend of Crichie 1	–	–	–	M	3835 ±33	Chalmers 1867		659	1433	N2(L)	5
Broomend of Crichie 1	–	–	–	M	3720 ±35	Chalmers 1867		660	1434	N3	5
Broomend of Crichie 2	L	E	S	M	3856 ±29	Davidson 1867		542	1435	N2	4
Chapelden, Tore of Troup, Aberdour	L	NE	SE	M	–	Greig *et al.* 1989	4	–	–	[N4]	4

Table 17.2: (this page and opposite) Data from burials with Beakers from north-east Scotland; orientation, side positioning, and sexed skeletal information. List ordered alphabetically by sex and orientation/side

*Notes: B&B = Beakers and Bodies Project; *Whitehouse, Skene: wrongly labeled Whitestone in Clarke 1970 and in subsequent publications*

Site	Side	Orient- ation	Line of sight	Sex	C14 BP	Reference	Illus ref	Clarke illus. no.	Clarke corpus no.	Clarke classifi- cation	L&v derW Step
Clinterty, Newhills, Kinellar	–	–	–	M	3813 ±30	Low 1902–4, 8–9		661	1443	N3	4
Ellon, Hillhead	L[ex]	–	–	M	3780±30	Reid 1924, 37		704	1541	N3(L)	6
Hatton Mill, Friockheim	L	NE	SE	M	3705 ±26	Wedderburn 1970	2	–	–	[AOC]	3?/?7
Keabog, Pitdrichie 1	–	–	–	M	3831 ±31 3816 ±29	Shepherd & Bruce 1987	2	–	–	[N3]	5
Keabog, Pitdrichie 2	L	E	S	M	3910 ±33	Shepherd & Bruce 1987	4	–	–	[N3(L)]	6
Lesmurdie B	L?	NNE	ESE	M	3770 ±33	Robertson 1851–4		678	1586	N3	4
Mains of Balnagowan	R	WSW	SSE	M?	3700 ±35	Shepherd & Bruce 1984	4	–	–	[N/NR]	4
Mains of Scotstown	L	E	S	M	3813 ±27	Ralston 1996	4	–	–	[N4]	4
Newlands, Oyne 1	L	NE	SE	M	3677 ±31	Callander 1933		691	1477	N3	6
Newlands, Oyne 2	L	NE	SE	M	3757 ⊥39	Low 1936		721	1478	N4	5 <Abdua
Upper Ord Auchindoir 3	L? [ex]	–	–	M	3854 ±31	Bryce & Low 1905		495	1480	N2	4 <Abdua
Parkhill 1	L?/ base [ex]	–	–	M	3723 ±28	Ferguson 1882		471	1484	N2	4 <Abdua
Parkhill 2	L or NP[ex]	–	–	M	3777 ±32	Ferguson 1882		585	1485	N3	4 <Abdua
Park Quarry 1	L	E	S	M	–	Unpub rep. *B&B*	ANS	–	–	–	3
Park Quarry 3	L	E	S	M	–	Unpub rep. *B&B*		–	–	–	>>
Persley Quarry	L [ex]	–	–	M	–	Reid & Fraser 1924		522	1486	N2	4 <Abdua
Sandhole, Fetterangus	L	E	S	M	3845 ±32	Ralston 1996	10	–	–	[N1/D or N/NR]	3/4
Tavelty Farm, Kintore	–	E	–	M	3710 ±70	Ralston 1996	12	–	–	[N2(L)]	4
Udny Green	L?	NE	SE	M	3795 ±28	Murray & Shepherd 2007	3	–	–	[N/NR]	3 5/6 <Abdua
Upper Boyndlie Tyrie (East Castlehill)	R?	SE	NE	M	3809 ±29	Callander 1909		725	1503	N3	4
Upper Mains of Catterline	L	NE	SE	M	3770 ±31	Reid & Fraser 1924		718	1692	N4	6
Uppermill Cruden Ardiffery	L? [ex]	–	–	M	–	Gray 1845		551–2	1423–4	N2 N2	>>
Whitehouse*, Skene	L	E	S	M	–	Callander 1906		317–8	1507–8	N/NR; N3	4, 4

A Beaker burial pattern from east Yorkshire

The evidence from east Yorkshire (Fig. 17.2; Table 17.1) of the 62 inhumations accompanied by Beakers for which adequate details of placement and orientation were recorded, reveals a close adherence amongst the majority of the burials to a specific system of orientation and concomitant side placement (Tuckwell 1975): the majority of bodies lain on their left (L) were orientated either directly east (E) or within the eastern quadrant, whilst those on their right (R) were principally orientated west (W) or within the western quadrant. The majority consequently lay with a line of sight to the south (S) or southern quadrant (Fig. 17.2). Where the sex of the skeleton was stated male burials accounted for all but one

Figure 17.2: Orientation and positioning data for crouched inhumations from east Yorkshire showing data for whole sample and for sexed burials only: a) with Beakers b) with Food Vessels (north to top)

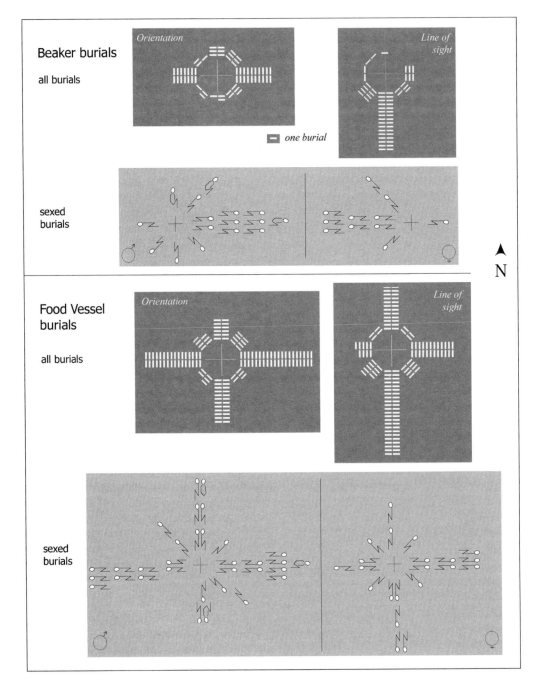

LES arrangement and the less numerous RWS burials were almost exclusively female (Fig. 17.2). Small though the numbers of known or designated sex were, the clear demarcation in arrangement for those where such a distinction was made allowed for the definition of a gender-defined prevailing Beaker burial rite of a 'male' pattern encoded as LES (LESM) and 'female' of RWS (RWSF). The overall pattern is designated LESM/RWSF while individual burials within 45° are expressed as,

for example, L/NE/SE or R/NW/SW.

A small number of sexed burials – all males – were laid partially on their backs, legs to left (back/left: B/L) with orientations varying between east (Garton Slack 161), north-east (Acklam Wold 124), and north (Garton Slack 37) and principally associated with large flint knives. From the record this seems a deliberate placement, ie not a result of post-depositional upper body collapse.

An additional minority did not conform to

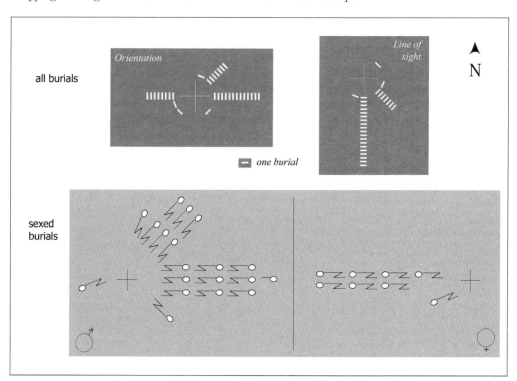

Figure 17.3: Orientation and positioning data for burials with Beakers from north-east Scotland showing data for whole sample and for sexed burials only (north to top)

the mainstream pattern, chiefly represented by those at either ends of the Beaker chronological spectrum. Of the three burials accompanied by early All-Over-Cord decorated (AOC) Beakers (Needham's Low Carinated; Lanting & van der Waals' Step 1/2) with orientation details (Aldro 116, Willerby 235, and Rudston 67) two were of R/NE/NW and LNE patterns; the only sexed burial was an R/NW/SW female, some indication that the LESM/RWSF pattern could have been in place, although not exclusively, from the earliest stage of Beaker appearance in the area. Within the patterning of burials with later Beakers, deviations from the mainstream arrangement increase. Of the 11 burials with Step 6 Beakers, three (Aldro 116, Painsthorpe Wold 4, and Garrowby Wold 104) were of LWN, L/SW/NW and RSE patterns; two of the five Step 7 burials (Rudston 63 and Acklam Wold 204), both unsexed, lay as RSE and RNW. These latter echo some of the tendencies visible within the Food Vessel burial assemblage which appears to have succeeded, but may also have overlapped chronologically with, later Beaker use (included in the illustration (Fig. 17.2(b)) to highlight the contrast with strict Beaker adherence). With Food Vessel graves, increasing orientation to the south and combinations of this and R-side positioning produce a mixed picture of line of

sight, with the pre-eminence of the south now balanced by both the north and east-orientated (RSE and REN) burials, and with regular placing of males on their right.

The Beaker burial pattern in north-east Scotland

The publication of a north-east Scottish LESM Beaker burial at Chapelden, near Banff, Aberdeenshire (Greig *et al.* 1989), prompted an examination of the 26 north-east Scottish Beaker burials for which some evidence of orientation was then available (A.N. Shepherd 1989; Fig 17.3; Table 17.2). The study revealed the existence of the same pattern as that present in east Yorkshire: a predominant east–west orientation combining with left/right side-positioning to produce a southerly line of sight, the LES/RWS pattern, and – where evidence for the sex of the skeleton was available – all LES burials were of males and all RWS, with one possible exception (Mains of Balnagowan, see below), females. A substantial proportion (*c.* 35%) of the 'LES' male burials were of L/NE/SE form, prompting re-assessment of whether these represent merely a 45° deviation from the cardinal point (due to, for example, time of day or year/season of the interment affecting

Figure 17.4: North-east Scotland: Beakers with males/male-pattern burials. Male/female gender symbols with pot indicate assessed sex of accompanying skeleton; burial pattern indicated with north to top of page. Principal accompanying artefacts shown. Ordered by radiocarbon years BP (where undated, by closest dated stylistic comparison)

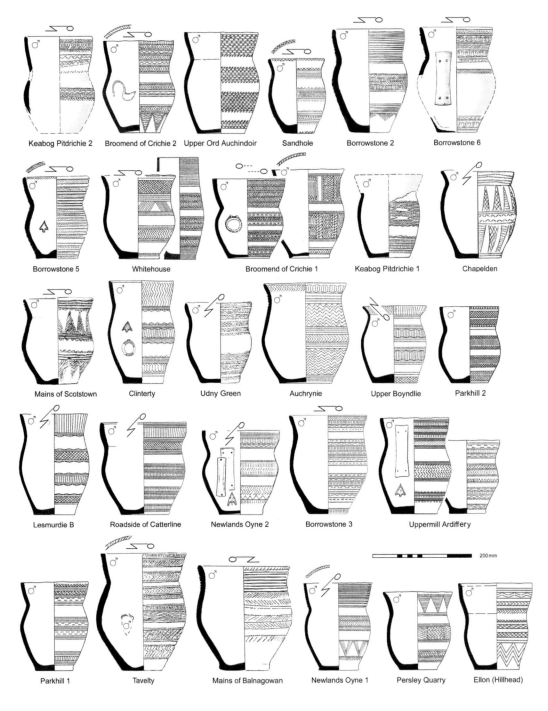

an exact line) or whether they demonstrate the existence of a deliberate subset or actual separate tradition. The evidence does not tend to support a separate tradition: there appears no geographical clustering and no discernible single Beaker style or decoration uniting them.

No orientation information survives for the small number of burials with the earlier AOC (Step 1/2) Beakers from north-east

Scotland to indicate whether the LESM/RWSF pattern was in place at this earlier stage. There is no indication of a later stage weakening of the pattern as had been noted for the Yorkshire graves: there were three Step 6 Beakers with orientation details, all male, one LES and two L/NE/SE. Unlike Yorkshire there are no true Step 7 (long-necked) examples in the core area of the north-east nor any subsequent body of Food Vessel burials to provide a comparable

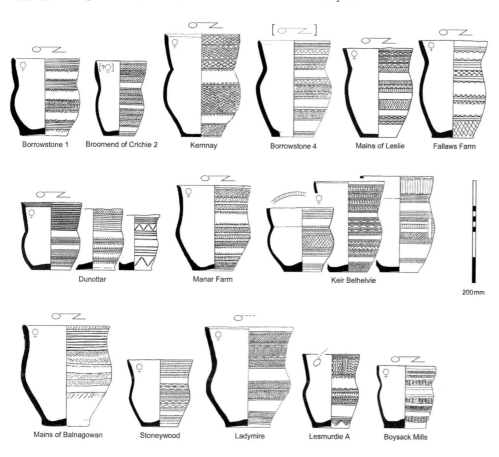

Figure 17.5: North-east Scotland: Beakers with females/female-pattern burials. Male/female gender symbols with pot indicate assessed sex of accompanying skeleton; burial pattern indicated with north to top of page. Ordered by radiocarbon years BP (where undated, by closest dated stylistic comparison)

pattern: with but one or two exceptions these only begin to appear further south into Angus (Sheridan 2007, 99). This situation/distribution is in itself of considerable interest and has been the subject of further study (in the *Beakers and Bodies Project*: N. Wilkin, pers. comm. and see Curtis & Wilkin this volume).

The picture, then, is of the LESM/RWSF pattern in place and rigidly adhered to for the core Beaker period – a shared burial tradition uniting disparate areas of the North Sea coastal Beaker polity.

Patterns in the patterns: male/female pots for male/female burials?

A further intriguing finding from the author's 1989 north-east Beaker study was the apparent clustering of Step 5 vessels with female burials and Step 4 (plus the three Step 3) with males (A.N. Shepherd 1989, table 1; Beakers categorised according to the Lanting & van der Waals Step system as developed

and applied by Ian Shepherd (1986)). The gender differentiation observable in the skeletal placing thus appeared to be amplified by a distinction in the pot form, with 'male' and 'female' pots being distinguishable. This tended to confirm the validity of the ceramic Step 3/4:Step 5 distinctions, whilst demanding a re-interpretation of these distinctions as deriving from socio-cultural factors rather than expressing stages in one continuous typochronological development (A.N. Shepherd 1989, 80). This presaged the emergent picture from radiocarbon dating programmes (Kinnes *et al.* 1991) of a lack of chronological support for the distinctions between previously established typological categories: 'No events, horizons or processes could be chronologically identified/disentangled by radiocarbon determinations' (*ibid.*, 39). The recognition of the synchronicity/coexistence of individual types within the Beaker assemblage has subsequently been more fully accepted and reinforced (see, in particular Needham 2005).

However this apparently clear correlation of male=Step 3/4:female=Step 5 required closer

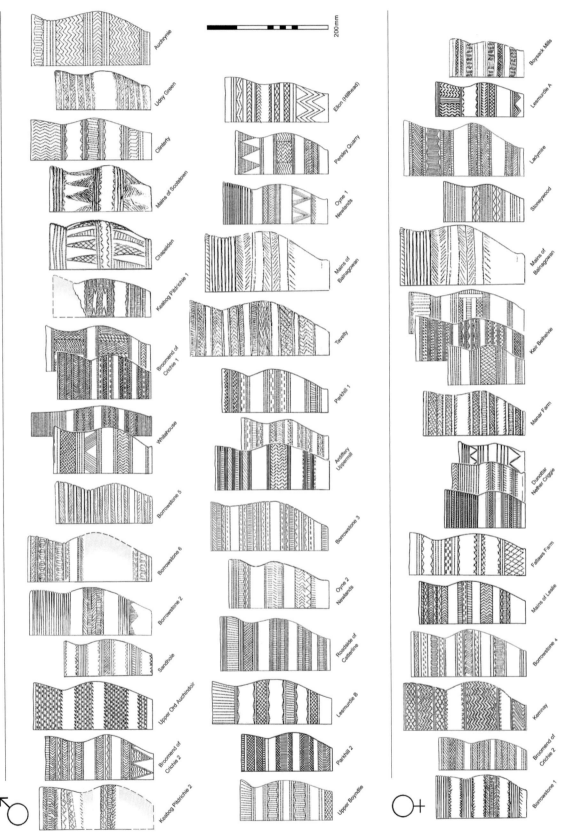

Figure 17.6: North-east Scotland: comparison of Beakers with males/male-pattern and females/female-pattern burials

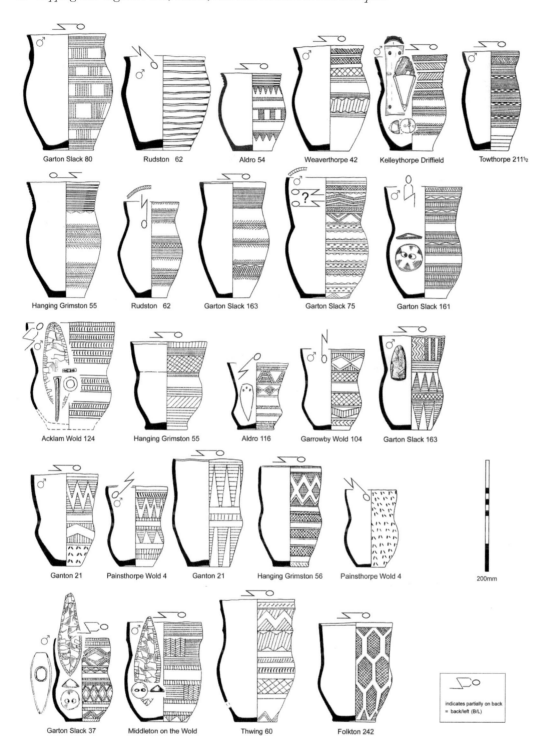

Figure 17.7: East Yorkshire: Beakers with males/male-pattern burials. Male/female gender symbols with pot indicate assessed sex of accompanying skeleton; burial pattern indicated with north to top of page. Principal accompanying artefacts shown. Ordered by typological Step attribution

Garton Slack 80

Rudston 62

Aldro 54

Weaverthorpe 42

Kelleythorpe Driffield

Towthorpe 211½

Hanging Grimston 55

Rudston 62

Garton Slack 163

Garton Slack 75

Garton Slack 161

Acklam Wold 124

Hanging Grimston 55

Aldro 116

Garrowby Wold 104

Garton Slack 163

Ganton 21

Painsthorpe Wold 4

Ganton 21

Hanging Grimston 56

Painsthorpe Wold 4

200mm

indicates partially on back
= back/left (B/L)

Garton Slack 37

Middleton on the Wold

Thwing 60

Folkton 242

examination, in particular to test whether this distinction held true in Yorkshire. To maximise the available information, for both the north-east and Yorkshire assemblages, in addition to data for Beakers accompanying burials of known sex, data for those deposited with unsexed burials of the 'male' LES and 'female' RWS pattern were also incorporated. The 1989 north-east material was augmented with additional data from the work of the *Beakers and Bodies Project* (Curtis & Wilkin this volume).

Figure 17.8: East Yorkshire: Beakers with females/female-pattern burials. Male/female gender symbols with pot indicate assessed sex of accompanying skeleton; burial pattern indicated with north to top of page. Principal accompanying artefacts shown. Ordered by typological Step attribution

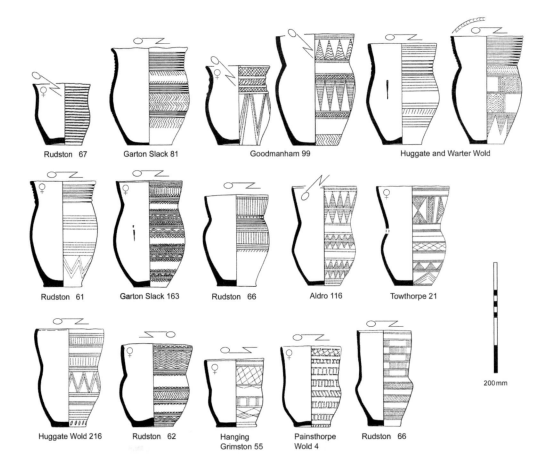

Rudston 67 Garton Slack 81 Goodmanham 99 Huggate and Warter Wold

Rudston 61 Garton Slack 163 Rudston 66 Aldro 116 Towthorpe 21

Huggate Wold 216 Rudston 62 Hanging Grimston 55 Painsthorpe Wold 4 Rudston 66

200mm

The data for Beakers with gender-defined burials in north-east Scotland

A closer analysis of the style and decoration of the north-east Scottish Beakers has in part upheld the Step 3/4:5 male:female distinction. Beakers with male or male-pattern burials (Fig. 17.4) show a clear preponderance of Step 4 features (I. Shepherd 1986, 24–7): differentiation of the neck with a sharp bend exaggerated by contrasting décor, in particular horizontal grooving (Borrowstone 2) and decoration in bands or pairs of bands in zones (Tavelty; Catterline). There are additionally some elements of Step 3 present such as the sinuous profile (Sandhole, Fetterangus) and some taller slender profiles (Clinterty & Lesmurdie B). There are also, however, a small number categorised as Step 5 (from Broomend of Crichie 1, Newlands Oyne 2 and Pitdrichie) that feature greater zone contraction and a broader width to height ratio. A distinctive group of male pots comprises

those characterised by raised horizontal neck ribs (Borrowstone 5 & 6; Tavelty) and an all-over-banded decoration (henceforth AOB); they are accompanied by artefacts that are traditionally assumed to be male, in particular 'high status' archers' equipment – arrowheads, bracers, and belt rings (although not all archers' burials are accompanied by this type of ribbed pot, *viz*. Newlands Oyne, Uppermill & Clinterty).

Beakers associated with female and female-pattern burials (Fig. 17.5) – fewer in number than those with male/male-pattern burials – do show a preponderance of Step 5 style: a broader width to height ratio (with a strand of particularly shorter squat examples, eg, Borrowstone 1; Keir, Belhelvie) and longer accentuated necks with characteristic sharp bend and lower belly (eg, Kemnay; Ladymire). Almost all show zone contraction into three or four zones – neck-belly-foot/lower belly. Unlike the male/male-pattern burials, none of the female/female-pattern examples included demonstrable 'high status' accompaniments. It

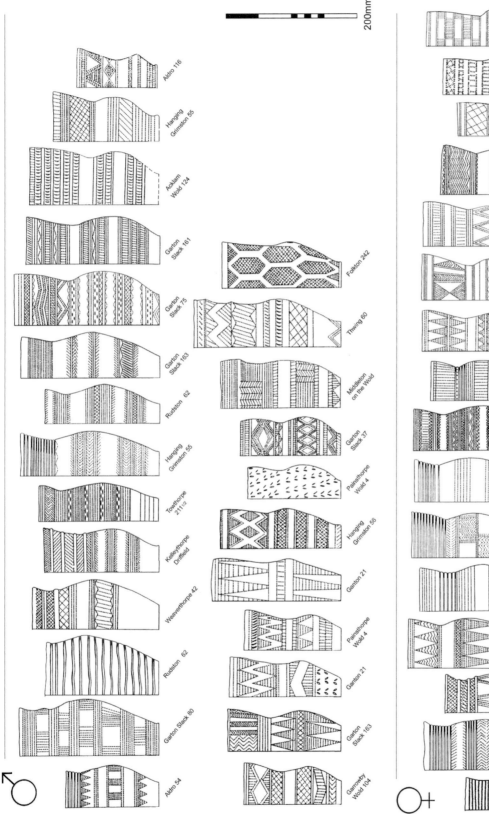

Figure 17.9: East Yorkshire: comparison of Beakers with males/male-pattern and females/female-pattern burials

Figure 17.10: Beakers with male and female paired and associated burials. Arrangement of burials within cist or grave indicated (north to top)

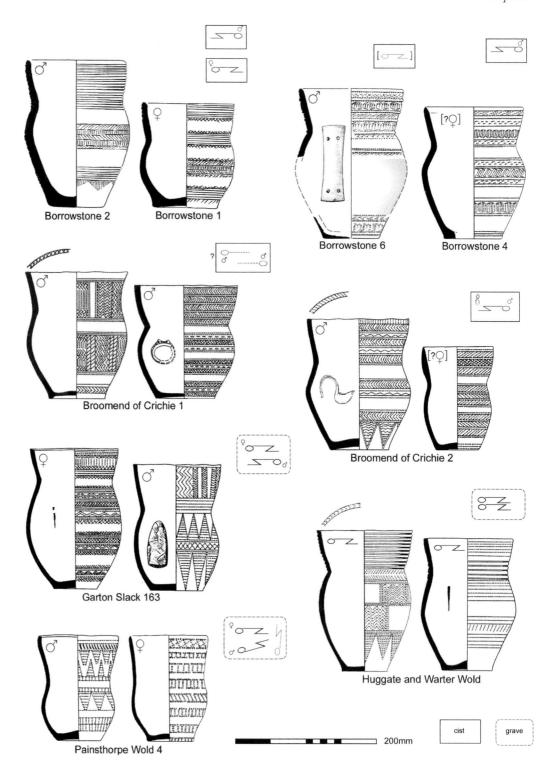

should be noted here, however, that almost all burials, of both sexes, were accompanied by one or more flint artefacts (mostly flakes) of greater or lesser sophistication/refinement. These offer another area of study to refine analysis, as Barfield's work on the Beaker-associated flint objects from Northern Italy has shown (2001a).

The combined presentation of the north-east Beakers (Fig 17.6) makes those aforementioned tendencies from both male and female burials apparent. There are definite male pots that are not found with females: those with high raised ribs, the tall and virtually AOB variety and a very short-necked globular strand (Neil Wilkin's VSN group, distinguished for the north-east Scottish assemblage: Curtis & Wilkin this volume). Equally there are pots that rarely appear within the male assemblage and which seem to have female associations: a group of very short and broad pots, and those with longer, cup-shaped neck. The decoration on female pots has a tendency to the 3-zone arrangement – neck, belly, and lower body/foot – although this arrangement is not entirely absent from the male assemblage. At a more detailed decorative level some aspects of male:female demarcation can be discerned. Opposed long triangles are found on male pots only (eg, the almost identical pots from Chapelden and Mains of Scotstown); likewise, only males have opposed triangles that cover or dominate the belly. Distinction in the treatment of the neck is a prominent factor in the assemblage: vertical motifs or designs on the necks (Clinterty; Lesmurdie B) and grooved 'collars' (Borrowstone 2; Newlands Oyne 1) appear to be a feature of male pots and are not represented on female pots (with the exception of the ambivalent Mains of Balnagowan). Likewise, the vertical zigzag fringes on the bellies of male pots (Clinterty; Upper Boyndlie) are found only on the necks of female pots (Keir Belhelvie; Ladymire); and cross-hatch fringing is found on three female pots (Borrowstone 1; Kemnay; Fallaws Farm). This motif appears on only two male Beakers (Sandhole; Udny Green); in comparison to 'mainstream' North-east male Beakers, these are smaller and they share similar S-shaped profiles.

The data for Beakers with gender-defined burials from east Yorkshire

Within the Yorkshire assemblage, as already noted, a wider range of Beakers was represented than in north-east Scotland, covering all categories of Steps 1–7 (Needham's LC, SN, and LN types). Among these there appeared no such clear male:female/Step 4:Step 5 distinction as had been seen in the north-east, with both male and female burials being accompanied by a range of Beakers. The Beakers with male and male-pattern burials (Fig. 17.7) do show a strong presence of those features

attributed to early (Step 3 and 4) Beakers: the presence of sinuous profiles (eg, Rudston 62) and tall, slender, profiles (eg, Garton Slack 163); a remnant of AOB at Towthorpe 211½ and to a lesser extent Kelleythorpe, Driffield, where there is some zone contraction. This last had raised ribs and, as with the north-east ribbed pots, it was accompanied by archer's material: a stone bracer and a bronze dagger together with two amber v-bored buttons and a hawk's skull. Most display motif zoning and neck differentiation with a sharp bend exaggerated by contrasting decoration, in particular grooving (eg, Hanging Grimston 55). However, there is a strong representation in the Yorkshire male assemblage of those Beakers categorised as Step 5 with a broader width to height ratio (eg, Garton Slack 75), longer neck and a generally lower belly (eg, Acklam Wold 124). Additionally in the Yorkshire assemblage almost 50% fall within Steps 6/7, which are barely present in the Scottish group. This is unsurprising, since these equate with Clarke's southern group (principally S2–S4) which does hold some degree of regional integrity.

As in the north-east Scottish assemblage, there are fewer female and female-pattern burials (Fig. 17.8), with confirmed males outnumbering females by roughly 2:1. These, unlike the north-east examples, include only 27% of Step 5 category (eg, Rudston 62 with an uncharacteristic or even unique LES female burial), and a much higher proportion (53%) of those of Steps 3 and 4, with sinuous profiles (eg, Huggate and Warter Wold 254) and a pronounced neck separated by banding. Again, as a contrast to their north-east Scottish counterparts, the Yorkshire female burials did include possible higher status accompaniments (copper awls at Huggate and Warter Wold 254 and Garton Slack 163 and a high ribbed pot from Goodmanham 99).

The combined male/female assemblage from Yorkshire (Fig. 17.9) shows the mixed, multi-stranded nature of the accompaniments. However, some individual details of decoration can be identified as having a male or female bias: for example, opposed long triangles were only present with male Beakers on the belly (Garton Slack 163) or covering the whole pot (Ganton 21), whereas on female pots they were located in the neck area (Goodmanham 99; Aldro 116). Within the decoration there appears a tendency for male motifs, zigzags and long triangles to be negative (ie, unfilled) (as at Ganton 21 and Painsthorpe Wold 4), by contrast with filled triangular and lozenge motifs on female Beakers (Goodmanham 99; Aldro 116). Cross-hatch fringing is not present on any male pots in the Yorkshire assemblage but is found on two female pots (Garton Slack 163; Rudston 62), the former from a paired male/female burial (see case studies below and on CD) and the latter also from a possible male/female linked pair (although with less secure association).

Patterns of burial gender differentiation in operation: case studies

From this review of the gender-attributable pots it is clear that although the generality of pot shape (amongst pots belonging to Step3/4–5) supports the suggestion that there was a gender distinction in pot design, this does not extend to the height and size of the pot, which cannot be taken as a reliable gender indicator. Only one extreme of the shape spectrum appears diagnostic: the shorter squatter form is invariably female (particularly when associated with a child: eg, Dunottar). Overall, male pots tend to be taller, but not exclusively so: some female/female-pattern pots are of some considerable height (*contra* the medium size for females posited by Brodie (1998, 48). Focusing in on the detail of motifs does not for the most part provide mutually exclusive male/female motifs or treatments that can be ascribed exclusively to one gender across either or any area. However, there is much that can be teased out to support a general sense of there being underlying male: female differentiation controls in operation. These controls appear to exist across both core areas examined, although the specific details of enforcement may have varied. To try and isolate the application of these strictures, examples of paired or associated male/female burials were examined in detail. These are shown in Figure 17.10 (and 17.11☺) and details of the case studies are presented in the accompanying CD.

The examples from north-east Scotland were the pair of adjacent RWSF and LESM burials from a cemetery at Borrowstone (cists 1 and 2; I. Shepherd 1986, 12–13); a further neighbouring pair of an LESM and

a female pattern RWS (Borrowstone cists 4 & 6); a double burial of LES male and an infant (described as 'female': Broomend of Crichie 2) and a double burial of two males, with possible opposing east–west orientations (Broomend of Crichie 1). The pots display both interesting similarities and links in decorative layout but clear distinctions in shape, eg, Borrowstone 1 and 2 where the 'male' pot (Borrowstone 2 LESM) has an elongated S-profile with distinct neck, defined by a 'collar' of grooving, while the 'female' pot (Borrowstone 1 RWSF) presents a strikingly different, almost dumpy shape and a cut-down version of the male design modified with cross-hatched fringing (Fig. 17.10; Fig. 17.11☺). Both are united with the same technique of grooving and white infill (incorporating ground burnt bone: see Curtis *et al.* 2010).

The Beakers accompanying the male and infant (?female) at Broomend of Crichie 2 present a pair of contrasting size and shape, with subtly differing design, the larger placed with the male, the smaller with the infant: it is notable that the cup-shaped neck of the smaller pot is an inverse of the everted rim of the larger, almost fitting into the latter's concave curve. The pots with the two males from Broomend 1 show the same contrast in size and opposing profiles. Also of note is the decoration of simple diagonal hatching on the rim of the larger male pot. Decorated rims are a comparatively common feature amongst these pairs (see also Fig. 17.10, Broomend 2; Huggate & Warter Wold 254) and are always found ornamenting the larger pot.

The same contrast in size and shape, combined with varied but linked design, is shown by the pairs from Yorkshire. At Garton Slack 163, unusually, the larger pot accompanies the RWS female although it displays the female cross-hatched fringing. In the case of Huggate and Warter Wold 254 we have two adult individuals buried in the female RWS pattern; no sex was stated but one was accompanied by an awl, an artefact type commonly associated with females in late 3rd and early 2nd millennium graves (Thomas & Ellwood 2005). Again, as with Broomend 1, two burials of apparently the same sex were accompanied by a combination of a larger and smaller pot, in this case the larger with a cup-shaped neck and the smaller, a sinuously profiled example. The Painsthorpe Wold 4 Beakers show less contrast in size although these are a later Step 6 and Step 5 pair; the burials show an unusual arrangement, the youth on his left orientated west (LWN), looking not just to the north but, possibly more importantly, towards the accompanying female RWS burial.

The reciprocity of shape within the large and small pot pairings that accompany the double male (Broomend 1) and double ?female (Huggate & Warter Wold 254) burials presents an additional possibility: that pot forms were used to express not merely a male: female distinction but possibly a senior:junior relationship or a male:'female'-equivalent association. Indeed, in all the pairings there is a sense of a 'senior' and 'junior', not just in size but also in style and treatment of the pot: contrasting use of motif and style produces one pot, usually accompanying the female, of reduced elaboration and more muted pattern. The sense is of motifs being used as a uniting factor, stressing links and continuity/similarities, while shape and treatment were used to underline differences in gender or status. There are also demonstrable links across groupings, such as the bands of running chevrons that are found both on the smaller Broomend 1 and the larger Broomend 2 pots; these project a sense of lineage in motif arrangement in the immediate geographical area.

The striking differences in size and shape were clearly an important factor in the way in which people observed the required formalities. Even if we allow the possibility that some pots may have been old, 'heirloom' items when buried (although see below regarding the manufacture of pots for the grave), the pairings nevertheless underline the synchronicity of otherwise very diverse styles – styles that were indicative of demarcations, simultaneously uniting and separating. These pairings highlight the importance of the requirement to choose one pot of each type for placement in the grave.

The case studies described here and on the CD convey a very complex picture of the nuances of Beaker burial patterns, both skeletal and ceramic, in full operation. They show a core LES/RWS pattern and its concomitant pottery forms, strictly adhered to in some cases (eg, the Borrowstone cists). However, these case studies also demonstrate, with the double burial data from the two males at Broomend of Crichie 1 and the youth and female at Painsthorpe Wold, that the expression of the relationship of the individuals – in particular a desire or requirement to have them face each other – could over-ride the standard single burial formality which would otherwise prescribe orientation in the accepted direction.

Although by focusing on the details of Beaker variation, the original emphatic male: female distinctions of Step 4 and 5 Beakers may have been rendered less clear and persuasive, the closer focus on the minutiae of these pairings has made more apparent the structure within which a range of options existed to satisfy the required observance of the formalities. The distinction has become less that of any prescribed, definitive 'male:female' pots – undeviating, slavishly followed – but rather of choices being made to suit a specific relationship or situation. These choices clearly carry complex and deep-rooted significance, forming part of the long-established prescribed formalities of burial.

Assessment and discussion: implications of the pattern

The foregoing studies have reinforced the sense that much of the perceived variability in Beaker design was the result not of typo-chronological development, but rather of the exercise of choice from amongst synchronous styles and forms, selected according to individual circumstances and criteria within a dense interconnection of governing rules. Respect for these rules was expressed through elements chosen from Boast's 'grab bag of signifiers' (2002, 97), combined to fulfil the requirements of the rites. What also emerges from this examination is a sense of those elements that linked and those that separated. The burial pattern itself appears as an overriding unifying factor; beneath its umbrella a mass of detailed demarcations and distinctions existed.

Previous sections have looked in detail at two core British Beaker areas. Here we look at the wider picture, examining the location and ramifications of the burial pattern, some significances in the patterning of Beaker diversity, and the mechanism of their transmission.

The Beaker burial pattern: universality and diversity

(Universality: a metaphysical entity that remains unchanged in character through a series of changing relations)

Yorkshire and north-east Scotland both offer comparatively large assemblages of Beaker grave information within which patterns can readily be observed; in comparison, the evidence for the adjacent areas of East Lothian and Northumberland is scanty but it does indicate (N. Wilkin, pers. comm.; Lanting & van der Waals 1972, 41) that the LESM/RWSF burial ritual was also observed in these areas, thereby reinforcing the picture of a universality of practice across much of the British northern east coast Beaker polity. There is, in contrast, no evidence that the LESM/RWSF pattern prevailed south of the Humber. In Wessex (Lanting & van der Waals 1972, 37) the dominant orientation is north–south, with a combination of left- and right-side placement (males on their left and females on their right, as in the north) producing a predominantly eastern line of sight, a LNEM/RSEF pattern. The burial pattern in operation thus amplifies the divisions between pottery forms north and south of the Humber that were encapsulated in Clarke's groupings and which were revisited, and refined, by Boast (2002, 99–104; figs 10.2–10.5)

In marked contrast there is extensive evidence for the LES/RWS pattern amongst Chalcolithic/Beaker period graves over substantial areas of continental Europe. In particular, the pattern is widespread in Corded Ware burials in central Europe (Benz *et al.* 1998, 311; Turek & Černý 2001, 604; Vander Linden 2007) but with one crucial difference: the gender differentiation is the reverse of the British Beaker practice, with males buried on their right, in the northern British female RWS position, and the females on their left, in the LES arrangement.

This existence of the same rite but with the gender distinction reversed is more striking when the Corded Ware pattern is compared with that prevalent within the central European Bell Beaker communities (Benz *et al.* 1998, 308; Müller 2001, 589; Heyd 2007; Turek & Černý 2001, 604). Here, unlike the Corded Ware arrangement, side placement matches the British Beaker practice of males on their left, females on their right, but the orientations are

primarily north–south, combining to produce the LNEM/RSEF pattern, with a primarily Eastern line of sight. As noted above, this was also prevalent in Wessex and appeared amongst some later Step 6/7 Beaker burials in Yorkshire.

The presence of two markedly different burial arrangements, both strictly observed, in adjacent areas of central and north-east Europe has been described by Benz *et al.* (1998, 312–3) as Bell Beaker [ideology] confronting Corded Ware ideology in a 'zone of tension'. It is tempting to speculate that somewhere in this zone, or close to it, in the same 'fusion corridor' which saw the marrying of Corded Ware and Bell Beaker pot traditions (Needham 2005, 177–8), these tensions were resolved and a similar marriage took place, this time of the burial traditions, with the Bell Beaker male: female/L:R side differentiation and the Corded Ware LES/RWS arrangement combining to form the pattern subsequently practised in the British east coast Beaker domains. This melding of the Corded Ware orientation pattern and Bell Beaker gender side distinction can be seen as representing the sealing of a new alliance or association through the adoption of this combined new set of formalities.

The conjecture that such a fusion took place prior to its transmission to, or appearance in, Britain is reinforced by the Dutch Beaker burial evidence. Here the LES/RWS pattern was in place amongst Beaker burials of the central Netherlands (Lanting 2008, 100) with the same gender differentiation (as far as it could be discerned from the small number of proven females) as that appearing in north Britain: males on their left, females on their right, ie, LESM/RWSF, the gender distinction of the side positioning of the Corded Ware burials reversed. Further to the north, in the North-east Netherlands, there was a prevailing orientation of north-west/south-east–north-east/south-west with 25% north/south, although the exact rules were unclear (Lanting 2008, 100); this suggests another possible transitional or otherwise distinct area with a separate tradition, or with particular subsets of rules (as for the L/NE/SE burials of north-east Scotland).

The existence of the LESM/RWSF pattern within the Dutch Beaker polity, with its close proximity and early links to the Scottish Beaker development in particular, is of considerable interest. Paradoxically the early Dutch-style burials in Scotland (Sheridan 2008) cannot offer any supporting evidence to attest to the pattern being observed here from that early Chalcolithic stage because they were not protected by burial in cists, and therefore virtually no skeletal evidence survived. Only the orientation of the grave pits, principally east–west, offers some indication that this may well have been the case.

That the same LESM/RWSF formalities were observed on the closest continental littoral to the north British east coast Beaker communities reinforces the evidence for strong links – ancestral or otherwise – with these groups. By contrast the evidence from Wessex (Lanting & van der Waals 1972, 37) points to a pattern closer to the Bell Beaker LNEM/RSEF arrangement, underlining the impression of there having been two very different strands of influence in northern and southern Britain in the Chalcolithic. It is also the case that a significant minority of the Wessex burials deviate from the prevailing LNEM/RSEF form, with some females buried as LSW (*ibid.*, 37–8). The majority of these LSWF burials are accompanied by Beakers of Steps 2/3, therefore assumed to be 'relatively early' (*ibid.*, 38). This points to another separate (and rare) tradition with a female left-side placement, only previously observed amongst Corded Ware burials. Although some of the apparent anomalies are clearly the result of specific modifying factors (eg, the presence of other burials) others may be responding to individual local factors or traditions which are indiscernible. Further analysis of the detail of these Wessex burials would be desirable (particularly given the recent additional data from the burials of the Amesbury Archer, his 'Companion' and the Boscombe Bowmen, which appear to represent a discrete grouping/subset of L/NW/NE males (Fitzpatrick 2011, 198). Whatever the explanation for these possible subsets in funerary practice there is a sense that here, as with the AOC Beaker burials in the north, there is the possibility that more than one pattern was in place amongst the earliest Beaker communities. These differing Beaker burial patterns in the north and south of Britain enhance the image of a complex of routes and waves of development encapsulated in Clarke's original 1970 analysis, now further amplified by the patterns of journeying indicated by

the recent isotope analysis (Fitzpatrick 2011, 204–207, 232–4).

As we have seen, there is no sizeable presence of AOC burials, and those that exist do not appear to present a Corded Ware LESF/RWSM pattern with reversed gender differentiation. Thus it would seem that the Corded Ware LES/RWS pattern arrived already *modified* through a melting pot, the possible mediation of Dutch Beaker groups indicated above. The AOC pot itself may represent the continued use of a strand from some Corded Ware ancestry, an iconic pot with a long survival, as fragments found apparently used as closure deposits at Neolithic sites across Scotland attest (A.N. Shepherd 1996, 47–8).

Why these extensive areas should be united by certain observances of crouched inhumation but differ in their interpretation raises the question of the relative importance of the governing factors of side, orientation, and line of sight. For male:female differentiation, side placement was a most useful instant indicator of demarcation. A left-side male placement could arguably be interpreted as an expression of the requirement for a man's weapon arm (in an assumed predominantly right-handed population) to be free instantly and at the ready to defend. But the Corded Ware male right-side placement, and its supremacy ultimately in Early Bronze Age burials, negates this, or else suggests that different criteria dictated the formalities.

There exists the possibility that once the pattern was set, the issue of *how* males and females were distinguished was of less importance than that they *were* (and in this regard, note the present-day, obsolete, survival of male garments buttoning left-over-right, female right-over-left). The demarcation would simply represent a subsidiary factor within what appears to be, across a swathe of territory extending across central and northern Chalcolithic Europe into Britain, a critical burial requirement of facing south. If such a pan-European ideology based on observance of orientation towards the sun did exist, then during the later stages of Beaker use it seems to have faded, or else was overwhelmed by more southern practices, or was not so overtly expressed in burial arrangement than hitherto.

Were orientation to be the fundamental factor then the east–west/male–female correspondence could be interpreted as the symbolic expression of the requirement of the male to aim towards the sunrise in readiness for departure on the day's hunting, and of the female to point west towards the sunset in readiness for the return of the hunter and preparation of the evening meal. Again, such an interpretation does not hold good for Corded Ware, continental Bell Beaker or more southern British Beaker arrangements. Any number of local topographical factors may have governed the orientational strictures of the pattern; in this respect it is remarkable that in its varied forms it was so clearly adhered to over such an extensive area.

In continental Europe the placement of Bell Beaker burials according to extremely strict rules has been interpreted as revealing a fundamental aspect of the Bell Beaker ideology (Benz *et al.* 1998, 311). That females should be given their own rules within that system has been taken to suggest a certain parity between men and women (*ibid.*). Clearly the distinction of male/female or male/'female' was important from a very early stage within a Chalcolithic/Beaker milieu, although there are still important limits to full male/female parity: for instance, we find no female burials with archers' equipment. This is unlikely to be due to a gap in the record and is more likely to represent a division, archery being considered a traditional male preserve. Yet, although the females may never have borne arms or hunted, they were still deemed worthy of burial in their own right.

That the distinction was already present (albeit reversed) in Corded Ware communities suggests that this male/female distinction was an embedded feature of Chalcolithic societies. The clear distinction made for females in burial ceased to be a requirement to be followed within the formalities of the fuller Bronze Age, with a more universal right-side placement, a factor already noted. Yet what social or religious factors produced the total reversal in male/female designated rite, probably in the Netherlands but possibly before that, it is impossible to say.

The pots: marking the person and making the distinction
(Marking: a mark or pattern of marks that ... can be used as a means of identification)
It is easy to see how the conformity to a

burial rite, based as it is on a limited number of variables (left or right, four/eight principal compass directions) could allow for prescriptive patterning which might readily be enforced. Standardisation of the ritual pot required to observe the formalities would have been more complex, with multiple variables of shape and design allowing for any number of statements to be made. It is harder here for us to separate the signal from the noise. Yet the fact that within our partial, fragmented, record any patterns are discernible at all indicates the strength of adherence to the prescribed formalities.

Burial is for reverencing the person being laid to rest and for the comfort and reassurance of those left behind. The formalities are required to fulfil these twin aims. The Beaker, chief amongst the grave goods, can be used to express the messages of reverence and re-affirmation. That it was not simply plucked from the deceased's hearth-side for deposition, but had instead been expressly 'made for the grave' (Boast 1995, 174), seems now to be accepted as a given. Support for this assumption comes not just from comparison with traditional ethnohistoric practices, where the production of specific ritual vessels for designated occasions is common practice (eg, central India: Miller 1985, 56, table 4), but more so from the regular survival of Beakers as whole pots. This suggests they cannot have been in daily use prior to deposition: the attrition from frequent use would be apparent, as noted by Salanova: for the standard Beaker product the 'rate of fracturing along joints [of coil-built vessels is] quite high' (2000, 92).

The sense, then, is one of the pot being 'ordered' for the interment, made specifically for inclusion and unlikely to be one used in life. Rather it was used to sum up a life, the nature and style of the pot offering statements that can express the deceased's status, role and position within family or society. Although it is not possible to assign meaning to individual motifs and read the pot as one might say a Native American wampum belt, it has been worthwhile to attempt to determine whether any aspects of pot design can be assigned to a specific gender. From this there seems to be less a specific set of gender-defined motifs than a gender-defined style and appropriate placement, so that a statement of maleness or femaleness can be seen to be made.

Needham has used the term 'lineage' to

describe Beaker categories (2005, 182). This term – although not necessarily in the sense that Needham intended – is indeed pertinent. Much as a grave-stone can indicate name, age, parentage, and status, the Beaker pot could, in the structured/formalised use of familial motifs, indicate similar descriptors of an individual. Where or how a band or motif was placed, and the nature of that motif, could have held as much significance as the placement of motifs within heraldic quartering. Similar rules may have applied to regulate the ordering of bands/zones at the pot's neck, belly, and lower body/foot. Not wishing to stretch the heraldic analogy too far, there nevertheless exists the possibility that the varied edging/fringing of zones (eg, plain bands, cross-hatching, zigzag) might not be expressions of simple decorative whim, but rather indicators of gender or status, used in their own right as distinguishing lines in much the same way as the heraldic *lines of partition* could be used in differencing family arms (Burnett & Dennis 1997, 24). In this way a limited range of motifs can be followed across time and transmitted through lineage.

People, patterns and pots: mechanisms of transmission

(Transmission: spread; communication; diffusion; conduction)

The universality of the northern British Beaker pattern shows on some level a unity/ideology, where the traditions of pot design went hand in hand with the cultural imperatives underpinning the burial pattern. What we see can only be snapshots of the numerous and complex mechanisms by which these motifs and patterns were transmitted or retained, imposed upon, and preserved within, familial groupings. We can, however, make some estimates as to how this was effected, how tribal identities and affiliations were reinforced through material culture, and how observation of the formalities could perhaps have aided the preservation of homeland memory.

The transmission and curation of the pot motifs has been posited as most likely taking place through the agency of the female (*inter alia* Brodie 2001, 492) although (*contra* Brodie) there need be no assumption that potting itself was purely 'a female craft': see, for example, central India (Miller 1985, 36) where actual pot production was a male preserve, the females being responsible for decoration (painting)

and cultural transmission. Possible suggested models for the diffusion of designs via female agency are exogamy or trade alliances, either consensual or through force: Brodie has discussed (2001, 492) the possibility of women stolen/abducted for their skills including language. Such female transference could have taken place within the Beaker network or by dealing with an existing indigenous population (Brodie 1998; Needham 2005, 208). The mobility demonstrated by strontium isotope analysis of south German Beaker graves shows overall more than 25% mobility, with 33% for females (Brodie 2001, 493). Again Miller's study of pot variation in Central India shows that changes in designs over distance could be quite gradual (Miller 1985, 110–13): different designs are used, yet there is underlying similarity in areas 200 km apart: this reflects reinforcement from the natal village, and/or the influence of the mother-in-law.

Reasons for movement have been seen as taking place under the impetus of the spread of metallurgy, a key factor in the development of the Beaker network (Salanova 2000, 100; Brodie 2001, 494). Expansion of Beaker metalwork to north Britain, Scotland in particular, through the medium of Dutch-style Beakers is discussed elsewhere in this volume (Sheridan; I. Shepherd). However this transmission took place, and by whatever route, the pattern was in existence within north-east Scotland from somewhere between 2470/2460 and 2340/2230 BC (Pitdrichie 2, Borrowstone 1, & Broomend of Crichie 2 dates) within the northern Chalcolithic and lasted through the main core period of Needham's *instituted,* one might say *embedded,* phase for at least one of Case's 'quarters of a millennium' (1977). Dating of more recently discovered LESM burials from the Ferrybridge henge (Roberts 2005) and from elsewhere on the A1M route (Brown *et al.* 2007) indicate similar date brackets for Yorkshire (2630–2130 to 2290–1940 cal BC). Within this range the 'internal' chronology of the Borrowstone cemetery provides a guide, indicating at least a two- (or even three-) stage history: a possible pioneering phase represented by the early cists 1 and 2 (with their unusual form of incised Beaker, neither AOC nor of the classic tooth-comb Northern Beaker), followed comparatively soon, probably no more than 30 years later (R. Kidd, pers. comm.), by a phase dominated by archers (and their women) (cists 4–6). After another possible 80 years, a final, settled, phase is represented by the burial in cist 3. There is a sense here, then, of the successive pulses in Beaker developments identified by Clarke being manifested in Yorkshire by successive use of barrows, and in north-east Scotland by returning to the same ridge. Throughout this process we see the use of a burial pattern that distinguishes male and female by the same strictures that were in play across the North Sea, in the Netherlands and beyond.

The question of what economy supported these Beaker-using societies has never been fully resolved; there is some indication from the Netherlands of both arable and pastoral farming (Fokkens 2001, 307). In this respect a small note/thought on archers can be offered: the suggestion by Piggott (1971, 89–92) that continental Beaker bow pendants indicate the use of a small composite bow says something further about the nature of Beaker archers. The rationale for the choice of the composite short bow over the lethal long bow is that this is usable for the mounted archer: 'the weapon par excellence of the eastern horse-archer' (Strickland & Hardy 2005, 97–112). This could indicate the use of the horse (enigmatically suggested by Barfield (2001b, 618)) and confers a mobility on the Beaker/Chalcolithic male that has yet to be fully discussed. Previous resistance (on whatever basis) to the acceptance of movement of peoples has begun to break down (Brodie 1998, 50) increasingly so in the face of isotope evidence. This may help broaden the view of rapid Beaker movement and dissemination: the 'Beaker Folk' may have legs again.

In conclusion

Incontrovertibly, the rigid adherence to a systematic placement of the dead, in accordance with imperatives of topographical positioning and gender distinction, across a wide geographic area and within a range of grave types, presents a form of social unity/conformity which has radical implications. The existence of a pattern so strictly observed, whose dictats can be seen to manifest themselves so clearly through the placement of the individual and the choice of grave goods, is a major factor in viewing the universality of the Beaker phenomenon in general and its place in pushing back the 'Chalcolithic frontier'. The changing way in which that pattern was adapted to discriminate between genders allows us to follow its movement and development within and across Europe.

The universality of the burial pattern along the north British east coastlands licenses us to speak of 'Beaker societies' in a way that we could not confidently propose on the basis of the ceramic evidence alone. It indicates a form of shared ideology or philosophy, a further factor underlining the homogeneity of the pot types themselves over such a broad area (exemplified in Salanova's European standard: 2000, 94).

To re-use Needham's terminology (2005), the burial pattern displays a fusion, a unity, while the pot variety shows not so much a fission as a polyglot multi-stranded heritage, expressive of the joint heritage of male and female. Perhaps it can be said that whilst the Beaker within the burial defines the individual, the form of the burial itself defines the tribe. The rites discussed are founded/embedded in the Chalcolithic; they continued to prescribe the rules governing the burial formalities for over two centuries until they faltered, died out or were overcome at the onset of those changes that mark the full Bronze Age.

Acknowledgements
Thanks are due to Neil Curtis, Meg Hutchison, Ray Kidd, Neil Wilkin, and Margot Wright for valuable data and insights drawn from the work of the *Beakers and Bodies Project* at Marischal Museum, Aberdeen. Thanks also to John Cruse and Terry Manby for their scouring of the post-1905 Yorkshire data for additional material, to Hilary Murray for all the philosophical and editorial support, and to Alison Sheridan for her lively and robust help in polishing up the text. Mike Allen has been a very patient and long-suffering editor and has helped make this paper a much better, trimmer, offering. Finally thanks and a dedication: to the tall, once gracile, male from this shorter, and increasingly dumpier, female.

Bibliography

Barfield, L. 2001a. Beaker lithics in northern Italy. In Nicolis (ed.) 2001, 507–18
Barfield, L. 2001b. Final discussion summarised. In Nicolis (ed.) 2001, 617–22
Benz, M., Strahm, C. & Willigen, S. van. 1998. Le

campaniforme: phénomène et culture archéologique. *Bulletin de la Société Préhistorique Française* 95, 305–14

Boast, R. 1995. Fine pots, pure pots, Beaker pots. In Kinnes, I. & Varndell, G. (ed.), *Unbaked Urns of Rudely Shape*, 69–80. Oxford: Oxbow Monograph 55

Boast, R. 2002. Pots as categories: British Beakers. In A. Woodward & J.D. Hill (ed.), *Prehistoric Britain: the ceramic basis*, 96–105. Oxford: Oxbow Books/ Prehistoric Ceramics Research Group Occasional Publication 3

Brodie, N. 1998. British Bell Beakers: twenty-five years of theory and practice. In M. Benz & S. van Willingen (ed.), *Some New Approaches to the Bell Beaker 'Phenomenon': lost paradise?*, 43–56. Oxford: British Archaeological Report S690

Brodie, N. 2001. Technological frontiers and the emergence of the Beaker culture. In Nicolis (ed.) 2001, 487–96

Brown, F., Howard-Davis, C., Brennard, M., Boyle, A., Evans, T., O'Connor, S., Spence, A., Heawood, R. & Lupton, A. 2007. *The Archaeology of the A1(M). Darrington to Dishforth DBFO Road Scheme.* Lancaster: Oxford Archaeology North

Bryce, T.H. & Low, A. 1905. Notes (I.) on a human skeleton found in a cist with a Beaker urn, at Acherole …etc. *Proceedings of the Society of Antiquaries of Scotland* 39, 418–38

Burnett, C.J. & Dennis, M.D. 1997. *Scotland's Heraldic Heritage; The Lion Rejoicing.* Edinburgh: The Stationery Office

Callander, J.G. 1906. Notices of (1) two stone cists each containing two drinking-cup urns … etc. *Proceedings of the Society of Antiquaries of Scotland* 40, 23–39

Callander, J.G. 1907. Notices of 1) a stone cist … etc. *Proceedings of the Society of Antiquaries of Scotland* 41, 116–29

Callander, J.G. 1909. Notice of the discovery in Aberdeenshire of five cists, each containing a drinking-cup urn. *Proceedings of the Society of Antiquaries of Scotland* 43, 81–7

Callander. J.G. 1933. a short cist containing a Beaker at Newlands, Oyne, Aberdeenshire, and sundry archaeological notes. *Proceedings of the Society of Antiquaries of Scotland* 67, 228–43

Case, H.J. 1977. The beaker culture in Britain and Ireland. In R.J. Mercer, (ed.), *Beakers in Britain and Europe: four studies*, 71–101. Oxford: British Archaeological Report S26

Chalmers, J.H. 1867. Notice of the discovery of a Stone Kist at Broomend, near Inverurie, Aberdeenshire. *Proceedings of the Society of Antiquaries of Scotland* 7, 110–14

Clarke, D.L. 1970. *Beaker Pottery of Great Britain and Ireland.* Cambridge: Cambridge University Press

Curtis, N. & Wilkin N. this volume. The Regionality of Beakers and Bodies in the Chalcolithic of North-East Scotland. In M.J. Allen, J. Gardiner & S. Sheridan (eds), *Is there a British Chalcolithic? Place, people and polity in the later 3rd millennium.* Oxford: Prehistoric Society Research Paper 4

Carlin, N. Popovic, L. Wilkin, N. & Wright, M. 2010. The moon, the bonfire and Beaker: Analysing white inlay from Beaker pottery in Aberdeenshire. *PAST* 63, 1–3

Coutts, H. 1966. Recent discoveries of short cists in Angus and East Perthshire. *Proceedings of the Society of Antiquaries of Scotland* 97, 157–65

Davidson, C.B. 1867. Notice of further Stone Kists found at Broomend, near Inverurie, Aberdeenshire. *Proceedings of the Society of Antiquaries of Scotland* 7, 115–8

Ferguson. W. 1882. Note on a cist, with an urn, discovered at Parkhill, near Aberdeen, in October 1881. *Proceedings of the Society of Antiquaries of Scotland* 16, 69–72

Fitzpatrick, A.P. 2011. *The Amesbury Archer and the Boscombe Bowmwn. Bell Beaker burials at Boscombe Down, Amesbury, Wiltshire.* Salisbury: Wessex Archaeology Report 27

Fokkens, H. 2001. 21 years after Oberreid: the 'Dutch Model' reconsidered. In Nicolis (ed.) 2001, 301–8

Gray, R. 1845. *The New Statistical Account of Scotland by the ministers of the respective parishes under the superintendence of a committee of the society for the benefit of the sons and daughters of the clergy* 12 (Aberdeenshire), 355. Edinburgh

Greenwell, W.G. 1877. *British Barrows.* Oxford: Clarendon Press

Greenwell, W.G. 1890. Recent researches in barrows in Yorkshire, Wiltshire, Berkshire etc. *Archaeologia* 52, 1–72

Greig, M.K., Greig, C., Shepherd, A.N. & Shepherd, I.A.G. 1989. A beaker cist at Chapelden, Tore of Troup, Aberdour, Banff and Buchan District. *Proceedings of the Society of Antiquaries of Scotland* 119, 73–81

Haughton, C. & Powlesland, D. 1999. *West Heslerton. The Anglian Cemetery.* Vol I *The Excavation and Discussion of the Evidence.* Yedingham: Landscape Research Centre Ltd

Heyd, V. 2007. Families, prestige goods, warriors and complex societies: Beaker groups of the 3rd Millennium cal BC along the Upper and Middle Danube. *Proceedings of the Prehistoric Society* 73, 321–70

Jay, M., Parker Pearson, M., Richards, M., Nehlich, O., Montgomery, J., Chamberlain, A. & Sheridan, A. this volume. The Beaker People Project: an interim report on the progress of the isotopic analysis of the organic skeletal material. In M.J. Allen, J. Gardiner & S. Sheridan (eds), *Is there a British Chalcolithic? Place, people and polity in the later 3rd millennium.* Oxford: Prehistoric Society Research Paper 4

Kinnes, I., Gibson, A., Ambers, J., Bowman, S., Leese, M. & Boast, R. 1991. Radiocarbon dating and British Beakers: the British Museum programme. *Scottish Archaeological Review,* 8, 35–68

Kirk, W. & McKenzie, J. 1955. Three Bronze age cist burials in NE Scotland. *Proceedings of the Society of Antiquaries of Scotland* 88, 1–14

Lanting, J. 2008. De NO-Nederlandse/NW-Duitse Klokbekergroep: culturele achtergrond, typologie van het aardewerk, datering, verspreiding en grafritueel. *Palaeohistoria* 49/50, 11–326

Lanting, J.N. & Waals, J.D. van der 1972. British beakers as seen from the continent: a review article. *Helinium* 12, 20–46

Low, A. 1902–4. On the contents of short cists found in Aberdeenshire and neighbouring counties. *Proceedings of Aberdeen University Anatomical and Anthropological Society* 1902–4, 8–36

Low, A. 1936. a short cist containing a Beaker and other relics at Newlands, Oyne, Aberdeenshire.

Proceedings of the Society of Antiquaries of Scotland 70, 326–31

Miller, D. 1985. *Artefacts as Categories. A Study of Ceramic Variability in Central India.* Cambridge: Cambridge University Press

Mortimer, J.R. 1905. *Forty Years Researches in British and Saxon Burial Mounds of East Yorkshire.* London: A. Brown & Sons

Müller, A. 2001. Gender differentiation in burial rites and grave-goods in the Eastern or Bohemian-Moravian Group of the Bell Beaker Culture. In Nicolis (ed.) 2001, 589–99

Murray, D. & Ralston. I. 1997. The excavation of a square-ditched barrow and other cropmarks at Boysack Mills, Inverkeilor, Angus. Proceedngs of the Society of Antiquaries of Scotland 127, 359–86

Needham, S. 2005. Transforming Beaker Culture in north-west Europe; processes of Fusion and Fission. *Proceedings of the Prehistoric Society* 71, 171–217

Nicolis, F. (ed.). 2001 *Bell Beakers Today: pottery, people, culture, symbols in prehistoric Europe.* Trento: Officio Beni Archeologici

Piggott, S. 1971. Beaker bows: a suggestion. *Proceedings of the Prehistoric Society* 37, 80–94

Ralston, I. 1996. Four short cists from north-east Scotland and Easter Ross. *Proceedings of the Society of Antiquaries of Scotland,* 126, 121–55

Reid, R.W. 1924. *Illustrated catalogue of specimens from prehistoric interments found in the north-east of Scotland and preserved in the Anthropological Museum, Marishal College, University of Aberdeen.* Aberdeen: University of Aberdeen

Reid, R.W. & Fraser, Rev. J.R. 1924. A short stone cist found in the parish of Kinneff and Catterline, Kincardineshire *Proceedings of the Society of Antiquaries of Scotland* 58, 27–30

Roberts, I. (ed.) 2005. *Ferrybridge Henge. The Ritual Landscape.* Leeds: Yorkshire Archaeology 10

Robertson, A. 1851–4. Notes of the discovery of stone cists at Lesmurdie, Banffshire containing primitive urns, &c, along with human remains. *Proceedings of the Society of Antiquaries of Scotland* 1, 205–11

Salanova, L. 2000. *La question du Campaniforme en France et dans les îles anglo-normandes: productions, chronologie et roles d'un standard ceramique.* Paris: Editions du Comité des Travaux Historiques et Scientifiques /Société Préhistorique Française

Shennan, S.J. 1976. Bell Beakers and their context in central Europe. In J. N. Lanting & J. van der Waals (eds), *Glockenbecker Symposium Oberried 1974,* 231–40. Haarlem: Fibula-Van Dishoek

Shepherd, A.N. 1989. A note on the orientation of Beaker burials in north-east Scotland, 79–80. In Greig *et al.* 1989, 73–81

Shepherd, A.N. 1996. A Neolithic ring-mound at Midtown of Pitglassie, Auchterless, Aberdeenshire. *Proceedings of the Society of Antiquaries of Scotland* 126, 17–51

Shepherd, I.A.G. this volume. Is there a Scottish Chalcolithic? In M.J. Allen, J. Gardiner & S. Sheridan (eds), *Is there a British Chalcolithic? Place, people and polity in the later 3rd millennium.* Oxford: Prehistoric Society Research Paper 4

Shepherd, I.A.G. 1986. *Powerful Pots: Beakers in north-east prehistory.* Aberdeen: Anthropological Museum, University of Aberdeen

Shepherd, I.A.G. Shepherd, A.N & Bruce, M.F. 1984. A Beaker burial at Mains of Balnagowan, Ardersier, Inverness District, *Proceedings of the Society of Antiquaries of Scotland* 114, 560–6; fiche 2, G8–G14

Shepherd, I.A.G. & Bruce, M. 1987. Two beaker cists at Keabog, Pitdrichie, near Drumlithie, Kincardine and Deeside. *Proceedings of the Society of Antiquaries of Scotland* 117, 33–40

Sheridan, A. this volume. A Rumsfield Reality Check: what we know, what we don't know and what we don't know we know about the Chalcolithic in Britain and Ireland. In M.J. Allen, J. Gardiner & S. Sheridan (eds), *Is there a British Chalcolithic? Place, people and polity in the later 3rd millennium.* Oxford: Prehistoric Society Research Paper 4

Sheridan, J.A. 2007. Scottish Beaker dates: the good, the bad and the ugly. In M. Larsson & M. Parker Pearson (eds), *From Stonehenge to the Baltic: living with cultural diversity in the third millennium BC,* 91–123. Oxford: British Archaeological Report S1692

Sheridan, J.A. 2008. Upper Largie and Dutch-Scottish connections during the Beaker period. In H. H Fokkens, B.J. Coles, J.P. Kleijne, H.H. Ponjee & C.G. Slappendel (eds), *Between Foraging and Farming. An Extended Broad Spectrum of Papers Presented to Leendert Louwe Kooijmans,* 247–60. *Analecta Praehistorica Leidensia 40*

Strickland, M. & Hardy, R. 2005. *The Great Warbow.* Stroud: Sutton

Thomas, N. & Ellwood, C. 2005. Early Bronze Age copper-alloy awls from Sites I and II, with metal analysis and classification. In N. Thomas, *Snail Down, Wiltshire. The Bronze Age Barrow Cemetery and Related Earthworks, in the Parishes of Collingbourne Ducis and Collingbourne Kingston. Excavations 1953, 1955 and 1957,* 219–22. Devizes: Wiltshire Archaeological & Natural History Society

Tuckwell, A.N. 1970. *The Possible Significances of the Orientation and Positioning of Skeletons in the Round Barrows of the Yorkshire Wolds.* Unpublished MA Thesis, University of Edinburgh.

Tuckwell, A.N. 1975. Patterns of burial orientation in the round barrows of East Yorkshire. *Bulletin of the Institute of Archaeology London* 12, 95–123

Turek, J. & Černý, V. 2001. Society, gender and sexual dimorphism of the Corded Ware and Bell Beaker populations. In Nicolis (ed.) 2001, 601–12

Vander Linden, M. 2007. Existe-t-il une archeology sociale? Complexité et structure sociale du complexe à Céramique Cordée. In J. Guilaine (ed.), *Le Chalcolithique et la Construction des Inegalités. Tome 1: Le continent européen,* 75–92. Paris: Editions Errance.

Wedderburn, L.M. Maclagan. 1970. A Short Cist Burial At Hatton Mill Farm, Friockheim, Angus. *Proceedings of the Society of Antiquaries of Scotland* 102, 82–6

Woodham, A.A. 1973. Ladymire, Logie Buchan. *Discovery & Excavation in Scotland,* 3

Woodham, A.A. 1974. Paradise Road, Kemnay: short cist. *Discovery & Excavation in Scotland,* 5–6

18

Chalcolithic Land-use, Animals, and Economy – a Chronological Changing Point?

Michael J. Allen and Mark Maltby

The Beaker period has been considered to be the start of full time farming and a review of the environmental and economic evidence to characterise this is long overdue. The authors attempt to examine the changes associated with the Beaker phase in terms of geoarchaeological and faunal evidence. Despite the surprising few assemblages, and the paucity of well-dated data, indications of increased farming and tillage and of changes in animal husbandry are suggested.

Other papers in this volume provide detailed accounts of the material culture assemblages and associations, metalwork, burial rites, and social and ideological aspects of the period *c.* 2500–2200 BC, constructing (*inter alia*) arguments for and against there being sufficient evidence to justify designation of a distinctive British Chalcolithic. While there can be no doubt that this chronologically restricted period was marked by the currency of very specific and innovative developments in all these areas, there has also grown up an assumption that it witnessed an increase and intensification in farming and sedentism, though few publications cite clear evidence for this on any scale in Britain (eg, Megaw & Simpson 1979; Barker 1985; Bradley 2007). It seems to be largely a default position, given the unequivocal evidence for such intensification in the subsequent millennium.

This paper set out to review the environ-mental evidence for economy, development of organised field systems, and land-use during the period in question and compare it with similar data from the later Neolithic. In so doing we wished to attempt to determine if changes in food economy and land-use went hand-in-hand with other cultural and social developments and represented an equally distinctive economic 'Package'.

Our principal sources of data comprised evidence of fields for cultivation and stock enclosure, the consequent deposits resulting from tillage, and evidence of remains from cereal production and of animal husbandry. The traditional premise is that the onset of farming and, particularly, of mixed farming systems as the primary source of food production led to increased sedentism, underlying, supporting, and enabling the development of social hierarchies articulated by the circulation of portable wealth and objects of display. These achieved their greatest expression in the later 3rd millennium. But can we demonstrate this to be the case?

Our initial expectation was that such a review would enable us to track the development in farming from the cultivation of small-scale plots and exploitation of herds, primarily of cattle on a partially mobile basis, in the later Neolithic through to the demonstrably more organised arable and pastoral farming systems that became widely established by the Middle Bronze Age. In reality, however, this was by no means an easy task to accomplish. It quickly became evident that, in spite of the wealth of archaeological data, there was a severe lack of good, non-funerary, well-dated palaeo-environmental datasets and, especially, datasets associated with clear evidence of domestic activity (cf. Allen 2005a). Alex Gibson (1982, 1), highlighted the difficulty of determining what might constitute 'domestic' evidence in non-monumental contexts and questioned how far the residues of activities performed within henge monuments, or in the later phases of causewayed enclosures, could truly be considered to reflect 'domestic' actions and discard rather than defined ceremonial or ritual acts involving highly selected materials. The picture has proven to be no clearer 30 years later. So, what is our starting point, archaeologically?

1. *Where are the settlements in southern England?* Leaving aside the, as yet not fully analysed, settlement evidence from Durrington Walls, which may have included Beaker-associated occupation in the later stages, much of the domestic evidence from southern England has come from sites dominated by pits, especially in East Anglia (eg, Gibson 1981) and there is little in the way of accompanying palaeo-environmental data. Elsewhere, in spite of postulated settlement inferences (Allen 2005a), no fully functioning, articulating settlement sites have been excavated. Even the well-known finds at Belle Tout (Bradley 1970; 1982) provide only rather ephemeral traces of settlement.

2. *Is there evidence of agriculture?* No field systems associated with Beaker pottery can be defined – but even if they did exist we might not expect them to become visually and archaeologically recognisable as lynchets until the later Early or Middle Bronze Age, when soil erosion had been prevalent for centuries and lynchets started to emerge as clear field monuments.

3. *Can we determine animal husbandry practices?* The dataset of animal remains for the later Neolithic–Early Bronze Age is quite extensive, but a large part of it comes from monumental sites and burial contexts where it may present a biased picture of animal exploitation, which may not provide coherent evidence for a change in relative importance of different species within farmed stock, or of their herd structure.

One of the major difficulties in addressing each of these questions is that of conflation and confusion in terms of the definition of what represents the Late Neolithic, Chalcolithic, and/or Early Bronze Age – and in acquiring environmental material with good dating and clear sequencing of deposits. This lack of chronological clarity renders it difficult to make many evidence-based constructive comments that outline the development of farming trends in terms of the excavated environmental material. What follows, therefore, is not the comprehensive review we had intended, but a series of observations, questions, and comments.

The two authors tackle the subject in different ways. Maltby examines the faunal data from selected sites from various parts of the British Isles to provide a broad regional review, highlighting some of the problems of interpretation. Allen examines the geoarchaeological and land snail evidence, mainly from southern England, in an attempt to provide markers that might then be detected elsewhere. The data for farming, land-use, and cereal cultivation proved to be so sparse and incomplete that no real patterning was immediately evident. Instead, proxy evidence of land-use (erosion products) was examined.

This review of the data is, then, primarily restricted to lowland Britain as that is the region where the majority of relevant datasets are available. Nevertheless, if the changes in economy are as dramatic and clear cut as many texts suggest (eg, Simpson 1971), then examination of a range of data obtained since the late 1970s should allow key features of the subsistence economy and environment of the period to be defined (at least for mainland Britain) and characterised in broad terms.

Land-use and Agriculture (an increase in farming? Farmers not farming?)

The Neolithic is ostensibly defined by progressive clearance of woodland for pasture (but see Allen & Gardiner 2009; 2012), and the presence of farming; that is of the cultivation of cereals and keeping of domestic animals (Parker Pearson 2008), as well as various other cultural traits. The palaeo-environmental evidence for this economic development is, however, surprisingly sparse, poorly-dated, and difficult to access. Most often in text books the Neolithic is considered in one chapter or section and the Bronze Age in another (often by different authors). The agricultural economic evidence, such as it might be, all too often falls between the two and is essentially overlooked (see Simmons & Tooley 1981). Megaw and Simpson (1979), for instance, discuss the 'Beaker Culture' under the headings: Beaker pottery (*c.* 12 pages), Beaker burials (*c.* 3 pages), Beaker domestic sites (*c.* 5½ pages), and material equipment (*c.* 11 pages) as the first section of their chapter on the Early Bronze Age. They pay only lip service to the agricultural economy and farming … and clearly struggled with the concept of the food economy:

> 'An economic argument that is that beaker societies were basically pastoral and nomadic, not requiring any permanent or substantial structures … is in part belied by other economic evidence from the pottery and from certain recognizable house forms' (*ibid.,* 192).

In some parts of Europe the appearance of Beakers occurs at the same time as a pronounced swing towards barley cultivation (Burgess & Shennan 1976, 311), but we do not have the data to be sure that this is broadly applicable to southern England (Dennell 1976). More detailed evidence of agriculture is often difficult to elucidate – mainly because suitable dated contexts have rarely been found containing charred grain (see below). Impressions of cereal grains could provide proxy data but are, again, extremely rare for this period: none was found on the many thousands of sherds of pottery from Northton, Scotland, for instance. Though both cereal cultivation and evidence of arding were recovered from the Beaker settlement at Rosinsh (Shepherd 1976; Shepherd & Tuckwell 1976/77), this remains an exceptional find. The Western Isles

as a whole seem to provide quite a different picture – one rich in Beaker settlement and economic evidence – as Sharples has recently reviewed (2009), falling outside the pattern, and on the geographical periphery, of the data we discuss here.

Since suitable environmental evidence from later 3rd millennium sites is still so difficult to come by, perhaps the examination of proxy-data from 'off-site' sequences may help. Here we can turn to a review of colluvial sequences (cf. Allen 2005a). If there was an increase in tillage and organised farming, and an expansion of clear-felled areas to accommodate this, might we not expect to see this represented in some form in increased colluvial or alluvial sedimentation on a regional, if not local, scale? No single deposit will necessarily provide the evidence, but a general review may detect some broad changes, many accompanied by palaeo-environmental (sediments, snails, and pollen) data. Numerous colluvial sequences have been examined across southern England (Bell 1982; 1983; Allen 1988; 1992; 1995; 2005a, etc.) and many have been dated via the occurrence and distribution of diagnostic archaeological artefacts. In order to make useful comparisons we need to review colluvial deposits which have been archaeologically excavated or from which artefacts have been recorded, and preferably along with another proxy palaeo-environmental indicator (eg, snails). This, by its very nature, means that most of the comparable sites are located on chalk substrates and have a southern distribution (see Bell 1981a, fig. 5.2).

We need, however, to consider which part of the colluvial sequence might correlate with Beaker-related activities rather than those prior or subsequent to them – such as later Neolithic woodland clearance for expansion of pasture for cattle (eg, Thomas 1999) or mature Bronze Age development of formal field systems and intensive agriculture (eg, Fowler 1983). Where would hypothetical sediment influx occur stratigraphically in relation to Beaker 'marker horizons'? Would it be colluvium prior to, or sealing, a Beaker-related buried soil that was a consequence of the hypothetical increase in farming?

Sites of Beaker finds encompassed within colluvium in southern England are indicated on Figure 18.1 and Table 18.1. The distribution, in part, reflects the work of two archaeologists then based in Brighton and Lewes (Martin

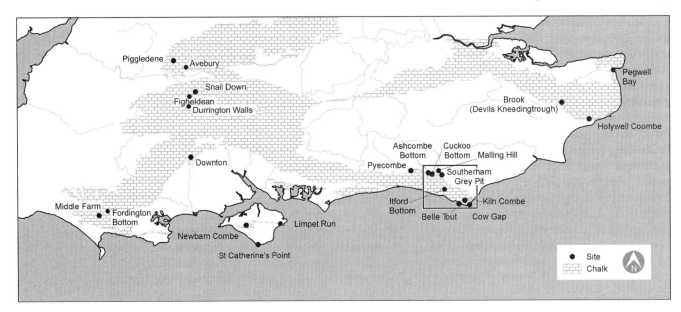

Figure 18.1: Location of Beaker find spots within colluvium and possible Beaker settlement sites on the Downlands of southern England (see Table 18.1 for details)

Bell and Mike Allen respectively), but serves to indicate the potential frequency of these sites. It is significant that many are contained *within* colluvium, indicating a phase of activity resulting in landscape destabilisation *prior to* the Beaker-associated activity. In most cases there is a lack of the survival of basal buried soils and of evidence of Neolithic woodland environments (eg, Allen 1992), as these had been removed by erosion and the surviving colluvium pre-dating Beaker activity may relate to the first phases of increased land-take for farming and of increased tillage. Similarly, many of the sites have been found preserved on or within distinct buried soils developed within the colluvial sequences.

Sites in colluvium associated with clearance
Was Beaker activity associated with expanding areas of clear-fell and opening of new land for agriculture? Very few of the colluvial sequences examined (see Allen 1994; 2005a) seem to indicate woodland clearance associated with dated later Neolithic or Early Bronze Age activity. In Sussex, at Southerham Grey Pit (Fig. 18.1), grassland buried soils containing Beaker pottery and flintwork lay on shallow colluvium that related to clearance of woodland, which may have occurred in the early Beaker period or, more probably, pre-dated it. From the colluvial evidence, therefore, there seems little indication of the establishment of new open landscapes. Even at Holywell Coombe (Bennett *et al.* 1998) where the Beaker

midden lay on early post-glacial muds which, themselves, overlay late glacial chalk marls, although early post-glacial woodland existed there is no indication of its clearance *for* the Beaker activity.

In Buckinghamshire at Pitstone/Marsworth, hillwash was initiated by clearance at 3010–1760 cal BC (3910±220BP, HAR-327), but there is no cultural evidence of Late Neolithic/Beaker activity (Evans & Valentine 1974; Evans 1966).

Sites in colluvium associated with pre-existing established open conditions of Late Neolithic–Early Bronze Age date
At most of the relevant sites where Beaker activity occurred, artefacts lay on and within colluvium, indicating that large erosive events had removed basal woodland soils (these cannot have been subsumed by gradual colluviation as even the molluscan evidence for former post-glacial woodland does not survive) and colluviation resulting from woodland clearance and the onset of farming and tillage had already occurred. Geographically these locations are spread right across the southern chalk from Dorset to Kent, and the Isle of Wight to Buckinghamshire.

In Kent the Beaker midden and occupation material sealed below colluvium at Holywell Coombe sat on early post-glacial chalk muds, into which were scored Beaker ard marks (see below). The land snail evidence indicated that the Beaker activity was, however, probably established in pre-existing open conditions but was, itself, associated with some local regeneration of scrub.

At Cow Gap, Kiln Combe, Ashcombe Bottom, Cuckoo Bottom, and Pyecombe (East and West Sussex) the Beaker-associated buried soils developed in colluvium that was a result of Beaker or pre-Beaker period tillage (and possibly older woodland clearance). Elsewhere, for instance at Newbarn Combe and St Catherine's Point (Isle of Wight), and Piggledene and Fighledean (Wiltshire), Beaker period or Early Bronze Age buried soils were developed in colluvium and, again, overlay, sometimes shallow, colluvial deposits resulting from tillage. This evidence certainly hints at a phase of increased land-use prior to Beaker-associated activity.

Sites on buried soils sealed by colluvium that may have been derived from Beaker or Early Bronze Age activity

Preservation of buried soils within colluvial sequences can, however, only occur if sediment deposition is not simply gradual and gently accumulatory, but included flushes of sediments which rapidly buried and sealed the soil (Allen 1991). But can we take the presence of relatively large numbers of Beaker finds *within* colluvial sequences to indicate the increased farming that we suggest may accompany the adoption of the Chalcolithic social economy, or even the burial of these sites *within* the Beaker/Chalcolithic period? There is no other period or cultural phase that seems to be represented this frequently within colluvial sequences (Bell 1983; Allen 1992; Allen & Scaife 2007 etc.). Although sites of Iron Age, Roman, and medieval date have been found engulfed by colluvium, Beaker finds seem to be more commonly found (or recognised) than those of other periods.

The important point to emphasise here is that these 'sites' were not identified from surface scatters of material, burials, or archaeological features, but as a consequence of environmental investigation and sampling. Two of the sites were subject to full archaeological excavation of trenches and extensive Beaker-related settlement evidence (Kiln Combe and Ashcombe Bottom). Ard marks were found on the Beaker period buried soils (Fig. 18.2). At Ashcombe Bottom tillage was confirmed by soil micromorphology. Ard marks are not very

common finds in British prehistory and have usually been found preserved beneath long barrows (eg, South Street) or round barrows. Ard marks associated with Beaker activity were recorded within dune sand at Rattray (Murray *et al.* 1992) and Rosinish (Shepherd & Tuckwell 1976/77) in Scotland, and at a number of other sites in the Western Isles (see Sharples 2009 – though he sees some of these as deliberate demarcation and symbolic acts occurring prior to creation of burial monuments), as well as at the base of the Beaker midden at Holywell Coombe, Kent (Bennett *et al.* 1998, 286–7, figs 6.16–17), but those at Gwithan, Cornwall, have recently been re-ascribed to the post-Beaker Early Bronze Age (Nowakowski *et al.* 2007). Examples at Brean Down, that score the Neolithic palaeosol and are sealed by Bronze Age blown sand (Bell 1990, figs 19 & 20), have been considered to be Early/Middle Bronze Age (unit 6b) but could conceivably relate to Beaker activity on the site (unit 7). Where ard marks are preserved, and especially where they are preserved in colluvial sequences, we need to consider what they represent. They often survive just as single lines of striation (eg, Fig. 18.2 & 18.3) at the base of buried soils, scoring the horizon below the soil. Are these merely deeper ard impacts that have not been erased by subsequent activity or do they represent deeper scoring as a consequence of rip arding and preparing land, rather than its annual tillage? That being the case then these few records may also be evidence of change in agricultural practices.

The fact that so many lie preserved and sealed by colluvium indicates an ensuing increase in cultivation, but we cannot, in most cases, discern if this related to later Beaker/Chalcolithic activity, Early or even Middle–Late Bronze Age farming.

Settlements: location, recognition, identification, and interpretation

With regard to the location of settlement activity, we could argue that other non-funerary Beaker-related sites occurred elsewhere other than in dry valley, footslope, and colluviated or sand-engulfed locations. Perhaps they have been destroyed by ploughing? The pottery is largely grog-tempered and not as robust as fabrics belonging to later periods, and buildings need not have required deep post-holes (cf. Belle Tout) or even, necessarily, have been post-

	Site	References	Description	Beaker events	Beaker sherds	min no. vessels	Beaker sherds per m³ excavated
	Kent						
1	Pegwell Bay	Weir *et al.* 1971; Kerney 1965; Pitcher *et al.* 1954	Colluvium over loess and chalk. Colluvium post-dates 5550–4490 BC (6120±250 BP) with Neolithic artefacts				
2	Brook, borehole V	Kerney *et al.* 1964		Beaker finds	1	1	40
3	Holywell Coombe	Kerney *et al.* 1980; Bennett *et al.* 1998	Complex colluvial sequence with Mesolithic, Beaker & Roman – but sealed Beaked buried soil & site.	Beaker settlement activity	505–540	*c.* 150	7.3–8.6
4	Devils Kneadingtrough, Brook	Kerney *et al.* 1964; Barker *et al.* 1971	Colluvium initiated by clearance at 3620–2920 cal BC (4540±105BP), Neolithic & Beaker artefacts	Beaker finds	–	–	–
	East Sussex						
5	Belle Tout	Bradley 1970; 1982	In dry valley but not sealed by or on hillwash	Beaker settlement	1180	175	7.9
6	Cow Gap	Bell 1981, 101–2; Allen unpubl.; 2005	Beaker pottery & flints found in buried soil separately by Bell, Allen, and Lovell	Beaker settlement activity	6	3+	40
7	Kiln Combe	Bell 1981, 120; 1983	Beaker pottery in complex buried soil with evidence of erosion during accumulation & ard marks 2280–1740 cal BC (3630±90BP, HAR–5469) from lower buried soil (layer 7)	Beaker settlement activity	101	10+	2.2
8	Malling Hill	Allen 1995	Neolithic pit sealed by Bronze Age lynchet	EBA cultivation	–	–	–
9	Ashcombe Bottom	Allen 1994; 2005b	Beaker buried soil & ard marks	Beaker settlement & cultivation activity	56	20	4.1
10	Cuckoo Bottom	Allen 2005c	Beaker pottery & buried soil	Beaker settlement activity	22	7	3.6
11	Grey Pit	Allen 1995	Beaker pottery & charcoal in buried soil beneath colluvium & associated with clearance	Beaker settlement activity	10	4	>18.2
12	Itford Bottom		Colluvium initiated by secondary clearance at 2480–1770 cal BC (3720±120BP, BM–1545)	Clearance & EBA cultivation	–	–	–
	West Sussex						
13	Pyecombe	Allen 2005a	Beaker pottery & buried soil (with Beaker barrow on skyline)	Beaker settlement activity	4	2	13
	Isle of Wight						
14	Newbarn Combe tr 2	Allen 2005a	Early Bronze Age flint scatter buried under hillwash	EBA knapping	0	0	0
15	St Catherine's Point	K. Trott, pers. comm.; Allen 2005a	Beaker pottery recorded in single layer in hillwash in cliff section	Beaker settlement activity	*c.* 200	n/a	n/a
16	Limpet Run	Allen 1994	EBA pottery & colluvial sequence		–	–	–

Table 18.1: (this page and on the opposite page) List of the main documented colluvial deposits with Beaker finds on the chalk of southern England. The location of these sites is shown in Figure 18.1 (after Allen 1992, table 4.1; 1994, table 4; 2005, tables 1 and 2). Detailed site locations and grid references are given for these in Allen 2005a, table 2; 1994, table 4, and more detailed maps of the area marked within the box is given in Allen 2005a)

	Site	References	Description	Beaker events	Beaker sherds	min no. vessels	Beaker sherds per m³ excavated
	Wiltshire						
17	Downton	Rahtz 1962	Beaker activity in Avon valley on river floodplain terrace	Beaker settlement	183	n/a	0.4
18	Piggledene 1	Fowler 1963; Swanton unpubl.	Beaker finds within colluvium	Beaker settlement activity	6	–	–
19	Piggledene 2	Allen 2005a; Allen 2000	Beaker finds within colluvium – possibly in a buried soil	Beaker settlement activity	4	2	71.4
20	Durrington Walls	Wainwright & Longworth 1971 Parker Pearson *et al.* 2006; 2009	Beaker activity under midden, bankwash & hillwash	Beaker settlement activity	?	?	?
21	Figheldean	Allen & Wyles 1993	Late Neolithic & Early Bronze Age buried soil sealed by prehistoric colluvium	EBA cultivation	–	–	–
22	Snail Down	Thomas 2005	Extensive Beaker finds below barrows in valley & footslope location	Beaker settlement activity	–	–	–
23	Avebury	Evans *et al.* 1993 Allen & Snashall 2009; pers. obs.	a) ?Neolithic–Bronze Age colluvium & alluvium b) ?Grooved Ware–Early Bronze Age colluvium	?Beaker settlement activity	–	–	–
	Dorset						
24	Middle Farm colluvium	Smith *et al.* 1997, 81–4	Beaker post-holes sealed by colluvium	Beaker settlement activity	1	1	0.3
25	Middle Farm excavation	Smith *et al.* 1997, 81–4	Possible settlement activity overlooking dry valley	?Beaker settlement activity	25	5	–
26	Fordington Bottom	Allen 1997b	Post-Early Bronze Age colluvial sequences	EBA cultivation	–	–	–

Figure 18.2: Ard marks on the Beaker buried soils buried by colluvium at Ashcombe Bottom, East Sussex (left) and Kiln Combe, East Sussex (right)

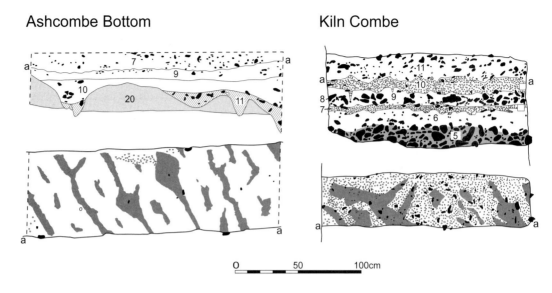

Figure 18.2: Ard marks on the Beaker buried soils buried by colluvium at Ashcombe Bottom, East Sussex (left) and Kiln Combe, East Sussex (right)

built. Further, where non-funerary Beaker remains do occur, finds are more commonly found in isolated or groups of pits with no structures, enclosures, or compounds that we typically associate with later settlements. Where Neolithic settlements have come to light recently, such as at Yarnton, Oxfordshire (Hey 1997), Horton, Berkshire (Gardiner pers. comm.), and Whitehorse Stone, Kent (Hayden 2006), had it not been for the presence of post-built structures, would they have been interpreted as settlements? Further, when Beaker pits are found, they are usually isolated with few other contemporaneous remains, and very rarely are they found in close proximity to a post-built round-house that we could even consider to be of Beaker date (eg, Fir Tree Field, Down Farm, Dorset (Green 2000, fig. 45). Usually the pits seem to contain special and structured deposits rather than what we might recognise as more 'normal' domestic or settlement waste (the same can be said for many animal bone assemblages, see below). At Fir Tree Field the pits yielded little in the way of charcoal or charred plant remains – and the land snail evidence only provided a record of long-established open country conditions. Rarely in southern England do we find sites which we can clearly define as Beaker domestic settlement sites with the typical accoutrements and features we might want, or expect, to find. One recently excavated site is at Wainscott, near Gillingham, Kent, where a saddle quern and charred *Hordeum vulgare* (barley) grain from a pit sealed by post-Roman colluvium have been recovered. The grain was dated

to 2410–2190 cal BC (3859±30 BP, SUERC-32989 and 3810±30 BP, SUERC-3331) and was associated with four Beakers but no other structural or settlement features (Cooke & Seager Smith forthcoming). Even Beaker 'sites' within colluvium that Allen has considered to indicate settlement evidence (2005a) are not proven, as none has been excavated in plan apart from Holywell Coombe, which was interpreted by the excavator as a 'midden'. Clearly more evidence existed beyond the limits of their excavation (Bennett *et al.* 1998).

The exploitation of animals

The faunal evidence from the later 3rd millennium is more extensive than are other palaeo-environmental remains, but it is hardly comprehensive. There are various mantras that have become entrenched in interpretations of the development of animal exploitation in prehistoric Britain. Cattle were the predominant species in the earlier Neolithic based largely on assemblages from causewayed enclosures (Thomas 1999; Ray & Thomas 2003; Serjeantson & Field 2006). This pattern changed in the later Neolithic when pigs become very well represented on a number of sites, often associated with Grooved Ware (Grigson 1982; Thomas 1999; Albarella & Serjeantson 2002). Sometime during the Bronze Age, and certainly by the latter part of this period, pigs generally declined and sheep became significantly more important (Serjeantson 2007; Hambleton 2009). This continued into the Iron Age where sheep dominated most faunal assemblages, although

Figure 18.3: photograph of ard marks on the Beaker soil at Ashcombe Bottom (photo: Mike Allen)

cattle were often well-represented (Maltby 1996; Hambleton 1999; 2009; Albarella 2007). Domestic horses began to appear in faunal assemblages in the later Neolithic (McCormick 2007a; Bendrey 2010), but they are generally relatively rare on Bronze Age sites (Hambleton 2009). The exploitation of wild animals does not appear to have been very important in any period. It is now widely believed that dairy production played a significant role in the exploitation of cattle from the Neolithic onwards (eg, Legge 1981; 1992; Parker Pearson 2008). Cattle may also have increased in importance as plough animals in the later prehistoric period (Hambleton 1999).

In many ways these impressions of animal exploitation have remained fairly constant for a relatively long period, partly because good faunal assemblages from the British Neolithic and Early Bronze Age are still rare. Time and again general statements about animal exploitation have relied on the same handful of, mostly monumental, sites. From southern Britain these include assemblages from the earlier Neolithic causewayed enclosures of Windmill Hill, Wiltshire (Whittle *et al.* 1999), Hambledon Hill, Dorset (Legge 1981; Mercer & Healy 2008) and Etton, Cambridgeshire (Armour-Chelu 1998). For the later Neolithic, there is nearly always a heavy reliance on the

assemblages from Durrington Walls (Harcourt 1971; Albarella & Serjeantson 2002; Albarella & Payne 2005). For the Beaker period, there is almost inevitably a reference to the settlement that developed around Newgrange in Ireland (Wijngaarden-Bakker 1975; 1986; McCormick 2007b), but very little from anywhere else. There is naturally a concern that there is a danger of over-generalising trends in species exploitation from information extrapolated from a sample that is so narrow in range and from a small number of possibly atypical assemblages..

Material from funerary monuments has always been treated with caution by zooarchaeologists as it is assumed that the animal bones deposited may not be representative of 'typical' subsistence strategies. Arguably this could be the case for other assemblages as well. The search for long-term trends has resulted in a lack of discussion of regional, or shorter chronological, variations, perhaps reflecting the impression that such refinements are impossible to achieve given the currently available data. Similarly, there has not been much debate about how rapidly the apparently widespread changes in animal exploitation between the latter half of the 3rd millennium BC and the latter part of the 2nd developed.

It is not surprising that, in recent years, the greatest interest in zooarchaeological assemblages from the Neolithic and Bronze Age periods have been concerned with deposition rather than production (eg, Parker Pearson 2003; Pollard 1995; 2001; 2006). The success of much of this research in demonstrating that many faunal assemblages are not simply random collections of surviving body parts has further discouraged confident interpretation about animal husbandry. Perhaps unexpectedly it has been ceramic residue analysis (eg, Copley *et al.* 2003), and stable isotope studies (eg, Towers *et al.* 2011; Viner *et al.* 2010; Montgomery *et al.* 2007) that have provided most insights into the history of animal exploitation and significantly enhanced our understanding about diet and animal exploitation.

This review focuses upon several faunal assemblages associated with Beaker ceramics from different areas of the British Isles. Do these assemblages contrast with (other) Late Neolithic assemblages? When and where do we get evidence for the beginnings of the emergence of sheep husbandry as a more dominant factor in animal exploitation? Are there regional variations? Can any of these trends be linked with changes or variations in other environmental archaeological data? It is, of course, recognised that comparisons of Grooved Ware, Beaker, and Food Vessel sites, for example, cannot be regarded as simple chronological comparisons, not least because many sites have mixed ceramic assemblages. It is also recognised that pottery production, use, deposition, and its social and symbolic significance need not be directly related to animal husbandry, consumption of their products, deposition of their bones, and their social and symbolic significance.

Southern England

Most known Beaker 'sites' are burials which rarely produce evidence for the deposition of animal bones within the graves themselves. Bones have been found in some of the associated ring-ditches, but are often not closely dated. Animal bones associated with Beaker pottery have been found in a few pits, and secondary ditch fills of some henges and earlier barrows.

The occasional deposition of animals in graves in Beaker and other late 3rd millennium BC burials in southern England has usually involved cattle. These include the so-called

head and hoof burials (Piggott 1962), the best known of which is from Hemp Knoll, near Avebury. The head and feet may have been attached to a hide which was deposited in the grave when the body and coffin were covered, perhaps marking the end of the body being on display (Robertson-MacKay 1980; Williams 2001). At Fordington Farm, near Dorchester, an adult male was laid out with a cattle scapula as a head-rest and a cattle atlas as a foot-rest. Three other filleted cattle scapulae and two scorched humerus fragments were found in the grave. These bones represent processed bones rather than food offerings, although there is no clear evidence that the scapulae were used as shovels (Bellamy 1991).

The animal bone sample from Mount Pleasant, Dorset is one of the largest available, but only consists of 630 bone fragments associated (mainly) with Grooved Ware pottery and 1946 with (mainly) Beaker sherds (Harcourt 1979). Species counts based on minimum numbers of individuals have high percentages of pig (53% and 52% of domestic species respectively), followed by cattle (25% and 27%) and sheep/goat (13% and 18%). Horse was also identified in the late Neolithic material. There is a slight increase in sheep/goat in the Beaker assemblage, but otherwise no real changes in the Beaker horizons. Bones of wild species of mammal and bird are found consistently, albeit in small numbers, in association with both Grooved Ware and Beaker pottery but these include species that are unlikely to have been eaten. As far as we can tell from the published information, deposition of bones and species representation was closely similar in the two horizons. It is the pottery that has changed not the associated activities (Bradley 2007, 152).

A similar phenomenon can be found in the ditch of Coneybury Henge, Wiltshire, where assemblages associated with later Neolithic and subsequent Beaker pottery were both dominated by cattle upper limb bones (Maltby 1990). This example also demonstrates that not all henges have produced high percentages of pig bones, contrasting with the vast assemblage recovered from nearby Durrington Walls in this respect (Alberella & Serjeantson 2002). Sheep/goat bones were, however, poorly represented at both sites.

At Snail Down, Wiltshire, Beaker settlement evidence was found beneath parts of the barrow cemetery. However, only 63 animal bones were identified to species (Clutton-Brock & Jewell 2005). Cattle (59%), sheep/goat (21%), pig (11%), dog (5%), roe deer (2%) and red deer (2%) were identified. No horse remains were found in these occupation deposits, although some were found associated with other sites within the Snail Down complex. Some of the bovid remains are from aurochsen but it is not clear how many of these were found in the settlement deposits.

At Yarnton, on the floodplain of the Upper Thames in Oxfordshire, 166 animal bones from later Neolithic and early Bronze Age middens and pits were identified (Mulville pers. comm.). Cattle (43%), pig (22%), sheep/goat (19%), horse (10%), red deer (5%) and pine marten (1%) were recorded. Sheep/goat became relatively more abundant in the later deposits. However interpretation is limited by the small sample, poor preservation (loose teeth predominated), and the presence of a partial cattle skeleton in a Grooved Ware pit.

A single pit containing Beaker pottery was discovered at Dean Bottom, on the Marlborough Downs. Sheep/goat provided 67% of the 546 fragments identified to species, followed by cattle (26%), pig (4%), roe (2%) and red deer (1%) (Maltby 1992). It is tempting to use this evidence to argue that extensive sheep pasture associated with the expansion of arable farming developed on the Downs at the end of the Neolithic. This assemblage, however, is derived from a deliberate deposit in a single feature and may not reflect the normal dietary regime. Animal bones from other Beaker settlement sites are sparse. At Brean Down, for example, a sample of only 29 identified elements was recovered (Levitan 1990).

Central and eastern England

East Anglia has provided an unusually large number of Beaker-associated domestic sites, particularly near the edges of the Fens, but evidence for animal exploitation is very limited (Bamford 1982). It appears that not all the bones from Hockwold-cum-Wilton on the fen edge in west Norfolk may have been retained. This is unfortunate as species representation from one occupation layer produced high percentages of sheep/goat (66% of domestic mammals). In contrast to many Neolithic faunal assemblages from southern Britain, cattle (24%) and pig (20%) were relatively poorly represented. There is no evidence for horse but roe deer are quite well represented, and also red deer and otter. Many of the sheep were apparently young animals. In contrast, another occupation layer from a neighbouring site was dominated by cattle (75% of domestic mammals) with only (21%) sheep/goat and (5%) pig, no horse and very few red and roe deer. At West Row Fen, another small sample was dominated by cattle, with some sheep/goat, pig, dog, deer antler, and fish (Martin & Murphy 1988).

The challenge of interpreting animal bone deposits in isolated Beaker features is illustrated by the assemblage from two pits from Biddenham Loop, near Bedford (Maltby 2009). One pit produced 646 animal bone fragments associated with a large quantity of Beaker pottery and worked flint. Over 100 fragments were burnt, many slightly eroded and several had been damaged by canid gnawing, indicating much of the mammalian material had been redeposited. At least four pigs were represented including a neonatal mortality, two animals of 6–12 months, and an adult male. A scapula bore filleting marks. Ten cattle bones included four phalanges and a butchered tibia. A section of red deer antler had evidence for working. Roe deer was represented by fragments of a femur and a butchered pelvis.

Fish have been rarely found on Beaker sites but bones from at least two perches and three chub were identified at Biddenham Loop, most of the other fishbones probably also coming from these species. These freshwater species are likely to have been available in the nearby river but there is no definite evidence that they were eaten.

It may be very significant that this unusually rich assemblage was located in fills immediately above a complete Beaker pot. The assemblage, however, provides only limited insights into animal exploitation patterns. Pig, cattle and roe deer were exploited for meat and red deer antler was worked. Most of the species represented are best suited to open woodland habitats, lowland pastures, or aquatic environments and the absence of sheep could reflect the lack of open grassland in the vicinity. However, it would be stretching the evidence to the extreme to extrapolate that the people that deposited material in this pit lived in dense woodland, and routinely subsisted on a diet of pork, beef and occasionally venison and belonged to a community that did not keep or eat sheep. What we have evidence for is the deposition of some of the fauna of these environments, possibly in a single episode, related to a particular significant event. The animals or parts of animals chosen for consumption and deposition may have symbolically represented those environments but they probably were not typical of the general diet.

Two Beaker graves in Northamptonshire, at Irthlingborough and Gayhurst Quarry, included exceptional deposits of cattle bones. At the former, the mound above a male inhumation was festooned with at least 184 cattle skulls along with other selected parts of cattle (scapulae, mandibles and pelves) (Davis 2009; Davis & Payne 1993). At Gayhurst Quarry, a complex sequence of deposition of at least 100, and potentially as many as 300, cattle was associated with another male inhumation, who was buried with a foreleg of a pig (Deighton & Halstead 2004; 2007). In both cases the dominance of cattle probably indicates their paramount importance in the regional pastoral economy and perhaps their association with individuals of high status and prestige. Cattle were obviously kept in sufficient numbers to permit such wholesale slaughter, even allowing for the probability that animals were acquired from many sources, not all of them local (Towers *et al.* 2010; Jay *et al.* this volume). It obviously does not mean, however, that the communities involved ate only beef. Nor do the ages of cattle selected for incorporation into these ceremonies necessarily reflect the typical slaughter patterns for the species. The problem is that we do not have sufficient material from contemporary sites in the region to determine whether the mortality profiles are typical or not. Many Neolithic and Bronze Age cattle assemblages include significant numbers of calf bones. Their presence has been taken to indicate that dairy production was of some importance (eg, Legge 1981), a premise supported by discoveries of ruminant dairy residues on pottery (eg, Copley *et al.* 2003; Craig *et al.* 2005). Calves are less well-represented in these assemblages compared with some other assemblages and young adults were preferentially selected for deposition at Irthlingborough (Davis & Payne 1993).

Scotland

Again there is limited evidence of animal

bones directly associated with Beakers from both settlement and burial contexts in mainland Scotland. Few burials have produced animals bones directly associated with human remains. The few exceptions include a pit from the Seafield West cemetery, Highland, that contained a late 3rd millennium cremation burial accompanied by a mandible of dog or fox (Cressey & Sheridan 2003, 53). Pig bones, usually consisting of forelimb joints, have been found associated with inhumations in at least eight Early Bronze Age graves, some of which also have Beakers (Lawson *et al.* 2002). Animal fats and ruminant dairy products were found during lipid analysis of beakers in a cist burial from Udny Green, Aberdeenshire (Mukherjee & Evershed 2007).

Ireland

McCormick's (2007b) survey of mammal remains from Irish prehistoric sites demonstrated that there has been a substantial increase in the amount of information available since Wijngaarden-Bakker's (1974; 1986) initial analyses of the Beaker material from Newgrange. Unfortunately, however, very few of the recently excavated sites belong to that period.

The assemblage from Newgrange amounted to over 12,000 identified mammal fragments. These were dominated by cattle (58%) followed by pig (34%). Sheep/goat was very poorly represented (3%). Dog (2%) included some associated groups. The site produced the first evidence for domestic horse in Ireland (McCormick 2007b). Wild mammals form only a small proportion of the assemblage, with red deer bones and antlers providing 0.8% of the mammal sample (Wijngaarden-Bakker 1986; McCormick 2007a 85).

Although the Beaker site at Newgrange is often described as a settlement, it would be surprising that, given its location near the entrance of the Neolithic passage grave, it was a typical occupation site. Much of the material may have been depositions associated with feasting (Bradley 2007, 147).

Discussion

We do not yet have the evidence to define changes in cereal cultivation from the later Neolithic into the putative Chalcolithic but, in terms of tillage, there are hints from the colluvial record that Beaker-associated activity may be linked with episodes of colluviation that occured prior to that activity (preparing he land), as well as during and after it (ie, in part, erosion from Beaker-associated tillage). Expectations would be for a systematic expansion of sheep plus cattle based economies at the expense of pig. The evidence, however, is extremely patchy since actual settlement sites are still rare, and those with well-sealed and dated environmental data rarer still.

Our hypotheses was, and in part still is, that the increased cultural wealth seen in the Chalcolithic period is predicated upon increased social economies that were more reliant on the systematic exploitation of domesticated food and farming than on more disparate food collection, gathering, and hunting practices. We see these actions perhaps not as environmental determinism, but environmental possibilism (cf. Bell & Walker 1992, 8) – a view that environments limit, but do not necessarily cause, patterns of human behaviour (Hardesty 1977). In fact, however, there may be no major economic change at the onset of the Chalcolithic, but perhaps the major changes we perceive in the palaeo-environmental data occurred *within* the Chalcolithic period and possibly date to Needham's (2005) *fission horizon* (2250–2150 BC), as Cleal and Pollard indicate for instance for the Stonehenge area (this volume).

With regards to the faunal data, evidence that the widespread expansion of sheep exploitation, largely at the expense of pig, occurred in the Chalcolithic period is extremely patchy. Sheep are well-represented on the occasional site in Wessex and East Anglia and in northern Scotland but continued to be found quite rarely on most sites in Wessex, the English Midlands, and at Newgrange. In many areas, it still seems more likely that this transformation did not take place until later, in the 2nd millennium. In contrast, there is no doubt that cattle husbandry continued to be of paramount importance in many areas – a phenomenon that continued from the earlier Neolithic in areas where assemblages from both periods can be compared. Cattle continued to be exploited for milk as well as meat throughout this period. They probably become one of the major commodities associated with individual power and wealth. On some Beaker sites, pigs formed a significant

and, occasionally, dominant component of the faunal assemblage. However, further work is required to compare these sites more thoroughly with Grooved Ware sites. Recent excavations have supported previous suggestions that domestic horses were introduced to Britain in the later 3rd millennium. They form only a small proportion of most assemblages, however, and are absent from several of the samples considered here. Their rarity and value in improving the speed of travel and possibly warfare would also have placed them within the realm of high status and prestige commodities. It is, however, worth emphasising that substantial faunal assemblages from small settlement sites are extremely rare. Most of the samples are from sites or features that were of special significance and are not necessarily ones which represent a true picture of animal exploitation in this period.

Although the chronological resolution for changes in artefacts and site events around the Neolithic–Bronze Age transition is clearly improving and becoming more precise, that for environmental sequences and economic data still lags woefully behind, despite pleas made over 15 years ago to improve this situation (Allen 1997a, 139). These explicitly included the acquisition of closely dated environmental data; the acquisition and careful dating of long sequences of non-site environmental data and radiocarbon dating to enable the construction of detailed site chronologies and their environmental data-sets to enable intra and extra-site comparisons (Allen 1997a, 139). These pleas still stand and without these data the resolution of the principal and fundamental questions posed in this paper will continue to be hindered.

Acknowledgements

We would principally like to thank Julie Gardiner for editing our text, suggesting revisions, and making improvements. We also thank the referees for pointing us towards data that we'd not been aware of.

Bibliography

Albarella, U. 2007. The end of the Sheep Age: people and animals in the late Iron Age. In C. Haselgrove & T. Moore (eds), *The Late Iron Age in Britain and beyond*, 389–402. Oxford: Oxbow Books

Albarella, U. & Serjeantson, D. 2002. A passion for pork: meat consumption at the British late Neolithic site of Durrington Walls. In P. Miracle & N. Milner (eds), *Consuming Passions and Patterns of Consumption*, 33–49. Cambridge: Monographs of the McDonald Institute

Albarella, U. & Payne, S. 2005. Neolithic pigs from Durrington Walls, Wiltshire, England: a biometrical database. *Journal of Archaeological Science* 32(4), 589–599

Allen, M.J. 1988. Archaeological and environmental aspects of colluviation in South-East England. In W. Groenmann-van Waateringe & M. Robinson (eds), *Man-Made Soils* 69–92, Oxford: British Archaeological Report S410

Allen, M.J. 1991. Analysing the landscape: a geographical approach to archaeological problems. In J. Schofield (ed.), *Interpreting Artefact Scatters; contributions to plough-zone archaeology,* 39–57. Oxford: Oxbow Monograph 4

Allen, M.J. 1992. Products of erosion and the prehistoric land-use of the Wessex chalk. On M. Bell & J. Boardman (eds), *Past and Present Soil Erosion: archaeological and geographical perspectives*, 37–52. Oxford: Oxbow Books

Allen, M.J. 1994.The Land-use History of the Southern English Chalklands with an Evaluation of the Beaker Period using Environmental Data: colluvial deposits as environmental and cultural indicators. Unpublished PhD thesis, University of Southampton

Allen, M.J. 1995. The prehistoric land-use and human ecology of the Malling-Caburn Downs; two late Neolithic/Early Bronze Age sites beneath colluvium, *Sussex Archaeological Collections* 133, 19–43

Allen, M.J. 1997a. Environment and land-use: the economic development of the communities who built Stonehenge (and economy to support the stones). In B. Cunliffe & C. Renfrew (eds), *Science and Stonehenge*, 115–144. Oxford: Proceedings of the British Academy 92

Allen, M.J. 1997b. Evidence of the environment and farming economy, 258–74. In R.J.C. Smith, F. Healy, M.J. Allen, E.L. Morris, I. Barnes & P.J. Woodward, *Excavations Along the Route of the Dorchester By-pass, Dorset, 1986–8*, 277–83. Salisbury: Wessex Archaeology Report 11

Allen, M.J. 2000. Piggledene Bottom: dry valley. In P.J. Fowler, *Landscape Plotted and Pieced; landscape history and local archaeology in Fyfield and Overton, Wiltshire*, 209–11. London: Society of Antiquaries of London

Allen, M.J. 2005a. Beaker settlement and environment on the chalk downs of southern England. *Proceedings of the Prehistoric Society* 71, 219–45

Allen, M.J. 2005b. Beaker occupation and development of the downland landscape at Ashcombe Bottom, near Lewes, East Sussex, *Sussex Archaeological Collections* 143, 7–33

Allen, M.J. 2005c. Beaker and Early Bronze Age activity, and a possible Beaker valley entrenchment, in Cuckoo Bottom, near Lewes, East Sussex. *Sussex Archaeological Collections* 143, 35–45

Allen, M.J. & Gardiner, J. 2009. If you go down to the woods today; a re-evaluation of the chalkland postglacial woodland; implications for prehistoric communities. In M.J. Allen, N. Sharples & T.P. O'Connor (eds), *Land and People; papers in memory of John G. Evans*, 49–66. Oxford: Prehistoric Society Research Paper 2

Allen, M.J & Gardiner, J. 2012. Not out of the woods yet: some reflections on Neolithic ecological relationships with woodland. In A.M. Jones & J. Pollard (eds), *Image, Memory and Monumentality: archaeological engagements with the material world*. Oxford: Prehistoric Society Research Paper 5, 93–107

Allen, M.J. & Scaife, R. 2007. A new downland prehistory: long-term environmental change on the southern English chalklands. In A. Fleming & R. Hingley (eds), *Prehistoric and Roman Landscapes; landscape history after Hoskins*, 16–32. Macclesfield: Windgather Press

Allen, M.J. & Snashall, N. 2009. New features at Avebury from hand coring: geoarchaeology in Action, *Past* 63, 12–13

Allen, M.J. & Wyles, S.F. 1993. The land-use history: the molluscan evidence. In Graham, A. and Newman, C., Excavations of Iron Age and Romano-British enclosures in the Avon Valley. *Wiltshire Archaeological & Natural History Magazine* 86, 45–50

Allen, M.J., Gardiner, J. & Sheridan, A. (eds), 2012. *Is there a British Chalcolithic? Place, people and polity in the later 3rd millennium*. Oxford: Prehistoric Society Research Paper 4

Armour-Chelu, M. 1998. The animal bone. In F. Pryor, *Etton: excavations at a Neolithic causewayed enclosure near Maxey, Cambridgeshire, 1982-77*, 273–88. London: English Heritage Archaeological Report 18

Bamford, H.A. 1982. *Beaker Domestic Sites in the Fen Edge and East Anglia*. Dereham: East Anglian Archaeology 16

Barker, G. 1985. *Farming in Prehistoric Europe*. Cambridge: Cambridge University Press

Barker, H., Burleigh, R. & Meeks, N. 1971. British Museum natural radiocarbon measurements VII. *Radiocarbon* 13, 103–113

Bell, M. 1981a. Valley sediments and environmental change. In M. Jones & G.W. Dimbleby (eds), *Environment of Man: the Iron Age to the Anglo-Saxon period*, 75–91. Oxford: British Archaeological Report 87

Bell, M.G. 1981b. Valley sediments as evidence of prehistoric land-use: a study based on dry valleys in south east England. Unpubl. Ph.D. thesis, London University, Institute of Archaeology

Bell, M.G. 1982. The effects of land-use and climate on valley sedimentation. In A.F. Harding (ed.), *Climatic change in later prehistory*. Edinburgh: University Press, 127–42

Bell, M.G. 1983. Valley sediments as evidence of prehistoric land-use on the South Downs. *Proceedings of the Prehistoric Society* 49, 119–50

Bell, M.G. 1990. *Brean Down excavations 1983–1987*. London: English Heritage Archaeological Report 15

Bell, M.G. & Walker, M.J. 1992. *Late Quaternary Environmental Change: physical and human perspectives*. Harlow: Longman Scientific & Technical

Bellamy, P. 1991. The excavation of Fordington Farm round barrow. *Proceedings of the Dorset Natural History & Archaeological Society* 113, 107–32

Bendrey, R. 2010. The horse. In T. O'Connor & N. Sykes (eds), *Extinctions and Invasions: a social history of British fauna*, 10–16. Oxford: Windgather

Bennett, P., Ouditt, S. & Rady, J. 1998. The prehistory of Holywell Coombe. In R. Preece & D.R. Bridgland,

Late Quaternary Environmental change in north-west Europe; excavations at Holywell Coombe, south-east England, 263–314. London: Chapman & Hall

Bradley, R.J. 1970. The excavation of a Beaker settlement at Belle Tout, East Sussex, England. *Proceedings of the Prehistoric Society* 36, 312–379

Bradley, R.J. 1982. Belle Tout – Revision and re-assessment. In P.L. Drewett, *The Archaeology of Bullock Down, Eastbourne. East Sussex: the development of a landscape,* 12–20. Lewes: Sussex Archaeological Society Monograph 1

Bradley, R. 2007. *The Prehistory of Britain and Ireland.* Cambridge: Cambridge University Press

Burgess, C. & Shennan, S. 1976. The Beaker phenomenon: some suggestions. In C. Burgess & R. Miket (eds), *Settlement and Economy in the Third Millennia B.C.,* 309–31. Oxford: British Archaeological Report 33

Clutton-Brock, J. & Jewell, P. 2005. Remains of the wild and domestic animals. In Thomas 2005, 236–43

Clarke, D.V., Cowie, T.G. & Foxan, A. 1985. *Symbols of Power at the Time of Stonehenge.* Edinburgh: Her Majesties Stationery office

Cleal, R. & Pollard, J, this volume. The Revenge of the Native: monuments, material culture, burial and other practices in the third quarter of the 3rd millennium BC in Wessex. In Allen *et al.* (eds)

Copley, M.S., Berstan, S.N., Dudd, G., Docherty, A.J., Mukherjee, V., Straker, V., Payne, S. & Evershed, R.P. 2003. Direct chemical evidence for widespread dairying in prehistoric Britain. *Proceedings of the National Academy of Science* 100, 1524–9

Craig, O.E., Taylor, G., Mulville, J., Collins, M.J. & Parker Pearson M. 2005. The identification of prehistoric dairying activities in the Western Isles of Scotland: an integrated biomolecular approach. *Journal of Archaeological Science* 32, 91–103

Cressey, M. & Sheridan, A. 2003. The excavation of a Bronze Age cemetery at Seafield West, near Inverness, Highland. *Proceedings of the Society of Antiquaries of Scotland* 133, 47–84

Cooke, N. & Seager Smith, R.H. forthcoming. Prehistoric and Romano-British activity and Saxon settlement at Hoo Road, Wainscott, Kent. *Archaeologia Cantiana*

Davis, S. 2009. The animal remains from Barrow 1. In J. Harding & F. Healy, *A Neolithic and Bronze Age landscape in Northamptonshire. vol 2: the Raunds Area Project Data,* 12–22. Swindon: English Heritage

Davis, S. & Payne, S. 1993. A barrow full of cow skulls. *Antiquity* 67, 12–22

Deighton, K. & Halstead, P. 2004. Reconstructing the burial rite of an Early Bronze Age lord. *Current Archaeology* 195, 114–18

Deighton, K. & Halstead, P. 2007. The cattle bone from Barrow 2, 152–75. In A. Chapman, A Bronze Age barrow cemetery and later boundaries, pit alignments and enclosures at Gayhurst Quarry, Newport Pagnell, Buckinghamshire. *Records of Buckinghamshire* 47, 81–211

Dennell, R.W. 1976. The economic importance of plant resources represented on archaeological sites. *Journal of Archaeological Science* 3, 229–47

Evans, J.G. 1986. Radiocarbon dates from the Pitstone soil at Pitstone, Buckinghamshire, in Gowlett, J.A.J. & Hedges, R.E.M. (eds), *Archaeological Results from Accelerator Dating,* 91–4. Oxford: Oxford University Committee for Archaeology Monograph 11

Evans J.G. & Valentine, K.W.G. 1974 Ecological changes induced by prehistoric man at Pitstone, Buckinghamshire *Journal of Archaeological Science* 1, 343–51

Evans, J.G., Limbrey, S., Maté, I. & Mount, R, 1993. An environmental history of the Upper Kennet valley, Wiltshire, for the last 10,000 years, *Proceedings of the Prehistoric Society* 59, 139–95

Fowler P.J. 1983. *The Farming of Prehistoric Britain.* Cambridge: Cambridge University Press

Fowler, P.J. 1963. The archaeology of Fyfield and Overton Down, Wilts. (second interim report), *Wiltshire Archaeological & Natural History Magazine* 58, 342–50

Garwood, P. this volume. The Present Dead: the Making of Past and Future Landscapes in the British Chalcolithic. In Allen *et al.* (eds)

Gibson, A.M. 1982. *Beaker Domestic Sites; a study of domestic pottery of the third and early second millennia BC in the British Isles.* Oxford: British Archaeological Report 102

Green, M, 2000. *A Landscape Revealed; 10,000 years on a downland farm.* Stroud: Tempus

Grigson, C. 1982. Porridge and pannage: pig husbandry in Neolithic England. In M. Bell & S. Limbrey (eds), *Archaeological Aspects of Woodland Ecology,* 297–314. Oxford: British Archaeological Report S315

Hambleton, E 1999. *Animal Husbandry Regimes in Iron Age Britain: a comparative analysis of faunal assemblages from British Iron Age sites.* Oxford: British Archaeological Report 282

Hambleton, E. 2009. *A Review of Animal Bone Evidence from Southern England.* Swindon: English Heritage

Harcourt, R.A. 1971. The animal bones. In Wainwright & Longworth 1971, 338–50

Harcourt, R.A. 1979. The animal bones. In G.J. Wainwright, *Mount Pleasant, Dorset: Excavations 1970–1971,* 214–23. London: Report of the Research Committee Society of Antiquaries of London 37

Hardesty, D.L. 1977. *Ecological Anthropology.* New York: John Wiley

Hayden, C. 2006. *The Prehistoric Landscape at White Horse Stone, Boxley, Kent.* HS1 Integrated Site report series. In Archaeologica Data Service, 2006. http// archaeologydataservice.ac.uk/archives/view/ctrl/ references.cfm

Hey, G. 1997. Neolithic settlement at Yarnton, Oxfordshire. In P. Topping (ed.), *Neolithic Landscapes,* 99–111. Oxford: Oxbow Books

Hey, G., Mulville, J. & Robinson, M. 2003. Diet and culture in southern Britain: the evidence from Yarnton. In Parker Pearson (ed.) 2003, 79–88

Lawson, J.A., Henderson, D. & Sheridan, A. 2002. An early Bronze Age short-cist burial at Abbey mains Farm, Haddington, East Lothian. *Proceedings of the Society of Antiquaries of Scotland* 132, 193–204

Kerney, M.P., Brown E.H. & Chandler, T.J. 1964. The Late-Glacial and Post-Glacial history of the chalk escarpment near Brook, Kent. *Philosophical Transactions of the Royal Society, London* B.248, 135–204

Kerney, M.P., Preece, R.C. & Turner, C. 1980. Molluscan and plant biostratigraphy of some Late Devensian and Flandrian deposits in Kent. *Philosophical Transactions of the Royal Society, London* B.291, 1–43

Legge, A.J. 1981. Aspecst of cattle husbandry. In R.J.

Mercer (ed.), *Farming Practice in British Prehistory*, 169–81. Edinburgh: Edinburgh University Press

Legge, A. 1992. *Animals, Environment and the Bronze Age Economy*. London: British Museum Press

Levitan, B. 1990. The animal bones. In Bell, 1990, 220–41

Maltby, M. 1990. The exploitation of animals in the Stonehenge Environs in the Neolithic and Bronze Age. In J. Richards, *The Stonehenge Environs Project*, 247–50, plus microfiche. London: English Heritage Archaeological Report 16

Maltby, M. 1992. The animal bone. In C. Gingell, *The Marlborough Downs: a late Bronze Age landscape and its origins*, 137–42. Devizes: Wiltshire Archaeological & Natural History Society Monograph 1

Maltby, M. 1996. The exploitation of animals in the Iron Age; the archaeozoological evidence. In T.C. Champion & J.C. Collis (eds), *The Iron Age in Britain: recent trends*, 17–27. Sheffield: J.R. Collis

Maltby, M. 2009. Animal bones. In M. Luke, *Life in the Loop: investigation of a prehistoric and Romano-British landscape at Biddenham Loop, Bedfordshire*, 16, 92, 118–19, 152–4, 189–92, 238–40, 283–4. Bedford: East Anglian Archaeology 125

McCormick, F. 2007a. The horse in early Ireland. *Anthropozoologica* 42, 85–104

McCormick, F. 2007b. Mammal bone studies from prehistoric Irish sites. In E.M. Murphy & N.J. Whitehouse (eds), *Environmental Archaeology in Ireland*, 77–101. Oxford: Oxbow Books

Martin, E.A. & Murphy, P. 1988. West Row Fen, Suffolk: a Bronze Age fen-edge settlement site. *Antiquity* 62, 353–8

Megaw, J.V.S., & Simpson, D.D.A. (eds), 1979. *Introduction to British Prehistory*. Leicester: Leicester University Press

Mercer, R. & Healy, F. 2008. *Hambledon Hill, Dorset: excavation and survey of a Neolithic monument complex and its surrounding landscape*. Swindon: English Heritage

Montgomery, J., Cooper, R. & Evans, J.A. 2007. Foragers, farmers or foreigners? An assessment of dietary strontium isotope variation in Middle Neolithic and early Bronze Age East Yorkshire. In L. Larsson & M. Parker Pearson (eds), *From Stonehenge to the Baltic: cultural diversity in the third millennium BC*, 65–75. Oxford: British Archaeological Report 1692

Mukherjee, A.J. & Evershed, R.P. 2007. Lipid residue analysis of surface and absorbed organic residues from the beaker, 41–2. In H.K. Murray & I.A.G. Shepherd, Excavation of a Beaker cist burial at Udny Green, Aberdeenshire. *Proceedings of the Society of Antiquaries of Scotland* 137, 35–58

Murray, H.K., Murray, J.C., Shepherd, A.N. & Shepherd, I.A.G. 1992. Evidence of agricultural activity of the later second millennium BC at Rattray, Aberdeenshire. *Proceedings of the Antiquaries of Scotland* 122, 113–25

Needham, S. 2005. Transforming Beaker culture in north-west Europe: processes of fusion and fission. *Proceedings of the Prehistoric Society* 71, 171–217

Needham, S. this volume. Case and Place for the British Chalcolithic. In Allen *et al.* (eds)

Nowakowski, J.A., Quinnell, H., Sturgess, J., Thomas, C. & Thorpe, C. 2007. Return to Gwithian; shifting sands of time, *Cornish Archaeology* 46, 13–76

Parker Pearson, M. (ed.), 2003. *Food, Culture and Identity in the Neolithic and Early Bronze Age*. Oxford: British Archaeological Report S1117

Parker Pearson, M. 2008. Chieftains and pastoralists in Neolithic and Bronze Age Wessex; a review. In P. Rainbird (ed.), *Monuments in the Landscape*, 34–53. Stroud: Tempus

Parker Pearson, M., Pollard, J., Richards, C., Thomas, J., Tilley, C., Welham, K. & Albarella, U. 2006. Materializing Stonehenge: the Stonehenge Riverside Project and new discoveries. *Journal of Material Culture* 11, 227–61

Parker Pearson, M., Pollard, J., Thomas, J. & Welham, K. 2009. Newhenge. *British Archaeology* 110, 14–21

Piggott, S. 1962. Heads and hoofs. *Antiquity* 36, 110–18

Pitcher, W.S., Shearman, D.J. and Pugh, D.C. 1954. The loess of Pegwell Bay, Kent. *Geological Magazine* 91, 308–14

Pollard, J. 1995. Selected deposition at Woodhenge. *Proceeding of the Prehistoric Society* 61, 137–56

Pollard, J. 2001. The aesthetics of depositional practice. *World Archaeology* 33, 315–33

Pollard, J. 2006. A community of beings: animals and people in the Neolithic of southern Britain. In Serjeantson & Field (eds) 2006, 135–48

Rahtz, P.A. 1962. Neolithic and Beaker Sites at Downton, near Salisbury, Wiltshire. *Wiltshire Archaeological & Natural History Magazine* 58, 116–41

Ray, K. & Thomas, J. 2003. In the kinship of cows: the social centrality of cattle in the earlier Neolithic of Southern Britain. In Parker Pearson (ed.) 2003, 37–44

Robertson-MacKay, M. 1980. A 'Head and Hooves Burial' beneath a round barrow, with other Neolithic and Bronze Age sites on Hemp Knoll, near Avebury. *Proceedings of the Prehistoric Society* 46, 123–76

Sharples, N. 2009 Beaker settlement in the Western Isles. In M.J. Allen, N. Sharples & T.P. O'Connor (eds), *Land and People; papers in memory of John G. Evans*, 147–58. Oxford: Prehistoric Society Research Paper 2

Serjeantson, D. 2007. Intensification of animal husbandry in the Late Bronze Age? The contribution of sheep and pigs. In C. Haselgrove & R. Pope (eds), *The Earlier Iron Age in Britain and the Near Continent*, 80–93. Oxford: Oxbow Books

Serjeantson, D. & Field, D. (eds), 2006. *Animals in the Neolithic of Britain and Ireland*. Oxford: Oxbow Books

Simmons, I.G. & M.J. Tooley (eds), 1981. *The Environment of British Prehistory*. London: Duckworth

Simpson, D.D.A. (ed.) 1971. *Economy and Settlement in Neolithic and Early Bronze Age Britain and Europe*. Leicester: Leicester University Press

Thomas, J. 1999. *Understanding the Neolithic*. London: Routledge

Thomas, N. 2005. *Snail Down, Wiltshire: the Bronze Age Barrow Cemetery and related Earthworks, in the Parishes of Collingbourne Ducis and Collingbourne Kingston: Excavations, 1953, 1955 and 1957*. Devizes: Wiltshire Archaeological & Natural History Society Monograph 3

Towers, J., Jay. M., Mainland, I., Nehlich, O. & Montgomery, J. 2011. A calf for all seasons? The potential of stable isotope analysis to investigate prehistoric husbandry practices. *Journal of Archaeological Science* 38, 1858–68

Shepherd, I.A.G. 1976. Preliminary results from the Beaker settlement at Rosinish, Benbecula. In C.

Burgess & R. Miket (eds), *Settlement and Economy in the Third Millennia B.C.* 209–20. Oxford: British Archaeological Report 33

Shepherd, A. this volume. Stepping out together: men, women and their Beakers in time and space. In Allen *et al.* (eds)

Shepherd, I.A.G. & Tuckwell, A.N. 1976/77. Traces of beaker-period cultivation at Rosinish, Benbecula, *Proceedings of the Antiquaries of Scotland* 108, 108–13

Smith, R.J.C., Healy, F., Allen, M.J., Morris, E.L., Barnes, I. & Woodward, P.J. 1997. *Excavations along the Route of the Dorchester By-pass, Dorset, 1986-8.* Salisbury: Wessex Archaeology Report 11

Viner, S., Evans, J., Albarella, U. & Parker Pearson, M. 2010. Cattle mobility in prehistoric Britain: strontium isotope analysis of cattle teeth from Durrington Walls. *Journal of Archaeological Science* 37, 2812–20

Wainwright, G.J. & Longworth, I.H. 1971. *Durrington Walls: excavations 1966–1968* 338–50. London: Report of the Research Committee Society of Antiquaries of London 29

Weir, A.H., Catt, J.A. & Madgett, P.A. 1971. Postglacial soil formation in the loess of Pegwell Bay, Kent (England), *Geoderma* 5, 131–49

Whittle, A., Pollard, J. & Grigson, C. 1999. *The Harmony of Symbols: the Windmill Hill causewayed enclosure.* Oxford: Oxbow Books

Wijngaarden-Bakker, L.H. van, 1974. The animal remains from the Beaker settlement at Newgrange, Co. Meath: first report. *Proceedings of the Royal Irish Academy* 74C, 313–383

Wijngaarden-Bakker, L.H. van, 1986. The animal remains from the Beaker settlement at Newgrange, Co. Meath: final report. *Proceedings of the Royal Irish Academy* 86C, 1–92

Williams, H. 2001. Lest we remember. *British Archaeology* 60, 20–3

19

The Present Dead: the making of past and future landscapes in the British Chalcolithic

Paul Garwood

The spatial distribution and frequency of early Beaker burial events in Britain are not well-understood. Prevailing interpretations of monuments, bodies, and artefacts as symbolic media for constructing identities in death are attractive, but it is altogether less clear how, why, and by whom these identities were created. This paper examines the nature of early Beaker burials from a landscape perspective, showing how a series of distinctive spatial strategies articulated relationships among monuments, spaces, people, and practices. These addressed tensions between past and present, foreign and native, reconfiguring past and present landscapes in efforts to delineate imagined landscapes of the future.

Beaker funerary practice in Britain is often treated in isolation as if this 'tradition' had a life of its own disengaged from other fields of cultural discourse. It is increasingly apparent, however, that the presence of Beakers was less pervasive and their significance more specific and contingent than is often portrayed (Bradley 2007, 142–53). At the same time, the assumed long-term continuity of the symbolic schemes represented in Beaker graves now appears questionable, especially in the light of the changing social and landscape contexts of such burials over time (Needham 2005; Garwood 2007a). We are confronted with not one but several different kinds of Beaker funerary expression during the Chalcolithic and Early Bronze Age.

Most studies of Beaker graves focus either on typo-chronological and contextual analyses of burials and grave goods, or large-scale regional and inter-regional patterns of cultural representation, in both cases seeking to draw general social-symbolic and cultural conclusions about the nature of the 'Beaker Phenomenon'. In contrast, it is remarkable how little work has been undertaken on the particular social circumstances and cultural landscape contexts of Beaker graves 'on the ground' (though see Thomas 1999, 162–220). The purpose of this paper is to examine the geography and character of early Beaker burials in Britain with respect to the distinctive cultural landscapes of funerary performance and memorialisation they helped to create.

New lands: visions of cultural interaction and dissemination

A two-stage process of Beaker dissemination is now widely recognised: an initial 'pioneering' or 'contact' phase lasting a few generations at most, followed by a long drawn-out process of consolidation and indigenous adoption (Needham 2005; 2007, 42–3). There is no question that the initial phase at least involved long-distance movements of people, as isotopic analysis of human bone from Beaker burials in several parts of Europe demonstrates (eg, Evans *et al.* 2006; Fitzpatrick 2003; Price *et al.* 1998; 2004). The scale and frequency of these movement are unknown but it is likely that such 'isotopic aliens' (Needham 2007) were not numerous and probably travelled from several different European regions (Sheridan 2008a, 63–4). Whilst current research in Britain, notably the *Beaker People Project* (Jay & Montgomery 2008), may yet prove otherwise, a general picture of movement by mostly small groups along pre-existing networks of social and economic interaction may be emerging (Bradley 2007, 143–4; Sheridan 2008b; Vandkilde 2001).

Far less certain, however, are the particular means by which 'foreign' Beaker social networks and modes of cultural representation penetrated native societies, and why some regions and not others attracted Beaker 'travellers' or adopted their practices (Bradley 2007, 142–4). The search for metal sources, the forging of new exchange networks (Needham 2005, 208), and the journeys of roving warriors or chiefs and their retinues (Needham 2000), are often seen as the prime-movers, while non-Beaker cultural worlds may themselves have offered attractions to 'foreigners' such as renowned ceremonial centres and shrines that drew pilgrims from far afield for cultic and medicinal reasons (Darvill 2006a, 151; Fitzpatrick 2009, 183–4). These explanations, however, rarely take full account of the particular spatio-temporal and cultural constitution of each 'Beaker society' at a regional level. In the Netherlands, pre-existing single grave traditions underpinned a high degree of cultural continuity, producing a fusion of Beaker and Corded Ware cultural repertoires during the mid-3rd millennium cal BC (van der Beek & Fokkens 2001). In Britain, in contrast, it is possible to suggest greater ethno-cultural distinctions, and more intense rivalries and possible ideological conflicts that resonated through a series of social transformations over a period of six or seven centuries (Needham 2005).

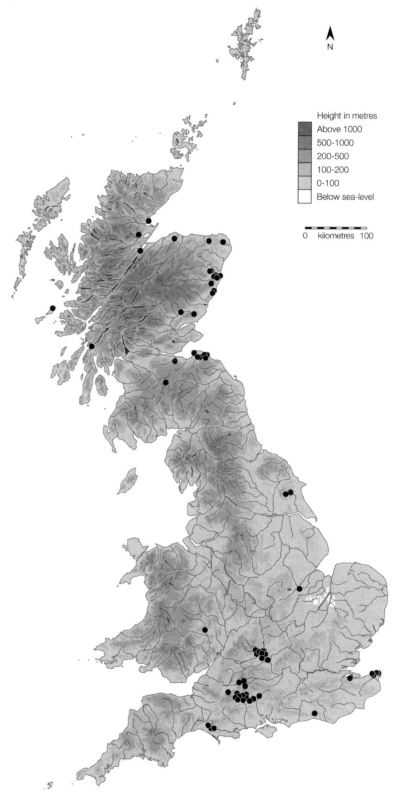

Figure 19.1: Distribution of early Beaker graves in southern Britain, c. 2500–2150 cal BC

It is evident, therefore, that the implantation of Beaker culture owed as much to the actions of 'native' groups as those of 'Beaker incomers' (Needham 2007, 42–3). In this context, ideas of prestige goods exchange (Shennan 1986) and 'cult package' transmission (Burgess & Shennan 1976), despite criticisms (eg, Fitzpatrick 2009, 178; Fokkens *et al.* 2008, 124–5), have proved resilient as ways of accounting for indigenous interest in acquiring 'things Beaker': without them, the various kinds of 'conversion', 'defection', and 'emulation' proposed as modes of acculturation lose their rationales and the *substance* of Beaker-related practices and beliefs that made them desirable becomes elusive. Marriage exchange systems involving female exogamy into expansive Beaker kin groups, either across a 'Chalcolithic frontier' (Brodie 1997; 1998) or among interjacent populations, is also a compelling explanation (Needham 2005, 208; Price *et al.* 1998, 410), although the marriage exchanges imagined are materially invisible and the strategies of ethnic transference are unexplained.

Whilst the spread of Beaker culture in Britain, as elsewhere, remains contentious, it is possible to recognise distinct patterns in the distribution of Beaker graves which may help to clarify the character and frequency of funerary events (Fig. 19.1). Well-dated burials are extremely rare before 2300 cal BC and only appear relatively common from *c.* 2150 cal BC (Needham 2005). It is also apparent that the distribution of early Beaker graves is very uneven (Case 2001; Sheridan 2008a, 65–6): although new discoveries will inevitably modify the overall picture, some regions appear to lack such graves entirely, including most parts of the West Midlands (Garwood 2007b), south-east England (Garwood 2003), east-central Scotland (Wilkin 2009), the south-west peninsular, and East Anglia. Most revealing, perhaps, is the clustering of Beaker graves close to Late Neolithic ceremonial complexes. This has been noted for some time, but the pattern seems to be an enduring one, and is all the more convincing considering the results of extensive developer-funded excavations throughout Britain over the last 20 years. These have taken place in a diverse range of geo-environmental zones, in areas both with and without Neolithic ceremonial monuments, yet for the most part these reinforce existing distributions of early Beaker burials. These observations highlight the critical importance of establishing the local, indigenous contexts of primary Beaker contact and the significance of early Beaker burials within specific *landscape* settings.

Identity, personhood, and early Beaker funerary ritual

Identification of the person-kinds present in Beaker burials is clearly important for understanding the significance of funerary events and the places of burial and memorialisation in the landscape. It is important to recognise, however, that funerary representations of society and personhood may bear little relation to everyday relationships but instead convey ideal social or sacred stereotypes (Thomas 1991; Fokkens *et al.* 2008, 124–5), while human bodies may be subject to such dramatic transformations of meaning in ritual acts that they cease to be 'people' at all (Garwood 2007c). Indeed, the rarity of burials of complete or articulated bodies in Britain during the 3rd millennium (Gibson 2007) suggests that mortuary practices *normally* involved body disaggregation and dissolution, which must cast doubt on the usual assumption of symbolic emphasis on 'individuality' in mortuary customs (Barrett 1988; cf. Thomas 2000). But this cuts both ways: if the majority of the people who comprised Chalcolithic populations never found their way after death into formal deposits, then the efforts made in Beaker burials to sustain the integrity of individual bodies as 'whole' things are all the more striking.

This issue has direct relevance to recent discussions of the relational construction of identity in prehistoric mortuary practices (eg, Brück 2004; Jones 2005). These offer some compelling new perspectives on aspects of identity construction, but rely heavily on a polemical dichotomisation of individualism/ modernity/us *versus* dividualism/pre-modernity/them. This seems overstated: whilst we idealise individuality we also embrace dividuality in our own lives, recognising that our expressions of identity are situational and relational constructs which change as we move from one social setting to another (depending on the context of interaction, motives, etiquettes, and other person-kinds present). Conversely, there is no reason to think that people in prehistory did not express *in*dividuality in their lives just as strongly as we do. Indeed, the technologies of remembrance implicated in early Beaker funerary rituals seem focused precisely on the maintenance of individual bodies and their outward appearances, perhaps to control dividuality and construct representations of ideal, bounded person-kinds in the specific circumstances of burial events (cf. Thomas 1991). This suggests not so much a concern with lived individuality or biography, but rather the iconic status of individual bodies as a means of mediating undivided and exclusive kinds of identity in death. The question that arises, of course, is what kinds of identities were created in this way and why.

Gender differentiation is often seen as the primary structuring principle in Beaker society (eg, Drenth & Hogestijn 2001; Mizoguchi 1993), probably ascribed from early childhood (Drenth & Lohof 2005; Garwood 2007c, 76), with precedence in Beaker burials usually given to adult males. In Britain, there are gendered contrasts in terms of body postures, orientations, and associated artefacts (Gibbs 1990; Sofaer Derevenski 2002; Thomas 1991), with males usually placed in central positions and primary contexts in grave sequences, perhaps to demonstrate cosmological primacy as the progenitors of the living, while the rarity and simplicity of women's graves, and their secondary positions in relation to males, may suggest a more 'subordinate' status (Mizoguchi 1993, 227; Lucas 1996, 108–9). Although the display of weapons in Beaker graves may point to 'aggressive male individualism' or a warrior ethos (Heyd 2007, 357–8), the idea of a distinct warrior elite is more debatable. Warrior/hunter symbolism, myths, and narratives may instead have projected an aesthetic of male prowess and of violent 'power over' living kinds, portrayed by archery equipment and daggers for the 'hunting' of animals, human foes, and perhaps 'monsters' (Case 2004b; Fokkens *et al.* 2008). Alongside or as an alternative to weapons, some male graves contain items that suggest productive and 'magical' processes that probably evoked power over the material world and human and animal reproductive capacities (Fitzpatrick 2009).

It is widely assumed, of course, that Beaker burials embodied a range of meanings other than gender, including ethnicity and status. The

significance of ethnicity in funerary symbolism is especially difficult to gauge. Whilst it may have been important for Beaker groups to sustain a sense of ethnic distinctiveness as their cultural networks became stretched (Needham 2007, 44), this may not have been represented as a single 'identity'. Contrasts between Beaker groups with different continental origins, for example, may have been carried over into Britain, resulting in many different expressions of 'Beaker' culture (Case 2004b; Needham 2005, 179). This has intriguing implications for our understanding of ethno-cultural diversity (Case 1993; Sheridan 2008b) as well as possible relations of exclusion and conflict *within* the wider Beaker *ecumene*. Interpretations of Beaker social organisation are just as ambiguous, ranging from 'egalitarian' communities headed by warrior sodalities (Sarauw 2007) to ranked societies with an elite stratum marked by rich graves (Case 2004a). Similarly, suggested Beaker social units range from 'families' (Turek & Černý 2001) to 'clans' (Healy & Harding 2004) or 'elite kin groups' (Case 2004a). The issue of hierarchy is particularly vexed: there is little evidence for centralisation, defended sites, or craft specialisation (Heyd 2007, 338–9; Vandkilde 2001, 353), yet the presence of 'prestige goods', rich graves, and – in some areas – ceremonial centres has encouraged recognition of social complexity (eg, chiefly polities: Shennan 1982; 1986; Thorpe & Richards 1984). In this context, Beaker funerals may have been a means to assert solidarity in the midst of larger numbers of potential enemies whose systems of authority were seen as threatening, while monument-building and ceremonies conducted by indigenous groups may have been a means to resist unsettling Beaker influences (Bradley 2007, 153; Needham 2007). The increasing number and diversity of Beaker burials in Britain in the late 3rd millennium could thus be seen as symptoms of *growing* tensions over religious authority, land, identity, and political leadership.

It is apparent, however, that all of these interpretative approaches – based primarily on readings of graves alone – risk confusing the meanings of funerary deposits because *in themselves* they usually provide no way to contextualise acts of burial in relation to the intentions of the people who 'made the dead'. In particular, these approaches tend to ignore a dimension of social practice critical to the

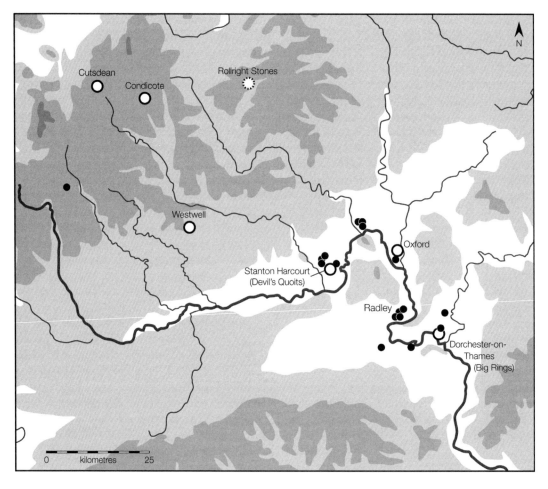

construction of meaning in funerary ritual – the *places* selected for burial events and their spatial relationships to other significant places and practices in the cultural landscape. Instead of using the evidence from burials to arrive at an understanding of 'Beaker society', it may be better to gain an understanding of the social significance of particular places of burial in the landscape in order to understand the meaningful construction of the dead and the materials surrounding them.

Beaker graves in the landscape

The very limited attention paid to the spatial contexts of Beaker graves may be due in part to the theorisation of Late Neolithic ceremonial landscapes as 'structured', synchronic expressions of cosmological order, with numerous variations on themes of structured opposition, concentric symbolic ordering, and relationships among the living, the dead, and the ancestors (eg, Darvill 1997; Field 1998; Parker Pearson & Ramilisonina 1998;

Parker Pearson 2000). Whilst not dismissing the value of these theoretical perspectives or the importance of prehistoric cosmography, these studies in some respects have had a baleful effect on Chalcolithic landscape studies. In particular, the application of essentially synchronic interpretative models to great swathes of time, conflating distinct stages of Beaker funerary practice within an even longer-term model of symbolic order, has led to unsubtle appreciations of the changing constitution of cultural and political space, the temporalities of beliefs and their representation, and the significance of practices in particular landscape settings. Such an approach seems less and less warranted, however, given increasingly precise radiocarbon timescales and growing recognition of the rapid changes that took place during the later 3rd millennium (eg, Bayliss *et al.* 2007). In any case, the validity of an all-encompassing symbolic-structural interpretation is arguable at best: it is better to assume that Late Neolithic/Chalcolithic cosmographic schemes were malleable from

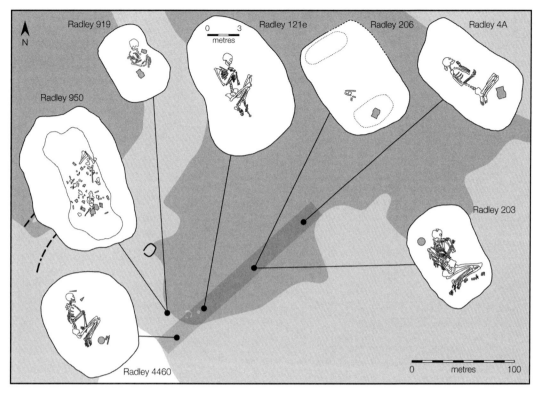

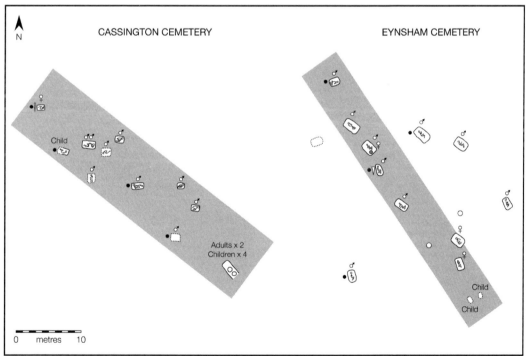

Figure 19.3: Linear arrangements of Beaker graves in the Upper Thames valley: Top: the Radley Beaker grave alignment; Bottom: the Eynsham and Cassington 'flat grave' cemeteries

one generation to the next, exposed to alternative visions of truth and order, and subject to a ceaseless play of changing, multiple meanings (Thomas 1999, 37–8).

The spatial locations of early Beaker graves are especially relevant to this debate. These burials were probably marked in most cases by small mounds that fixed and made visible the places of the dead in the landscape, giving the past a material presence to guide future memories, perceptions and, action (Barrett 1994, 112; Garwood 1991). Their presence

Figure 19.4: Beaker graves located at Late Neolithic monument sites in the Upper Thames valley: Top: Dorchester-on-Thames: Big Rings henge and Site XII; Bottom: Stanton Harcourt Site XXI (Linch Hill Corner)

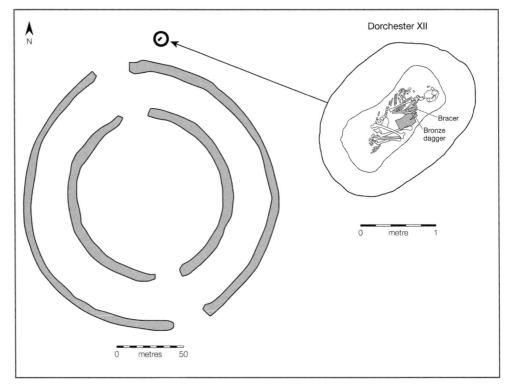

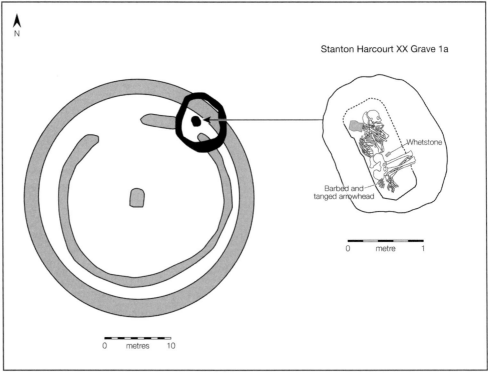

in many cases close to existing ceremonial monuments also suggests the creation of particular relationships with other elements of the built landscape. The meanings attached to burials, the dead persons present, and

artefact selection and placement were thus bound up with the specific locales chosen for funerary deposition and monument building: we need to investigate where and when these took place and the ways in which intended

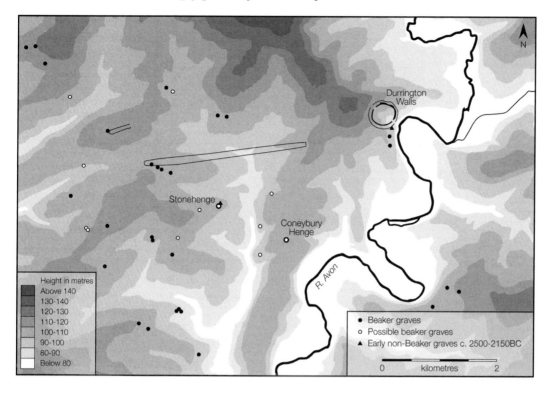

Figure 19.5:
Distribution of Beaker
graves in the Stonehenge
landscape

meanings were conveyed. Investigation of the landscape contexts of Beaker graves is thus crucial, being the principle means we have to explore how their creators construed their actions in relation to the wider world in which they lived. The evidence from the upper Thames valley, Stonehenge, and the other areas discussed below suggests that each Chalcolithic landscape saw complex interplays between political, social, and religious beliefs and agendas, with varied but comparable use of practical and architectural media to realise particular strategic objectives.

The upper Thames valley

A recent review of the evidence from the upper Thames valley (Garwood 2011; cf. Healy 2004) reveals some striking patterns in the frequency, distribution, and location of Beaker burials (Fig. 19.2). Although the dating evidence is often imprecise, early Beaker graves appear to be absent before *c.* 2350/2300 cal BC (especially if the date from Radley grave 919 is unreliable: A. Barclay, pers. comm.; Barclay 1999a, 55–7). Most are clustered close to Late Neolithic ceremonial monuments, with earlier burials occurring mainly on the river terraces between Dorchester-on-Thames and Stanton Harcourt, followed by later expansion

upstream after *c.* 2100 cal BC (eg, burials at Lechlade and Shorncote: Barclay & Glass 1995; Darvill 2006b). Overall, nearly all of the burials are of adults, the majority male, although it is notable that about half of the earliest Beaker graves are those of women, contrary to usual expectations about male primacy in terms of their supposed 'status' and 'leading' role in early Beaker society.

Most of the adult male inhumations lie on their left sides, heads to north/north-west and facing east (see Fig. 19.3). These include early burials at Radley 4A (Barclay 1999b), probably Radley 4660 and 950 (Barclay 1999a), and Stanton Harcourt XXI ring ditch 1a (Linch Hill: Barclay 1995, 99), all probably dating to *c.* 2350–2100 cal BC. Radley burial 607 shares most of these attributes although it lacks a Beaker (Barclay 1999a). There are also a few well-equipped adult male burials dating to the period *c.* 2200–2000 cal BC on their left sides, heads to the north-east/east, facing south-east, including graves at Dorchester-on-Thames XII (Whittle *et al.* 1992) and Gravelly Guy X6 (Lambrick & Allen 2004). The predominantly male graves in the flat cemeteries at Cassington (Leeds 1934) and Eynsham (Leeds 1938) probably also belong to this phase (Fig. 19.3). Female Beaker graves are rarer and

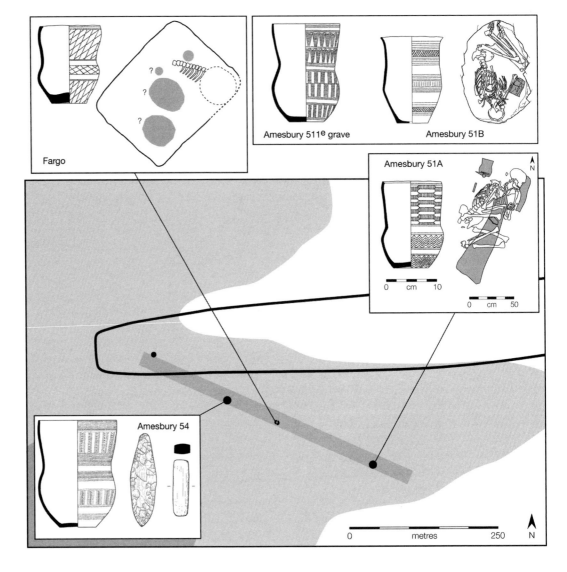

less consistent in lay-out: these include Gene Function Centre grave 204, Oxford (Boston *et al*. 2003), a Beakerless burial with a copper awl at Abingdon (Allen & Kamash 2008) both dating to the period *c*. 2350–2100 cal BC, and later graves such as Mount Farm 618 (Lambrick 2010), and Stanton Harcourt 1054 and Grave II.2 (Lambrick & Allen 2004; Barclay 1995). Unlike adult males, these almost never have their heads towards the north and are more likely to lie on their right sides, but otherwise they share few features in common. It is also notable that all the individuals with large artefact sets are male, while female graves contain fewer items selected from a limited range of categories (Gibbs 1990, 72–133; Sofaer Derevenski 2002).

Most of these burials were located close to pre-existing ceremonial monument groups at Stanton Harcourt (Barclay 1995; Lambrick & Allen 2004), Oxford (Dodd 2003, 7–10; Boston *et al*. 2003, 179–82), Radley (Garwood 1999), and Dorchester-on-Thames (Whittle *et al*. 1992), suggesting deliberate attempts to make use of landscape settings that were already resonant with religious or political significance. Two striking spatial patterns stand out: the organisation of burials in lines and the positioning of graves immediately beside Late Neolithic monuments. The alignment of early Beaker-associated burials at Radley (Fig. 19.3; Garwood 1999, 304, fig. 9.7) indicates careful spatial inter-referencing of burial events, perhaps in sequence from north-east (Barrow 4A: 2470–2200 cal BC) to south-west (Grave 607: 2210–2030 cal BC). It is possible these were positioned along an existing route which ran past ring ditch 611, several Grooved

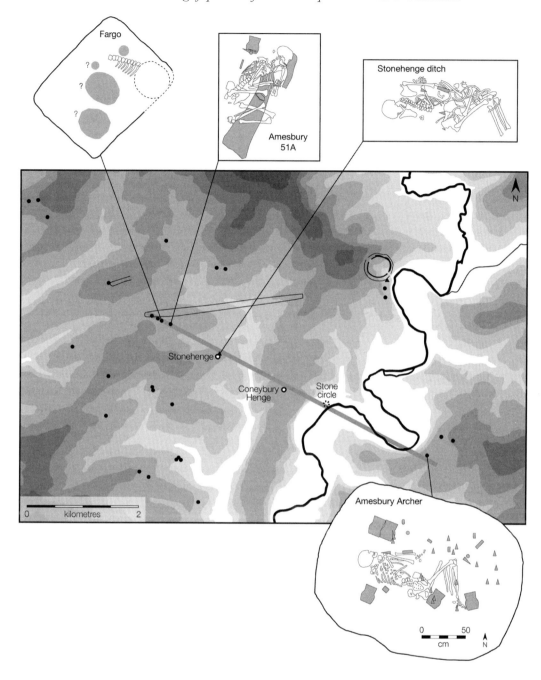

Ware pits, and a probable Late Neolithic segmented ring ditch. The more densely clustered linear arrangements of Beaker flat graves at Cassington and Eynsham, in both cases oriented broadly north-west to south-east, again suggest deliberate alignment, possibly parallel to routes or boundaries. At Radley it is notable that the line of graves ran between and past the Neolithic monuments rather than towards them, which may indicate that these evoked only ambiguous or remote interest. There are also two examples of Beaker graves located immediately beside or superimposed on pre-existing monuments (Fig. 19.4): Site XII beside the Big Rings henge at Dorchester-on-Thames (Whittle *et al.* 1992), and Stanton Harcourt Site XXI/1 cutting the Late Neolithic double ring ditch at Linch Hill Corner (Barclay 1995, 99–100). Neither of these burials is radiocarbon dated but, on the basis of artefact associations and grave forms, it is likely that they belong to the period *c.* 2300–2000 cal BC.

These contrasting ways of positioning

Beaker graves in the landscape may not be contemporaneous, it is possible that *earlier* single graves and linear groups were located some distance from the larger still-used Late Neolithic monuments, while *later* intrusive burial events took place immediately adjacent to or were imposed directly on the physical forms of earlier structures. Alternatively, decisions about the locations of Beaker graves may have been dictated throughout the period by the specific histories and interactions of different communities and the significance they attached to monuments and the ritual performances enacted at them. Whether contemporaneous or not, the different kinds of burial location clearly suggest different perceptions of the built environment, things of the past and relationships with other 'communities', living and dead, the potential significance and meanings of which are discussed below.

The Stonehenge landscape

The spatial distribution and chronology of early Beaker burials in the Stonehenge landscape are especially revealing (Fig. 19.5). Our knowledge of these is considerable, based on recent summaries of the site evidence (Cleal *et al.* 1995; Darvill 2006a; Exon *et al.* 2000; Grinsell 1957; 1979; Lawson 2007), assessments of artefact assemblages in major catalogues and site reports (eg, Annable & Simpson 1964; Clarke 1970; Green & Rollo-Smith 1984), and recent discoveries of Beaker graves to the south-west of Stonehenge (Leivers & Moore 2008) and at Boscombe on the east side of the Avon (Evans *et al.* 2006; Fitzpatrick 2003; A. Barclay, pers. comm.). Although it is important to recognise that antiquarian and archaeological investigation across the landscape has been uneven and selective, especially in relation to the lack of excavation of truncated barrows close to Stonehenge, and more general biases reflected in the lack of attention given to areas such as the hills to the east of the Avon and the military estates to the north of the Cursus (Lawson 2007, 363–84), several aspects of known early Beaker burial location stand out.

It is noticeable, for example, that the small number of graves probably dating to the period before 2300 cal BC, found to the south and west of Stonehenge at Wilsford G1, G2b, and G54, and just north of Wilsford

G1 in trench 15 beside the A303 (dated to 2460–2290 cal BC; Leivers & Moore 2008), are all located at least 1 km from Stonehenge in places that were not visible from the central sarsen monument. The early Beaker graves to the east of the Avon, including the Amesbury Archer, and to the west at Shrewton 5k, were spatially distanced from Stonehenge and again out of sight. In contrast, several graves dating to the period *c.* 2300–2100 cal BC are intervisible with Stonehenge, notably the burials on the ridge to the north-west at Amesbury 51 (Ashbee 1975/6) and Fargo Plantation (Stone 1938), which form part of a linear alignment of monuments (Fig. 19.6) including at least three more Beaker-associated round barrows, Amebury 54, 56, and Winterbourne Stoke 30 (also noted by Lawson: 2007, 154, fig. 5.23).

It is especially notable that extension of this alignment south-eastwards connects together some of the most impressive ceremonial monuments and burials in this landscape, including Stonehenge (Fig. 19.7). From north-west to south-east, this alignment runs from the west end of the Cursus, beside the linear Beaker barrow group and Fargo henge, past the north-west entrances of both the Stonehenge enclosure (beside the Heel Stone) and Conebury Henge, to a point on the River Avon just south of the stone circle site (dating to *c.* 2470–2200 cal BC; Parker Pearson *et al.* 2009) at the starting point of the Avenue, and – if continued to the east of the Avon – it runs just to the south of the Amesbury Archer burial (2470–2280 cal BC; Fitzpatrick 2009). Moreover, the only known inhumation burial with Beaker-associated material (wristguard and barbed and tanged arrowheads) situated close to Stonehenge, dating to *c.* 2200–2000 cal BC, was found in the ditch on the north side of the Stonehenge enclosure (Evans 1984) at its closest point to this line. It is just conceivable that this spatial pattern is coincidental, but it seems extraordinary that so many prominent monuments and graves datable to the period *c.* 2500–2000 cal BC, including the 'centrepiece' of the ceremonial landscape and several artefact-rich Beaker-related burials, should all be situated along an exactly straight corridor traversing some 5 km of the Stonehenge landscape, unless linked in some way. The most straightforward explanation is they were situated with reference to an important route across the landscape.

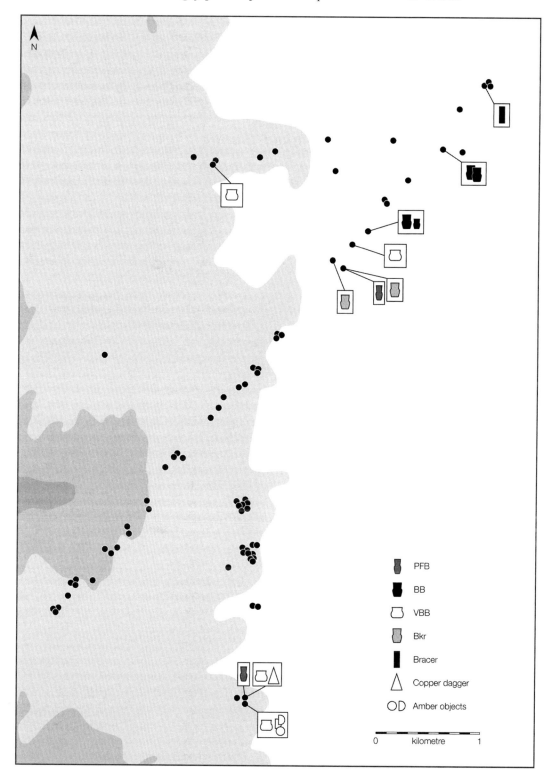

Figure 19.8: The Epe-Vaassen 'barrow road', north-east Veluwe, central Netherlands

Legend:
- PFB
- BB
- VBB
- Bkr
- Bracer
- Copper dagger
- Amber objects

0   kilometre   1

This does, however, present some major interpretative challenges: for example, the monuments and Beaker graves forming this alignment date to several different phases of activity in the Stonehenge landscape, and the 'route' cuts across the line of the Avenue, which is usually assumed to be the only ceremonial path to Stonehenge.

Moreover, such an alignment of monuments contradicts the concentric cosmographic structuring of the landscape proposed in recent interpretations (Darvill 1997; Parker Pearson & Ramilisonina 1998). These now seem less tenable as the *only* way of conceiving of landscape order and signification during the Chalcolithic. It is not a question of the concentric symbolic scheme and its suggested meanings necessarily being 'wrong' (cf. Barrett & Fewster 1998; Whittle 1998), but rather that more complex spatial structuring of the Stonehenge landscape can be imagined. It is possible that different religious and symbolic schemes (and distinctive modes of ceremonial performance) operated at different times, or that a series of reorganisations (and perhaps restorations) of particular kinds of cosmological and political order took place in the course of struggles over possession, rights of access, and ideological or moral 'truths' that drew on competing or contradictory visions of the cosmos. Rapid shifts in the dominance of one scheme over another, with short episodes of monument construction and modification, including occasional iconoclastic acts, could conceivably have been played out over centuries. We may be seeing a landscape as much the creation of social disharmony as symbolic order. Uncertainty over dating, however, still presents the greatest problem for unravelling these relationships, especially with regard to Stonehenge itself, which has recently been the subject of several conflicting chronological schemes (see Darvill 2006a; Bayliss *et al.* 2007, 46–7; Parker Pearson *et al.* 2007).

Other landscapes of early Beaker burial in Britain and beyond

Less is known about the landscape contexts of early Beaker burials elsewhere in Britain, either because of a lack of concerted landscape-scale studies or significant gaps in dating evidence. Even so, it is possible to recognise similar patterns to those observed in the upper Thames valley and around Stonehenge. At Avebury, for example, early Beaker funerary and occupation sites, which appear at about the same time as the first phase of construction at Silbury Hill (*c.* 2400–2200 cal BC: Bayliss *et al.* 2007), and perhaps also the building of the West Kennet palisade enclosures (*ibid.*, 45; Whittle 1997, table 1), were spatially separated

and mostly invisible from the arenas and avenues that comprise the ceremonial complex (Cleal 2005; Gillings *et al.* 2008, 193–8). At Raunds, Northamptonshire, whilst neither of the lavish Beaker graves at the centres of Barrows 1 and 6, dating to *c.* 2200–1900 cal BC, was located close to contemporary ceremonial monuments, Barrow 6 was clearly positioned to refer to several much older monuments (Harding & Healy 2007, 60–4). It is also notable that the location of the early 'Dutch-style' Beaker grave at Upper Largie, Argyll, about 3.5 km to the north of the henge at the heart of the Kilmartin Glen monument complex (Sheridan 2008b), is similar to the spatial distancing of the Amesbury Archer burial from Stonehenge. Overall, it would seem that early Beaker graves were located to avoid Late Neolithic monuments while later graves were not.

Linear arrangements of Beaker burials are also present on the continent. These include short alignments of flat graves at Öberau in Bavaria (Heyd 2007, 365, fig. 24) similar to the Cassington and Eynsham groups, and the line of graves and barrows at Eext, Drenthe, north-east Netherlands (Jager 1985, 190, fig. 3). In the same area (*gemeente* of Anloo), far longer 'beaded' distributions of Single Grave Culture and Beaker barrows in sinuous and angled lines across the landscape have been interpreted as prehistoric 'roads' (*ibid.*; Bakker 1991). Most striking of all is the extraordinary dead-straight alignment of barrows which extends for over 6 km north-east to south-west from Epe to Vaassen on the east side of the Veluwe, central Netherlands (Fig. 19.8). This has been described by Jan-Albert Bakker (1976, 77–9, fig. 11; 1991, 517; 2008), with site details summarised by Klok (1988, app. 2) and Lanting and van der Waals (1976, table 4). Although many of the monuments forming this alignment are unexcavated, one section is firmly dated to the mid-3rd millennium and it is likely that the whole route originated in the period *c.* 2700–2400 cal BC. Although it would be unwise to draw a direct analogy between this 'barrow road' and the alignment of monuments and graves at Stonehenge, especially because of the presence of ceremonial monuments in one case and not the other, nonetheless it is evident that Late Neolithic and Chalcolithic communities sometimes structured funerary events in linear forms that were 'mapped out' across the landscape on an impressive scale.

Changing landscapes of cosmological order and political discourse

Recent interpretations of Late Neolithic and Chalcolithic cultural worlds imagine consistent, long-lasting kinds of historical consciousness bound up with the dead, and an all-pervasive concern with the past and above all 'ancestors' (eg, Parker Pearson & Ramilisonina 1998). Yet different people can have divergent and often opposed perceptions of their 'past', with diverse narratives of their history (-ies) that can change quickly over time (Garwood 1991; Bradley 2002). Moreover, use of the idea of 'ancestors' as a universal and unitary cultural phenomenon is arguable at best (eg, Whitley 2002; Whittle 2003; cf. Pitts 2003). Rather than a celebration of ancient ancestral communities, the 'single grave' practices widely adopted in the mid-3rd millennium are better understood as media for constituting 'individual' sacralised identities (Barrett 1988). Indeed, one of the striking features of early Beaker graves is the *absence* of things of the past (and indigenous present): although a few objects appear old and worn, the majority were in good condition or even 'pristine' when buried. What they share, instead, is novelty, distant origins, and an otherness with respect to local material repertoires. We can discern a strategy of funerary expression that sought power and legitimacy not by referring to ancestors, personal biographies, or 'history', but rather by presencing a domain that transcended all these things, reified by exotic materials and symbols from 'other worlds'. Early Beaker burials thus suggest commitment to a cosmological scheme, and networks of social interaction, that were far more extensive than regional religious or cult affiliations, through which alliances and acquisitions of valued sacred resources from afar could be made to escape the constraints of local political or religious hegemony (and quite possibly 'ancestors' too).

There are, of course, many instances of multiple Beaker burials (for instance at Barnack: Last 1998), the presence of old objects in graves (eg, at Raunds Barrow 1: Healy & Harding 2004) and the redeposited remains of both the ancient dead (eg, at Raunds Barrow 6: Harding & Healy 2007, 96–7) and the recent dead (eg, at Raunds Barrow

5: *ibid.*, 100–1). These practices do suggest concerns with biographical, historical, and mythological pasts but, on present evidence, they mostly date to the period *after c.* 2150 cal BC. By this time, new agendas prevailed in the way Beaker and non-Beaker practices were co-related, and in the way that people acted in their constructed landscapes of death and memorialisation (Garwood 2007a). The error in some previous interpretations has been to extend understandings of Beaker burials of the period *c.* 2150–1800 cal BC, when concerns with family, lineage, and ancestral belonging in the landscape *were* prominent, to the earlier – Chalcolithic – phase of Beaker funerary practice, when they were not.

In this light, and considering the landscape evidence discussed above, Needham's view that 'Beaker people' quickly developed a sense of rightful place in the landscape by marking out their ancestral presence (2007, 42), needs some qualification. Beaker burials and their memorials were creations of 'inscriptive' practices (Rowlands 1993): the dead being 'written into' the grave, and their presence inscribed on the land through monument building (Bradley 2002, 11–12). The 'present dead' and their monuments, created in this way, were media for the construction of 'future pasts' by projecting what is believed to be right and true into the cultural landscape of the future. In the early Beaker case this was not a simple matter of 'making the ancestral dead', but a consequence of more complex engagements with multiple religious and political agendas, both exogenous and indigenous, which burial events addressed in strategic ways. These rare but dramatic acts in making 'future-history' were indeed quick to appear, but seem more concerned with identity, origins and remote times/places than ancestry *per se*, in forms that realised a *break* with the indigenous past.

Yet, as the chronology and spatial contexts of early Beaker burial events demonstrate, this was not a matter of immediate 'conquest' or replacement of pre-existing cosmographies. Quite the reverse: it is possible to discern initial avoidance of conflict in the distancing of Beaker graves from ceremonial monuments, and subtleties in the way that structures of the past were treated. Where 'ancient monuments', such as long mounds and causewayed enclosures (at Radley for instance), were no longer used for social acts in the present, referencing seems to have been more allusive than direct, perhaps intended to situate present practices within a naturalised or mythic order of things. In these cases, neither the past times imagined nor the places associated with them were a threat to the beliefs or social agendas reified in Beaker burials. In contrast, structures which were still in use for ceremonial purposes, which evoked still-powerful emotions and visions of cosmos and identity, could have been foci for continued religious commitment and resistance to new values and beliefs. The positioning of Beaker graves at such locales seems to occur only commonly from *c.* 2150 cal BC, when deliberate attempts may have been made to appropriate and reconfigure the significance of ancient places by inscribing new meanings into them.

From this perspective, the positioning of monuments beside paths seems an especially apposite way of celebrating the early Beaker dead – metaphorically recalling the journeys past and future of people from 'distant lands', positioned on significant routes to guarantee/oversee the successful travels of their descendants. Lines of barrows alongside paths may also have been a means by which a kind of local historical narrative was constructed, but one which was extended into the far distance and beyond, into the unchanging cosmological 'background' of the cultural landscape where sacred, timeless sources of power and authority resided (Hirsch 1990). Such 'avenues' could have been seen as conduits for the transfer of materials and substances from sacred domains into the world of the living, managed by travellers moving betwixt and between, as well as paths of the dead. It is also striking that these form *unbounded* avenues: roads without end, paths to nowhere – and everywhere – that in a sense could be followed both forwards and backwards in time. These can be contrasted with the monumentalised avenues of Late Neolithic ceremonial architecture, with their hard boundaries and specific beginnings and ends, designed to control practices and meanings within the landscape in far more prescriptive ways (Thomas 1993).

It is likely, of course, that the routes beside which Beaker graves were located already existed, and certainly there is good evidence for long distance journeying, pilgrimage, and linear structuring of monuments during the Late Neolithic (Harding 2003, 98). A concern with paths and mobility may also relate to the importance of stock-breeding and transhumance as major economic and social dimensions of Chalcolithic society in north-west Europe (Fokkens 1999). The positioning and monumentalisation of the Beaker dead along routes, however, not only suggests the sacralisation of these pathways but also – by cutting across the cosmographic structures of Neolithic ceremonial landscapes – attempts to penetrate and perhaps subvert 'indigenous' cultural order. Indeed, implied violence pervades much Beaker funerary symbolism, in the form of weaponry such as daggers, battleaxes and archery equipment (Thomas 1991), with daggers sometimes held in the hands of the dead (Fowler 2004, 74), and wristguards possibly worn as 'warrior insignia' (Fokkens *et al.* 2008). There is also growing evidence for the practical use of weapons causing injury and death (Thorpe 2006; Vandkilde 2006). Yet the sense of violent potency embodied in these images of the dead may be more a product of metaphorical allusions bound up with the specific landscape contexts, histories, and substance of Beaker funerary rituals than a simple expression of social conflict: the dead being *portrayed* as wayfarers, sentinels (guarding the continuing passage of people, animals, objects, and perhaps spirits), or as warriors who had seized the paths of success and power. Moreover, symbolic violence may be an intrinsic property of ritual – a means to convey the inevitable 'conquest' of the everyday world by the sacred (Maurice Bloch's 'rebounding violence'; 1992). The Beaker dead, in this light, could have been seen not only as iconic figures but also as the very agents of supernatural domination.

The highly evocative – and provocative – qualities of early Beaker burials perceived by prehistorians thus appear to be an effect not only of their symbolic coherence and striking imagery, but also because they mark a unique conjuncture of vividly expressed, mutually reinforcing sets of ideals, myths, values, and anxieties that could, perhaps, *only* be expressed together in funerary performances. At the same time, this was not an unchanging cultural phenomenon. Needham has argued that the Beaker funerary 'package' was already established by the time it appeared in Britain (2005, 182): indeed so, but perhaps only just.

Bell Beaker graves in the Netherlands date no earlier than the 25th century cal BC (Lanting & van der Plicht 1999/2000), as do those along the Danube (Heyd 2007). The creation of distinctive 'Beaker' burial rites may therefore have happened barely one or two generations before their first performance in Britain. It is difficult to see these as 'traditional' (in the sense of repeated customary practice with a long history of performance), but rather as something novel; an invented 'tradition' that served to articulate new political and cultural ends. In contrast, Beaker burial events by 2150 cal BC took place in landscapes marked by the presence of the 'old' Beaker dead and the abandonment or reworking of earlier ceremonial monuments. Formerly people without a local past, the users of Beakers appear increasingly in the course of the later 3rd millennium to have made their own histories: in lines of burial mounds, 'cemetery barrows', manipulation of ancient objects and human remains, and the mythologising of ancient monuments.

In this light, while the concept of a 'British Chalcolithic' is an attractive one because of the way it describes a genuinely distinctive cultural world that was neither 'Late Neolithic' nor 'Early Bronze Age', it would be a great mistake to imagine that the cultural repertoires, forms of social action and meaning that such a 'period' encompasses must therefore have been consistent. The changing significance of Beaker burials in the Chalcolithic landscape shows us again that we must not become prisoners of our own constructions of the past.

Acknowledgments

I am very grateful to Lis Dyson, the volume editors, and anonymous referees for their helpful comments on the first draft of the text. Thanks also to Alistair Barclay for providing me with information about unpublished data. The interpretations presented are, of course, my own. Finally, I am especially grateful to Henry Buglass for his work on the illustrations.

Bibliography

Allen, T.G. & Kamash, Z. 2008. *Saved from the Grave: Neolithic to Saxon discoveries at Spring Road Municipal Cemetery, Abingdon, Oxfordshire, 1990–2000.* Oxford: Thames Valley Landscape 28

Annable, F.K. & Simpson, D.D.A. 1964. *Guide Catalogue of the Neolithic and Bronze Age Collections in Devizes Museum.* Devizes: Wiltshire Archaeological & Natural History Society

Ashbee, P. 1975/6. Amesbury Barrow 51: excavation 1960. *Wiltshire Archaeological & Natural History Magazine* 70/1, 1–60

Bakker, J.A. 1976. On the possibility of reconstructing roads from the TRB period. *Berichten van de Rijksdienst voor het Oudheidkundig Bodemonderzoek* 26, 63–91

Bakker, J.A. 1991. Prehistoric long-distance roads in North-West Europe. In J. Lichardus (ed.), *Die Kupferzeit als Historische Epoche*, 505–28. Bonn: Habelt

Bakker, J.A. 2008. A note on prehistoric routes on the Veluwe and near Uelzen. In H. Fokkens, B.J. Coles, A.L. van Gijn, J.P. Kleijne, H.H. Ponjee & C.G. Sappendel (eds), *Between Foraging and Farming: an extended broad spectrum of papers presented to Leendert Louwe Kooijmans*, 281–6. *Analecta Praehistorica Leidensia* 40)

Barclay, A. 1995. A review of Neolithic and Bronze Age sites in the Devil's Quoits area. In A. Barclay, M. Grey & G. Lambrick, *Excavations at the Devil's Quoits, Stanton Harcourt, Oxfordshire, 1972–3 and 1988*, 78–105. Oxford: Thames Valley Landscapes, the Windrush Valley 3

Barclay, A. 1999a. Final Neolithic/Early Bronze Age. In Barclay & Halpin (eds) 1999, 35–148

Barclay, A. 1999b. Summary and reassessments of monuments excavated before 1983–4. In Barclay & Halpin (eds) 1999, 149–66

Barclay, A. & Glass, H. 1995. Excavations of Neolithic and Bronze Age ring ditches, Shorncote Quarry, Somerford Keynes, Gloucestershire. *Transactions of the Bristol & Gloucestershire Archaeological Society* 113, 21–60

Barclay, A. & Halpin, C. (eds). 1999. *Excavations at Barrow Hills, Radley, Oxfordshire. Vol I: the Neolithic and Bronze Age monument complex.* Oxford: Thames Valley Landscapes, Monograph 11

Barrett, J.C. 1988. The living, the dead and the ancestors: Neolithic and early Bronze Age mortuary practices. In J. Barrett & I. Kinnes (eds), *The Archaeology of Context in the Neolithic and Bronze Age: recent trends*, 30–41. Sheffield: Department of Archaeology & Prehistory, University of Sheffield

Barrett, J.C. 1994. *Fragments from Antiquity: an archaeology of social life in Britain, 2900–1200 BC.* Oxford: Blackwell

Barrett, J.C. & Fewster, K.J. 1998. Stonehenge: is the medium the message? *Antiquity* 72, 847–52

Bayliss, A., McAvoy, F. & Whittle, A. 2007. The world recreated: redating Silbury Hill in its monumental landscape. *Antiquity* 81, 26–53

Beek, Z. van der & Fokkens, H. 2001. 24 years after Oberreid: the 'Dutch model' reconsidered. In Nicolis (ed.) 2001, 301–8

Bloch, M. 1992. *Prey into Hunter: the politics of religious experience.* Cambridge: University Press

Boston, C., Bowater, C., Boyle, A. & Holmes, A. 2003. Excavation of a Bronze Age barrow at the proposed Centre for Gene Function, South Parks Road, Oxford, 2002. *Oxoniensia* 68, 179–200

Bradley, R. 2002. *The Past in Prehistoric Societies.* London: Routledge

Bradley, R. 2007. *The Prehistory of Britain and Ireland.* Cambridge: University Press

Brodie, N. 1997. New perspectives on the Bell-Beaker culture. *Oxford Journal of Archaeology* 16(3), 297–314

Brodie, N. 1998. British Bell Beakers: twenty-five years of theory and practice. In M. Benz & S. van Willigen (eds), *Some New Approaches to the Bell Beaker 'Phenomenon': lost paradise?*, 43–56. Oxford: British Archaeological Report S690

Brück, J. 2004. Material metaphors: the relational construction of identity in early Bronze Age burials in Ireland and Britain. *Journal of Social Archaeology* 4(3), 307–33

Burgess, C. & Shennan, S. 1976. The Beaker phenomenon: some suggestions. In C. Burgess & R. Miket (eds), *Settlement and Economy in the Third and Second Millennia BC*, 309–27. Oxford: British Archaeological Report 33

Case, H.J. 1993. Beakers: deconstruction and after. *Proceedings of the Prehistoric Society* 59, 241–68

Case, H.J. 2001. The Beaker culture in Britain and Ireland: groups, European contacts and chronology. In Nicolis (ed.) 2001, 361–77

Case, H.J. 2004a. Beaker burial in Britain and Ireland: a role for the dead. In M. Besse & J. Desideri (eds), *Graves and Funerary Rituals During the Late Neolithic and the Early Bronze Age in Europe (2700–2000 BC)*, 195–201. Oxford: British Archaeological Report S1284

Case, H.J. 2004b. Bell Beaker and Corded Ware culture burial associations: a bottom-up rather than top-down approach. In A. Gibson & A. Sheridan (eds), *From Sickles to Circles: Britain and Ireland at the time of Stonehenge*, 201–14. Stroud: Tempus

Clarke, D.L. 1970. *Beaker Pottery of Great Britain and Ireland.* Cambridge: Cambridge University Press

Cleal, R.M.J. 2005. 'The small compass of a grave': Early Bronze Age burial in and around Avebury and the Marlborough Downs. In G. Brown, D. Field & D. McOmish (eds), *The Avebury Landscape: aspects of the field archaeology of the Marlborough Downs*, 115–32. Oxford: Oxbow Books

Cleal, R.M.J. & Walker, K. with Montague, R. 1995. *Stonehenge in its Landscape.* London: English Heritage Archaeological Report 10

Darvill, T. 1997. Ever increasing circles: the sacred geographies of Stonehenge in its landscape. In B. Cunliffe & C. Renfrew (eds), *Science and Stonehenge*, 167–202. *Proceedings of the British Academy* 92

Darvill, T. 2006a. *Stonehenge: the biography of a landscape.* Stroud: Tempus

Darvill, T. 2006b. Early prehistory. In N. Holbrook & J. Juřica (eds), *Twenty-five Years of Archaeology in Gloucestershire: a review of new discoveries and new thinking in Gloucestershire, South Gloucestershire and Bristol 1979–2004*, 5–60. Cirencester: Bristol & Gloucestershire Archaeological Report 3

Dodd, A. 2003. Synthesis and discussion. In A. Dodd (ed.), *Oxford Before the University*, 7–12. Oxford: Thames Valley Landscapes 17

Drenth, E. & Hogestijn, W.J. 2001. The Bell Beaker culture in the Netherlands: the state of research in 1998. In Nicolis (ed.) 2001, 309–32

Drenth, E. & Lohof, E. 2005. Mounds for the dead: funerary and burial ritual in Beaker period, Early and Middle Bronze Age. In L.P. Louwe Kooijmans, P.W. van den Broeke, H. Fokkens & A.L. van Gijn (eds), *The Prehistory of the Netherlands*, I, 433–54. Amsterdam: University Press

Evans, J.G. 1984. Stonehenge – the environment in the Late Neolithic and Early Bronze Age and a Beaker-age burial. *Wiltshire Archaeological & Natural History Magazine* 78, 7–30

Evans, J., Chenery, C. & Fitzpatrick, A. 2006. Bronze Age childhood migration of individuals near Stonehenge, revealed by strontium and oxygen isotope analysis. *Archaeometry* 48, 309–22

Exon, S., Gaffney, V., Woodward, A. & Yorston, R. 2000. *Stonehenge Landscapes. Journeys through Real-and-imagined Worlds.* Oxford: Archaeopress

Field, D. 1998. Round barrows and the harmonious landscape: placing Early Bronze Age burial monuments in south-east England. *Oxford Journal of Archaeology* 17, 309–26

Fitzpatrick, A. 2003. The Amesbury Archer. *Current Archaeology* 16(4), 146–52

Fitzpatrick, A. 2009. In his hands and in his head: the Amesbury Archer as a metalworker. In P. Clark (ed.), *Bronze Age Connections: cultural contact in prehistoric Europe*, 176–88. Oxford: Oxbow Books

Fokkens, H. 1999. Cattle and martiality: changing relations between man and landscape in the Late Neolithic and the Bronze Age. In C. Fabech & J. Ringtved (eds), *Settlement and Landscape: proceedings of a conference in Aarhus, Denmark, May 4–7, 1998*, 35–43. Aarhus: Aarhus University Press

Fokkens, H., Achterkamp, Y. & Kuijpers, M. 2008. Bracers or bracelets? About the functionality and meaning of Bell beaker wrist-guards. *Proceedings of the Prehistoric Society* 74, 109–40

Fowler, C. 2004. *The Archaeology of Personhood.* London: Routledge

Garwood, P. 1991. Ritual tradition and the reconstitution of society. In P. Garwood, D. Jennings, R. Skeates & J. Toms (eds), *Sacred and Profane. Archaeology, Ritual and Religion*, 10–32. Oxford: Oxford University Committee for Archaeology Monograph 32

Garwood, P. 1999. Radiocarbon dating and the chronology of the monument complex. In Barclay & Halpin (eds) 1999, 293–309

Garwood, P. 2003. Round barrows and funerary traditions in Late Neolithic and Bronze Age Sussex. In D. Rudling (ed.), *The Archaeology of Sussex to AD 2000*, 47–68. Great Dunham: Heritage Marketing & Publications

Garwood, P. 2007a. Before the hills in order stood: chronology, time and history in the interpretation of early Bronze Age round barrows. In J. Last (ed.), *Beyond the Grave: new perspectives on round barrows*, 30–52. Oxford: Oxbow Books

Garwood, P. 2007b. Regions, cultural identity and social change, *c.* 4500–1500 cal BC: the West Midlands in context. In P. Garwood (ed.), *The Undiscovered Country: the earlier prehistory of the West Midlands*, 194–215. Oxford: Oxbow Books

Garwood, P. 2007c. Vital resources, ideal images and virtual lives: children in Early Bronze Age funerary ritual. In S.E.E. Crawford & G.B. Shepherd (eds), *Children and Social Identity in the Ancient World*, 63–82. Oxford: Archaeopress/Institute of Archaeology & Antiquity Interdisciplinary Series 1

Garwood, P. 2011. Making the dead (with a contribution by A. Barclay). In A. Morigi, D. Schreve, M. White,

G. Hey, P. Garwood, M. Robinson, A. Barclay and P. Bradley, *Thames Through Time: the archaeology of the gravel terraces of the Upper and Middle Thames. Volume 1, Early Prehistory to 1500 BC*, 383–432. Oxford: Oxford Archaeology

Gibbs, A.L. 1990. *Sex, Gender and Material Culture Patterning in Later Neolithic and Early Bronze Age England.* Unpublished Ph.D. thesis, University of Cambridge

Gibson, A. 2007. A Beaker veneer? Some evidence from the burial record. In Larsson & Parker Pearson (eds) 2007, 47–64

Gillings, M., Pollard, J., Wheatley, D. & Peterson, R, 2008. *Landscape of the Megaliths: excavation and fieldwork on the Avebury monuments, 1997–2003.* Oxford: Oxbow Books

Green, C. & Rollo-Smith, S. 1984. The excavation of eighteen round barrows near Shrewton, Wiltshire. *Proceedings of the Prehistoric Society* 50, 255–318

Grinsell, L.V. 1957. Archaeological gazetteer. In R.B. Pugh (ed.), *The Victoria History of the Counties of England: Wiltshire, Vol 1, Pt 1*, 21–279. London: Institute of Historical Research

Grinsell, L.V. 1979. *The Stonehenge Barrow Groups.* Salisbury: Salisbury & South Wiltshire Museum

Harding, J. 2003. *Henge Monuments of the British Isles.* Stroud: Tempus

Harding, J. & Healy, F. 2007. *The Raunds Area Project: a Neolithic and Bronze Age landscape in Northamptonshire.* Swindon: English Heritage

Healy, F. 2004. Gravelly Guy in the context of the Stanton Harcourt ceremonial complex. In Lambrick & Allen 2004, 64–5

Healy, F. & Harding, J. 2004. Reading a burial: the legacy of Overton Hill. In A. Gibson and A. Sheridan (eds), *From Sickles to Circles: Britain and Ireland at the time of Stonehenge*, 176–93. Stroud: Tempus

Heyd, V. 2007. Families, prestige goods, warriors and complex societies: Beaker groups of the 3rd millennium cal BC along the middle and upper Danube. *Proceedings of the Prehistoric Society* 73, 327–79

Hirsch, E. 1995. Introduction. Landscape: between place and space. In E. Hirsch, & M. O'Hanlon (eds), *The Anthropology of Landscape: perspectives on place and space*, 1–30. Oxford: Oxford University Press

Jager, S. 1985 A prehistoric route and ancient cart-tracks in the gemeente of Anloo (Province of Drenthe). *Palaeohistoria* 27, 185–245

Jay, M. & Montgomery, J. 2008. The Beaker People Project. *British Archaeology* 101, 26

Jones, A. 2005. Lives in fragments? Personhood and the European Neolithic. *Journal of Social Archaeology* 5(2), 193–224

Klok, R.H.J. 1988. Prehistoric barrows on the Veluwe. *Berichten van de Rijksdienst voor het Oudheidkundig Bodemonderzoek* 38, 9–61

Lambrick, G. 2010. *Neolithic to Saxon Settlement at Mount Farm, Berinsfield, Dorchester.* Oxford: Oxford Archaeology Occasional Paper 19

Lambrick, G. & Allen, T. 2004. *Gravelly Guy, Stanton Harcourt: the development of a prehistoric and Romano-British community.* Oxford: Thames Valley Landscapes 21

Lanting, J.N. & Plicht, J. van der 1999/2000. De ¹⁴C-chronologie van de Nederlandse pre- en protohistorie, III: Neolithicum. *Palaeohistoria* 41/2, 1–110

Lanting, J.N. & Waals, J.D. van der. 1976. Beaker culture relations in the Lower Rhine basin. In N. Lanting & J.D. van der Waals (eds), *Glockenbecher Symposion Oberried 1974*, 1–80. Haarlem: Fibula-van Dishoek

Larsson, L. & Parker Pearson, M. (eds). 2007. From Stonehenge to the Baltic: living with cultural diversity in the third millennium BC, 41–6. Oxford: British Archaeological Report S1692

Last, J. 1998. Books of life: biography and memory in a Bronze Age barrow. *Oxford Journal of Archaeology* 17, 43–53

Lawson, A.J. 2007. *Chalkland: an archaeology of Stonehenge and its region.* Shaftesbury: Hobnob Press

Leeds, E.T. 1934. Recent Bronze Age discoveries in Berkshire and Oxfordshire. *Antiquaries Journal* 14, 264–76

Leeds, E.T. 1938. Beakers of the Upper Thames district. *Oxoniensia* 3, 7–30

Leivers, M. & Moore, C. 2008. *Archaeology on the A303 Stonehenge Improvement.* Salisbury: Wessex Archaeology

Lucas, G.M. 1996. Of death and debt: a history of the body in Neolithic and Bronze Age Yorkshire. *Journal of European Archaeology* 4, 99–118

Mizoguchi, K. 1993. Time in the reproduction of mortuary practices. *World Archaeology* 25, 223–35

Müller, A. 2001. Gender differentiation in burial rites and grave goods in the eastern or Bohemian-Moravian group of the Bell-Beaker culture. In Nicolis (ed.) 2001, 589–99

Needham, S. 2000. Power pulses across a cultural divide: cosmologically driven acquisition between Armorica and Wessex. *Proceedings of the Prehistoric Society* 66, 151–207

Needham, S. 2005. Transforming Beaker culture in north-west Europe: processes of fusion and fission. *Proceedings of the Prehistoric Society* 71, 159–70

Needham, S. 2007. Isotopic aliens: Beaker movement and cultural transmission. In Larsson & Parker Pearson (eds) 2007, 41–6

Nicolis, F. (ed.). 2001. *Bell Beakers Today: pottery, people, culture, symbols in prehistoric Europe.* Trento: Officio Beni Archeologici

Parker Pearson, M. 2000. Ancestors, bones and stones in Neolithic and Early Bronze Age Britain and Ireland. In A. Ritchie (ed.), *Neolithic Orkney in its European Context*, 203–14. Cambridge: McDonald Institute for Archaeological Research

Parker Pearson, M. & Ramilisonina. 1998. Stonehenge for the ancestors: the stones pass on the message. *Antiquity* 72, 308–26

Parker Pearson, M., Cleal, R., Marshall, P., Needham, S., Pollard, J., Richards, C., Ruggles, C., Sheridan, A., Thomas, J., Tilley, C., Welham, K., Chamberlain, A., Chenery, C., Evans, J., Knüsel, C., Linford, N., Martin, L., Montgomery, J., Payne, A. & Richards, M. 2007. The age of Stonehenge. *Antiquity* 81, 617–39

Parker Pearson, M., Pollard, J., Thomas, J. & Welham, K. 2009. Newhenge. *British Archaeology* 110, 14–21

Pitts, M. 2003 Don't knock the ancestors. *Antiquity* 77, 172–8

Price, T., Grupe, G. & Schroter, P. 1998. Migration in the bell beaker period of central Europe. *Antiquity* 72, 405–11

Price, T., Knipper, G., Grupe, G. & Smrcka, V. 2004. Strontium isotopes and prehistoric migration: the Bell beaker period in central Europe. *European Journal of Archaeology* 7, 9–40

Richards, J. 1990. *The Stonehenge Environs Project*. London: English Heritage Archaeological Report 16

Rowlands, M. 1993. The role of memory in the transmission of culture. *World Archaeology* 25(2), 141–51

Sarauw, T. 2007. Male symbols or warrior identities? The 'archery burials' of the Danish Bell Beaker Culture. *Journal of Anthropological Anthropology* 26, 65–87

Shennan, S. 1982. Ideology, change and the European Early Bronze Age. In I. Hodder (ed.), *Symbolic and Structural Archaeology*, 155–61. Cambridge: Cambridge University Press

Shennan, S. 1986. Interaction and change in third millennium cal BC western and central Europe. In C. Renfrew & J.F. Cherry (eds), *Peer Polity Interaction and Socio-Political Change*, 137–48. Cambridge: Cambridge University Press

Sheridan, A. 2008a. Towards a fuller, more nuanced narrative of Chalcolithic and Early Bronze Age Britain 2500–1500 cal BC. Bronze Age Review 1, 57–78. (www.britishmuseum.org/bronzeagereview/1)

Sheridan, A. 2008b. Upper Largie and Dutch-Scottish connections during the Beaker period. In H. Fokkens, B.J.Coles, A.L. van Gijn, J.P. Kleijne, H.H. Ponjee & C.G. Sappendel (eds), *Between Foraging and Farming: an extended broad spectrum of papers presented to Leendert Louwe Kooijmans*, 247–60. *Analecta Praehistorica Leidensia* 40

Sofaer Derevenski, J. 2002. Engendering context: context as gendered practice in the Early Bronze Age of the Upper Thames valley, UK. *European Journal of Archaeology* 5(2), 191–211

Stone, J.F.S. 1938. An early Bronze Age grave in Fargo Plantation, near Stonehenge. *Wiltshire Archaeological & Natural History Magazine* 48, 357–70

Thomas, J. 1991. Reading the body: Beaker funerary practice in Britain. In P. Garwood, D. Jennings, R. Skeates & J. Toms (eds), *Sacred and Profane. Archaeology, Ritual and Religion*, 33–42. Oxford: Oxford University Committee for Archaeology Monograph 32

Thomas, J. 1993. The politics of vision and the archaeologies of landscape. In B. Bender (ed.), *Landscape: politics and perspectives*, 19–48. Oxford: Berg

Thomas, J. 1999. *Understanding the Neolithic*. London: Routledge

Thomas, J. 2000. Death, identity and the body in Neolithic Britain. *Journal of the Royal Anthropological Institute* 6, 653–68

Thorpe, I.J. & Richards, C. 1984. The decline of ritual authority and the introduction of Beakers into Britain. In R .Bradley & J. Gardiner (eds), *Neolithic Studies: a review of some current research*, 67–84. Oxford: British Archaeological Report 133

Thorpe, N. 2006. Fighting and feuding in Neolithic and Bronze Age Britain and Ireland. In T. Otto, H. Thrane & H. Vandkilde (eds), *Warfare and Society: archaeological and social anthropological perspectives*, 141–66. Aarhus: Aarhus University Press

Turek, J. & Černý, V. 2001. Society, gender and sexual dimorphism of the Corded Ware and Bell Beaker populations. In Nicolis (ed.) 2001, 601–12

Vander Linden, M. 2007. What linked the Bell Beakers in third millennium cal BC Europe? *Antiquity* 81, 343–52

Vandkilde, H. 2001. Beaker representation in the Danish Late Neolithic. In Nicolis (ed.) 2001, 333–60

Vandkilde, H. 2006. Warriors and warrior institutions in Copper Age Europe. In T. Otto, H. Thrane & H. Vandkilde (eds), *Warfare and Society: archaeological and social anthropological perspectives*, 393–422. Aarhus: Aarhus University Press

Whitley, J. 2002. Too many ancestors. *Antiquity* 76, 119–26

Whittle, A. 1997. *Sacred Mound, Holy Rings. Silbury Hill and the West Kennet Palisade Enclosures: a later Neolithic complex in north Wiltshire*. Oxford: Oxbow Monograph 74

Whittle, A. 1998. People and the diverse past: two comments on 'Stonehenge for the ancestors'. *Antiquity* 72, 852–54

Whittle, A. 2003. *The Archaeology of People: dimensions of Neolithic life*. London: Routledge

Whittle, A., Atkinson, R.J.C., Chambers, R. & Thomas, N. 1992. Excavations in the Neolithic and Bronze Age complex at Dorchester–on-Thames, Oxfordshire, 1947–52 and 1981. *Proceedings of the Prehistoric Society* 58, 143–201

Wilkin, N.C.A. 2009. *Regional Narratives of the Early Bronze Age: a contextual and evidence-led approach to the funerary practices of east-central Scotland*. Unpublished M. Phil. thesis, University of Birmingham

The Revenge of the Native: monuments, material culture, burial and other practices in the third quarter of the 3rd millennium BC in Wessex

Rosamund Cleal and Joshua Pollard

Reviewing sequences present in the regions of Avebury and Stonehenge, in the heartland of the Wessex chalk, it is asked whether the term Chalcolithic has sufficient heuristic value to validate its adoption for the period c. 2500–2200 BC. A key problem exists in the identification of 'Chalcolithic' as a term that privileges metal over other material culture and concepts: it implies that metal is the catalyst and medium of change and that the change brought about by its adoption is so profound and rapid that it requires the relabelling of a period as short as 200–300 years. In contrast, an argument is here presented for the 'long view' – that the appearance of Beaker-associated metal needs to be understood in the context of a series of changes and developments with their origins in the preceding centuries, and which continue into the full Early Bronze Age.

If the concept of a Chalcolithic is to be a useful one for the British Isles it must facilitate a better understanding of the complex developments that characterise the 3rd millennium BC, and particularly of the later part of it when renewed and sustained contact with continental Europe is materialised in the appearance of metal and the Beaker 'package'. If the concept does not help in understanding those complexities, or if it is clear that significant changes were not driven by the appearance of metal or intimately bound up in it, then labelling part of the 3rd millennium as 'the Chalcolithic' is probably not going to advance our understanding, and might even hinder it.

In looking for places where the usefulness of the concept would seem most likely to be apparent, Wessex must be a prime contender. In the southern English chalklands of Wiltshire and Dorset in particular, monuments of the 3rd millennium are frequent and complex, and there is a rich funerary record for the last centuries of that millennium (Lawson 2007). The third quarter of that millennium is becoming an increasingly important period – one in which we know copper objects were in circulation,

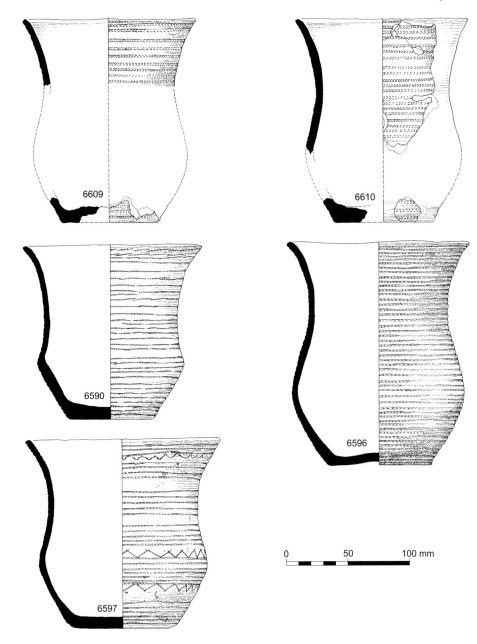

albeit perhaps in limited numbers, alongside other components of novel material culture often associated with early Beaker pottery and individual inhumation burial. The emergence of new long-distance networks might also be interpolated from recent stable isotope analysis of certain burials. However, this is still a time in which Grooved Ware remains in currency, and characteristically 'Late Neolithic' monuments continue to be constructed or modified, and certainly used.

This paper examines some of the, admittedly familiar, monuments and associated sites and finds in the light of the better refined

chronology of the 3rd millennium BC which has been emerging for the last decade or so. Through micro-regional case studies of the Avebury and Stonehenge landscapes, it discusses whether the record of seemingly varied practices, objects and traditions are consistent with a recognisable 'Copper Age'. Throughout, our focus is on material practices, local trajectories of monument construction and use, settlement, and burial. We investigate whether major social and ideological transformations can be identified coincident with the appearance of early copper objects and Beaker pottery, or if, culturally, later Neolithic traditions of practice

Technique	Dated examples	References
Plaited cord impression & techniques of multiple cord impression	'Amesbury Archer' Lower Camp, Boscombe Down	Fitzpatrick 2011
All-over cord (AOC) impressions	'Amesbury Archer'	Fitzpatrick 2011
Triangle fringe motif Zones of comb-impression defined by twisted cord (Cord Zoned Maritime Beakers (CZM))	'Amesbury Archer' Lower Camp, Boscombe Down	Fitzpatrick 2011
All Over Comb on squat, low carinated vessels	'Amesbury Archer'	Fitzpatrick 2011
Ermine motif *	Shrewton 5k 2480–2200 cal BC (BM 3017)	Green & Rollo Smith 1984
	Thomas Hardye School, Dorchester, 2460–2190 cal BC	Gardiner *et al.* 2007

Table 20.1: Features identifiable on dated early Beakers in Wessex

*There is a potentially earliest Beaker from the Stonehenge area, from barrow Shrewton 5k, associated with a single radiocarbon date which places it within this period. Needham (2005, 191) points out that it is a 'statistical outlier' for short-necked Beakers, but if accurate is one of the earliest Beakers in the country, and the dagger should also not be later than around the 22nd century BC (Green & Rollo Smith 1984, fig. 21, P1 and C1, p. 295; Needham 2005, 191, table 4). A more recent find of a Beaker from Thomas Hardye School, Dorchester, with an ermine motif and an unusual mid-carinated but relatively squat profile loosely related to short necked forms, also has a date within this period (Gardiner *et al.* 2007, 38, table 7). Although both are single dates, this may indicate an early start for ermine motifs and, potentially, some short-necked forms

are resilient. This will be a look in detail at an area where, if anywhere, a Chalcolithic ought to be identifiable. But is it?

Looking for early metal-users

Quite when the first copper objects were introduced into the British Isles remains unclear. Copper artefacts were exchanged over considerable distances from Carpathian Basin sources during the 4th millennium, reaching as far north as southern Scandinavia (Ottaway 1973; Midgley 1992, 294–302). Their presence a boat journey away, on the other side of the North Sea, raises the possibility that a few of these earliest metal objects *may* have reached the British Isles during the 4th or early 3rd millennia, but in such small numbers as to be currently archaeologically invisible. Proxy evidence for the use of early copper axes in a pre-Beaker horizon may derive from the

sudden increase in the use of substantial quantities of large timber in monumental constructions otherwise unassociated with stone axes and axe fragments close to 2500 BC, notably at the Durrington Walls Southern Circle (Wainwright & Longworth 1971; Parker Pearson 2011, 59). The argument is compelling, but the evidence equivocal, and at present the earliest copper remains firmly associated with Beaker grave assemblages. On the basis of new dating programmes, the appearance of the Beaker 'package' (pots, single burials, metal knives and ornaments, and so forth) in the British Isles is placed in the second or third quarter of the 25th century BC (Needham 2005; Sheridan 2007; Parker Pearson *et al.* 2007, 634). It follows that if a British 'Copper Age' were to be envisaged, it would span the period 2500–2200BC.

If any attempt is to be made to look for activity which might represent early metal

Figure 20.2. Major late Neolithic sites in the Avebury region

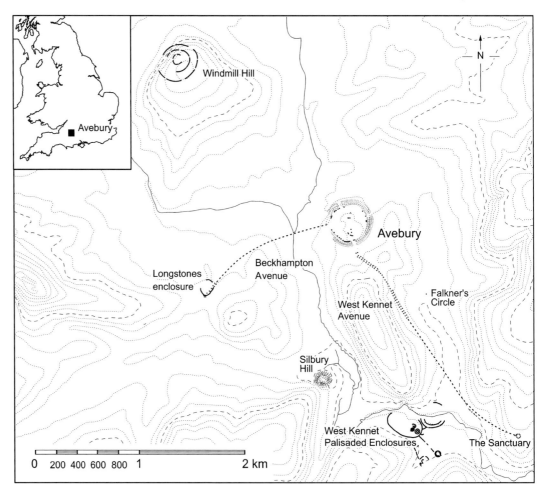

users, apart from the fortunate few who were buried with identifiably early copper artefacts, it is clearly necessary to extrapolate from known early grave groups and other datable contexts and for this Wessex is well-placed. Radiocarbon dating of potentially early and earliest Beakers is ongoing, and the picture may change, but there are sufficient dates available to form an outline picture. To ignore finds which are undatable by radiocarbon dating would be to risk under-estimating the impact of earliest Beakers. Key finds here are the well-known burials from Boscombe Down, near Amesbury in Wiltshire, including the 'Amesbury Archer', which have some of the earliest secure radiocarbon dates from Beaker associated burials in the country (Fig. 20.1). The 'Amesbury Archer' (Fitzpatrick 2011) has a series of dates placing his death and burial in the period 2440–2290 cal BC (68% confidence: Barclay & Marshall 2011); while the earliest of the primary burials of the 'Boscombe Bowmen' group from Lower

Camp, Boscombe, may be slightly earlier (2460–2280 cal BC at 79% confidence: *ibid.*). They are all, therefore, well within the putative 'Chalcolithic'. Table 20.1 indicates the formal and decorative features which can be identified from these and other datable early finds which will be used for extrapolation. In this paper we attempt to identify the earliest appearances of Beakers – in Needham's terms those certainly pre-dating his 'fission horizon' (from *c.* 2250 cal BC: Needham 2005, 209) – in areas where there is an established tradition of 'Neolithic' activity, and to regard these in the light of whether they suggest such a shift in ideology and practice as to constitute a major change which requires a new label. In order to achieve this we look first at the longer 3rd millennium sequences of activity in each region, followed by a review of earliest Beaker occurrences.

	All over Cord	All over Comb	Cord Zoned Maritime	Triangle Fringe motif	Ermine motif
Windmill Hill	✗	–	✗	✗	✗
South Street long barrow ditch	✗	? ✗	–	–	✗
Horslip long barrow ditch	✗	–	–	–	–
West Kennet long barrow filling	✗	–	–	–	–
The Sanctuary	✗	–	–	–	–
West Kennet Avenue Beaker burials	–	–	✗	–	–
Bishop's Cannings Down (surface find)	–	–	–	✗	–
Avebury G55 pre-barrow	✗	–	–	–	–

Table 20.2: Decoration motifs of potentially early Avebury Beakers

✗ - presence

Avebury

Monument sequence

Participation in the construction of earthen and chambered long mounds, the enclosure at Windmill Hill and the Greater Cursus, illustrates the degree of ceremonial pre-eminence that the Avebury and Stonehenge regions had gained during the course of the 4th millennium (Whittle 1993; Cleal *et al.* 1995; Darvill 2006; Parker Pearson *et al.* 2006; Lawson 2007; Gillings *et al.* 2008). We contend that the creation of major ceremonial centres in these regions during the later Neolithic – here encompassing some of the most labour-intensive and architecturally creative monuments of the north-west European Neolithic – was driven by this earlier legacy; whether conceived as emulation of ancestral achievements, a reaffirmation of the perceived sacredness of these landscapes (inherent in the cosmological status of their easterly and southerly flowing rivers, distinctive chalk and stone geology, and topography), a political appropriation of the pre-eminent historical status of these areas, or a combination of all these factors.

The later Neolithic was to witness the emergence of new forms of monument (henges, stone and timber circles, palisades, and so forth), and most likely different structures of social power to those that existed during the earlier part of the period. However, the incorporation of earlier constructions into new monument complexes, and material practices which positively evoked the past, created lines of connection to the past, and a perceived continuity of sorts. It is through the resources of the past that future projects are

taken forward (Barrett 1994). This is especially evident in the Avebury region (Fig. 20.2), where certain places persisted in significance through repeated acts of occupation, modification and deposition. Around the turn of the 4th and 3rd millennia part of the outer circuit of the Windmill Hill enclosure was redefined (Whittle *et al.* 2011, 96–7). Following a hiatus after the formation of primary mortuary deposits, deliberately introduced artefact-rich chalk spreads and soils accumulated within the chambers of the West Kennet long barrow (Piggott 1962), probably being introduced at regular intervals of three or four generations from 3620–3240 BC until the second half of the 3rd millennium BC (Bayliss *et al.* 2007, 95). The succession of ceramic styles (Neolithic bowl, Peterborough Ware, Grooved Ware, and Beaker) at the long-lived midden sites on the West Kennet Avenue and under Avebury G55 and West Overton G6b, and at Windmill Hill (Smith 1965a; 1965b; Smith & Simpson 1966, Whittle *et al.* 1999), shows a similar persistence of place values (Pollard 2005), ones that could explicitly have drawn upon notions of ancestral sanction.

It should, therefore, come as little surprise that the earliest of the 3rd millennium monuments in the region either referenced, through architectural form, earlier traditions or were located in places with lengthy histories of prior activity. Created probably between 2820 and 2660 BC, the Longstones enclosure in the west of the region was situated adjacent to two earlier Neolithic long mounds, and its discontinuous ditched form looks to deliberately evoke that of mid-4th millennium enclosures such as Windmill Hill (Gillings *et al.* 2008). The earliest components of the Avebury henge, notably the innermost megalithic settings such as the Cove and a primary earthwork (Avebury 1), could belong to this horizon, or even close to 3000 BC (Pollard & Cleal 2004). They were themselves created in a landscape location that had witnessed settlement and other activities extending back to the early 4th millennium (Smith 1965a). At Avebury, there then follows a lengthy, if punctuated, series of structural changes and elaborations, that, more in terms of sequence of event than architectural detail, matches the long sequence of construction and reworking seen to the south at Stonehenge (Pollard & Cleal 2004; Cleal et al. 1995).

There is no doubt that the period under particular scrutiny here, the three centuries between 2500 and 2200 BC, witnessed the most intensive phase of monument construction during the course of the Neolithic (Gillings et al. 2008). It was immediately preceded by the second phase earthwork at Avebury, dated to the 26th century BC. Given its artefactual associations – with Durrington style Grooved Ware and chisel arrowheads – the multiple timber circle at the Sanctuary might also be placed in this century, or at least close to 2500 BC (Pollard 1992); this reinforced by the secure chronology for the analogous monument of the Southern Circle at Durrington Walls (Parker Pearson et al. 2007). The scale of work then increases rapidly. Available radiocarbon dates and structural associations place the creation of the Outer Circle at Avebury, the West Kennet and Beckhampton Avenues, the lithicisation of the Sanctuary, the West Kennet palisade enclosures and the start at least of Silbury Hill within the 25th–23rd centuries BC (Bayliss et al. 2007; Gillings et al. 2008, 202–4). There are, admittedly, problems with the available dates from the West Kennet palisades which, if taken at face value and their full two-sigma ranges, could imply a very long chronology extending c. 2900–1800 BC, and so parallel to the attenuated sequence at Avebury itself (Whittle 1997). Taking dates on samples from primary contexts alone, both Enclosure 1 and Outer Radial Ditch 1, which abuts Enclosure 2, are weighted towards the period 2500–2200 BC. Activity here, as at the Avebury henge, may continue much later given the early 2nd millennium dates on bone from the Trench H midden spread in Enclosure 1.

Available chronologies suggest that these constructions overlap with the earliest Beakers and metalwork, Silbury Hill certainly so; though none can be considered a 'Beaker monument'. At the risk of making essentialising links between material forms, practices, and identities, all this activity looks, culturally, Late Neolithic. Latest Neolithic construction projects were directed towards the integration of the formerly separate monuments of Avebury, the Longstones enclosure, and the Sanctuary into a unified complex, via linkage performed by the two megalithic avenues. Creating the avenues, the Longstones Cove and stone circles at the Sanctuary – lithicising these sites – was a way of memorialising locations of extreme significance and potency, relocating them into a domain closely associated with the ancestral dead, and sanctifying the past rather than new forms of ideological order. In the riverside zone, Grooved Ware is the only ceramic style that was in use at the West Kennet enclosures, along with lithic forms such as oblique arrowheads that firmly belong to an insular Late Neolithic repertoire. Even the pig-dominated faunal assemblage was generated through practices of aggregation and feasting that find greater reference in the communal practices of the Neolithic than the framework of projects structured around close lineage relations that was to emerge in the last quarter of the 3rd millennium. Silbury Hill is without clear material culture associations, perhaps because of proscriptions on the deposition of certain kinds of artefact here. It is too early for its mounded form to be influenced by early round barrows, and it is more plausible to envisage either inspiration from earlier large mounds such as the Boyne Valley tombs (Whittle 1997, 150), or just local generation of a novel monumental form, here connected with the source of the Kennet (Leary & Field 2010).

Earliest Avebury Beakers

There are, then, many indications that activity around later Neolithic Avebury was heavily referencing the past, so the question of where Beakers were first used is vital to understanding the degree to which their appearance marks, or does not mark, a real break with that past. Use and deposition involving new practices in novel places hints at marked change, perhaps fully meriting the identification of a 'Chalcolithic'. The retention of traces of older practices in

	All over Cord	All over Comb	Cord Zoned Maritime	Triangle Fringe motif	Ermine motif
Stonehenge Q&R dismantling	–	? ✕	–	–	–
Stonehenge nr Sarsen Circle	✕	? ✕	–	–	✕
Nr Heelstone	–	? ✕	–	–	–
Amesbury Archer	✕	✕	–	✕	–
Lower Camp Boscombe	✕	–	✕	–	–
Winterbourne Gunner	✕	✕	–	–	–
Wilsford G54	✕	–	✕	–	–
Shrewton 5k	–	–	–	–	✕
Coneybury Henge	–	–	–	–	✕
Durrington Walls (1966-68)	✕	–	–	–	–
Durrington Walls (2004-2007)	–	–	–	✕	–
Woodhenge Ditch	–	✕	–	–	–

Table 20.3: Decoration motifs of potentially early Stonehenge Beakers

✕ - presence

places apparently imbued with a remembered hinterland of past associations would rather indicate a gentler transition.

Table 20.2 summarise the occurrence of types of Beaker and Beaker motif discussed as being possibly indicative of early use, within the Avebury area. The clearest example of potentially earliest Beakers with no later material is at South Street long barrow: sherds of an AOC Beaker, a probable All Over Comb Beaker, and a short-necked Beaker with ermine motif are all present in the 'Beaker clearance horizon' in the barrow ditches (Smith 1979, 273, fig. 30: 6–8). These were associated with cross-ploughing marks on the weathered sides of the ditch which the excavators were confident in identifying as representing an episode of cultivation associated with some woodland clearance (Evans 1979, 289, 298).

At Windmill Hill in the upper ditch fills of the causewayed enclosure, intermittent use of the ditch circuits during the 3rd millennium is indicated by sherds of Peterborough Ware, Grooved Ware, potentially earliest Beakers, with later Beakers also present (Hamilton 1999). The early Beaker sherds – CZM, AOC, and one vessel with triangle fringing (Smith 1965a, 80, fig. 35) – were concentrated in the outer circuit, where Fengate Ware and Grooved Ware were also quite frequent, while potentially later Beakers were more widespread (Hamilton 1999, figs 198–9). Although, therefore, a slight change to the pattern of use is identifiable, it does not suggest that the use of earliest Beakers was markedly different to the intermittent use of the site which had

taken place over at least the previous five or six centuries.

Two other monuments of the Early Neolithic have evidence of use associated with potentially earliest Beakers: West Kennet and Horslip long barrows. At the latter there are AOC Beaker sherds, including one with complex cord (Ashbee 1979, fig. 8, P13), in this case of two lines of cord impressed together. There is also long-necked Beaker. No clear sequence is discernible, but the occurrence of these two types suggests separate, probably short, episodes of use. West Kennet long barrow is an altogether more complex case. The latest interpretation, informed by new radiocarbon dates, suggests repeated episodes of deposition of material culture into the chambers and passage of the monument (Bayliss *et al.* 2007, 97) which may have gone on, intermittently, until the late 3rd millennium At least one sharply carinated AOC Beaker was deposited in pieces, including into three of the chambers and into the stone-hole of one of the blocking stones (Piggott 1962, 45, fig. 14, B7), apparently dating the blocking to the period of early Beaker use or later. Clearly later Beakers, with long necks, however, were also deposited, although they were found only in the western chamber, excavated in the 19th century (Case 1995, fig. 8). Once again, as at Windmill Hill, it seems that there was a pattern of repeated use which involved the deposition of Peterborough Ware, Grooved Ware, and Beakers (including potentially earliest Beakers) which extends over 1000 years.

If these potentially earliest Beakers are

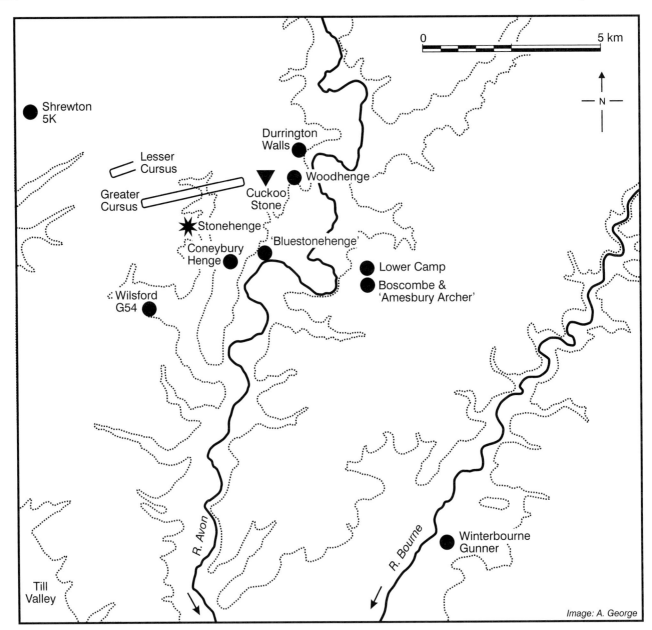

Figure 20.3. Major Late Neolithic sites and early Beaker burials in the Stonehenge region

indicative of use during the centuries of the putative Chalcolithic they provide no evidence of marked change in the ways this landscape was inhabited. Small episodes of clearance had occurred at South Street before the Beaker 'horizon', associated with Peterborough Ware; Windmill Hill had seen many short episodes of occupation throughout the centuries; and by the third quarter of the 3rd millennium the sequence at West Kennet long barrow was one which had been punctuated by episodes of activity including deposition of pottery for more than a millennium, and Beakers appear to have been used in much

the same way as preceding ceramics. Nor can the occurrence of potentially early Beaker associated episodes in the same places as earlier episodes be written off simply as the result of these contexts constituting 'traps' – such as ditches – which were fortuitously preserving remnants of settlement patterns which were in other respects different. A crude measure of this is the location of diagnostically Beaker flint arrowheads as compared to other types, as the robustness of the material means that it would survive whether or not protected by burial in a negative feature. Around Windmill Hill barbed-and-tanged arrowheads occur in similar numbers to transverse and leaf-shaped forms (Holgate 1988, table 4). Lack of chronological discrimination means that very early Beaker associated use cannot be distinguished from that associated with later Beakers in lithic scatters, and the use of Windmill Hill by users of Beakers is a long one, but this does strengthen the argument that the introduction of Beakers did not disrupt a well-established settlement pattern. Neither can the argument of clearances being preferentially chosen because of ease of use be argued convincingly. By the centuries in which early Beakers were in use it is generally accepted that the landscape around Avebury was cleared to a great extent (Whittle 1993); old clearings would have long since become indistinguishable among a mosaic of scrub, short grassland, and areas in various stages of regeneration.

Turning to the funerary record, the single example of a potentially earliest Beaker in a funerary context is a Cord Zoned Maritime Beaker from a grave next to a stone of the West Kennet Avenue accompanying an adult probably male inhumation (Smith 1965a, 229–30, fig. 78, P350; Brothwell 1965, 231). It is worth noting that although the *type* of use is novel, the *location* chosen for the grave with the CZM Beaker is one already marked by long use. The adult male buried here was interred within the area of an already ancient spread of artefacts and features known as the West Kennet Avenue 'occupation site' (Smith 1965a, fig. 73). This contained many hundreds of sherds of Peterborough Ware and Grooved Ware, some features, and its location appears to have been respected by the builders of the Avenue as one stone was omitted from its course in this area. One of us has considered in detail the possibility that the use of this area may have been 'monumentalised', first by the erection of posts and, later, taken a step further when the Avenue was laid out both to incorporate it and to mark it by omitting one stone (Pollard 2005, 110–11). Rather than a break with the past, the choice of location for this very early grave with its novel ceramic grave good suggests that the past was very much in the minds of the people making that choice.

The West Kennet Avenue has also produced a unique vessel which may also belong to this period. This is a small bowl, decorated with grooves and impressions and was also found with the burial of an adult male next to a standing stone (Smith 1965a, 229–30, fig. 78, P352; Brothwell 1965, 230). The decoration, while appearing to owe something to Grooved Ware of the Clacton sub-style (in that it has a dot-filled zone), also includes a motif similar to an ermine motif (Table 20.3). Isobel Smith suggested that its relations lay with handled cups which appear to be related to the Beaker tradition (Smith 1965a, 229). It seems more likely now, however, that the handled cups lie at the other end of the Beaker time frame to this vessel (Green *et al.* 1982) and that, as the West Kennet Avenue bowl was found in a similar context to the CZM Beaker, it dates very early in the period of Beaker use and is a unique object combining motifs from both the Beaker and Grooved Ware traditions.

At Avebury, then, we contend that in neither the sequences of monument development, nor in the occurrence of the potentially earliest Beakers, is there evidence of a discontinuity in the trajectories or practice of monument building and use, or in the ways in which the landscape in which they are situated was exploited and inhabited. Even new burial traditions associated with Beakers were enacted in a fashion that respected pre-existing monuments. If the introduction of copper as to have had such an impact on the social contexts into which it and associated artefacts first trickled, such that it requires formal recognition as a new temporal period, it would be reasonable to expect at the very least that its effects would be recognisable in both the monuments and settlement.

Stonehenge

Monument sequence

The complex of Neolithic monuments around Stonehenge lies 25 km to the south of Avebury, on a chalk plateau in the centre of Salisbury Plain between the rivers Till and Avon (Fig. 20.3). The sequence of monument building here follows a broadly similar course of events to that outlined for the Avebury landscape, though critical differences are apparent, particularly in the range of monument forms present (Darvill 2006). Notable by their absence in the Avebury region, two cursus monuments were created in the Stonehenge landscape during the mid-4th millennium (Thomas *et al.* 2009). Both may have memorialised or reinstated an important east–west axis of movement across the chalk plateau between the two river systems (Tilley *et al.* 2007). At nearly 3 km long, the Greater or Stonehenge Cursus was the most significant monumental intervention in this landscape during the earlier part of the Neolithic. Once constructed (at 3630–3370 BC) its presence was to structure later activity in the region: providing an axis upon which the Cuckoo Stone monolith and Woodhenge would later be sited; and establishing a north–south division across the landscape that was respected throughout much of the 3rd millennium, seen especially in the 'containment' of Grooved Ware associated settlement in the zone to the south of the Cursus (Darvill 1997). As with events in the Avebury region, during the later Neolithic the past mattered and provided an important symbolic resource that sanctioned subsequent gatherings and acts of monument creation.

At least two, probably three, new monuments were constructed during the first quarter of the 3rd millennium. Pre-eminent is the first phase of Stonehenge itself, dated to 3015–2935 BC and comprising a circular earthwork enclosure with southern and north-eastern (solstitial) entrances (Cleal *et al.* 1995). Excavations by the Stonehenge Riverside Project in 2008 demonstrated both that the monument was located at the end of a periglacial 'earthwork' that was later to be inscribed as the initial length of a ditched avenue, and that the ring of 56 Aubrey Holes immediately inside the henge bank most likely held Welsh bluestones in the first phase. Large numbers of cremations and deposits of disarticulated human bone were incorporated within the monument from the time of its construction until *c.* 2400 BC (Parker Pearson *et al.* 2009); the Beaker 'archer' burial interred in the western ditch terminal flanking the main entrance (at *c.* 2440–2140 cal BC: Barclay & Marshall 2011, table 30) perhaps representing a final element in the site's long-standing use as a cemetery.

Also belonging to this earliest 3rd millennium horizon is the henge monument at Coneybury, located on high ground to the south-east of Stonehenge (Richards 1990). It enclosed a series of pit and post features reminiscent of the later Neolithic 'square-in-circle' wooden structures known from the Durrington-Woodhenge zone (see below). Artefactual associations suggest the smaller river-side stone circle at Bluestonehenge may

have been constructed around the same time (Parker Pearson *et al.* 2009). By the end of the first quarter of the 3rd millennium there existed a group of three circular monuments in stone, earth, and timber in the zone to the south of the Cursus.

Events during the middle of the millennium saw dramatic modifications at Stonehenge and the creation of a new monument group in the riverside zone to the east of the Cursus. Developments in the eastern riverside zone began with the creation of several square-in-circle timber shrines in the valley later enclosed by the Durrington Walls henge earthwork and along the ridge to the south (Thomas 2007, Pollard 2009). One of these was reworked to create the second phase Southern Circle in the decades centred on 2500 BC, which was linked to the Avon via a metalled and embanked avenue. Available evidence suggests that the analogous multiple timber circle at Woodhenge was broadly contemporaneous. It now seems likely that the Q- and R- settings of bluestones at Stonehenge are integral with the sarsen circle and trilithons of phase 3, and should be placed in the 26th–early 25th centuries BC (Parker Pearson *et al.* 2007, and M. Parker Pearson, pers. comm.). Telling of its enduring significance, the ditch of the Greater Cursus was also reinstated as a circuit of pits around this time (Thomas *et al.* 2009).

This scaling-up of constructional activity around the middle of the 3rd millennium, and the physical integration of various monuments both new and pre-existing into coherent complexes via the creation of avenues to/from the Avon, mirrors the situation seen at Avebury. In the most coherent interpretation to date, for a period of time around 2500 BC, the Stonehenge-Bluestonehenge-Durrington-Woodhenge complex provided the setting for rites surrounding the translation of the newly dead into ancestors (Parker Pearson & Ramilisonina 1998). The timber monuments at Durrington Walls and Woodhenge were intimately linked with periodic gathering and feasting, timed to coincide with the winter solstice; while the lithic settings at Stonehenge and Bluestonehenge retained their close association with funerary and ancestral domains.

Contemporary with earliest Beaker burials in the wider region, but seemingly resilient to the presence of any novel ideologies that these might represent, the 25th–23rd centuries saw on-going constructional activity and modification of the region's major monuments. By the middle of the 25th century the henge earthworks had been created at Durrington Walls (Parker Pearson *et al.* 2007). The stone settings at Bluestonehenge were removed and taken, most likely, to be re-erected at Stonehenge in the period 2400–2300 BC, and their former position then enclosed by a henge earthwork. Linked to this was the extension of the Stonehenge Avenue to the Avon riverside. Broadly contemporary is the henge earthwork at Woodhenge (at 2480–2030 BC), which probably goes with the megalithic cove constructed in the southern part of that monument after the timber settings had rotted (Pollard & Robinson 2007). Pits were cut into the tops of major post-holes at the Southern Circle, Woodhenge, and the Durrington 68 and 70 timber settings, and incorporated deposits of animal bone, flint, Grooved Ware, and some Beaker (Thomas 2007). This activity may have continued into the early 2nd millennium (Parker Pearson *et al.* 2009). All of these actions – enclosure, the selected erection of stones, pit digging, and deposition – were bound up in strategies of marking and memorialisation. Once again, the past was to the fore, and connections were being established to the traditions and achievements of earlier generations, and to the forms of long-standing sacred authority that was materialised in these monuments.

As Richard Bradley has cogently argued, nowhere is this sense of continuity in sacred tradition so evident than as at Stonehenge itself (Bradley 1991). While the earliest barrow cemeteries were being constructed in the region, some in sight of the great monument, Stonehenge continued to be visited, the bluestones were reset on at least two separate occasions, and the Y and Z Holes (equivalents, perhaps, to the pits cut into the tops of the former post-holes at Woodhenge and the Southern Circle) dug (Cleal *et al.* 1995). On the basis of available radiocarbon dates, this sequence of events spans the 23rd–16th centuries BC, and so well into the Early Bronze Age.

Earliest Stonehenge Beakers

There are some differences between the appearance of earliest Beakers in the Stone-henge landscape to their appearance in the Avebury area. In the Stonehenge landscape it seems that potentially earliest Beakers are 'trickling in' in small quantities to Woodhenge, Stonehenge and Coneybury henge (Fig. 20.3), in contrast to Avebury where no potentially early Beaker has yet been identified from the henge interior, bank or ditch. In terms of funerary use, however, the novel ceramic seems largely confined to locations at some distance from Stonehenge. Table 20.3 summarises the occurrence of types of Beaker and Beaker motif discussed as possibly indicative of early use, within the Stonehenge area.

The appearance of Beakers within the sequence at Stonehenge is not, however, clear. Only a very small amount of material, no more than about five or six potentially early vessels, are represented by very few sherds and this paucity seems to continue a reluctance to leave ceramics at the site which is attested earlier by the limited Grooved Ware assemblage (of only 11 sherds; Cleal 1995, 350–3). Two comb-impressed sherds were found in the Q/R-hole setting, but only in a position related to dismantling rather than erection, and other sherds are not stratified.

Potentially earliest Beakers are present in the wider Stonehenge landscape but appear to be thinly distributed and not closely clustered around the monument. The Amesbury Archer and other Boscombe Down Beakers, which have been taken as the starting point for the discussion of Beakers, above (Table 20.1), are 5 km from Stonehenge, and other potentially early groups may be present at Wilsford G54 and Winterbourne Gunner, in both cases as disturbed burials in which the existence of a group can only be suggested (Cleal in Fitzpatrick 2011). At Winterbourne Gunner, 10 km from Stonehenge (Fig. 20.3), this is of an AOC and an All Over Comb Beaker, both in disturbed contexts (Musty 1963), and at Wilsford G54 of a CZM, AOC and a Beaker with comb-defined and filled zones in a form which is potentially squatter than shown in the illustration (which is modelled on the Wessex/Middle Rhine Beaker from Winterslow Hut: Smith 1991, 27, fig. 12 P6–P8). The ermine-motif decorated vessel from Shrewton, discussed above, is also situated at a similar distance.

Within Woodhenge, Durrington Walls, and Coneybury earliest Beakers are also sparse. Excavations at Coneybury produced a single sherd with an ermine motif among other sherds which may be early but not necessarily earliest (Ellison 1990, 146, fig. 108, P73). This was from the ditch but was recorded as very worn so may have been on the site some time before reaching its final context. The Durrington Walls 1966–8 excavations produced only two potentially earliest Beakers, both AOC sherds, from the interior (on the platform) (Longworth 1971, fig, 65, P568 and P569). The recent excavations of Durrington Walls have produced a single triangle fringe piece (from the Southern Circle) but analysis of the assemblage is not complete at the time of writing. At Woodhenge several sherds of an AOC Beaker were found within the secondary fill of the ditch, on the west side of the entrance. Although the reconstruction is described as conjectural it is reconstructed as fairly squat and it seems possible that it is of very early Beaker date (Cunnington 1929, pl. 41, 4).

Finally, the locations of the potentially earliest Beakers used in a funerary context are worth considering in the light of the use made of an 'old' place at the West Kennet Avenue. At Wilsford G54 the excavations produced Early Neolithic pottery, Peterborough Ware, and Grooved Ware (Smith 1991); at Shrewton the excavations produced one sherd of Grooved Ware; and at Boscombe Down there was considerable activity associated with Grooved Ware, including a pit circle (Wessex Archaeology in prep.) within 450 m of the 'Amesbury Archer'. Common locations for Beaker, and later, burials, and Grooved Ware deposition is a well-recognised feature (Cleal 1999, 6). For sites a millennium earlier it could be argued that concentration on particular places was in large part because areas which had already been cleared of trees offered a natural advantage to new occupiers, but, as noted for Avebury, above, by the late 3rd millennium BC this argument hardly applies as the landscape is generally recognised as largely open by then (Allen 1997): ancient clearances would not have stood out.

Themes and discussion

To summarise the regional sequences outlined above, it is evident that events in the Avebury and Stonehenge landscapes display similar 3rd millennium BC trajectories, even if the details of individual monument forms differ to a degree. There exists a varied tempo to monument construction, with a notable increase in the scale of activity during the period *c.* 2600–2200 BC. This applies to megalithic settings especially, which may relate to their primarily memorialising role. While this period of enhanced constructional activity is broadly coincident with the earliest Beakers and single grave burials, events at the core monument complexes very much represent developments that drew upon earlier practices and traditions; and probably long-drawn out and complex political-religious histories structured around inter-complex competition. Even 'lithicisation' can be seen as a technology of marking in stone structures and routeways of extraordinary pre-existing value. Reference back to the past remained an important part of ceremonial practice; and we would argue this is also seen in the deployment of Beakers in places already well known and used, including by then ancient long mounds.

The dates from the West Kennet palisades demonstrate that, for a time, Grooved Ware and Beaker ceramics must have circulated simultaneously, being deployed in very different spheres of practice. Material components of the early Beaker package frequently accompanied burials; in the case of the pre-eminent ceremonial centre around Stonehenge sited at a respectful distance. By contrast, Grooved Ware and associated lithic forms, such as oblique arrowheads, retained an association with timber earthwork monuments, and a usage as part of aggregation and feasting events that underpinned corporate monument construction and use, and time-sanctioned forms of authority. Early Beakers are also present in non-funerary contexts, though in tellingly low numbers, often represented by sherds from single or a handful of vessels, as at Stonehenge, Woodhenge, and Durrington Walls. On Boscombe Down, to the south-east of Stonehenge, where the Amesbury Archer and Boscombe Bowmen burials are located, a rapid succession from Grooved Ware to Beaker during the late 25th or early 24th centuries BC is argued (Barclay & Marshall 2011, fig. 62). However, set *c.* 5 km from Stonehenge and on the opposite side of the River Avon, events on Boscombe Down may have been less structured by the established religious and social order manifest by Stonehenge and the riverside monument complex. Perhaps here there was more room to experiment with new forms of material practice.

Taken together, the picture is one of low numbers of earliest Beakers and associated material, their frequently peripheral occurrence, or apparently respectful placement in earlier monuments, alongside the absence of evidence for wholesale change in ceremonial practice (and so, perhaps a conservatism in social and political structure). This chimes well with Needham's analysis of the Beaker social network during the third quarter of the 3rd millennium as 'poorly integrated within the social fabric of the Final Neolithic' (2005, 207). If there *is* a real 'horizon' of ideological change identifiable within the 3rd millennium this might come in the Early Bronze Age proper (after *c.* 2200 BC), seen in the emergence of barrow cemeteries. This corresponds to Needham's (2005) *fission horizon* (placed at 2250–2150BC), following which there was diversification of grave groups in Beaker funerary practice and a general up-take of Beaker associated material culture in domestic as well as funerary domains of practice. Even following this horizon, key monuments such as Avebury and Stonehenge remained important foci. Periodic modifications, such as the resetting of stones and the digging of the Y and Z holes at Stonehenge, were worked in relation to established architectural formats; while the deposition of human bone in the ditch at Avebury (Gillings & Pollard 2004, 72–3) bespeaks of an on-going relationship with ancestral/deep-time realms.

We are not in a position to suggest that the sequences we outline here for Wessex are either typical or atypical of the rest of the British Isles. Our chronological resolution is too poor for many regions to be able to establish that. Nor do we imply that Wessex was at the heart of earliest Beaker adoption, nor necessarily peripheral. We can note in passing a similar absence of 'cultural dislocation' in regions such as the Upper Thames Valley to the north-east, where the few earliest Beaker burials are found around pre-existing monument complexes (Thomas 1999, 197–8; Garwood 2011, 404), and where their presence need not indicate significant ideological contestation. Much the same is true of the area around Dorchester, Dorset, to the south of the regions considered here, where the most dramatic transformations

occur at the start of the Early Bronze Age proper (after *c.* 2200 BC), centred on events at the Mount Pleasant complex (Wainwright 1979; Cleal & Pollard in prep.).

Do we really need a Chalcolithic?

It will have become apparent that we do not consider the invention of a British Chalcolithic to be a particularly useful heuristic device, at least not when applied to the 3rd millennium BC of central southern England. This opinion stems from our reading of events and processes during this time, and also from engagement with archaeological philosophies that seek to escape from the essentialism of culture-history. It is curious that further periodisation might even be desired given the problematic legacy that our existing systems of chronological division present. This is an old debate. Writing in the early 1950s, Stuart Piggott pertinently observed that 'many of us today feel that our archaeological terminology is in serious need of revision and that such phrases as 'Neolithic' or 'Bronze Age' periods have a rather dubious validity' (Piggott 1954, xvii). We know that periodisation is problematic: it creates narrative structures that bind rather than assist; it essentialises; it brings with it implicit notions of directionality and progress; and leads to images of stasis within period boundaries, contrasted with radical change at the points of origin and demise – after all, transition of state can only come about through change (Lucas 2005, 49–53). To rustle up a Chalcolithic would seem a step more in tune with the days of Lubbock and Pitt Rivers than today's sophisticated, nuanced, and reflexive prehistory.

Rather than adopting a hard-edge Chalcolithic, and connotations of radical social and ideological change brought about by the sudden presence of metals and other exotic goods linked to the Beaker package, would it not be better to seek to understand events within this temporal horizon in terms of 'culture contact' (though without the asymmetric power relations that characterise such during the European age of exploration)? This would focus attention on the varied and contingent outcomes of exposure to new people, new ideas and new material realms as Late Neolithic networks within the British Isles were gradually drawn into those of adjacent regions of continental Europe. Thinking in terms of contact scenarios offers the possibility of envisioning situations of cultural resistance or up-take of practices within local frames of cosmological reference, without *a priori* privileging of either side. The local scale matters, because it is through the actions of individuals and small groups that even global processes must be enacted. To return to the Wessex chalk, we do not know whether at the moment of contact those few visiting individuals such as the Amesbury Archer were perceived as powerful, rather than exotic or radically 'other' and dangerous. Perhaps they were welcomed as curious and interesting outsiders, rather than role models that should be emulated. While in the long term the Beaker 'package' of material and practices was to take hold, in the third quarter of the 3rd millennium its presence did not disrupt the trajectory of events at the major ceremonial centres in Wessex, nor seemingly existing structures of authority. To regard the eventual widespread uptake of Beaker material and values as pre-ordained at the outset is simply teleological.

We are not, of course, denying that change happened during the course of the 3rd millennium BC. We are simply wary about the effects of isolating and reifying those periods of transformation. If periodisation was allowed to take hold then why stop with the Chalcolithic? It is perhaps illuminating, by contrast, to consider the appearance of Grooved Ware and its associated material culture, the appearance of henges and stone circles, and the apparent speed at which these phenomena spread across the British Isles. If a striking shift or discontinuity in existing practices and trajectories was to be identified, surely this is a clearer example than the early stages of metal-using. The emergence of novel monument forms during the first half of the 3rd millennium cal, combined with the apparently rapid take-up in southern Britain of novel ceramic and lithic forms, including some striking changes in the nature of the stone-working technologies and pottery 'recipes' (Cleal 1995), could be indicative of a shift or change in world-view so fundamental that it could equally require a new period title. But, if that is the way we conclude, are we better able to understand the past?

Finally, and turning to the etymological core of the issue, we can ask why should copper matter? Why should its appearance have a dramatic impact on social life, or at least any more dramatic impact than the appearance of lathe-turned wooden bowls or woven cloth? The obsession we have with metal technology and its implications might be misleading, and perhaps says more about our recent obsession with 'hard technologies' that are routinely and implicitly associated with the male domain than past realities. Setting so much in store by the appearance of metal may disguise other more subtle changes, represented in particular by the burial record, and is curiously reflective of our very secular present time. This is far too complex a subject to form much of the discussion here, but it is undoubtedly worth noting that the widespread change in burial practice post *c.* 2200 BC may indeed represent a fundamental shift in how the majority of the population viewed their world. A recurrent concern in the historic period has been that of the existence of life after death and the nature of the afterlife for the soul. Graslund, in a paper on the nature of soul beliefs in prehistoric Europe, argues that burial customs of the metal ages in northern Europe are consistent with historically attested soul beliefs among peoples who believe in a soul which is released from the body not on death but on dissolution or destruction of the body, and in which objects are required for the journey of the soul after its release from the body (Graslund 1994, 21). Although grave goods are occasionally found in late 4th–early 3rd millennium burials the widespread adoption of them is not then or during the putative Chalcolithic, but later, during the 'full' Bronze Age. Perhaps, in focusing on metal, the term does us a real disservice, in that it distracts us from concerns which go to the heart of what it was to be an individual alive in the later part of the 3rd millennium cal BC.

Bibliography

Allen, M.J. 1997. Environment and land-use: the economic development of the communities who built Stonehenge (and economy to support the stones). In B. Cunliffe & C. Renfrew (eds), *Science and Stonehenge*, 115–44. *Proceedings of the British Academy* 92

Ashbee, P. 1979. The finds [Horslip] 218–25. In Ashbee, P, Smith, I.F., & Evans, J.G., Excavation of three long barrows near Avebury, Wiltshire. *Proceedings of the Prehistoric Society* 45, 207–300

Barclay, A. & Marshall, P. 2011. Chronology and the radiocarbon dating programme. In Fitzpatrick 2011, 167–84

Barrett, J. 1994. *Fragments from Antiquity: an archaeology of social life in Britain, 2900–1200 BC*. Oxford: Blackwell

Bayliss, A., McAvoy, F. & Whittle, A.W.R. 2007. The world recreated the date of Silbury Hill. *Antiquity* 81, 26–53

Bradley, R. 1991. Ritual, time and history. *World Archaeology* 23(2), 209–19

Brothwell, D. 1965. Human remains [West Kennet Avenue]. In Smith 1965, 230–1

Case, H. 1995 Some Wiltshire Beakers and their contexts, *Wiltshire Archaeological & Natural History Magazine* 88, 1–17

Cleal, R.M.J., 1995. Pottery fabrics in Wessex in the fourth to second millennia BC. In I. Kinnes & G. Varndell (eds), *Unbaked Urns of Rudely Shape: essays on British and Irish pottery for Ian Longworth*, 185–94. Oxford: Oxbow Books

Cleal, R.M.J. 1999 Introduction: the what, where, when and why of Grooved Ware. In R.M.J. Cleal & A. Macsween (eds), *Grooved Ware in Britain and Ireland*, 1–8. Oxford: Oxbow Books

Cleal, R.M.J. & Walker, K. with Montague, R. 1995. *Stonehenge in its Landscape: twentieth-century excavations*. London: English Heritage

Cunnington, M. 1929. *Woodhenge*. Devizes: George Simpson

Darvill, T. 1997. Ever increasing circles: the sacred geographies of Stonehenge in its landscape. In B.W. Cunliffe & A.C. Renfrew (eds), *Science and Stonehenge*, 167–202. *Proceedings of the British Academy* 92

Darvill, T. 2006. *Stonehenge: the bibliography of a landscape*. Stroud: Tempus

Ellison, A. 1990. The prehistoric pottery [Coneybury henge], in Richards 1990, 144–9

Evans, J.G. 1979. The environment [Horslip, South Street and Beckhampton Road long barrows], 275–98. In P. Ashbee, I.F. Smith & J.G. Evans, 'Excavation of three long barrows near Avebury, Wiltshire', *Proceedings of the Prehistoric Society* 45, 207–300

Fitzpatrick, A.P. 2011. *The Amesbury Archer and the Boscombe Bowmen: Bell Beaker burials at Boscombe Down, Amesbury, Wiltshire*. Salisbury: Wessex Archaeology Report 27

Garwood, P. 2011. Making the Dead. In A. Morigi, D. Schreve, M. White, G. Hey, P. Garwood, M. Robinson, A. Barclay & P. Barclay, *The Archaeology of the Gravel Terraces of the Upper and Middle Thames: early prehistory to 1500BC*, 383–432. Oxford: Oxford Archaeology

Gillings, M. & Pollard, J. 2004. *Avebury*. London: Duckworth

Gillings, M., Pollard, J., Wheatley, D. & Peterson, R. 2008. *Landscape of the Megaliths: excavation and fieldwork on the Avebury monuments, 1997–2003*. Oxford: Oxbow Books

Gräsland, B. 1994 Prehistoric soul beliefs in northern Europe. *Proceedings of the Prehistoric Society* 60, 15–26

Green, C., Lynch, F. & White, H. 1982. The excavation of two round barrows on Launceston Down, Dorset (Long Crichel 5 & 7). *Proceedings of the Dorset Natural History & Archaeological Society* 104, 39–58

Hamilton, M. 1999. Late Neolithic and Bronze Age [pottery], and, Secondary use of causewayed enclosures in the region and beyond: Peterborough Ware, Beaker pottery and round barrows. In Whittle *et al.* 1999, 292–310, and 373–5

Larsson, M. & Parker Pearson, M. (eds). 2007. *From Stonehenge to the Baltic: living with cultural diversity in the third millennium BC*. Oxford: British Archaeological Report S1692

Lawson, A.J. 2007. *Chalkland: an archaeology of Stonehenge and its region*. East Knoyle: Hobnob Press

Leary, J. & Field, D. 2010. *The Story of Silbury Hill*. London: English Heritage

Longworth, I.H. 1971. The Neolithic pottery. In Wainwright & Longworth 1971, 48–155

Lucas, G. 2005. *The Archaeology of Time*. London: Routledge

Midgley, M. 1992. *TRB: the first farmers of the North European Plain*. Edinburgh: Edinburgh University Press

Musty, J. 1963. Beaker finds from south Wiltshire. *Wiltshire Archaeological & Natural History Magazine* 58, 414–6

Needham, S. 2005. Transforming Beaker culture in north-west Europe: processes of fusion and fission. *Proceedings of the Prehistoric Society* 71, 171–217

Ottaway, B. 1973. Earliest copper ornaments in northern Europe. *Proceedings of the Prehistoric Society* 39, 294–331

Parker Pearson, M. 2011. The Bronze Age: beyond the barrow mounds. In R. Whimster (ed.), *The New Antiquarians: 50 years of archaeological innovation in Wessex*, 56–69. York: Council for British Archaeology Research Report 166

Parker Pearson, M. & Ramilisonina, 1998. Stonehenge for the ancestors: the stones pass on the message. *Antiquity* 72, 308–26

Parker Pearson, M., Chamberlain, A., Jay, M., Marshall, P., Pollard, J., Richards, C., Thomas, J., Tilley, C. & Welham, K. 2009. Who was buried at Stonehenge? *Antiquity* 83, 23–39

Parker Pearson, M., Cleal, R., Marshall, P., Needham, S., Pollard, J., Richards, C., Ruggles, C., Sheridan, A., Thomas, J., Tilley, C., Welham, K., Chamberlain, A., Chenery, C., Evans, J., Knüsel, C., Linford, N., Martin, L., Montgomery, J., Payne, A. & Richards, M. 2007. The age of Stonehenge. *Antiquity* 81, 617–39

Parker Pearson, M., Pollard, J., Richards, C., Thomas, J., Tilley, C., Welham, K. & Albarella, U. 2006. Materializing Stonehenge: the Stonehenge Riverside Project and new discoveries. *Journal of Material Culture* 11, 227–61

Parker Pearson, M., Pollard, J., Thomas, J. & Welham, K. 2009. Newhenge. *British Archaeology* 110, 14–21

Piggott, S. 1954. *Neolithic Cultures of the British Isles*. Cambridge: Cambridge University Press

Piggott, S. 1962. *The West Kennet long barrow: excavations 1955–56*. London: HMSO

Pollard, J. 1992. The Sanctuary, Overton Hill, Wiltshire: a re-examination. *Proceedings of the Prehistoric Society* 58, 213–26

Pollard, J. 2005. Memory, monuments and middens in the Neolithic Landscape. In G. Brown, D. Field, & D. McOmish (eds), *The Avebury Landscape: aspects of the field archaeology of the Marlborough Downs*, 103–14. Oxford: Oxbow Books

Pollard, J. 2009. The materialization of religious structures in the time of Stonehenge. *Material Religion* 5(3), 332–53

Pollard, J. & Cleal, R.M.J. 2004. Dating Avebury. In R. Cleal & J. Pollard (eds), *Monuments and Material Culture: papers in honour of an Avebury archaeologist: Isobel Smith*, 120–9. East Knoyle: Hobnob Press

Pollard, J. & Robinson, D. 2007. A return to Woodhenge: the results and implications of the 2006 excavations. In Larsson & Parker Pearson (eds) 2007, 159–68

Richards, J. 1990. *The Stonehenge Environs Project*. London: English Heritage

Smith, I.F. 1965a. *Windmill Hill and Avebury: excavations by Alexander Keiller 1925–1939*. Oxford: Clarendon Press

Smith, I.F. 1965b. Excavation of a Bell Barrow, Avebury G55. *Wiltshire Archaeological & Natural History Magazine* 60, 24–46

Smith, I.F. 1979. The prehistoric finds [South Street long barrow], 269–274. In P. Ashbee, I.F. Smith and J.G. Evans, 'Excavation of three long barrows near Avebury, Wiltshire', *Proceedings of the Prehistoric Society* 45, 207–300

Smith, I.F. 1991. Round barrows Wilsford-cum-Lake G51–54. Excavations by Ernest Greenfield in 1958. *Wiltshire Archaeological & Natural History Magazine* 84, 11–39

Smith, I.F. & Simpson, D.D.A. 1966. Excavation of a round barrow on Overton Hill, north Wiltshire. *Proceedings of the Prehistoric Society* 32, 122–55

Sheridan, A. 2007. Scottish Beaker dates: the good, the bad and the ugly. In Larsson & Parker Pearson (eds) 2007, 91–123

Thomas, J. 1999. *Understanding the Neolithic*. London: Routledge

Thomas, J. 2007. The internal features at Durrington Walls: investigations in the Southern Circle and Western Enclosures 2005–6. In Larsson & Parker Pearson (eds) 2007, 145–57

Thomas, J., Marshall, P., Parker Pearson, M., Pollard, J., Richards, C., Tilley, C. & Welham, K. 2009. The date of the Greater Stonehenge Cursus. *Antiquity* 83, 40–53

Tilley, C., Richards, C., Bennett, W. & Field, D. 2007. Stonehenge– its landscape and its architecture: a reanalysis. In Larsson & Parker Pearson (eds) 2007, 183–204

Wainwright, G.J. 1979. *Mount Pleasant, Dorset: excavations 1970–1971*. London: Report of the research committee of the Society of Antiquaries of London 37

Wainwright, G.J. & Longworth, I.H. 1971. *Durrington Walls: excavations 1966–1968*. London: Report of the Research Committee of the Society of Antiquaries of London 29

Whittle, A. 1993. The Neolithic of the Avebury area: sequence, environment, settlement and monuments. *Oxford Journal of Archaeology* 12, 29–53

Whittle, A. 1997. *Sacred Mound, Holy Rings. Silbury Hill and the West Kennet Palisade Enclosures: a Later Neolithic complex in North Wiltshire*. Oxford: Oxbow Books

Whittle, A., Healy, F. & Bayliss, A. 2011. *Gathering Time: dating the Early Neolithic enclosures of southern Britain and Ireland*. Oxford: Oxbow Books

Whittle, A., Pollard, J. & Grigson, C. 1999. *The Harmony of Symbols: the Windmill Hill causewayed enclosure*. Oxford: Oxbow Books

Index